JUS COGENS

One of the most complex doctrines in contemporary international law, *jus cogens* is the immediate product of the socialization of the international community following the Second World War. However, the doctrine resonates in a centuries-old legal tradition which constrains the dynamics of voluntarism that characterize conventional international law. To reconcile this modern iteration of individual-oriented public order norms with the traditionally State-based form of international law, Thomas Weatherall applies the idea of a social contract to structure the analysis of *jus cogens* into four areas: authority, sources, content, and enforcement. The legal and political implications of this analysis give form to *jus cogens* as the product of interrelation across an individual-oriented normative framework, a State-based legal order, and values common to the international community as a whole.

THOMAS WEATHERALL holds a J.D. from Georgetown University, a Ph.D. in International Law from the University of Cambridge, an M.Sc. in Global Governance and Diplomacy from the University of Oxford, and a B.A. in International Studies from The Johns Hopkins University. This book is based on the doctoral thesis completed by the author as an International Scholar of the Cambridge Overseas Trust at the University of Cambridge.

JUS COGENS

International Law and Social Contract

THOMAS WEATHERALL

CAMBRIDGE
UNIVERSITY PRESS

CAMBRIDGE
UNIVERSITY PRESS

University Printing House, Cambridge CB2 8BS, United Kingdom

Cambridge University Press is part of the University of Cambridge.

It furthers the University's mission by disseminating knowledge in the pursuit of education, learning and research at the highest international levels of excellence.

www.cambridge.org
Information on this title: www.cambridge.org/9781107081765

First published 2015

A catalogue record for this publication is available from the British Library

Library of Congress Cataloguing in Publication data
Weatherall, Thomas, author.
Jus cogens : international law and social contract / Thomas Weatherall.
pages cm
ISBN 978-1-107-08176-5 (Hardback)
1. Jus cogens (International law) I. Title.
KZ1261.W43 2015
341′.1–dc23 2014043410

ISBN 978-1-107-08176-5 Hardback

CONTENTS

FOREWORD

The history of political thought is marked by a constant tension between the universal and the parochial. Ever since the formation of the first city states, political organization was conceived of as a form of governance focused on the self. But it was also defined in terms of governance free from the other—free from control of those political organizations that had formed themselves beyond the city walls.

True, among the Greek city states there was a sense of a broader Hellenic identity. Large threats, such as Persian invasion, required the otherwise bickering microstates of the Hellenic world to engage in temporary alliances. But whatever united them, the Greek *polis* as an individual unit was seen as the natural focus and principal or exclusive unit of governance.[1]

Similarly, when Rome absorbed much of the Western world, it still defined itself, its Roman core, in contrast to those barbarians to whom the civilizing mission of the Empire was sadly denied.

However, throughout history, starting with the influential school of the Stoa, this parochial view was of course balanced by the recognition of common bonds of humanity. Just like the physical laws of nature that apply equally everywhere on the globe or throughout the universe, human characteristics were seen to exhibit similar, universal features that make humans human. These could be inherent in human nature, such as the will to survive, the capacity to love, or the need for a metaphysical grounding of life and of the inexorable drive towards death consciously experienced.

For some, shared humanity meant that there were also shared principles relating to rules of human conduct that apply universally. As

[1] Aristotle famously noted that a state should only be as large as was necessary to fulfil its function of security, a good life for its citizens, and not more than can be 'taken in at a single view'. Artistotle, The Politics 163 (Stephen Everson, ed., Cambridge University Press 1988).

Cicero observed, human laws would differ from community to community. However, true law, and justice, are universal and eternal:

> But of all the things which are a subject of philosophical debate there is nothing more worthwhile than clearly to understand that we are born for justice and that justice is established not by opinion but by nature. That will be clear if you examine the common bonds among human beings. There is no similarity, no likeness of one thing to another, so great as the likeness we all share.[2]

Cicero also laid the groundwork for subsequent natural law theory in emphasizing that 'True law is right reason, consonant with nature, spread through all people.'[3] Anticipating to an extent the discussion about *jus cogens*, he added:

> It is wrong to pass laws obviating this law; it is not permitted to abrogate any of it; it cannot be totally repealed. We cannot be released from this law by the senate or the people. . . . There will not be one law at Rome and another at Athens, and now and another later, but all nations at all times will be bound by this one eternal and unchangeable law.[4]

As natural law theory advanced from the period of scholasticism and the Renaissance towards modernity, the manifestations of eternal rules of human behaviour became more varied. Indeed, they are altogether too varied to be summarized in a few short points. However, one might perhaps roughly distinguish four types of natural law:

- There were those rules that flowed directly or indirectly from religious text or precepts. It is divine will re-cast into mandatory rules of conduct, into divine law. While these rules applied principally to the circle of believers, some principles might also be applied to those who had not yet been converted—a debate that erupted with particular vigour in the context of the 'discovery' of the native population of the Americas by Spain.
- There was the assumption that all human beings, made in the image of God, share certain attributes, including in particular human dignity. Hence, all human societies would similarly share common features. Among them were the eternal principles of natural law. These could be

[2] Marcus Tulius Cicero, On the Commonwealth and On the Laws 115 (James E. G. Zetzel ed., Cambridge University Press 1999).

[3] Id. at 71. [4] Id.

identified through the application of right reason by those capable of applying reason right.

- Referring back to Roman law, there was also reference to a more positive expression of these principles, through the concept of *jus gentium*. These were voluntary or necessary rules shared by the civilized in-group (Rome) and the barbarians outside of the civilizational system of the empire.
- Finally, there was the *jus inter gentes*—international law. This could be voluntary or contractarian law, or it could be natural law. The latter assumed that states were collectivities of persons, and they would therefore behave like natural persons. Hence, states, too, were subject to the natural rules that necessarily govern any human society.

These different types of law shared a number of common characteristics. First, as natural law was related to traits of human nature, and therefore of human societies, it was pre-ordained or inherent. It could be discovered through biblical exegesis or the application of right reason, but it did not need to be created through an act of will. It was necessary law, rather than voluntary law.

Second, the principles of natural law were eternal, or at least as stable as the perennial characteristics of human nature.

Third, natural law, being based in the universal reach of God or the universally shared characteristics of human beings, applied universally. This could be true universality, applying to all human beings. Or there could be relative universality, extending to those seen to be part of the community of mankind, but excluding others. In previous ages this might for instance have excluded women, slaves, or in some respects the infidels.

Fourth, natural law principles applied directly to the conduct of individuals, whether acting for themselves, or as agents of a social organization including the state. Natural law was therefore perfect law in itself, rather than a pre-cursor of law. No additional step was necessary to enact natural law to render it binding.

Fifth, the content of natural law tended to be dominated by values. Natural law generally aimed at a perfecting society, a social organization arranged according to universal core values that would channel human conduct towards ethically and socially desirable ends.

When Jean Bodin proclaimed the principle of state sovereignty in his *Six livres de la republique* of 1576, this did not spell the end of natural law. Instead, natural law theories and approaches coexisted with the increasing emphasis on voluntary law, as is most famously evident in the work of Hugo Grotius.[5] Universal values that could command the force of law without positive enactment persisted. This included values relating to the worth and dignity of the human person. Indeed, the communitarian vision of a *civitas maxima* found its high point in the writings of Christian Wolff, reaching well into the 'Westphalian age'. His *Grundsaetze des Natur- und Voelkerrchts* appeared in 1754. He postulated that the *obligatio universalis* 'connects all human beings as they are human beings. General law (*jus universale*) flows from this and consists of that which is owed to all human beings, because they are human beings.'[6]

However, only four years after the appearance of Wolff's book, Emer de Vattel published his own text on the *Laws of Nations or the Principles of Natural Law*. Vattel accepted that there existed a natural law of nations, or a necessary law of nations. Nevertheless, he expressly opposed Wolff's vision of a *civitas maxima* united under one law. Instead, in substantive terms, Vattel's treatise emphasized the voluntary law of nations. He argued that nations were born free and equal, and endowed with the fullest freedom of action. So long as they had not voluntarily submitted to other men or other nations, they 'remain absolutely free and independent'.[7]

Vattel is generally seen as the harbinger of unrestrained positivism—as the man who broke the common bond of mankind and helped bury the remnants of what had been an unbroken adherence to universalism and natural law argument since antiquity.[8] And yet he accepted that the voluntary law of nations was circumscribed by natural law. Hence, there was a distinction between 'lawful and unlawful treaties or conventions and between customs which are innocent and reasonable and which are unjust and deserving of condemnation'.[9] States would only be 'permitted' by the necessary law of nations to conclude agreements or establish rules of customary law that complied with the necessary law of nations.[10] While Vattel acknowledged that individuals had formed themselves into

[5] Hugo Grotius, De Jure Belli ac Pacis Libri Tres (James B. Scott ed., Francis Kelsey trans., 1925) (1646).

[6] Christian Wolff, Grundsaetze des Natur-und Voelkerrechts 43 (1754) translation by author.

[7] Emer de Vattel, Le Droit des gens, ou, Principes de la loi naturelle appliqués a la conduite et aux affaires des nations er des souverains 3 (James B. Scott ed., Charles G. Ferwick trans., 1916) (1797).

[8] Phillip Allott, *Josephine Onoh Memerial Lecture* (Hull University Press 1989).

[9] *Ibid.* at 4. [10] *Ibid.*

sovereign states, he did not accept that this process had broken the bonds of common humanity. He asserted that 'no convention or special agreement can release' man from the duty to comply with the requirements of the 'universal society of the human race'.[11]

It is true though that the subsequent turn towards positivism emphasized state sovereignty at the expense of the recognition of the individual as a holder of rights at the international level. The rights of individuals were increasingly submerged within the metaphysical person of the state. The state was no longer seen as being embedded in a naturalist legal order circumscribing its competences and conduct. Instead of universal rules, international law could increasingly only reach as far as the consent of individual states would carry it.

It was only after World War II and the horrors visited upon countless populations that the concept of human dignity as a principle of law started to surface again. And, it took the hard slog of establishing human rights in positive law to give meaning to the 'elementary principles of humanity' that had been boldly proclaimed by the International Court of Justice in 1949.[12] That hard slog during the years of ideological division of the Cold War commenced with the adoption of the Universal Declaration of Human Rights in 1948, and reached its zenith with the entry into force of the 'Bill' of Human Rights of the two UN Covenants in 1976. The UN Declaration, and with it the Bill of Rights, were clearly dedicated to the universal protection of human dignity.

The end of the Cold War was celebrated in human rights terms with the 1993 Vienna *World Conference on Human Rights*. The conference was somewhat side-tracked by the attempt of some Asian and developing states to argue that human rights were not, after all, fully universal, but in fact, subject to what was called 'national particularities'. However, in the end, the Conference adopted a Declaration which confirmed, in its opening Article, that 'the universal nature of these rights and freedoms is beyond question'.[13] The Preamble echoed the wording of the Universal Declaration, confirming that 'all human rights derive from the dignity and worth inherent in the human person, and that the human person is the central subject of human rights and fundamental freedoms'.

[11] *Ibid.* at 5.

[12] The *Corfu Channel Case* (*United Kingdom of Great Britain and Northern Ireland v. Albania*), Judgment, ICJ Reports 1949, p. 4) 22.

[13] The World Conference on Human Rights, Vienna Declaration and Programme of Action, *adopted* 25 June 1993.

Arguably, at this point the legal community of mankind had returned to a fully universal belief in common characteristics of human beings. That belief supported the claim of universal rights and fundamental freedoms—a claim directly based on the inherent dignity of the human person.

By this time, the international legal system had undergone a number of structural developments. The International Court of Justice had recognized since 1970 that there exist legal obligations owed to the international community as a whole.[14] These '*erga omnes*' obligations give all states a legal interest in the performance of key obligations of international constitutional standing by all other states.

In addition, the 1969 Vienna Convention on the Law of Treaties had recognized the doctrine of *jus cogens*. A rule of *jus cogens*, or a peremptory norm of general international law, was defined as:

> a norm accepted and recognized by the international community of States as a whole as a norm from which no derogation is permitted and which can be modified only by a subsequent norm of general international law having the same character.[15]

Hence, states cannot exempt themselves from having to comply with rules of *jus cogens,* which require compliance under all circumstances. In addition, the *Articles on State Responsibility* put forward by the International Law Commission introduced the concept of serious violations of peremptory norms (*jus cogens*). Such serious violations would trigger an obligation by all other states not to recognize the outcome of the transgression, not to assist the offender in keeping it in place, and to cooperate with a view to overturning it.[16] Moreover, under the doctrine of universal criminal jurisdiction, the commissioning of such violations might trigger individual criminal responsibility directly under international law.

In short, as rules of general international law, *jus cogens* rules are universal. They must be complied with by all under all circumstances. An infraction legally affects all other members of the organized international community as a whole. Indeed, they are legally obliged to

14 *Barcelona Traction, Light and Power Company, Limited (Belgium v. Spain)*, Judgment, ICJ Reports 1970, p. 3, 32.

15 Vienna Convention on the Law of Treaties, *opened for signature* 23 May 1969, 1155 UNTS 331, Article 53 (*entered into force* 27 January 1980).

16 International Law Commission, Draft Articles on Responsibility of States for Intentionally Wrongful Acts, Report of the International Law Commission on the Work of its Fifty-Third Session, [2001] II(2) YBILC 26 *et seq*., Articles 40–41.

oppose serious violations. Moreover, individual perpetrators face criminal sanction.

It might be argued that the 19th and early 20th centuries something of an aberration. They key elements of natural law doctrine described above appear to have resurfaced:

Item	300 BC–late 18th century	19th to mid 20th century	Mid 20th century to present
Reach	Universal	Binds only consenting states	Universal
Made by	*A priori*, inherent rule of natural law	Strict state consent	Universal consensus
Stability of the Rule	Eternal	Changes frequently, according to changing interests of states	Can change/expand if a new rule is recognized as a rule of *jus cogens* by the international community as a whole
Substantive Content	Transports values	Advances interests	Transports values
Applies to	All levels	States only	States and individuals
Legal Effect	Cannot be contracted out of	Inferior to state sovereignty	*Jus cogens, erga omnes, etc.*

The exact catalogue of *jus cogens* rules is subject to controversy. They are generally believed to include the prohibition of the threat or use of force, or of aggression, the prohibitions of slavery, genocide, ethnic cleansing, apartheid, torture, crimes against humanity including sexual violence, grave breaches of humanitarian law and fundamental human rights law. Self-determination and the protection of diplomatic agents are also at times proposed for inclusion in the list.

All of the items listed are focused on the protection of the human person from acts of war or from grave abuse in times of peace. With the exception of the final item, these protections apply to all persons. One might see in this development the positive enactment of previous natural law thinking at the international level. Alternatively, one might content oneself with the observation that a minimum catalogue of legal rules for the protection of the human person now enjoys the protection of the international legal order as a matter of positive law, without the need to refer back to any natural law roots connected with the idea of human dignity.

A third, and exciting, explanation is proposed in the present book. This is the idea of a social contract as the source of, or explanation for, the elevation of elementary human rights to the level of *jus cogens*. This idea implies a global social compact made by humanity as such with a view to safeguarding a common set of rights flowing directly from the concept of human dignity shared by all.

Of course, the concept of the social contract has been put forward in a number of different variants. To Hobbes, the social contract described the process whereby individuals gave up all their rights in exchange for protection from life in a brutal state of nature. An almighty state would provide security, but demanded unquestioned obedience.

To Rousseau, the social contract offered an opportunity to secure radically direct democratic governance. The individual would renounce his or her autonomy and subject him or herself to the 'general will' of society. Rather than denying their own identity by subjecting it to majority governance, Rousseau thought that individuals can only fulfil themselves through such action within a greater collective.

Rawls has proposed more recently that a social contract can aim to establish greater social or material equality among individuals. In addition to security from one's fellow human beings, to direct democracy or to egalitarian aims, a fourth type of social contract was of course proposed by John Locke. According to Locke, human beings do not enter an organized society with a view to abandoning all their rights, or to achieve equality among all. Instead, the very essence of the social contract is that individuals subscribe to societal organizations precisely because they wish to see their rights protected by a central authority, and because they wish to be able to accumulate unequal levels of wealth.

For Locke, pre-state societies were inherently unstable as all its members enjoyed the power to enforce their own rights. Opting into the state meant a certain loss of freedom on the part of individuals, but it also meant that the organs of the state would now ensure stable and predictable relations with the society. In particular, individuals could be confident in their right to hold property and not to be arbitrarily deprived of it.

Locke's conception was therefore not quite the same as modern arguments concerning human rights. The struggles for human rights and fundamental freedoms of the 19th century and the first half of the

20th century have led to a concept of human rights as a defence against arbitrary and abusive action of the state. While Locke would also oppose such action, his principal aim was to preserve and protect individuals from arbitrary or violent action among themselves.

But can we see the operationalization of the concept of human dignity, and the enshrinement of key human rights among the highest order rules of the positive system of international law, as a modern form of social contract? This view is certainly an attractive one from a number of angles.

Liberal international law scholars tend to focus on what happens within states when considering how international law works. The idea of the self-constituting of mankind through a global social contract, and through invisible and highly complex global networking, seems consistent with such an approach.

Those interested in constructing a constitutional or public law view of international law will also likely applaud this concept. Constitutions tend to promote certain core values, and provide mechanisms to entrench and privilege these within the legal system. The global social contract can help explain this function at the international level.

The advance in social contract theory offered in this book must also strike a chord with those who take a cosmopolitan view of the international system. The universal values they seek to defend can finally be grounded in an act of positive will. As this is a general and universal will, the global social contract theory helps cosmopolitans to extricate themselves from the allegation that they contribute to value-imperialism.

Finally, strictly positivist international lawyers, and international relations 'realists', can maintain that the state remains relevant and indeed dominant within the international system. However, it is now impossible to deny the reality of the existence of a concept of the organized international community 'as a whole'. Social contract theory can help clarify the somewhat murky identity of that concept. The international community 'as a whole' consists of all global constituents. They may often, or indeed, mainly, continue to act through the medium of the state. However, increasingly, these constituencies will demand that states and other dominant actors at the international level will deliver to them what they demand.

It is certain that this book will be received with great anticipation. This is not only due to the recently revived interest in the doctrine of *jus cogens*. The value of this splendid book lies in the originality of thought and in the clarity and depth of the presentation by its author.

Marc Weller
Cambridge, England

ACKNOWLEDGMENTS

This book is based on my doctoral thesis completed at the University of Cambridge in 2012 under the supervision of Professor Marc Weller. The project was possible only through a great deal of support.

First and foremost, I owe the privilege of undertaking this project to Professor Weller, who gave me the opportunity to study at Cambridge. From the moment he took me on as his doctoral student, Professor Weller remained confident in my ability to carry this project to fruition. I also owe a debt of gratitude to those who were kind enough to read my work at various stages of completion and provide commentary, most notably Professors John Dunn, Mads Andenas, and Philip Allott. I also wish to thank Judge Cançado-Trindade, who kindly met with me at The Hague during the final stages of my doctoral studies.

I wish to thank my thesis examiners, James Crawford and Alexander Orakhelashvili, for their genuine interest in seeing that this work might make the greatest possible contribution to the study of *jus cogens*. I am also grateful to the anonymous reviewers of this book, whose feedback was invaluable in preparing it for publication.

During my time at Georgetown University, I benefited greatly from a diversity of perspectives that influenced the contours of this work. In this respect, Professors David Stewart, Don Wallace, and Michel Paradis deserve special recognition; so too Judge Francis Allegra and Representative Eleanor Holmes Norton. Each had occasion to comment on various topics related to this book, and I am grateful that their influences have found expression at various points.

My three years in Cambridge were generously supported by the Cambridge Overseas Trust, to which I am deeply grateful for making my research possible. I must also thank King's College for supporting me in various ways throughout my time at Cambridge, and the Lauterpacht Centre for International Law, which supported me as a research assistant.

The production of this book would not have been possible without the expertise and professionalism of the team at Cambridge University Press.

Richard Woodham and David Mackenzie ensured that the book moved smoothly through its various stages of production, and I thank them for making that process a painless one. I am grateful to Maureen MacGlashan for her meticulous compilation of the index, and to Jacqueline French for her thorough copy-editing. Most of all, Elizabeth Spicer was instrumental in shepherding my manuscript through its early stages at the Press, and remained positive and encouraging throughout that process – I am indebted to her for that support, without which this book might not exist.

Finally, I am grateful for my friends in Cambridge, especially Josh Keeler, and the Cambridge University Cycling Club. I also wish to recognize Dr Gleider Hernandez, who supervised my first course in public international law at Oxford, and Mr G. H. L. LeMay, whose tutorials at Worcester College will forever shape my intellectual endeavours. Lastly, I am grateful to the unending support and encouragement of my dad Dr James Weatherall, my mom Kate, my sister Claire, and, of course Emily.

Thomas Weatherall
Washington, D.C.

TABLE OF CASES

Decisions of international courts and tribunals

Permanent Court of International Justice (PCIJ)

The Case of the S.S. 'Lotus' (France v. Turkey), Judgment, 1927 PCIJ (ser. A) No. 10 (7 Sept.).

Jurisdiction of the Courts of Danzig, Advisory Opinion, 1928 PCIJ (ser. B) No. 15 (3 March).

Settlers of German Origin in Poland, Advisory Opinion, 1923 PCIJ (ser. B) No. 6 (10 Sept.).

International Court of Justice (ICJ)

Accordance with International Law of the Unilateral Declaration of Independence in Respect of Kosovo, Advisory Opinion, ICJ Reports 2010, p. 403.

Ahmadou Sadio Diallo (Republic of Guinea v. Democratic Republic of the Congo), Compensation, Judgment, ICJ Reports 2012, p. 324.

Ahmadou Sadio Diallo (Republic of Guinea v. Democratic Republic of the Congo), Merits, Judgment, ICJ Reports 2010, p. 639.

Application of the Convention on the Prevention and Punishment of the Crime of Genocide (Bosnia and Herzegovina v. Serbia and Montenegro), Judgment, ICJ Reports 2007, p. 43.

Application of the Convention on the Prevention and Punishment of the Crime of Genocide (Bosnia and Herzegovina v. Serbia and Montenegro), Preliminary Objections, Judgment, ICJ Reports 1996, p. 595.

Application of the Convention on the Prevention and Punishment of the Crime of Genocide (Bosnia and Herzegovina v. Serbia and Montenegro), Provisional Measures, Order of 8 April 1993, ICJ Reports 1993, p. 3.

Application of the International Convention on the Elimination of All Forms of Racial Discrimination (Georgia v. Russian Federation), Preliminary Objections, Judgment, ICJ Reports 2011, p. 70.

Armed Activities on the Territory of the Congo (New Application: 2002) (Democratic Republic of the Congo v. Rwanda), ICJ Reports 2006, p. 3.

Arrest Warrant of 11 April 2000 (Democratic Republic of the Congo v. Belgium), Judgment, ICJ Reports 2002, p. 3.
Asylum Case (Colombia v. Peru), Judgment, ICJ Reports 1950, p. 266.
Barcelona Traction, Light and Power Company, Limited (Belgium v. Spain), ICJ Reports 1970, p. 3.
Continental Shelf (Libyan Arab Jamahiriya v. Malta), Judgment, ICJ Reports 1985, p. 13.
The Corfu Channel Case (United Kingdom of Great Britain and Northern Ireland v. Albania), Judgment, ICJ Reports 1949, p. 4.
East Timor (Portugal v. Australia), Judgment, ICJ Reports 1995, p. 90.
Fisheries Case (United Kingdom v. Norway), Judgment, ICJ Reports 1951, p. 116.
Gabčíkovo-Nagymaros Project (Hungary v. Slovakia), Judgment, ICJ Reports 1997, p. 7.
Jurisdictional Immunities of the State (Germany v. Italy: Greece Intervening), Judgment, ICJ Reports 2012, p. 99.
LaGrand (Germany v. United States of America), Judgment, ICJ Reports 2001, p. 466.
Legal Consequences for States of the Continued Presence of South Africa in Namibia (South West Africa) Notwithstanding Security Council Resolution 276 (1970), Advisory Opinion, ICJ Reports 1971, p. 16.
Legal Consequences of the Construction of a Wall in the Occupied Palestinian Territory, Advisory Opinion, ICJ Reports 2004, p. 136.
Legality of the Threat or Use of Nuclear Weapons, Advisory Opinion, ICJ Reports 1996, p. 226.
Legality of Use of Force (Yugoslavia v. Spain), Provisional Measures, Order of 2 June 1999, ICJ Reports 1999, p. 761.
Legality of Use of Force (Yugoslavia v. United States of America), Provisional Measures, Order of 2 June 1999, ICJ Reports 1999, p. 916.
Military and Paramilitary Activities in and against Nicaragua (Nicaragua v. United States of America), Jurisdiction and Admissibility, Judgment, ICJ Reports 1984, p. 392.
Military and Paramilitary Activities in and against Nicaragua (Nicaragua v. United States of America), Merits, Judgment, ICJ Reports 1986, p. 14.
North Sea Continental Shelf (Federal Republic of Germany v. Denmark / Federal Republic of Germany v. Netherlands), Judgment, ICJ Reports 1969, p. 3.
Nottebohm Case (Liechtenstein v. Guatemala) (Second Phase), Judgment, ICJ Reports 1955, p. 4.
Obligation to Negotiate Access to the Pacific Ocean (Bolivia v. Chile), Application Instituting Proceedings, 24 April 2013.
Questions Relating to the Obligation to Prosecute or Extradite (Belgium v. Senegal), Judgment, ICJ Reports 2012, p. 422.
Questions Relating to the Obligation to Prosecute or Extradite (Belgium v. Senegal), Provisional Measures, Order of 28 May 2009, ICJ Reports 2009, p. 139.
Reservations to the Convention on the Prevention and Punishment of Genocide, Advisory Opinion, ICJ Reports 1951, p. 15.

South West Africa Cases (Ethiopia v. South Africa / Liberia v. South Africa) (Second Phase), Judgment, ICJ Reports 1966, p. 6.

International Centre for Settlement of Investment Disputes (ICSID)

Azurix Corporation v. Argentina, Decision on Application for Annulment, No. ARB/01/12 (2009).

CMS Gas Transmission Company v. Argentina, Award, No. ARB/01/8, IIC 65 (2005).

Continental Casualty Company v. Argentina, Decision on Application for Partial Annulment, No. ARB/03/9 (2011).

Phoenix Action Limited v. Czech Republic, Award, No. ARB/06/5 (2009).

Sempra Energy International v. Argentina, Decision on Argentina's Application for Annulment of the Award, No. ARB/02/16 (2010).

International Criminal Court (ICC)

Prosecutor v. Al Bashir, Decision on the Cooperation of the Democratic Republic of the Congo Regarding Omar Al Bashir's Arrest and Surrender to the Court, No. ICC-02/05-01/09–195 (2014).

Prosecutor v. Al Bashir, Decision on the Prosecution's Application for a Warrant of Arrest against Omar Hassan Ahmad Al Bashir, No. ICC-02/05–01/09–3 (2009).

Prosecutor v. Al Bashir, First Warrant of Arrest, No. ICC-02/05–01/09–1 (2009).

Prosecutor v. Al Bashir, Second Decision on the Prosecution's Application for a Warrant of Arrest against Omar Hassan Ahmad Al Bashir, No. ICC-02/05–01/09–94 (2010).

Prosecutor v. Al Bashir, Second Warrant of Arrest, No. ICC-02/05–01/09–95 (2010).

Prosecutor v. Gaddafi et al., Decision to Terminate the Case against Muammar Mohammed Abu Minyar Gaddafi, No. ICC-01/11–01/11–28 (2011).

Prosecutor v. Gbagbo, Decision on the Confirmation of Charges, No. ICC-02/11–01/11-656 (2014).

Prosecutor v. Gbagbo, Decision Pursuant to Article 15 of the Rome Statute on the Authorisation of an Investigation into the Situation in the Republic of Côte d'Ivoire, No. ICC-02/11–14 (2011).

Situation in the Libyan Arab Jamahiriya, Decision on the 'Prosecutor's Application Pursuant to Article 58 as to Muammar Mohammed Abu Minyar Gaddafi, Saif Al-Islam Gaddafi and Abdullah Al-Senussi', No. ICC-01/11–01/11–1 (2011).

Situation in the Libyan Arab Jamahiriya, Warrants of Arrest in respect of Muammar Gaddafi, Saif Al-Islam Gaddafi and Abdullah Al-Senussi, Nos. ICC-01/11–01/11–2, ICC-01/11–01/11–3, ICC-01/11–01/11–4 (2011).

International Tribunal for the Law of the Sea (ITLOS)

Responsibilities and Obligations of States Sponsoring Persons and Entities with Respect to Activities in the Area, Advisory Opinion (Seabed Disputes Chamber), Case No. 17 (2011).

Permanent Court of Arbitration (PCA)

Dispute Concerning Access to Information Under Article 9 of the OSPAR Convention (Ireland v. United Kingdom), Final Award, 42 ILM 1118 (2003).

United Nations Human Rights Committee (UNHRC)

Wackenheim v. France, No. 854/1999, CCPR/C/75/D/854/1999 (2002).

United Nations Committee Against Torture (UNCAT)

Agiza v. Sweden, No. 233/2003, UN Doc. CAT/C/34/D/233/2003 (2005).
M.B.B. v. Sweden, No. 104/1998, UN Doc. CAT/C/22/D/104/1998 (1999).
Tapia Paez v. Sweden, No. 39/1996, UN Doc. CAT/C/18/D/39/1996 (1997).

Decisions of special tribunals

International Criminal Tribunal for the former Yugoslavia (ICTY)

Prosecutor v. Aleksovski, Judgment, IT-95-14/1-T (1999).
Prosecutor v. Blaškić, Appeals Chamber Judgment, IT-95-14-A (1997).
Prosecutor v. Blaškić, Judgment on the Request of Croatia for Review of the Decision of Trial Chamber II of 18 July 1997, IT-95–14-AR108bis (1997).
Prosecutor v. Brđanin, Judgment, IT-99-36-T (2004).
Prosecutor v. Delalić et al., Judgment, IT-96-21-T (1998).
Prosecutor v. Furundžija, Judgment, IT-95-17/1-T (1998).
Prosecutor v. Galić, Judgment, IT-98-29-T (2003).
Prosecutor v. Jelisić, Judgment, IT-95-10-T (1999).
Prosecutor v. Karadžić, Third Amended Indictment, IT-95-5/18-PT (2009).
Prosecutor v. Kristić, Judgment, IT-98-33-T (2001).
Prosecutor v. Kupreškić, Judgment, IT-95-16-T (2000).
Prosecutor v. Kunarac et al., Judgment, IT-96-23-T & IT-96-23/1-T (2001).
Prosecutor v. Nikolić, Decision on Interlocutory Appeal Concerning Legality of Arrest, Appeals Chamber Judgment, IT-94-2-AR73, (2003).
Prosecutor v. Popović et al., Judgment, IT-05-88-T (2010).
Prosecutor v. Simić, Judgment, IT-95-9/2-S (2002).
Prosecutor v. Tadić, Appeals Chamber Judgment, IT-94-1-A (1999).
Prosecutor v. Tadić, Decision on the Defence Motion for Interlocutory Appeal on Jurisdiction, IT-94-1-A (1995).
Prosecutor v. Tadić, Opinion and Judgment, IT-94-1-T (1997).

International Criminal Tribunal for Rwanda (ICTR)

Prosecutor v. Akayesu, Judgment, ICTR-96-4-T (1998).
Prosecutor v. Bikindi, Judgment, ICTR-01-72-T (2008).

Prosecutor v. Kambanda, Judgment and Sentence, ICTR-97–23-S (1998).
Prosecutor v. Kayishema and Ruzindana, ICTR-95–1-T (1999).
Prosecutor v. Setako, Judgment and Sentence, ICTR-04–81-T (2010).

International Military Tribunal at Nuremberg (IMT)

United States v. List et al. (The Hostage Case), in 11 Trials of War Criminals before the Nuernberg Military Tribunals under Control Council Law No. 10 759 (Washington: GPO 1950).
Nazi Conspiracy and Aggression, Opinion and Judgment, International Military Tribunal at Nuremberg (1946).

Special Court for Sierra Leone (SCSL)

Prosecutor v. Fofana and Kondewa, Judgment, SCSL-04-14-J (2007).
Prosecutor v. Gbao, Decision on Preliminary Motion on the Invalidity of the Agreement between the United Nations and the Government of Sierra Leone on the Establishment of the Special Court for Sierra Leone, SCSL-04-15-PT-141 (2004).
Prosecutor v. Kallon and Kamara, Decision on Challenge to Jurisdiction: Lomé Accord Amnesty, SCSL-04-15-PT-060-I (2004).
Prosecutor v. Kondewa, Decision on Lack of Jurisdiction/Abuse of Process, Amnesty Provided by the Lomé Accord, SCSL-04-14-T-128-7347 (2004).
Prosecutor v. Sesay et al., Judgment, SCSL-04-15-T (2009).
Prosecutor v. Norman et al., Judgment, SCSL-04-14-T (2007).
Prosecutor v. Taylor, Decision on Immunity from Jurisdiction, No. SCSL-03-01-I-059 (2004).
Prosecutor v. Taylor, Judgment, SCSL-03-01-T-1283 (2012).

Special Tribunal for Lebanon (STL)

Prosecutor v. Ayyash et al., No. STL-11-01/I/AC/R17bis, Interlocutory Decision on the Applicable Law: Terrorism, Conspiracy, Homicide, Perpetration, Cumulative Charging, 145 ILR 232 (2011).

Decisions of regional courts

African Commission of Human and Peoples' Rights (ACHPR)

Modise v. Botswana, Comm. No. 97/93, 2000 AHRLR 25 (1996).

African Court of Human and Peoples' Rights (ACtPHR)

African Commission on Human and Peoples' Rights v. Great Socialist People's Libyan Arab Jamahiriya, Order for Provisional Measures, Application No. 004/2011 (2011).

European Court of Human Rights (ECtHR)

A. v. United Kingdom, No. 25599/94 (1998).
Ahmed v. Austria, No. 25964/94 (1996).
Al-Adsani v. United Kingdom, No. 35763/97 (2001).
Chahal v. United Kingdom, No. 22414/93 (1996).
Demir and Baykara v. Turkey, No. 34503/97 (2008).
Jones v. United Kingdom, Nos. 34356/06 & 40528/06 (2014).
Kalogeropoulou and Others v. Greece and Germany, No. 59021/00 (2002).
Othman v. United Kingdom, No. 8139/09 (2012).
Ould Dah v. France, No. 13113/03 (2009).
Soering v. United Kingdom, No. 14038/88 (1989).
S.W. v. United Kingdom / C.R. v. United Kingdom, Nos. 20166/92 & 20190/92 (1995).
Z. and Others v. United Kingdom, No. 29392/95 (2001).

European Court of Justice (ECJ)

Kadi et al. v. Council of the European Union et al., C-402/05 P / C-415/05 P, [2008] ECR I-6351 (2008).
Omega Spielhallen-und Automatenaufstellungs-GmbH v. Oberbürgermeisterin der Bundesstadt Bonn, C-36/02, [2004] ECR I-9609 (2004).

Inter-American Commission of Human Rights (IACHR)

Thomas v. United States, Case 12.240, Report No. 100/03 (2003).
Roach and Jay Pinkerton v. United States, Case 9647, Res. 3/87 (1987).
Domingues v. United States, Case 12.285, Report No. 62/02 (2002).
Romero y Galdámez v. El Salvador, Case 11.481, Report No. 37/00 (1999).

Inter-American Court of Human Rights (IACtHR)

Almonacid Arellano et al. v. Chile, Judgment, Series C No. 154 (2006).
Aloeboetoe et al. v. Suriname, Judgment, Series C No. 15 (1993).
Baldeón García v. Peru, Judgment, Series C No. 147 (2006).
Barrios Altos Case, Judgment, Series C No. 75 (2001).
Bayarri v. Argentina, Judgment, Series C No. 187 (2008).
Brothers Gomez Paquiyauri v. Peru, Judgment, Series C No. 110 (2004).
Bueno Alves v. Argentina, Judgment, Series C No. 164 (2007).
Ceaser v. Trinidad and Tobago, Judgment, Series C No. 123 (2005).
Gelman v. Uruguay, Judgment, Series C No. 221 (2011).
Gomes-Lund et al. (Guerrilha do Araguaia) v. Brazil, Judgment, Series C No. 219 (2010).

The Juridical Condition and the Rights of Undocumented Migrants, Advisory Opinion, OC-18/03, Series A No. 18 (2003).
La Cantuta v. Peru, Judgment, Series C No. 162 (2006).
Miguel Castro-Castro Prison v. Peru, Judgment, Series C No. 160 (2006).
Ramírez v. Guatemala, Judgment, Series C No. 126 (2005).
Servellón García and ors v. Honduras, Judgment, Series C No. 152 (2006).
Tibi v. Ecuador, Judgment, Series C No. 114 (2004).
Velásquez-Rodríguez v. Honduras, Judgment, Series C No. 4 (1988).
Ximenes-Lopes v. Brazil, Judgment, Series C No. 149 (2006).
Yatama v. Nicaragua, Judgment, Series C No. 127 (2005).

National court decisions

Argentina

Chile v. Arancibia Clavel, Supreme Court of Justice (Argentina), A/533/XXXVIII, ILDC 1082 (2004).
Office of the Prosecutor v. Priebke, Supreme Court of Justice (Argentina), P/457/XXXI, ILDC 1599 (1995).
Riveros v. Office of the Public Prosecutor, Supreme Court of Justice (Argentina), M/2333/XLII, ILDC 1084 (2007).
Simón v. Office of the Public Prosecutor, Supreme Court of Justice (Argentina), S/1767/XXXVIII, ILDC 579 (2005).
Washington Cabrera J. E. c. Comisión Técnica Mixta de Salto Grande, Supreme Court of Justice (Argentina), Fallas 1993-305-2150 (1983).

Australia

Habib v. Australia, Federal Court of Australia, [2010] FCAFC 12, ILDC 1518 (2010).
Nulyarimma and Others v. Thompson / Buzzacott v. Minister for the Environment and Others, Federal Court of Australia, [1999] FCA 1192, 120 ILR 353 (1999).
R. v. Tang, High Court of Australia, [2008] HCA 39 (2008).
Zhang v. Zemin, New South Wales Court of Appeal (Australia), [2010] NSWCA 255 (2010).

Austria

A.A. v. Austria, Supreme Court (Austria), No. 1Ob225/07f (2008).
Anita W. v. John Adam II (Prince of Liechtenstein), Supreme Court (Austria), No. 7Ob316/00x, ILDC 1 (2001).
Decision No. 11Os139/98, Supreme Court (Austria) (1998).

Belgium

Jugoslovenski Aerotransport v. Belgium, Court of Appeal (Bruxelles) (Belgium), No. 1998/KR/528 (1999).

R.D. v. Belgium, Court of Cassation (Belgium), No. P.04.1211.N, JT 2005, 322, ILDC 6 (2004).

Re Sharon and Yaron, Court of Cassation (Belgium), No. P.02.1139.F/2, JT 2003, 243, ILDC 5 (2003); Court of Appeal (Bruxelles), 127 ILR 110 (2002).

Société Anonyme des Chemins de Fer Liégeois-Luxembourgeois v. The Netherlands, Supreme Court (Belgium), Pasicrisie Belge, I, p. 294 (1903).

Bosnia and Herzegovina

Prosecutor's Office v. Anić, Court of Bosnia and Herzegovina (Section I for War Crimes), S1 1 K 005596 11 Kro, ILDC 1907 (2011).

Canada

Bouzari v. Islamic Republic of Iran, Court of Appeal for Ontario (Canada), 71 OR (3d) 675 (2004).

R. v. Finta, Supreme Court (Canada), [1994] 1 SCR 701 (1994).

R. v. Munyaneza, Montreal Superior Court (Criminal Division) (Canada), [2009] QCCS 2201 (2009).

Suresh v. Canada (Minister of Citizenship and Immigration), Supreme Court (Canada), [2002] 1 SCR 3 (2002).

Victoria (City) v. Adams, Supreme Court of British Columbia (Canada), [2008] BCSC 1363 (2008).

Zrig v. Canada (Minister of Citizenship and Immigration), Federal Court of Appeal (Canada), [2003] FCA 178, [2003] 3 F.C. 761 (2003).

Chile

Peru v. Chile, Supreme Court (Chile), No. 2242-06, ILDC 1443 (2007).

Re Víctor Raúl Pinto v. Relatives of Tomás Rojas, Supreme Court (Chile), Decision on Annulment, No. 3125-04, ILDC 1093 (2007).

Colombia

Constitutional Case No. C-225/95, Constitutional Court (Colombia), No. C-225/95 (1995).

Gallón Giraldo y Otros v. Colombia, Constitutional Court (Colombia), No. C-370/2006, ILDC 660 (2006).

Review of the Constitutionality of the Rome Statute of the International Criminal Court, Constitutional Court (Colombia), No. C-578/2002 (2002).

Segovia Massacre Case, Supreme Court of Justice (Colombia), No. 156 (2010) (*reproduced in Gomes-Lund et al. (Guerrilha do Araguaia) v. Brazil*, IACtHR Series C No. 219 (2010)).

Czech Republic

Novotný v. Ministry of Justice, Constitutional Court of the Czech Republic, No. I ÚS 601/04, ILDC 990 (2007).

France

AFP and PLO v. Alstom and Veolia, Versailles Court of Appeal (France), No. 11-05331, 52 ILM 1161 (2013).

Bucheron v. Germany, Court of Cassation (France), No. 02-45961, Bull. Civ., 2003, I, No. 258 (2003).

Ely Ould Dah Case, Gard Assizes Court (France), No. 70/05 (Arrêt de condamnation) / No. 71/05 (Arrêt statuant sur les intérêts civils) (2005).

Gaddafi Case, Paris Court of Appeal (*Chambre d'accusation*) (France), RGDIP 1999, p. 464 (2000), Court of Cassation (Criminal Chamber), RGDIP 2001, p. 473 (2001), 152 ILR 490.

Lydienne X v. Prosecutor, Court of Cassation (Criminal Chamber) (France), No. 12-81676, ILDC 2035 (2013).

Réunion Aérienne v. Socialist People's Libyan Arab Jamahiriya, Court of Cassation (Civil Chamber I) (France), No. 09-14743, 150 ILR 630 (2011).

Rwanda Genocide Case, Court of Cassation (Criminal Division) (France), No. 96-82491 (1998).

Spanish Government v. Lambege et Pujol, Court of Cassation (France), D. 1849 1 (1849).

Germany

Attorney of the Federal Armed Forces v. Anonymous (a Major of the Armed Forces), Federal Administrative Court (Germany), 2 WD 12:04, ILDC 483 (2005).

East German Expropriation Case, Mr von der M, BVerfG [Constitutional Court] (Germany), 2 BvR 955/00, ILDC 66 (2004).

Former Syrian Ambassador to the German Democratic Republic, BVerfG [Constitutional Court] (Germany), 2 BvR 1516/96, 115 ILR 596 (1997).

Jorgic Case, BVerfG [Constitutional Court] (Germany), 2 BvR 1290/99, ILDC 132 (2000).

Proceedings on the Constitutionality of §211 of the Criminal Code (Life Imprisonment Case), BVerfG [Constitutional Court] (Germany), 45 BVerfGE 187 (1977).

Greece

Margellos and Others v. Federal Republic of Germany, Special Supreme Court (*Anotato Eidiko Dikastirio*) (Greece), No. 6/2002, 129 ILR 525 (2007).

Prefecture of Voiotia v. Federal Republic of Germany (Distomo Massacre Case), Court of Cassation (*Areios Pagos*) (Greece), No. 11/2000, 129 ILR 513 (2000).

Guatemala

Guatemala Genocide Case, Constitutional Court (Guatemala), No. 3380-2007 (2007).

Hong Kong (China)

C v. Director of Immigration, Court of First Instance (Hong Kong), HCAL 132/2006, [2008] 2 HKC 165, ILDC 1119 (2008).

C, KMF and BF v. Director of Immigration and Secretary for Security, Court of Final Instance (Hong Kong), FACV Nos. 18/19/20 2011 (2013).

Israel

Attorney-General (Israel) v. Eichmann, Supreme Court (Israel), 36 ILR 5 (1962).

Italy

Ferrini v. Germany, Court of Cassation (Civil Section) (Italy), No. 5044/2004, ILDC 19 (2004).

Frascà v. Germany and Giachini (Guardian of Priebke) and Italy (joining), Court of Cassation (Italy), No. 4284/2013, ILDC 1998 (2013).

Germany v. De Guglielmi et al., Court of Appeal (Italy), No. 941/2012, ILDC 1905 (2012).

Germany v. Mantelli and ors, Court of Cassation (Italy), No. 14201/2008, ILDC 1037 (2008).

Germany v. Milde, Court of Cassation (First Criminal Section) (Italy), No. 1072/2009, ILDC 1224 (2009).

Italy v. Abdelaziz and ors, Court of Cassation (First Criminal Section) (Italy), No. 1072, ILDC 559 (2007).

Lozano v. Italy, Court of Cassation (First Criminal Section) (Italy), No. 31171/2008, ILDC 1085 (2008).

Military Prosecutor v. Albers, Court of Cassation (First Criminal Section) (Italy), No. 32139/2012, ILDC 1921 (2012).

Kenya

Kenya v. Aid Mohamed Ahmed et al., Chief Magistrate Court (Kenya), CR 3486/2008 (2008).

Kenya Section of the International Commission of Jurists v. Attorney General et al., High Court (Kenya), [2011] eKLR, ILDC 1804 (2011).

R.M. v. Attorney General, High Court (Kenya), Civil Case 1351, AHRLR 256 (KeHC 2006), ILDC 699 (2006).

R. v. Abdirahnam Isse Mohamud et al., High Court (Kenya), CR 72/2011 (2011).

Latvia

Kariņš and ors v. Parliament of Latvia and Cabinet of Ministers of Latvia (Border Treaty), Constitutional Court (Latvia), No. 2007–10–0102, ILDC 884 (2007).

Mexico

Decision on the Extradition of Ricardo Miguel Cavallo, Supreme Court (Mexico), No. 712/2003, 42 ILM 888 (2003).

Namibia

Minister of Defence v. Mwandinghi, High Court (Namibia), 1991 (1) SA 851 (Nm), 91 ILR 343 (1990), *affirmed by* Supreme Court (Namibia), 1992 (2) SA 355 (NmS), 91 ILR 35 (1991).

The Netherlands

Association of Lawyers for Peace (Vereniging van Juristen voor de Vrede) and ors v. Netherlands, Supreme Court (Netherlands), LJN: AN8071, ILDC 152 (2004).

Bouterse Case, Amsterdam Court of Appeal (Netherlands), Nos. R 97/163/12 Sv & R 97/176/12 Sv (2000), *abrogated on other grounds by Bouterse Case*, Supreme Court (Netherlands), LJN: AB1471, ILDC 80 (2001).

Samanyolu Case, Rotterdam District Court (Netherlands), CR 10/600012-09 (2010).

Stichting Mothers of Srebrenica and ors v. Netherlands and United Nations, Supreme Court (Netherlands), LJN: BW1999, ILDC 1760 (2012).

New Zealand

Attorney General v. Ahmed Zaoui and ors, Supreme Court (New Zealand), SC CIV 19/2004, [2005] NZSC 38, ILDC 81 (2005).

Fang v. Jiang, High Court (New Zealand), CIV 2004-404-5843, [2007] NZAR 420, ILDC 1226 (2006).

Mansouri-Rad v. Department of Labour, Refugee Status Appeals Authority (New Zealand), No. 74665/03, [2005] NZAR 60, ILDC 217 (2005).

Peru

Case of Santiago Martín Rivas, Supreme Court (Constitutional and Social Chamber) (Peru), No. 679-2005-PA/TC, ILDC 960 (2007).

Fujimori Case, Supreme Court (Specialized Criminal Law Chamber) (Peru), No. 19-2001 AV, ILDC 1516 (2009).

Rivera Lazo and ors, Superior Court (Third Criminal Chamber) (Peru), No. 28-2001, ILDC 1887 (2010).

The Philippines

Muna et al. v. Romulo et al., Supreme Court (Philippines), GR No. 159618, ILDC 2059 (2011).

Poland

Natoniewski v. Germany, Supreme Court (Poland), No. IV CSK 465/09, 2010 POLISH YEARBOOK OF INTERNATIONAL LAW 299, ILDC 1996 (2010).

Russia

H. v. Prosecutor General Office, Supreme Court (Russia), N KAS06-129, ILDC 1361 (2006).

Seychelles

R. v. Mohamed Ahmed Dahir & Ten (10) Others, Supreme Court of Seychelles, CR 51/2009 (2010).

Slovenia

A.A. v. Germany, Constitutional Court (Slovenia), Up-13/99-24 (2001).

Arbitration Agreement Opinion Procedure, Constitutional Court (Slovenia), Rm-1/09-26, ILDC 1485 (2010).

One Third of the National Assembly Deputies, Constitutional Court (Slovenia), Rm-1/00-29, ILDC 402 (2001).

South Africa

Azanian Peoples Organization ('AZAPO') and ors v. President of South Africa and ors, Constitutional Court (South Africa), No. CCT 17/96, 1996 (4) SA 671 (CC), ILDC 648 (1996).

Azanian Peoples Organization and ors v. Truth and Reconciliation Commission and ors, Cape Provincial Division of the Supreme Court (South Africa), 1996 (4) SA 562 (C) (1996).

Kaunda v. President of South Africa and ors, Constitutional Court (South Africa), No. CCT 23/04, 2005 (4) SA 235 (CC), ILDC 89 (2004).

Mthembu v. State, Supreme Court of Appeal (South Africa), No. 379/07, (2008) ZASCA 51, ILDC 958 (2008).

The State v. Walter Basson, Constitutional Court (South Africa), No. CCT 30/03, 2005 (1) SA 171 (CC) (2004).

Van Zyl and ors v. Government of South Africa and ors, North Gauteng High Court (South Africa), No. 20320/02, [2005] ZAGPHC 70, ILDC 171 (2005).

South Korea

Yeo and ors v. Nippon Steel & Sumitomo Metal, High Court (South Korea), 2012 Na 44947, ILDC 2104 (2013).

Spain

Criminal Law Chamber of the Supreme Court et al. v. Garzón Real, Supreme Court (Spain), No. 101/2012, ILDC 1855 (2012).

Decision (Auto) of the Full Penal Chamber Confirming Spanish Jurisdiction to Investigate Crimes of Genocide and Terrorism Committed during the Chilean Dictatorship, National Court (*Audiencia Nacional*) (Spain), No. 173/98, 119 ILR 331 (1998).

Decision (Auto) of the Full Penal Chamber Confirming Spanish Jurisdiction over the Crimes of Genocide and Terrorism committed during the Argentine Dictatorship, National Court (*Audiencia Nacional*) (Spain), No. 84/98 (1998).

Guatemala Genocide Case (Menchú Tumn and ors v. Two Guatemalan Government Officials and Six Members of the Guatemalan Military), Constitutional Court (Criminal Chamber) (Spain), No. 237/2005, ILDC 137 (2005).

Guatemala Genocide Case (Menchú Tumn and ors v. Two Guatemalan Government Officials and Six Members of the Guatemalan Military), Constitutional Court (Criminal Chamber) (Spain), No. 327/2003, 42 ILM 686 (2003).

Public Prosecutor's Office and ors v. Scilingo Manzorro, National Court (*Audiencia Nacional*) (Criminal Chamber) (Spain), No. 16/2005, ILDC 136 (2005).

Sánchez and ors v. Gibson and ors, Supreme Court (Spain), No. 1240/2006, ILDC 993 (2006).

Scilingo Manzorro v. Spain, Supreme Court (Spain), No. 798/2007, ILDC 1430 (2007).

Switzerland

A. v. Federal Department of Economic Affairs, Federal Supreme Court (Switzerland), No. 2A 783/2006, ILDC 1200 (2008).

A. (Kahled Nezzar) v. Office of the Attorney General, Federal Criminal Court (Switzerland), No. BB.2011.140 (2012).

A. v. State Secretariat for Economic Affairs and Federal Department of Economic Affairs, First Public Law Chamber (Switzerland), No. 1A 48/2007, ILDC 1201 (2008).

Nada v. State Secretariat for Economic Affairs and Federal Department of Economic Affairs, Federal Supreme Court (Switzerland), No. 1A 45/2007, ILDC 461 (2007).

United Kingdom

A. and Others v. Secretary of State for the Home Department (No. 2), House of Lords (UK), [2005] UKHL 71 (2005).

Campaign for Nuclear Disarmament v. Prime Minister of the United Kingdom and ors, High Court of Justice (UK), [2002] EWHC 2777 (Admin.) (2002).

Jones v. Ministry of the Interior of Saudi Arabia and Lieutenant Colonel Abdul Aziz, House of Lords (UK), [2006] UKHL 26 (2006).

K. v. Secretary of State for the Home Department, House of Lords (UK), [2006] UKHL 46 (2006).

Kuwait Airways Corporation v. Iraqi Airways Company, House of Lords (UK), [2002] UKHL 19 (2002).

R. v. Bow Street Metropolitan Stipendiary Magistrate and Others, Ex parte Pinochet Ugarte (No. 3), House of Lords (UK), [2000] 1 A.C. 147, 38 ILM 581 (1999).

R. v. Gul, [2012] EWCA Crim 280, 152 ILR 568 (2012).

R. (on the application of Al-Jedda) v. Secretary of State for Defence, House of Lords (UK), [2007] UKHL 58 (2007).

R. (on the application of Al Rawi and ors) v. Secretary of State for Foreign and Commonwealth Affairs et al., Court of Appeal (UK), [2006] EWCA Civ 1279 (2006).

R. (on the application of Al-Skeini and ors) v. Secretary of State for Defence, High Court of Justice (UK), [2004] EWHC 2911 (Admin.) (2004).

R. (on the application of European Roma Rights Centre) v. Immigration Officer at Prague Airport, House of Lords (UK), [2004] UKHL 55 (2004).

R. (on the application of Hilal Abdul-Razzaq Ali Al-Jedda) v. Secretary of State for Defence, Court of Appeal (UK), [2006] EWCA Civ 327 (2006).

United States

Abelesz v. Magyar Nemzeti Bank, 692 F.3d 661 (7th Cir. 2012).
Adamu v. Pfizer, Inc., 399 F. Supp. 2d 495 (SDNY 2005) *rev'd and remanded sub nom. Abdullahi v. Pfizer, Inc.*, 562 F.3d 163 (2d Cir. 2009).
Adhikari v. Daoud & Partners, 697 F. Supp. 2d 674 (SD Tex. 2009).
Al–Bihani v. Obama, 619 F.3d 1 (DC Cir. 2010).
Almog v. Arab Bank, PLC, 471 F. Supp. 2d 257 (EDNY 2007).
Alvarez-Machain v. United States, 331 F.3d 604 (9th Cir. 2003) *rev'd sub nom. Sosa v. Alvarez-Machain*, 542 U.S. 692 (2004) and *vacated*, 374 F.3d 1384 (9th Cir. 2004).
Argentine Republic v. Amerada Hess Shipping Corp., 488 US 428 (1989).
Ashcroft v. Iqbal, 556 US 662 (2009).
Beanal v. Freeport-McMoran, Inc., 197 F.3d 161 (5th Cir. 1999).
Belhas v. Ya'alon, 515 F.3d 1279 (DC Cir. 2008).
Bell Atlantic Corp. v. Twombly, 550 US 544 (2007).
Benas v. Baca, No. CV-00-11507 LGB (SHX), 2001 WL 485168 (CD Cal. 2001) *aff'd*, 30 F. App'x 753 (9th Cir. 2002).
Bivens v. Six Unknown Named Agents of the Federal Bureau of Narcotics, 403 US 388 (1971).
Buell v. Mitchell, 274 F.3d 337 (6th Cir. 2001).
Chuidian v. Philippine National Bank, 912 F.2d 1095 (9th Cir. 1990).
Committee of US Citizens Living in Nicaragua v. Reagan, 859 F.2d 929 (DC Cir. 1988).
Doe v. Saravia, 348 F. Supp. 2d 1112 (ED Cal. 2004).
Doe v. Qi, 349 F. Supp. 2d 1258 (ND Cal. 2004).
Doe I v. State of Israel, 400 F. Supp. 2d 86 (DDC 2005).
Doe I v. Unocal Corp., 395 F.3d 932 (9th Cir. 2002) *on reh'g en banc sub nom. John Doe I v. Unocal Corp.*, 403 F.3d 708 (9th Cir. 2005).
Ewing v. California, 538 US 11 (2003)
Filártiga v. Peña-Irala, 630 F.2d 876 (2nd Cir. 1980).
Flatow v. Islamic Republic of Iran, 999 F. Supp. 1 (DDC 1998).
Habyarimana v. Kagame, 696 F.3d 1029 (10th Cir. 2012) *cert. denied*, 133 S. Ct. 1607 (US 2013).
Hain v. Gibson, 287 F.3d 1224 (10th Cir. 2002).
Hawkins v. Comparet-Cassani, 33 F. Supp. 2d 1244 (CD Cal. 1999) *rev'd in part*, 251 F.3d 1230 (9th Cir. 2001).
Hilton v. Guyot, 159 US 113 (1895).
In re Doe, 860 F.2d 40 (2nd Cir. 1988).
In re Estate of Ferdinand Marcos, Human Rights Litigation, 25 F.3d 1467 (9th Cir. 1994).
*In re Estate of Ferdinand E. Marcos Human Rights Litig*ation, 978 F.2d 493 (9th Cir. 1992).
In re Islamic Republic of Iran Terrorism Litigation, 659 F. Supp. 2d 31 (DDC 2009).

In re South African Apartheid Litigation, 617 F. Supp. 2d 228 (SDNY 2009).

Institute of Cetacean Research v. Sea Shepherd Conservation Society, 725 F.3d 940 (9th Cir. 2013).

Kadic v. Karadžić, 70 F.3d 232 (2nd Cir. 1995).

Kiobel v. Royal Dutch Petroleum Co., 133 S. Ct. 1659 (2013).

Kiobel v. Royal Dutch Petroleum Co., 621 F.3d 111 (2nd Cir. 2010) *aff'd*, 133 S. Ct. 1659 (US 2013).

Lafontant v. Aristide, 844 F.Supp. 128 (EDNY 1994).

Manoharan v. Rajapaksa, 845 F. Supp. 2d 260 (DDC 2012) *aff'd*, 711 F.3d 178 (DC Cir. 2013).

Matar v. Dichter, 563 F.3d 6 (2nd Cir. 2009).

Mehinovic v. Vuckovic, 198 F. Supp. 2d 1322 (ND Ga. 2002).

The Paquete Habana, 175 US 677 (1900).

Princz v. Federal Republic of Germany, 26 F.3d 1166 (DC Cir. 1994).

Samantar v. Yousuf, 560 US 305 (2010).

Sampson v. Federal Republic of Germany, 250 F.3d 1145 (7th Cir. 2001).

Sandhu v. Burke, No. 97 CIV. 4608 (JGK), 2000 WL 191707 (SDNY 2000).

Sarei v. Rio Tinto, PLC, 487 F.3d 1193 (9th Cir. 2007) *on reh'g en banc*, 550 F.3d 822 (9th Cir. 2008).

Sarei v. Rio Tinto, PLC, 671 F.3d 736 (9th Cir. 2011) *cert. granted, judgment vacated sub nom. Rio Tinto PLC v. Sarei*, 133 S. Ct. 1995 (2013).

Schooner Exchange v. McFaddon, 11 US 116 (1812).

Siderman de Blake v. Argentina, 965 F 2d 699 (9th Cir. 1992).

Smith v. Libya, 101 F.3d 239 (2nd Cir. 1996).

Sosa v. Alvarez-Machain, 542 US 692 (2004).

Tachiona v. Mugabe, 169 F. Supp. 2d 259 (SDNY 2001) *aff'd in part, rev'd in part* and *remanded sub nom. Tachiona v. United States*, 386 F.3d 205 (2nd Cir. 2004).

Taveras v. Taveraz, 477 F.3d 767 (6th Cir. 2007).

Tel-Oren v. Libyan Arab Republic, 726 F.2d 774 (DC Cir. 1984).

Trials of Major Bonnet and others for Piracy, 5 George I (1718), *in* 15 A Complete Collection of State Trials and Proceedings for High Treason and Other Crimes and Misdemeanors from the Earliest Period to the Year 1783 (London: T. C. Hansard, Thomas Howell ed., 1819).

Underhill v. Hernandez, 168 US 250 (1897).

United States v. Dire, 680 F.3d 446 (4th Cir. 2012) *cert. denied*, 133 S. Ct. 982 (2013).

United States v. Hasan, 747 F. Supp. 2d 599 (ED Va. 2010) *aff'd sub nom. United States v. Dire*, 680 F.3d 446 (4th Cir. 2012).

United States v. The La Jeune Eugenie, 26 F. Cas. 832 (CCD Mass. 1822).

United States v. Robins, 27 F. Cas. 825 (DSC 1799).

United States v. Smith, 18 US 153 (1820).

United States v. Yunis, 924 F.2d 1086 (DC Cir. 1991).

White v. Paulsen, 997 F. Supp. 1380 (ED Wash. 1998).

Xuncax v. Gramajo, 886 F. Supp. 162 (D. Mass. 1995).
Ye v. Zemin, 383 F.3d 620 (7th Cir. 2004).
Yousuf v. Samantar, 699 F.3d 763 (4th Cir. 2012) *cert. denied*, 134 S. Ct. 897 (US 2014).

Uruguay

Case of de Nibia Sabalsagaray Curutchet, Supreme Court of Justice (Uruguay), No. 365/09 (2009).

Zimbabwe

Mann v. Republic of Equatorial Guinea, High Court (Zimbabwe), No. CA 507/07, [2008] ZWHHC 1, 153 ILR 697 (2008).

INTRODUCTION

> The concept of *jus cogens* had existed in international law for a long time, even if in inchoate form. There were, however, profound differences of opinion as to the reasons for its existence and the foundations on which it rested; some based it on positive law, others on natural law, while yet others attributed to it a higher or even divine origin. But on one point there was general agreement – namely, that the concept of *jus cogens* expressed some higher social need. In principle, all legal rules were equal; the very concept of *jus cogens*, therefore, was a derogation from a fundamental legal principle. Ultimately, it was more society and less the law itself which defined the content of *jus cogens*.
>
> –Excerpt from the 685th Meeting of the International Law Commission[1]

What does it mean for acts to be universally condemned as offensive to the conscience of mankind? To issue global arrest warrants for atrocities carried out against a civilian population? Or for the international community to use force to suppress violations of basic human dignity within the borders of a recalcitrant State? Such actions, increasingly commonplace in contemporary international relations, are expressions of the twin developments of a common morality of the international community and its realization through a universal legal framework. These developments are part and parcel of a regime of international *ordre public* that has crystallized since the middle of the twentieth century, conceived in the wake of the two world wars and increasingly deployed since the end of the Cold War. This public order is evocative of a particular conceptualization of the international community that recasts the way in which sovereignty functions in international law and politics.

The *ordre public* of international order has evolved through the corpus of peremptory norms of general international law (*jus cogens*). A peremptory norm is 'accepted and recognized by the international

[1] [1963] I YbILC 73, para. 4 (685th Meeting, statement by Mr Rosenne).

community of States as a whole as a norm from which no derogation is permitted'. The legal category of *jus cogens* (compelling law) was codified with the intent of establishing a public order in international law by explicitly incorporating considerations of morality into norms that cannot be modified by the conventional sources of international law. The inviolable status of a peremptory norm is a feature of the subject matter of the rule, rather than the legislative process through which it was codified, and is therefore intrinsic to the norm itself. From peremptory norms arise obligations *erga omnes* (against all), duties of enforcement that extend to all States a general legal interest in their fulfilment. Claims are increasingly voiced in support of a nascent *actio popularis* (popular action) affording States the authority to respond to violations of peremptory norms. Violations of peremptory norms are classified as international crimes that give rise to individual criminal responsibility, and the extension of sovereign immunity to shield such conduct from prosecution has waned. Universal jurisdiction extends to all States the legal capacity to prosecute such violations pursuant to a duty *aut dedere aut judicare* (extradite or prosecute).

Of course, all of this represents a marked contrast to the distinctly Statist tradition of international legal order that has defined the post-Westphalian world since Vattel. After 1648, sovereignty endowed the State with an almost metaphysical quality through which it became a discrete, inviolable political entity in both its internal and its external affairs. The international legal system personified States as legal persons, sovereign individuals among purported equals, in a global arena shaped by the dynamics of power politics. It is against this backdrop that the legal philosophy of positivism adopted the law of nations, transforming an order formerly rooted in natural law into the exclusive domain of the sovereign State. Because international law came to be recognized as the product of the explicit consent of the State and a manifestation of its interests, it followed that international legal obligation could be undertaken only by the will of the State. This conceptualization dominated the discourse of international law until 1945 and has since endured as the traditional approach to international law.

In some ways, the post-1945 international public order can be cast as an admonishment of the Westphalian system, a refutation of its political philosophy and rejection of its legal structures. Violations of State sovereignty, where necessitated by the dictates of humanity, have been authorized time and again by the governance organs of the international community. This runs against the Statist rejoinder that subjugation to international obligations under universal humanitarian law violates the principle that the State cannot be legally compelled against its sovereign will: that intervention, even in cases of grave humanitarian crisis, is simultaneously a contravention of sovereignty, a breach of the principle of non-intervention, and a violation of fundamental legal norms prohibiting the use of force. On the contrary a precedent has emerged according to which State sovereignty is contingent upon respect for fundamental norms of good governance, alongside the expectation that grave violations of basic principles of humanity will be met with an international response. This premise is reflected in the 'responsibility to protect', a principle that has gained currency at the United Nations over the past decade as a safeguard against mass atrocities. The peremptory norms driving this evolution confer protections directly upon the individual, and in principle, accountability for their violation can be enforced against whomever perpetrates them, wherever they occur. Recognition of the individual as the recipient of rights and duties is a departure from an international legal philosophy that admits the State as the sole subject of law. State sovereignty, the fundamental ordering principle of the Westphalian system, can no longer be considered in isolation from the rule of law and basic considerations of humanity.

To be sure, international law fundamentally remains a legal system emanating from States, notwithstanding the stark contrast between the post-Westphalian and post-world war legal orders. The goal of this book is to reconcile the development of public order norms of *jus cogens* with the traditionally State-based structure of international law. It will demonstrate that contemporary developments in international law are consistent with a positivist legal framework, a proposition that requires a critical view of the concept of *jus cogens* to understand the way in which peremptory norms develop and operate through the international community.

Resolution of this tension resides in a Liberal approach to international law and politics. The task reflects normative individualism, a deontological, individual-oriented perspective that maintains the fundamental purpose of all law to be the good of the human being. It also appeals to the school of international constitutionalism, which recognizes core values common to the international community, admits basic rights and duties that bind the State beyond the traditional requirement of consent, and embraces extra-State legal interests and mechanisms. Finally, a Liberal approach conceives of international public order as an expression of cosmopolitanism, a progressive political theory that refers to the most basic and fundamental rights, moral in origin yet legal in nature, which transcend the boundaries of the State and accrue to the individual directly. According to this approach to international law, the State is best understood as an instrument for the fulfilment of individual wellbeing, a premise that casts sovereignty in a sense of basic responsibility rather than absolute unaccountability.

The proposition highlighted by this Liberal approach is that values matter in international law. This position illuminates the key distinction between the international law preceding the Second World War and a contemporary international legal order, and links the present epoch of international law with the classical tradition of the law of nations. While such an acknowledgment requires moving beyond a strictly positivist approach to international law and politics, it in no way amounts to a rejection of positivism. Instead, considerations of morality have been authoritatively incorporated into positive international law as peremptory norms of general international law. These fundamental norms are very much in force as positive law and have been reaffirmed on a regular basis: for example, in international condemnation of atrocities committed against the dignity of human beings in times of peace and war; in global non-recognition of the effects of aggression, discrimination, and violence against civilians; in multilateral responses by the international community to prevent and suppress widespread violations of humanitarian norms; and by the prosecution of individuals before international criminal courts and tribunals. While it is clear that a normative branch of peremptory international law is recognized, accepted, and implemented by the international community, what is far from obvious is how these public order norms are formed or how they delineate legal subjects and objects.

These legal issues confronting *jus cogens* are inexorably connected with political questions of the most basic kind. While peremptory norms serve the common interests of the international community of States as a whole, interests in some way oriented in basic considerations of humanity, what remains to be explained is precisely how these considerations are expressed as positive law. Peremptory norms, as a product of the socialization of the post-war era, do not conform to the dynamics of State voluntarism that characterize conventional international law. One way of elucidating such a public order is through the idea of the social contract, a political theory that for centuries has been employed to provide a narrative for the social origin of fundamental political and legal structures. The appropriateness of the social contract underlies one early interpretation of *jus cogens* during its incorporation into international law by the International Law Commission:

> [M]embership of a community required the respect of certain rules. If that were not so, society would remain in the condition of savagery described by the phrase *homo homini lupus*, which had lasted until the First World War and had prevailed almost unchallenged in the inter-war period. By becoming members of the international society, States recognized the existence of a minimum international order, which was none other than *jus cogens*.[2]

The social contract is a theoretical construct that explains governance structures as the product of the recognition of common rules, with correlative duties, to protect the most basic common interests of a community.

In the context of *jus cogens*, the idea of a social contract offers a compelling narrative of the confluence of an individual-oriented normative structure, a State-based legal order, and values common to the international community as a whole. Classical contractarianism is designed to provide an explanation of the legitimacy of political authority by accounting for the existence of civil society in terms of the interests of the individual. It invokes the social contract as a device through which elemental rights and duties are established in order to maximize individual wellbeing in the context of social coexistence. Consequently, the social contract can be implemented to cognize the interplay of sources, authority, content, and enforcement of the public order norms of civil society. It should be noted, explicitly at the outset, that it is the relevant aspects of law under consideration, and not the social contract itself, that bear the conceptual weight of the issues in question. It is to this end that contractarianism is employed as an ordering framework for this book: to guide an examination of particular legal aspects of public order norms that, in turn, expresses a political vision that reconciles the development of an individual-oriented *jus cogens* within a State-based international legal order.

[2] [1966] I(1) YbILC 39, para. 40 (828th Meeting, statement by Mr Bartoš). *See* [1963] I YbILC 76, para. 33 (685th Meeting, statement by Mr Bartoš) ('the international public order was merely the superstructure of the international community which resulted from the evolution of international society. It was the minimum of rules of conduct necessary to make orderly international relations possible').

OVERVIEW

The jurisprudence of *jus cogens* reveals a range of unresolved substantive and systemic issues. A contractarian assessment of these issues – applying elements of the social contract to frame an examination of *jus cogens* – orients *jus cogens* in the familiar discourse of the social contract. Ultimately, probing these discontents of *jus cogens* makes it possible to conceive of peremptory norms with greater lucidity and, in turn, forge a better understanding of international public order.

The first part of this book, Peremptory Norms of General International Law (*Jus Cogens*), presents the core concepts that will be relied upon throughout the analysis. Chapter 1 introduces peremptory norms of general international law (*jus cogens*), obligations *erga omnes*, and international responsibility, which are elements of international law necessary to understand the operation of peremptory norms. Next, Chapter 2 discusses the theory of social contract and how the idea serves as an ordering framework for the present analysis by drawing attention to four principal areas of *jus cogens*: authority, sources, content, and enforcement.

Part II of this book, The Authority of *Jus Cogens*, negotiates philosophical principle and legal practice to develop an explanation of the authority of peremptory norms of international law. Chapter 3 confronts the idea of authority through a critical assessment of the juridical construction *the international community of States as a whole*, that entity which accepts and recognizes peremptory norms. History and practice reveal that the interests of the international community, implicated by the relations of States, are represented by the protection of human dignity. Chapter 4 examines the distinct role of human dignity as a general principle of law across four domains: domestic constitutional law, European Union law, public international law, and *jus cogens*. Chapter 5 applies the normative aspect of human dignity to account for considerations of morality in the doctrine of peremptory norms, ultimately leading to an explanation of the effect of morality in *jus cogens*.

This part concludes with Chapter 6, which relates the authority of *jus cogens* as a product of the interests of the international community to the starting point of the theory of social contract.

Jurisprudence is the focus of Part III, Material and Formal Sources of *Jus Cogens*, the aim of which is to elucidate the sources of peremptory norms in international law. Chapter 7 examines historical considerations relevant to understanding the normativity implicit in *jus cogens* as a category of non-derogable norms in international law. In this context, Chapter 8 considers the formal source of peremptory norms indicated by Article 53 of the Vienna Convention and the way in which normativity is formally incorporated into positive international law. Chapter 9 then accesses the interplay of the material and formal sources of peremptory norms to support an understanding by which normative elements akin to the natural law tradition contribute to the emergence of *jus cogens* through formal, positive sources of law in a way that resembles the mechanics of the social contract.

Part IV, Peremptory Norms and the Individual, develops a substantive conceptualization of the form of peremptory norms as they concern rights and duties incumbent upon the individual. The part begins with Chapter 10, which discusses the development of individual legal personality in international law, and the subsequent crystallization of individual rights and duties in the international sphere. Against this backdrop, and through application of the understanding of the formal source of peremptory norms developed in the previous part, Chapter 11 surveys the material content of *jus cogens* to identify the peremptory norms accepted and recognized by the international community of States as a whole. Chapter 12 examines aspects of individual responsibility, both criminal and civil, for violations of peremptory norms as the principal locus of responsibility arising from *jus cogens* under international law, and also considers the complicated erosion of sovereign immunity and amnesty in the context of *jus cogens* violations. The final chapter of this part, Chapter 13, considers implications of the individual as the primary subject of peremptory norms and the way in which the content of *jus cogens* reflects the emergence of the social contract through historical exigencies.

Part V of this book, Peremptory Norms and the State, concerns the legal effects of peremptory norms with respect to the State, an examination framed by obligations *erga omnes* arising from peremptory norms and responsibility for their breach. Chapter 14 discusses the performance of obligations *erga omnes* as the concept has evolved in contemporary practice. This includes consideration of the consequences for breaches of these obligations and the way in which these effects reflect structures that have emerged pursuant to the enforcement of peremptory norms. Chapter 15 then assesses the nature of State responsibility arising under *jus cogens* and its divergence from that of the individual, characterized by the principle of 'dual responsibility'; it also considers the effect of the *erga omnes* status of obligations for purposes of standing before the International Court of Justice, as well as the jurisdictional immunity of the State before domestic courts in cases concerning State responsibility for *jus cogens* violations. Chapter 16 consists of a case study of the crisis in Libya, which illustrates how the legal regime of obligations *erga omnes* arising from peremptory norms harmonizes with the governing institutions of the international community. Finally, Chapter 17 considers how the enforcement of *jus cogens* through obligations *erga omnes* reflects the operational elements of the social contract.

The conclusion of this book is Part VI, International Law and Social Contract, which consolidates the findings of the previous chapters as they concern the purpose of this book – to reconcile an individual-oriented normative structure of public order with a State-based international legal order. Chapter 18 discusses the legal observations that are the primary focus of the book by reviewing understandings of the sources, authority, content, and enforcement of *jus cogens* developed herein, and the way in which the effects of peremptory norms occupy a coherent, State-based legal order. Based on these legal findings, Chapter 19 considers the broader theoretical implications of this book. This entails a summary of academic frameworks related to *jus cogens*, a review of the way features of *jus cogens* are consistent with the social contract, and an evaluation of public order exhibiting characteristics of a social contract in international law.*

* Chapter 20 provides an index surveying domestic *jus cogens* jurisprudence in greater detail than permitted in the main text of the book.

PART I

Peremptory norms of general international law (*jus cogens*)

The doctrine of *jus cogens* can be understood as the confluence of international law and social contract. This part presents these core concepts as referred to throughout this book. Chapter 1 consists of a discussion of interrelated elements of international law – peremptory norms of general international law (*jus cogens*), obligations *erga omnes*, and the international law of responsibility – that give definition to *jus cogens*. Chapter 2 provides an introduction to the theory of the social contract and explains how the idea is applied to *jus cogens* to frame the analysis of this book. The analysis of the elements of international law set out in Chapter 1, in the parts of this book to follow, are guided by the framework set out in Chapter 2.

1

International law

This book comes into contact with three interrelated areas of international law: peremptory norms of general international law (*jus cogens*), obligations *erga omnes*, and the international law of responsibility. An understanding of *jus cogens* requires consideration of each of these convergent elements, and it serves to introduce them at the outset.

A Peremptory norms of general international law (*jus cogens*)

Translating from Latin to mean 'compelling law', the concept of *jus cogens* is of Roman law origin, though the term itself only first arises in nineteenth-century works regarding pandects.[1] The principle of *jus cogens* originates from the municipal law of obligations, with reference to those particular rules and principles whose application cannot be compromised by the will of parties to a contract.[2] Formally, *jus cogens* constitutes a form of public order by delineating the boundaries within which positive law may be concluded.[3] As a legal concept, the notion of *jus cogens* is regarded to be universal: it is found in all major forms of domestic legal order.[4] The proposal to introduce a provision on *jus cogens* into international law is found in the First Report on the Law of Treaties by *special rapporteur* Hersch Lauterpacht. Lauterpacht, the second of four *special rapporteurs* appointed by the International Law

[1] Manfred Lachs, *The Development and General Trends of International Law in our Time*, 169 RECUEIL DES COURS 202 (1980); Jerzy Sztucki, JUS COGENS AND THE VIENNA CONVENTION ON THE LAW OF TREATIES 6 (Vienna: Springer-Verlag 1974).

[2] Egon Schwelb, *Some Aspects of International Jus Cogens as Formulated by the International Law Commission*, 61 AMERICAN JOURNAL OF INTERNATIONAL LAW 946, 948–9 (1967).

[3] Alexander Orakhelashvili, PEREMPTORY NORMS IN INTERNATIONAL LAW 19 (Oxford University Press, 2006).

[4] Karen Parker & Lyn Beth Neylon, *Jus Cogens: Compelling the Law of Human Rights*, 12 HASTINGS INTERNATIONAL & COMPARATIVE LAW REVIEW 411, 423 (1989).

Commission (ILC) on the matter, posited in 1953 that there must be recognized boundaries beyond which the State may not conclude law:

> It would thus appear that the test whether the object of the treaty is illegal and whether the treaty is void for that reason is not inconsistency with customary international law pure and simple, but inconsistency with such overriding principles of international law which may be regarded as constituting principles of international public policy (*ordre international public*). These principles need not necessarily have crystallized in a clearly accepted rule of law such as prohibition of piracy or of aggressive war. They may be expressive of rules of international morality so cogent that an international tribunal would consider them as forming part of those principles of law generally recognized by civilized nations[.][5]

The inception of a category of international law expressive of the higher interests and values of the international community, one from which conventional law could not deviate, is often contextualized as a reaction to the excesses of unbridled State sovereignty that reached a zenith during the Second World War.[6] It represents a departure from theories of international law that hold State practice to be the exclusive source of international law.

The notion of international public policy was further developed during the drafting of the law of treaties by the ILC. Gerald Fitzmaurice, the third *special rapporteur* on the law of treaties, postulated that the establishment of such a category in international law necessarily gave rise to a distinction between two classes of rules in international law, 'those which are mandatory and imperative in any circumstances (*jus cogens*) and those (*jus dispositivum*) . . . the variation or modification of which under an agreed régime is permissible'.[7] Echoing the commentary by Lauterpacht, Fitzmaurice alluded to the normativity implicit in the material content of *jus cogens*:

> It is not possible – nor for the present purposes necessary – to state exhaustively what are the rules of international law that have the character of *jus cogens*, but a feature common to them, or to a great many of them, evidently is that they involve not only legal rules but considerations of morals and of international good order.[8]

[5] Hersch Lauterpacht, First Report on the Law of Treaties, [1953] II YbILC 154–6, para. 4.

[6] Mark Janis, *The Nature of* Jus Cogens, 3 Connecticut Journal of International Law 359, 362 (1987–8).

[7] Gerald Fitzmaurice, Third Report on the Law of Treaties, [1958] II YbILC 40, para. 76.

[8] *Ibid.*, 40–1, para. 76 (Fitzmaurice distinguishes *jus cogens* from morals or good order not incorporated as 'an actual legal rule').

Humphrey Waldock, the fourth and final *special rapporteur* on the law of treaties, similarly affirmed the notion of public order norms in international law:

> Imperfect though the international legal order may be, the view that in the last analysis there is no international public order – no rule from which States cannot at their own free will contract out – has become increasingly difficult to sustain.[9]

Although no explicit reference to 'international public order' was included in the final draft of the law of treaties,[10] its effect is manifest in the establishment of a normative category of inviolable rules of such importance to the international community that no derogation is permitted. Broad consensus in support of this conceptualization of *jus cogens* among the drafters of the law of treaties is reflected in a statement by the Soviet member of the ILC:

> [T]here was no disagreement on the juridical nature of *jus cogens*. The important point was that all members agreed on the practical issues that a rule having the character of *jus cogens* was one from which States could not contract out, *and that such rules existed.*[11]

The formal recognition of *jus cogens* in the law of treaties was therefore conceived to have broad structural implications in international law.[12]

The category of *jus cogens* formally entered into international law in Articles 53 and 64 of the Vienna Convention on the Law of Treaties (1969),[13] which establish the illegality of treaties conflicting with a peremptory norm of general international law:

Article 53. Treaties conflicting with a peremptory norm of general international law ('_jus cogens_')

> A treaty is void if, at the time of its conclusion, it conflicts with a peremptory norm of general international law. For the purposes of the

[9] Humphrey Waldock, Second Report on the Law of Treaties, [1963] II YbILC 52, para. 1 (noting that the limitation of the use of force and development of international criminal law 'presupposes the existence of an international public order containing rules having the character of *jus cogens*').

[10] [1966] I(1) YbILC 38, para. 25 (828th Meeting, statement by Mr Tunkin).

[11] [1963] I YbILC 76, para. 28 (685th Meeting, statement by Mr Tunkin) (emphasis added).

[12] *See, e.g.*, [1963] I YbILC 62–78 (683rd–686th Meetings); [1966] I(1) YbILC 36–41 (828th Meeting).

[13] Vienna Convention on the Law of Treaties, *opened for signature* 23 May 1969, 1155 UNTS 331 (*entered into force* 27 Jan. 1980).

present Convention, a peremptory norm of general international law is a norm accepted and recognized by the international community of States as a whole as a norm from which no derogation is permitted and which can be modified only by a subsequent norm of general international law having the same character.

...

Article 64. Emergence of a new peremptory norm of general international law ('*jus cogens*')

If a new peremptory norm of general international law emerges, any existing treaty which is in conflict with that norm becomes void and terminates.[14]

The 'Vienna Convention' effects of peremptory norms are clear: a treaty is null and void upon its conclusion that conflicts with a norm belonging to *jus cogens*, and should a peremptory norm emerge with which a treaty in force conflicts, that treaty 'becomes void and terminates'. No treaty is valid in international law that derogates from a peremptory norm.[15]

Although the Vienna Convention concerns the law of treaties and binds only signatories – notwithstanding that its provisions are considered to be declaratory of customary international law[16] – Article 53 reflected a concept with legal effect beyond the treaty context. As much was indicated by the Chairman of the drafting committee at the first session of the UN Conference on the Law of Treaties at Vienna in 1968:

> The article expressed a reality by setting forth the consequences in the realm of treaty law of the existence of rules of *jus cogens*. The existence of such rules was beyond dispute. No jurist would deny that a treaty which violated such rules as prohibition of the slave-trade was null and void. Article 5[3], however, did not purport to deal with the whole broad problem of the rule of *jus cogens*: its sole purpose was to set forth the effect of those rules on treaties.[17]

[14] *Ibid.*, Articles 53 and 64.

[15] *See* Fitzmaurice, Third Report, [1958] II YbILC 26, para. 2 (Article 16. Legality of the object (general)) ('It is essential to the validity of a treaty that it should be in conformity with or not contravene, or that its execution should not involve an infraction of those principles and rules of international law which are in the nature of *jus cogens*'); Waldock, Second Report, [1963] II YbILC 52 (a treaty is void 'if its object or its execution involves the infringement of a general rule or principle of international law having the character of *jus cogens*').

[16] *See, e.g.*, Restatement (Third) of Foreign Relations Law of the United States, Introductory Note (1987) (quoting the US Department of State) (The Vienna Convention 'is already generally recognized as the authoritative guide to current treaty law and practice ... codifying existing international law').

[17] United Nations Conference on the Law of Treaties, Vienna, 26 March – 24 May 1968, A/CONF.39/11 (1969), First Session 295, para. 21 (statement by Mr Yasseen).

The contemporary practice of international and domestic judicial organs, to refer to Article 53 for any consideration of *jus cogens*, is consistent with this view of a concept existing outside the treaty context.[18] As the best available textual guidance to *jus cogens* in international law, Article 53 provides the logical starting point from which to analyze the formal source of peremptory norms.[19] And, as the first codification of the concept of *jus cogens* in international law, the *travaux préparatoires* of Article 53 provides a rich resource documenting understandings of the ILC during drafting, positions of governments present at the UN Conference on the Law of Treaties at Vienna, and the views of States ratifying the Vienna Convention.

Since its codification in the law of treaties, the concept of *jus cogens* has evolved dramatically.[20] Although the first codified consequence of public order norms in international law is to invalidate contrary law concluded between States, there is virtually no instance in which Article 53 has been invoked to invalidate a treaty.[21] Moreover, in practice, peremptory norms are violated by individual conduct rather than international agreements between States. This suggests that the inclusion of a provision concerning peremptory norms in the law of treaties was primarily structural: if international law admits the existence of non-derogable norms that bind

[18] *See, e.g., Military Prosecutor v. Albers*, Court of Cassation (Italy), No. 32139/2012, ILDC 1921, para. 2.3 (2012); *Habib v. Australia*, Federal Court of Australia, [2010] FCAFC 12, para. 83, ILDC 1518 (2010); *C v. Director of Immigration*, Court of First Instance (Hong Kong), HCAL 132/2006, [2008] 2 HKC 165, para. 77, ILDC 1119 (2008); *A. v. Federal Department of Economic Affairs*, Federal Supreme Court (Switzerland), No. 2A 783/2006, para. 8.1, ILDC 1200 (2008); *Re Víctor Raúl Pinto v. Relatives of Tomás Rojas*, Supreme Court (Chile), Decision on Annulment, No. 3125-04, ILDC 1093, para. 32 (2007); *Fang v. Jiang*, High Court (New Zealand), [2007] NZAR 420, para. 26 (2006); *Jones v. Ministry of the Interior of Saudi Arabia and Lieutenant Colonel Abdul Aziz*, House of Lords (United Kingdom) [2006] UKHL 26, 21, para. 42 (Hoffmann, L.) (2006); *Suresh v. Canada (Minister of Citizenship and Immigration)*, Supreme Court (Canada), 2002 SCC 1, para. 61 (2002); *Prosecutor v. Kupreškić*, IT-95-16-T, para. 520, note 771 (2000); *Office of the Prosecutor v. Priebke*, Supreme Court (Argentina), P/457/XXXI, para. 70, ILDC 1599 (1995); *Siderman de Blake v. Republic of Argentina*, 965 F.2d 699, 714–15 (9th Cir. 1992).

[19] *See, e.g.*, Vladimir Degan, Sources of International Law, 217–18 (The Hague: Martinus Nijhoff 1997) ('The starting point of any discussion on *jus cogens* in general international law is Article 53 of the 1969 Vienna Convention on the Law of Treaties').

[20] To suggest that *jus cogens* has merely been '[s]eized upon by idealists, who would extend it beyond the narrow context of treaty making', demonstrates unawareness of a depth of *jus cogens* jurisprudence: *Compare* David Armstrong, Theo Farrell & Hélène Lambert, International Law and International Relations 14–15 (Cambridge University Press 2nd edn, 2012), *with* discussion *infra*, Chapter 8.D (Judicial Organs).

[21] See discussion *infra*, Chapter 5.C.i (Non-Derogation).

States apart from their consent, *a fortiori*, these norms cannot be abrogated by treaty agreements between States. The unilateral aspect of peremptory norms, rather than the treaty dimension articulated in Article 53, has assumed the greatest practical importance,[22] as illustrated by jurisprudence of the International Court of Justice (ICJ).[23]

B Obligations *erga omnes*

The concept of obligations *erga omnes* in international law is closely related to *jus cogens* norms. Literally translating to mean 'against all', *erga omnes* refers to an obligation owed by each State to the international community as a whole.[24] The doctrine of obligations *erga omnes* was first articulated by the International Court of Justice in *Barcelona Traction,*

[22] Orakhelashvili, PEREMPTORY NORMS IN INTERNATIONAL LAW 205–8; Andrea Bianchi, *Human Rights and the Magic of* Jus Cogens, 19(3) EUROPEAN JOURNAL OF INTERNATIONAL LAW 491, 495–6 (2008); Bruno Simma, *From Bilateralism to Community Interest in International Law*, 250 RECUEIL DES COURS 288 (1994); Theodor Meron, HUMAN RIGHTS LAW-MAKING IN THE UNITED NATIONS 196–7 (Oxford: Clarendon Press 1986); Egon Schwelb, *Some Aspects of International Jus Cogens as Formulated by the International Law Commission*, 61 AMERICAN JOURNAL OF INTERNATIONAL LAW 946, 955 (1967).

[23] *Questions Relating to the Obligation to Prosecute or Extradite (Belgium v. Senegal)*, Judgment, ICJ Reports 2012, p. 422, para. 99 (finding *erga omnes* obligations arising from *jus cogens* prohibition of torture sufficient under Torture Convention to grant third-State standing before the court); *Jurisdictional Immunities of the State (Germany v. Italy: Greece Intervening)*, Judgment, ICJ Reports 2012, p. 99, para. 93 (finding *jus cogens* prohibitions of war crimes and slavery substantive rules with no impact on the procedural rule of State immunity under customary international law); *Accordance with International Law of the Unilateral Declaration of Independence in Respect of Kosovo*, Advisory Opinion, ICJ Reports 2010, p. 403, para. 81 (noting illegality of declarations of independence connected with 'the unlawful use of force', as among 'egregious violations of norms of general international law, in particular those of a peremptory character (*jus cogens*)'); *Application of the Convention on the Prevention and Punishment of the Crime of Genocide (Bosnia and Herzegovina v. Serbia and Montenegro)*, Judgment, ICJ Reports 2007, p. 43, para. 161 (finding international responsibility of Serbia for breach of *erga omnes* obligations arising from *jus cogens* prohibition of genocide); *Armed Activities on the Territory of the Congo (New Application: 2002) (Democratic Republic of the Congo v. Rwanda)*, ICJ Reports 2006, p. 3, paras. 64, 78, 125 (finding *jus cogens* status of prohibitions of genocide and racial discrimination at issue insufficient to engage the jurisdiction of the court); *Arrest Warrant of 11 April 2000 (Democratic Republic of the Congo v. Belgium)*, ICJ Reports 2002, p. 3, paras. 56–60 (finding no exception to immunity *ratione personae* of foreign minister for *jus cogens* violations of war crimes and crimes against humanity).

[24] *See* Christian Tams, ENFORCING OBLIGATIONS *ERGA OMNES* IN INTERNATIONAL LAW (Cambridge University Press 2005); Maurizio Ragazzi, THE CONCEPT OF INTERNATIONAL OBLIGATIONS *ERGA OMNES* (Oxford University Press 1997); André De Hoogh, OBLIGATIONS *ERGA OMNES* AND INTERNATIONAL CRIMES (The Hague: Martinus Nijhoff 1996).

Light and Power Company, Limited (Belgium v. Spain) (1970) and has since been revisited on numerous occasions.[25] In *Barcelona Traction*, the ICJ distinguished State obligations owed to another State from those 'towards the international community as a whole' and interpreted such obligations to arise from peremptory norms:

> In particular, an essential distinction should be drawn between the obligations of a State towards the international community as a whole, and those arising vis-à-vis another State in the field of diplomatic protection. By their very nature the former are the concern of all States. In view of the importance of the rights involved, all States can be held to have a legal interest in their protection; they are obligations *erga omnes*.
>
> Such obligations derive, for example, in contemporary international law, from the outlawing of acts of aggression, and of genocide, as also from the principles and rules concerning the basic rights of the human person, including protection from slavery and racial discrimination. Some of the corresponding rights of protection have entered into the body of general international law . . . others are conferred by international instruments of a universal or quasi-universal character.[26]

This conceptualization was interpreted by the ILC to refer to 'a number, albeit a small one, of international obligations which, by reason of the importance of their subject-matter for the international community as a whole, are – unlike the others – obligations in whose fulfillment all States have a legal interest'.[27]

Structurally, as obligations owed to the international community as a whole, the classification *erga omnes* denotes a general legal interest in

[25] *Questions Relating to the Obligation to Prosecute or Extradite (Belgium v. Senegal)*, Judgment, ICJ Reports 2012, p. 422, 450, paras. 68–9; *Application of the Convention on the Prevention and Punishment of the Crime of Genocide (Bosnia and Herzegovina v. Serbia and Montenegro)*, Judgment, ICJ Reports 2007, p. 43, 104, 111, paras. 147, 162; *Armed Activities on the Territory of the Congo (New Application: 2002) (Democratic Republic of the Congo v. Rwanda)*, Judgment, ICJ Reports 2006, p. 6, 32, 51–2, paras. 64, 125; *Legal Consequences of the Construction of a Wall in the Occupied Palestinian Territory*, Advisory Opinion, ICJ Reports 2004, p. 136, 172, 199, paras. 88, 155–7; *East Timor (Portugal v. Australia)*, Judgment, ICJ Reports 1995, p. 90, 102, para. 29; *Legal Consequences for States of the Continued Presence of South Africa in Namibia (South West Africa) notwithstanding Security Council Resolution 276 (1970)*, Advisory Opinion, ICJ Reports 1971, p. 16, para. 126; *Barcelona Traction, Light and Power Company, Limited (Belgium v. Spain)*, Judgment, ICJ Reports 1970, p. 3, 32, paras. 33–4.

[26] ICJ Reports 1970, p. 3, 32, paras. 33–4.

[27] Report of the International Law Commission on the Work of its Twenty-Eighth Session, [1976] II(2) YbILC 99, para. 10 (Commentary to Draft Article 19 adopted by the ILC at its 28th Session).

their fulfilment. This means that, simultaneously, each State is bound by *erga omnes* obligations and every State has a legal interest in their performance. This *erga omnes* status is an effect of the importance of the maintenance of norms from which such obligations derive, as noted by *special rapporteur* Robert Ago in his Fifth Report on State Responsibility (1976):

> The specially important content of certain international obligations and the fact that respect for them in fact determines the conditions of the life of international society are factors which, at least in many cases, have precluded any possibility of derogation from the rules imposing such obligations by virtue of special agreements. These are also the factors which render a breach of these obligations more serious than failure to comply with other obligations.[28]

It is from this seriousness of compliance to the public order of the international community that a general legal interest in the performance of obligations *erga omnes* arises, an importance rendering the legal obligations arising therefrom 'indivisible'. *Special rapporteur* Gaetano Arangio-Ruiz set out this relationship in his Fourth Report on State Responsibility (1992):

> It is well known ... that the concept of *erga omnes* obligation is not characterized by the importance of the interest protected by the norm (as is typical of *jus cogens*) but rather by the 'legal indivisibility' of the content of the obligation, namely by the fact that the rule in question provides for obligations which bind simultaneously each and every State concerned with respect to all the others.[29]

This general legal interest in the performance of obligations to the international community departs from the bilateralization that traditionally characterizes obligations in international law.

Functionally, obligations *erga omnes* concern the enforcement norms of *jus cogens*, as indicated by *special rapporteur* James Crawford in his

[28] Robert Ago, Fifth Report on State Responsibility, [1976] II(1) YbILC 33, para. 101.

[29] Gaetano Arangio-Ruiz, Fourth Report on State Responsibility, [1992] II(1) YbILC 34, para. 92; see Robert Ago, Fifth Report on State Responsibility, [1976] II(1) YbILC 29, para. 89; *Prosecutor v. Furundžija*, IT-95-17/1-T, para. 151 (1998) ('Furthermore, the prohibition of torture imposes upon States obligations *erga omnes*, that is, obligations owed towards all the other members of the international community, each of which then has a correlative right. In addition, the violation of such an obligation simultaneously constitutes a breach of the correlative right of all members of the international community and gives rise to a claim for compliance accruing to each and every member, which then has the right to insist on fulfilment of the obligation or in any case to call for the breach to be discontinued').

Fourth Report on State Responsibility (2001).[30] And, beyond this correlative association, a causal relationship links *jus cogens* and obligations *erga omnes* by which the latter derive from the former. This, the position of the International Court in *Barcelona Traction*,[31] was reiterated before the ILC in 1996: 'It was clear that there were *jus cogens* rules which, though not themselves *erga omnes*, had *erga omnes* effects.'[32] *Erga omnes* obligations derive from *jus cogens* as obligations, concerning the enforcement of peremptory norms, owed by each State to the international community as a whole. Sustaining these distinctions, obligations *erga omnes* are 'virtually coextensive' with peremptory norms of *jus cogens*.[33]

C The international law of responsibility

International law conceives of distinct, though often concurrent, forms of responsibility arising for the individual and the State under *jus cogens*. The term international crime has evolved to refer exclusively to individual conduct in violation of a peremptory norm. 'A crime in this sense is seen as a violation of basic rules of *jus cogens*.'[34] Conversely, international law does not admit crimes of States.[35] Thus, the classification of an offence as an international crime refers at once to the seriousness of

[30] James Crawford, Fourth Report on State Responsibility, [2001] II(1) YbILC 13, para. 49 ('In the context of peremptory norms the emphasis is on the primary rule itself and its non-derogable or overriding status. By contrast, the emphasis with obligations to the international community is on the universality of the obligation and the persons or entities to whom it is owed, specifically all States and other legal entities which are members of that community').

[31] ICJ Reports 1970, p. 3, 32, para. 34.

[32] [1996] I YbILC 26, para. 26 (2436th Meeting, statement by Mr Villagrán Kramer) ('It was clear that there were *jus cogens* rules which, though not themselves *erga omnes*, had *erga omnes* effects: a breach of them could result in an international crime, namely, a serious act prejudicial to an essential interest of the community of States').

[33] James Crawford, Third Report on State Responsibility, [2000] II(1) YbILC 34, para. 106 (a); James Crawford, Fourth Report on State Responsibility, [2001] II(1) YbILC 13, para. 49 ('even if the two are not different aspects of the one underlying idea, the two substantially overlap'). However obligations *erga omnes* are not necessarily the exclusive domain of *jus cogens* and may also concern other 'essential principles of contemporary international law', such as the right of peoples to self-determination: *see* discussion *infra*, Chapter 11 (The Material Content of *Jus Cogens*).

[34] Jochen Frowein, *Jus Cogens, in* III Encyclopedia of Public International Law 65, 68 (Amsterdam: North-Holland, Rudolf Bernhardt ed., 1997).

[35] James Crawford, *International Crimes of States, in* The Law of International Responsibility 405, 405–14 (Oxford University Press, James Crawford, Alain Pellet & Simon Olleson eds., 2009).

the law violated – a norm belonging to *jus cogens* – and the subject of criminal responsibility for the breach – the individual.[36] In addition to criminal responsibility, a precedent of individual civil liability for violations of peremptory norms has emerged, notably in the jurisprudence of the United States.[37] By contrast, the international responsibility of the State is engaged by an internationally wrongful act – conduct attributable to the State in breach of its obligations under international law[38] – which may in principle include breaches of obligations *erga omnes* and individual conduct in violation of a peremptory norm.[39] Importantly, State responsibility is not itself criminal or civil in nature: as an 'undifferentiated regime', State responsibility knows no such distinction and conceives only of international responsibility.[40] This accounts, for example, for the omission of the concept of international crimes of States from the Rome Statute. It is in this sense that there exists a duality of responsibility under international law for violations of peremptory norms.

[36] This is distinct from the notion of transnational crime, which refers to the scope of a crime rather than its gravity, as in espionage, counterfeiting currency, illicit traffic in drugs, slave trading, trading in women and children, pollution of the seas, damaging submarine cable, offences against persons protected by international law, unlawful dispatch of explosives through post, pirate broadcasting, and theft of national and archaeological treasures.

[37] *See* discussion *infra*, 12.B (Individual Civil Responsibility) and 12.C (Immunities).

[38] International Law Commission, Responsibility of States for Internationally Wrongful Acts, Report of the International Law Commission on the Work of its Fifty-Third Session, [2001] II(2) YbILC 26 *et seq.*, Articles 1–3.

[39] *See* discussion *infra*, Chapter 15 (State Responsibility and *Jus Cogens*).

[40] James Crawford, *The System of International Responsibility*, *in* THE LAW OF INTERNATIONAL RESPONSIBILITY 17, 22 (Crawford *et al.* eds.).

2

The social contract

For the past five centuries, the concept of the 'social contract' has been utilized by political philosophers to explain the establishment and legitimacy of political order and civil society. Implementing the theory involves deconstructing a political structure to understand how its component elements operate to form a complete political system.[1] It has been observed that there is 'no single unified tradition' of contractarianism, a point evidenced by the myriad forms and functions contained within social contract theory.[2] For example, a social contract theory may be analytical, whereby it provides an account of the origin and maintenance of political authority or moral principles, or normative, whereby it establishes that some form of political authority or moral principles is justified, legitimate, or ought to be adopted.[3] One pair of scholars identifies the three varieties of contract theory as moral, civil, and constitutional, each with its own distinct character and specific ends;[4] another suggests contract theory may be categorized by its particular discipline: constitutional, philosophical, or integrated.[5] A slightly different proposition divides contract theory into two types depending on whether it concerns the foundation of social cooperation or the source of political obligation.[6] Perhaps most generally, contractarianism can simply be

[1] Gregory Kavka, HOBBESIAN MORAL AND POLITICAL THEORY 19–22 (Princeton University Press 1986) (describing this 'resolutive-compositive' method in greater detail).

[2] David Boucher and Paul Kelly, *The Social Contract and its Critics: An Overview*, *in* THE SOCIAL CONTRACT FROM HOBBES TO RAWLS 1 (London: Routledge, David Boucher & Paul Kelly eds., 1994).

[3] Jody Kraus, THE LIMITS OF HOBBESIAN CONTRACTARIANISM 2–3 (Cambridge University Press 1993).

[4] Boucher and Kelly, *The Social Contract and its Critics*, 1–10.

[5] Martyn Thompson, *Locke's Contract in Context*, *in* THE SOCIAL CONTRACT FROM HOBBES TO RAWLS 77 (Boucher & Kelly eds.).

[6] Dario Castiglione, *History, Reason and Experience*, *in* THE SOCIAL CONTRACT FROM HOBBES TO RAWLS 95–6 (Boucher & Kelly eds.).

classified as either political or moral.[7] While there are undoubtedly discernible themes across this variation, the lack of external continuity in social contract theory is clear. The main point to draw from this variation is that the social contract is 'a flexible tool in the hands of the theorist'.[8] Contractarian thought of the Enlightenment era was concerned primarily with explaining the emergence and authority of public order, making this form of social contract theory particularly suitable for structuring an analysis of *jus cogens* in international law.

The fundamental premise of the social contract of Enlightenment vintage is that it predicates the emergence of political order upon the protection of societal values necessary to safeguard individual wellbeing within a community. Consequently, its existence is manifest by society itself, and it may be studied from this vantage point. While the most prominent social contract theorists of the Enlightenment era remain the trio of Thomas Hobbes,[9] John Locke,[10] and Jean-Jacques Rousseau,[11] the theory developed by Immanuel Kant is associated with the same tradition.[12] Many other prominent political and legal philosophers of the period developed their own social contract theories, including Fernando Vasquez, Francisco Suárez, Hugo Grotius, and Samuel Pufendorf.[13] Four general elements of the contractarian narrative structure this book:

1. Common interests and values of a community.
2. A legislative expression of the social need to protect these interests.

[7] Kraus, The Limits of Hobbesian Contractarianism 2.

[8] Boucher and Kelly, *The Social Contract and its Critics* 2.

[9] Thomas Hobbes, Leviathan (London: Penguin Books, C. B. Macpherson ed., 1985 [1651]).

[10] John Locke, Two Treatises of Government (London: Everyman 2003 [1689]).

[11] Jean-Jacques Rousseau, The Social Contract (*Du contract social ou Principes du droit politique*) (London: Everyman 2003 [1762]); Jean-Jacques Rousseau, The State of War, *in* Rousseau on International Relations (Oxford: Clarendon Press, Stanley Hoffmann & David Fidler eds., 1991); Jean-Jacques Rousseau, Discourse on the Origin and the Foundations of Inequality among Men [1754], *in* Victor Gourevitch, Rousseau: The Discourses and other Early Political Writings 131 (Cambridge University Press 1997).

[12] Immanuel Kant, Metaphysics of Morals [1797], *in* The Cambridge Edition of the Works of Immanuel Kant (Cambridge University Press, Mary Gregor ed., 1996) [hereinafter, Kant, Metaphysics]; Immanuel Kant, Groundwork of the Metaphysics of Morals [1795], *in* The Cambridge Edition of the Works of Immanuel Kant (Gregor ed.); Immanuel Kant, On the Common Saying: That May Be Correct in Theory, But it is of No Use in Practice [1793], *in* The Cambridge Edition of the Works of Immanuel Kant (Gregor ed.) [hereinafter, Kant, Theory and Practice].

[13] *See* Michael Lessnoff (ed.), Social Contract (London: Macmillan 1986); Michael Lessnoff (ed.), Social Contract Theory (Oxford: Basil Blackwell 1991).

3. Normative rights, and correlative duties, delineated through this social need.
4. The establishment of civil society pursuant to the enforcement of these norms.

These elements, which in effect frame Enlightenment social contract theory, delineate the relationship between individuals and political order such that the origin and authority of the latter is based squarely in safeguarding the common interests of the former.[14] The burden of

[14] Enlightenment social contract theory is distinguishable from its contemporary counterparts, which focus chiefly on distributive justice within an existing domestic political order. John Rawls is the most prominent contemporary social contract theorist, whose theory is an exemplar of the social justice brand of contract theory that dominates modern discourse. This approach to the social contract conceives of a series of thought experiments specifically addressing the US political system that are designed to identify principles that assign 'rights and duties in the basic institutions of society and . . . define the appropriate distribution of the benefits and burdens of social cooperation'. Rawls's own application of his theory to international law reveals how theories of social justice lose their persuasive appeal when removed from the domestic context to which they have been tailored and applied to international politics. Rawls proposes applying the identical domestic framework of justice a second time, at the international level, after its adoption at the domestic level. To overcome the prevailing political reality across the international community, which frequently falls short of the Rawlsian standard of 'domestic justice', 'Peoples' not classed as liberal or decent are excluded from this process because they are not 'well ordered'. The second iteration of the Rawlsian thought experiment produces a 'Law of Peoples' consisting of eight fundamental principles: (1) 'Peoples are free and independent, and their freedom and independence are to be respected by other peoples'; (2) 'Peoples are to observe treaties and undertakings'; (3) 'Peoples are equal and are parties to the agreements that bind them'; (4) 'Peoples are to observe a duty of non-intervention'; (5) 'Peoples have the right of self-defense but no right to instigate war for reasons other than self-defence'; (6) 'Peoples are to honour human rights'; (7) 'Peoples are to observe certain specified restrictions in the conduct of war'; (8) 'Peoples have a duty to assist other peoples living under unfavorable conditions that prevent their having a just or decent political and social regime'. These principles offer 'an integrated solution, a just and stable institutional scheme preserving a distribution of basic rights, opportunities, and index goods that is fair both globally and within each nation'. The modern, social justice branch of social contract theory is clearly distinct in its normative task from classical social contract theory, and its obstacles are illuminated upon application of the Rawlsian scheme to *jus cogens*. At the outset, the way in which Rawls himself has applied his social contract theory to international law makes it difficult to reframe his own approach to account for *jus cogens* in particular; perhaps one solution would be to advocate expansion of *jus cogens* to include Rawls's eight principles of the 'Law of Peoples' pursuant to social justice. Assuming instead that it is appropriate to begin anew, application of a Rawlsian framework to account for *jus cogens* depends upon its original position, where the initial choice is made, which is difficult to identify in contemporary international relations. Rawls himself determined that such a 'realistic' initial choice, from which to launch the second iteration of the thought experiment, required excluding States

social contract theory in this book is modest: it serves as an analytical framework that informs which questions to ask of *jus cogens* in order to better understand the mechanics of international society. This approach rests on the presupposition that *jus cogens* norms are cognizable as an expression of the social contract of the international community.

There is already support for the application of social contract theory to the doctrine of *jus cogens*.[15] The historic appeal of Enlightenment-era social contract theory as a means by which to translate precepts characteristic of the natural law tradition into universal individual rights of liberal political order makes the application of social contract theory to *jus cogens* attractive. To this end, Louis Henkin notes:

> Currents of natural law and natural rights run deep in human rights even today. Politically as well as intellectually, however, human rights today trace their authentic origins to seventeenth- and eighteenth-century concepts . . . The American and French Revolutions, and the declarations that expressed the principles that inspired them, took 'natural rights' and made them secular, rational, universal, individual, democratic, and radical. For divine foundations for the rights of man they substituted (or perhaps only added) a social-contractual base.[16]

It is especially appropriate to apply the methodology of contractarianism to understand *jus cogens* if one views *jus cogens* as the most recent expression of this centuries-old intellectual and political tradition.

deemed not 'well ordered', a premise that chafes against contemporary international relations. The product of the experiment is a prescriptive set of concepts and principles against which international law is to be judged. By Rawls's application, the breadth of these eight prescriptive principles provides too much against the limited content of *jus cogens*; as a self-proclaimed thought experiment, any iteration of this exercise does too little to explain *jus cogens*. This version of social contract theory is ill-suited to elucidate the authority of existing structures of international law, and while it might provide a tool to advocate their liberalization, that is not the task of the present work. *See* John Rawls, The Law of Peoples (Cambridge, MA: Harvard University Press 2001); John Rawls, A Theory of Justice (Oxford University Press 1973); Thomas Pogge, Realizing Rawls (Ithica, NY: Cornell University Press 1989); David Gauthier, *Justice as a Social Choice*, *in* Morality, Reason and Truth (Totowa, NJ: Rowman & Allanheld, David Copp & David Immerman eds., 1985), *reproduced in* Social Contract Theory 251–69 (Lessnoff ed.); James Buchanan, The Limits of Liberty (Chicago University Press 1975), *reproduced in* Social Contract Theory 53–86 (Lessnoff ed.).

15 *See, e.g.*, Loius Henkin, *The Mythology of Sovereignty*, *in* Essays in Honour of Wang Tieya 351 (London: Martinus Nijhoff, Ronald St John Macdonald ed., 1994) (discussing the 'international social contract').

16 Louis Henkin, The Rights of Man Today 3–13 (London: Stevens & Sons 1978).

In this same vein, enforcing *jus cogens* has been conceived as a requirement of an 'implied' social contract of international law, through which the enforcement of peremptory norms is delegated to the international community.[17] M. Cherif Bassiouni characterizes the enforcement of *jus cogens* through principles of international criminal law as an 'essentially retributive' mechanism grounded in the 'inherent and inalienable' rights of victims.[18]

> The 'social contract' theory requires international criminal justice to pursue the goal of accountability for those who commit transgressions of certain norms of international criminal law. These norms apply particularly to *jus cogens* international crimes because of their universal condemnation, and the large-scale harm they produce.[19]

Although social contract theory has yet to be applied *in toto* to deconstruct the doctrine of *jus cogens*, its appeal as a way of envisaging the emergence and enforcement of *jus cogens* norms in international law has not gone unnoticed.

The applicability of social contract theory to *jus cogens* is not uncontested. Opposition arises largely from misapprehension of the complex nature of consent in both social contract theory and *jus cogens*. In short, it is said that the 'social contract depends on consent or at least the fiction of consent ... [while] [*j*]*us cogens* norms do not depend on consent'.[20] This rejection oversimplifies the function of consent in both social contract theory and *jus cogens*, the subject of Part III. It bears noting briefly that the social contract need not refer to a historical instrument based upon consent:[21] Kant for one explicitly cautioned against this,[22] while others refigured consent in various ways. Moreover, *jus cogens*, as a category of norms accepted and

[17] M. Cherif Bassiouni, *The Philosophy and Policy of International Criminal Justice*, *in* MAN'S INHUMANITY TO MAN 108–18 (The Hague: Martinus Nijhoff, Antonio Cassese & Lal Chand Vohrah eds., 2003).

[18] *Ibid.*, 115, 119. [19] *Ibid.*, 117–18 (footnote omitted).

[20] Mary Ellen O'Connell, Jus Cogens: *International Law's Higher Ethical Norms*, *in* THE ROLE OF ETHICS IN INTERNATIONAL LAW 86 (Cambridge University Press, Donald Childress ed., 2011) (quoting and addressing Henkin *supra*).

[21] *Cf.* Henkin, *The Mythology of Sovereignty*, 351, 357 ('The international system has had a social contract at least since the seventeenth century, reflected in a network of international law ... The end of the Second World War saw a new social contract represented in the UN Charter. The Charter (I note) is a social contract of States').

[22] Kant, THEORY AND PRACTICE 8:297; Kant, METAPHYSICS 6:315–16; 6:318–19.

recognized by the whole of the international community of States, cannot be said to be entirely independent of consent. The inquiry in either case depends on the expression of legislative will, and the process in each instance is not simple. For present purposes, deconstructing international society offers a window to its social contract, and the methodology of contractarianism provides a guide to this analysis.

PART II

The authority of *jus cogens*

Understanding the authority of *jus cogens* begins with *the international community of States as a whole*, that entity which, according to the Vienna Convention on the Law of Treaties, accepts and recognizes peremptory norms. Chapter 3 deconstructs *the international community of States as a whole* in a way that permits an assessment of its higher interests. Finding human dignity to represent the higher interests and values of the international community of States a whole, Chapter 4 explores human dignity as a general principle of law, from its origin in antiquity to its articulation in *jus cogens*. As a concept with moral implications, Chapter 5 contemplates the role of morality in the doctrine of *jus cogens*. Chaper 6 concludes this part by considering the emergence of an international social contract, arising from the shared interests and values of the international community, expressed through general principles necessary to the maintenance of social coexistence, and whose moral quality reflects a particular relation of the individual to governance structures through norms from which no derogation is permitted.

3

The interests of the international community

In international law, it is possible to ascertain higher interests of the international community enshrined as norms of public order. In principle, public order constitutes an expression of the primacy of values and interests common to society, from which its members may not deviate due to their importance to the community. The practical effect of public order is to regulate the relationship between the individual and society in such a way as to establish the preeminence of the general interest of the latter over the particular interests of the former. As duties owed to others in society, public order necessarily reflects a moral character.[1] In the law of contracts, public order is expressed as a restriction of the contractual will of the individual by the common interests of a community.[2] As applied to international law, the construction 'public order of the international community' is credited to Judge Hermann Mosler, who postulated the illegality and non-recognition of State conduct contrary to the foundations of international law and society.[3] According to Judge Mosler,

> In any legal community there must be a minimum of uniformity which is indispensable in maintaining the community. This uniformity may relate to legal values which are considered to be the goal of the community or it may be found in legal principles which it is the duty of all members to realise. It may relate to legal rules which are binding within the community. The whole of this minimum can be called a common public order (ordre public international). The international community cannot dispense with this minimum of principles and rules as without them it would cease to exist.[4]

[1] *See* discussion *infra*, Chapter 7.D (*Jus Cogens* as Public Order in International Law).

[2] Alexander Orakhelashvili, PEREMPTORY NORMS IN INTERNATIONAL LAW 19 (Oxford University Press 2006).

[3] *See* Theodor Meron, HUMAN RIGHTS LAW-MAKING IN THE UNITED NATIONS 197–8 (Oxford: Clarendon Press 1986).

[4] Herman Mosler, *The International Society as a Legal Community*, 140 RECUEIL DES COURS 33 (1974) ('International Public Order' and *Ius Cogens*).

It is widely accepted that *jus cogens* constitutes a form of public order in international law, as indicated by one representative observation by a member of the ILC during the drafting of the law of treaties:

> *Jus cogens* was the indispensable minimum for the existence of the international community; it was positive law created by States, not as individuals but as organs of the international community, in order to safeguard the community's existence.[5]

This proposition can be traced back to the earliest stages of drafting of the law of treaties by the ILC.[6] In the First Report on the Law of Treaties by *special rapporteur* Lauterpacht in 1953, where the concept of *jus cogens* was introduced into the drafting of the law of treaties, it was proposed that peremptory norms reflect 'principles of international public policy *(ordre international public)*'.[7] Waldock, the fourth and final *special rapporteur* on the law of treaties, observed this quality of *jus cogens* in the Commentary to his 1963 Report:

> Imperfect though the international legal order may be, the view that in the last analysis there is no international public order – no rule from which States cannot at their own free will contract out – has become increasingly difficult to sustain.[8]

As one delegation to the UN Conference on the Law of Treaties (UNCLOT) aptly stated in reference to the draft article, '[t]he individual and reciprocal rights and duties of contracting parties were subjected to the supreme and unanimously recognized interests of the international community'.[9] The public order character of *jus cogens* is substantiated by its prescribed legal effect: the invalidation of contrary law concluded by States. By the formal codification of the Vienna Convention, Article 53

[5] [1966] I(1) YbILC 39, para. 34 (828th Meeting, statement by Mr De Luna) (this formulation preceded Judge Mosler's statement immediately above by nearly a decade.).

[6] *See* Arnold McNair, The Law of Treaties 213–14 (Oxford: Clarendon Press 1961) ('It is difficult to imagine a society, whether of individuals or of States, whose law sets no limit whatever to freedom of contract. In every civilized community there are some rules of law and some principles of morality which individuals are not permitted by law to ignore or to modify by their agreements').

[7] Hersch Lauterpacht, First Report on the Law of Treaties, [1953] II YbILC 154–6, para. 4.

[8] Humphrey Waldock, Second Report on the Law of Treaties, [1963] II YbILC 52, para. 1.

[9] United Nations Conference on the Law of Treaties, Vienna, 26 March–24 May 1968, A/CONF.39/11 (1969), First Session [hereinafter, UNCLOT, First Session (1968)] 317, para. 21 (statement by Brazil).

articulated *jus cogens* in terms of the invalidating effect of norms 'from which no derogation is permitted'.[10]

Public order, by its nature, reflects the protection of values fundamental to the social coexistence of its members, a conceptualization that may be applied to the international community. That *jus cogens* reflects the higher interests of the international community of States as a whole is implicit in the text of Article 53 of the Vienna Convention itself, which identifies a peremptory norm as a norm 'accepted and recognized by *the international community of States as a whole*'.[11] Admitting *jus cogens* as a form of public order in the international community implies that its substantive content relates to the common interests of this body. The ILC indicated the natural consequence of this public order conceptualization in its commentary to the final draft of the law of treaties, that '[i]t is not the form of a general rule of international law but the particular nature of the subject-matter with which it deals that may, in the opinion of the Commission, give it the character of *jus cogens*'.[12] This subject matter was understood to constitute 'the interests ... of the international community as a whole',[13] a point reinforced by obligations *erga omnes* arising from such norms expressing a general legal interest in their fulfilment by virtue of their importance to international society.[14] Judge Dugard referred to the public order character of *jus cogens* in these terms in his separate opinion in *Armed Activities on the Territory of the Congo* (2006), stating that peremptory norms 'give legal form to the most fundamental policies or goals of the international community... This explains why they enjoy a hierarchical superiority to other norms in the international legal order.'[15] To elucidate the authority of *jus cogens* as public order

[10] 1155 UNTS 331, Article 53 (1969). [11] *Ibid.* (emphasis added).

[12] Humphrey Waldock, Fifth Report on the Law of Treaties, [1966] II YbILC 248, para. 2 (Commentary to Draft Article 50).

[13] [1963] I YbILC 62–78 (683rd–686th Meetings); Alfred Verdross, Jus Dispositivum *and* Jus Cogens *in International Law*, 60 American Journal of International Law 55, 57–8 (1966). *See* Gordon Christenson, Jus Cogens: *Guarding Interests Fundamental to International Society*, 28 Virginia Journal of International Law 585, 585–648 (1998); Karen Parker and Lyn Beth Neylon, *Jus Cogens: Compelling the Law of Human Rights*, 12 Hastings International & Comparative Law Review 411, 428 (1989); Lauri Hannikainen, Peremptory Norms (*Jus Cogens*) in International Law 180 (Helsinki: Finnish Lawyers' Publishing Company 1988); Gennady Danilenko, *International* Jus Cogens: *Issues of Law-Making*, 2(1) European Journal of International Law 42, 42–65 (1991).

[14] *See* discussion *supra*, Chapter 1.B (Obligations *Erga Omnes*).

[15] *Armed Activities on the Territory of the Congo (New Application: 2002) (Democratic Republic of the Congo v. Rwanda)*, Sep. Op. Dugard, ICJ Reports 2006, p. 86, para. 10.

norms, it is helpful to begin with an analysis of *the international community of States as a whole* from which these norms arise.

A The international community of States as a whole

Article 53 of the Vienna Convention indicates that *the international community of States as a whole* is the author of *jus cogens*.[16] This proposition appears uncontroversial, as the whole of the international community of States is the presumptive organ that provides voice and substance to public order norms in international law. To identify the higher interests of this entity given form through *jus cogens*, it is necessary first to understand the meanings conveyed by the construct. To this end, the expression may be distilled into its component clauses to elucidate the concept. Particular attention is paid here to distinct procedural and substantive aspects depicted by the construct, and its constituent clauses, which reflect complementary and mutually reinforcing dimensions of the international community.

i. 'The international community'

In a literal sense, the existence of a *community*, as an entity or group, is defined and constituted by interaction among its members as well as shared purpose, the pursuit of which unites the group and defines its interests.[17] An implication of a 'community' is that its common good is directed towards the good of its members. In the context of a community of individuals, Jacques Maritain expresses this sense of common good as embodying,

> as its chief value, the highest possible attainment (that is the highest compatible with the good of the whole) of persons to their lives as

[16] *See* discussion *supra*, Chapter 1, text accompanying *nn.* 16–19 (on Article 53 as a textual authority for *jus cogens*).

[17] *See, e.g.*, Black's Law Dictionary (West Group 9th edn, 2009) (defining 'community' as (1) A neighborhood, vicinity, or locality. (2) A society or group of people with similar rights or interests. (3) Joint ownership, possession, or participation); *see International Community, in* The New Oxford Companion to Law (Oxford University Press, Peter Cane & Joanne Conaghan eds., 2008) ('Community denotes commonality, fellowship, sharing. At a general level community expresses a plurality of individuals who are held together by some common initiative or enterprise . . . At a normative level community is the space where individuals might cohere or be drawn together by shared values, principles, norms, common objectives, or a sense of fraternity').

> persons, and to their freedom of expression or autonomy – on to the gifts of goodness which in their turn flow from it.[18]

The institution of law, in turn, is conceived as the instrument through which a community promotes common good, hence, *ubi societas, ibi jus* (where there is society, there is law).[19] This same understanding of 'community' can be seen to underly the 'international community'.[20] The law of the 'international community' exists most basically to promote the goals and values of this community.[21] Arguably, the interaction and interdependence of a globalized world has enabled – and necessitated – the evolution of law of the international community in order to preserve values and interests common to its members implicated by contemporary inter-State relations.[22]

The 'international community' in this sense has 'a juridical connotation' related to mankind, which itself is 'a concept describing a factual phenomenon'.[23] The idea of 'community' introduces the conceptualization of a collective with shared interests and values; that this collective is 'international' in scope suggests that it encompasses the whole of mankind. Such an understanding may be drawn, for example, from omitted Draft Article 19 of the Articles on State Responsibility, which addressed the elevated status of international crimes.[24] Tomuschat observed in this

[18] Jacques Maritain, THE RIGHTS OF MAN AND NATURAL LAW 9 (New York: Charles Scribner's Sons, Doris Anson trans., 1943), *quoted in* Andrew Clapham, HUMAN RIGHTS OBLIGATIONS OF NON-STATE ACTORS 546, *n.* 49 (Oxford University Press 2006).

[19] *See* James Crawford, *Responsibility for Breaches of Communitarian Norms: An Appraisal of Article 48 of the ILC Articles on Responsibility of States for Internationally Wrongful Acts, in* FROM BILATERALISM TO COMMUNITY INTEREST: ESSAYS IN HONOR OF BRUNO SIMMA 224, 240 (Oxford University Press, Ulrich Fastenrath ed., 2011) (suggesting a recasting of the maxim in the context of the international community as an international society, *ibi ius gentium, ubi societas*).

[20] *See* Andreas Paulus, *International Community, in* MAX PLANCK ENCYCLOPEDIA OF PUBLIC INTERNATIONAL LAW (Oxford University Press 2013) ('The international community is a shortcut for the direct and indirect dealings of State authorities, non-State organizations, and businesses, as well as individual citizens, beyond State boundaries, and for the endeavor to tackle common problems ... for which States alone are unwilling, incapable, or illigitimate to act unilaterally').

[21] *Ibid.*, paras. 1–3; Mosler, *The International Society as a Legal Community*, 11–12; Fernando Tesón, A PHILOSOPHY OF INTERNATIONAL LAW 1 (Boulder, CO: Westview Press 1998).

[22] *See, e.g.*, Hedley Bull, THE ANARCHICAL SOCIETY 12 (New York: Columbia University Press 1977).

[23] Christian Tomuschat, *Obligations Arising for States Without or Against their Will*, 241 RECUEIL DES COURS 226 (1993).

[24] *See* discussion *infra*, Chapter 12.A (Individual Criminal Responsibility).

context that, while the international community may be conceived as a community of States,

> [o]n the other hand, the text of Article 19 of the Draft Articles would also permit a reading to the effect that the international community has been chosen as a synonym for mankind, namely the human beings who in fact suffer injury when grave violations of rules of fundamental importance are committed.[25]

The international community not only connotes a socialized collective with shared goals and interests but also introduces the subject of these values as the whole of mankind. Substantively, *the international community* may be seen to represent shared interests and values that arise from mankind, the unit of which is the individual human being.

ii. 'of States'

Procedurally, the international community is conceived as one *of States*, a reality evidenced throughout international relations. The membership of the United Nations organization, the most prominent organ of the international community, exclusively comprises States.[26] And international law is law 'inter-nations' in the first instance: its evolution paralleled that of a system of competing, sovereign States with the purpose of stabilizing their mutual relations.[27] Unsurprisingly, the creation of international law remains the domain of the State, which persists as the primary subject of international law; the Vienna Convention on the Law of Treaties, for example, is explicit in its application to States.[28] With specific relevance to the provisions on *jus cogens*, Article 53 of the Vienna Convention refers to peremptory norms as norms 'accepted and recognized by the international community *of States* as a whole'.[29] Subsequent commentary on the codification of *jus cogens* in the law of treaties has consistently conceived the international community to be one constituting States and, indeed, comprising all States.[30] This corresponds to the source of peremptory norms, namely, their customary formation

[25] Tomuschat, *Obligations Arising for States Without or Against their Will*, 224.

[26] Charter of the United Nations, Chapter II, Article 4 (1945).

[27] *See* Leo Gross, *The Peace of Westphalia, 1648–1948*, 42(1) American Journal of International Law 20–41 (1948).

[28] 1155 UNTS 331, Article 1 (1969). [29] *Ibid.*, Article 53 (emphasis added).

[30] Hannikainen, Peremptory Norms (*Jus Cogens*) in International Law 58; Mosler, *The International Society as a Legal Community*, 4.

and articulation through State practice.[31] In this procedural sense, the clause *of States* may be taken to refer to the formal source of peremptory norms as oriented in the practice of States.[32]

A substantive interpretation of the clause arises when conceiving of the State in an existential sense. It serves presently to recall the origin and purpose of the State as a point of departure. In classical philosophy, Aristotle considered the *polis* to be a complete community charged with, and capable of, providing for the wellbeing of its members. Accordingly, 'the end of the state is not mere life; it is, rather, a good quality of life', and it is this elemental purpose that government, in whatever form, is directed to fulfil.[33] That the ultimate purpose of law and society is the good of its members is sometimes obscured behind the façade of the State. However, the principle is expressed in contemporary discourse on law and society,[34] and although novel to the international law of the early twentieth century,[35] the proposition has found significant traction in contemporary international law.[36] Human rights discourse has increasingly depicted the sovereignty of the State to be contingent upon its fulfilment of the basic wellbeing of the individual, reinforcing the premise that 'States are no more than instruments whose inherent function it is to serve the interests of their citizens . . .'[37]

31 *See* discussion *infra*, Chapter 8.B (Article 53 of the Vienna Convention).

32 This understanding was shared by members of the ILC throughout the drafting of Article 53: *see, e.g.*, [1966] I(1) YbILC 39, para. 34 (828th Meeting, statement by Mr De Luna). This understanding was also expressed by Governments upon submission of the draft articles. *See, e.g.*, Waldock, Fifth Report, [1966] II YbILC 21–2 (recalling statements by Algeria, Brazil, and Indonesia).

33 Aristotle, POLITICS OF ARISTOTLE III.xi.6 (Oxford University Press, Ernest Barker trans., 1973 [*c.* 350 BC]).

34 *See, e.g.*, Steven Vago, LAW AND SOCIETY 21 (London: Prentice Hall 9th edn, 2009) (citing Roscoe Pound, AN INTRODUCTION TO THE PHILOSOPHY OF LAW, 98–9 (New Haven, CT: Yale University Press 1922)).

35 *See, e.g.*, Clyde Eagleton, *Some Questions as to the Place of the Individual in the International Law of the Future*, 37(4) AMERICAN JOURNAL OF INTERNATIONAL LAW 642 (1943); Phillip Brown, *The Individual in International Law*, 18(3) AMERICAN JOURNAL OF INTERNATIONAL LAW 532, 536 (1924).

36 Anne Peters, *Humanity as the* Alpha *and* Omega *of Sovereignty*, 20(3) EUROPEAN JOURNAL OF INTERNATIONAL LAW 513, 513–44 (2009); Rhoda Howard and Jack Donnelly, *Dignity, Human Rights, and Political Regimes*, 80(3) THE AMERICAN POLITICAL SCIENCE REVIEW 801, 803–4 (1986); Wolfgang Friedmann, *The Changing Dimensions of International Law*, 62(7) COLUMBIA LAW REVIEW 1147, 1148 (1962).

37 Christian Tomuschat, *General Course on Public International Law*, 281 RECUEIL DES COURS 161–2, para. 2 (1999); *see* James Brierly, THE LAW OF NATIONS 55 (Oxford: Clarendon Press 6th edn, 1963).

If the purpose of the State, in the most basic sense, is to promote the wellbeing of its members, then it is conceivable that the *international community of States* should be oriented in this common purpose: the wellbeing of the individuals who constitute the community of mankind residing in political subdivisions of States. Put differently, *of States* can be seen to align the interests of a community encompassing all States with their *raison d'être* as States. In a similar sense, the qualifier *of States* can be seen to have a limiting effect upon the scope of the interests of the international community as a whole cognizable through *jus cogens*. The US Supreme Court described the law of nations, the analogue of *jus cogens* in US jurisprudence, as 'a sphere in which [the] rules binding individuals for the benefit of other individuals overlapped with the norms of state relationships'.[38] From this view, *of States* can be seen to focus the interests of an international community of human-oriented States on those particular such interests implicated by the relations of States as interacting and interdependent units within that community.

iii. 'as a whole'

The clause *as a whole* refers to singularity in the interests and values from which peremptory norms emerge. Procedurally, the placement of the clause immediately after *of States* qualifies the way in which State practice contributes to the emergence of peremptory norms. This literal interpretation of the clause was explained by the Chairman of the Drafting Committee at the Vienna Conference:

> [B]y inserting the words 'as a whole' ... the Drafting Committee had wished to stress that there was no question of requiring a rule to be accepted and recognized as peremptory by all States. It would be enough if a very large majority did so[.][39]

Consistent with this interpretation is the modern emphasis placed upon *opinio juris*, rather than universality in the practice of every State, in the formation of customary international law.[40] This holism is especially appropriate with respect to *jus cogens* because the category is understood to constitute 'positive law created by States, not as individuals but as organs of the international community'.[41]

[38] *Sosa v. Alvarez-Machain*, 542 US 692, 715 (2004).
[39] UNCLOT, First Session (1968) 472, para. 12 (statement by Mr Yasseen).
[40] *See* discussion *infra*, Chapter 8.B.ii (State Practice).
[41] [1966] I(1) YbILC 39, para. 34 (828th Meeting, statement by Mr De Luna).

Underlying this procedural dimension, by which peremptory norms emerge through acceptance and recognition by States *as a whole*, is the substantive implication of the clause: *as a whole* emphasizes the commonality of values and interests of the international community which transcend the individual State. In this sense, the clause is invocative of an international community as a singular entity whose values and interests reflect holism rather than aggregation. It is in this sense that the International Court of Justice observed, in the context of the Genocide Convention, that 'States do not have any interests of their own; they merely have, one and all, a common interest'.[42] *As a whole* can be considered in this sense as a qualifier that substantively distinguishes interests and values articulated through the international community from those incidentally common to States.

***

Taken together, *the international community of States as a whole* depicts a layered concept. It contains both procedural and substantive elements of a juridical entity expressing the interests and values of an international community organized as States, advancing the collective social needs of mankind, made necessary by the subdivision of the international community into interrelated States. Procedurally, the construct describes the way in which peremptory norms emerge from States, acting collectively as organs of the international community. Substantively, the construct reflects the collective social need of mankind, arising from the relations of States and defined by their common interests and values, in furtherance of a common good based upon individual wellbeing, pursuant to which States are themselves organized. This bifurcated understanding of the concept, hereinafter referred to in shorthand as 'the international community', can be understood in terms of complementary aspects by which its procedural dimension promotes its substantive end. This is to suggest that the collective social need of mankind is advanced through the practice of States acting collectively as organs of the international community to establish peremptory norms of general international law.

B Individual-oriented interests

This interpretation of the international community is consistent with the prevailing understanding of the subject matter of *jus cogens*. In its

42 *Reservations to the Genocide Convention*, Advisory Opinion, ICJ Reports 1951, p. 15, 23.

commentary to an earlier draft of the Vienna Convention, the ILC observed that '[i]t is not the form of a general rule of international law but the particular nature of the subject-matter with which it deals that may, in the opinion of the Commission, give it the character of *jus cogens*'.[43] This subject matter has been understood to embody 'extra-State' interests, or 'the higher interest of the whole international community', a point advanced by Alfred Verdross in both his scholarly work and his capacity as a member of the drafting committee of the ILC:

> The criterion for these rules consists in the fact that they do not exist to satisfy the needs of the individual states but the higher interest of the whole international community. Hence these rules are absolute.[44]

Verdross explicitly drew this connection during the drafting of the law of treaties by asserting that 'norms having the character of *jus cogens*' are those 'related to the interests of the international community, in other words, to those of all mankind'.[45] In this view, the interests of the international community reflect those of mankind as distinct from those understood in terms of States. These interests may be understood through the same procedural and substantive lenses implicit in the construct *international community of States as a whole.*

The interests of the international community reflect 'extra-State' interests in the sense that they transcend those of the individual State. This aspect of interests of the international community conforms to the procedural conceptualization of the construct developed above, according to which peremptory norms emerge from States acting as organs of the international community as a whole in furtherance of its common interests. Substantively, these interests are those that explicitly concern the social need of mankind. During the drafting of the ILC Articles on State Responsibility, *special rapporteur* Willem Riphagen highlighted these dimensions by reference to:

> . . . the tendencies in modern international law to recognize and protect interests which are 'extra-State' interests in the sense that their ultimate beneficiaries are entities which are not States, but individual human beings, peoples or even humanity as a whole.[46]

[43] [1966] II YbILC 248, para. 2 (Commentary to Draft Article 50).
[44] Verdross, Jus Dispositivum *and* Jus Cogens *in International Law* 55, 58.
[45] [1966] I(1) YbILC 37, para. 9 (828th Meeting, statement by Mr Verdross) (noting also 'that nearly all the governments had accepted the basic principle').
[46] Willem Riphagen, Second Report on State Responsibility, [1981] II(1) YbILC 86, para. 61.

Riphagen proceeded to describe these 'extra-State' interests as given to States through rights and obligations 'in trust'.[47] The Inter-American Commission of Human Rights echoed this sentiment in the *Michael Domingues* case:

> Norms of *jus cogens* ... derive their status from fundamental values held by the international community, as violations of such [peremptory] norms are considered to shock the conscience of humankind and therefore bind the international community as a whole, irrespective of protest, recognition or acquiescence.[48]

As with the interpretation of 'international community' above, the procedural and substantive aspects of its 'interests' are complementary: the interests of the international community are extra-State insofar as they transcend the State and concern the benefit of mankind.

The substantive element of the interests of the international community indicates that the beneficiary of the interests protected by *jus cogens* is, in the first instance, the individual. In his Third Report on the Law of Treaties, Fitzmaurice, in one of the earliest articulations of the concept of *jus cogens* in international law, referred for illustrative purposes to 'cases where the position of the individual is involved, and where the rules contravened are rules instituted for the protection of the individual'.[49] Waldock, the next and final *special rapporteur* on the law of treaties, similarly linked the interests of the international community to protections of the individual:

> [T]he more the international community became integrated, the more its attention would be directed to the position of the individual. Significant *jus cogens* developments could therefore by expected in the direction of the protection of the rights of the individual in the interests of the world community as a whole.[50]

These observations are consistent both with the discussion above and with the later articulation of *special rapporteur* Riphagen during the drafting of the Articles on State Responsibility, who posited the beneficiaries of such norms to be 'human beings, peoples, or humanity as a whole'.[51] Verdross

[47] *Ibid.*
[48] *Domingues v. United States*, No. 12.285, Inter-American Commission on Human Rights, Report No. 62/02, para. 49 (2000).
[49] Gerald Fitzmaurice, Third Report on the Law of Treaties, [1958] II YbILC 40, para. 76.
[50] [1966] I(1) YbILC 40, para. 56 (828th Meeting, statement by Mr Waldock).
[51] Willem Riphagen, Second Report on State Responsibility, [1981] II(1) YbILC 86, para. 61.

goes further to propose that 'all rules of general international law created for a humanitarian purpose' constitute *jus cogens*.[52]

Conversely, if the interests of the international community are 'extra-State' in character, it would be a *non sequitur* to conceive of such interests in terms of States. This is particularly so considering the way in which the practice of States pursuant to these interests reflects their capacity to act as organs of the international community and does not depend upon a uniformity of practice of each individual State.[53] States are instrumental to a procedural understanding of the articulation of higher interests of the international community as peremptory norms, yet these interests are not those of States *qua* States, except in the most abstract sense of the State's *raison d'être*.[54] Rather, as a construct referring to shared interests and values of mankind, it follows that the higher interests of the community refer to those of the human being. Identifying the individual, the unit of mankind, as the ultimate beneficiary of peremptory norms accepted and recognized by the international community is supported by the conceptualization of international community depicted above and, in turn, the interests of the international community.

From the perspective of this *travaux préparatoires* and relevant commentary, the interests of the international community of States as a whole, which give rise to *jus cogens*, are oriented in safeguarding the most basic values and interests of mankind, the beneficiary of which is the individual. This understanding of the interests of the international community is pervasive throughout the discourse of international law. Judge Hermann Mosler observes that the 'common interest of mankind to which international law is devoted, includes the protection of the dignity of man'.[55] Judge Bruno Simma suggests that the conceptualization of 'community interest' departs from the bilateralism that traditionally characterizes international law, and it represents values that transcend the individual interests of States to concern all States.[56] The consequence of this conceptualization is to draw attention to the interests of an international community composed not only of States, 'but in the

[52] Verdross, Jus Dispositivum *and* Jus Cogens, 55, 59. (This is one of three groups of *jus cogens* proposed by Verdross, the others being the prohibition of treaties infringing upon the rights of third-States and rules regarding the use of force in the UN Charter.)

[53] *See* discussion *infra*, Chapter 8.B.ii (State Practice).

[54] *See* discussion *infra*, Chapter 8.B.i (*Opinio Juris Sive Necessitatis*).

[55] Mosler, *The International Society as a Legal Community*, 70.

[56] Bruno Simma, *From Bilateralism to Community Interest in International Law*, 250 Recueil des Cours 233–4 (1994).

last instance all human beings'.[57] Similarly, Judge A. A. Cançado Trindade notes the increasing importance of 'basic considerations of humanity' in the formation of international law as delimiting interests beyond the will of the State, deriving 'from human conscience', which are 'shared by the international community as a whole and humankind'.[58] C. Wilfred Jenks posits that the will of the international community 'reflects human nature and human aspirations' and that its binding force flows from its expression of 'the fundamental law of our being, the brotherhood of man'.[59] And Andreas Paulus identifies the emergence of 'a newer, community interest régime [that] covers human or community interests ... [whose] ultimate beneficiaries are human beings, groups, and humanity-at-large rather than States as such'.[60] What is common across each of these accounts, which represent an increasingly accepted position in contemporary international law, is that the common interests of the international community as a whole are not State interests per se. Rather, these interests concern mankind as a whole and are best conceived in terms of the individual as the unit of mankind rather than by the metrics of the State.

The individual-oriented character of the interests of the international community is often presented through concepts – basic considerations of humanity, the fundamental wellbeing of the individual, and the juridical conscience of mankind – which lack precision.[61] One resolution to this issue lies in the identification of a more refined principle that subsumes these other concepts while effectively representing the interests of the international community. The general legal principle of human dignity, which itself is frequently invoked to represent the interests of the

57 *Ibid.* ('Thus, a rising awareness of the common interests of the international community, a community that comprises not only States, but in the last instance all human beings, has begun to change the nature of international law profoundly.')

58 Antônio Augusto Cançado Trindade, *International Law for Humankind: Towards a New Jus Gentium (II) – General Course on Public International Law*, 317 Recueil des Cours 19–20, 272 (2005).

59 C. Wilfred Jenks, Law, Freedom and Welfare 99–100 (London: Stevens & Sons 1963).

60 Andreas Paulus, Jus Cogens *in a Time of Hegemony and Fragmentation*, 74(2) Nordic Journal of International Law 297, 309 (2005).

61 *See, e.g.*, Ian Brownlie, Principles of Public International Law 27 (Oxford: Clarendon Press 5th edn, 1998) (suggesting that 'considerations of humanity', as a source of law, 'may be related to human values already protected by positive legal principles which, taken together, reveal certain criteria of public policy and invite the use of analogy. Such criteria have obvious connections with general principles of law and with equity, but they need no particular justification').

international community,[62] satisfies this role by capturing each of these other articulations of 'higher interests'. In this capacity, human dignity is a term of art that has served as a general principle of law since antiquity and throughout the Enlightenment period; it is expressed by modern constitutionalism, provides the basis for the law of the European Union, and informs the content of universal instruments in public international law. Today, the dignity of the human being can be found as an animating principle of *jus cogens*, which may be seen as the most recent development in this intellectual and political tradition. To utilize human dignity as a proxy for the interests of the international community of States as a whole, it is necessary first to discuss the philosophy of the concept, before turning to its political history as a general principle of law.

C The philosophy of human dignity

The concept of human dignity derives from antiquity and the tradition of natural law. The underlying idea of 'human' originates in Greek philosophy and has been attributed to Aristotle's conceptualization of the wholeness of the human person.[63] The Roman Law notion of 'dignity', or *dignitas*, captures ideas of rank and status belonging to the individual.[64] *Dignitas hominis*, commonly attributed to Cicero, unites these two concepts to denote the inherent status of 'worthiness' of every individual by virtue of his being human.[65] In his first articulation of the concept, Cicero defines the dignity of the human being as 'the honourable authority of a person, combined with attention and honour and worthy respect paid to him',[66] a conceptualization that reveals two distinct elements.[67]

62 *See* discussion *infra*, Chapter 4.D (Peremptory Norms of General International Law (*Jus Cogens*)).

63 Michael Smith, Human Dignity and the Common Good in the Aristotelian-Thomistic Tradition 7–13 (Lewiston, NY: Mellen University Press 1995).

64 Don Chalmers and Ryuichi Ida, *On the International Legal Aspects of Human Dignity*, *in* Perspectives on Human Dignity: A Conversation 158 (Dordrecht: Springer, Jess Malpas & Norelle Lickiss eds., 2007).

65 Hubert Canick, *'Dignity of Man' and 'Persona' in Stoic Anthropology: Some Remarks on Cicero, De Officiis I 105–107*, *in* The Concept of Human Dignity in Human Rights Discourse 19 (The Hague: Klewer Law International, David Kretzmer & Klein Eckart eds., 2002).

66 Marcus Tullius Cicero, De Inventione, De Optimo Genere Oratorum, Topica, II.LV.166 (*'dignitas est alicuius honesta et cultu et honore et verecundia digna auctoritas'*) (London: William Heinemann Ltd., H. M. Hubbell trans., 1968 [*c.* 46 BC]).

67 David Feldman, *Human Dignity as a Legal Value: Part I*, Public Law 682, 686–7 (1999); Canick, *'Dignity of Man' and 'Persona in Stoic Anthropology*, 129, 23; Guy Green, *Human*

The first is human dignity as an inward quality of the individual, to whom dignity is inalienably endowed by virtue of his human being. It is in this sense that human dignity operates as a general principle of law that gives rise to basic rights and freedoms of the individual deriving from humanity. The second is an outward quality that informs relations towards other individuals in society in the form of duties. As such, human dignity is a morally prescriptive principle of respect that defines its imperative precepts to be afforded to all human brings. These two aspects of human dignity are expressed in Cicero's later articulation of the concept:

> It is important too to realize that each of us is endowed by nature with two characteristics: the first is common to all, in that we share that reason and dignity which is the mark of our superiority over the animal kingdom, and from which is derived all that is good and fitting as well as the capacity for discovering our duty; the second is particular to each individual, for just as bodies differ enormously, some being able to move quickly, others being strong in combat, some having an impressive presence, others possessing an endearing charm, so in characters there are just as many, or rather even more, differences.[68]

In this passage, human dignity is taken to be a quality that distinguishes human beings from animals, and the previous definition of dignity is expanded in detail. The two aforementioned aspects are elaborated upon, noting human dignity as both a quality of the individual and a common duty based in reason. Taken together, Cicero's articulations of human dignity bear the hallmarks of the natural law tradition of the Stoics, according to which universal realities of mankind's humanity, freedom, and direction by reason establish a law common to all of mankind.[69] The first aspect of human dignity, as a quality of the individual, is addressed at present.

Since its inception in Stoic philosophy, the concept of human dignity has time and again guided normative development and shaped social expectations. Several prominent iterations illustrate this recurrent influence of human dignity. In the context of religion, Christianity, more than

Dignity and the Law, *in* PERSPECTIVES ON HUMAN DIGNITY: A CONVERSATION 151 (Malpas & Lickiss eds.); Doron Shultziner, HUMAN DIGNITY: FUNCTIONS AND MEANINGS, *in* PERSPECTIVES ON HUMAN DIGNITY: A CONVERSATION 74–92 (Malpas & Lickiss eds.).

68 Marcus Tullius Cicero, ON MORAL OBLIGATION (DE OFFICIIS), Book I, para. 107 (London: Faber and Faber Ltd., John Higginbotham, trans., 1967 [*c.* 44 BC]).

69 *See* discussion *infra*, Chapter 7.A (Ancient Law).

any other, places significant weight upon human dignity as a foundational principle that emphasizes the worth of the human person.[70] The expression of human dignity in Christian thought was articulated by Thomas Aquinas, according to whom the dignity of human beings derives from their creation in God's image.

> Man is made to God's image, and since this implies, so Damascene tells us, that he is intelligent and free to judge and master of himself, so then, now that we have agreed that God is the exemplar cause of things and that they issue from his power through his will, we go on to look at this image, that is to say, at man as the source of actions which are his own and fall under his responsibility and control.[71]

Freedom and reason, those qualities of the individual regarded as the basis of human dignity, follow in this view from man's creation in the image of God. This Thomistic depiction of autonomy accounts for the worth of the human person. Aquinas presents just such a conceptualization of the dignity of man, in the context of violating the premises of dignity:

> A man who sins deviates from the rational order, and so loses his human dignity [dignitate humana] in so far as a man is naturally free and an end unto himself.[72]

Here, though developing the concept of human dignity through Christianity by accounting for dignity in the context of God, Aquinas retains the classical notions of freedom and reason as the basis for respect; this dignity is similarly taken to be that quality of human beings which distinguishes Man from beast.[73] The continuity is significant notwithstanding the distinction applied by some scholarship to segregate human dignity in its specifically religious context.[74] Its significance lies in its

[70] Smith, Human Dignity and the Common Good in the Aristotelian-Thomistic Tradition 1; Robert Kraynak, *'Made in the Image of God': The Christian View of Human Dignity and Political Order, in* In Defense of Human Dignity: Essays for Our Times 81 (University of Notre Dame Press, Robert Kraynak & Glenn Tinder eds., 2003).

[71] Thomas Aquinas, Summa Theologiae 1a2a3, Prologus (London: Blackfriars ed. 1969 [*c.* 1265–1274]).

[72] Thomas Aquinas, Summa Theologiae 2a2ae, 64.2.3 (London: Blackfriars ed. 1975 [*c.* 1265–1274]).

[73] *Ibid.*, 64.3.2.

[74] *Cf.* Christopher McCrudden, *Human Dignity and Judicial Interpretation of Human Rights*, 19(4) European Journal of International Law 655, 658–9 (2008) (distinguishing between religious, philosophical, and historical approaches to human dignity, while recognizing a 'bridge' between ancient law and Catholicism).

indicia that human dignity is a consistent, rather than merely recurring, concept in the discourse of humanity.

Renaissance Humanism, an intellectual movement that championed the 'self-emancipation of man', embraced human dignity as its central premise.[75] The seminal articulation of the period is the renowned *Oratio* of Giovanni Pico Della Mirandola, delivered at Rome in 1486. The famously erudite Mirandola is credited with 'the most succinct expression of the mind of the Renaissance', and his *Oration on the Dignity of Man* (as it is now commonly called) is regarded as 'the manifesto of humanism'.[76] The conceptualization of human dignity depicted by Mirandola continues in the tradition established during the Greek Enlightenment and embraced by Aquinas:

> The nature of all other creatures is defined and restricted within laws which We have laid down; you, by contrast, impeded by no such restrictions, may, by your own free will, to whose custody We have assigned you, trace for yourself the lineaments of your own nature. I have placed you at the very center of the world, so that from that vantage point you may with greater ease glance round about you on all that the world contains. We have made you a creature neither of heaven nor of earth, neither mortal nor immortal, in order that you may, as the free and proud shaper of your own being, fashion yourself in the form you may prefer. It will be in your power to descend to the lower, brutish forms of life; you will be able, through your own decision, to rise again to the superior orders whose life is divine.[77]

The human dignity depicted by Mirandola contains the principal elements of classical and ecclesiastical articulations. Here, again, dignity is recognized as that quality which distinguishes human beings from all other living beings. It is based in the free will of the individual, a self-determination which presupposes the possession of reason to guide man's actions.

Human dignity is a cornerstone of Enlightenment thought, as exemplified by the philosophy of Immanuel Kant, who implements the classical principle as the guiding force of his categorical imperative. In doing so,

[75] Don Chalmers and Ryuichi Ida, *On the International Legal Aspects of Human Dignity*, *in* PERSPECTIVES ON HUMAN DIGNITY: A CONVERSATION 159 (Malpas & Lickiss eds.).

[76] Russell Kirk, *Introductory Remarks*, *in* Giovanni Pico Della Mirandola, ORATION ON THE DIGNITY OF MAN *(DE HOMINIS DIGNITATE)* xi and xiii (Washington, DC: Regnery Publishing, A. Robert Caponigri trans., 2006 [1496]).

[77] Pico Della Mirandola, ORATION ON THE DIGNITY OF MAN (*DE HOMINIS DIGNITATE*) 7–8.

Kant adds a particular depth to a concept that continues to shape contemporary law and morality.[78] Kant's theory is oriented in a view of man and his nature which conceives that humanity is to be used, both in one's own person and in others, always as an end and never merely a means.[79] The influence of Stoic philosophy on Kant's categorical imperative is evident, and both the individual and social aspects of human dignity are expressed by the categorical imperative. In its first formulation, the categorical imperative is understood as the directive to 'act in accordance with a maxim that can at the same time make itself a universal law', meaning normative prescriptions must be applicable to the service of all members of society.[80] The second formulation emphasizes the ultimate value of the rational being as 'the subject of ends', which requires that the individual is always treated as an end only and never merely as a means.[81] These first two formulations contribute to the third and final formulation of the categorical imperative, the 'formal principle':

> [A]ct as if your maxims were to serve at the same time as a universal law (for all rational beings). A kingdom of ends is thus possible only by analogy with a kingdom of nature; the former, however, is possible only through maxims, that is, rules imposed upon oneself, the latter only through laws of externally necessitated efficient causes.[82]

A kingdom, in this sense, is conceived to be 'a systematic union of various rational beings through common laws', and it is one of ends by virtue of its laws, which 'have as their purpose . . . the relation of these beings to one another as ends and means'.[83] This last expression of the categorical imperative unites the previous two while drawing attention to their divergent foci upon the individual and society. Universal laws are those that capture both elements, the individual as an end in himself and the social aspect of this quality that demands universal respect.

According to Kant, the dignity of the human person derives from the capacity to act in accordance with the categorical imperative. As a

[78] *See* Susan Shell, *Kant on Human Dignity*, *in* In Defense of Human Dignity: Essays for Our Times 53–80 (Kraynak & Tinder eds.).

[79] Immanuel Kant, Groundwork of the Metaphysics of Morals [1795], *in* The Cambridge Edition of the Works of Immanuel Kant 4:429 (Cambridge University Press, Mary Gregor ed., 1996) [hereinafter, Kant, Groundwork].

[80] *Ibid.*, 4:437–8; Immanuel Kant, Metaphysics of Morals [1797], *in* The Cambridge Edition of the Works of Immanuel Kant 6:225–6 (Gregor ed.) [hereinafter, Kant, Metaphysics].

[81] Kant, Groundwork 4:438. [82] *Ibid.*, 4:438. [83] *Ibid.*, 4:433.

rational being, man is capable of formulating universal laws, which require him to think in terms of both himself as an individual and society as a whole, comprising other individuals, for whom universal law must necessarily also be conceivable. Dignity in this sense is dependent upon freedom, 'the only original right belonging to every man by virtue of his humanity',[84] and reason, through which universal laws guiding conduct are formulated in accordance with the categorical imperative.[85] This dignity, which sets man apart from other beings,[86] denotes that 'he must always take his maxims from the point of view of himself, and likewise every other rational being, as lawgiving beings (who for this reason are also called persons)'.[87] It is in this context that Kant articulates the idea of respect found in Cicero's classical interpretation of dignity:

> Our own will insofar as it would act only under the condition of a possible giving of universal law through its maxims – this will possible for us in idea – is the proper object of respect; and the dignity of humanity consists just in this capacity to give universal law, though with the condition of also being itself subject to this very lawgiving.[88]

Thus, the ability of the individual to act in accordance with the categorical imperative, which is to formulate and apply universal laws, is the source of the respect owed to human dignity in both its inward and its outward aspects; put differently, human dignity is, at once, the subject and object of respect. This ability to exercise reason according to the categorical imperative is the capacity for morality. Kant summarizes the relation of these various aspects of human dignity as follows:

> With the idea of freedom the concept of autonomy is now inseparably combined, and with the concept of *autonomy* the universal principle of morality, which in idea is the ground of all actions of *rational beings*, just as the law of nature is the ground of all appearances.[89]

Dignity depicts the value attached to the human being by virtue of these qualities, which Kant describes in a literal sense as having no price.[90]

***

84 Kant, Metaphysics 6:237. 85 Kant, Groundwork 4:434. 86 *Ibid.*, 4:452.
87 *Ibid.*, 4:438. 88 *Ibid.*, 4:440. 89 *Ibid.*, 4:452.
90 Kant, Groundwork 4:434–5 ('What is related to general human inclinations and needs has a *market price*; that which, even without presupposing a need, conforms with a certain taste, that is, with a delight in the mere purposeless play of our mental powers, has a *fancy price*; but that which constitutes the condition under which alone something can be an end in itself has not merely a relative worth, that is, a price, but an inner worth, that is, *dignity*').

Human dignity is a concept defined by rich classical, ecclesiastical, and philosophical traditions. Notwithstanding their expansive diversity, these overlapping sources reveal a common foundation that refutes the charge that the concept lacks substantive meaning. On the contrary, human dignity is a term of art that has retained a basic philosophical core throughout its intellectual history denoting the inalienable worth of the individual as a human being, deserving of respect from other human beings, in society.[91] The power of human dignity lies in the way in which the principle influences law and morality in society. It is nonsensical, however, to conceive of human dignity as a right in itself; it is more correctly taken to be a functional expression of humanity. In this view, human dignity represents the worth of the individual that must be protected if society is to fulfil its purpose of promoting the wellbeing of the individual. It is in this sense that human dignity operates as a general legal principle to inform the content of the most basic norms and laws of society. The next chapter examines the influence of human dignity across political systems as a general principle of law.[92]

[91] *See, e.g.*, McCrudden, *Human Dignity and Judicial Interpretation of Human Rights*, 655, 679 (2008) (referring to a 'basic minimum content' or 'minimum core' of human dignity).

[92] *Cf. ibid.* (suggesting that human dignity operates merely as a 'placeholder' devoid of substance, which forfeits the intrinsic power of the concept).

4

Human dignity as a general principle of law

In a structural sense, human dignity is conceived to serve a foundational role in the maintenance of society that justifies the existence and authority of the institution of law. It has been observed that the dignity of the human being becomes truly purposeful only when recognized and protected by law.[1] In this sense, human dignity is posited to represent 'a supreme value that bestows moral justification upon the concrete instructions' of fundamental laws of society, laws that conventionally take the form of a constitution.[2] This implies, broadly, that human dignity is a purpose of law, given that the dignity of the individual as a free and autonomous being can be realized only in the context of a community where it is protected by the institution of law.[3] Consequently, the rule of law is necessary for the respect of the dignity of the human person and, as a corollary, to disregard the rule of law is to violate human dignity.[4] Therefore, safeguarding the dignity of the human being represents the ultimate goal of legal and social order.[5] The interrelation of law,

[1] Michael Smith, HUMAN DIGNITY AND THE COMMON GOOD IN THE ARISTOTELIAN-THOMISTIC TRADITION 166 (Lewiston, NY: Mellen University Press 1995); *see* Dominique Rousseau, *Concluding Report*, EUROPEAN COMMISSION FOR DEMOCRACY THROUGH LAW, Proceedings of the UniDem Seminar organized in Montpellier (France) from 2 to 6 July 1998 (1999).

[2] Doron Shultziner, *Human Dignity: Functions and Meanings*, *in* PERSPECTIVES ON HUMAN DIGNITY: A CONVERSATION 76 (The Hague: Kluwer Law International, David Kretzmer & Klein Eckart eds., 2007).

[3] John Finnis, NATURAL LAW AND NATURAL RIGHTS 272 (Oxford: Clarendon Press 1980).

[4] Joseph Raz, THE AUTHORITY OF LAW 221 (Oxford: Clarendon Press 1983).

[5] Michael Reisman et al., *The New Haven School: A Brief Introduction*, 32 YALE JOURNAL OF INTERNATIONAL LAW 575, 580 (2007); William Morison, *Myres S. McDougal and Twentieth-Century Jurisprudence: A Comparative Essay*, *in* TOWARD WORLD ORDER AND HUMAN DIGNITY 48 (New York: Free Press, Myres McDougal & Burns Weston eds., 1976); Herman Mosler, *The International Society as a Legal Community*, 140 RECUEIL DES COURS 98 (1974).

society, and human dignity thus provides an explanation for the basic authority of the institution of law.[6]

The proposition that law is essential to the maintenance of society oriented in the protection of human dignity is a conceptualization as old as written history itself. Before the International Criminal Tribunal for the former Yugoslavia (ICTY), Judge Shahabuddeen evoked the writings of Thucydides to establish the pedigree of considerations of humanity in the foundation of ancient law and illustrate their relevance to law imperative to present-day international society. In his Separate Opinion in *Tadić*, Judge Shahabuddeen begins with the following passage borrowing from *The Peloponnesian War*:

> Some time ago, yet not far from where the events in this case happened, a 'breakdown of law and order' occurred. There 'were savage and pitiless actions into which men were carried not so much for the sake of gain as because they were swept away into an internecine struggle by their ungovernable passions'. The turmoil saw 'the ordinary conventions of civilised life thrown into confusion'. Sadly, it seems, people took 'it upon themselves to begin the process of repealing those general laws of humanity which are there to give a hope of salvation to all who are in distress, instead of leaving those laws in existence, remembering that there may come a time when they, too, will be in danger and will need their protection'.
>
> That last reflection of a great thinker of antiquity was later expressed in the saying by Westlake 'that the mitigation of war must depend on the parties to it feeling that they belong to a larger whole than their respective tribes or states, a whole in which the enemy too is comprised, so that the duties arising out of that larger citizenship are owed even to him'. The development of a sense of that 'larger citizenship' has been disappointingly slow. Since the ancient chronicler spoke of the 'general laws of humanity', then lacking legal force but still recognisable, it has taken over two thousand years for those 'laws' to assume the shape of binding norms applying world-wide.[7]

Shahabuddeen's introductory statement draws attention to two particular points, the first of which is the continuity of law based in humanity and its role in the 'ordinary conventions of civilised life'. Since time

[6] This is distinct from legal positivism, which concerns the legitimacy of laws within a legal system, rather than the authority of the legal system itself, which necessarily precedes positive sources of law.

[7] *Prosecutor v. Tadić*, Sep. Op. Shahabuddeen, IT-94-1-A, 150, paras. 1–2 (1999) (footnotes omitted) (The quotations in the first paragraph are taken from Thucydides, The Peloponnesian War 211 (Hereford: Penguin, Rex Warner trans., 1961) (regarding the island of Corcyra); those in the second appear in Lassa Oppenheim (ed.), The Collected Papers of John Westlake on Public International Law 274 (Cambridge University Press 1914).)

immemorial, human society has been predicated upon the preservation of the basic dignity of the human being, considerations forming a 'law of humanity' binding notwithstanding the absence of formal legal authority.[8] The authority of norms protecting the dignity of the human being is therefore derived not from the institution of law, but rather, from the intrinsic importance of human dignity to the maintenance of human coexistence. The second point to which Shahabuddeen draws attention is particularly salient: that the laws of humanity have come to 'assume the shape of binding norms applying world-wide'. Thus, not only is the institution of law based upon the dignity of the human person, but also this common value of human dignity has been articulated through norms of international law.

Human dignity has broadly been expressed as a general principle of law necessary for social coexistence,[9] one that informs the content of fundamental legal norms across the domains of domestic, regional, and public international law. However, notwithstanding this common general principle of law, its manifestations are diverse and particular to the exigencies of various domains which, in turn, prohibits any general conclusion about common substantive expression.[10] As a representation of the higher interests of the international community, it is unsurprising that the general legal principle of human dignity should permeate other strata of law: if the fundamental goal of legal order is the protection of human dignity,[11] then such pervasion is to be expected. The influence of human dignity across various domains of fundamental law reflects its importance to the maintenance of society and reinforces the way in which the principle reflects, in practice, interests common to the international community as a society encompassing the whole of mankind. To illuminate the application of human dignity as a general principle, its influence is demonstrated across four domains of law of fundamental character: domestic constitutional law, European Union law, public international law, and finally, *jus cogens*.

Importantly, the ubiquity of human dignity as a general legal principle across domains of law does not prove a singularity of legal

[8] This is essentially the premise of the natural law tradition: *see* discussion *infra*, Chapter 7.A (Ancient Law).

[9] David Feldman, *Human Dignity as a Legal Value: Part I*, PUBLIC LAW 682–702 (1999).

[10] This conclusion is consistent with the value as a general principle of law, the application of which generates relevant norms particular to the context of its application. *See* David Feldman, *Human Dignity as a Legal Value: Part II*, PUBLIC LAW 61, 75 (2000); Christopher McCrudden, *Human Dignity and Judicial Interpretation of Human Rights*, 19(4) EUROPEAN JOURNAL OF INTERNATIONAL LAW 655, 710–12 (2008).

[11] *See* discussion *supra*, text accompanying *nn.* 1–6.

systems. Although a monist legal order is implicit in later parts of this book,[12] interaction between systems does not equate to an implication that the various domains examined constitute a continuous legal order. While it is posited that human dignity has influenced the evolution of public order norms across constitutional, European Union, and public international law, the particular norms of these discrete systems are a product of their social and historical considerations that deny singularity. This reflects the Kantian proposition that human dignity generates rights and duties through the categorical imperative in the form of laws of 'public right' at the various domestic, inter-State, and cosmopolitan (global) levels.[13] Although public right denotes a distinct form and quality of the law as public order in kind, its diverse manifestations are peculiar to the dictates of the protection of human dignity required in their various domains. Consequently, although the intrinsic worth of the human person is expressed in public order norms across distinct areas of law, its substantive expression across these domains varies according to the diversity of legal systems considered, variation arising from historical, social, and systemic exigencies. The commonality of human dignity as a general principle of law is a broader reflection of the nature of the principle as one necessary to the maintenance of social coexistence and expressive of the higher interests of a community. The examination of human dignity across different legal domains is intended to demonstrate the nature and scope of the principle's practical influence. This perspective, in turn, suggests how it is possible to conceive of the role of human dignity as a general principle of law informing *jus cogens*, and places *jus cogens* into the context of a particular legal category.

A Constitutional law

Human dignity has played a central role in the jurisprudence of constitutional law since the American and French revolutions that marked the culmination of the Enlightenment period.[14] From the late eighteenth

[12] *See* discussion *infra*, text accompanying Ch. 5, *n.* 114 (quoting *Prosecutor v. Furundžija*, IT-95-17/1-T, paras. 153–5 (1998)).

[13] Charles Covell, THE LAW OF NATIONS IN POLITICAL THOUGHT 165 (New York: Palgrave Macmillan 2009).

[14] McCrudden, *Human Dignity and Judicial Interpretation of Human Rights*, 655, 664–5, 672–3 (2008); Andrew Clapham, HUMAN RIGHTS OBLIGATIONS OF NON-STATE ACTORS 534 (Oxford University Press 2006); Arthur Chaskalson, *Human Dignity as a Constitutional*

century onward, the legitimacy of constitutional instruments – the nexus of law and society – has been increasingly oriented in the dignity of the human person. It was noted above that domestic constitutions are taken to be expressions of the basic dignity of the human person and its realization in the context of society.[15] The consequently peremptory nature of constitutional law was expounded succinctly by Alexander Hamilton during the great constitutional debates of the United States in 1788: 'No legislative act, therefore, contrary to the Constitution, can be valid.'[16] Relating constitutional instruments to a general principle represented by human dignity reflects both the power of dignity as a concept and the common expectation of modern political society to promote the human dignity of its citizens.

This function of dignity is perhaps most overtly expressed by the constitutional instrument of Germany, the 1949 Basic Law, which in its first Article states that 'Human dignity shall be inviolable. To respect and protect it shall be the duty of all state authority.'[17] In the context of the German Constitution, the function of human dignity is understood as a general principle of law, or a fundamental legal norm, 'which inspires the interpretation and application of all other norms of the basic law'.[18] Importantly, the conceptualization of dignity evoked in the German experience is understood to be the very same as that elaborated in the previous chapter, as evidenced by the German Constitutional Court in the *Life Imprisonment* case:

> The constitutional principles of the Basic Law embrace the respect and protection of human dignity. The free human person and his or her dignity are the highest values of the constitutional order. The state in all of its forms is obliged to respect and defend it. This is based on the conception of human persons as spiritual-moral beings endowed

Value, *in* THE CONCEPT OF HUMAN DIGNITY IN HUMAN RIGHTS DISCOURSE 133–44 (The Hague: Kluwer Law International, David Kretzer & Klein Eckart eds., 2002).

15 Covell, THE LAW OF NATIONS IN POLITICAL THOUGHT 165 (attributing this position to Kant); Shultziner, *Human Dignity: Functions and Meanings*, 76.

16 THE FEDERALIST No. 78, at 466 (Alexander Hamilton) (New York: Penguin, Charles Kelser & Clinton Rossiter eds., 2003).

17 Basic Law for the Federal Republic of Germany, Article 1 ([1949] Christian Tomuschat & Donald Kommers trans., 2010).

18 Christian Walter, *Human Dignity in German Constitutional Law*, *in* THE PRINCIPLE OF RESPECT FOR HUMAN DIGNITY, European Commission for Democracy through Law (Proceedings of the UniDem Seminar, Montpelier 2–6 July 1998); *see* Edward Eberle, DIGNITY AND LIBERTY 41–5 (Westport, CT: Praeger 2002).

> with the freedom to determine and develop themselves. This freedom within the meaning of the Basic Law is not that of an isolated and self-regarding individual but rather that of a person related to and bound by the community. In the light of this community-boundedness, personal liberty cannot be "unlimited in principle." The individual must accept those limits on freedom of action that the legislature deems necessary in the interest of the community's social life; yet the autonomy of the individual also has to be protected. This means that the state must regard every individual within society with equal worth.[19]

That the principal elements of the concept of human dignity are presented in such clarity might be attributed to the particular influence of Christian and Kantian thought in the formulation of the German Basic Law.[20] However contemporary European constitutionalism would suggest otherwise; as a whole, European law is demonstrative of the way in which human dignity operates as the basis of constitutional norms.[21] It has been observed that 'the law in Europe (that is to say both the national legislation of the various states and European law) regards the human being as its '*raison d'être*',[22] and the majority of European constitutions lay claim, either explicitly or implicitly, to human dignity as a general legal principle.[23]

While the Western experience demonstrates human dignity to be an inherently liberal principle,[24] its recognition is by no means limited to the constitutional instruments of liberal States. Indeed, human dignity is evoked in the constitutional instruments of non-liberal States with a frequency matching, if not surpassing, that of constitutions of the West.

19 *Proceedings on the Constitutionality of §211 of the Criminal Code (Life Imprisonment Case)*, BVerfGE [Constitutional Court] (Germany), 45 BVerfGE 187, II.1 (1977), *in* Donald Kommers and Russell Miller, The Constitutional Jurisprudence of the Federal Republic of Germany 365 (Durham, NC: Duke University Press 3rd edn, 2012).

20 McCrudden, *Human Dignity and Judicial Interpretation of Human Rights*, 655, 665.

21 *See, e.g.*, Catherine Dupré, *Unlocking Human Dignity: Towards a Theory for the 21st Century*, 14(2) European Human Rights Law Review 190 (2009) (describing human dignity as the 'standard ingredient of European constitutions').

22 Christos Giakoumopoulos, *Opening Speech*, *in* The Principle of Respect for Human Dignity, European Commission for Democracy through Law.

23 *See* The Principle of Respect for Human Dignity, European Commission for Democracy through Law.

24 Rhoda Howard and Jack Donnelly, *Dignity, Human Rights, and Political Regimes*, 80(3) The American Political Science Review 801, 803 (1986); David Walsh, *Are Freedom and Dignity Enough?*, *in* In Defense of Human Dignity: Essays for Our Times (University of Notre Dame Press, Robert Kraynak & Glenn Tinder eds., 2003).

The Constitutions of Syria,[25] Cuba,[26] and Russia,[27] for example, each establish the State to be the guarantor of the non-derogable value of human dignity; the Cuban instrument goes so far as to identify human dignity as the general principle underpinning all law. The Basic Law of Saudi Arabia maintains that 'All acts that . . . detract from man's dignity and rights shall be prohibited',[28] and the Constitution of Côte d'Ivoire states that '[a]ll human beings are born free and equal before the law . . . and [enjoy] respect of their dignity.'[29] The Constitution of the People's Republic of China holds that '[t]he personal dignity of citizens . . . is inviolable'.[30] The Constitution of the Democratic Republic of Congo affirms that '[a]ll human beings are born free and equal in dignity and rights'.[31] What these instances demonstrate is a consistent practice of incorporating human dignity in constitutional instruments as some form of basic legal value or existential premise of the State, even where the State is in practice unwilling or unable to fulfil such expectations. This prevalence of human dignity, irrespective of contradiction with the prevailing political system of a State or its actual record of respect for individual rights, indicates the general recognition of the concept as a foundational principle of political order.

A study by the Constitutional Design Group demonstrates the veracity of the trend that human dignity operates as a general legal principle in constitutional instruments globally.[32] In its report entitled *Human Dignity*,[33] the group presents a statistical analysis on written constitutions entered into force since 1789, based upon a data set including 701 of the approximately 800 constitutions established during this period and more than 90 per cent of those codified since the Second World War. In essence, the report provides statistics on the recurrence of the phrase

[25] The Constitution of Syria, Article 25(1) (1973).
[26] The Constitution of the Republic of Cuba, Preamble, Article 9(a) (1992).
[27] The Constitution of the Russian Federation, Article 21 (1993).
[28] The Basic Law of Saudi Arabia, Article 39 (1992).
[29] The Constitution of Côte d'Ivoire, Article 2 (2000).
[30] The Constitution of the People's Republic of China, Article 38 (2004).
[31] The Constitution of the Democratic Republic of the Congo, Article 11 (2005).
[32] The Constitutional Design Group is an academic group sponsored by the Comparative Constitutions Project (CCP), whose stated objective is to 'investigate the sources and consequences of constitutional choices' through data on formal written constitutions since 1789.
[33] Constitutional Design Group, *Human Dignity*, Option Reports (2011) *accessed at* www.constitutionmaking.org/files/human_dignity.pdf (no longer available).

'human dignity' during this span to glean a sense of the historical trends of constitutional development throughout the period. The report finds that, while 38 per cent of all of the constitutions examined reference 'human dignity',[34] in 2000, roughly 70 per cent of the constitutions in force explicitly refer to human 'dignity' or the 'dignity of man'.[35] Of course, weight must only be given to such statistics with the greatest caution.[36] Nevertheless, such statistical findings are indicative of the extent to which human dignity is expressly invoked as a legal principle across regions and cultures, in the majority of constitutional instruments presently in force. The conclusion lends credence to the power and prevalence of human dignity in the practical discourse of constitutional law.

B European Union law

Although its law is inherently constitutional in nature, the European Union (EU) bears separate mention as a unique geopolitical entity with its own jurisprudence. Given that the constitutional law of its individual member States is oriented in the general principle of human dignity, it follows that the core law of the EU should similarly reflect the guiding principle of its constituent parts. This is the implication of the observation cited above, that 'the law in Europe (that is to say both the national legislation of the various states and European law) regards the human being as its "*raison d'être*"'.[37] Such a claim may be traced back to the objectives of the European Convention on Human

[34] *Ibid.*, 1. [35] *Ibid.*, 2.

[36] Statistical analysis does not capture the effective implementation of human dignity in constitutional instruments, which would require detailed scrutiny of every constitutional document and the content and intent of its provisions. For example, when assessing the regional variation of constitutions in force as of 2000, the report finds references to human dignity most common in Eastern Europe, Latin America, Sub-Saharan Africa, and the Middle East, and least common in Oceana, Western Europe, South and East Asia, and North America. Basing conclusions purely on explicit reference to 'human dignity' in constitutional documents would wrongly suggest the absence of commitment to human dignity in the founding instruments of the United States and Western Europe. On the contrary, human dignity is 'implicit' in the Constitution of the United States, *see* Eberle, Dignity and Liberty 46–8, a point demonstrated in the constitutional law of Europe above. Moreover, the recurrence of 'human dignity' fails to incorporate variance in the context in which the concept is referenced. Even so, the statistical evidence cited here supports the currency of human dignity as a general legal principle in constitutional instruments worldwide.

[37] Giakoumopoulos, *Opening Speech*.

Rights (1950),[38] 'the very essence of which', as the European Court of Human Rights has reiterated on numerous occassions, 'is respect for human dignity and freedom'.[39] More explicit codification of the general principle is found in the preamble of the Charter of Fundamental Rights of the European Union (2000):

> Conscious of its spiritual and moral heritage, the Union is founded on the indivisible, universal values of human dignity, freedom, equality and solidarity ... It places the individual at the heart of its activities[.][40]

The instrument leaves little question as to the place of human dignity in the constitutional order of the EU, placing it first in the general principles upon which the organization is based. The Charter proceeds to provide particular expressions of human dignity in its first Chapter, titled 'Dignity', in which Article 1 holds that 'Human dignity is inviolable. It must be respected and protected.'[41] The subsequent articles of the Chapter articulate protections of the right to life, the right to the integrity of the person, the prohibition of torture and inhumane or degrading treatment or punishment, and the prohibition of slavery or forced labour.[42] There is an unmistakable continuity between these provisions and several accepted and recognized norms of *jus cogens*.[43] It is a continuity that supports a common basis of these fundamental norms, which arise in both European law and general international law, as protections of human dignity.

Two oft-cited examples illustrate the role of human dignity in the jurisprudence of European law. The first instance concerns a French ban on 'dwarf tossing', a case that was ultimately decided by the United Nations Human Rights Committee (UNHRC), with respect to the International Covenant on Civil and Political Rights (ICCPR).[44] In *Manuel Wackenheim v. France* (2002), the claimant contended that the ban on dwarf throwing constituted discrimination, thereby violating the prohibition of discriminatory acts under Article 26 of the ICCPR. The

[38] European Convention for the Protection of Human Rights and Fundamental Freedoms, as amended by Protocols Nos. 11 and 14, ETS No. 5 (4 November 1950, *entered into force* 3 September 1953).

[39] *See, e.g., S.W. v. United Kingdom / C.R. v. United Kingdom*, No. 20166/92, 21 European Human Rights Reports 363, 44/42 (1996).

[40] Charter of Fundamental Rights of the European Union, 2000/C 364/01, Preamble (2000).

[41] *Ibid.*, Article 1. [42] *Ibid.*, Articles 2–5.

[43] *See* discussion *infra*, Chapter 11.A (Identifying Peremptory Norms).

[44] *Manuel Wackenheim v. France*, No. 854/1999, CCPR/C/75/D/854/1999 (2002).

contention was weighed against the position of the State, which held the ban to be consistent with the requisites of public policy, and in turn the principles underlying the Covenant more generally. Explicitly acknowledging the overriding value of human dignity, the Committee upheld the legality of the ban:

> The Committee considers that the State party has demonstrated, in the present case, that the ban on dwarf tossing as practised by the author did not constitute an abusive measure but was necessary in order to protect public order, which brings into play considerations of human dignity that are compatible with the objectives of the Covenant. The Committee accordingly concludes that the differentiation between the author and the persons to whom the ban ordered by the State party does not apply was based on objective and reasonable grounds.[45]

In context of the ICCPR, human dignity was implicitly identified by the Committee as a general legal principle. And, as the principle upon which the Covenant is based, human dignity provided the basis upon which the ban was upheld and the claim of differential treatment was rejected.

A second example in European jurisprudence is the *Omega* case (2004),[46] which concerned a German ban on a particular game in a British-made 'laserdrome', a 'killing game', in which participants simulate shooting one another with laser beams. The Bundesverwaltungsgericht endorsed the decision of the Oberverwaltungsgericht, which held that 'the commercial exploitation of a "killing game" . . . constituted an affront to human dignity', a value at the core of the German Basic Law.[47] In its Judgment, the court repeated with approval a statement by the Advocate General:

> [T]he Community legal order undeniably strives to ensure respect for human dignity as a general principle of law. There can therefore be no doubt that the objective of protecting human dignity is compatible with Community law, it being immaterial in that respect that, in Germany, the principle of respect for human dignity has a particular status as an independent fundamental right.[48]

Here, then, human dignity is recognized explicitly as a general principle of law, one upon which the legal order of the EU is based, the protection

[45] *Ibid.*, para. 7.4.

[46] *Omega Spielhallen-und Automatenaufstellungs-GmbH v. Oberbürgermeisterin der Bundesstadt Bonn*, Judgment, European Court of Justice (First Chamber), C-36/02, [2004] ECR I-9609 (2004).

[47] *Ibid.*, para. 11.

[48] *Ibid.*, para. 34.

of which is consistent with the basic policy goals of the European Community. The European Court of Justice (ECJ) goes so far as to hold that respect for fundamental rights, which derive from human dignity, justifies restrictions upon the free movement of goods and provision of services,[49] a remarkable finding in light of the historical origins of the EU as an economic community. On the basis of this reasoning, the Court upheld the legality of the ban as 'protecting public policy by reason of the fact that that activity is an affront to human dignity'.[50] In doing so, the court affirmed that human dignity is a general principle of law with an overriding value in the normative hierarchy of EU law.

C Public international law

Since the end of the Second World War, a catalogue of instruments enshrining basic human rights has been codified by States as public international law. Such instruments, the most prominent of which are the United Nations Charter (1945), the 1948 Universal Declaration of Human Rights (UDHR), the 1966 International Covenant on Civil and Political Rights (ICCPR), and the 1966 International Covenant on Economic, Social and Cultural Rights (ICESCR), are widely regarded as constitutional in nature by virtue of their expression of fundamental human rights protections.[51] Like constitutional and EU law, the provisions of universal instruments of international law derive from human dignity as a general principle of law. It is uncontroversial that human rights, especially those most basic rights enshrined in universal legal

[49] *Ibid.*, para. 35. [50] *Ibid.*, para. 41.

[51] *See, e.g.*, Marc Weller, *The Struggle for an International Constitutional Order*, *in* ROUTLEDGE HANDBOOK OF INTERNATIONAL LAW (London: Routledge, David Armstrong ed., 2009); Stephen Gardbaum, *Human Rights as International Constitutional Rights*, 19(4) EUROPEAN JOURNAL OF INTERNATIONAL LAW 749–68 (2008); Anne Peters, *Compensatory Constitutionalism: The Function and Potential of Fundamental International Norms and Structures*, 19 LEIDEN JOURNAL OF INTERNATIONAL LAW 579–610 (2006); Pavlos Eleftheriadis, *Cosmopolitan Law*, 9(2) EUROPEAN LAW JOURNAL 241–63 (2003); Marc Weller, *The Reality of the Emerging Universal Constitutional Order: Putting the Pieces of the Puzzle Together*, 10(2) CAMBRIDGE REVIEW OF INTERNATIONAL AFFAIRS 40–63 (1997); Luigi Ferrari-Bravo, *International and Municipal Law: The Complementarity of Legal Systems*, *in* THE STRUCTURE AND PROCESS OF INTERNATIONAL LAW 718 (The Hague: Martinus Nijhoff, Ronald St John Macdonald & Douglas Johnston eds., 1983); Taslim Elias, NEW HORIZONS IN INTERNATIONAL LAW 390 (The Hague: Martinus Nijhoff 1979).

instruments, represent expressions of the dignity of man.[52] Indeed, it is easily argued that there are no human rights *not* connected to human dignity.[53]

The United Nations organization is itself oriented in human dignity, as articulated in the preambular passage of its Charter.[54] Its second sentence constitutes a pledge 'reaffirm[ing] faith in fundamental human rights, in the dignity and worth of the human person, in the equal rights of men and women and of nations large and small'.[55] In this context, the concept serves at once as a theoretical basis for the direction of the organization as well as a practical principle around which universal consensus for the organization is based.[56] The precedence of human dignity in the Charter is demonstrative of its importance to the international community as well as the institution's overarching commitment to human dignity, which provided the foundation upon which the human rights legislation of the twentieth century would unfold. In an explicit statement to this effect, a 1986 General Assembly Resolution established human dignity as the general legal principle from which new human rights instruments should be based. Titled 'Setting International Standards in the Field of Human Rights', the Resolution contains a set of guidelines to be considered in the development of international instruments in the field of human rights, which includes that codified human rights should 'derive from the inherent dignity and worth of the human person'.[57]

It is against this backdrop that the three landmark human rights instruments of the twentieth century – the Universal Declaration and the two Covenants – evolved. In each case, human dignity is the general

52 *See, e.g.*, Clapham, HUMAN RIGHTS OBLIGATIONS OF NON-STATE ACTORS 534; Rosalyn Higgins, PROBLEMS AND PROCESS: INTERNATIONAL LAW AND HOW WE USE IT 96 (Oxford: Clarendon Press 1994); Bruno Simma, *From Bilateralism to Community Interest in International Law*, 250 RECUEIL DES COURS 242 (1994); Jack Donnelly, *Human Rights as Natural Rights*, 4(3) HUMAN RIGHTS QUARTERLY 391, 404–5 (1982).

53 *See, e.g.*, Feldman, *Human Dignity as a Legal Value: Part I*, 682, 690.

54 Yehoshua Arieli, *On the Necessary and Sufficient Conditions for the Emergence of the Doctrine of the Dignity of Man and His Rights*, *in* THE CONCEPT OF HUMAN DIGNITY IN HUMAN RIGHTS DISCOURSE 2–3 (Kretzmer & Eckart eds.)(identifying this is crucial to the distinction between the United Nations and the League of Nations, which was based principally upon State sovereignty).

55 Charter of the United Nations, Preamble (1945).

56 McCrudden, *Human Dignity and Judicial Interpretation of Human Rights*, 655, 675–7.

57 Setting International Standards in the Field of Human Rights, UNGA Res. 41/120, A/RES/41/120, para. 4(b) (1986).

legal principle informing the content and authority of the instrument and its provisions.[58] The first line of the Preamble of the Universal Declaration declares that the 'recognition of the inherent dignity and of the equal and inalienable rights of all members of the human family is the foundation of freedom, justice and peace in the world' and that violations of this recognition '[outrage] the conscience of mankind'.[59] The Preambles of the ICCPR and the ICESCR contain similar references to the dignity of man, whilst expressly adding that the rights contained in each instrument 'derive from the inherent dignity of the human person'.[60] Such preambular statements directly identify human dignity as the operative general principle of law, thereby invoking a source of authority of the derivative provisions contained by the instruments. Human dignity is implemented beyond the preambular language of the Universal Declaration, providing in Article 1:

> All human beings are born free and equal in dignity and rights. They are endowed with reason and conscience and should act towards one another in a spirit of brotherhood.[61]

This article is significant for two reasons. First, it articulates the major features of the concept of human dignity developed in the previous chapter, affirming the application of the philosophical principle depicted above in practice. Second, as a positive codification of the concept of human dignity, the article affirms that, as a general principle of law that inspires legal development (its typical preambular role), human dignity contributes directly to the corpus of actionable positive law. Additionally, human dignity functions as a general legal principle in myriad regional instruments articulating fundamental rights,[62] and

58 Arieli, *On the Necessary and Sufficient Conditions for the Emergence of the Doctrine of the Dignity of Man and His Rights*, 1–2; Klaus Dicke, *The Founding Function of Human Dignity in the Universal Declaration of Human Rights*, *in* The Concept of Human Dignity in Human Rights Discourse 111–20 (Kretzmer & Eckart eds.); Chaskalson, *Human Dignity as a Constitutional Value*, 133.

59 Universal Declaration of Human Rights, UNGA Res. 217 A (III), A/RES/217 (III), Preamble (1948) [hereinafter, Universal Declaration (1948)].

60 International Covenant on Civil and Political Rights, 99 UNTS 171, Preamble (1966) (*entered into force* 23 March 1976); International Covenant on Economic, Social and Cultural Rights, 993 UNTS 3, Preamble (1966) (*entered into force* 3 January 1976).

61 Universal Declaration (1948), Article I.

62 Arab Charter on Human Rights, Preamble (2004) (*entered into force* 15 March 2008), *in* 12 International Human Rights Report 893 (2005); Cairo Declaration on Rights in Islam, UN Doc. A/CONF.157/PC/62/Add.18, Article 1(a) (1993); African [Banjul] Charter on Human and Peoples' Rights, OAU Doc. CAB/LEG/67/3, Preamble and Article 5

operates in judicial practice as a way in which to interpret the application of fundamental rights.[63]

D Peremptory norms of general international law (*jus cogens*)

While the expression of human dignity in domestic constitutional law, EU law, and public international law is widely recognized and well developed, its connection to peremptory norms has not been thoroughly studied. For example, although the introduction to the seminal work of the New Haven School postulates that 'the basic values of human dignity' are 'authoritatively incorporated' as *jus cogens* in international law, this link is never further discussed in a volume exceeding one thousand pages; in fact, *jus cogens* receives only a cursory eleven-page treatment.[64] One implicit indication that human dignity underpins *jus cogens* is found in the Third Restatement of Foreign Relations Law of the United States (1987), which states that 'some rights are fundamental and intrinsic to human dignity',[65] and then observes that '[n]ot all human rights are peremptory norms (*jus cogens*)', but only a particular subset.[66] However, the Restatement does not complete the connection between *jus cogens* and norms fundamental and intrinsic to human dignity. The following paragraphs consider the depth of the connection between *jus cogens* and the general legal principle of human dignity.

At the first session of the ILC in 1949, the law of treaties was adopted as a priority for formal codification. The *travaux préparatoires* of the ILC's drafting of the law of treaties demonstrates a rapid evolution of the concept of *jus cogens* in international law as well as the general principle of law underpinning its development. The proposal to introduce a provision on *jus cogens* into international law, it may be recalled, originated with Lauterpacht's First Report on the Law of Treaties, which

(1981) (*entered into force* 21 October 1986); American Convention on Human Rights, OAS TS No. 36, Articles 5(2), 6(2), 11(1) (1969) (*entered into force* 18 July 1978); The Final Act of the Conference on Security and Cooperation in Europe [Helsinki Declaration], Principle VII (1975), 14 ILM 1292; American Declaration of the Rights and Duties of Man, OAS Res. XXX, Preamble (1948).

63 McCrudden, *Human Dignity and Judicial Interpretation of Human Rights*, 655–724.

64 Myres McDougal, Harold D. Lasswell, and Lung-chu Chen, Human Rights and World Public Order: The Basic Policies of an International Law of Human Dignity, xx, 339–50 (New Haven, CT: Yale University Press 1980).

65 Restatement (Third) of Foreign Relations Law of The United States § 702, cmt. *m* (1987).

66 *Ibid.*, cmt. *n*.

envisaged such norms to be those 'expressive of rules of international morality so cogent that an international tribunal would consider them as forming part of the principles of law generally recognized by civilized nations'.[67] Fitzmaurice, the subsequent *special rapporteur*, expanded upon the basis of *jus cogens* in his commentary to Draft Article 17:

> Most of the cases in this class are cases where the position of the individual is involved, and where the rules contravened are rules instituted for the protection of the individual ... they involve not only legal rules but considerations of morals and of international good order.[68]

As the ILC's work on the law of treaties evolved from a statement on treaty law to the formulation of a formal convention, the comments by members of the Commission depict a consistent perception of the nature of *jus cogens*. Norms of *jus cogens* were identified as 'necessary to international life and deeply rooted in the international conscience'[69] and, as such, function as 'constitutional rules of the international community'.[70] Judge Radhabinod Pal placed *jus cogens* in the specific context of the United Nations and the principle of human dignity:

> [T]here could be no doubt that an international public order existed now and that certain principles of international law had the character of *jus cogens*. The whole perspective of United Nations policy could be characterized as a value-orientated jurisprudence, directed towards the emergence of a public order in the international community under the rule of law. The Charter sought to establish a process by which the world community could regulate the international abuse of naked force and promote a world public order embodying values of human dignity in a society[.][71]

According to Judge Pal, the norms enshrined by *jus cogens* derive from the same general principle of law upon which the United Nations institution is based. By 1966, such sentiments were widely expressed in the meetings of the ILC on the law of treaties,[72] and the draft article was 'met

67 Hersch Lauterpacht, First Report on the Law of Treaties, [1953] II YbILC 154–6, para. 4; *see* discussion *infra*, Chapter 5, text accompanying *n.* 22.

68 Gerald Fitzmaurice, Third Report on the Law of Treaties, [1958] II YbILC 40–1, para. 76.

69 [1963] I YbILC 63, para. 39 (683rd Meeting, statement by Mr Yasseen).

70 *Ibid.*, 72, para. 65 (685th Meeting, statement by Mr de Luna).

71 *Ibid.*, 65, para. 64 (683rd Meeting, statement by Mr Pal).

72 [1966] I(1) YbILC 37, para. 9 (828th Meeting, statement by Mr Verdross), 39, para. 29 (statement by Mr Yasseen), para. 34 (statement by Mr De Luna), 40, para. 56 (statement by Mr Waldock) ('the more the international community became integrated, the more its attention would be directed to the position of the individual. Significant *jus cogens*

with a large measure of approval' by Governments in their initial comments.[73] In the context of a general principle of law generating peremptory norms, the work of the ILC points to a basis in the wellbeing of the individual and considerations of morality – in effect, defining the parameters of human dignity.

Under the auspices of Resolution 2287 (XXII), the UN General Assembly convened the first of two sessions of the UN Conference on the Law of Treaties (UNCLOT) in March 1968, at which representatives from more than one hundred countries considered ratification of the articles adopted by the ILC. In the absence of a catalogue of norms defined by the drafting committee, statements regarding the substance of *jus cogens* were generally limited to expressions of the general principle of law upon which norms of the legal category were thought to derive. The official record of the conference demonstrates that, across regions, cultures, and even delegations opposing the principle, considerations of humanity were understood to be the basis of *jus cogens*. A number of delegations referred to respect for the equality and rights of the human person as underpinning *jus cogens*,[74] one of which explicitly identified human dignity as 'the whole basis of *jus cogens*'.[75] Interestingly the French delegation, which ultimately voted against the Vienna Convention citing concerns over the ambiguity surrounding the article on peremptory norms, nevertheless stated:

> The substance of *jus cogens* was what represented the undeniable expression of the universal conscience, the common denominator of what men of all nationalities regarded as sacrosanct, namely, respect for and protection of the rights of the human person.[76]

developments could therefore be expected in the direction of the protection of the rights of the individual in the interests of the world community as a whole'); Humphrey Waldock, Fifth Report on the Law of Treaties, [1966] I(2) YbILC 229, para. 25 (877th Meeting, statement by Mr Tunkin); 230, para. 38 (statement by Mr Ruda) ('the reason for giving the character of *jus cogens* to a rule ... [is] that the rule in question safeguarded values of vital importance to all mankind'); 232, para. 59 (statement by Mr Jiménez de Aréchaga) ('the essence of *jus cogens* was that it comprised those rules of general international law which affected the vital interests and moral values of the international community as a whole'), para. 61 (statement by Mr Ago).

[73] Waldock, Fifth Report, [1966] II YbILC 23, para. 1; *see* 20–3 (statements by Luxembourg, Algeria, Brazil, the Phillipines).

[74] United Nations Conference on the Law of Treaties, Vienna, 26 March–24 May 1968, A/CONF.39/11 (1969), First Session [hereinafter UNCLOT, First Session (1968)], 300, para. 9 (Sierra Leone), 311, para. 41 (Italy), 321, para. 1 (United Republic of Tanzania).

[75] *Ibid.*, 322, para. 3 (United Republic of Tanzania).

[76] *Ibid.*, 309, para. 32 (France).

A significant number of delegations drew similar attention to this concept of the 'legal conscience of mankind', or various parallel constructions, from which *jus cogens* was conceived to derive.[77] Some went so far as to directly appeal to elements of natural law and principles of morality, or the 'common heritage of all peoples', as the basis of *jus cogens.*[78] Others described *jus cogens* as a form of international constitutional law[79] and invoked the United Nations Charter, its principles, purposes, and particular provisions, to attach substance to the content of *jus cogens.*[80] The record of the Conference testifies to a distinct impression, building upon the work of the ILC, that *jus cogens* was oriented, explicitly or otherwise, in human dignity.

More than a decade later, Judge Mosler articulated a similar sentiment during the proceedings of the Institute of International Law concerning the Institute's Resolution, *New Problems of Extradition.* The matter arose in the context of Article IV of the Resolution permitting the refusal to extradite on the basis of human rights concerns. The title of Article IV (Article III of the Draft Resolution) was changed at the behest of Judge Mosler from 'The Protection of *Human Rights* in Matters of Extradition' to 'The Protection of the *Basic Rights of the Human Person*'.[81] Critical of the imprecision of the term 'human rights', Mosler favoured replacing it with the expression 'basic rights of the human person' on the ground that the latter construction 'took account of the dignity of the human person and the needs closely linked with the development of man as a human being'.[82] Protections

77 *Ibid.*, 258, para. 75 (Holy See); 294, para. 7 (Mexico); 296, para. 23 (Iraq); 299, para. 61 (Chile); 301, para. 22 (Madagascar); 301, para. 26 (Colombia); 302, para. 33 (Poland); 309, para. 32 (France); 311, para. 42 (Italy); 318, para. 25 (Czechoslovakia); 320–1, para. 49 (Ivory Coast); 323, para. 20 (The Philippines); 327, para. 74 (Mali); 387, para. 11 (Cuba); United Nations Conference on the Law of Treaties, Vienna, 9 April–22 May 1969, A/CONF.39/11/Add.1 (1970), Second Session [hereinafter UNCLOT, Second Session (1969)] 103, para. 28 (Bulgaria); 104, paras. 37–9 (Italy); 124, para. 72 (Spain); 204, para. 24 (El Salvador).

78 UNCLOT, First Session (1968) 302, para. 33 (Poland); 303, para. 48 (Uruguay); 301, para. 26 (Colombia); 312, para. 55 (Romania); 320, para. 43 (Ecuador); 324, para. 26 (Switzerland); 327, para. 73 (Mali); UNCLOT, Second Session (1969) 104, para. 37 (Italy); 105, paras. 51–2 (Costa Rica); 106, para. 55 (Belgium).

79 UNCLOT, First Session (1968), 297, para. 43 (Lebanon); 324, para. 36 (Norway).

80 *Ibid.*, 297, para. 34 (Cuba); 297, para. 43 (Lebanon); 313, para. 66 (Bulgaria).

81 Institute of International Law, *Deliberations of the Institute During Plenary Meetings (Cambridge Session)*, 60(II) YEARBOOK OF THE INSTITUTE OF INTERNATIONAL LAW 214, 234–5, 306 (1983) (emphasis added).

82 *Ibid.*

of this nature, according to Mosler, constitute *jus cogens* which, in turn, warrant overriding conventional treaty obligations (in this instance extradition obligations), while the same cannot be extended to human rights more generally.[83] Implicit in Mosler's reasoning is the presupposition that the protection of human dignity distinguishes norms of *jus cogens* from the broader category of human rights.

From this standpoint it is unsurprising that, in a number of the conventions codifying specific peremptory norms, human dignity is expressly identified as the operative general legal principle giving rise to the codified norm. While the content of *jus cogens* will be the subject of Chapter 11, it is illustrative for the present discussion to gloss a number of instruments codifying peremptory norms – the prohibitions of slavery, apartheid, torture, and war crimes (serious violations of humanitarian law) – which indicate their derivation from human dignity. The Preamble of the Supplementary Convention on the Abolition of Slavery, the Slave Trade, and Institutions and Practices Similar to Slavery (1956) begins by orienting the content of the instrument upon the consideration 'that freedom is the birthright of every human being' and that 'the peoples of the United Nations reaffirmed in the Charter their faith in the dignity and worth of the human person'.[84] The Preamble of the International Convention on the Suppression and Punishment of the Crime of Apartheid (1973) provides that 'colonialism and all practices of segregation and discrimination associated therewith' must be halted 'in the interests of human dignity, progress, and justice'.[85] The Preamble of the Convention against Torture and Other Cruel, Inhuman or Degrading Treatment or Punishment (1984) bases the condemnation of such acts on 'the equal and inalienable rights of all members of the human family', which 'derive from the inherent dignity of the human person'.[86] In each of these examples, human dignity is explicitly articulated as the general principle of law from which the relevant norm, accepted and recognized as a peremptory norm of general international law, derives.

[83] *Ibid.*, 234.

[84] Supplementary Convention on the Abolition of Slavery, the Slave Trade, and Institutions and Practices Similar to Slavery, 226 UNTS 3 (7 September 1956, *entered into force* 30 April 1957).

[85] International Convention on the Suppression and Punishment of the Crime of Apartheid, 1015 UNTS 243 (30 November 1973, *entered into force* 18 July 1976).

[86] Convention against Torture and Other Cruel, Inhuman or Degrading Treatment or Punishment, UN Doc. A/39/51, 1465 UNTS 85 (10 December 1984, *entered into force* 26 June 1987).

The humanitarian principles contained in the Geneva Conventions (1949) constitute protections of the dignity of the human person in particularly vulnerable situations. The General Commentary to the instruments reflects that their significance lies in introducing 'into the sphere of States interests ... moral ideas touching the human person', namely 'the safeguarding of the lives and dignity of human beings'.[87] According to the ICRC Commentary to Article 3, common to the four Geneva Conventions, the guarantee of 'humane treatment' is intended to ensure that the individual is treated 'as a fellow human being and not as a beast or a thing',[88] a construction that echoes the philosophy of human dignity developed above.[89] The Commentary to Article 7 concerning the non-renunciation of rights explicitly employs human dignity:

> The initiators of the 1864 and following Conventions wished to safeguard the dignity of the human person, in the profound conviction that imprescriptible and inviolable rights were attached to it even when hostilities were at their height.[90]

Interestingly, however, the Geneva Conventions each lack a substantive preamble where an articulation of such a relevant general principle would normally be found. This is especially unusual given the nature and importance of the Conventions and the lengthy preambular statements of other such instruments.[91] The Commentary reveals that the ICRC had proposed a preamble at the Geneva Conference, to be identical in each of the four Conventions:

> Respect for the personality and dignity of human beings constitutes a universal principle which is binding even in the absence of any contractual undertaking.
>
> Such a principle demands that, in time of war, all those not actively engaged in the hostilities and all those placed *hors de combat* by reason of sickness, wounds, capture, or any other circumstance, shall be given due respect and have protection from the effects of war, and that those

[87] Jean Pictet (ed.), I THE GENEVA CONVENTIONS OF 12 AUGUST 1949 11–12 (Geneva: International Committee of the Red Cross 1952).

[88] *Ibid.*, 53. [89] *See* discussion *supra*, Chapter 3.C (The Philosophy of Human Dignity).

[90] Pictet (ed.), I THE GENEVA CONVENTIONS OF 12 AUGUST 1949 82.

[91] *Ibid.*, 18–23 (The instrument begins simply with the following text: 'The undersigned Plenipotentiaries of the Governments represented at the Diplomatic Conference held at Geneva from April 21 to August 12, 1949, for the purpose of revising the Geneva Convention for the Relief of the Wounded and Sick in Armies in the Field of July 27, 1929, have agreed as follows').

> among them who are in suffering shall be succoured and tended without distinction of race, nationality, religious belief, political opinion or any other quality[.][92]

In the face of debate over proposed additions to the preambular statement and failure to successfully reach a compromise, the decision was made to remove the preamble altogether. Consequently, as lamented in the Commentary, 'the essential motive which had brought sixty-four nations together at Geneva, was left unexpressed solely on account of non-essential additions that parties on both sides were resolved to make'.[93] Notwithstanding this omission, the humanitarian law enshrined by the Geneva Conventions – regarded to belong to *jus cogens* – is seen to derive from the general principle of human dignity.[94]

One relevant example from domestic jurisprudence that highlights the connection between *jus cogens* and human dignity is the *Milde* decision by the Italian Court of Cassation.[95] The case concerned reparations for atrocities perpetrated by German forces against Italian citizens during the occupation of Italy between October 1943 and the end of the Second World War.[96] Italian courts, in a series of similar cases, viewed such matters as calling for a balancing of State immunity against the obligation

[92] *Ibid.*, 21 (from *Remarks and Proposals submitted by the International Committee of the Red Cross*, Document for the consideration of Governments invited by the Swiss Federal Council to attend the Diplomatic Conference of Geneva (21 April 1949), Geneva, February 1949, 8).

[93] *Ibid.*, 22.

[94] *See* Protocol Additional to the Geneva Conventions of 12 August 1949, and relating to the Protection of Victims of Non-International Armed Conflicts (Protocol II), Preamble (8 June 1977, *entered into force* 7 December 1978) (Additional Protocol II does contain a preamble, which provides in part: 'in cases not covered by the law in force, the human person remains under the protection of humanity and the dictates of the public conscience').

[95] *Germany v. Milde*, Court of Cassation (First Criminal Section) (Italy), No. 1072/2009, ILDC 1224 (2009) (The case concerned the 2006 conviction of Max Josef Milde, a former member of the Hermann Goering Division of the Third Reich Army, by the Military Tribunal of La Spezia for his involvement in an operation in Italy resulting in the deaths of more than 200 civilians. Germany was found liable for civil damages due to the criminal conduct of its military forces and ordered to pay compensation in the order of 1 million euros. Germany unsuccessfully challenged Italian jurisdiction in the case before both the Military Court of Appeal in Rome and the Italian Court of Cassation primarily on the basis of sovereign immunity, yet prevailed before the International Court of Justice in *Jurisdictional Immunities of the State (Germany v. Italy: Greece Intervening)*, Judgment, ICJ Reports 2012, p. 99). *See infra*, *n.* 104.

[96] *Germany v. Milde*, Court of Cassation (First Criminal Section) (Italy), No. 1072/2009, ILDC 1224 (2009).

of reparation arising from international crimes resulting from the violation of peremptory norms:

> International rules on State immunity from jurisdiction cannot but be balanced against respect for this principle. The restriction of immunity in cases of individuals bringing lawsuits to obtain redress for a grave breach of the most fundamental principles of human dignity granted by *jus cogens* rules seems to be a reasonably balanced solution.[97]

Consistent with this approach, the Italian Court of Appeal in *Milde* perceived a conflict between sovereign immunity and respect for peremptory norms, one resolved with reference to the respective general principles underlying State sovereignty and *jus cogens*.

> Compliance with each person's inviolable rights is a fundamental principle of international law. It has the effect of reducing the scope of other traditional principles based on the sovereign equality of States, such as the customary norm granting every State immunity from the civil jurisdiction of foreign States. In fact, the jurisdictional immunity of foreign States is not absolute and cannot be invoked in proceedings relating to acts amounting to international crimes, i.e. acts violating the universal values based on respect for human dignity which transcend, as such, the interests of a particular State community.[98]

In a judgment rendered on 21 October 2008, following its prior reasoning in *Ferrini* (2004),[99] the Court of Cassation upheld the jurisdiction of Italian courts over the sovereign immunity of Germany on the basis of the peremptory nature of the norms violated.[100] The Court of Cassation endorsed the reasoning of the Court of Appeal, linking *jus cogens* to 'respect for liberty and dignity as inherent values of every human person'.[101] It reaffirmed its earlier articulation that human dignity is 'a fundamental principle due to its axiological content as a meta-value'.[102]

[97] *Jurisdictional Immunities of the State (Germany v. Italy: Greece Intervening)*, Counter-Memorial of Italy, 79, para. 4.101 (2009).

[98] *Germany v. Milde*, Court of Cassation (First Criminal Section) (Italy), No. 1072/2009, ILDC 1224, *reproduced in* Massimo Iovane, *States and Other Subjects of International Law*, 18 Italian Yearbook of International Law 325, 326 (2008).

[99] *Ferrini v. Germany*, Court of Cassation (Civil Section) (Italy), No. 5044/2004, ILDC 19 (2004).

[100] *Germany v. Milde*, Court of Cassation (First Criminal Section) (Italy), No. 1072/2009, ILDC 1224, *reproduced in* Iovane, *States and Other Subjects of International Law*, 330–1 ('the real question to be decided is whether customary rules protecting fundamental values inherent to every human being should prevail over the rule on the jurisdictional immunity of foreign States').

[101] *Ibid.*, 328. [102] *Ibid.*, 329.

In *Milde* and similar cases before Italian courts, the doctrine of *jus cogens* was evoked precisely because human dignity, the general principle of law underpinning peremptory norms, was perceived to produce overriding procedural and juridical effects.[103] The reasoning in *Milde* recognizes human dignity to be the general principle of law from which norms of *jus cogens* emerge, that this general principle is of legal relevance, and that it is the source of legal effects of peremptory norms. The Italian jurisprudence here tested, and exceeded,[104] the legal effect of human dignity as a general principle of law. Nevertheless, the reasoning by the Court of Cassation serves as a valuable articulation of the general principle of law underlying *jus cogens*.

Where the International Court of Justice has affirmed the legal effects of peremptory norms, it has demonstrated a readiness to recognize principles of humanity as the basis of *jus cogens*. Relevant jurisprudence of the International Court demonstrates a preference on the part of the Court to refer to 'elementary considerations of humanity' as the basis of peremptory norms. The expression seems to convey the same meaning as human dignity, and the two are taken here to refer, in effect, to the same principle.[105] In its first contentious case, *Corfu Channel* (1949), the International Court affirmed the obligation incumbent upon Albania to inform ships traversing Albania's territorial waters of the existence of a minefield, which in this specific instance entailed the duty to warn approaching British ships of the danger. Such obligations, according to the Court, derive not from the laws of war codified in the Hague

[103] *Ibid.*, 332–3.

[104] *See Jurisdictional Immunities of the State (Germany v. Italy: Greece Intervening)*, Judgment, ICJ Reports 2012, p. 99 (In response to this decision, Germany filed an application to initiate proceedings against Italy with the International Court in 2009 concerning the repeated failure of Italian courts to recognize the sovereign immunity of the German State before its civil courts in cases concerning remedies for violations of peremptory norms. In its Judgment in the case, the International Court rejected Italy's balancing of general principles on the grounds that it conflated jurisdiction over a dispute with its merits. The Court found that Italy had violated its obligations to respect the jurisdictional immunity of Germany under international law. Although the Court rejected the Italian courts' interpretation of the interaction between substantive rules of *jus cogens* and the procedural rule of sovereign immunity, by restricting its judgment to the issue of jurisdiction and neglecting general principles altogether, it avoided compromising human dignity as the general principle of law underlying *jus cogens*.). *Cf.* ICJ Reports 2012, Dis. Op. Cançado Trindade, 83 (drawing attention to the 'central principles' of the case, which center on 'the principle of humanity and the principle of human dignity').

[105] *See* discussion *supra*, Chapter 3, text accompanying *nn.* 61–2.

Convention of 1907 themselves, but rather, from 'certain general and well-recognized principles, namely: elementary considerations of humanity'.[106]

The International Court struck a similar tone in its 1951 Advisory Opinion, *Reservations to the Genocide Convention*, where it denounced reservations to the Convention on the basis of the nature of the codified norm. In its Opinion, the Court noted that genocide is a crime which 'shocks the conscience of mankind and results in great losses to humanity, and which is contrary to moral law and to the spirit and aims of the United Nations'. It further observed that the Convention itself was 'adopted for a purely humanitarian and civilizing purpose ... since its object on the one hand is to safeguard the very existence of certain human groups and on the other to confirm and endorse the most elementary principles of morality'.[107] Later in its decision, the Court refered to 'the moral and humanitarian principles which are its basis'.[108] The Court restated this position with respect to the prohibition of genocide more than a half-century later, in *Armed Activities on the Territory of the Congo* (2002),[109] explicitly linking these considerations of morality and humanity with *jus cogens*.

The International Court of Justice made similar pronouncements regarding 'elementary considerations of humanity' as a general principle of law in a series of later cases concerning humanitarian law. In *Military and Paramilitary Activities in and against Nicaragua* (1986), the Court found the Geneva Conventions applicable to the dispute in question irrespective of formal reservations by the United States:

> [I]n the event of international armed conflicts, these rules also constitute a minimum yardstick, in addition to the more elaborate rules which are also to apply to international conflicts; and they are rules which, in the Court's opinion, reflect what the Court in 1949 called 'elementary considerations of humanity'.[110]

[106] *The Corfu Channel Case (United Kingdom of Great Britain and Northern Ireland v. Albania)*, Judgment, ICJ Reports 1949, p. 4, 22 (as well as two other principles).

[107] *Reservations to the Genocide Convention*, Advisory Opinion, ICJ Reports 1951, p. 15, 23.

[108] *Ibid.*, 24.

[109] *Armed Activities on the Territory of the Congo (New Application: 2002) (Congo v. Rwanda)*, ICJ Reports 2006, p. 3, para. 64 (applying the language and reasoning of the Court in 1951 to the prohibition of genocide as *jus cogens*).

[110] *Military and Paramilitary Activities in and against Nicaragua (Nicaragua v. United States of America)*, Judgment, ICJ Reports 1986, p. 14, para. 218.

To this end, the Court invoked an article echoing the Martens Clause of The Hague Conventions,[111] common to all four of the Geneva Conventions,[112] which establishes the applicability of the provisions of the Conventions irrespective of reservation or denunciation, by virtue of their basis in obligations deriving from 'the principles of the law of nations, as they result from the usages established among civilized peoples, from the laws of humanity and the dictates of public conscience'.[113]

In *Legality of the Threat or Use of Nuclear Weapons* (1996), the International Court of Justice referred again to this character of humanitarian law as 'fundamental to the respect of the human person and "elementary considerations of humanity"', a reference to its pronouncement in *Corfu Channel*.[114] Judge Weeramantry, in his Dissenting Opinion, held that the Court should have gone further to declare the illegality of the use or threat of use of nuclear weapons in any circumstances, as it 'contradicts the fundamental principle of the dignity and worth of the human person on which all law depends'.[115] In *Legal Consequences of the Construction of a Wall in the Occupied Palestinian Territory* (2004), the Court reiterated these positions.[116] It should be noted that the Court invoked 'elementary considerations of humanity' with some regularity long before it referenced the category of *jus cogens* itself.[117] Even so, the

111 *See* discussion *infra*, Chapter 5, text accompanying *n.* 58.

112 Geneva Convention (I) for the Amelioration of the Condition of the Wounded and Sick in Armed Forces in the Field, 75 UNTS 31, Article 63 (12 August 1949, *entered into force* 21 October 1950); Geneva Convention (II) for the Amelioration of the Condition of Wounded, Sick and Shipwrecked Members of Armed Forces at Sea, 75 UNTS 85, Article 62 (12 August 1949, *entered into force* 21 October 1950); Geneva Convention (III) Relative to the Treatment of Prisoners of War, 75 UNTS 135, Article 142 (12 August 1949, *entered into force* 21 October 1950); Geneva Convention (IV) Relative to the Protection of Civilian Persons in Time of War, 75 UNTS 287, Article 158 (12 August 1949, *entered into force* 21 October 1950).

113 *Military and Paramilitary Activities in and against Nicaragua (Nicaragua v. United States of America)*, Judgment, ICJ Reports 1986, p. 14, para. 218.

114 *Legality of the Threat or Use of Nuclear Weapons*, Advisory Opinion, ICJ Reports 1996, p. 226, paras. 79, 95.

115 *Ibid.*, Dis. Op. Weeramantry, 433; *see also* Dis. Op. Schwebel, 318–19.

116 *Legal Consequences of the Construction of a Wall in the Occupied Palestinian Territory*, Advisory Opinion, ICJ Reports 2004, p. 136, para. 157 (referring to the resultant obligations as 'of an *erga omnes* character').

117 *Armed Activities on the Territory of the Congo (New Application: 2002) (Congo v. Rwanda)*, Judgment, ICJ Reports 2006, p. 3, para. 64 (as the first instance in which the court expressly addressed *jus cogens*).

jurisprudence of the Court is indicative of a common general legal principle underling fundamental norms of international law.

Other international courts have expressly associated *jus cogens* with the general principle of human dignity. For example, in *Furundžija* (1998), the ICTY Trial Chamber justified its decision to adopt a broad definition of torture as punishable under the jurisdiction of the Tribunal on the basis of 'the general spirit of international humanitarian law', adding that 'the primary purpose of this body of law is to safeguard human dignity'.[118] The Trial Chamber continued:

> The general principle of respect for human dignity is the basic underpinning and indeed the very *raison d'être* of international humanitarian law and human rights law; indeed in modern times it has become of such paramount importance as to permeate the whole body of international law.[119]

The Trial Chamber similarly considered, in *Aleksovski* (1999), that 'the purpose of Common Article 3 [of the Geneva Conventions] is "to uphold and protect the inherent human dignity of the individual"'.[120] The ICTY Appeals Chamber reiterated the role of human dignity as a general legal principle in its 2000 Judgment in the same case, stating generally that where 'outrages upon personal dignity' are defined as a criminal offence, 'it was the broader concept of human dignity that was emphasized' as 'the important value protected by the offence' at issue.[121] The jurisprudence of the ICTY thus supports the proposition that human dignity is viewed to be the general principle of law underlying peremptory norms, even beyond those at issue before that Tribunal. A similar position is found in the jurisprudence of the Special Court for Sierra Leone (SCSL), most notably in *Kallon and Kamara*, where the Court denied recognition of amnesty for international crimes subject to universal jurisdiction.[122] The Court justified its conclusion on the basis that, in the first instance, all States may prosecute such offences pursuant to an 'obligation to protect human dignity' with relation to *jus cogens* which gives rise to obligations *erga omnes*.[123]

***

[118] *Prosecutor v. Furundžija*, IT-95–17/1-T, para. 162 (1998).

[119] *Ibid*., para. 183.

[120] *Prosecutor v. Aleksovski*, IT-95–14/1-T, paras. 47–57 (1999).

[121] *Prosecutor v. Aleksovski*, IT-95–14/1-A, paras. 24–5 (2000).

[122] *Prosecutor v. Kallon and Kamara*, Decision on Challenge to Jurisdiction: Lomé Accord Amnesty, SCSL-04-15-PT-060-I, para. 71 (2004).

[123] *Ibid.* (the Court identified the 'obligation to protect human dignity' as a peremptory norm in a less-than-precise relation of those elements).

The development and application of *jus cogens* testifies to its expression of the higher interests of the international community represented by the general legal principle of human dignity. From the inception of the concept of *jus cogens* in international treaty law, the drafting of the law of treaties, and the formal ratification of the Vienna Convention, to the codification of specific peremptory norms, their adjudication by the International Court, and their enforcement against individuals, there is a clear convergence over time and across fora around a central premise and purpose underlying such norms. Although human dignity is not explicitly identified as a general legal principle in every instance, there is substantial jurisprudence in support of the proposition that respect for the intrinsic worth of the human person is, in practice, the basis of the higher interests of the international community which give rise to *jus cogens*.

Admitting a linkage of *jus cogens* with human dignity implies that peremptory norms hold a legal status akin to constitutional law in domestic legal orders, core EU law, and some of the most widely recognized rules codified in public international law. In those latter instances, law deriving from the general principle of human dignity was conceived to enjoy a hierarchically superior normative position by virtue of the values enshrined by those rules and, in turn, their importance to the maintenance of social order within those domains. It follows, in this sense, to consider the normativity of *jus cogens* and the degree to which the general principle of human dignity might provide an explanation for the legal effects of *jus cogens* in the same way that the principle is often invoked to account for the imperative law of other legal domains.

5

The authority of *jus cogens*

Lauterpacht introduced the concept of *jus cogens* as norms 'expressive of rules of international morality', an understanding that has endured throughout the evolution of peremptory norms.[1] That morality has been pervasive in *jus cogens* since its inception may be viewed with reference to human dignity. Recall that Cicero's definition of human dignity, as 'the honourable authority of a person, combined with attention and honour and worthy respect paid to him',[2] contains two distinct aspects. The first is a quality of the individual, to whom dignity is inalienably endowed by virtue of his human being. It is in this sense that the dignity of the human person, as a general principle of law, defines protections of the individual deriving from basic considerations of humanity. The second aspect of human dignity, a corollary of the first, is a social, externally oriented aspect that generates duties deriving from its normative prescriptions which inform relations towards other individuals in society. The value of the human person connotes respect to be afforded to every human being by virtue of his or her humanity, respect that takes the form of a doctrine of morality. Consequently, the law generated by human dignity as a legal principle imposes moral obligations to respect its prescriptions alongside their legal codification, thereby accounting for the morally compelling nature of such law. This chapter looks first to the moral dimension of the principle of human dignity and then considers the role of morality in the doctrine of *jus cogens*; it concludes by assessing the peremptory legal effects of *jus cogens*.

A Human dignity as a moral concept

Morality is a social idea with an outward-oriented focus that prescribes standards of conduct that, in effect, define obligations owed to others.

[1] Hersch Lauterpacht, First Report on the Law of Treaties, [1953] II YbILC 154–6, para. 4.
[2] Marcus Tullius Cicero, De Inventione, De Optimo Genere Oratorum, Topica, II.LV.166 (H. M. Hubbell trans. [46 BC] 1968).

A 'moral reason' for action is therefore 'one that relates to the wellbeing of others, what is owed to them or will serve their interests in some way'.[3] The basic upshot of this understanding is to regard morality as a limiting principle that constrains the pursuit of individual wellbeing in order to protect the wellbeing of others. It is in this capacity that morality enters into the philosophy of human dignity. Agency, it may be recalled, is the source of the inherent value and worth of the human person circumscribed by dignity.[4] Freedom and reason, as qualities unique to human beings and endowed to all human beings, constitute the sense of 'human' operative in *dignitas hominis*.[5] Dignity depicts the value attached to the human being by virtue of these qualities, whose agency is worthy of basic respect. Respect, in turn, is the basis of morality.

Respect is central to the second aspect of human dignity, a corollary to the first, which accounts for the moral dimension of human dignity. According to Kant, human dignity is the 'proper object of respect',[6] and it is only through respect that human dignity is actualized.

> [Dignity] is, an unconditional, incomparable worth; and the word *respect* alone provides a becoming expression for the estimate of it that a rational being must give. *Autonomy* is therefore the ground of the dignity of human nature and of every rational nature.[7]

Human dignity, which is based in individual autonomy (freedom and reason), is therefore the source of both individual worth as well as the recognition of the worth of others. This is to say that human dignity, as the capacity to exercise through will the categorical imperative and formulate universal laws, is at once the subject and object of respect. Or, to use Kant's terminology, '[m]orality consists, then, in the reference of all action to the lawgiving by which alone a kingdom of ends is possible.'[8] Consequently, morality reflects the aspect of human dignity

[3] Bernard Williams, Morality 88 (Cambridge University Press 1972), cited in Kent Greenwalt, Conflicts of Law and Morality 27 (Oxford University Press 1987).

[4] *See, e.g.*, Joseph Raz, The Authority of Law 221 (Oxford: Clarendon Press 1983); John Finnis, Natural Law and Natural Rights 272 (Oxford: Clarendon Press 1980).

[5] Jess Malpas, *Human Dignity and Human Being*, *in* Perspectives on Human Dignity: A Conversation 19 (Dordrecht: Springer, Jess Malpas & Norelle Lickiss eds., 2007).

[6] Immanuel Kant, Groundwork of the Metaphysics of Morals [1795], *in* The Cambridge Edition of the Works of Immanuel Kant 4:440 (Cambridge University Press, Mary Gregor ed., 1996) [hereinafter, Kant, Groundwork].

[7] *Ibid.*, 4:436. [8] *Ibid.*, 4:434.

whereby the exercise of reason in individual agency respects the dignity of others.[9] Kant is clear in this sense:

> Now, morality is the condition under which alone a rational being can be an end in itself, since only through this is it possible to be a lawgiving member in the kingdom of ends. Hence morality, and humanity insofar as it is capable of morality, is that which alone has dignity.[10]

The inward and outward aspects of dignity are practically inseparable, placing human dignity at the heart of both the fundamental rights of the individual and the basic moral duties owed to other individuals in society. Kant articulates this conclusion while implicitly drawing upon the classical formulation of dignity:

> [I]t also follows that this dignity (prerogative) he has over all merely natural beings brings with it that he must always take his maxims from the point of view of himself, and likewise every other rational being, as lawgiving beings (who for this reason are also called persons) . . . the dignity of humanity consists just in this capacity to give universal law.[11]

With this conclusion, the inward and outward dimensions of human dignity are inextricably connected through respect, a linkage that establishes a clear, yet complex, conceptualization of morality.

A practical understanding of morality takes form in the maxim, 'we know our right only through our duty'. In practice, morality as respect owed to others takes the form of duties, a point mused by Kant, who reflects that the doctrine of morals is, especially by Cicero, referred to as a doctrine of *duties* and never as a doctrine of *rights*.[12] Kant provides the following explanation:

> The reason is that we know our own freedom (from which all moral laws, and so all rights as well as duties proceed) only through the *moral imperative*, which is a proposition commanding duty, from which the capacity for putting others under obligation, that is, the concept of right, can afterwards be explicated.[13]

Put differently, this means that one realizes freedom only through the duty to respect that freedom of others. It is, moreover, in this sense that

[9] Morton Kaplan, ON FREEDOM AND HUMAN DIGNITY 22 (Morristown, NJ: General Learning Press 1973); Tibor Machan, *Metaphysics, Epistemology, and Natural Law Theory*, 31 AMERICAN JOURNAL OF JURISPRUDENCE 65, 70 (1986).

[10] Kant, GROUNDWORK 4:435. [11] *Ibid.*, 4:438–40.

[12] Immanuel Kant, METAPHYSICS OF MORALS [1797], *in* THE CAMBRIDGE EDITION OF THE WORKS OF IMMANUEL KANT 6:239 (Gregor ed.) [hereinafter, Kant, METAPHYSICS].

[13] *Ibid.*

morality is conceived as a limiting principle imposing absolute duties of respect while rights are naturally limited.[14] Therefore, human dignity is actualized by individuals, as autonomous actors, making decisions guided by the dictates of reason in such a way as to respect the dignity of others.[15] This notion of duty is, for practical purposes, an expression of moral obligation.

In practice, this moral aspect of human dignity as a doctrine of duties is borne out by the link between human dignity and the institution of law. Recall the proposition above that the dignity of the human being becomes truly purposeful only when recognized and protected by the institution of law.[16] This is precisely because human dignity is realized only through respect which, though expressed as moral duty, is reinforced through codification as fundamental law.[17]

Public order norms are the expression of such moral duties, as legal rules, necessary to the maintenance of social coexistence of individuals within a community. Law thereby creates a source of obligation through rules that prescribe and reinforce standards of moral conduct. Morality and law remain distinct spheres of obligation, even where they share common normative objects, and each exerts disparate (internal and external) pressures to conform to the conduct in question.[18]

Far from revolutionary, the idea of law derived from considerations of morality is the bedrock of the classical tradition of natural law. The natural law tradition is characterized predominantly by two key elements – a universal order governing all human beings, and the inalienable rights of the individual[19] – which culminate in principles of common morality that constitute a universal order mediating the social existence of human beings. These elements of natural law are each reflected in the conceptualization of human dignity and, more to the

[14] *See e.g.*, Universal Declaration, Articles 28–30 (expressing this limitation on rights).

[15] This is, more or less, a tenet of natural law: *See, e.g.*, Robert George, IN DEFENSE OF NATURAL LAW 104–5 (Oxford: Clarendon Press 1999).

[16] Dominique Rousseau, *Concluding Report*, *in* THE PRINCIPLE OF RESPECT FOR HUMAN DIGNITY, European Commission for Democracy through Law (Proceedings of the Uni-Dem Seminar, Montpellier 2–6 July 1998); Michael Smith, HUMAN DIGNITY AND THE COMMON GOOD IN THE ARISTOTELIAN-THOMISTIC TRADITION 166 (Lewiston, NY: Mellen University Press 1995).

[17] The idea of 'natural duties' as 'moral requirements' is an element of natural law: John Simmons, MORAL PRINCIPLES AND POLITICAL OBLIGATIONS 13 (Princeton University Press 1979).

[18] *See* Lon Fuller, THE MORALITY OF LAW (New Haven, CT: Yale University Press 1969).

[19] Wolfgang Friedman, LEGAL THEORY 96 (London: Stevens & Sons 1967).

point, the concept of human dignity provides an articulation of natural law based in, and flowing from, humanity itself. By elucidating the way in which moral considerations enter into law through human dignity as a general legal principle, the present discussion introduces the generally accepted yet ambiguous normativity of *jus cogens*. The discourse of law deriving from human dignity regularly considers the principle in the context of morality, which takes the practical form of respect as its 'core value' and in turn confers upon that law normative distinction within legal hierarchy.[20] Therefore, where morality arises in the doctrine of *jus cogens*, it may be viewed in this way as a corollary of the general principle of human dignity underpinning the norms of that category.

B Morality and peremptory norms

Human dignity can be seen as providing a vessel through which to introduce moral elements into positive law. It was discussed above that the two aspects of human dignity, its inward and outward aspects that respectively generate protections and duties, complete a whole formulation of the concept. Consequently, consideration of human dignity as a general legal principle underlying *jus cogens* provokes analysis of the corollary moral quality of peremptory norms. While morality is not law per se, the legal prescriptions derived from human dignity carry a moral quality that obligates beyond conventional legal codification. This relation is consistent with the understanding that the peremptory status of *jus cogens* is a function of its normative content rather than its formal source.[21] To assess this dynamic in practice, it is necessary first to examine considerations of morality in the doctrine of *jus cogens*.

i. Travaux préparatoires

In his First Report on the Law of Treaties, Lauterpacht described *jus cogens* as a category of norms 'expressive of rules of international

[20] David Feldman, *Human Dignity as a Legal Value: Part I*, PUBLIC LAW 682, 687–8 (1999); Myres McDougal, Harold D. Lasswell, and Lung-chu Chen, Human Rights and World Public Order: The Basic Policies of an International Law of Human Dignity, xviii, 7, 451 (New Haven, CT: Yale University Press 1980); Jack Donnelly, *Human Rights as Natural Rights*, 4(3) HUMAN RIGHTS QUARTERLY 391, 399 (1982).

[21] *See, e.g.*, [1966] II YbILC 248, para. 2 (Commentary to Draft Article 50) ('It is not the form of a general rule of international law but the particular nature of the subject-matter with which it deals that may, in the opinion of the Commission, give it the character of *jus cogens*').

morality' which, in the context of his broader statement, indicates a conceptualization of morality corollary to a general legal principle reflecting human dignity:

> It would thus appear that the test whether the object of the treaty is illegal and whether the treaty is void for that reason is not inconsistency with customary international law pure and simple, but inconsistency with such overriding principles of international law which may be regarded as constituting principles of international public policy (*ordre international public*). These principles need not necessarily have crystallized in a clearly accepted rule of law such as prohibition of piracy or of aggressive war. They may be expressive of rules of international morality so cogent that an international tribunal would consider them as forming part of those principles of law generally recognized by civilized nations which the International Court of Justice is bound to apply by virtue of Article 38[c] of its Statute. Although it is not possible to cite any judicial decision in support of that view, there are occasional interesting observations of individual judges to that effect. Thus in his individual opinion in the *Oscar Chinn* case Judge Schücking asserted that 'the Court would never . . . apply a convention the terms of which were contrary to public morality'.[22]

Despite the absense of judicial opinion demonstrating the effect of *jus cogens* upon a conflicting treaty, the principle underlying Lauterpacht's conceptualization of peremptory norms was articulated by the International Court two years earlier in its *Reservations to the Genocide Convention* Advisory Opinion.[23]

Fitzmaurice, the subsequent *special rapporteur*, followed Lauterpacht in his later Report on the Law of Treaties by identifying *jus cogens* to be rules oriented in morality in the same sense:

> The rules of international law in this context fall broadly into two classes – those which are mandatory and imperative in any circumstances (*jus cogens*) and those (*jus dispositivum*) which merely furnish a rule for application in the absence of any other agreed régime, or, more correctly, those the variation or modification of which under an agreed régime is permissible, provided the position and rights of their States are not affected . . . [Most *jus cogens*] are cases where the position of the individual is involved, and where the rules contravened are rules instituted for the protection of the individual . . . It is not possible – nor for present purposes necessary – to state exhaustively what are the rules of

[22] Lauterpacht, First Report, [1953] II YbILC 155, para. 4.

[23] *Reservations to the Genocide Convention*, Advisory Opinion, ICJ Reports 1951, p. 15, 23. *See* discussion *infra*, text accompanying *n.* 64.

> international law that have the character of *jus cogens*, but a feature common to them, or to a great many of them, evidently is that they involve not only legal rules but considerations of morals and of international good order.[24]

Although avoiding such explicit reference to morality, Waldock, the final *special rapporteur*, acknowledges the same quality of the concept by reference to the emergence of an international public order in his Second Report on the Law of Treaties.[25] The understanding of peremptory norms submitted by the final three *special rapporteurs* on the law of treaties is one expressive of a distinct moral quality to *jus cogens*. This perceived moral aspect is linked to general principles of individual well-being and elements of public order understood to form the basis of the concept of *jus cogens*.

The perception that considerations of morality underlie the concept of *jus cogens* was clearly received by governments upon submission of the 1966 ILC Draft Articles for their observations. Prior to submission, Spanish Ambassador Antonio De Luna, as a member of the ILC, drew attention to precedent for recognizing moral considerations in international law, citing the *Oscar Chinn* case and quoting Lord Arnold McNair in applying this precedent to the law of treaties:

> It is difficult to imagine any society, whether of individuals or of States, whose law sets no limit whatever to freedom of contract. In every civilized community there are some rules of law and some principles of morality which individuals are not permitted by law to ignore or to modify by their agreements.[26]

This perception seems to have been shared by governments, who overwhelmingly favoured the concept of *jus cogens* in their observations, even if its contours remained to be determined by subsequent practice. The Portuguese delegation, for example, conceived of reference to moral consideration in the context of a prevailing trend in international law:

> [D]octrine has been moving with increasing force towards acceptance of the rule that every convention violating international law, rules of universal morality and fundamental human rights must be considered null

24 Gerald Fitzmaurice, Third Report on the Law of Treaties, [1958] II YbILC 40–1, para. 76.

25 Humphrey Waldock, Second Report on the Law of Treaties, [1963] II YbILC 52, para. 1; *see* discussion *supra*, Chapter 1, text accompanying *n*. 9 (Commentary to draft Article 13); *see also* Humphrey Waldock, Fifth Report the Law of Treaties, [1966] II YbILC 247, para. 1 (Commentary to Draft Article 50).

26 [1966] I(1) YbILC 39, para. 31 (828th Meeting, statement by Mr De Luna) (quoting Arnold McNair, THE LAW OF TREATIES 213–14 (Oxford: Clarendon Press 1961)).

> owing to the unlawful character of its purpose. Even those authors who, keeping in mind the possibility of a treaty modifying international custom, recognize the difficulty of solving the question, and ask if all treaties which affect principles which are essential to the structure of international society should not be considered null, as for example, those providing for recourse to piracy or disrespect for the human person.[27]

Several delegations took note of the hierarchical implications of *jus cogens* in international law,[28] while another analogized the concept to domestic principles of social justice.[29] The delegation from Algeria suggested that this trend follows in the spirit of the United Nations, through which moral considerations had already found legal expression:

> [W]hile it may be difficult to find an exact criterion for defining rules having a *jus cogens* character, the United Nations has already developed a number of peremptory norms of morality and public policy in international relations – norms which will be defined and developed in State practice.[30]

The Algerian statement intelligently linked the development of peremptory norms to customary international law by drawing attention to the way in which these legal norms take form through State practice.[31] By deferring to the future development of general international law, this comment also responded to reservations owing to the lack of a defined content of peremptory norms.

The delegation from Luxembourg based its objection to the concept of *jus cogens* in the law of treaties upon this understanding of an introduction of moral considerations into international law:

> [Luxembourg] interprets the Commission's object as being to introduce as a cause of nullity criteria of morality and 'public policy' such as are used in internal law to determine the compatibility of private contracts with fundamental concepts of the social order; and it questions whether such concepts are suitable for transfer to international relations which are characterized by the lack of any authority, political or judicial, capable of imposing on all States standards of international justice and morality. Consequently, in the view of the Luxembourg Government, it is not possible in the present state of international relations to define in legal terms the substance of peremptory international law.[32]

27 Waldock, Fifth Report, [1966] II YbILC 327 (statement by Portugal).

28 *Ibid.*, 23 (statements by Thailand, Uruguay).

29 *Ibid.*, 22 (statement by Panama).

30 *Ibid.*, 21 (statement by Algeria).

31 *See ibid.*, 21 (statement by Brazil), 22 (statement by Indonesia); *see* discussion *infra*, Chapter 8.B (Article 53 of the Vienna Convention).

32 Waldock, Fifth Report, [1966] II YbILC 20 (statement by Luxembourg).

Importantly, Luxembourg's challenge to the article was not opposition to the concept of peremptory norms per se, but rather arose from a lack of definition and questions of enforcement. These statements represent reception by Governments of the *special rapporteurs*' introduction of moral considerations into international law through *jus cogens*, which was generally endorsed by members of the ILC during the drafting of the law of treaties.

When the final report of the ILC was brought before the UN Conference on the Law of Treaties for ratification in 1968–9, the influence of morality through *jus cogens* had gained momentum. That peremptory norms embodied considerations of morality was explicitly recognized by a range of representatives to the Conference,[33] as observed by the delegation from Brazil:

> [A]t the stage of development now reached by international law, no one could deny the truth of Lord McNair's dictum 'It is difficult to imagine any society, whether of individuals or of States, whose law sets no limit whatever to freedom of contract. In every civilized community there are some rules of law and some principles of morality which individuals are not permitted by law to ignore or to modify by their agreements.' Thus, when the question of including a provision on *jus cogens* had arisen in the International Law Commission, an extraordinary concordance of views had emerged among members of widely differing personality and legal background.[34]

Many delegations invoked the notion of 'international legal conscience' as the basis of *jus cogens*,[35]and some appealed directly to elements of natural law, or the 'common heritage of all peoples', as the basis of *jus*

[33] United Nations Conference on the Law of Treaties, Vienna, 26 March–24 May 1968, A/CONF.39/11 (1969), 1st Session [hereinafter, UNCLOT, First Session (1968)] 295, para. 15 (United States); 297, para. 43 (Lebanon); 298, para. 48 (Nigeria); 301, para. 26 (Colombia); 303, para. 48 (Uruguay); 305, para. 60 (United Kingdom); 315, para. 1 (Spain); 317, para. 20 (Brazil); 318, para. 25 (Czechoslovakia); 319, para. 37 (Ceylon); 321, para. 50 (Ivory Coast); 323, para. 17 (The Philippines); 327, para. 73 (Mali); 333, para. 86 (Central African Republic); United Nations Conference on the Law of Treaties, Vienna, 9 April–22 May 1969, A/CONF.39/11/Add.1 (1970), 2nd Session [hereinafter, UNCLOT, Second Session (1969)] 95, para. 24 (The Philippines); 98, para. 58 (Cameroon); 100, para. 75 (Ukrainian Soviet Socialist Republic); 105, para. 51(Costa Rica); 201, para. 40 (Monaco).

[34] UNCLOT, First Session (1968) 317, para. 20 (Brazil) (internal citation omitted).

[35] *Ibid.*, 258, para. 75 (Holy See); 294, para. 7 (Mexico); 296, para. 23 (Iraq); 299, para. 61 (Chile); 301, para. 22 (Madagascar); 301, para. 26 (Colombia); 302, para. 33 (Poland); 309, para. 32 (France); 311, para. 42 (Italy); 318, para. 25 (Czechoslovakia); 320–1, para. 49 (Ivory Coast); 323, para. 20 (The Philippines); 327, para. 74 (Mali); 387, para. 11

cogens.[36] The diversity in the breadth of explicit support for the moral dimension of *jus cogens* across regions and cultures lends credence to the incorporation of moral considerations into law as a global movement rather than an exclusively Western phenomenon.[37]

Interestingly, as with Luxembourg's cautionary statement above, opposition to the inclusion of *jus cogens* generally remained based not solely on discomfort over the formal incorporation of morality into international law, but rather, the failure to adequately circumscribe the precise content of this normative category.[38] These concerns, resulting chiefly from the failure to define the content of *jus cogens*, can begin to be assuaged by demonstrating the particular effect of morality on *jus cogens*.[39] Moreover, the position of Luxemburg appears to contemplate that *jus cogens* refers to bare morality itself, rather than the codification of law based on moral considerations which, in turn, retains a moral quality. On this point, René-Jean Dupuy had offered clarification earlier in the first session of the Conference, noting the distinction between morality (as natural law) and moral considerations arising in codified positive law:

> Of course, *jus cogens* must not be confused with natural law, since its rules were not immutable, although it contained natural law. Principles such as the prohibition of slavery and genocide had entered positive law; but those rules of natural law had been ratified and sanctioned by positive law without losing their value as fundamental dictates of the universal conscience. It could even be said that such progressive integration of natural into positive law was highly desirable, because of the increased precision it gave to positive law.[40]

(Cuba); UNCLOT, Second Session (1969) 103, para. 28 (Bulgaria); 104, paras. 37–9 (Italy); 124, para. 72 (Spain); 204, para. 24 (El Salvador).

[36] UNCLOT, First Session (1968) 302, para. 33 (Poland); 303, para. 48 (Uruguay) 301, para. 26 (Colombia); 312, para. 55 (Romania); 320, para. 43 (Ecuador); 324, para. 26 (Switzerland); 327, para. 73 (Mali); UNCLOT, Second Session (1969) 104, para. 37 (Italy); 105, paras. 51–2 (Costa Rica); 106, para. 55 (Belgium).

[37] *See* discussion *supra*, Chapter 4, text accompanying *nn*. 67–80.

[38] UNCLOT, First Session (1968) 309, para. 26 (France); UNCLOT, Second Session (1969) 103, para. 30 (Switzerland) ('From the human or moral point of view, it was reassuring to hear so many similar statements concerning the priority which should be given to rules to safeguard respect for human rights. His own Government, for example, considered that the various Geneva conventions for the protection of war victims constituted a milestone in international law. Morality, however, was one thing, but law was another; even natural law, by virtue of a few convincing examples, did not authorize a leap into the unknown.').

[39] See discussion *infra*, Chapter 5.C (The Expression of Morality in *Jus Cogens*).

[40] UNCLOT, First Session (1968) 258, para. 74 (Holy See).

According to this view, codification of *jus cogens* only recognizes that there are legal consequences that arise from residual moral duties where moral considerations are codified as positive law. By 1968 this position was far from radical, as the 1951 Advisory Opinion by the International Court concerning reservations to the Genocide Convention had already reached that conclusion regarding the effect of moral considerations on positive law.[41] Ultimately, the Committee of the Whole endorsed the Drafting Committee's text of Article 50 (Article 53 in the final text) by 72 votes to 3, with 18 abstentions,[42] and the Conference adopted the article by vote of 87 to 8, with 12 abstentions,[43] thereby formally codifying the doctrine of *jus cogens* in international law.

Attempts have been made to circumvent the moral underpinning of *jus cogens*. One proposal is that the concept of *jus cogens* 'had been modified' during the drafting process in such a way as to remove the moral element of *jus cogens*.[44] First, this proposition seems to imply that language pertaining to morality had been removed from earlier drafts of Article 53.[45] The draft articles concerning *jus cogens* prepared by *special rapporteurs* Lauterpacht,[46] Fitzmaurice,[47] and

[41] *Reservations to the Genocide Convention*, Advisory Opinion, ICJ Reports 1951, p. 15, 23. *See* discussion *infra*, Chapter 5, text accompanying *n*. 58.

[42] UNCLOT, First Session (1968) 472, para. 16.

[43] UNCLOT, Second Session (1969) 106–7, para. 65.

[44] Arthur Weisburd, *American Judges and International Law*, 36 Vanderbilt Journal of Transnational Law 1475, 1490 (2003).

[45] *Ibid.*; Artuhr Weisburd, *The Emptiness of the Concept of* Jus Cogens, *as Illustrated by the War in Bosnia-Herzegovina*, 17 Michigan Journal of International Law 1, 14 (1995) ('By 1966, however, the ILC had moved away from this type of thinking on the subject. By this time, the draft language of the renumbered article on *jus cogens* was as follows').

[46] Lauterpacht, First Report, [1953] II YbILC 154 (*Article 15. Consistency with International Law*: A treaty, or any of its provisions, is void if its performance involves an act which is illegal under international law and if it is declared so to be by the International Court of Justice.).

[47] Fitzmaurice, Third Report, [1958] II YbILC 27 (*Article 17. Legality of the object (conflict with international law)*: It being always open, *prima facie*, to any two or more States to agree, for application *inter se*, upon a rule or regime varying or departing from the rules of customary international law in the nature of *jus dispositivum*, a treaty embodying such an agreement cannot be invalid on that ground. Hence it is only if the treaty involves a departure from or conflict with absolute and imperative rules or prohibitions of international law in the nature of *jus cogens* that a cause of invalidity can arise. Since the treaty is in any event *res inter altos acta*, and without force as against non-parties, the invalidity as such of the treaty only affects directly the relations between the parties to it and means that neither or none of the parties can claim compliance with it on the part of the other or others.).

Waldock[48] contained no reference to moral rules, so no such reference could have been removed from subsequent draft articles. To be sure, a formal source of *jus cogens* took clearer form by the final draft article.[49] However, like the introduction of *jus cogens*, reference to formal sources of international law can also be traced back to the commentary by Lauterpacht in his First Report and does not itself mark a transformation in understanding from earlier drafts.[50]

Second, the proposition that the concept of *jus cogens* had been changed during drafting presumes that, by 1966, the ILC 'had moved away from' a concept of *jus cogens* based in public policy and considerations of morality.[51] However, the records of proceedings before the ILC and subsequent UN Conference suggest the contrary.[52] To this end, one

[48] Waldock, Second Report, [1963] II YbILC 52 (*Article 13. Treaties void for illegality*:

1. A treaty is contrary to international law and void if its object or its execution involves the infringement of a general rule or principle of international law having the character of *jus cogens.*
2. In particular, a treaty is contrary to international law and void if its object or execution involves –
   (a) the use or threat of force in contravention of the principles of the Charter of the United Nations;
   (b) any act or omission characterized by international law as an international crime; or
   (c) any act or omission in the suppression or punishment of which every State is required by international law to co-operate.
3. If a provision, the object or execution of which infringes a general rule or principle of international law having the character of *jus cogens,* is not essentially connected with the principal objects of the treaty and is clearly severable from the remainder of the treaty, only that provision shall be void.
4. The provisions of this article do not apply, however, to a general multilateral treaty which abrogates or modifies a rule having the character of *jus cogens.*).

[49] *Compare,* Waldock, Fifth Report, [1966] II YbILC 247 (*Article 50. Treaties Conflicting with a Peremptory Norm of General International Law (jus cogens)*: A treaty is void if it conflicts with a peremptory norm of general international law from which no derogation is permitted and which can be modified only by a subsequent norm of general international law having the same character), *with* UNCLOT, First Session (1968) 471, para. 2 (*Article 50:* A treaty is void if, at the time of its conclusion, it conflicts with a peremptory norm of general international law. For the purposes of the present Convention, a peremptory norm of general international law is a norm *accepted and recognized by the international community of States as a whole* as a norm from which no derogation is permitted and which can be modified only by a subsequent norm of general international law having the same character (emphasis added)).

[50] *See* discussion *infra*, Chapter 8.B (Article 53 of the Vienna Convention).

[51] Weisburd, *The Emptiness of the Concept of* Jus Cogens, 1, 14.

[52] *See* discussion *supra*, Chapter 5.B.i (*Travaux Préparatoires*).

commentator refers to the three-Power amendment of Greece, Finland, and Spain of then draft Article 50, which proposed clearer language relating to a formal source of peremptory norms, to be illustrative of a departure from the basis of *jus cogens* in considerations of morality.[53] Yet members of the ILC itself did not appear to perceive identifying a formal source of peremptory norms based in State practice to represent a departure from the moral considerations underlying *jus cogens*.[54] For example, as Ambassador De Luna of Spain noted before the ILC in 1966:

> In every civilized community there are some rules of law and some principles of morality which individuals are not permitted by law to ignore or to modify by their agreements ... *Jus cogens* was the indispensable minimum for the existence of the international community; it was positive law created by States, not as individuals but as organs of the international community, in order to safeguard the community's existence.[55]

De Luna's remarks leave unanswered the question of how such principles of morality are incorporated through formal sources into legal norms, and what legal effect this element of morality might have. But his observation undermines the proposition that positive law and considerations of morality are mutually exclusive. However desirable such a 'modification' might be in the context of *jus cogens*, it does not appear attributable to the ILC from 1966 onward, or the subsequent UN Conference at Vienna, where moral considerations remained the premise of *jus cogens*.[56]

ii. Jurisprudence

The invocation of moral considerations where international law addresses the protection of human dignity precedes the codification of *jus cogens* in the Vienna Convention. One early example is the Martens Clause of The Hague Conventions of 1899 and 1907, instruments

[53] Weisburd, *The Emptiness of the Concept of* Jus Cogens, 1, 15.

[54] *See, e.g.*, Waldock, Fifth Report, [1966] II YbILC 21 (statement by Algeria), *supra* at *n*. 30.

[55] [1966] I(1) YbILC 39, paras. 31–4 (statement by Mr De Luna) (internal quotation marks omitted).

[56] *See, e.g.*, Andrea Bianchi, *Human Rights and the Magic of* Jus Cogens, 19(3) European Journal of International Law 491, 495–6 (2008) (observing instead that *jus cogens* introduced moral considerations into international law 'for the first time in an overt manner').

codifying the laws and customs of war.[57] The Martens Clause expressly invokes moral obligations deriving from the humanitarian values that the instruments codified:

> Until a more complete code of the law of war has been issued, the High Contracting Parties deem it expedient to declare that, in cases not included in the Regulations adopted by them, the inhabitants and the belligerents remain under the protection and the rule of the principles of the law of nations, as they result from the usages established among civilized peoples, from the laws of humanity, and the dictates of the public conscience.[58]

The clause poses obvious problems from the standpoint of positive law by blurring the distinction between law and morality in the very way that would give pause to some drafters of the law of treaties.[59] The Martens Clause ostensibly attempts to overcome the absence of a developed corpus of law safeguarding human dignity by directly invoking the laws of humanity, the public conscience, and usages of civilized people as authorities that ought to guide both conduct and judicial consideration.[60] In doing so, the clause exposes the gap in international law that the category of *jus cogens* filled by 'positivising' the dictates of morality deriving from considerations of human dignity. Notwithstanding its shortcomings,[61] the Martens Clause evidences both the willingness of the international community to introduce considerations of morality into international law and the point at which such considerations enter law through the protection of human dignity. The Geneva Conventions share a common denunciation clause, which borrows from the Martens Clause of the Hague Conventions,[62] and 'inspired' the drafting of provisions

57 Hague Convention (II) with Respect to the Laws and Customs of War on Land and its annex, 32 Stat. 1803, 1 Bevans 247, Preamble (1899); Hague Convention (IV) respecting the Laws and Customs of War on Land and its annex, 36 Stat. 2277, 1 Bevans 631, Preamble (1907).

58 *Ibid.*

59 *See* Lauterpacht, First Report, [1953] II YbILC 154–6, para. 4 (suggesting the possibility that *jus cogens* would include binding rules of international morality not necessarily crystallized as positive law).

60 Theodor Meron, Human Rights and Humanitarian Norms as Customary Law 41–2 (Oxford: Clarendon Press 1989).

61 *See* Antonio Cassese, *The Martens Clause: Half a Loaf or Simply Pie in the Sky?*, 11(1) European Journal of International Law 187–216 (2000).

62 *See infra*, Chapter 11, *nn.* 81–2 ('The denunciation ... shall in no way impair the obligations which the Parties to the conflict shall remain bound to fulfil by virtue of the principles of the law of nations, as they result from the usages established among civilized peoples, from the laws of humanity and the dictates of the public conscience').

concerning *jus cogens* in the Vienna Convention on the Law of Treaties by *special rapporteur* Waldock.[63]

Two cases before the International Court of Justice evidence the evolution of the moral dimension of *jus cogens*. The first is the 1951 *Reservations to the Genocide Convention* Advisory Opinion, which also preceded codification of the Vienna Convention. In its opinion, the Court accounts for 'special characteristics' of the prohibition against genocide by drawing upon the moral quality of the norm to explain its binding force irrespective of its codification in the Genocide Convention:

> The origins of the Convention show that it was the intention of the United Nations to condemn and punish genocide as 'a crime under international law' involving a denial of the right of existence of entire human groups, a denial which shocks the conscience of mankind and results in great losses to humanity, and which is contrary to moral law and to the spirit and aims of the United Nations. The first consequence arising from this conception is that the principles underlying the Convention are principles which are recognized by civilized nations as binding on States, even without any conventional obligation. A second consequence is the universal character both of the condemnation of genocide and of the co-operation required 'in order to liberate mankind from such an odious scourge'. The Genocide Convention was therefore intended by the General Assembly and by the contracting parties to be definitely universal in scope. It was in fact approved on December 9th, 1948, by a resolution which was unanimously adopted by fifty-six States.
>
> The objects of such a convention must also be considered. The Convention was manifestly adopted for a purely humanitarian and civilizing purpose. It is indeed difficult to imagine a convention that might have this dual character to a greater degree, since its object on the one hand is to safeguard the very existence of certain human groups and on the other to confirm and endorse the most elementary principles of morality. In such a convention the contracting States do not have any interests of their own; they merely have, one and all, a common interest, namely, the accomplishment of those high purposes which are the *raison d'être* of the convention. Consequently, in a convention of this type one cannot speak of individual advantages or disadvantages to States, or of the maintenance of a perfect contractual balance between rights and duties. The high ideals which inspired the Convention provide, by virtue of the common will of the parties, the foundation and measure of all its provisions.[64]

63 [1963] I YbILC 131, para. 31 (693rd Meeting, statement by *special rapporteur* Waldock); *see* Egon Schwelb, *Some Aspects of International Jus Cogens as Formulated by the International Law Commission*, 61 American Journal of International Law 946, 957 (1967).

64 *Reservations to the Genocide Convention*, Advisory Opinion, ICJ Reports 1951, p. 15, 23.

The passage adopts language that tracks the concept of human dignity as a general principle of law defining protections of the individual and corollary moral duties. The passage also employs the same vocabulary as the definition of general principles found in Article 38(1)(c) of the ICJ Statute by reference to 'principles which are recognized by civilized nations', which are later defined as 'the most elementary principles of humanity'.[65] Although this Advisory Opinion preceded the formal codification of the Vienna Convention by nearly two decades, it is contemporary with the introduction of the concept of *jus cogens* in the drafting of the law of treaties.[66] And the prohibition against genocide was subsequently recognized as belonging to *jus cogens* by express reference to the 1951 Advisory Opinion.[67]

The importance of the 1951 Advisory Opinion by the International Court is that is provides perhaps the earliest account of the *effect* of the moral quality of norms deriving from basic considerations of humanity. That effect is to render the norm peremptory, binding upon all members of the international community and inviolable by precepts of positive law. This suggests that considerations of morality account not for the substance of positive law per se, as was feared during the drafting of the Vienna Convention, but instead, inform the legal effects of positive law codifying such moral considerations. Given that the legal effects of international law norms arising from considerations of morality were already being contemplated by the Court as early as 1951, it is unsurprising that the drafters of the Vienna Convention were then inclined to include reference to the concept as it impacted the law of treaties.

More than half a century later, the International Court revisited the prohibition against genocide in *Armed Activities on the Territory of the Congo* (2006).[68] Here, the Court acknowledged the existence of *jus cogens* for the first time, a departure from jurisprudence which had theretofore been limited to the *erga omnes* effects of such norms.[69] The case concerned Congo's request for provisional measures against Rwanda in response to human rights violations and breaches of humanitarian law. As a basis for jurisdiction, Congo relied in part on the *jus cogens* status of

[65] See discussion *infra*, 8.B (Article 53 of the Vienna Convention).
[66] Lauterpacht, First Report, [1953] II YbILC 154–6, para. 4.
[67] *Armed Activities on the Territory of the Congo (New Application: 2002) (Congo v. Rwanda)*, ICJ Reports 2006, p. 3, para. 64.
[68] *Ibid.* [69] *Ibid.*, para. 64.

the norm at issue, rather than the consent of the parties to the dispute.[70] The Court found that it did not have jurisdiction to entertain the application, rejecting the proposition that a dispute concerning *jus cogens* was sufficient to engage the Court's jurisdiction.[71] Nevertheless, the Court quoted from its 1951 Advisory Opinion regarding the universality of the prohibition against genocide, 'as binding on States, even without any conventional obligation', in the express context here of *jus cogens*.[72] By doing so, the 2006 Judgment linked the line of jurisprudence preceding codification of the Vienna Convention – concerning norms arising from moral considerations in international law, as evidenced by the 1951 Advisory Opinion – with the contemporary doctrine of *jus cogens*.

Judge Dugard, in his Separate Opinion in the case, elaborated on the nature of *jus cogens*, observing that a 'blend of principle and policy' accounts for the peremptory status of *jus cogens* norms:

> Norms of *jus cogens* are a blend of principle and policy. On the one hand, they affirm the high principles of international law, which recognize the most important rights of the international order – such as the right to be free from aggression, genocide, torture and slavery and the right to self-determination; while, on the other hand, they give legal form to the most fundamental policies or goals of the international community – the prohibitions on aggression, genocide, torture and slavery and the advancement of self-determination. This explains why they enjoy a hierarchical superiority to other norms in the international legal order.[73]

By this account, moral considerations inform the content of *jus cogens* insofar as norms of positive law 'affirm the high principles of international law'; however, unlike the Martens Clause, for example, moral considerations are not themselves taken to constitute substantive international law.[74] Instead, according to Dugard, this moral aspect confers the peremptory status of *jus cogens* norms and thus their 'hierarchical superiority' in international law. *Jus cogens* is notable in this sense for introducing moral considerations into international law 'for the first time in an overt manner'.[75]

[70] *Ibid.*, paras. 1, 15. [71] *Ibid.*, paras. 64, 125. [72] *Ibid.*, para. 64.
[73] *Ibid.*, Sep. Op. Dugard, p. 86, para. 10.
[74] *See* discussion *supra*, text accompanying *n*. 58.
[75] Bianchi, *Human Rights and the Magic of* Jus Cogens, 491, 495–6.

C The expression of morality in *jus cogens*

The incorporation of moral considerations into international law through the doctrine of *jus cogens* is widely accepted in doctrine on the subject.[76] The influence of considerations of morality in the development and application of *jus cogens* in international law is consistent with a basis in the general legal principle of human dignity.[77] In this view, the moral dimension of human dignity explains the perceived 'peremptory' force associated with *jus cogens* as norms expressive of that general principle. Difficulty arises in explaining the effect of morality within the doctrine of *jus cogens*, and reconciling morality with a category of positive international law more generally.

That morality may account for the 'peremptory' legal effects of *jus cogens* is not affirmed with approval in every instance.[78] Indeed, one early treatise on *jus cogens* not only dismisses the role of morality and social considerations in accounting for the peremptory effects of *jus cogens* but denies the existence of a hierarchy of international law altogether.[79] One alternative explanation proffered for the legal effects of *jus cogens*, which purports to sidestep the morality element, is that States simply have accepted and recognized peremptory norms to be universal and non-derogable.[80] But

[76] *Compare, e.g.*, Bionchi, *Human Rights and the Magic of* Jus Cogens, 491, 495–6; Alexander Orakhelashvili, Peremptory Norms in International Law 49 (Oxford University Press 2006); Fernando Tesón, A Philosophy of International Law 93 (Boulder, CO: Westview Press 1998); Meron, Human Rights and Humanitarian Norms as Customary Law 9; Theodor Meron, Human Rights Law-Making in the United Nations 202 (Oxford: Clarendon Press 1986); Manfred Lachs, *The Development and General Trends of International Law in our Time*, 169 Recueil des Cours 204 (1980); Taslim Elias, New Horizons in International Law 15 (The Hague: Martinus Nijhoff 1979), *with* Weisburd, *The Emptiness of the Concept of* Jus Cogens, 1, 14–16 (1995); Lauri Hannikainen, Peremptory Norms (*Jus Cogens*) in International Law 20 (Helsinki: Finnish Lawyers' Publishing Company 1988).

[77] *See* discussion *supra*, 5.A (Human Dignity as a Moral Concept).

[78] Hannikainen, Peremptory Norms (*Jus Cogens*) in International Law 20. In a review of Orakhelashvili's *Peremptory Norms in International Law*, Byers quiped that, '[n]ot surprisingly, Orakhelashvili favors the idea that *jus cogens* is rooted in natural law'. *See* Michael Byers, *Recent Books in International Law*, 101 American Journal of International Law 913, 915 (2007). To this Orakhelashvili responded the following year with a short letter to the Editors in Chief of the *American Journal* expressing his dissatisfaction with Byers' review. *See* Alexander Orakhelashvili, *Correspondence*, 102(2) American Journal of International Law 309 (2008) ('*mentioning* an idea is obviously different than *favoring* it').

[79] Hannikainen, Peremptory Norms (*Jus Cogens*) in International Law 11–12, 20.

[80] Weisburd, *American Judges and International Law*, 1475, 1490. *See* UNCLOT First Session (1968) 472, para. 12 (statement by Mr Yasseen) (referring to 'a rule to be accepted and recognized as peremptory by all States').

this does not sufficiently resolve the matter, given that there is substantial evidence in *opinio juris* and the practice of States to suggest that morality is perceived to account for the peremptory effect of *jus cogens* norms, notwithstanding their expression as positive law.[81] The relevant question remains, therefore, not whether morality is an element of *jus cogens*, but rather, what effect this moral foundation has as a matter of international law.

When assessing the role of morality in *jus cogens*, the distinction between considerations of morality and the institution of law must be reiterated. The differentiation between moral and legal rules is presented lucidly by Professor MacCormick, who proposes the following formulation:

> To ascribe to all members of a class C a right to treatment T is to presuppose that T is, in all normal circumstances, a good for every member of C, and that T is a good of such importance that it would be wrong to deny it to or withhold it from any member of C. That as for moral rights; as for legal rights I should say this: when a right to T is conferred by law on all members of C, the law is envisaged as advancing the interests of each and every member of C, and the law has the effect of making it legally wrongful to withhold T from any member of C.[82]

This presentation clearly demonstrates the divergent syntax of moral and legal rules concerning the same object. By this depiction, moral considerations arising from human dignity reflect the first relation, while their codification as law takes the form of the second relation. In *South West Africa Cases*, the International Court of Justice drew attention to the importance of maintaining this distinction through a positivist approach to the substance and application of law, even where moral considerations inform the content of that law:

> [I]t has been suggested, directly or indirectly, that humanitarian considerations are sufficient in themselves to generate legal rights and obligations, and that the Court can and should proceed accordingly. The Court does not think so. It is a court of law, and can take account of moral principles only in so far as these are given a sufficient expression in legal form. Law exists, it is said, to serve a social need; but precisely for that reason it can do so only through and within the limits of its own discipline. Otherwise, it is not a legal service that would be rendered.[83]

81 *See* discussion *supra*, 5.B (Morality and Peremptory Norms).

82 Donald MacCormick, *Rights in Legislation*, *in* LAW, MORALITY, AND SOCIETY 204 (Oxford: Clarendon Press, P. M. S. Hacker & Joseph Raz eds., 1977).

83 *South West Africa Cases (Ethiopia v. South Africa / Liberia v. South Africa) (Second Phase)*, Judgment, ICJ Reports 1966, p. 6, paras. 49–50 (The court continued:

The Court was quite right to preserve this distinction between law and morality, and the Court does not propose that moral considerations have no impact on their parallel positive legal forms. There is a body of literature dedicated to the subject, with one pervasive understanding being that the obligatory force of morality provides additional pull to comply with what is otherwise proscribed by the law.[84] The question for purposes of this section is what effect moral considerations have upon their expression in legal form as *jus cogens*. Because peremptory norms are conceived by contemporary international law to have two peculiar legal effects that distinguish them from the rest of international law, non-derogability and universality, it serves to begin with a discussion of those effects.

i. Non-derogation

According to Articles 53 and 64 of the Vienna Convention on the Law of Treaties, a treaty conflicting with a peremptory norm at the time of its conclusion 'is void', and a treaty in conflict with the emergence of a new peremptory norm 'becomes void and terminates'.[85] This legal effect of *jus cogens* reflects the resistance of peremptory norms to modification or repeal by the particular will of individual States. A 1983 case decided by the Argentine Supreme Court, *Washington Cabrera J. E. c. Comisión Técnica Mixta de Salto Grande*, provides a rare example of the effect of non-derogation in the treaty context.[86] The case concerned the constitutionality of a headquarters agreement between Argentina and the *Comisión Técnica Mixta de Salto Grande* that granted the latter judicial immunity. A majority of the Court held that an immunity agreement lacking alternative dispute settlement remedies for private parties violated the right to judicial protection under the National Constitution.[87] The Court reasoned that the National Constitution was superior to a

'Humanitarian considerations may constitute the inspirational basis for rules of law, just as, for instance, the preambular parts of the United Nations Charter constitute the moral and political basis for the specific legal provisions thereafter set out. Such considerations do not, however, in themselves amount to rules of law').

84 *See, e.g.*, Greenwalt, CONFLICTS OF LAW AND MORALITY; Fuller, THE MORALITY OF LAW; H. L. A. Hart, THE CONCEPT OF LAW 181–207 (Oxford: Clarendon Press 1961).

85 1155 UNTS 331, Articles 53 and 64 (1969).

86 *Washington Cabrera J. E. c. Comisión Técnica Mixta de Salto Grande*, Supreme Court of Justice (Argentina), Fallas 1993-305-2150 (1983).

87 *Ibid.*

treaty, and its due process protections could not be abrogated through a bilateral agreement. Justices Gustavino and Gabrielli, writing in dissent, further determined that this defect violated Article 53 of the Vienna Convention on the Law of Treaties by running afoul of the *jus cogens* right of access to justice, rendering Article 4 null and void, an opinion endorsed by the majority of the Court.[88] While due process is more accurately characterized as a general principle of law 'accepted by all nations in *foro domestico*' rather than a peremptory norm,[89] the example illustrates how non-derogation might operate to invalidate a treaty.

Article 64 of the Vienna Convention provides that the non-derogation principle applies to invalidate treaties codified prior to the crystallization of 'new' *jus cogens* norms.[90] It would seem also that the principle of non-derogation applies to treaties concluded prior to the Vienna Convention that contravene *jus cogens*. In 1993, the Inter-American Court of Human Rights ordered Suriname to pay reparations in a case concerning indigenous persons assaulted and killed by State military forces believing them to belong to a Jungle Commando.[91] In assessing how to measure reparations, the Court was confronted with a disagreement regarding the family law applicable to the case: Surinamese law, or the law of the Saramaka tribe.[92] The autonomy of the Saramakas, which had been granted by treaty on 19 September 1762 was invoked before the Court in support of the legislative autonomy of the Saramakas.[93] The Court, while ultimately finding that Suriname had recognized Saramaka customary law, considered the treaty to be null and void because it violated *jus cogens*.[94] Specifically, the instrument required the Saramakas to capture and return escaped slaves to the Governor of Suriname, and empowered the Saramakas to sell other prisoners to the Dutch as slaves, in violation of the *jus cogens* prohibition of slavery.[95] The treaty could not, therefore, be invoked before the Inter-American Court.

[88] *See ibid.*, Minority Opinion of Guastavino and Gabrielli, paras. 9–11.

[89] *See, e.g.*, Bardo Fassbender, TARGETED SANCTIONS AND DUE PROCESS 7, para. 5; 15, para. 1.17 (New York: United Nations 2006) (Study Commissioned by the United Nations); RESTATEMENT (THIRD) OF FOREIGN RELATIONS LAW OF THE UNITED STATES (1987) § 102, cmt. l (referring to 'rules of fair procedure generally' as among general principles common to the major legal systems); PCIJ Advisory Committee of Jurists, PROCÈS-VERBAUX OF THE PROCEEDINGS OF THE COMMITTEE 335 (The Hague: Van Langenhuysen Brothers 1920) (statement by Lord Phillimore) (identifying 'certain principles of procedure' as among the general principles of law).

[90] 1155 UNTS 331, Article 64 (1969).

[91] *Aloeboetoe et al. v. Suriname*, IACtHR Series C No. 15, paras. 1–6 (1993).

[92] *Ibid.*, paras. 55–8. [93] *Ibid.* [94] *Ibid.* [95] *Ibid.*, paras. 57–8.

Instances of treaty invalidation are, however, exceedingly uncommon,[96] and in practice, violations of peremptory norms involve unilateral acts rather than impermissible international agreements.[97] The principle of non-derogability therefore applies to unilateral State conduct. Article 4 of the ICCPR provides an illustration of this proposition. According to Article 4(1) of the Covenant, States Parties may derogate from their obligations under the instrument in times of public emergency.[98] No derogation is permitted according to Article 4(2), however, from certain provisions of the ICCPR,[99] which in one sense are non-derogable 'by the very fact that they are listed in article 4, paragraph 2'.[100] More broadly, however, the UNHRC acknowledged that the non-derogability provision of Article 4(2) 'may not be resorted to in a way that would result in derogation from non-derogable rights'.[101] The Committee then addressed the relation between Article 4(2) of the ICCPR and *jus cogens*:

> The enumeration of non-derogable provisions in article 4 is related to, but not identical with, the question whether certain human rights obligations bear the nature of peremptory norms of international law. . . [T]he category of peremptory norms extends beyond the list of non-derogable provisions as given in article 4, paragraph 2. States parties may in no circumstances invoke article 4 of the Covenant as justification for acting in violation of humanitarian law or peremptory norms of international law[.] [102]

[96] This remains so even where Articles 53 and 64 are invoked to invalidate a treaty: *see R.D. v. Belgium*, Court of Cassation (Belgium), No. P.04.1211.N, JT, 2005, 322, ILDC 6, para. 24 (2004) (finding that the 1962 Treaty on Extradition and Mutual Assistance in Criminal Matters Between Belgium, Luxembourg, and the Netherlands had not been invalidated by emergence of a peremptory norm under Article 64 of the Vienna Convention).

[97] *See* discussion *supra*, Chapter 1, text accompanying *nn.* 20–1.

[98] ICCPR, Article 4(1) ('In time of public emergency which threatens the life of the nation and the existence of which is officially proclaimed, the States Parties to the present Covenant may take measures derogating from their obligations under the present Covenant to the extent strictly required by the exigencies of the situation, provided that such measures are not inconsistent with their other obligations under international law and do not involve discrimination solely on the ground of race, colour, sex, language, religion or social origin').

[99] ICCPR, Article 4(2) ('No derogation from articles 6, 7, 8 (paragraphs 1 and 2), 11, 15, 16 and 18 may be made under this provision').

[100] UN Human Rights Committee, CCPR General Comment 29: Article 4: Derogations during a State of Emergency (2001), *in* I Compilation of General Comments and General Recommendations Adopted by Human Rights Treaty Bodies 234, 236, para. 7, UN Doc. HRI/GEN/1/Rev.9 (Vol. I) (2008).

[101] *Ibid.*, 239, para. 15.

[102] *Ibid.*, 237–8, para. 11; *see ibid.*, 238, para. 12 ('In assessing the scope of legitimate derogation from the Covenant, one criterion can be found in the definition of certain human rights violations as crimes against humanity. If action conducted under the authority of a

In an earlier General Comment, the UNHRC explained that, 'in times of emergency, the protection of human rights becomes all the more important, particularly those rights from which no derogation can be made'.[103] And, in a General Comment concerning the prohibition of torture, the HRC related non-derogability to the general principle of human dignity:

> The Committee recalls that even in situations of public emergency such as are envisaged by article 4 (1) this provision is non-derogable under article 4 (2). Its purpose is to protect the integrity and dignity of the individual.[104]

The UNHRC further indicated, in the same paragraph, that simply criminalizing such forbidden conduct is insufficient, and that it is incumbent upon the State to 'ensure an effective protection through some machinery of control'.[105] Although State obligations arising from peremptory norms will be addressed in Part V, it suffices at present to note that one effect of the peremptory status of norms belonging to *jus cogens* is to render those norms non-derogable by any State conduct.[106]

ii. Universality and normative hierarchy

The corollary of the non-derogability of peremptory norms is the universal application of those norms. This understanding found virtually unanimous support during the drafting of the Vienna

State constitutes a basis for individual criminal responsibility for a crime against humanity by the persons involved in that action, article 4 of the Covenant cannot be used as justification that a state of emergency exempted the State in question from its responsibility in relation to the same conduct. Therefore, the recent codification of crimes against humanity, for jurisdictional purposes, in the Rome Statute of the International Criminal Court is of relevance in the interpretation of article 4 of the Covenant').

103 UN Human Rights Committee, General Comment 5: Article 4: Derogations (1981), *in* I Compilation of General Comments and General Recommendations Adopted by Human Rights Treaty Bodies 176, para. 3, UN Doc. HRI/GEN/1/Rev.9 (Vol. I) (2008).

104 UN Human Rights Committee, General Comment 7: Article 7 (Prohibition of Torture or Cruel, Inhuman or Degrading Treatment or Punishment) (1982), *in* Compilation of General Comments and General Recommendations Adopted by Human Rights Treaty Bodies 178, para. 1, UN Doc. HRI/GEN/1/Rev.9 (Vol. I) (2008) (replaced by General Comment 20 (1992)).

105 *Ibid. See* Chapter 14 (The Enforcement of *Jus Cogens*: Obligations *Erga Omnes*).

106 *See Bueno Alves v. Argentina*, IACtHR Series C no. 164, para. 76 (2007) (finding *jus cogens* 'remains valid even under the most difficult circumstances, such as war, threat of war, the fight against terrorism and other crimes, state of siege, or a state of emergency, civil commotion or domestic conflict, suspension of constitutional guarantees, domestic political instability or other public emergencies or catastrophes').

Convention,[107] reflecting a common understanding, even among dissenting delegations,[108] that *jus cogens* norms are universal in nature. The universality of *jus cogens* is implicit in non-derogability, and both effects are viewed to arise from the subject matter of *jus cogens*.[109] This relation results in a distinct category of law contributing to the oft-observed contrast by which *jus cogens* is defined in opposition to *jus dispositivum*.[110] This juxtaposition is clearly expressed in Judge Tanaka's Separate Opinion in the *South West Africa Cases*, where he referred to

> a category of law, namely *jus cogens*, recently examined by the International Law Commission, a kind of imperative law which constitutes the contrast to the *jus dispositivum*, capable of being changed by way of agreement between States[.][111]

This normative distinction introduces an element of hierarchy into international law. The overriding effect of this hierarchy is implicitly

[107] *See, e.g.*, UNCLOT, First Session (1968) 293–334; UNCLOT, Second Session (1969) 93–107 (Note that these statements pertain to the conception of *jus cogens* as a category of peremptory norms submitted by the ILC in its Draft Articles on the Law of Treaties (1966): Waldock, Fifth Report, [1966] II YbILC 247–9).

[108] *See, e.g.*, Waldock, Fifth Report, [1966] II YbILC 20–1 (statement by Luxembourg).

[109] *Ibid.*, 248, para. 2 (Commentary to Draft Article 50) ('It is not the form of a general rule of international law but the particular nature of the subject-matter with which it deals that may, in the opinion of the Commission, give it the character of *jus cogens*'); Robert Ago, Fifth Report on State Responsibility, [1976] II(1) YbILC 32, para. 99 ('The content of the rules of international *jus cogens* is so important to the community of States that derogation from those rules . . . has in fact been prohibited'). *See, e.g.*, Bianchi, *Human Rights and the Magic of* Jus Cogens, 491, 494; Martti Koskenniemi, *Hierarchy in International Law: A Sketch*, 8 European Journal of International Law 566 (1997); Meron, Human Rights Law-Making in the United Nations 200; Jerzy Sztucki, Jus Cogens and the Vienna Convention on the Law of Treaties 89 (Vienna: Springer-Verlag 1974); Herman Mosler, *The International Society as a Legal Community*, 140 Recueil des Cours 84 (1974).

[110] Fitzmaurice, Third Report, [1958] II YbILC 40, para. 76 (Commentary to draft article 17); *see* [1966] I(1) YbILC 37, para. 9 (828th Meeting, statement by Mr Verdross); [1963] I YbILC 73, para. 63 (685th Meeting, statement by Mr De Luna). *See, e.g.*, Ago, Fifth Report, [1976] II(1) YbILC 32, para. 99 (referring to 'a "normative" differentiation' between *jus cogens* and other rules of international law); Orakhelashvili, Peremptory Norms in International Law 47; Ian Sinclair, The Vienna Convention on the Law of Treaties 204 (Manchester University Press 1984); Mosler, *The International Society as a Legal Community*, 35; Schwelb, *Some Aspects of International Jus Cogens*, 946, 948; Alfred Verdross, Jus Dispositivum *and* Jus Cogens *in International Law*, 60 American Journal of International Law 55, 55–63 (1966).

[111] *South West Africa Cases (Ethiopia v. South Africa / Liberia v. South Africa) (Second Phase)*, Judgment, ICJ Reports 1966, Sep. Op. Tanaka, p. 250, 298.

set out in Article 53 of the Vienna Convention with respect to the relation between *jus cogens* and *jus dispositivum*. Moreover, unlike *jus dispositivum* that runs between States, *jus cogens* is distinct from 'individual advantages or disadvantages to States',[112] and therefore, 'could not be made dependent on a reciprocal or corresponding performance . . . by other States'.[113]

More broadly, universality suggests a monist legal order with *jus cogens* as a hierarchically elevated sphere of law. An authoritative expression of the practical effect of this hierarchy is found in the ICTY *Furundžija* Judgment:

> Because of the importance of the values it protects, this principle has evolved into a peremptory norm or *jus cogens*, that is, a norm that enjoys a higher rank in the international hierarchy . . . The fact that torture is prohibited by a peremptory norm of international law has other effects at the inter-state and individual levels. At the inter-state level, it serves to internationally de-legitimise any legislative, administrative or judicial act authorising torture. It would be senseless to argue, on the one hand, that on account of the *jus cogens* value of the prohibition against torture, treaties or customary rules providing for torture would be null and void *ab initio*, and then be unmindful of a State say, taking national measures authorising or condoning torture or absolving its perpetrators through an amnesty law. If such a situation were to arise, the national measures, violating the general principle and any relevant treaty provision, would produce the legal effects discussed above and in addition would not be accorded international legal recognition . . . What is even more important is that perpetrators of torture acting upon or benefiting from those national measures may nevertheless be held criminally responsible for torture, whether in a foreign State, or in their own State under a subsequent regime. In short, in spite of possible national authorisation by legislative or judicial bodies to violate the principle banning torture, individuals remain bound to comply with that principle. As the International Military Tribunal at Nuremberg put it: 'individuals have international duties which transcend the national obligations of obedience imposed by the individual State'.[114]

112 *Reservations to the Genocide Convention*, Advisory Opinion, ICJ Reports 1951, p. 15, 23; *see Armed Activities on the Territory of the Congo (New Application: 2002) (Congo v. Rwanda)*, ICJ Reports 2006, p. 3, para. 64 (applying the language and reasoning of the Court in 1951 to the prohibition of genocide as *jus cogens*).

113 *Prosecutor v. Kupreškić*, IT-95-16-T, para. 518 (2000).

114 *Prosecutor v. Furundžija*, IT-95-17/1-T, paras. 153–5 (1998) (internal citations omitted).

This passage articulates the hierarchical effect of universality in a monist system that encompasses both domestic and international law.[115] Such a hierarchy is expressive of a gradient of specificity to generality, from the particular rules governing local relations, to more general laws between States, and ultimately a small corpus of universal norms contained by *jus cogens*. These strata of law – domestic law and the *jus dispositivum* and *jus cogens* of international law – exist in an order of preeminence by which laws of a higher level permeate those of the tiers below; as a corollary, laws of a lower level cannot derogate from those of a higher tier. The recognition of such stratification is implicit in the universality and non-derogability of peremptory norms, legal effects that distinguish *jus cogens* from the broader *jus dispositivum* of international law.

***

The 'peremptory' legal effects of *jus cogens* – non-derogability and universality – may be understood with reference to the morality underlying the doctrine of *jus cogens*. In principle, the peremptory character of *jus cogens* follows logically from the operative conceptualization of morality oriented in human dignity, which holds that fundamental rights can be realized only through duties of universal application.[116] In the previous section, morality was defined as a *social* idea with an outward-oriented focus that prescribes standards of conduct that, in effect, define obligations owed to others.[117] Respect, in this sense, is the basis of human dignity, and only when human dignity is respected by an entire community is it actualized by its individual members. The same relation can be seen in the legal precepts derived from human dignity.[118] In the context of *jus cogens*, this would suggest that only when its normative expressions are respected by the international community of States as a whole can these protections of human dignity be realized fully by mankind. To this

[115] *Cf.* Hannikainen, Peremptory Norms (*Jus Cogens*) in International Law 11–12 (denying that *jus cogens* constitutes a hierarchical category of norms in international law).

[116] *See* discussion *supra*, text accompanying *nn.* 12–20.

[117] *See* discussion *supra*, 5.A (Human Dignity as a Moral Concept).

[118] *See* M. Cherif Bassiouni, *The Philosophy and Policy of International Criminal Justice, in* Man's Inhumanity to Man 115–16 (The Hague: Martinus Nijhoff, Antonio Cassese & Lal Chand Vohrah eds., 2003) ('Punishment for *jus cogens* international crimes helps restore the human dignity of the specific victim and symbolically reaffirms the value of human dignity of humene genre and, in the Kantian sense, it restores the human dignity of the perpetrator').

end, it follows that peremptory norms are regarded as non-derogable rules of a public order character, inviolable by contrary rules of positive international law, and universal in application. In practice, peremptory norms are conceived by contemporary international law to have precisely these legal effects.

That morality is linked to human dignity, in the context of the higher interests of the international community, is therefore not merely rhetorical. Human dignity, it may be recalled, represents the shared values and interests of the international community as a representation of mankind: it is a social principle. *Jus cogens* gives legal effect to these higher interests through public order norms necessary for the maintenance of international coexistence, and it is in this sense that human dignity accounts for the moral authority of peremptory norms. Put differently, human dignity serves as the basis of morality in the international community by representing its higher interests, incorporated as peremptory norms of international law, required as a matter of social necessity for international coexistence. The interests of the international community implicated by the relations of States centre on the intrinsic worth of the human person because respect for this value is fundamental to social coexistence. It is by virtue of this link to social coexistence that the principle of human dignity retains a moral quality, and legal precepts arising from its protection in international law permeate all strata of legal order while permitting no derogation.

The role of morality should not be overstated. As a material source of peremptory norms, the general principle of human dignity reflects the higher interests of the international community as a whole and in turn informs the content of the category of *jus cogens*. Even so, as discussed in Chapter 8, the formal source by which peremptory norms of international law are evidenced as a matter of positive law remains customary international law.[119] The role of morality in this process is therefore modest: it explains why particular legal effects are associated with the category of *jus cogens*. Considerations of morality arise from the way in which peremptory norms are 'accepted and recognized' by the international community of States as a whole, thereby distinguishing *jus cogens* from the broader *jus dispositivum* of international law. The 'peremptory' legal effects of *jus cogens*, to the extent they are

[119] *See* discussion *infra*, Chapter 8 (The Formal Source of Peremptory Norms).

associated with morality, are nevertheless features established as a matter of positive law.[120] Thus, while the doctrine of morality may account for the authority of peremptory norms as non-derogable and universal, these effects remain legal in nature.[121]

[120] Grigory Tunkin, Jus Cogens *in Contempoary Internaitonal Law*, 3 TOLEDO LAW REVIEW 107, 117 (1971) ('international law and international morality are different systems of social norms and in spite of a close connection between principles of *jus cogens* and principles of international morality, a principle of general international law is a principle of *jus cogens* on the basis of international law, not on the basis of international morality').

[121] *South West Africa Cases (Ethiopia v. South Africa / Liberia v. South Africa) (Second Phase)*, Judgment, ICJ Reports 1966, p. 6, para. 49 ('a court of law [] can take account of moral principles only in so far as these are given a sufficient expression in legal form').

6

Expression of an international social contract

The authority of *jus cogens*, as a product of the interests of the international community of States as a whole, can be understood as the starting point for a theory of social contract. The impetus behind the organization of civil society through social contract is conceived to be the insecurity, in the absence of society, of principles necessary for coexistence within a community. Social contract theory regards this to be the 'state of nature', that 'state in which men are set by God'.[1] It is the natural condition of pre-political man, without or preceding government.[2] The origin of the idea of the state of nature rests with the pre-Socratic classical Greek thinker Protagoras, whose 'origin of cities', part of a theory of progress, depicts the law of the State as the means by which men escape an uncoordinated, self-destructive natural state.[3] In this insecure, immoral condition, the most basic and fundamental norms of a community – often conceived as natural law – are secured only by exiting the state of nature and entering into a civil state guarded by law. This notion of unstable interaction is the common starting point of contractarian narratives depicting the emergence of civil society; however, there is no more detailed common depiction of the state of nature. Rather, the account of the state of nature varies across even the Enlightenment social contract theorists in accordance with divergent conceptualizations of the nature of man. As the justifications for political order, and the various depictions of government, derive from the state of nature and the nature of pre-political man (which vary according to the political contexts in which they are conceived), what follows are vastly different images of political order.[4] Yet a cursory gloss of prominent

[1] John Dunn, *The State of Nature, in* John Dunn (ed.), THE POLITICAL THOUGHT OF JOHN LOCKE 97 (Cambridge University Press 1983).

[2] Michael Lessnoff (ed.), SOCIAL CONTRACT 20 (London: Macmillan 1986).

[3] *Ibid.*, 20–1.

[4] Jean Hampton, HOBBES AND THE SOCIAL CONTRACT TRADITION 273 (Cambridge University Press 1986).

conceptualizations of the state of nature reveals fundamental similarities notwithstanding philosophical differences.

Hobbes penned *Leviathan* in 1651, towards the end of the English Civil War. It is in this context that Hobbes depicted the natural relation of man as competitive, limited only by death, and underpinned by an unlimited right to liberty in a state of perpetual insecurity. The natural state of mankind, in the absence of political society and the coercive authority necessary to secure peaceful relations among individuals, is therefore a condition of war 'of every man, against every man'.[5] In this natural state there is but one Right of Nature: the liberty to use force to preserve one's life.[6] As a rational creature, man chooses to leave this state of nature and enter into a civil state by following the three laws of nature: to seek peace, lay down rights to this end as necessary, and perform covenants made.[7] Consequently, a social contract between man and sovereign establishes a leviathan charged with providing security for the commonwealth. The laws of nature, which constitute equity, justice, gratitude, and other moral virtues, become formal laws through incorporation into civil law, a process common to every political society of the world.[8] While it is acknowledged that natural laws are not laws proper and need not be published to bind men, these basic laws can only be fully realized through the formation of civil society, because the passions of man are contrary to natural law (as demonstrated by the state of nature).[9]

Locke's writings on the social contract in his *Two Treatises of Government*, though often cast as a rationalization of the Glorious Revolution of 1688 in England, are more recently thought to have been 'a demand for a revolution to be brought about'.[10] As a foundation for his Liberal conceptualualization of the establishment of civil society, Locke depicts the natural state of man in the second volume of *Two Treatises of Government* as one of perfect freedom and equality, a cooperative social condition

[5] Thomas Hobbes, LEVIATHAN I.13.62 (London: Penguin Books, C. B. McPherson ed., 1985 [1651]).

[6] *Ibid.*, I.14.64. [7] *Ibid.*, I.14.64–5, I.15.71.

[8] *Ibid.*, II.26.4 (Hobbes states that these natural laws may be summarized by the statement, 'Do not that to another, which thou thinkest unreasonable to be done by another to thy selfe', a remarkable parallel to Kant's categorical imperative discussed below).

[9] *Ibid.*, II.17.85.

[10] Peter Laslett, *Two Treatises of Government and the Revolution of 1688*, *in* John Locke, TWO TREATISES OF GOVERNMENT 45, 45–51 (Cambridge University Press, Peter Laslett ed., 1988) (this despite Locke's Preface to the contrary in his 1689 edition) [hereinafter Locke, TWO TREATISES].

guided by a single Law of Nature: to preserve the state of nature and to 'put into every man's hands, whereby everyone has a right to punish the transgressors of that law to such a degree, as may hinder its violation'.[11] A consequence of this natural freedom, however, is that the state of nature, although a condition of natural peace, mutual assistance, and good will, is punctuated by lapses into a state of war during which the law of nature is freely enforced: man is at liberty to preserve his property, judge the transgressions of others, and punish violations, all through the use of force.[12] This intrinsically insecure condition is understood to be the consequence of the absence of a common judge or superior, which necessitates man's escape from the state of nature by establishing civil society through the social contract.[13] By concluding a social contract, man enters into civil society, thereby establishing the authority necessary to preserve his natural rights: life, liberty, and estate.[14] Importantly, this is understood to be the 'great and chief end' of civil society: the preservation of the natural rights of man, which is guaranteed by establishing political order capable of enforcing the law of nature.

Rousseau, in *Du contract social ou Principes du droit politique*, provides 'a response to the specific historical conditions of institutional and societal instability' unique to the French monarchic tradition that orients sovereign will in the 'permanent and common interests of the entire nation'.[15] Rousseau depicts the state of nature as a condition of 'peace and innocence' in which no man has legitimate authority over another. In his essay *The State of War*, Rousseau depicts natural man as a 'peaceful and timid' being whose initial inclination is to flee rather than fight; man's propensity to fight derives from the habit and experience of the social condition, which corrupts man and drives him to unite into artificial associations to wage war upon one another.[16] Consequently, the

[11] Locke, Two Treatises II.2.7. [12] *Ibid.*, II.3.19. [13] *Ibid.*, II.3.21.

[14] *Ibid.*, II.7.87, II.9.124.

[15] Jeremy Jennings, *Rousseau, Social Contract and the Modern Leviathan*, *in* The Social Contract from Hobbes to Rawls 118 (London: Routledge, David Boucher & Paul Kelly eds., 1994). *See* Jean-Jacques Rousseau, The Social Contract (Du Contract Social ou Principes du Droit Politique) (London: Everyman 2003 [1762]) [hereinafter, Rousseau, Social Contract]; Jean-Jacques Rousseau, Discourse on the Origin and the Foundations of Inequality among Men [1754], in Victor Gourevitch, Rousseau: The Discourses and Other Early Political Writings 131 (Cambridge University Press 1997) [hereinafter, Rousseau, Discourse on Inequality].

[16] Jean-Jacques Rousseau, The State of War, *in* Rousseau on International Relations (Oxford: Clarendon Press, Stanley Hoffmann & David Fidler eds., 1991) [hereinafter, Rousseau, State of War].

lack of security in the unfettered state of nature, corrupted by the social state, creates a condition resembling the Hobbesian state of nature that requires man to protect the first law of nature, self-preservation, by uniting through the social contract.[17] Civil society is established to provide security unknown in the state of nature and alleviate the negative passions of the social state, ultimately creating a condition conducive to the development of 'rational natural law'.[18] This connection is articulated explicitly in Rousseau's conceptualization of a general will of the human race:

> It is certain that the words 'human race' bring to mind a purely collective idea which does not imply any real union among the individuals which constitute it. To this let us add the following supposition: let us think of the human race as a corporate person having, together with a feeling of common existence which gives it individuality and makes it a unity, a universal motive force which makes each part act for a general end relative to the whole. Let us assume that this common feeling is that of humanity and the natural law is the active principle of the whole machine. Then let us observe what results from the constitution of man in his relations with his fellows. Entirely contrary to what we have supposed we shall find that the progress of society stifles humanity in men's hearts by arousing personal interest, and that the notions of natural law, which it would be more appropriate to call the law of reason, only begin to develop when the earlier development of the passions is making all its precepts powerless.[19]

By this conceptualization, the fundamental laws of nature common to all men can be preserved only through the formation of civil society. The social contract is the means to this end.

Kant's theory of the social contract, depicted first in *Metaphysics of Morals*, closely follows that developed by Rousseau. According to Kant, the state of nature is not a rightful condition because it lacks distributive justice,[20] and as such it comes to resemble the Hobbesian natural state of man.[21] Consequently, man must enter not a social state but a civil state

[17] John Noone, *Rousseau's Theory of Natural Law as Conditional*, 33(1) Journal of the History of Ideas 23, 31 (1972).

[18] Rousseau, State of War xlii–xliii.

[19] Rousseau, Social Contract (Omitted second Chapter of the 1759 'Geneva Manuscript', entitled 'The General Society of the Human Race', para. 8) (Though this is not an optimistic picture, the statement effectively demonstrates the place of natural law in Rousseau's presentation of social contract theory).

[20] Immanuel Kant, Metaphysics of Morals [1797], *in* The Cambridge Edition of the Works of Immanuel Kant 6:306 (Cambridge University Press, Mary Gregor ed., 1996) [hereinafter, Kant, Metaphysics].

[21] Howard Williams, *Kant on the Social Contract*, *in* The Social Contract from Hobbes to Rawls 133 (Boucher & Kelly eds.).

through the original contract (distinguished as expressing the ends individuals *ought* to share from social contracts more generally),[22] the only relation of individuals through which man is able to enjoy his rights.[23] Establishing the civil constitution is envisaged by Kant to be a law of natural right, an objectively necessary duty of man.[24] The original contract is, therefore, taken to be an *a priori* idea of pure practical reason – that is, an idea necessary to make experience possible – without which civil society would be impossible.[25] The condition generated by the civil state under the original contract is described by Kant as a rightful condition of 'public right':

> The sum of the laws which need to be promulgated generally in order to bring about a rightful condition is *public right*. – Public right is therefore a system of laws for a people, that is, a multitude of human beings, or for a multitude of peoples, which, because they affect one another, need a rightful condition under a will uniting them, a *constitution* (*constitutio*), so that they may enjoy what is laid down as right.[26]

Importantly, a natural right is understood to be one 'which can be derived from *a priori* principles for a civil constitution', a relation that directly links the public right defined by the original contract to natural law.[27] This is unsurprising given the depiction of the original contract as an exceptional union that reflects not only the shared will of a group of individuals, but also 'an end . . . that each *ought to have*'.[28] By introducing the 'ought' qualification in addition to the 'is' with respect to the social contract, and identifying its principles as *a priori*, Kant explicitly denotes a normative character to the rules established by civil society.

***

As a narrative that accounts for the establishment of society through the historical exigencies of a community, the social contract offers a perspective through which to understand the development of *jus cogens* in international law. *Jus cogens* constitutes norms accepted and recognized

22 Immanuel Kant, On the Common Saying: That May Be Correct in Theory, But It Is of No Use in Practice [1793], *in* The Cambridge Edition of the Works of Immanuel Kant 8:289, 8:295 (Gregor ed.) [hereinafter, Kant, Theory and Practice].

23 *Ibid.*, 8:289; Kant, Metaphysics 6:306.

24 Kant, Theory and Practice 8:289; Kant, Metaphysics 6:264.

25 Kant, Theory and Practice 8:297; Kant, Metaphysics 6:355.

26 Kant, Metaphysics 6:311.

27 Kant, Theory and Practice 8:290; Kant, Metaphysics 6:256.

28 Kant, Theory and Practice 8:289.

by the international community as a whole, from which no derogation is permitted by virtue of their importance to international society. A contractarian understanding of the international community begins with its organization in terms of the higher interests common to its members. The social contract may be seen as a response to the state of nature and the conditions prevailing prior to the establishment of civil society. The higher interests of a community articulated through the social contract reflect those particular values and interests deemed necessary for a community to establish peaceful, social coexistence. The doctrine of *jus cogens* invites just such a conceptualization as a category of norms necessary to the social coexistence of the international community. Variation across social contract theories attests to distinct historical circumstances conceived to give rise to their respective articulations,[29] conditions necessitating the protection of particular values. By analogy, the values and interests common to the international community may be interpreted from expressions of social necessity that give rise to *jus cogens*.

Consequently, the concept of *jus cogens* can be seen to reflect a genesis similar to that of the social contract. The peremptory character of *jus cogens* norms is a product of their importance to the maintenance of the international community. The Criminal Chamber of the High Court of Spain relied upon this quality of *jus cogens* to explain how peremptory norms could apply as law in Spain even prior to their formal codification in its Criminal Code:

> We believe that the *ius cogens* status of the international law . . . prevents [. . .] going against its essential content or limiting its intended temporal, subjective or territorial scope of application . . . [D]ue to its characteristics and universal nature, this law is organised, not in one specific State, but in all of humanity and all States in order to protect higher values of humanity[.][30]

[29] 'Historical' is used here in reference to the state preceding, and necessitating, social organization, not the historicity of a social contract. However, variation across social contract theorists often does reflect particular historical conditions in response to which those theorists were writing. Hobbes is an obvious example of this 'historical contextualism', which remains distinguishable from any presumption of the social contract itself as a historical fact or artefact. *See* Quentin Skinner, Reason and Rhetoric in the Philosophy of Hobbes (Cambridge University Press 1996).

[30] *Public Prosecutor's Office et al. v. Scilingo Manzorro*, National Court (*Audiencia Nacional*) (Criminal Chamber) (Spain), Case No. 16/2005, Aranzadi JUR 2005/132318, ILDC 136, paras. B.1–B.2, B.4–B.5 (2005) (conviction for crimes against humanity, by exercise of universal jurisdiction, as customary international law part of the Spanish legal order prior to codification of that crime in the Criminal Code of Spain).

The German Constitutional Court made a similar observation with respect to the incorporation of *jus cogens* in the Basic Law of Germany:

> [T]he Basic Law also adopts the gradual recognition of the existence of mandatory provisions ... not open to disposition by the states (*jus cogens*). These are rules of law which are firmly rooted in the legal conviction of the community of states, which are indispensable to the existence of public international law, and the compliance with which all members of the community of states may require.[31]

The nature of the international community underlying the concept of *jus cogens*, and in turn its higher interests, is gleaned from the construct *the international community of States as a whole*, the entity which, according to Article 53 of the Vienna Convention, accepts and recognizes peremptory norms. The layered construct depicts both procedural and substantive elements expressing the interests and values of an organized society comprising States representing the collective social need of mankind. The complementarity of these aspects suggests that the social need of mankind is realized through the practice of States acting collectively as organs of the international community to establish peremptory norms of general international law.

Contractarianism indicates that shared values and interests necessary to social coexistence are expressed through principles regarded to be moral in character and as such evoke elements of natural law.[32] From physical security to freedom and equality, Enlightenment contract theory depicts a social contract that gives rise to civil society through the protection of 'natural rights', which reflect the particular values and interests essential to the existence of society in the context of particular historical exigencies.[33] In the context of *jus cogens*, the higher interests of the community are 'extra-State', concerning the whole of mankind, and designate the individual human being as their ultimate beneficiary. These interests are represented by the general legal principle of human dignity which, like the natural law principles identified variously by Enlightenment contractarians, reflects shared values and interests, in this instance,

[31] *East German Expropriation Case, Mr von der M*, BVerfG [Constitutional Court] (Germany), 2 BvR 955/00, ILDC 66, paras. 97–8, 116 (2004) (finding *jus cogens* to be incorporated into the Basic Law of Germany, but that the protection of property of a State's citizens is not part of *jus cogens*).

[32] *See* discussion *infra*, Chapter 7.A-B (Ancient Law, The Development of International Law).

[33] *See* discussion *infra*, Chapter 13.B (Social Contract through Historical Exigencies).

of the international community as a whole. Human dignity denotes the intrinsic worth of the individual as a human being, deserving of respect from other human beings.[34] That the principle represents a general principle of law is reflected in space – its expansive global expression across various domains of fundamental legal and social order[35] – and reinforced by time – the consistency with which it has been articulated over the course of more than two millennia.[36] Its expression through the interests of the international community as *jus cogens* places the doctrine, and international law more generally, into this tradition of legal and political history. While the social contract conceives of civil society as the product of shared social need, its moral authority derives from the expression of values and interests shared by the community, necessary to the maintenance of society, which denotes duties owed to other individuals as a matter of common humanity. Similarly, the morality underlying *jus cogens* expresses the worth of the human person, and it is because norms expressing this value are necessary to social coexistence – as evidenced by the interests of the international community – that a moral quality distinguishes *jus cogens* from *jus dispositivum*.

Notwithstanding the moral quality of the principles enshrined by the social contract, the normative expression of these values and interests is a product of history and experience that inform the social need of a community. The broad variation of principles essential to social coexistence across the spectrum of Enlightenment contract theory is a manifestation of this historical contextualism, which shapes social need and thus the values necessary to the maintenance of society.[37] For contractarians, this social need is a response to the state of nature, the pre-political condition of man, the escape from which is the basis of the social contract.[38] A similar historical foundation is demonstrable in the establishment of the category of *jus cogens* in international law and the particular general principle from which peremptory norms derive. Prior to the Second World War, international law was concerned primarily with the rules and legal structures facilitating

[34] *See* Christopher McCrudden, *Human Dignity and Judicial Interpretation of Human Rights*, 19(4) European Journal of International Law 655, 679 (2008) (referring to these elements of human dignity as the 'basic minimum content', or 'minimum core', of the principle of human dignity).

[35] *See* discussion *supra*, Chapter 4 (Human Dignity as a General Principle of Law).

[36] *See* discussion *supra*, Chapter 3.C (The Philosophy of Human Dignity).

[37] *See* discussion *infra*, Chapter 13.B (Social Contract through Historical Exigencies).

[38] *Ibid.*

inter-State relations.[39] It has been suggested that it is precisely this State-oriented 'science' of international law that permitted the outbreak of the world wars.[40] Consequently, the aftermath of the Second World War saw a reaction against the absolute Statism that had previously defined the international system. Natural law elements of morality and humanity were incorporated into positive international law in the form of *jus cogens*. This constituted a break from international law of the previous period indicative of a kind of international social contract, as noted by one member of the ILC during the drafting of the Vienna Convention:

> While not opposed to the idea that the sovereignty of States was the basis of the international community ... sovereignty could [not] be absolute now that the international community had become organized ... There was not necessarily a surrender of national sovereignty, but membership of a community required the respect of certain rules. If that were not so, society would remain in the condition of savagery described by the phrase *homo homini lupus*, which had lasted until the First World War and had prevailed almost unchallenged in the inter-war period. By becoming members of the international society, States recognized the existence of a minimum international order, which was none other than *jus cogens*. The abstract notions of absolute freedom and absolute sovereignty were not compatible with the existence of international society.[41]

The establishment of *jus cogens* in international law can be viewed in this way as a reaction to the social need to qualify State sovereignty through membership in an emergent international community. The response to this 'state of nature' was a legal category drawing its authority from the general principle of human dignity, which was seen to represent the higher interests of the international community as a whole, and justify the emergence of norms that transcend the interests of the individual State, by virtue of the importance of this value to the existence of international society. *Jus cogens* may therefore be conceived as a product of social and historical necessity, which was observed by the German delegation to the UN Conference on the Law of Treaties in 1969:

> The emergence of the notion of *Jus cogens* in international law was a direct consequence of social and historical evolution, which had had a far-reaching influence on the development of international law.[42]

[39] Wolfgang Friedman, Legal Theory 551 (London: Stevens & Stevens 1967).
[40] Walter Schiffer, The Legal Community of Mankind 257 (New York: Columbia University Press 1954).
[41] [1966] I(1) YbILC 39, para. 40 (828th Meeting, statement by Mr Bartoš).
[42] United Nations Conference on the Law of Treaties, Vienna, 9 April–22 May 1969, A/CONF.39/11/Add.1 (1970), 2nd Session, 95, paras. 25–6 (statement by Federal Republic of Germany).

In historical context, it seems appropriate to conceive of *jus cogens* as a response to the absense of international society structures intended to prevent the recurrence of international conduct abhorrent to the conscience of mankind by enshrining the higher interests of the international community as *jus cogens*. Of course, when looking to the sources of *jus cogens* and particular norms belonging to the category, it becomes clear that the formal concept of *jus cogens* was preceded by – and in some sense merely codified – earlier expressions of international socialization.

In a related way, contractarianism establishes a particular relation of the individual to civil society by which the authority of civil society derives from its protection of interests and values necessary to the well-being of the individual within a community.[43] The protection of these principles is conceived to be necessary to social coexistence because they are of such importance to the human being that coexistence with other individuals in a community requires their minimum respect.[44] Consequently, these principles shape the social contract, and their protection is the source of authority of civil society and corresponding governance structures. A commensurate link may be deduced from *jus cogens*, which reflects the higher interests of the international community as 'extra-State' in kind. The relation denoted by this conceptualization is one that places the individual atop a normative hierarchy in international law, above the State, as the subject of non-derogable protections of *jus cogens* distinct from the *jus dispositivum* concluded between States. In this sense, in the aftermath of the two world wars, the emergence of *jus cogens* refocused the ultimate end of political order, through the socialization of the international community, to uphold values and interests common to mankind.

With the emergence of *jus cogens* in international law, it becomes possible to cognize a social contract of the international community. This social contract reveals the individual human being, as the unit of mankind, to be the subject of the interests of the international community implicated by the relations of States. These interests are represented by the general legal principle of human dignity, which expresses the social need of the international community in a way that refocuses the highest authority of the international system from the unbridled sovereignty of the State to the shared values and interests of humanity.

[43] *See* discussion *supra*, Chapter 3.A.ii ('of States') (discussing this proposition in the context of the State).

[44] *See* discussion *supra*, text accompanying *nn*. 1–28.

Through the international community, the State acts as its organ pursuant to these higher interests, with its own interests subordinated by the social need of mankind. *Jus cogens* thereby establishes a relation of the individual to the State through the international community by which the intrinsic worth of the human being is authoritatively expressed as a societal principle through peremptory norms. *Jus cogens* constitutes peremptory norms accepted and recognized by the international community, necessary to the maintenance of international society, from which no derogation is permitted. It is through this relation of States to mankind by socialization of the international community that the origin and authority of a social contract can be seen in international law.

PART III

Material and formal sources of *jus cogens*

Questions relating to the material and formal sources of peremptory norms obscure the place of *jus cogens* in the tradition of international law and compromise the justiciability of peremptory norms. These issues, raised in the previous part, centre on the formal incorporation of moral considerations as positive law. This part begins with a history of the philosophical and juridical sources of the concept of *jus cogens* in Chapter 7, from the foundations of natural law to the emergence of public order norms in international law. Chapter 8 consists of a positivist assessment of the formal source of peremptory norms, one that accounts for the incorporation of normative elements into international law as *jus cogens*. Finally, the formal source of *jus cogens* is analogized to the legislative mechanism of the social contract in Chapter 9 as a reconciliation of the naturalist and positivist dimensions of *jus cogens*.

7

Historical antecedents

The previous chapter drew attention to the way elements characteristic of the natural law tradition inform the authority of *jus cogens* in international law. To elucidate this connection between *jus naturale* and *jus cogens*, it is instructive to begin with an assessment of natural law and its historic linkage to international law through the law of nations (*jus gentium*). The tradition of natural law has played a constant role throughout the evolution of international law. Lauterpacht submits that this influence of natural law reflects the moral authority required to safeguard fundamental rights in contemporary international law:

> The rights of man cannot, in the long run, be effectively secured except by the twin operation of the latent forces of the law of nature and the compelling force of the law of nations – both conceived as a power superior to the supreme power of the State.[1]

Fitzmaurice recognizes Lauterpacht's premise that, in the absence of any overriding legal authority, it is necessary for stable international relations that reason and morality assert themselves as a legal source through natural law:

> The fact is that while within the State it is not essential to give the idea of a higher law – of natural law – a function superior to that of providing the inarticulate ethical premise underlying judicial decisions ... in international society the position is radically different. There – in a society deprived of normal legislative and judicial organs – the function of natural law, whatever may be its form, must approximate more closely to that of a direct source of law. In the absense of the overriding authority of the judicial and legislative organs of the State there must assert itself – unless anarchy or stagnation are to ensue – the persuasive but potent authority of reason and principle derived from the fact of the necessary coexistence of a plurality of States. This explains the pertinacity, in the international sphere, of the idea of natural law as a legal source.[2]

[1] Hersch Lauterpacht, International Law and Human Rights 93 (London: Praeger 1950).

[2] Gerald Fitzmaurice, *Some Problems Regarding the Formal Sources of International Law, in* Symbolae Verzijl 153 (The Hague: Martinus Nijhoff, Jan Hendrik Willem Verzijl &

More generally, Brierly finds that such an admission of elements of 'reason', analogous to natural law, as a source of international law need not pose a threat to the rule of law, as no legal order consists purely of positive rules:

> [N]o system of law consists only of formulated rules, for these can never be sufficiently detailed or sufficiently foreseeing to provide for every situation that may call for a legal decision; those who administer law must meet new situations not precisely covered by a formulated rule by resorting to the principle which medieval writers would have called natural law, and which we generally call reason.[3]

With respect to *jus cogens*, it was widely viewed during codification of the doctrine that it had its conceptual origins in considerations of morality and the tradition of natural law.[4] It bears observing that Lauterpacht, Fitzmaurice, and Brierly were the first of the four *special rapporteurs* of the ILC responsible for drafting the law of treaties, where *jus cogens* was formally codified. As such, they are largely responsible for the formal inclusion of *jus cogens* in international law and the way in which the concept was framed in the Vienna Convention. Their affirmations of the role of natural law as a source of international law are particularly salient when considering the incorporation of normativity into positive law.

Waldock, the final *special rapporteur* on the law of treaties, considered in his capacity as Expert Consultant to the Conference on the Law of Treaties at Vienna 'that the International Law Commission had based its approach to the question of *jus cogens* on positive law much more than on natural law'.[5] This is certainly so, and it remains necessary to identify precisely how, and to what extent, normative considerations related to natural law enter into international law as a material source of *jus cogens*.[6] As Phillip Allott observes, 'in international law, there is really only one problem, what to do about natural law'.[7] To address this issue,

F. M. van Asbeck eds., 1958) (quoting Hersch Lauterpacht, *The Grotian Tradition in International Law*, 23 British Yearbook of International Law 1, 22–3 (1946)).

3 James Brierly, The Law of Nations 66 (Oxford: Clarendon Press, 6th edn. 1963).

4 *See* discussion *supra*, Chapter 5.B.i (*Travaux Préparatoires*).

5 United Nations Conference on the Law of Treaties, Vienna, 26 March–24 May 1968, A/CONF.39/11 (1969), First Session [hereinafter, UNCLOT, First Session (1968)] 327, para. 77 (statement by Expert Consultant Waldock).

6 *See* discussion *supra*, Chapter 5 (The Authority of *Jus Cogens*) (discussing normativity and *jus cogens*).

7 Philip Allott, *Language, Method, and the Nature of International Law*, 45 The British Yearbook of International Law 78, 100 (1971).

this chapter elucidates the material source of *jus cogens* by contemplating the origin of natural law in classical Greek philosophy and Roman law, the way in which this tradition shaped the development of international law, the waning of natural law during the rise of legal positivism, and the reemergence of normativity in international law through *jus cogens*.

A Ancient law

In contrast to positive law, which is regarded as historical, natural law is conceived to be constant. Three particular tenets define natural law and find expression throughout its theoretical development. The first is that human beings, as individuals capable of free will and judgment, possess reason, and that the law of nature is accessible through this 'right reason' common to mankind. The principles contained in the law of nature guide human interaction and govern the social existence of human beings. This social dimension is the second component of natural law theory, by which natural law informs a morality common to mankind. As natural law constitutes a moral order determined by right reason common to humanity, it is by consequence universal; this is the third element common to natural law theory. Thus natural law consists of the principles of common morality based in right reason which constitute a universal order that mediates the social existence of human beings. These ideas have remained at the core of natural law theory since its inception in Greek thought, resulting in a particular influence on the individual and his relation with society. The State initially came to be defined in terms of this objective order derived from nature, and in turn, the establishment of society as well as the individual's place in it could be derived from the rational nature of men. Social contract theory reflects these aspects of natural law, and in some respects the social contract may be understood to provide an explanation of natural law in relation to society and its governance.[8]

The origin of *jus naturale* can be traced to Greek philosophers who distinguished between nature and that which is created by man, and thus between natural law (*physei dikaion*) and dispositive law (*nomo dikaion*).[9] Forming the basis of the philosophy of the Sophists, early

[8] *See* discussion *supra*, Chapter 6 (Expression of an International Social Contract).

[9] Alfred Verdross and Herbert Koeck, *Natural Law: The Tradition of Universal Reason and Authority*, *in* The Structure and Process of International Law: Essays in Legal Philosophy, Doctrine and Theory 17–18 (The Hague: Martinus Nijhoff, Ronald St John Macdonald & Douglas Johnston eds., 1983).

natural law entailed the principles that ought to govern the behaviour of man derived from the nature of man as a rational, social being. The Stoics placed great emphasis on the role of reason as the foundation of natural law, which arises from the universal realities of man's common origin and his possession of, and thus direction by, reason. Aristotelian natural law, by contrast, is conceived to derive from the nature of man, one defined not as a 'static fact' but rather as a tendency of man to pursue self-preservation and the fulfilment of basic needs. Although substantively dissimilar to the natural law of the Stoics, Aristotle similarly distinguished natural law – which is common, universal, and valid everywhere – from law created by man.[10] This general division of law into two distinct parts, commonplace among early natural law theorists, is a central feature of natural law. Through the advent of Roman jurisprudence just prior to the first millennium, natural law was transformed from a philosophical ideal into a legal system with expansive application. A formative stage of this process was the adoption of elements of Greek philosophy into Roman law and thought by Cicero. Cicero shared Aristotle's belief in the universality of natural law, similarly observing that this universality is evidence of its validity as natural law. Moreover, these aspects of natural law were taken to establish an imperative law that could not be compromised or altered by the laws of man.[11] Importantly, Cicero links natural law with the law common to all mankind (*jus gentium*) and contends that *jus gentium* should be incorporated into the law of every State (*jus civile*). From this flows the notion of a worldwide society of man governed by a common law derived from nature, which Cicero termed *civitas humana*.[12]

The convergence of natural law with the concept of *jus gentium* is the reflection of a process born out of practical necessity during the expansion of the Roman Empire. The *jus civile* of Rome, according to classical history, applied exclusively to citizens of Rome, leaving foreigners bereft of both rights and duties. However as Rome expanded, acquiring new jurisdiction over foreign peoples, it became increasingly necessary to construct a system of law through which to govern an empire.[13] Consequently, a broad system of law applicable across a plurality of peoples

[10] Herbert Jolowicz, Historical Introduction to the Study of Roman Law 103 (Cambridge University Press 1939).
[11] *Ibid.*
[12] Verdross and Koeck, *Natural Law: The Tradition of Universal Reason and Authority*, 19.
[13] Jolowicz, Historical Introduction to the Study of Roman Law 100–3.

emerged, and this system came to be understood as *jus gentium*, the common law of mankind. Although this *jus gentium* was Roman in practical origin, much of the formality of Roman law was distilled away, leaving a more general law influenced by Greek natural law.[14] Natural law thus allowed Roman and foreign peoples to coexist under a common law representative of 'general good sense'.[15] This *jus gentium*, which existed and functioned alongside *jus civile*, necessarily embodied key elements of natural law doctrine enumerated above. Thus, through historical necessity, the philosophy of natural law was embodied in the practical development of *jus gentium*, and the two have come to synonymously represent the idea of a general law, based upon reason, common to mankind.

The Roman application of natural law principles to construct a system of general law governing different peoples marks the first true example of a system of 'supranational' law. The subsequent influence of natural law upon the development of international law in the Middle Ages entailed reference to, and indeed the incorporation of, Roman law in a similar sense, which had already conceived a functioning system of *jus gentium*. Thus throughout the Middle Ages, Roman law was held to be 'written reason' (*ratio scripta*).[16] Consequently, reference to Roman law provided access to the contents of natural law and was relied upon heavily throughout the development of a system of international law where the interaction of princes mirrored that of private individuals.[17]

Natural law continued to have a distinct influence throughout the evolution of early international relations, illustrating a common reliance upon natural law thinking, the consistent structural distinction between natural and positive law, and constant reference to elements of reason, morality, and universality. During the Middle Ages, natural law endured through ecclesiastical endorsement. As a 'higher law', natural law was conceived as divine law and held to be the nearest to the law of God realizable by man.[18] It is testament to its perceived power and universality that natural law was adopted in medieval Church doctrine, where it shaped the 'just war' (*bellum justum*) tradition expounded by religious scholars. While Saints Ambrose and Augustine, Christian theologians and philosophers, are credited with the earliest articulations of just war doctrine in the fourth and fifth centuries,[19] it was the thirteenth-century

[14] *Ibid.* [15] Wolfgang Friedman, LEGAL THEORY 101–2 (London: Stevens & Stevens 1967).
[16] Brierly, THE LAW OF NATIONS 19–20. [17] *Ibid.* [18] Friedman, LEGAL THEORY 107.
[19] Paul Christopher, THE ETHICS OF WAR & PEACE 7 (Upper Saddle River, NJ: Pearson/Prentice Hall 2004).

scholarship of Thomas Aquinas that reformulated natural law as a system to guide the conduct of States. Aquinas is recognized as the principal natural law thinker of the period, and his writings on natural law and just war influenced international legal scholars for centuries. The natural law doctrine expounded by Aquinas constitutes basic moral norms derived from reason: he identifies the corpus as natural as it entails rules that can be known by individuals through human reason, and as law given that it constitutes behavioural prescriptions.[20] The distinction between natural and positive law that featured prominently in early natural law scholarship finds expression again: the law of nations, as a human construct, is regarded as positive law (even if influenced by natural law).[21] The influence of Aquinas features prominantly in the sixteenth-century writings of Spanish clergymen Francisco Suárez and Francisco de Vitoria; the former is credited with introducing for the first time 'the modern concept of a society or community of sovereign states, tied together by a body of laws applying to their mutual relations'.[22]

B The development of international law

It has been observed that '[o]ne of the factors which in the seventeenth and eighteenth centuries gave new vitality to the law of nature was the need for a law of nations'.[23] A modern school of natural law took shape after the Reformation that transformed the international system in such a way as to relocate moral authority from the feudal vestiges of Church and Empire to the common humanity of mankind. It is during this period that the doctrine of natural law came to conceive of the individual, rather than their rulers (princes) or groupings (States), as the bearer of fundamental rights and duties. Lauterpacht observes in this respect that '[w]e can trace the same mutuality of influence in the relations of

[20] Joseph Boyle, *Natural Law and International Ethics*, *in* Traditions of International Ethics 113 (Princeton University Press, Terry Nardin & David Mapel eds., 1992).

[21] Charles Covell, The Law of Nations in Political Thought 6 (New York: Palgrave Macmillan 2009).

[22] *See* John Doyle, Collected Studies on Francisco Suárez, S. J. (1548–1617) 315 (Leuven University Press 2010) (quoting Gerhard von Glahn, Law Among the Nations: An Introduction to Public International Law 38–9 (London: Macmillan 2nd edn, 1970)).

[23] Hersch Lauterpacht, An International Bill of the Rights of Man 41 (New York: Columbia University Press 1945).

international law and the law of nature'.[24] The modern tradition of natural law is thought to originate with Hugo Grotius, the Dutch lawyer and philosopher who published his seminal work *The Law of War and Peace* during the Thirty Years War in 1625.[25] Grotius relies heavily on scripture and classical texts to forcefully advocate the application of predominantly Christian principles of law and justice to the conduct of warfare and preservation of peace. The universal moral order construed for this purpose is framed by natural law. It is presupposed that man is a social animal and that the maintenance of social order is the fundamental end of law,[26] at the heart of which lies the law of nature. Grotius identifies the authority of natural law to follow from right reason,[27] and it is through this reason common to all mankind that morality is conceived.[28] As this rational and social nature of man is universal, the natural law deriving therefrom is similarly universal and proved by its universality.[29] Like the philosophers of natural law who preceded him, Grotius maintains a distinction between the law of nature (*jus naturale*) and volitional law (*jus voluntarium*).[30] The critical distinction between these two forms is that the former derives from universal principles of nature deduced through right reason, while the latter originates from the will of man and constitutes positive law subject to change.[31] The law of nations, which derives from the mutual consent of many or all nations for the benefit 'of the great society of states',[32] is made possible by the law of nature.[33]

It was the aim of German philosopher and statesman Samuel Pufendorf to advance the modern school of natural law set into motion by Grotius. Consequently, his main works on the subject – *On the Law of*

[24] *Ibid.*

[25] Hugo Grotius, De Jure Belli Ac Pacis Libri Tres II (Oxford: Clarendon Press, Francis Kelsey trans., James B. Scott ed., 1925 [1646]).

[26] *Ibid.*, Prologomena.6–8.

[27] *Ibid.*, I.I.X.1 ('The law of nature is a dictate of right reason, which points out that an act, according as it is or is not in conformity with rational nature, has in it a quality of moral baseness or moral necessity; and that, in consequence, such an act is either forbidden or enjoined by the author of nature, God').

[28] *Ibid.*, I.II.I.2. [29] *Ibid.*, I.I.XII.1.

[30] *Ibid.*, Prologomena.30, I.I.IX.2 (referencing Aquinas on this point).

[31] *Ibid.*, Prologomena.40, I.I.XIII–I.I.XIV (Volitional law is categorized as either human or divine, with human law constituting both municipal law as well as the law of nations).

[32] *Ibid.*, Prologomena.17, I.I.XIV.

[33] Grotius identifies structural principles of international law – *pacta sunt servanda, rebus sic stantibus*, and the prohibition of leonine (unequal) treaties – as flowing from the law of nature, principles that remain at the core of the contemporary international legal order: *See ibid.*, Prologomena.15, II.XI.2, II.XII.VIII.

Nature and Nations (1672),[34] and *On the Duty of Man and Citizen According to Natural Law* (1673)[35] – are carried out largely in relation to the writings of Grotius, as well as Hobbes, and break from the idea of nature as a teleological, purposeful realm which had characterized the natural law theories of Aristotle and Aquinas.[36] Natural law, according to Pufendorf, constitutes universal social duties arising from the common character and condition of mankind.[37] The precepts of natural law are known by right reason common to all mankind,[38] which renders men capable of social relations with other men; as such they are essential to sociability and comprise the basis of society.[39] It is in this sense that natural law constitutes the 'laws of sociability' from which morality derives when realized through reason and carried out by the free will of the individual.[40] Its basis in human reason is taken to be evidence that God is the author of natural law and, in turn, the source of obligation under natural law.[41] Throughout his works, Pufendorf employs the classical distinction between natural (*naturalem*) and positive (*positivam*) law,[42] and further maintains that natural law (*lex naturalis*) 'should be measured and defined in terms of its opposition to positive laws' (*jus positivum*).[43] Pufendorf indicates that hierarchy defines the relationship between the two kinds of law: it is a presupposition of civil law, which constitutes the positive law of the State, that it ought not establish

34 Samuel Pufendorf, De Jure Naturae et Gentium Libri Octo (Oxford: Clarendon Press, C.H. Oldfather & W.A. Oldfather trans., James B. Scott ed., 1934 [1688]) [hereinafter, Pufendorf, De Jure Naturae].

35 Samuel Pufendorf, De Officio Hominis et Civis Juxta Legem Naturalem (Cambridge University Press, Michael Silberthorne trans., James Tully ed., 2006 [1682]) [hereinafter, Pufendorf, De Officio].

36 Pufendorf, De Officio xvii (James Tully, Introduction).

37 Pufendorf, De Jure Naturae Preface, 7; I.3.1, I.3.13.

38 *Ibid.*, II.iii.24; Pufendorf, De Officio Preface, 7.

39 Pufendorf, De Jure Naturae II.iii.13, 15; Pufendorf, De Officio Preface, 12.

40 Pufendorf, De Jure Naturae I.ii.5; Pufendorf, De Officio I.3.8.

41 Pufendorf, De Jure Naturae I.ii.6, II.iii.20; Pufendorf, De Officio I.3.11.

42 Pufendorf, De Jure Naturae I.vi.18.

43 *Ibid.*, I.ii.6, I.vi.18; Pufendorf, De Officio I.2.15 ('With respect to its author, law is divided into divine and human; the one was made by God, the other by man. But if it is viewed in the light of whether it has, or has not, a necessary and universal congruence with men, it is divided into natural and positive. Natural law is law which is so congruent with the rational and social nature of man that there cannot be a good and peaceful society for the human race without it. Hence too it can be traced out and known by the light of man's native reason and by reflection on human nature in general. Positive law is law which does not derive from the common condition of human nature, but proceeds solely from the will of the legislator').

anything contrary to natural law given that the two have at their foundation a common end.[44] With respect to international law, Pufendorf holds that natural law is binding upon all men and all nations.[45] Consequently, the natural law that applies to men and that which applies to States differs 'only in their external denomination'; they are substantively the same and the two are referred to commonly as the law of nations (which accounts for the title of Pufendorf's 1672 work).[46] Concurrent with the early establishment of the modern State system, then, is the vision of a natural law of universal reason governing the relations of States.

The Enlightenment period, particularly the middle decades of the eighteenth century, was the height of the secular natural law tradition. As the international system developed through increasing interaction and interdependence, made possible and necessary by developments in commerce, technology, and warfare, the application of natural law to the relations of States became evermore evolved and institutionalized. It is during this period that the work of Emerich de Vattel, a Swiss diplomat and legal scholar, contributed to the formation of an actual system of jurisprudence by which natural law was transcribed into a law of nations of general application and judicial validity.[47] In *The Law of Nation's, or Principles of the Law of Nature, Applied to the Conduct and Affairs of Nations and Sovereigns* (1758),[48] Vattel presupposes that the law of nature, constituting fundamental obligations which man necessarily observes in his relations with other men, is applicable to relations between States.[49] In the convention of natural law theorists preceding him, Vattel understands natural law as universal law discoverable through reason which derives from 'the essence and nature of man and things in general';[50] it is directly connected in practice to moral

44 *Ibid.*, VIII.i.2. 45 *Ibid.*, Preface, iii. 46 *Ibid.*, II.iii.23.

47 Covell, THE LAW OF NATIONS IN POLITICAL THOUGHT 11.

48 Emer de Vattel, THE LAW OF NATIONS OR PRINCIPLES OF THE LAW OF NATURE, APPLIED TO THE CONDUCT AND AFFAIRS OF NATIONS AND SOVEREIGNS (Indianapolis, IN: Liberty Fund, Béla Kapossy & Richard Whatmore eds., 2008 [1797]) [hereinafter, Vattel, LE DROIT DES GENS].

49 Implicit in this application is a differentiation between the systems of natural law applied respectively to the individual and to the State, one that would develop into the dualist distinction between separate legal orders concerning individuals and States in international law.

50 Emer de Vattel, ESSAY ON THE FOUNDATION OF NATURAL LAW AND ON THE FIRST PRINCIPLE OF THE OBLIGATION MEN FIND THEMSELVES UNDER TO OBSERVE §§ VI, IX–X (Indianapolis, IN: Liberty Fund, T. J. Hochstrasser trans., Béla Kapossy & Richard Whatmore eds., 2008 [1797]).

science.[51] Applying the doctrine of natural law to international law required Vattel to employ the familiar Roman law distinction between natural and positive law, under the guise of the necessary law of nations (*droit des gens nécessaire*) and the voluntary law of nations (*droit des gens volontaire*).[52] In articulating the relationship between the necessary and voluntary law of nations, Vattel employs a construction akin to the contrast between *jus cogens* and *jus dispositivum* implicit in the Vienna Convention:

> Whence, as this law is immutable, and the obligations that arise from it necessary and indisposable, nations can neither make any changes in it by their conventions, dispense with it in their own conduct, nor reciprocally release each other from the observance of it.[53]

Consequently (and remarkably similar to Article 53 of the Vienna Convention codified centuries later), 'every treaty, every custom, which contravenes the injunctions or prohibitions of the necessary law of nations, is unlawful'.[54] Here Vattel provides a coherent articulation of the practical effect of the non-derogability of necessary law in relation to voluntary law in the very way in which peremptory norms are conceived in contemporary international law. Moreover, Vattel contemplates a form of obligations *erga omnes* arising from necessary law in the context of the requirements of a 'universal society of the human race',[55] one corresponding to what contemporary international law has come to recognize as a general legal interest in the performance of obligations arising from peremptory norms, and the positive duty of third-States to respond to serious breaches of these obligations.[56]

[51] *Ibid.*, §§ I–IV.

[52] Vattel, Le Droit des Gens *Preliminaries* §§ 7–8, 27–28 (for original French, *see* Emer de Vattel, I Le droit des gens, ou, principes de la loi naturelle appliqués à la conduite et aux affaires des nations et des souverains, *Preliminaries* xxi (Oxford: Clarendon Press, Charles G. Fenwick trans., James B. Scott, ed., 1916 [1797])) (The 'necessary law of nations' constitutes the application of natural law to States and is identified as necessary 'because nations are absolutely bound to observe it'. By contrast, the 'voluntary law of nations', or the 'positive law of nations', constitutes all international law – voluntary, conventional, and customary – that expresses the will of the State).

[53] *Ibid.*, § 9. [54] *Ibid.*

[55] *Ibid.*, §§ 11, 22 (internal citation omitted) ('The laws of natural society are of such importance to the safety of all states, that . . . [a]ll nations have therefore a right to resort to forcible means for the purpose of repressing any one particular nation who openly violates the laws of society which nature has established between them, or who directly attacks the welfare and safety of that society').

[56] *See* discussion *infra*, Chapter 14.A (Prevention and Consequences for Third-States).

In effect, Vattel's treatise provides an early sketch of the modern *jus cogens* regime arrived at through the application of natural law to the system of States. However, nearly two centuries would pass before the framework of *necessary* and *voluntary* law would take the form of Article 53 of the Vienna Convention. To be sure, during the nineteenth century, principal political theorists and philosophers including Bentham, Hegel, and Kant each, to varying degrees, conceived of a law of nations in part derived from principles of natural law.[57] But more importantly, and not without some irony, the recognition of a legal order of States distinct from that of individuals, commonly attributed to Vattel, culminated in a system in which the State was personified as a sovereign individual in what would become a predominantly voluntary and formal international law. In the course of the nineteenth and early twentieth centuries, the natural law that had shaped the history of international law was increasingly eroded and supplanted by a system of positive law whose sources were increasingly circumscribed and defined exclusively by the practice and consent of States.

C The science of legal positivism

Legal positivism is the philosophy of jurisprudence that adopts an empirical approach to the study of law.[58] Positivism accesses law through the scientific method in an attempt to discern and describe actual law apart from *a priori* principles, ethics, and moral considerations. Such a distinction of what the law *is* from what the law *ought to be* is the central philosophical tenet of legal positivism,[59] thereby divorcing legal science from the philosophy of law and separating legality from morality. John Austin writes, '[*t*]*he science of jurisprudence* (or, simply and briefly, *jurisprudence*) is concerned with positive laws, or with laws strictly so called, as considered without regard to their goodness or badness'.[60] Positivism, as an approach concerned with gaining knowledge of the material reality of law rather than evaluating the law on a normative

[57] Covell, THE LAW OF NATIONS IN POLITICAL THOUGHT 11.

[58] John Austin, LECTURES ON JURISPRUDENCE OR THE PHILOSOPHY OF POSITIVE LAW (London: John Murray Albemarle Street, Robert Campbell ed., 3rd edn. 1869); Hans Kelsen, GENERAL THEORY OF LAW AND STATE (Cambridge, MA: Harvard University Press 1949); H. L. A. Hart, THE CONCEPT OF LAW (Oxford: Clarendon Press 1961). *See* Hans Morgenthau, *Positivism, Functionalism, and International Law*, 34 AMERICAN JOURNAL OF INTERNATIONAL LAW 260 (1940).

[59] Friedman, LEGAL THEORY 257.

[60] Austin, LECTURES ON JURISPRUDENCE V, 176–7.

basis, professes to constitute a divergent approach to the study of law from that of the natural law tradition. Consequently, the term positivism has become synonymous with the existence or description of law as opposed to abstract, ideal, or theoretical law. The fundamental systemic requirement implicated by positivism is that law is created by a formal source that accounts for the historicity of positive law, from which it derives its validity.[61] The source of law refers to the active process or means by which law is created, as opposed to morality or reason as material sources of law, or where the law is physically found. This is to say that the positive character of law – its legitimacy as valid law – is a result of its creation by a political superior vested with the authority to create law: a sovereign. As the product of a formal source, the legitimacy of law originates externally rather than from a metaphysical source.[62] In this sense, positivism takes its name from this creative act of 'positing' the law, emphasizing its human origin.[63] This notion of the source of law is intended to achieve certainty over the content of the law by providing a methodology through which to distinguish the law in force (*lex lata*) from the law that ought to be (*lex ferenda*).

When the doctrine of legal positivism rose to prominence in the nineteenth century, international law was rejected by positivists from the realm of authentic law.[64] Given the influence of the naturalist tradition throughout the development of international law, this is perhaps unsurprising. In the absence of a superior law-maker or sovereign as the source of valid law, the law governing the international sphere could not be endowed with the requisite historicity from which the legitimacy of positive law derives. This led early positivists, most notably Austin, to conclude that international law is more rightly characterized as a field of

[61] *Ibid.*, Introduction, I, 81, 88 ('Laws proper, or properly so-called, are commands. Laws which are not commands, are laws improper or improperly so called . . . The matter of jurisprudence is positive law; law, simply and strictly so called: or law set by political superiors to political inferiors').

[62] Consequently, a corollary is that, unlike legal obligation, which is conceived as an 'external' pressure, moral obligation derives its force 'internally'; it is principally this divergent source of obligation that differentiates natural from positive law. *See* Sergio Cotta, *Positive Law and Natural Law*, 37(2) The Review of Metaphysics 265, 272 (1983).

[63] Joseph Raz, The Authority of Law 38 (Oxford: Clarendon Press 1983).

[64] *See* Hart, The Concept of Law 231 (Jeremy Bentham is the notable exception to this trend; he coined the term *international law* at the end of the eighteenth century and perceived international law to be analogous to municipal law).

'positive morality' than law proper.[65] However, the requirement that law reflect a relation between political superiors and inferiors was gradually abandoned by positivists. According to Hans Kelsen, law is not 'a rule', but rather, 'a set of rules having the kind of unity we understand by a system', and legal order is conceived to derive from a basic norm (*grundnorm*).[66] And for H. L. A. Hart, law is understood as social custom, a system constituting both 'primary rules' of conduct and 'secondary rules' of recognition that cannot be reduced to 'orders backed by threats'.[67] These later depictions of positive law expressly depart from Austin's emphasis on the command of a superior.

Consequently, the absence of a single international sovereign no longer barred the law of nations from legal positivism, which accepted international law through the doctrine of consent.[68] Positive international law came to be understood as the product of the sovereignty of the State, this providing the necessary historicity of a formal source of law, thereby constituting a kind of 'auto-limitation' among States.[69] This voluntarism conceived of a system based upon the power and will of the State that replaced one adapted from natural law, discounted by Austin and other early positivists, which had heretofore governed international behaviour through moralistic norms.[70]

D *Jus cogens* as public order in international law

By the middle of the twentieth century, the philosophies of natural law and positivism converged in international law through the emergence of *jus cogens* as norms of international public order. In principle, public order constitutes an expression of the primacy of values and interests

[65] Austin, Lectures on Jurisprudence V, 175–7 ('By distinctive names *law* and *morality*, I denote the difference between the human sources from which the two classes respectively emanate . . . Now, by the name "*positive* morality," I mean the human laws which I mark with that expression, as considered without regard to their goodness or badness').

[66] Kelsen, General Theory of Law and State 3, 115. [67] Hart, The Concept of Law.

[68] Walter Schiffer, The Legal Community of Mankind 79 (New York: Columbia University Press 1954).

[69] *See, e.g.*, Stephen Hall, *The Persistent Spectre: Natural Law, International Order and the Limits of Legal Positivism*, 12(2) European Journal of International Law 269, 282 (2001).

[70] Oscar Schachter, *The Nature and Process of Legal Development in International Society*, *in* The Structure and Process of International Law 762–3 (St John Macdonald & Johnston eds.); Friedman, Legal Theory 256; Leo Gross, *The Peace of Westphalia, 1648–1948*, 41(1) American Journal of International Law 20, 29 (1948).

common to the whole of a community from which its individual members may not deviate because of their importance to society.[71] While public order refers more directly to the role norms serve in society than their naturalist or positivist origins,[72] an element of normativity is explicit. This is indicated most obviously by the categorical distinction between *jus cogens* and *jus dispositivum*, one mirroring the naturalist distinction between universal, moral rules governing international standards of conduct (*jus naturale*) and positive law created by legal subjects (*jus positivum*).[73] This distinction arises from the subject matter of *jus cogens*, which is understood to express values and interests common to the international community as a whole.[74] Implicit in the concept of *jus cogens* are normative elements of morality,[75] and universalism,[76] both characteristic of the tradition of natural law. Moreover, this normativity has particular legal consequences for States indicative of the public order character of *jus cogens*: peremptory norms bind all States, irrespective of dissent or objection, and resist modification by the will of individual subjects.[77] These legal effects echo a natural law tradition that has had a virtually constant influence upon the development of international law, of which *jus cogens* may be seen as the most recent iteration.

What is unique about this modern iteration of the natural law tradition is its formal incorporation into positive law. For naturalist elements to retain their currency in international law, this formal inclusion in the international legal order was necessary given contemporary adherence to a positivist approach to law. As noted by Judge Alvarez in the *Fisheries Case*, '[f]or the principles of law resulting from the juridical conscience of peoples to have any value, they must have a tangible manifestation, that is to say, they must be expressed by authorized bodies.'[78] The International Court restated as much in the *South West Africa Cases*, where it observed that it 'can take account of moral principles only in so far as

[71] *See* discussion *supra*, Chapter 1, text accompanying *nn.* 1–12.

[72] Alexander Orakhelashvili, Peremptory Norms in International Law 48 (Oxford University Press 2006).

[73] *See* discussion *supra*, Chapter 5, text accompanying *n.* 110.

[74] *See* discussion *supra*, Chapter 3, text accompanying *n.* 13.

[75] *See* discussion *supra*, Chapter 5.B (Morality and Peremptory Norms).

[76] *See* discussion *supra*, Chapter 5.C.ii (Universality and Normative Hierarchy).

[77] *See* discussion *supra*, Chapter 5.C.i (Non-Derogation); *see* discussion *infra*, Chapter 8, *nn.* 110–24 (discussing *jus cogens* and customary international law).

[78] *Fisheries Case (United Kingdom v. Norway)*, Judgment, ICJ Reports 1951, p. 116, Ind. Op. Alvarez, 148.

these are given a sufficient expression in legal form'.[79] In this sense, *jus cogens* represents a deviation from the traditional influence of naturalism in international law, hitherto an independent source of international law. During the drafting of the law of treaties, it was noted that the explicitly positive codification of *jus cogens* was an attempt by its framers to 'relieve it from its naturalist bias', thereby permitting an acceptable expression of normativity in international law.[80] However positivism is not apt to explain normativity in law, and indeed, such normativity was unknown to the positivist international legal order prevailing at the time of the drafting of the Vienna Convention: 'In principle, all legal rules were equal; the very concept of *jus cogens*, therefore, was a derogation from a fundamental legal principle.'[81] Introducing naturalist elements into positive international law created a doctrinal paradox.

The principal site of convergence of opposing legal doctrines is the source of peremptory norms in international law: whether they express principles and values oriented in a naturalist approach to law, or constitute the positivist product of States. The virtue of a naturalist approach is its ability to account for the normativity implicit in the public order function of *jus cogens*. However, contemporary international law conceives of its formal sources exclusively through positivism, no longer admitting natural law as an independent source.

As it stands, peremptory norms do exist in international law; the tension between naturalism and positivism has neither precluded the development of the material content of *jus cogens* nor muted its peremptory legal effects. In the previous chapter, the origin and authority of *jus cogens* was linked to the interests of the international community of States as a whole, a layered concept encapsulating both procedural and substantive elements of an entity expressing the interests and values of international society. By this construction, peremptory norms emerge through the practice of States acting collectively as organs of the international community. How States express these values and principles in such a way as to generate positive legal norms of a public order character is the key issue to be resolved. The following discussion examines how the contemporary legal order has accommodated the natural law elements of *jus cogens* through formal sources of positive international law.

79 *South West Africa Cases (Ethiopia v. South Africa / Liberia v. South Africa) (Second Phase)*, Judgment, ICJ Reports 1966, p. 6, 34, paras. 49–50.

80 Jerzy Sztucki, JUS COGENS AND THE VIENNA CONVENTION ON THE LAW OF TREATIES 75 (Vienna: Springer-Verlag 1974).

81 [1963] I YbILC 73, para. 4 (685th Meeting, statement by Mr Rosenne).

8

The formal source of peremptory norms

A Positive sources of international law

As discussed above, positivism requires law to be created by a formal source, which accounts for the historicity of positive law, from which it derives its validity.[1] In international law, it follows, law is a product of the law-making authority of the sovereign State. The challenge facing a positivist account of *jus cogens* was articulated during the drafting of the law of treaties by the ILC:

> It was generally acknowledged that *jus cogens* formed part of positive law; it was disagreement over the content of positive law which was the source of the difficulty. If the term 'positive law' was understood to mean rules laid down by States, then *jus cogens* was by definition not positive law. But if 'positive law' was understood to mean the rules in force in the practice of the international community, then *jus cogens* was indeed positive law.[2]

This observation by De Luna offers insight into the challenge of codifying *jus cogens* precisely because legal positivism requires that law originate from the State. The most authoritative statement of the formal sources of international law is found in Article 38(1) of the Statute of the International Court of Justice (1945)[3]:

> *Article 38*
>
> 1. The Court, whose function is to decide in accordance with international law such disputes as are submitted to it, shall apply:
>   a. international conventions, whether general or particular, establishing rules expressly recognized by the contesting states;

[1] *See* discussion *supra*, Chapter 7.C (The Science of Legal Positivism).

[2] [1963] I YbILC 75, para. 19 (685th Meeting, statement by Mr de Luna).

[3] *See, e.g.*, Ian Brownlie, Principles of Public International Law 3 (Oxford: Clarendon Press, 5th edn. 1998); Malcolm Shaw, International Law 67 (Cambridge University Press, 5th edn. 2003) (attributing this as a consequence of the membership of all States to the United Nations who, by virtue of Article 93 of the Charter, are therefore all parties to the ICJ Statute).

b. international custom, as evidence of a general practice accepted as law;
c. the general principles of law recognized by civilized nations;
d. subject to the provisions of Article 59, judicial decisions and the teachings of the most highly qualified publicists of the various nations, as subsidiary means for the determination of rules of law.[4]

The drafters of Article 53 oriented *jus cogens* in the formal sources of international law, even if *jus cogens* was seen by some members of the ILC to be 'positive law created by States, not as individuals but as organs of the international community'.[5] The task at hand is to account for *jus cogens* through the positive sources articulated in Article 38(1) of the ICJ Statute.

i. *Treaty law*

In the hierarchy of sources articulated in Article 38, treaties constitute the clearest form of positive international law.[6] Article 2(a) of the Vienna Convention defines a treaty as 'an international agreement concluded between States in written form and governed by international law, whether embodied in a single instrument or in two or more related instruments and whatever its particular designation'.[7] Treaties are thus understood to be the 'creation of written agreements whereby the states participating bind themselves legally to act in a particular way or to set up particular relations between themselves'.[8] As a product of the will of States, treaties constitute the most deliberate mode of international law creation through the direct undertaking of commitments and obligations. While treaties are demonstrative of the horizontal structure of international law, they are not exclusively concluded bilaterally; the prevalence of multilateral treaties is reflected by the drafting of a second instrument on the law of treaties, the Vienna Convention on the Law of Treaties between States and International Organizations or between International Organizations (1986).[9] Treaty law is representative of *jus*

[4] Statute of the International Court of Justice, 15 UNCIO 355 (1945).
[5] [1966] I(1) YbILC 39, para. 34 (828th Meeting, statement by Mr De Luna).
[6] *See, e.g.*, Shaw, International Law 88–92; Vladimir Degan, Sources of International Law 355 (The Hague: Martinus Nijhoff 1997); Herman Mosler, *The International Society as a Legal Community*, 140 Recueil des Cours 99 (1974).
[7] 1155 UNTS 331, Article 2(A) (1969). [8] Shaw, International Law 88.
[9] Vienna Convention on the Law of Treaties between States and International Organizations or between International Organizations, UN Doc. A/CONF.129/15 (*opened for signature* 21 March 1986).

dispositivum against which *jus cogens* is juxtaposed, and whatever role treaties may play in the crystalization of peremptory norms, they are not themselves the formal source of peremptory norms.[10]

ii. Customary international law

'[I]nternational custom, as evidence of a general practice accepted as law',[11] derives from two discernible elements: a quantitative element, defined by State practice, and a qualitative element, reflecting the 'belief of law or necessity' (*opinio juris sive necessitatis*).[12] The International Court of Justice clearly articulated this two-part formulation in *Continental Shelf* (1985): 'It is of course axiomatic that the material of customary international law is to be looked for primarily in the actual practice and *opinio juris* of States.'[13] Early pronouncements by the Court looked principally to State practice, the quantitative element, as evidencing the formation of custom through 'constant and uniform usage practiced by the States in question'.[14] This depiction of customary law is captured by Corbett's analogy that '"usage" becomes "custom" just as footsteps across a common eventually become a "path" habitually followed by all'.[15] By 1969, however, in *North Sea Continental Shelf*, the Court

[10] *See, e.g.*, Alexander Orakhelashvili, Peremptory Norms in International Law 57–8 (Oxford University Press 2006); Michael Byers, *Conceptualising the Relationship between* Jus Cogens *and* Erga Omnes *Rules*, 66 Nordic Journal of International Law 211, 221 (1997); Degan, Sources of International Law 219; Jerzy Sztucki, Jus Cogens and the Vienna Convention on the Law of Treaties 75 (Vienna: Springer-Verlag 1974); N. G. Onuf and Richard Birney, *Peremptory Norms of International Law: Their Source, Function and Future*, 4 Denver Journal of International Law and Policy 187, 191–2 (1974); *cf.* Christos Rozakis, The Concept of *Jus Cogens* in the Law of Treaties 93 (Amsterdam: North-Holland 1976).

[11] 15 UNCIO 355, Article 38(1)(b) (1945).

[12] Brian Lepard, Customary International Law: A New Theory with Practical Applications 6 (Cambridge University Press 2010); Shaw, International Law 66–88; Brownlie, Principles of Public International Law 5–9; Mark Villiger, Customary International Law and Treaties 42–47 (The Hague: Kluwer Law International 1997); Michael Akehurst, *Custom as a Source of International Law*, 47 British Yearbook of International Law 1, 31, 53 (1977); Anthony D'Amato, The Concept of Custom in International Law 47–72 (London: Cornell University Press 1971).

[13] *Continental Shelf (Libyan Arab Jamahiriya v. Malta)*, Judgment, ICJ Reports 1985, p. 13, para. 27.

[14] *Asylum Case (Colombia v. Peru)*, Judgment, ICJ Reports 1950, p. 266, 276; *Fisheries Case (United Kingdom v. Norway)*, Judgment, ICJ Reports 1951, p. 116, 131, 138.

[15] D'Amato, The Concept of Custom in International Law 63 (quoting Percy Corbett, Leading Cases on International Law 5 (London: Sweet and Maxwell Ltd. 1922)).

concluded that the mere aggregation of State practice was insufficient to evidence the emergence of customary international law:

> Not only must the acts concerned amount to a settled practice, but they must also be such, or be carried out in such a way, as to be evidence of a belief that this practice is rendered obligatory by the existence of a rule requiring it. The need for such a belief, i.e., the existence of a subjective element, is implicit in the very notion of the *opinio juris sive necessitatis*. The States concerned therefore feel that they are conforming to what amounts to a legal obligation. The frequency, or even habitual character of the acts is not in itself enough. There are many international acts, e.g., in the field of ceremonial and protocol, which are performed almost invariably, but which are motivated only by considerations of courtesy, convenience or tradition, and not by any sense of legal duty.[16]

Arguably, this initial construction of *opinio juris sive necessitatis* in the formulation of customary international law presupposes relience upon the belief of pre-existing law to which State practice conforms and thereby gives form.[17] While the Court's formulation of the elements of customary international law in the 1985 *Continental Shelf* case is decidedly neutral,[18] pronouncements since *Continental Shelf* have emphasized the primacy of the subjective element, *opinio juris sive necessitatis*, when assessing evidence of customary international law: 'The Court must satisfy itself that the existence of the rule in the *opinio juris* of States is confirmed by practice.'[19] In *Military and Paramilitary Activities in and against Nicaragua* (1986), the Court 'determine[d], first, the substance of the customary rules' relating to the use of force by assessing the *opinio juris* giving form to the legal rule,[20] and then considered whether 'State practice justifie[d]' such a finding.[21]

16 *North Sea Continental Shelf (Federal Republic of Germany v. Denmark / Federal Republic of Germany v. Netherlands)*, Judgment, ICJ Reports 1969, p. 3, para. 77.

17 Jörg Kammerhofer, *Uncertainty in the Formal Sources of International Law: Customary International Law and Some of Its Problems*, 15(3) European Journal of International Law 523, 534 (2004) (referring to this as 'necessarily, not just ordinarily, a mistaken belief'); Philip Allott, *Language, Method, and the Nature of International Law*, 45 British Yearbook of International Law 78, 103 (1971) (same).

18 *Continental Shelf (Libyan Arab Jamahiriya v. Malta)*, Judgment, ICJ Reports 1985, p. 13, para. 27.

19 *Military and Paramilitary Activities in and against Nicaragua (Nicaragua v. United States of America)*, Judgment, ICJ Reports 1986, p. 14, paras. 184–6 ('the Court deems it sufficient that the conduct of States should, in general, be consistent with such rules').

20 *Ibid.*, paras. 185–205. 21 *Ibid.*, paras. 206–9.

The outcome of the contemporary methodology of assessing customary international law turns squarely on *opinio juris sive necessitatis.* Either *opinio juris sive necessitatis* evidences the existence of a rule of customary international law, which is substantiated by consistent State practice, as the Special Tribunal for Lebanon (STL) determined in its 2011 Interlocutory Decision with respect to terrorism:

> The conclusion is therefore warranted that a customary rule has evolved in the international community concerning terrorism ... it can be said that there is a settled practice concerning the punishment of acts of terrorism ... [which] is evidence of a belief of States that the punishment of terrorism responds to a social necessity *(opinio necessitatis)* and is hence rendered obligatory by the existence of a rule requiring it *(opinio juris).*[22]

Or, the absence of a rule in the *opino juris sive necessitatis* of States renders State practice ostensibly consistent with the asserted norm lacking the requisite *opinio juris* to evidence customary international law, as the International Court found in *Legality of the Threat or Use of Nuclear Weapons,*[23] and *Jurisdictional Immunities of the State.*[24] In either case, this contemporary formulation depends in the first instance upon *opinio juris sive necessitatis*, which is evidenced by the practice of States. The positive source of peremptory norms is commonly related to the mechanics of customary international law.[25]

[22] *Prosecutor v. Ayyash et al.*, No. STL-11-01/I/AC/R17bis, Interlocutory Decision on the Applicable Law: Terrorism, Conspiracy, Homicide, Perpetration, Cumulative Charging, 145 ILR. 232, para. 102 (2011) [hereinafter, STL Interlocutory Decision (2011)].

[23] *Legality of the Threat or Use of Nuclear Weapons*, Advisory Opinion, ICJ Reports 1996, p. 226, paras. 64–7.

[24] *Jurisdictional Immunities of the State (Germany v. Italy: Greece Intervening)*, ICJ Reports 2012, p. 99, para. 55.

[25] *Questions Relating to the Obligation to Prosecute or Extradite (Belgium v. Senegal)*, Judgment, ICJ Reports 2012, p. 422, para. 99 ('the prohibition of torture is part of customary international law and it has become a peremptory norm (*jus cogens*). That prohibition is grounded in a widespread international practice and on the *opinio juris* of States. It appears in numerous international instruments of universal application ... and it has been introduced into the domestic law of almost all States; finally, acts of torture are regularly denounced within national and international fora'); *Legality of the Threat or Use of Nuclear Weapons*, Advisory Opinion, ICJ Reports 1996, p. 226, para. 79 (referring to rules of international humanitarian law as 'observed by all States whether or not they have ratified the conventions that contain them, because they constitute intransgressible principles of international customary law'); *North Sea Continental Shelf* (*Federal Republic of Germany v. Denmark / Federal Republic of Germany v. Netherlands*), Judgment, ICJ Reports 1969, Sep. Op. Padilla Nervo, 97 (referring to 'customary rules belonging to the category of *jus cogens*'); *Domingues v. United States*, No. 12.285, Inter-American

iii. *General principles of law*

Article 38(1) of the ICJ Statute introduces 'the general principles of law recognized by civilized nations' as a formal source of international law.[26] The notion contains several interpretations in international legal doctrine.[27] One approach to general principles regards them as a vehicle through which to introduce moral considerations and elements of natural law into international law.[28] Another takes general principles to refer to precepts 'accepted by all nations in *foro domestico*', which are essentially 'maxims of law' adapted from domestic orders to fill gaps in international law to avoid *non liquet*.[29] It is conceivable that general

Commission on Human Rights, Report No. 62/02, paras. 49–50 (2000) (citing RESTATEMENT (THIRD) OF FOREIGN RELATIONS LAW OF THE UNITED STATES § 102 and *n.* 6 (1987)); [1963] I YbILC 71, para. 50 (684th Meeting, statement by Mr Ago) ('the general rules from which no departure was permitted were either customary rules or rules which, while embodied in a treaty, were still valid as customary rules for States not bound by the treaty, and hence for States in general'). *See, e.g.*, Brownlie, PRINCIPLES OF PUBLIC INTERNATIONAL LAW 514–17; Degan, SOURCES OF INTERNATIONAL LAW 219; Michael Byers, *Conceptualising the Relationship between* Jus Cogens *and* Erga Omnes *Rules*, 66 NORDIC JOURNAL OF INTERNATIONAL LAW 211, 239 (1997); Rosalyn Higgins, PROBLEMS AND PROCESS: INTERNATIONAL LAW AND HOW WE USE IT 20–2 (Oxford: Clarendon Press 1994); Lauri Hannikainen, PEREMPTORY NORMS (*JUS COGENS*) IN INTERNATIONAL LAW 242 (Helsinki: Finnish Lawyers' Publishing 1988).

26 15 UNCIO 355, Article 38(1)(c) (1945).

27 *See* Bin Cheng, GENERAL PRINCIPLES OF LAW AS APPLIED BY INTERNATIONAL COURTS AND TRIBUNALS 2–5 (Cambridge University Press 1994) ('Some writers consider that the expression refers primarily to general principles of international law and only subsidiarily to principles obtaining in the municipal law of various States. Others hold that [that] would have been redundant ... A difference of opinion also exists as to whether "the general principles of law recognized by civilised nations" are or are not principles of natural law'); Martti Koskenniemi, *General Principles: Reflexions on Constructivist Thinking in International Law*, 18 OIKEUSTIEDE-JURISPRUDENTIA 120–63 (1985) (identifying four discrete meanings that attach to the term 'principle' in international law).

28 *See, e.g.*, *South West Africa Cases (Ethiopia v. South Africa / Liberia v. South Africa) (Second Phase)*, Judgment, ICJ Reports 1966, p. 6, Sep. Op. Tanaka 250, 298 ('it is undeniable that in Article 38, paragraph 1(c), some natural law elements are inherent'); Robert Kolb, *Principles as Sources of International Law*, 23 NETHERLANDS INTERNATIONAL LAW REVIEW 1, 29 (2006); Antônio Augusto Cançado Trindade, *International Law for Humankind: Towards a New Jus Gentium (II) - General Course on Public International Law*, 317 RECUEIL DES COURS 157 (2005); Stephen Hall, *The Persistent Spectre: Natural Law, International Order and the Limits of Legal Positivism*, 12(2) EUROPEAN JOURNAL OF INTERNATIONAL LAW 292, 292–8 (2001); James Brierly, THE LAW OF NATIONS 63 (Oxford: Clarendon Press, 6th edn. 1963).

29 *See, e.g.*, PCIJ Advisory Committee of Jurists, PROCÈS-VERBAUX OF THE PROCEEDINGS OF THE COMMITTEE 335 (1920) (Statement by Lord Phillimore) ('such as certain principles of procedure, the principle of good faith, and the principle of *res judicata*, etc.'); Ulrich

principles common to all domestic legal orders would also constitute expressions of, or otherwise reflect, natural law.[30] A solution to this dichotomy is an inclusive concept of 'general principle of law' that captures both senses of the term, as articulated by Fitzmaurice in his General Course before The Hague Academy:

> By a principle, or general principle, as opposed to a rule, even a general rule, of law is meant chiefly something which is not itself a rule, but which underlies a rule, and explains or provides the reason for it. A rule answers the question 'what': a principle in effect answers the question 'why'. In the event of any dispute as to what the correct rule is, the solution will often depend on what principle is regarded as underlying the rule.[31]

This conceptualization is compatible with the alternative understandings of general principles and contemplates the introduction of subjective considerations into the formation of law. Indeed, it conforms to the particular formulation of 'general principles of law' in the ICJ Statute, which itself is deliberately constructed as a compromise between the divergent interpretations of general principles as constituting principles of 'objective justice' and 'common law'.[32]

B Article 53 of the Vienna Convention

Article 53 of the Vienna Convention, as the point of formal codification of *jus cogens* in international law, provides the best available textual guidance to the formal source of the concept.[33] Notwithstanding the circularity of utilizing the law of treaties to interpret a provision of the law of treaties, the Vienna Convention provides that terms of a treaty are to be interpreted with consideration of their context and the object and

Fastenrath, *Relative Normativity in International Law*, 4(1) European Journal of International Law 305, 320 (1993); Christian Tomuschat, *Obligations Arising for States Without or Against Their Will*, 241 Recueil des Cours 312 (1993); Wolfgang Friedmann, *The Uses of 'General Principles' in the Development of International Law*, 57(2) American Journal of International Law 279, 282–4 (1963).

[30] Jonathan Charney, *Universal International Law*, 87(4) American Journal of International Law 529, 535 (1993); Louis Henkin, *General Course on Public International Law*, 216 Recueil des Cours 61–2 (1989).

[31] Gerald Fitzmaurice, *The General Principles of International Law Considered from the Standpoint of the Rule of Law*, 92(II) Recueil des Cours 7 (1957).

[32] Cançado Trindade, *International Law for Humankind: Towards a New Jus Gentium (II)*, 157–8.

[33] *See* discussion *supra*, Chapter 1, text accompanying *nn.* 7–12.

purpose of the treaty,[34] and permits recourse to supplementary means of interpretation, including preparatory works.[35] This section looks to the text of Article 53 and its *travaux préparatoires* for guidance to the formal source of *jus cogens* indicated by the article, and then discusses evidence of this interpretation in jurisprudence.

According to Article 53 of the Vienna Convention, 'a peremptory norm of general international law is a norm *accepted and recognized* by the international community of States as a whole'.[36] This language parallels the construction of legal sources in Article 38(1) of the ICJ Statute,[37] which defines international custom 'as evidence of a general practice *accepted* as law' and general principles of law as '*recognized* by civilized nations'.[38] This terminological linkage to the sources of international law articulated in Article 38(1) was a deliberate effort on the part of the drafting committee of the Vienna Convention to provide guidance as to the formal source of *jus cogens*.[39] The language 'accepted and recognized' was added in response to a three-Power amendment to the draft article, which proposed to include 'recognized' in the text to refer to a formal source of peremptory norms of general international law.[40] The Chairman of the Drafting Committee at the UN Conference noted that, ultimately, 'the Drafting Committee had added the word "accepted" because it was to be found, together with the word "recognized", in Article 38 of the Statute of the International Court of Justice'.[41]

In the analysis of formal sources of *jus cogens*, attention has been drawn to the commentary of *special rapporteur* Waldock to the final clause of Article 53, which provides that a peremptory norm 'can be

[34] 1155 UNTS 331, Article 31 (1969). [35] *Ibid.*, Article 32.

[36] *Ibid.*, Article 53 (emphasis added).

[37] 15 UNCIO 355, Article 38 (1945) (emphasis added).

[38] While 'recognized' is used to refer to both treaties in Article 38(1)(a) of the ICJ Statute as well as to general principles in 38(1)(c), 'recognized' is best understood in the present context to refer to general principles. Treaty law is the conventional expression of *jus dispositivum* against which *jus cogens* is defined; it is a *non sequitur* to conceive of peremptory norms as a product of treaty law. *See* discussion *supra*, text accompanying *n.* 10.

[39] *See* Maurizio Ragazzi, The Concept of International Obligations *Erga Omnes* 52–3 (1997); Gennady Danilenko, *International* Jus Cogens: *Issues of Law-Making*, 2(1) European Journal of International Law 42, 53 (1991); Ian Sinclair, The Vienna Convention on the Law of Treaties 219 (Manchester University Press 1984).

[40] United Nations Conference on the Law of Treaties, Vienna, 26 March–24 May 1968, A/CONF.39/11 (1969), First Session [hereinafter, UNCLOT, First Session (1968)], 471, para. 4 (statement by Mr Yasseen).

[41] *Ibid.*

modified only by a subsequent norm of general international law having the same character'.[42] Here, Waldock suggested that such 'a modification of a rule of *jus cogens* would to-day most probably be effected through a general multilateral treaty'.[43] The comment raises the obvious question of whether a 'general multilateral treaty' may therefore be the source of *jus cogens*.[44] The matter is perhaps most clearly settled by the fate of the concept 'general multilateral treaty'. The term had been introduced by *special rapporteur* Waldock into Draft Article 1 of the Vienna Convention in reference to a treaty that, unlike other multilateral treaties, 'concerns general norms of international law or deals with matters of general interest to States as a whole'.[45] The potential relevance to *jus cogens* of such a treaty, conceived 'in the interest of the international community as a whole to be of universal application', is clear.[46] Owing to opposition from the governments present, to which the draft article was submitted, the provision on 'general multilateral treaties' was removed from the final draft.[47] Instead, the Vienna Convention provides that a multilateral treaty might become binding on third-States through customary international law.[48] According to Grigory Tunkin, a member of the ILC who at that time envisaged treaties to be a source of *jus cogens*,[49] this final construction effectively conveyed the meaning of 'general multilateral treaty'.[50] It seems therefore that, under the Vienna Convention, the idea of a 'general multilateral treaty' came to be subsumed by

[42] 1155 UNTS 331, Article 53 (1969). *See* Arthur Weisburd, *American Judges and International Law*, 36 Vanderbilt Journal of Transnational Law 1475, 1490 (2003).

[43] Humphrey Waldock, Fifth Report the Law of Treaties, [1966] II YbILC 248, para. 4 (Commentary to Draft Article 50).

[44] While the question of modification will not be taken up at present, it bears noting that some Governments at the UN Conference expressed scepticism for the proposition that a peremptory norm could be modified as such. *See, e.g.*, UNCLOT First Session (1968) 321, para. 2 (statement by United Republic of Tanzania) ('It was hard to see how "future developments" could modify the condemnation of the crime of genocide, the slave trade, or the use of force').

[45] Report of the Commission to the General Assembly, [1962] II YbILC 161 (Article 1(1)(c)).

[46] Humphrey Waldock, Fourth Report on the Law of Treaties, [1965] II YbILC 13–14 (Article 1(c)) (Observations and proposals of the Special Rapporteur).

[47] Grigory Tunkin, *Is General International Law Customary Law Only?*, 4 European Journal of International Law 534, 536–7 (1993).

[48] 1155 UNTS 331, Article 38 (1969) (Rules in a treaty becoming binding on third States through international custom).

[49] [1963] I YbILC 69, para. 26 (684th Meeting, statement by Mr Tunkin).

[50] Tunkin, *Is General International Law Customary Law Only?*, 534, 538–9 (The alternative to this conceptualization was a multilateral treaty to which all States are parties).

customary international law. In this sense, whether a multilateral treaty is considered a form of State practice evidencing the emergence of customary international law, or declaratory of existing customary international law,[51] conventional provisions articulating norms of *jus cogens* are not themselves peremptory,[52] and *jus cogens* norms exist independently of such conventional expressions.[53]

The construction of *jus cogens* in Article 53 of the Vienna Convention may therefore be interpreted to indicate the formal source of peremptory norms of general international law to be customary international law and general principles of law.[54] Importantly, 'accepted' and 'recognized' are linked in the Article by the non-contrasting connector 'and', rather than an alternative connector (e.g. 'or'), suggesting that peremptory norms are conceived to arise through some interrelation of customary international law and general principles, rather than from a plurality of possible alternative sources. This formulation was initially advanced by Lauterpacht in his First Report on the Law of Treaties (1953), in which he proposed that *jus cogens* are:

> [Not] customary international law pure and simple, but . . . such overriding principles of international law which may be regarded as constituting principles of international public policy (*ordre international public*). These principles . . . may be expressive of rules of international morality so cogent that an international tribunal would consider them as forming part of those principles of law generally recognized by civilized nations

[51] *Continental Shelf (Libyan Arab Jamahiriya v. Malta)*, Judgment, ICJ Reports 1985, p. 13, para. 27 ('It is of course axiomatic that the material of customary international law is to be looked for primarily in the actual practice and *opinio juris* of States, even though multilateral conventions may have an important role to play in recording and defining rules deriving from custom, or indeed in developing them'); Richard Baxter, *Multilateral Treaties as Evidence of Customary International Law*, 41 British Yearbook of International Law 275–300 (1968).

[52] *See supra*, *n.* 10.

[53] *See, e.g.*, *Application of the Convention on the Prevention and Punishment of the Crime of Genocide (Bosnia and Herzegovina v. Serbia and Montenegro)*, Judgment, ICJ Reports 2007, p. 43, para. 161; *Armed Activities on the Territory of the Congo (New Application: 2002) (Congo v. Rwanda)*, ICJ Reports 2006, p. 3, para. 64; *Reservations to the Genocide Convention*, Advisory Opinion, ICJ Reports 1951, p. 15, 23 ('The first consequence arising from this conception is that the principles underlying the [Genocide] Convention are principles which are recognized by civilized nations as binding on States, even without any conventional obligation').

[54] This is not to suggest that any or every custom expressive of any general principle of law constitutes peremptory norms of general international law, as will become clear in the section to follow.

> which the International Court of Justice is bound to apply by virtue of Article 38[c] of its Statute.[55]

Lauterpacht suggests that *jus cogens*, though based in customary international law, is not 'pure and simple' customary law but requires something more.[56] By this formulation, public order norms of general international law emerge as customary international law expressive of particular general principles of law within the meaning of Article 38(c) of the ICJ Statute. This construction is reinforced by the meaning of 'general international law' as 'international custom as evidence of a general practice accepted as law *and* the general principles of law recognized by the community of nations'.[57] This interpretation of 'general international law'[58] is consistent with the final text of Article 53 of the Vienna

[55] Hersch Lauterpacht, First Report on the Law of Treaties, [1953] II YbILC 155, para. 4 (Omited is the sentence, 'These principles need not necessarily have crystallized in a clearly accepted rule of law such as the prohibition of piracy of aggressive war. They . . .').

[56] *See, e.g.*, United Nations Conference on the Law of Treaties, Vienna, 9 April–22 May 1969, A/CONF.39/11/Add.1 (1970), Second Session [hereinafter, UNCLOT, Second Session (1969)] 102, paras. 20–1 (statement by the United States) ('To give a norm of customary international law a peremptory character, State practice must be unambiguous and, as set forth in the present text of article 5[3], its peremptory character must be accepted and recognized as a matter of legal obligation by the international community of States as a whole'). A basis in customary international law was widely shared by States at the UNCLOT: *see* UNCLOT First Session (1968) 301, para. 19 (Ghana); 302, paras. 33–4 (Poland); 305, para. 60 (United Kingdom); 318, para. 25 (Czechoslovakia); 319, para. 33 (Germany); 321, para. 52 (Ivory Coast), 325, para. 50 (Malaysia), 388, para. 16 (Australia); UNCLOT Second Session (1969) 102, para. 25 (Bulgaria); 103, para. 38 (Italy).

[57] *See* UNCLOT First Session (1968) 319, para. 33 (Federal Republic of Germany) (emphasis added) ('In order to become a peremptory norm of international law binding on all States, a rule required general recognition that went beyond the criteria developed by doctrine and practice. It must reflect international practice accepted as law and must also have uniform validity within the various legal systems'). No other State appears to have proferred a formal definition of 'general international law', but some alluded to its features: *see* 323, para. 16 (Philippines) ('The word "general" was probably intended to emphasize the acceptance of the norm by the entire community of nations'); 330, para. 26 (United States) ('a principle of general international law could become *jus cogens* only upon general acceptance as such throughout all regions of the world'); UNCLOT Second Session (1969) 185, para. 2 (Hungary) (defining general international law as 'the law which should prevail all over the world'); 238, para. 17 (Bulgaria) (defining general international law as 'rules of universal application'); 344, para. 7 (Ecuador) ('The universality of norms of general international law was closely linked with the universal dimensions of the international community').

[58] *Compare* Tunkin, *Is General International Law Customary Law Only?*, 534–41 (1993) (considering alternative modes of development of general international law), *with* Ian Brownlie, *Problems Concerning the Unity of International Law*, *in* International Law in the Time of its Codification: Essays in Honour of Robert Ago 154 (Milan:

Convention, which provides that peremptory norms of general international law are 'accepted and recognized', and suggests that the formal source of *jus cogens* can be conceived as custom *accepted* as law expressing *recognized* general principles related to the interests of the international community.

This construction of peremptory norms as 'general international law', 'accepted and recognized' by the international community, has been borne out in practice. The Inter-American Commission on Human Rights (IACHR) articulated with clarity the way in which peremptory norms crystallize through customary international law influenced by general principles in *Domingues v. United States*.[59]

> It has been said that the principal distinguishing feature of [peremptory] norms is their 'relative indelibility,' in that they constitute rules of customary law which cannot be set aside by treaty or acquiescence but only by the formation of a subsequent customary rule of contrary effect. More particularly, [while] customary international law rests on the consent of nations ... [n]orms of *jus cogens*, on the other hand, derive their status from fundamental values held by the international community, as violations of such peremptory norms are considered to shock the conscience of humankind and therefore bind the international community as a whole, irrespective of protest, recognition or acquiescence ... Therefore, while based on the same evidentiary sources as a norm of customary

Multa Paucis AG, A. Guiffrè ed., 1987) (referring to 'customary (or general) international law' interchangeably). During the UNCLOT, some delegations decried the vagueness of the term: UNCLOT First Session (1968) 316, para. 7 (Spain) (the term 'might, for instance, be held to refer only to geographical scope'); UNCLOT Second Session (1969) 246, para. 35 (United States) ('it was hard to see what difference there was between general international law and plain international law'). The term appears distinguishable from customary international law: *See, e.g.*, 334, para. 44 (Cyprus) (referring to either 'customary international law or general international law'). Not all general international law constitutes *jus cogens*: *See, e.g.*, 45, para. 10 (Ecuador) (*pacta sunt servanda*, 'was certainly part of general international law, [yet] it could not be regarded as a rule of *jus cogens*, since it admitted of exceptions').

59 *Domingues v. United States*, No. 12.285, Inter-American Commission on Human Rights, Report No. 62/02, paras. 47–50 (2000). Incidentally, while the norm identified by the Court in this instance (the prohibition of the death penalty) is contested in international law, the mechanism identified by the Inter-American Commission is not: *See, e.g.*, *Hain v. Gibson*, 287 F.3d 1224, 1243–4 (10th Cir. 2002) ('It is far from certain that abolition of the death penalty for juveniles is a customary norm of international law that has risen to the level that the international community as a whole recognizes it as *jus cogens*') (internal quotation marks omitted); *Buell v. Mitchell*, 274 F.3d 337, 373 (6th Cir. 2001) ('since the abolition of the death penalty is not a customary norm of international law, it cannot have risen to the level that the international community as a whole recognizes it as *jus cogens*').

> international law, the standard for determining a principle of *jus cogens* is more rigorous, requiring evidence of recognition of the indelibility of the norm by the international community as a whole.[60]

Consistent with the formulation provided in Article 53 of the Vienna Convention, the IACHR indicated that the formal source of *jus cogens* is customary international law deriving from 'fundamental values held by the international community'. In this view, *jus cogens* shares the evidentiary sources of customary international law yet is differentiated by the influence of particular general principles reflecting the interests of the international community.[61] The following subsections assess this formal source of *jus cogens* interpreted from Article 53 of the Vienna Convention, taking in turn the constituent evidentiary elements of customary international law – *opinio juris sive necessitatis* and State practice – and considering their interaction with general principles of law to give rise to peremptory norms of general international law.

i. Opinio juris sive necessitates

Law, as an expression of the goals and values of society, is a 'social fact', and this relation is exemplified in international law by *opinio juris sive necessitatis*. The expression, initially articulated as *opinio juris seu necessitatis*, derives from the 1899 work *Méthode d'interprétation et sources en droit privé positif* by François Gény, the first to postulate a subjective element to the formation of customary law.[62] The prevailing formulation of custom in contemporary international law places prominence upon the belief of obligation of law, *opinio juris*, or social need, *sive necessitatis*.[63] State practice is relied upon to evidence *opinio juris sive necessitatis*, meaning that *opinio* is determinative of customary international law, rather than State practice. In the context of customary international law rights attaching to the individual, it has been suggested that this relation arises out of practical necessity, because the element of State practice is often scarce in the emergence of such norms, so the search for

60 *Ibid.*, paras. 49–50 (internal citations omitted).

61 This formulation is consistent with findings in the previous chapter: *See* discussion *supra*, Chapter 5 (The Authority of *Jus Cogens*).

62 David Bederman, Custom as a Source of Law 142 (Cambridge University Press 2010). The construction *opinio juris seu necessitatis* finds expression in the 2011 Interlocutory Decision by the STL: *see* STL Interlocutory Decision (2011).

63 *See* discussion *supra*, Chapter 8.A.ii (Customary International Law).

'constant and uniform usage' would be fruitless.[64] However, the primacy of *opinio* in the identification of customary international law also reflects the community-oriented nature of custom as the product of social and historical forces that shape the needs of the international community. This normative aspect of the formation of customary law was observed by de Visscher, who writes:

> No custom is established until the moment when human thought comes to regard a way of social behavior as an element of order important enough to be observed henceforth as legally binding. The inductive reasoning that establishes the existence of custom is 'tied' reasoning: the matter is one not only of counting the observed regularities, but of weighing them, of evaluating them in terms of social ends considered desirable.[65]

According to de Visscher, this social element elevates customary law above conventional international law, which is strictly *dispositive* in nature.[66] This aspect of social need is implicitly expressed by *opinio juris sive necessitatis* in the emergence of customary international law.

This social and historical nature of *opinio juris sive necessitatis* is reflected in *jus cogens*, which may be understood to constitute public order norms of customary origin in international law arising from the needs and values of society. An observation before the ILC drew particular attention to this societal aspect of *jus cogens*:

> [M]embership of a community required the respect of certain rules. If that were not so, society would remain in the condition of savagery described by the phrase *homo homini lupus*, which had lasted until the First World War and had prevailed almost unchallenged in the inter-war period. By becoming members of the international society, States recognized the existence of a minimum international order, which was none other than *jus cogens*.[67]

64 Theodor Meron, *The Continuing Role of Custom in the Formation of International Humanitarian Law*, 90(2) American Journal of International Law 238, 240 (1996) ('In both human rights and humanitarian law, emphasis on *opinio juris* helps to compensate for scarcity of supporting practice'); Oscar Schachter, International Law in Theory and Practice 336 (The Hague: Martinus Nijhoff 1991); Bruno Simma and Philip Alston, *The Sources of Human Rights Law: Custom,* Jus Cogens, *and General Principles*, 12 Australian Yearbook of International Law 82, 99–100 (1988).

65 Charles de Visscher, Theory and Reality in Public International Law 156–7 (Princeton University Press, Percy Corbett trans., 1968).

66 *Ibid.*, 161.

67 [1966] I(1) YbILC 39, para. 40 (828th Meeting, statement by Mr Bartoš); [1963] I YbILC 76, para. 33 (685th Meeting, statement by Mr Bartoš) ('the international public order was

In this sense, *jus cogens* can be viewed as the basis of social order of the international community, an expression of its interests and values arising from, and applied to, social and historical exigencies. Consequently, as observed by a member of the ILC, because 'the concept of *jus cogens* expressed some higher social need . . . it was more society and less the law itself which defined the content of *jus cogens*'.[68] This sentiment is captured in a statement by the German delegation to the UN Conference on the Law of Treaties, in which the representative observed,

> that his delegation, like many others, recognized the existence of a category of peremptory norms of international law. It was definitely a new category in the structure of international law and its emergence called for reconsideration of the positivist theory and of the relations between the various sources of international law as enumerated in Article 38 of the Statute of the International Court of Justice. The emergence of the notion of *jus cogens* in international law was a direct consequence of social and historical evolution, which had had a far-reaching influence on the development of international law.[69]

In this instance, the qualities of the whole are a reflection of its parts: peremptory norms of general international law emerge through a customary process in which *opinio juris sive necessitatis* reflects the necessity for public order governing conduct of concern to international society. The intrinsically social character of *opinio* is manifest in the category of *jus cogens* and the peremptory norms therein. The basic premise underlying this proposition was widely expressed by both the ILC and States participating in the UN Conference on the Law of Treaties.[70]

The way in which normative aspects of *jus cogens*, discussed earlier in this and the previous chapters, enter into positive international law may be understood through the concept of *opinio juris sive necessitatis*. Applied to these normative elements, the perception of social need manifest in *opinio* is capable of expressing general principles of law (i.e. human dignity) taken to represent the higher interests of the international community as a whole. In the context of *jus cogens*, then, the social need of the international community expressed by *opinio juris sive*

merely the superstructure of the international community which resulted from the evolution of international society. It was the minimum of rules of conduct necessary to make orderly international relations possible').

68 [1963] I YbILC 73, para 4 (685th Meeting, statement by Mr Rosenne).

69 UNCLOT Second Session (1969) 95, paras. 25–6 (Statement by Federal Republic of Germany).

70 *See* discussion *supra*, Chapter 5.B.i (*Travaux Préparatoires*).

necessitatis is informed by the general legal principle of human dignity. It is through this *opinio* that the general legal principles expressing the higher interests of the international community – articulated variously as basic considerations of humanity, the fundamental wellbeing of the individual, and the juridical conscience of mankind – can be viewed to govern the emergence of peremptory norms in international law. In essence, what the international community expresses to be necessary to societal coexistence, the basis of *opinio juris sive necessitatis*, is determined by the higher interests of the international community, represented by the general principle of human dignity.[71]

Jurists have repeatedly proposed that *jus cogens* is a category of customary international law expressing general principles of law related to humanity and human dignity. As noted above, this conceptual understanding is implicit in Lauterpacht's depiction of the concept of *jus cogens* in international law as custom 'expressive of rules of international morality', a formulation that has endured throughout the evolution of peremptory norms.[72] Lord Steyn, writing much later for the House of Lords, observed with respect to a norm belonging to *jus cogens* that 'the international community has signed up to it. The moral norm has ripened into a rule of customary international law. It is binding on all states.'[73] The Special Court for Sierra Leone (SCSL) suggested that 'the obligation to protect human dignity' underlies *jus cogens* as 'a peremptory norm' and accounts for legal effects of the category.[74] Following the first formal recognition of *jus cogens* by the International Court of Justice, Judge Dugard observed that norms 'of *jus cogens* are a blend of principle and policy'.[75] Similarly, Judge Cançado Trindade was explicit about the role of general principles of law, particularly the principles of humanity and human dignity, in defining *opinio juris sive necessitatis* in the context of *jus cogens*, and cautioned against divorcing them:

> The invocation of 'elementary considerations of humanity' cannot be rhetorical, failing to guard coherence in not anticipating nor addressing

[71] *See* discussion *supra*, Chapter 3 (The Interests of the International Community).

[72] Lauterpacht, First Report on the Law of Treaties, [1953] II YbILC 155, para. 4.

[73] *R. et al. v. Immigration Officer at Prague Airport*, [2004] UKHL 55, para. 46 (2004) (Steyn, J.) (finding British immigration officers at Prague Airport violated the Race Relations Act, and prohibition against systematic racial discrimination as *jus cogens*).

[74] *Prosecutor v. Kallon and Kamara*, Decision on Challenge to Jurisdiction: Lomé Accord Amnesty, SCSL-04-15-PT-060-I, para. 71 (2004).

[75] *Armed Activities on the Territory of the Congo (New Application: 2002) (Democratic Republic of the Congo v. Rwanda)*, Sep. Op. Dugard, ICJ Reports 2006, p. 86, para. 10.

> the consequences of the application of those considerations in practice. Moreover, one should not pursue a very restrictive view of *opinio juris*, reducing it to the subjective component of custom and distancing it from the general principles of law, up to a point of not taking account of it at all.[76]

Given that *opinio juris sive necessitatis* is an expression of the social need of the international community, and that the general legal principle of human dignity represents the higher interests of the international community as a whole, recognition that the two concepts should be related in the formation of *jus cogens* corroborates the understanding of the formal source of *jus cogens* developed above.

The confluence of *opinio juris* and general legal principles (i.e. human dignity), in the context of public order norms and *jus cogens*, has been referred to recurrently in terms of legal or juridical 'conscience'. In the *Fisheries Case* (1951), Judge Alvarez referred to this social force linked with general principles and the way in which it influences the formation of 'necessary' legal norms in international law:

> In the first place, many of the principles, particularly the great principles, have their origin in the legal conscience of peoples ... This conscience results from social and international life; the requirements of this social and international life naturally give rise to certain norms considered necessary to govern the conduct of States *inter se*[.][77]

In the Opinion of the Judge, socialized international relations give rise to a common legal conscience manifest in general principles of law, which informs 'norms considered necessary' to such relations. While preceding the codification of *jus cogens* in the Vienna Convention, the Opinion by Judge Alvarez is contemporary with the Advisory Opinion of the Court in *Reservations to the Genocide Convention*,[78] and similarly articulates the parameters of *jus cogens*. At the UN Conference on the Law of Treaties, many delegations invoked this notion of 'international legal

[76] *Jurisdictional Immunities of the State (Germany v. Italy: Greece Intervening)*, Judgment, ICJ Reports 2012, p. 99, Dis. Op. Cançado Trindade, 283–4, paras. 290–1 (footnotes omitted). *See* Cançado Trindade, *International Law for Humankind: Towards a New Jus Gentium (II)*, 344 ('*jus cogens* presents itself as the juridical expression of the very international community as a whole, which, at last, takes conscience of itself, and of the fundamental principles and values which guide it').

[77] *Fisheries Case (United Kingdom v. Norway)*, Judgment, ICJ Reports 1951, p. 116, Ind. Op. Alvarez, 148.

[78] *Reservations to the Genocide Convention*, Advisory Opinion, ICJ Reports 1951, p. 15, 23.

conscience' as the material source of *jus cogens*,[79] as exemplified by the Czechoslovakia delegation:

> The content of *jus cogens* would be defined progressively by the practice of States and international jurisprudence. Rules of *jus cogens* were indispensable for the protection of public order, the community of States and the maintenance of the standards of public morality, and ... in order to acquire the character of *jus cogens*, a rule of international law must not only be accepted by a large number of States, it must also be regarded as indispensable for international life and be deeply rooted in the international conscience.[80]

More recently, Judge Cançado Trindade took note of the 'universal juridical conscience' that gives rise to *jus cogens* norms,[81] which underpins *opinio juris sive necessitatis* guided by general principles expressive of the higher interests of the international community, as *opinio juris communis necessitatis*:

[79] UNCLOT Official Records, First Session (1968) 258, para. 74 (Holy See) ('Principles such as the prohibition of slavery and genocide had entered positive law; but those rules of natural law had been ratified and sanctioned by positive law without losing their value as fundamental dictates of the universal conscience'); 294, para. 7 (Mexico) ('the rules of *jus cogens* were those rules which derived from principles that the legal conscience of mankind deemed absolutely essential to coexistence in the international community at a given stage of its historical development'); 296, para. 23 (Iraq); 299, para. 61 (Chile); 301, para. 22 (Madagascar); 301, para. 26 (Colombia); 302, para. 33 (Poland); 309, para. 32 (France) ('The substance of *jus cogens* was what represented the undeniable expression of the universal conscience, the common denominator of what men of all nationalities regarded as sacrosanct, namely, respect for and protection of the rights of the human person'); 311, para. 42 (Italy); 318, para. 25 (Czechoslovakia); 320–1, para. 49 (Ivory Coast); 323, para. 20 (The Philippines); 327, para. 74 (Mali); 387, para. 11 (Cuba) ('*jus cogens*, which was the expression of the conscience of the international community at any given moment'); UNCLOT Second Session (1969) 103, para. 28 (Bulgaria); 104, paras. 37–9 (Italy) ('norms of general international law acknowledged by the international community as a whole, that was to say they were based on the legal conscience of the whole of mankind'); 124, para. 72 (Spain); 204, para. 24 (El Salvador) ('The provisions on *jus cogens* would provide judges and arbitrators with a sensitive and delicate instrument which, if used with prudence, could serve to reflect the legal conscience of mankind at every stage of its development').

[80] UNCLOT First Session (1968) 318, para. 25 (Czechoslovakia).

[81] Cançado Trindade, *International Law for Humankind: Towards a New Jus Gentium (I)*, 316 ('It is my view that there is, in the multicultural world of our times, an irreducible minimum, which, in so far as international law-making is concerned, rests on its ultimate material source: human conscience. This may admittedly have distinct forms of expression, in distinct cultures, but I believe they all mean, ultimately, that which is common to all human beings (and distinguishes them from other species), which guides their actions, which identifies their values, which assists them in searching the meaning of their lives, individually and in socially organized collectivities: human conscience').

> It has, at last, been recognized that conscience refers to superior values which stand above the 'will', and that Law emanates from the common conscience of what is juridically necessary (*opinio juris communis necessitatis*). Distinctly from the formal 'sources' of International Law, which are nothing more than the means or vehicles of formation of its norms, conscience (expressed in the *opinio juris communis*) appears distinctly, in my understanding, as its *material* 'source' *par excellence*, affirming the binding character of such norms. It is therefrom, i.e., from the universal juridical conscience, that the peremptory norms of International Law (*jus cogens*) ultimately emanate.[82]

The construction *opinio juris communis necessitatis* captures the social need reflected by *opinio juris sive necessitatis* arising from the higher interests of the international community as a whole conceived in terms of the juridical conscience of mankind. It depicts the incorporation of normative considerations, inherent in the general legal principle of human dignity, into positive law through *opinio juris sive necessitatis* as peremptory norms of *jus cogens*. While *opinio juris sive necessitatis* is recognized to have a determinative role in the formation of customary international law, this may be especially so where the *opinio* in question derives from the juridical conscience of mankind with respect to *jus cogens*, as noted by the International Criminal Tribunal for the former Yugoslavia (ICTY) in *Kupreškić*:

> Admittedly, there does not seem to have emerged recently a body of State practice consistently supporting the proposition that one of the elements of custom, namely [State practice] has taken shape. This is however an area where *opinio iuris sive necessitatis* may play a much greater role than [State practice], as a result of the aforementioned Martens Clause. In the light of the way States and courts have implemented it, this Clause clearly shows that principles of international humanitarian law may emerge through a customary process under the pressure of the demands of humanity or the dictates of public conscience, even where State practice is scant or inconsistent. The other element, in the form of *opinio necessitatis*, crystallising as a result of the imperatives of humanity or public conscience, may turn out to be the decisive element heralding the emergence of a general rule or principle of humanitarian law.[83]

[82] *Ibid.*, 176 (footnotes omitted).

[83] *Prosecutor v. Kupreškić*, IT-95-16-T, para. 527 (2000) (finding the prohibitions of genocide, war crimes, and crimes against humanity as norms of international humanitarian law that are also *jus cogens*).

This proposition suggests the primacy *opinio juris sive necessitatis* in the customary formation of peremptory norms, notwithstanding any broader emphasis on *opinio* in the crystallization of customary international law more generally.

The identification of *opinio juris sive necessitatis* in international law frequently resides in pronouncements by international judicial organs.[84] Judicial practice indicates a plurality of potential forms in which *opinio juris sive necessitatis* may be articulated pursuant to the emergence of peremptory norms. Experience indicates that such expressions are most frequently affirmed and reinforced by, or through, authoritative organs of the international community.[85] To this end, the International Court of Justice has looked to resolutions of the UN General Assembly as indicia of *opinio juris sive necessitatis*, which in principle constitute authoritative expressions of the position of the international community as a whole.[86] The ICTY has stated that Security Council resolutions are '[o]f great relevance to the formation of *opinio juris*'.[87] The International Military Tribunal (IMT) at Nuremberg relied upon near-universal instruments of public international law, and the drafting of such instruments, as 'expressions of opinion'

84 [1966] II YbILC 248, para. 3 (Commentary to Draft Article 50) (considering the content of *jus cogens* to be determined by 'State practice and . . . the jurisprudence of international tribunals').

85 *South West Africa Cases (Ethiopia v. South Africa / Liberia v. South Africa) (Second Phase)*, Judgment, ICJ Reports 1966, p. 6, Sep. Op. Tanaka 250, 291–4 (With reference to the League of Nations, the United Nations, and their affiliated institutions and agencies, a 'State, instead of pronouncing its view to a few States directly concerned, has the opportunity, through the medium of an organization, to declare its position to all members of the organization and to know immediately their reaction on the same matter . . . each resolution, declaration, etc., being considered as the manifestation of the collective will of individual participant States, the will of the international community can certainly be formulated more quickly and more accurately as compared with the traditional method of the normative process . . . Briefly, the method of the generation of customary international law is in the stage of transformation from being an individualistic process to being a collectivistic process').

86 *Military and Paramilitary Activities in and against Nicaragua (Nicaragua v. United States of America)*, Judgment, ICJ Reports 1986, p. 14, para. 188 ('*opinio juris* may, though with all due caution, be deduced from, *inter alia*, the attitude of the Parties and the attitude of States towards certain General Assembly resolutions'); Lepard, Customary International Law; Yoram Dinstein, *The Interaction Between Customary International Law and Treaties*, 322 Recueil des Cours 303–12 (2007).

87 *Prosecutor v. Tadić*, Decision on the Defence Motion for Interlocutory Appeal on Jurisdiction, IT-94-1-A, para. 133 (1995) (referring particularly to unanimous Security Council resolutions).

of 'the conscience of the world' indicative of custom of universal recognition prohibiting aggressive war.[88] The ICJ has consistently drawn similar conclusions, generally with reference to 'elementary considerations of humanity'.[89] The STL observed that treaties, UN resolutions, and the legislative and judicial practice of States may 'evince the formation of a general *opinio juris seu necessitatis* in the international community'.[90] Judicial pronouncements on *opinio juris sive necessitatis* illustrate its preeminent role in the practical determination of customary international law, particularly norms of *jus cogens* (the above-cited opinions concern aggression, international humanitarian law, and terrorism).[91] Articulations of *opinio juris sive necessitatis* referred to by the IMT, ICJ, ICTY, and STL are each manifestations of the social need of the international community expressed through community-oriented channels.

ii. State practice

As indicated by the International Court of Justice, determining the existence of a customary rule in international law depends upon the confirmation of *opinio juris sive necessitatis* in the practice of States.[92] State practice constitutes any statement or act on the part of a State that

88 *Nazi Conspiracy and Aggression*, Opinion and Judgment, International Military Tribunal at Nuremberg 51–2 (1946) ('it must be remembered that international law is not the product of an international legislature, and that such international agreements as the [Kellogg–Briand] Pact of Paris have to deal with general principles of law, and not with administrative matters of procedure. The law of war is to be found not only in treaties, but in the customs and practices of states which gradually obtained universal recognition, and from the general principles of justice applied by jurists and practiced by military courts. This law is not static, but by continual adaptation follows the needs of a changing world. Indeed, in many cases treaties do no more than express and define for more accurate reference the principles of law already existing').

89 *Legal Consequences of the Construction of a Wall in the Occupied Palestinian Territory*, Advisory Opinion, ICJ Reports 2004, p. 136, para. 157; *Legality of the Threat or Use of Nuclear Weapons*, Advisory Opinion, ICJ Reports 1996, p. 226, paras. 79, 95; *Military and Paramilitary Activities in and against Nicaragua (Nicaragua v. United States of America)*, Judgment, ICJ Reports 1986, p. 14, para. 218; *Reservations to the Genocide Convention*, Advisory Opinion, ICJ Reports 1951, p. 15, 23; *The Corfu Channel Case (United Kingdom of Great Britain and Northern Ireland v. Albania)*, Judgment, ICJ Reports 1949, p. 4, 22.

90 STL Interlocutory Decision 49, para. 85 (2011).

91 *See* Meron, *The Continuing Role of Custom in the Formation of International Humanitarian Law*, 238, 239–40.

92 *See* discussion *supra*, Chapter 8.A.ii (Customary International Law).

pertains to a rule of international law,[93] and it is conceivable that a broad range of actions contribute to practice. For example, the catalogue proposed by Brownlie includes

> diplomatic correspondence, policy statements, press releases, the opinions of official legal advisors, official manuals on legal questions, e.g. manuals of military law, executive decisions and practices, orders to naval forces etc., comments by governments on drafts produced by the International Law Commission, state legislation, international and national judicial decisions, recitals in treaties and other international instruments, a pattern of treaties in the same form, the practice of international organs, and resolutions relating to legal questions in the United Nations General Assembly.[94]

Practically, as noted above, the emphasis in identifying customary international law resides principally in evidence of *opinio juris sive necessitatis*, with State practice utilized to substantiate such a determination.[95]

Evidence of *opinio juris sive necessitatis* expressing the higher interests of the international community is to be found in practice most commonly where States act as members of the international community. Such practice was envisaged to be the controlling source of *jus cogens* by one member of the ILC during the drafting of the law of treaties:

> *Jus cogens* was the indispensable minimum for the existence of the international community; it was positive law created by States, not as individuals but as organs of the international community, in order to safeguard the community's existence.[96]

The clearest example of such practice is the codification of multilateral instruments of international law, which reflects the general consensus of the international community and serves as an indicator of State practice evidencing *opinio*.[97] This process, it may be recalled, was implicit in the concept of a 'general multilateral treaty' considered by the ILC during the

93 Dinstein, *The Interaction Between Customary International Law and Treaties*, 269.

94 Brownlie, Principles of Public International Law 5.

95 Theodor Meron, Human Rights and Humanitarian Norms as Customary Law 94 (Oxford: Clarendon Press 1991) ('It is, of course, to be expected that those rights which are most crucial to the protection of human dignity and of the universally accepted values of humanity, and whose violation triggers broad condemnation by the international community, will require a lesser amount of confirmatory evidence').

96 [1966] I(1) YbILC 39, paras. 31–4 (statement by Mr De Luna) (internal quotation marks omitted).

97 Brownlie, Principles of Public International Law 5; Akehurst, *Custom as a Source of International Law*, 43.

drafting of the law of treaties, a concept best understood as contributory to, or declaratory of, customary international law.[98] In the context of *jus cogens*, each peremptory norm has been codified by multilateral instruments.[99] In these instances, multilateral instruments reflect the general principles underlying *opinio juris sive necessitatis*, thereby contributing to the emergent norms themselves; however, conventional provisions articulating peremptory norms are not themselves peremptory,[100] and peremptory norms exist independently from such conventional expressions.[101] The *opinio juris sive necessitatis* reflected by such instruments was articulated by the International Court of Justice in *Reservations to the Genocide Convention*:

> In such a convention the contracting States do not have any interests of their own; they merely have, one and all, a common interest, namely, the accomplishment of those high purposes which are the *raison d'être* of the convention. Consequently, in a convention of this type one cannot speak of individual advantages or disadvantages to States, or of the maintenance of a perfect contractual balance between rights and duties. The high ideals which inspired the Convention provide, by virtue of the common will of the parties, the foundation and measure of all its provisions.[102]

The Judgment of the Court indicates that the social need and values of the international community are expressed through the codification of multilateral instruments concerning *jus cogens*. As a practical consequence in that case, the Court found that the prohibition of genocide is not limited in its application to States by consent to the Genocide Convention.[103]

Other relevant practice expressive of *opinio juris* may be found in international organizations and institutions,[104] where States act in effect through collective practice as organs of the international community. In its *East Timor* Advisory Opinion, the International Court relied in part upon 'United Nations practice' as evidence of the *erga omnes* character of the principle of self-determination.[105] Similarly, in *Legal Consequences of*

[98] *See* discussion *supra*, text accompanying *nn*. 45–53 (regarding the concept 'General Multilateral Treaty').

[99] *See* discussion *infra*, Chapter 11.A (Identifying Peremptory Norms).

[100] *See supra*, *n*. 10. [101] *See supra*, *n*. 53.

[102] *Reservations to the Genocide Convention*, Advisory Opinion, ICJ Reports 1951, p. 15, 23.

[103] *See Armed Activities on the Territory of the Congo (New Application: 2002) (Congo v. Rwanda)*, ICJ Reports 2006, p. 3, para. 64.

[104] Brownlie, Principles of Public International Law 5; Akehurst, *Custom as a Source of International Law*, 1, 11.

[105] *East Timor (Portugal v. Australia)*, Judgment, ICJ Reports 1995, p. 90, para. 29.

the Wall, the Court looked to the 'constant practice of the UN Human Rights Committee' in its assessment of the 'extra-territorial' (customary) application of the ICCPR.[106] Additionally, domestic legislation and judgments, with particular reference to the higher interests of the international community, may similarly constitute relevant State practice, and the same considerations ventured above apply.[107] As peremptory norms are of such a nature that they effectively reflect custom 'by omission', many of the most obvious forms of State practice that exhibit literal 'custom' by usage may be of particularly limited relevance to their emergence.[108] Consequently, ascendance to multilateral instruments and the practice of international organizations (e.g. through their resolutions, declarations, and statements) are among the best available indicators of practice evidencing *opinio juris sive necessitatis* in relation to *jus cogens*.[109]

Given that State practice is relied upon only insofar as necessary to evidence *opinio juris sive necessitatis*, it follows that the expression of *opinio* need not rely upon universal practice to indicate the emergence of customary international law.[110] This proposition is especially relevant to the formation of *jus cogens*.[111] According to Article 53 of the Vienna

[106] *Legal Consequences of the Construction of a Wall in the Occupied Palestinian Territory*, Advisory Opinion, ICJ Reports 2004, p. 136, para. 109.

[107] Brownlie, PRINCIPLES OF PUBLIC INTERNATIONAL LAW 5; Akehurst, *Custom as a Source of International Law*, 1, 8–10.

[108] *See* Schachter, INTERNATIONAL LAW IN THEORY AND PRACTICE 336; Simma and Alston, *The Sources of Human Rights Law*, 82, 99–100; Meron, *The Continuing Role of Custom in the Formation of International Humanitarian Law*, 238, 240–1 (quoting Richard Baxter, *Multilateral Treaties as Evidence of Customary International Law*, 41 BRITISH YEARBOOK OF INTERNATIONAL LAW 275, 300 (1968)).

[109] Baxter, *Multilateral Treaties as Evidence of Customary International Law*, 300 ('The firm statement by the State of what it considers to be the rule is far better evidence of its position than what can be pieced together from the actions of that country at different times and in a variety of contexts'). *See* discussion *supra*, Chapter 8.A.ii (Customary International Law).

[110] Akehurst, *Custom as a Source of International Law*, 26–7; Eduardo Jiménez de Aréchaga, *International Law in the Past Third of a Century*, 159 RECUEIL DES COURS 7, 29 (1978) (Custom is 'the product of general consensus, not of individual State consent, express or implied'); Charney, *Universal International Law*, 536–8; Tomuschat, *Obligations Arising for States Without or Against Their Will*, 290; Dinstein, *The Interaction Between Customary International Law and Treaties*, 282 ('The requirement that the practice of States be general does not mean that the practice has to be shared by all nations: custom is not grounded on unanimity').

[111] Gennady Danilenko, *International* Jus Cogens*: Issues of Law-Making*, 2(1) EUROPEAN JOURNAL OF INTERNATIONAL LAW 42, 49–50 (1991); Hannikainen, PEREMPTORY NORMS (*JUS COGENS*) IN INTERNATIONAL LAW 216; Rozakis, THE CONCEPT OF *JUS COGENS* IN

Convention, peremptory norms are accepted and recognized by the international community *as a whole*. The meaning of this clause, it may be recalled, was explained by the Chairman of the Drafting Committee at the UN Conference on the Law of Treaties:

> [B]y inserting the words 'as a whole' ... the Drafting Committee had wished to stress that there was no question of requiring a rule to be accepted and recognized as peremptory by all States. It would be enough if a very large majority did so; that would mean that, if one State in isolation refused to accept the peremptory character of a rule, or if that State was supported by a very small number of States, the acceptance and recognition of the peremptory character of the rule by the international community as a whole would not be affected.[112]

This is consistent with the primary emphasis placed upon *opinio juris sive necessitatis* in the emergence of customary international law.[113] What this means, in effect, is that the State may be bound by a customary norm without its consent. Although attempts have been made to reconcile this binding aspect of custom within the rubric of State consent, through doctrines of 'implied consent' or 'consent through acquiescence',[114] the Vienna Convention on Succession of States in Respect of Treaties (1978) effectively quashed such theories.[115] There is no way a 'new State' can be imagined to have consented to a customary norm that emerged before it, to which it is nevertheless bound. The consequence of this reasoning was applied in the context of *jus cogens* by the Arbitration Committee of the Conference on Yugoslavia in 1992: '[T]he peremptory norms of general international law and, in particular, respect for the fundamental rights of the individual and the rights of peoples and

THE LAW OF TREATIES 77–78; Sztucki, JUS COGENS AND THE VIENNA CONVENTION ON THE LAW OF TREATIES 99.

112 UNCLOT First Session (1968) 472, para. 12 (statement by Mr Yasseen).

113 *See* discussion *supra*, Chapter 8.A.ii (Customary International Law).

114 *See* Jonathan Charney, *The Persistent Objector Rule and the Development of Customary International Law*, 56 BRITISH YEARBOOK OF INTERNATIONAL LAW 1, 16–21 (1985) (rejecting such theories); Gerald Fitzmaurice, *The Law and Procedure of the International Court of Justice, 1951–54: General Principles and Sources of Law*, 30 BRITISH YEARBOOK OF INTERNATIONAL LAW 1, 68–9 (1953) (identifying such theories as imprecise representations of *opinio juris*).

115 Vienna Convention on Succession of States in Respect of Treaties, 1946 UNTS 3, Article 5 (1978) ('The fact that a treaty is not considered to be in force in respect of a State by virtue of the application of the present Convention shall not in any way impair the duty of that State to fulfil any obligation embodied in the treaty to which it is subject under international law independently of the treaty').

minorities, are binding on all the parties to the succession.'[116] An explanation that appears to adhere more closely to practice is provided by the social need of the international community as a whole, expressed by *opinio juris sive necessitatis*, which is evidenced by State practice but not dependent upon it for purposes of consent to be bound by customary international law:

> When the question of consent is directly addressed, most writers argue that States do not have the free will to decide whether or not to be bound by rules of international law. The obligation to conform to rules of international law is not derived from the voluntary decision of a State to accept or reject the binding force of a rule of law. Rather, it is the societal context which motivates States to have an international law and obligates them to conform to its norms.[117]

This treatment of consent to norms of customary international law conforms to both the contemporary formulation of custom by the International Court and the prevailing function of *opinio juris sive necessitatis* in contemporary jurisprudence.[118] It supports the interpretation of State practice as declaratory of *opinio*, not its exclusive determinant, and thereby not necessary for a particular State to be bound by the norm that emerges from it.

This secondary reliance upon State practice, in the context of *jus cogens*, highlights an important corollary, which is that the individual State lacks the capacity to affect its legal obligations arising from a peremptory norm of general international law. As much is indicated in the statement by the Chairman of the Drafting Committee at the UN Conference on the Law of Treaties cited above.[119] The emergence of a norm of customary international law does not depend upon the universal practice or consent of each individual State.[120] A norm emerging through a customary process which is accepted and recognized by the international community as a whole as a peremptory norm permits no derogation.[121] Implicit in these two elements of *jus cogens* – customary formation and non-derogability – is application of the rule in the

[116] Conference on Yugoslavia Arbitration Committee, Opinions on Questions Arising from the Dissolution of Yugoslavia (11 January and 4 July 1992), Opinion No. 1, 31 ILM 1488, 1496 (1992).

[117] Charney, *The Persistent Objector Rule and the Development of Customary International Law*, 16.

[118] *See* discussion *supra*, Chapter 8.A.ii (Customary International Law).

[119] UNCLOT First Session (1968) 472, para. 12 (statement by Mr Yasseen).

[120] *See supra*, *n.* 110. [121] 1155 UNTS 331, Article 53 (1969).

broadest possible sense: to all States.[122] Therefore persistent objection, the theory according to which a State might evade customary legal obligation by consistent denunciation, is not applicable to *jus cogens*.[123] To this effect, the clearest examples of the inefficacy of the persistent objector exemption to legal obligations arising under a norm of *jus cogens* is found in the international response to policies of apartheid imposed by South Africa and Rhodesia.[124]

The inability of the State to affect its obligations arising under a peremptory norm is reflected in the restriction of its freedom to make reservations when acceding to an instrument concerning the enforcement of a peremptory norm. In 1950, the UN General Assembly submitted to the International Court three questions of a theoretical nature concerning reservations to the Genocide Convention, which were subsequently answered in the Advisory Opinion, *Reservations to the Genocide Convention* (1951).[125] In its Opinion, the Court found it relevant to consider the object and purpose of the Convention when contemplating the validity of reservations, observing that the 'principles underling the Convention are principles which are recognized by civilized nations as binding on States, even without any conventional obligation'.[126] Consequently, the Court concluded that the 'object and purpose of the Convention thus limit both the freedom of making reservations and that of objecting to them'.[127] The Court explicitly articulated the implication of its statement for State sovereignty:

> It has nevertheless been argued that any State entitled to become a party to the Genocide Convention may do so while making any reservation it chooses by virtue of its sovereignty. The Court cannot share this view. It is obvious that so extreme an application of the idea of State sovereignty could lead to a complete disregard of the object and purpose of the Convention.[128]

[122] *See* discussion *supra*, Chapter 5.C.ii (Universality and Normative Hierarchy).

[123] Dinstein, *The Interaction Between Customary International Law and Treaties*, 285–7; Anthea Roberts, *Traditional and Modern Approaches to Customary International Law: A Reconciliation*, 95 American Journal of International Law 757, 765, 784 (2001); Byers, *Conceptualising the Relationship between* Jus Cogens *and* Erga Omnes *Rules*, 217; Tomuschat, *Obligations Arising for States Without or Against their Will*, 276, 284–90; Charney, *The Persistent Objector Rule and the Development of Customary International Law*, 19 *n*. 81 (1985).

[124] Charney, *The Persistent Objector Rule and the Development of Customary International Law*, 15.

[125] *Reservations to the Genocide Convention*, Advisory Opinion, ICJ Reports 1951, p. 15, 16.

[126] *Ibid*., 23. [127] *Ibid*., 24. [128] *Ibid*.

Since its Advisory Opinion, the Court has formally admitted reservations to procedural aspects of the Convention, notably to the dispute settlement mechanism included under Article IX. Such reservations have been permitted on the basis that they do 'not affect substantive obligations relating to acts of genocide themselves under that Convention' and are thereby not incompatible with its object and purpose.[129] Of course, the principle that a treaty reservation may not be inconsistent with the object and purpose of the treaty itself has since been codified in the Vienna Convention on the Law of Treaties.[130] The importance of this principle to *jus cogens* is that, just as the ability of the State to evade customary obligations arising from peremptory norms through persistent objection is invalid, so too is the freedom of the State to contract out of parallel obligations through reservations to treaties articulating peremptory norms.

The overall limitation of State practice in the context of *jus cogens* is explained by an *opinio juris sive necessitatis* that expresses the social need and values of the international community as a whole, and overrides the particular will and interests of the individual State, in the customary emergence of peremptory norms. In this view, non-derogation, the distinguishing legal effect of *jus cogens* as defined in Article 53 of the Vienna Convention, and which establishes a category of norms independent of the contractual will of the individual State, is expressed also in the emergence and bindingness of peremptory norms. Deference towards the higher interests of the international community over the will of the individual State is indicative of the normative force of the general legal principle from which peremptory norms derive and the social need of the international community that *jus cogens* reflects. It is, therefore, possible to account for the incorporation of this normativity into positive international law through the mechanics of customary international law as the product of social need, expressed as *opinio juris sive necessitatis*, and evidenced by the practice of States.

[129] *Armed Activities on the Territory of the Congo (New Application: 2002) (Congo v. Rwanda)*, ICJ Reports 2006, p. 3, paras. 67–8 (citing *Legality of Use of Force (Yugoslavia v. Spain)*, Provisional Measures, Order of 2 June 1999, ICJ Reports 1999, p. 761, paras. 32–3; *Legality of Use of Force (Yugoslavia v. United States of America)*, Provisional Measures, Order of 2 June 1999, ICJ Reports 1999, p. 916, paras. 24–5).

[130] 1155 UNTS 331, Article 19 (1969) (Forumulation of Reservations).

iii. Shortcomings of customary international law

A minority position deems customary international law insufficient to serve the evidentiary function of a formal source of international law in the context of *jus cogens*.[131] This position requires contemplating the elements of customary international law, State practice and *opinio juris sive necessitatis*, in isolation. This approach problematically neglects that a jurist looks to *opinio juris sive necessitatis*, evidenced by the practice of States, to determine the emergence of customary international law.[132] At the very least, *opinio* necessarily informs which State practice contributes to the emergence of customary international law because, as the International Court noted in *North Sea Continental Shelf*:

> There are many international acts, e.g., in the field of ceremonial and protocol, which are performed almost invariably, but which are motivated only by considerations of courtesy, convenience or tradition, and not by any sense of legal duty.[133]

Apart from this important selection function, *opinio* serves to distinguish customary international law from the incidental amalgamation of congruent State practice. It signifies the norm supported by the practice of States and, according to the International Court, '[i]t is therefore in light of this "subjective element" . . . that the Court has to appraise the relevant practice'.[134] Therefore, it is not possible to contemplate State practice in the absence of *opinio juris sive necessitatis* for the purpose of identifying customary international law.

Nevertheless, one pillar of the critique of a customary source of *jus cogens* is that peremptory norms constitute rules of abstention and,[135] therefore, do not readily emerge from the practice of States.[136] This

[131] Orakhelashvili, PEREMPTORY NORMS IN INTERNATIONAL LAW 113–25; Simma and Alston, *The Sources of Human Rights Law* 103–4; Mark Janis, *The Nature of* Jus Cogens, 3 CONNECTICUT JOURNAL OF INTERNATIONAL LAW 359, 360–1 (1987–8); Onuf and Birney, *Peremptory Norms of International Law* 193.

[132] *See* discussion *supra*, Chapter 8.A.ii (Customary International Law).

[133] *North Sea Continental Shelf (Federal Republic of Germany v. Denmark / Federal Republic of Germany v. Netherlands)*, Judgment, ICJ Reports 1969, p. 3, para. 77.

[134] *Military and Paramilitary Activities in and against Nicaragua (Nicaragua v. United States of America)*, Judgment, ICJ Reports 1986, p. 14, para. 185.

[135] *See* discussion *infra*, Chapter 11.A (Identifying Peremptory Norms).

[136] *See* Orakhelashvili, PEREMPTORY NORMS IN INTERNATIONAL LAW 114; Simma and Alston, *The Sources of Human Rights Law*, 103–4; *cf.* Kammerhofer, *Uncertainty in the Formal Sources of International Law*, 529 (citing Gennady Danilenko, *The Theory of International Customary Law*, 31 GERMAN YEARBOOK OF INTERNATIONAL LAW 9 (1988)

proposition is on its face persuasive, particularly in isolation from *opinio juris sive necessitatis*. However, affirmative State practice may reflect the prohibition of certain conduct. The jurisprudence of the Perminant Court of International Justice, in the *S.S. Lotus* case, conceived of customary international law emerging through the omissions of States.[137] The prohibition against terrorism in international law – recognized to belong to customary international law in 2011 by the Special Tribunal for Lebanon – is a recent example of a prohibitory norm that has crystallized through an abundance of State practice evidencing *opinio juris sive necessitatis*.[138] Moreover, once *opinio juris sive necessitatis* is reintroduced as the basis of customary international law, evidenced by the practice of States, it is clear that abstention may evidence the *opinio* of prohibition; there is no obvious rationale to preclude *opinio juris sive necessitatis* from being evidenced by negative State practice, i.e. abstentions and omissions.[139]

Alternatively, this line of reasoning observes that State practice concerning norms protecting the human person 'does not "run between" States in any meaningful sense' and thereby lacks an element of interaction necessary under international law to constitute State practice.[140] While a State's policy, for example, not to torture may not seem to constitute the clearest form of State practice, and does not 'run between' States, the universe of State practice provides a multitude of opportunities for State practice to evidence such a prohibition – for example, in 'diplomatic correspondence, policy statements, press releases, the opinions of official legal advisors, official manuals on legal questions ... executive decisions and practices, orders ... comments by governments on [ILC] drafts ... state legislation, international and national judicial decisions, recitals in treaties and other international instruments, a pattern of treaties in the same form, the practice of international organs,

(distinguishing between 'abstention from acts' and 'passive practice')) (noting that this issue is really one concerning the function of *opinio juris*).

137 *The Case of the S.S. Lotus*, 1927 PCIJ Series A, No. 10, 28 ('Even if the rarity of the judicial decisions to be found among the reported cases were sufficient to prove in point of fact the circumstance alleged ... it would merely show that States had often, in practice, abstained ... and not that they recognized themselves as being obliged to do so; for only if such abstention were based on their being conscious of having a duty to abstain would it be possible to speak of an international custom').

138 STL Interlocutory Decision (2011), para. 100.

139 *See* discussion *supra*, Chapter 8.A.ii (Customary International Law).

140 Simma and Alston, *The Sources of Human Rights Law* 99; *see* Orakhelashvili, Peremptory Norms in International Law 115.

and [certain UN General Assembly resolutions]'.[141] A restrictive view of State practice that admits certain of these forms of State-to-State interaction to the exclusion of others, and to the detriment of protections of the human person, is not clearly supported by contemporary international jurisprudence concerning customary international law.[142]

If State practice is effectively disqualified from evidencing the emergence of peremptory norms of abstention concerning State conduct toward the human person, so it goes, then the framework of customary international law must inappropriately rest solely on *opinio juris sive necessitatis* without account of State practice.[143] This conclusion presupposes again that *opinio* can be determined in isolation of State practice by which it is evidenced, a proposition undermined by the role of State practice in the emergence of peremptory norms discussed above,[144] and evidenced in practice below.[145] It is unclear how *opinio juris sive necessitatis* might be distilled in isolation from practice. Pronouncements by the International Court since *Continental Shelf* have relied chiefly upon 'the *opinio juris of States* [as] confirmed by practice' to determine the crystallization of a customary norm.[146] States are the authors of *opinio juris sive necessitatis* as well as the practice that evidences it, even where that *opinio* reflects the interests of the international community of States as a whole. Therefore *opinio juris sive necessitatis* is itself inextricably linked to State practice and is unintelligible in isolation from the practice of States, which remains so where primacy is placed upon the subjective expression of *opinio juris sive necessitatis* rather than the objective practice evidencing it.

Even so, this proposition leads neatly to the claim that peremptory norms do not emerge through the consent of States, which a basis in State practice would otherwise ensure.[147] This non-consensual nature,

[141] Brownlie, PRINCIPLES OF PUBLIC INTERNATIONAL LAW 5; *see* Akehurst, *Custom as a Source of International Law*, 4–11, 53.

[142] *See* discussion *supra*, Chapter 8.A.ii (Customary International Law) (the 1950 *Asylum Case* is cited for this proposition; however, it does not necessarily reflect contemporary jurisprudence).

[143] *See, e.g.*, Simma and Alston, *The Sources of Human Rights Law*, 100.

[144] *See* discussion *supra*, Chapter 8.A.ii (Customary International Law).

[145] *See* discussion *infra*, Chapter 11.A (Identifying Peremptory Norms).

[146] *Military and Paramilitary Activities in and against Nicaragua (Nicaragua v. United States of America)*, Judgment, ICJ Reports 1986, p. 14, para. 184 (emphasis added); *see Legality of the Threat or Use of Nuclear Weapons*, Advisory Opinion, ICJ Reports 1996, p. 226, para. 64.

[147] *See, e.g.*, Charney, *Universal International Law*, 536–8.

discussed below,[148] is manifest in the universal, non-derogable qualities of *jus cogens*, and provides the foundation for the proposition that consent-based formal sources of law are unsuitable to account for norms not dependent upon State consent. As also discussed below, this claim may overextend the evidentiary function of formal sources of international law. Moreover, because peremptory norms belong to general international law, it is far from clear that such norms would in any event depend upon individual State consent for evidentiary or authoritative purposes.[149]

Perhaps most compelling is the observation that the imperative legal effects of peremptory norms are fatal to an account of the formal source of *jus cogens* based on customary international law, because customary international law can be modified by subsequent State practice and is subject to persistent objection.[150] However, subsequent modification of peremptory norms is not foreclosed as a matter of law. Article 53 of the Vienna Convention indicates that 'a peremptory norm ... can be modified only by a subsequent norm of general international law having the same character'.[151] While such modification may be limited in practice to the point of impossibility,[152] peremptory norms are at least in theory subject to modification by the same evidentiary method that gives rise to them in the first instance. What is more, as discussed below, the legal effects of peremptory norms that preclude persistent objection (universality and non-derogation) result from the material source of *jus cogens* and are severable from the evidentiary function of the formal source of peremptory norms.[153] The supposed shortcomings of an account of the formal source of *jus cogens* based in customary international law do not appear to outweigh the evidence in support of that formal source.

148 *See* discussion *infra*, Chapter 8.C (A New Source of International Law).
149 *See* discussion *supra*, Chapter 8.A.ii (Customary International Law).
150 Weisburd, *The Emptiness of the Concept of* Jus Cogens, 35.
151 1155 UNTS 331, Article 53 (1969).
152 Since the drafting of the Vienna Convention, scepticism has been expressed for the proposition that a peremptory norm would ever in practice be modified as such. *See, e.g.*, UNCLOT Official Records (1968) 321, para. 2 (statement by United Republic of Tanzania) ('It was hard to see how "future developments" could modify the condemnation of the crime of genocide, the slave trade or the use of force').
153 *See* discussion *supra*, 5.C.ii (Universality and Normative Hierarchy).

C A new source of international law

The case has been forcefully made that *jus cogens* evidences the existence of a 'new source' of international law,[154] particularly by scholars who find customary international law unable to serve as the formal source of peremptory norms.[155] This proposition arises principally from two grounds. The first relates to the reality that peremptory norms do not depend upon the consent of every State to have a legally binding effect. If the State can be so bound notwithstanding the absense of consent, then 'consensual' sources of international law are not sufficient to account for *jus cogens*. The second ground draws upon the legal effects of universality and non-derogability that characterize norms belonging to *jus cogens*. Specifically, the legal effects of peremptory norms cannot be accounted for through existing sources of international law because no existing source of law, dependent upon State consent, can immunize a norm based upon that consent from subsequent State practice by rendering it universal and non-derogable.[156] Each of these propositions is considered in turn.

i. Consent

The formal sources of international law satisfy evidentiary considerations pursuant to the ascertainment of rules of international law.[157] The assertion that norms belonging to *jus cogens* do not depend on consent and therefore cannot emerge through existing sources of law relies upon an understanding of the formal sources of international law defined by parameters of consent. It is true enough that evidence of a rule typically coincides with consent to that rule and its binding force; however, these

[154] *See* Orakhelashvili, PEREMPTORY NORMS IN INTERNATIONAL LAW 109; Bruno Simma, *From Bilateralism to Community Interest in International Law*, 250 RECUEIL DES COURS 292 (1994) (concluding that the formal source of peremptory norms is of little significance); Hannikainen, PEREMPTORY NORMS (*JUS COGENS*) IN INTERNATIONAL LAW 11–12; Simma and Alston, *The Sources of Human Rights Law*, 99.

[155] *See* discussion *supra*, Chapter 8.B.iii (Shortcomings of Customary International Law).

[156] *See* Orakhelashvili, PEREMPTORY NORMS IN INTERNATIONAL LAW 108 ('The conceptual difficulty thus arising is how consensual sources can give rise to norms that apply to States despite their consent and are concerned with the *a priori* hierarchy of norms which can operate despite and above the will of States expressed in traditional sources of law').

[157] *See* Jean d'Aspremont, FORMALISM AND THE SOURCES OF INTERNATIONAL LAW 12–14 (Oxford University Press 2011).

elements remain separate and distinct.[158] The formal sources of international law should not be conflated with voluntarism,[159] as illustrated by brief consideration of the formal sources of international law and their binding force.

A treaty evinces a binding agreement between acceding States as a formal source of law and as such provides evidence of the rule running between States; however, it binds those parties not because of their consent per se, but by the principle of *pacta sunt servanda*.[160] Therefore the source of legal obligation to uphold the agreement is distinct from the evidence of the agreement itself, although the two are undoubtedly interrelated and fully overlap in the treaty context. With respect to customary international law, *opinio juris sive necessitatis* and State practice are elements of the formal source of customary international law that evidence the crystallization of a customary rule. Ultimately, however, legal obligation arises from the general consensus of States, which in turn binds members of the international community, rather than consent – express or tacit – to the rule itself.[161] The fact that new States are not permitted upon recognition to select which norms of customary international law to which they agree to be bound illustrates the reality that the binding force of a rule of customary international law is not dependent upon individual consent to the rule.[162] General principles of international law by their very nature are not dependent upon individual State consent for their bindingness; instead, the commonality of 'maxims of law' to legal systems evidences the existence of general principles of

158 *See, e.g.*, Fitzmaurice, *The General Principles of International Law Considered from the Standpoint of the Rule of Law*, 36–47.

159 d'Aspremont, Formalism and the Sources of International Law 21–4.

160 1155 UNTS 331 (1969), Preamble, Article 26 (*pacta sunt servanda* is a 'universally recognized' rule requiring the 'good faith' performance of treaties); *see, e.g.*, Charney, *Universal International Law*, 534; Thomas Franck, The Power of Legitimacy Among Nations 187 (Oxford University Press 1990); C. Wilfred Jenks, Law, Freedom and Welfare 85 (London: Stevens & Sons 1963); Gerald Fitzmaurice, *Some Problems Regarding the Formal Sources of International Law*, *in* Symbolae Verzijl 153, 164 (The Hague: Martinus Nijhoff, Jan Hendrik Willem Verzijl & F. M. van Asbeck eds., 1958).

161 *See, e.g.*, Higgins, Problems and Process 34 ('custom is obligation involuntarily undertaken – that is, not based on the consent of any given state. No state has a veto over the emergence of a customary norm, which attains its status as such through repeated practice accompliched by *opinio juris*'); Charney, *Universal International Law*, 545; D'Amato, The Concept of Custom in International Law 187–99; Fitzmaurice, *Some Problems Regarding the Formal Sources of International Law*, 164.

162 D'Amato, The Concept of Custom in International Law 191–3.

law.[163] With respect to each formal source of international law,[164] consent to varying degrees overlaps with evidence of the existence of a rule; however, the binding force of those sources as a matter of legal obligation is strictly distinct from individual consent and derives from other principles.

Although the claim that *jus cogens* is non-consensual ostensibly implies the need to define a new formal source of international law due to its departure from State voluntarism,[165] the effective role of consent in the existing sources of international law belays that presumption. The formal source of norms belonging to *jus cogens* need only satisfy the evidentiary function required of a formal source to ascertain a rule of international law.[166] As with any other rule of international law, the binding force of the norm implicates a conceptually distinct issue from its existence as a norm of international law. Moreover, a basis of *jus cogens* in customary international law also undercuts the presupposition that peremptory norms emerge independent of the consent of States. Conversely, the critique that peremptory norms are not evidenced by the consent of States – and bind apart from individual State consent – applies equally against customary international law more broadly.[167] The presumption that the formal source of peremptory norms must account for their binding force against non-consenting States relies either upon overextension of the function of the formal sources of international law, or a conflation of the formal sources of international law with State voluntarism. The binding force of *jus cogens* is, in any event, better explained by its materials source, and does not undermine its basis in the existing sources of international law.

ii. Hierarchy

The second pillar in support of a new source of international law is that the imperative legal effects of peremptory norms directly impede the

[163] *See, e.g.*, Kolb, *Principles as Sources of International Law*, 29; Tomuschat, *Obligations Arising for States Without or Against Their Will*, 312; Friedmann, *The Uses of 'General Principles' in the Development of International Law*, 282–4; Fitzmaurice, *The General Principles of International Law Considered from the Standpoint of the Rule of Law*, 7; PCIJ Advisory Committee of Jurists, Procès-Verbaux of the Proceedings of the Committee 335 (1920) (Statement by Lord Phillimore).

[164] 15 UNCIO 355, Article 38 (1945). [165] Danilenko, *International* Jus Cogens 48.

[166] d'Aspremont, Formalism and the Sources of International Law 12–14.

[167] *See* Kammerhofer, *Uncertainty in the Formal Sources of International Law*, 533.

law-making capacity of the State in a way that cannot be accounted for through traditional sources of international law.[168] As discussed above, peremptory norms constrain the State in various ways: a norm belonging to *jus cogens* applies to all States,[169] denies persistent objection,[170] and permits no derogation.[171] An existing source of international law must account for the emergence of norms with these hierarchical effects, otherwise the concept of *jus cogens* may be seen as irreconcilable with those traditional sources.[172]

As discussed in Chapter 5, the material source of *jus cogens* gives rise to its legal effects of non-derogability and universality, those features characteristic of a normative hierarchy in international law.[173] It was observed in this sense by the ILC,[174] at the UN Conference on the Law of Treaties,[175] and following codification of the Vienna Convention,[176] that the subject matter of *jus cogens*, rather than its formal source, gives a norm of that category its peremptory character. The material source of *jus cogens*, which reflects the interests of the international community of States as a whole, finds expression in positive law through *opinio juris sive necessitatis*, an element of the formal source of customary international law.[177] In one illustrative example excerpted above, the Inter-American Commission on Human Rights commented on this point:

> Turning to the rules which govern the establishment of rules of *jus cogens* ... the principal distinguishing feature of these norms is their 'relative indelibility,' in that they constitute rules of customary law which

[168] Orakhelashvili, Peremptory Norms in International Law 108; Ulrich Scheuner, *Conflict of Treaty Provisions with a Peremptory Norm of General International Law*, 29(4) Zeitschrift für auslandisches offentlisches Recht und Volkerrecht 28, 30 (1969).

[169] *See* discussion *supra*, Chapter 5.C.ii (Universality and Normative Hierarchy).

[170] *See* discussion *supra*, *nn.* 119–24.

[171] *See* discussion *supra*, Chapter 5.C.i (Non-Derogation).

[172] Orakhelashvili, Peremptory Norms in International Law 114.

[173] *See* discussion *supra*, Chapter 5.C (The Expression of Morality in *Jus Cogens*).

[174] Waldock, Fifth Report, [1966] II YbILC 248, para. 2 (Commentary to Draft Article 50) ('It is not the form of a general rule of international law but the particular nature of the subject-matter with which it deals that may, in the opinion of the Commission, give it the character of *jus cogens*').

[175] UNCLOT First Session (1968) 297, para. 36 (statement by Cuba) ('The essential difference between *jus cogens* rules and other rules of international law lay not in their source but in their content and effects').

[176] *See, e.g.*, Sztucki, Jus Cogens and the Vienna Convention on the Law of Treaties 89; Mosler, *The International Society as a Legal Community*, 84.

[177] *See* discussion *supra*, Chapter 8.B.i (*Opinio Juris Sive Necessitatis*).

> cannot be set aside by treaty or acquiescence but only by the formation of a subsequent customary rule of contrary effect. More particularly, as customary international law rests on the consent of nations, a state that persistently objects to a norm of customary international law is not bound by that norm. Norms of *jus cogens*, on the other hand, derive their status from fundamental values held by the international community, as violations of such peremptory norms are considered to shock the conscience of humankind and therefore bind the international community as a whole, irrespective of protest, recognition or acquiescence . . . Therefore, while based on the same evidentiary sources as a norm of customary international law, the standard for determining a principle of *jus cogens* is more rigorous, requiring evidence of recognition of the indelibility of the norm by the international community as a whole. This can occur where there is acceptance and recognition by a large majority of states, even if over dissent by a small number of states.[178]

By this view, the evidentiary function of customary international law need not account for the legal effects of a rule belonging to *jus cogens* that emerges through a customary process. Instead, the explanation of these peremptory legal effects lies with the material source of *jus cogens*, which itself may find expression through an existing formal source of international law as *opinio juris sive necessitatis*.

***

Advocating a new source of international law is a radical proposition.[179] The schema of formal sources of international law articulated in Article 38 of the ICJ Statute – treaty, custom, and general principles of law – is centuries old.[180] The opposite extreme, that there are simply no specific sources or procedures that inform the establishment of peremptory

[178] *Domingues v. United States*, No. 12.285, Inter-American Commission on Human Rights, Report No. 62/02, paras. 49–50 (2000).

[179] *See, e.g.*, Orakhelashvili, Peremptory Norms in International Law 109–11 ('Therefore, it may be suggested that *jus cogens* is based on an autonomous body of superior rules, independent of any source of international law').

[180] *See* Emer de Vattel, The Law of Nations, or, Principles of the Law of Nature, Applied to the Conduct and Affairs of Nations and Sovereigns, Preliminaries § 27 (Indianapolis, IN: Liberty Fund, Bela Kapossy & Richard Whatmore eds., 2008 [1797]) ('three kinds of law of nations, the *voluntary*, the *conventional*, and the *customary*, together constitute the *positive law of nations*'); *see, e.g.*, *United States. v. The La Jeune Eugenie*, 26 F. Cas. 832 (CCD Mass. 1822) (Story, J.) ('Now the law of nations may be deduced, first, from the general principles of right and justice, applied to the concerns of individuals, and thence to the relations and duties of nations; or, secondly, in things indifferent or questionable, from the customary observances and recognitions of civilized nations; or, lastly, from the conventional or positive law, that regulates the intercourse between states').

norms,[181] is similarly undesirable. The fundamental problem with these propositions is that they untether *jus cogens* from a formal basis in existing international law. Perhaps a compromise position would simply excuse the relevance of the formal source of norms accepted and recognized to belong to *jus cogens* because no evidentiary function is really necessary.[182] This approach does not, however, provide a guide to the future identification of peremptory norms through evidentiary sources. More worryingly, a methodology of identifying peremptory norms independent of formal sources of international law risks eroding the doctrine, or worse, reducing it to a tool of judicial policy-making.

The codification of *jus cogens* in Article 53 of the Vienna Convention was expressly intended to avoid this outcome by delineating a formal source of peremptory norms based on Article 38 of the ICJ Statute, an intent reflected in both the text and the drafting history of the article.[183] An account of the formal source of *jus cogens* consistent with the long-standing sources of international law not only is desirable for the legitimacy of the doctrine itself, but is also consistent with any reasonable canon of interpretation. Although it has been suggested that no institution is capable of announcing or enforcing peremptory norms,[184] courts and tribunals have squarely refuted this claim.[185] Moreover, in so doing, domestic,[186] regional,[187]

181 Hannikainen, Peremptory Norms (*Jus Cogens*) in International Law 11–12.

182 Simma, *From Bilateralism to Community Interest in International Law*, 292 ('once recognition by the "international community as a whole" can be established, the question from which formal source rules of peremptory law can flow is more or less irrelevant'); *cf. Jacobellis v. Ohio*, 378 US 184, 197 (1964) (Stewart, J., Concurring) ('I know it when I see it').

183 *See* discussion *supra*, Chapter 8.B (Article 53 of the Vienna Convention).

184 Weisburd, *The Emptiness of the Concept of* Jus Cogens, 26.

185 *See* discussion *supra*, Chapter 8.D (Juridical Organs).

186 This is the prevailing view, for example, in US jurisprudence: *Ye v. Zemin*, 383 F.3d 620, 625 (7th Cir. 2004); *Buell v. Mitchell*, 274 F.3d 337, 373 (6th Cir. 2001); *Princz v. Fed. Republic of Germany*, 26 F.3d 1166, 1180 (DC Cir. 1994) (Wald, J., Dissenting); *Siderman de Blake v. Republic of Argentina*, 965 F.2d 699, 715 (9th Cir. 1992); *Committee of US Citizens Living in Nicaragua v. Reagan*, 859 F.2d 929, 940 (DC Cir. 1988). *See R. v. Bow Street Metropolitan Stipendiary Magistrate and Others, Ex parte Pinochet Ugarte (No. 3)*, House of Lords (UK), [2000] 1 A.C. 147, 38 ILM 581, 589 (Browne-Wilkinson, L.), 622 (Hope, L.) (1999); *C v. Director of Immigration*, Court of First Instance (Hong Kong), HCAL 132/2006, [2008] 2 HKC 165, ILDC 1119, para. 133 (2008); *Kenya Section of the International Commission of Jurists v. Attorney General et al.*, High Court (Kenya), [2011] eKLR, ILDC 1804, para. 67 (2011).

187 *See, e.g., Al-Adsani v. United Kingdom*, ECtHR, No. 35763/97, paras. 30, 60 (2001); *Domingues v. United States*, No. 12.285, IACHR, Report No. 62/02, paras. 49–50 (2000) (citing Restatement (Third) of Foreign Relations Law of the United States § 102 and *n*. 6 (1987).

ad hoc,[188] and international[189] courts have affirmed that customary international law is the formal source of *jus cogens*. Support for a new source of international law, based on the legal effects of *jus cogens* or shortcomings of customary international law, misapprehends the function of formal sources of international law and falls short of compelling a departure from the text and drafting history of Article 53 of the Vienna Convention.

D Judicial organs

Courts and tribunals are instrumental to the recognition of peremptory norms in their adjudicatory capacity. The jurisprudence of *jus cogens* has evolved through the judgments of domestic and international judicial organs as a kind of international common law,[190] and courts and tribunals generally look to assessments by other judicial organs to determine whether a peremptory norm has crystallized in international law. In practice, such pronouncements have proven to be the most authoritative expressions of the existence of particular peremptory norms as well as their legal effects.[191]

The International Court of Justice has identified most peremptory norms either explicitly or by reference to obligations *erga omnes* deriving therefrom, including the prohibitions of slavery,[192] war crimes (grave violations of humanitarian law),[193] crimes against

[188] *See, e.g., Prosecutor v. Furundžija*, IT-95-17/1, paras. 153–4 (1998).

[189] *Questions Relating to the Obligation to Prosecute or Extradite (Belgium v. Senegal)*, Judgment, ICJ Reports 2012, p. 422, para. 99; *Legality of the Threat or Use of Nuclear Weapons*, Advisory Opinion, ICJ Reports 1996, p. 226, para. 79; *North Sea Continental Shelf (Federal Republic of Germany v. Denmark / Federal Republic of Germany v. Netherlands)*, Judgment, ICJ Reports 1969, Sep. Op. Padilla Nervo, 97.

[190] *See, e.g., Al-Bihani v. Obama*, 619 F.3d 1, 17 (DC Cir. 2010) (Kavanaugh, J., concurring in denial of reh'g *en banc*) (describing customary international law as best understood as 'a kind of international common law').

[191] *See* [1966] II YbILC 248, para. 3 (Commentary to Draft Article 50) (considering the content of *jus cogens* to be determined by 'State practice and ... the jurisprudence of international tribunals').

[192] *Jurisdictional Immunities of the State (Germany v. Italy: Greece Intervening)*, Judgment, ICJ Reports 2012, p. 99, para. 93; *Barcelona Traction, Light and Power Company, Limited (Belgium v. Spain)*, Judgment, ICJ Reports 1970, p. 3, paras. 33–4.

[193] *Jurisdictional Immunities of the State (Germany v. Italy: Greece Intervening)*, Judgment, ICJ Reports 2012, p. 99, para. 95 (noting that the *Arrest Warrant Case* concerned 'criminal violations of rules which undoubtedly possess the character of *jus cogens*'); *Legal Consequences of the Construction of a Wall in the Occupied Palestinian Territory*, Advisory Opinion, ICJ Reports 2004, p. 136, para. 157; *Arrest Warrant of 11 April 2000 (Democratic Republic of the Congo v. Belgium)*, ICJ Reports 2002, p. 3, para. 13;

humanity,[194] aggression,[195] genocide,[196] systematic racial discrimination,[197] and torture.[198] The Court has consistently related obligations *erga omnes* arising from such norms to 'elementary considerations of humanity',[199] and observed as a consequence that, although codified by instruments of positive law, such obligations are not territorially limited to the scope of those instruments.[200] The Court has generally referred to

Military and Paramilitary Activities in and against Nicaragua (Nicaragua v. United States of America), Judgment, ICJ Reports 1986, p. 14, para. 79; *The Corfu Channel Case (United Kingdom of Great Britain and Northern Ireland v. Albania)*, Judgment, ICJ Reports 1949, p. 4, 22; *The Case of the S.S. Lotus*, 1927 PCIJ Series A, No. 10, 106 (Dis. Op. Altamira).

194 *Jurisdictional Immunities of the State (Germany v. Italy: Greece Intervening)*, Judgment, ICJ Reports 2012, p. 99, para. 95 (noting that the *Arrest Warrant Case* concerned criminal violations of rules which undoubtedly possess the character of *jus cogens*'); *Arrest Warrant of 11 April 2000 (Democratic Republic of the Congo v. Belgium)*, ICJ Reports 2002, p. 3, para. 13.

195 *Accordance with International Law of the Unilateral Declaration of Independence in Respect of Kosovo*, Advisory Opinion, ICJ Reports 2010, p. 403, para. 81 (finding 'the unlawful use of force' as among 'egregious violations of norms of general international law, in particular those of a peremptory character (*jus cogens*)'); *Barcelona Traction*, ICJ Reports 1970, p. 3, para. 33 (by inference).

196 *Application of the Convention on the Prevention and Punishment of the Crime of Genocide (Bosnia and Herzegovina v. Serbia and Montenegro)*, Judgment, ICJ Reports 2007, p. 43, para. 161; *Armed Activities on the Territory of the Congo (New Application: 2002) (Congo v. Rwanda)*, ICJ Reports 2006, p. 3, paras. 64, 125; *Reservations to the Genocide Convention*, Advisory Opinion, ICJ Reports 1951, p. 15, 23 (by later reference).

197 *Armed Activities on the Territory of the Congo (New Application: 2002) (Congo v. Rwanda)*, ICJ Reports 2006, p. 3, para. 78; *Barcelona Traction*, ICJ Reports 1970, p. 3, para. 33 (by inference).

198 *Questions Relating to the Obligation to Prosecute or Extradite (Belgium v. Senegal)*, Judgment, ICJ Reports 2012, p. 422, para. 99; *Ahmadou Sadio Diallo (Republic of Guinea v. Democratic Republic of the Congo)*, Merits, Judgment, ICJ Reports 2010, p. 639, para. 87 (by inference).

199 *Legal Consequences of the Construction of a Wall in the Occupied Palestinian Territory*, Advisory Opinion, ICJ Reports 2004, p. 136, para. 157; *Legality of the Threat or Use of Nuclear Weapons*, Advisory Opinion, ICJ Reports 1996, p. 226, paras. 79, 95; *Military and Paramilitary Activities in and against Nicaragua (Nicaragua v. United States of America)*, Judgment, ICJ Reports 1986, p. 14, para. 218; *Reservations to the Genocide Convention*, Advisory Opinion, ICJ Reports 1951, p. 15, 23; *The Corfu Channel Case (United Kingdom of Great Britain and Northern Ireland v. Albania)*, Judgment, ICJ Reports 1949, p. 4, 22.

200 *See Armed Activities on the Territory of the Congo (New Application: 2002) (Congo v. Rwanda)*, ICJ Reports 2006, p. 3, para. 64; *Reservations to the Genocide Convention*, Advisory Opinion, ICJ Reports 1951, p. 15, 23 ('The first consequence arising from this conception is that the principles underlying the [Genocide] Convention are principles which are recognized by civilized nations as binding on States, even without any conventional obligation').

jus cogens in contentious cases only, illustrating the practical limitation of reliance upon the Court to authoritatively articulate peremptory norms: it principally has occasion to refer to the category only where a dispute arises pertaining to the legal effects of *jus cogens*.[201] In this capacity, however, the Court is uniquely positioned to not only develop a jurisprudence of *jus cogens*, but also resolve discordance across the practice of other courts and tribunals, as it did with respect to the effect of *jus cogens* on the jurisdictional immunity of the State.[202]

Other international tribunals have contributed to the jurisprudence of *jus cogens* through decisions concerning both the content and the legal effects of the category. Though preceding the nomenclature of *jus cogens*, the IMT at Nuremberg observed that the prohibitions of aggression, war crimes, and crimes against humanity reflected customs of universal recognition arising from the practice of States and general principles of law.[203] The norms identified by the IMT at Nuremberg have been considered to

[201] *Questions Relating to the Obligation to Prosecute or Extradite (Belgium v. Senegal)*, Judgment, ICJ Reports 2012, p. 422, para. 99 (finding *erga omnes* obligations arising from *jus cogens* prohibition of torture sufficient under Torture Convention to grant third-State standing before the court); *Jurisdictional Immunities of the State (Germany v. Italy: Greece Intervening)*, Judgment, ICJ Reports 2012, p. 99, para. 93 (finding *jus cogens* prohibitions of war crimes and slavery substantive rules with no impact on the procedural rule of State immunity under customary international law); *Accordance with International Law of the Unilateral Declaration of Independence in Respect of Kosovo*, Advisory Opinion, ICJ Reports 2010, p. 403, para. 81 (noting illegality of declarations of independence connected with 'the unlawful use of force', as among 'egregious violations of norms of general international law, in particular those of a peremptory character (*jus cogens*)'); *Application of the Convention on the Prevention and Punishment of the Crime of Genocide (Bosnia and Herzegovina v. Serbia and Montenegro)*, Judgment, ICJ Reports 2007, p. 43, para. 161 (finding international responsibility of Serbia for breach of obligations *erga omnes* arising from *jus cogens* prohibition of genocide); *Armed Activities on the Territory of the Congo (New Application: 2002) (Congo v. Rwanda)*, ICJ Reports 2006, p. 3, paras. 64, 78, 125 (finding *jus cogens* status of prohibitions of genocide and racial discrimination at issue insufficient to engage the jurisdiction of the court); *Arrest Warrant of 11 April 2000 (Democratic Republic of the Congo v. Belgium)*, ICJ Reports 2002, p. 3, paras. 56–60 (finding no exception to immunity *ratione personae* of foreign minister for *jus cogens* violations of war crimes and crimes against humanity).

[202] *Jurisdictional Immunities of the State (Germany v. Italy: Greece Intervening)*, Judgment, ICJ Reports 2012, p. 99, para. 93; *see* discussion *infra*, Chapter 15.D (Jurisdictional Immunity of the State).

[203] *Nazi Conspiracy and Aggression*, International Military Tribunal at Nuremberg, Opinion and Judgment, 51 (1946) ('The law of war is to be found not only in treaties, but in the customs and practices of states which gradually obtained universal recognition, and from the general principles of justice applied by jurists and practiced by military courts. This law is not static, but by continual adaptation follows the needs of a changing world. Indeed, in many cases treaties do no more than express and define for more accurate reference the principles of law already existing').

be 'the direct ancestors of the universal and fundamental norms recognized as *jus cogens*'.[204] Since the codification of the Vienna Convention, the *ad hoc* international criminal tribunals for the former Yugoslavia and Rwanda have recognized *jus cogens*: the ICTY articulated the peremptory status of the prohibitions of genocide,[205] war crimes,[206] crimes against humanity,[207] torture,[208] and terrorism[209] as belonging to *jus cogens*, and found domestic amnesties inapplicable to *jus cogens* violations.[210] The International Criminal Tribunal for Rwanda (ICTR) has recognized the prohibition of genocide to belong to *jus cogens*.[211] The STL pronounced on the emergence of a customary norm prohibiting terrorism (presumably *jus cogens* in nature, but the Tribunal did not employ this language).[212] And the SCSL invoked the duty of States to prosecute *jus cogens* violations as justification for the prosecution of genocide, war crimes, and crimes against humanity, notwithstanding broad amnesty granted by the Lomé Agreement.[213] The SCSL further found that a domestic amnesty law covering *jus cogens* violations 'would not be accorded international legal recognition'[214] and could not deprive the court or other States of the power to prosecute international crimes by application of universal jurisdiction.[215]

In the jurisprudence of regional courts, the European Court of Human Rights (ECtHR) has acknowledged the *jus cogens* status of the prohibitions of torture and crimes against humanity as well as certain legal

204 *Siderman de Blake v. Republic of Argentina*, 965 F.2d 699, 715 (9th Cir. 1992) (quoting *Barcelona Traction*, ICJ Reports 1970, p. 3, para. 33).

205 *Prosecutor v. Brđanin*, IT-99-36-T, para. 680 (2004); *Prosecutor v. Kristic*, IT-98-33-T, para. 541 (2001); *Prosecutor v. Jelisić*, IT-95-10-T, para. 60 (1999).

206 *Prosecutor v. Kupreškić*, IT-95-16-T, paras. 519–20 (2000) (referring to prohibitions of genocide, war crimes, and crimes against humanity as norms of international humanitarian law that are also *jus cogens*).

207 *Ibid.*

208 *Prosecutor v. Simić*, IT-95-9/2-S, para. 34 (2002); *Prosecutor v. Kunarac et al.*, IT-96-23-T / IT-96-23/1-T, para. 466 (2001); *Prosecutor v. Delalić et al.* IT-96-21-T, para. 454 (1998); *Prosecutor v. Furundžija*, IT-95-17/1-T, paras. 153–4 (1998).

209 *Prosecutor v. Galić*, Judgment, IT-98-29-T, paras. 98, 769 (2003).

210 *Prosecutor v. Furundžija*, IT-95-17/1-T, paras. 155–6 (1998).

211 *Prosecutor v. Kayishema and Ruzindana*, ICTR-95-1-T, para. 88 (1999).

212 STL Interlocutory Decision (2011), para. 102.

213 *Prosecutor v. Gbao*, Decision on Preliminary Motion on the Invalidity of the Agreement between the United Nations and the Government of Sierra Leone on the Establishment of the Special Court for Sierra Leone, SCSL-04-15-PT-141, paras. 9–10 (2004).

214 *Prosecutor v. Kondewa*, Decision on Lack of Jurisdiction/Abuse of Process, Amnesty Provided by the Lomé Accord, SCSL-04-14-T-128-7347, paras. 45–52 (2004) (quoting *Prosecutor v. Furundžija*, IT-95-17/1, para. 155 (1998)).

215 *Prosecutor v. Kallon and Kamara*, Decision on Challenge to Jurisdiction: Lomé Accord Amnesty, SCSL-04-15-PT-060-I, paras. 60, 66–71 (2004).

effects of this status,[216] and the European Court of Justice (ECJ) examined other parameters of the concept, such as the compatibility of UN Security Council Resolutions with *jus cogens*.[217] The IACtHR has acknowledged the prohibitions of slavery,[218] torture,[219] crimes against humanity,[220] and racial discrimination[221] as belonging to *jus cogens*; the Inter-American Commission on Human Rights has extended *jus cogens* to other humanitarian concepts.[222] The IACtHR has also articulated

[216] *Jones v. United Kingdom*, ECtHR, Nos. 34356/06 & 40528/06, paras. 210–14 (2014) (finding interaction between sovereign immunity and *jus cogens* in 'a state of flux'); *Othman v. United Kingdom*, ECtHR, No. 8139/09 paras. 253–5, 266–7 (2012) (finding *jus cogens* prohibition of torture absolutely precludes admission of evidence obtained by torture, and threat of such admission at applicant's retrial upon deportation to Jordan sufficient to engage ECHR Article 6 (denial of justice)); *Ould Dah v. France*, No. 13113/03, 48 ILM 884, 894–6 (2009) (endorsing denial of immunity *ratione materiae* by French courts for *jus cogens* violation of torture); *Demir and Baykara v. Turkey*, ECtHR, No. 34503/97, para. 73 (2009) (recognizing *jus cogens* prohibition of torture); *Kalogeropoulou v. Greece and Germany*, ECtHR, No. 59021/00 (2002) (recognizing jurisdictional immunity of the State notwithstanding *jus cogens* status of prohibition of crimes against humanity); *Al-Adsani v. United Kingdom*, ECtHR, No. 35763/97 (2001) (recognizing jurisdictional immunity of the State notwithstanding *jus cogens* status of prohibition of torture).

[217] *Kadi et al. v. Council of the European Union et al.*, C-402/05 P / C-415/05 P, [2008] ECR I-6351, paras. 281–2, 286–8 (finding European Community judicature could not review compatibility of UN Security Council Resolution with *jus cogens*, but endorsing review of lawfulness of implementing European Community measures. This judgment overturned the General Court's prior finding that *jus cogens* had not been violated by a Security Council resolution that identified Kadi as a possible supporter of Al-Qaeda, and associated sanctions.).

[218] *Aloeboetoe et al. v. Suriname*, IACtHR Series C No. 15, paras. 56–7 (1993) (finding that Article 53 of the Vienna Convention would void a 1762 treaty granting Surinamese tribe, the Saramankas, autonomy because it provided for capture and sale of slaves). *See* discussion *supra*, Chapter 5, text accompanying *nn.* 91–5.

[219] *See, e.g.*, *Bayarri v. Argentina*, IACtHR Series C No. 187, para. 81 (2008); *Servellón García and ors v. Honduras*, IACtHR Series C No. 152, paras. 89–97 (2006); *Ximenes-Lopes v. Brazil*, IACtHR Series C No. 149 (2006); *Baldeón García v. Peru*, IACtHR Series C, No. 147, para. 117 (2006); *Ramírez v. Guatemala*, IACtHR Series C No. 126, para. 117 (2005); *Ceaser v. Trinidad and Tobago*, IACtHR Series C, No. 123, para. 100 (2005); *Tibi v. Ecuador*, IACtHR, Series C, No. 114, para. 143 (2004); *Brothers Gomez Paquiyauri v. Peru*, IACtHR Series C, No. 110, paras. 111–12 (2004).

[220] *Miguel Castro-Castro Prison v. Peru*, IACtHR Series C No. 160, paras. 402–4 (2006); *Almonacid Arellano et al. v. Chile*, IACtHR Series C No. 154, paras. 99, 128–9 (2006).

[221] *See, e.g.*, *Servellón García and ors v. Honduras*, IACtHR Series C No. 152, paras. 89–97 (2006); *Yatama v. Nicaragua*, IACtHR Series C No. 127, para. 184 (2005); *The Juridical Condition and the Rights of Undocumented Migrants*, IACtHR, Advisory Opinion OC-18/03, Series A No. 18, paras. 97–101, 110–11 (2003).

[222] *Domingues v. United States*, No. 12.285, IACHR Report No. 62/02, para. 49 (2000) (in reference to prohibition of the death penalty).

other effects related to *jus cogens*, such as the non-applicability of statutes of limitations,[223] the invalidity of amnesties,[224] and the duty of the State to prevent and punish violations of *jus cogens*.[225] And international arbitral bodies, including the Permanent Court of Arbitration,[226] and the International Centre for Settlement of Investment Disputes (ICSID),[227] have recognized various effects and constraints of *jus cogens*.

Finally, a range of domestic judgments have articulated the *jus cogens* status of various norms in international law and explored the contours of their legal effects across a diverse jurisprudence. This jurisprudence includes pronouncements by the national courts of Argentina,[228]

223 *Almonacid Arellano et al. v. Chile*, IACtHR Series C No. 154, paras. 99, 128–9 (2006).

224 *Gelman v. Uruguay*, IACtHR Ser. C No. 221, paras. 99, 183, 223, 240 (2011); *Gomes-Lund et al. (Guerrilha do Araguaia) v. Brazil*, IACtHR Series C No. 219, paras. 134–7 (2010); *Almonacid Arellano et al. v. Chile*, IACtHR Series C No. 154, paras. 28–9 (2006); *Barrios Altos Case*, IACtHR Series C No. 75, para. 41 (2001).

225 *La Cantuta v. Peru*, IACtHR Series C No. 162, para. 160 (2006); *Miguel Castro-Castro Prison v. Peru*, IACtHR Series C No. 160, paras. 402–4 (2006).

226 *Dispute Concerning Access to Information Under Article 9 of the OSPAR Convention (Ireland v. United Kingdom)*, Permanent Court of Arbitration, Final Award, 42 ILM 1118, paras. 84, 100–3 (2003).

227 *Continental Casualty Company v. Argentina*, Decision on Application for Partial Annulment, ICSID Case No. ARB/03/9, para. 117 (2011) (finding principle of necessity can be invoked in any context against any international obligation apart from a norm of *jus cogens*); *Sempra Energy International v. Argentina*, Decision on Argentina's Application for Annulment of the Award, ICSID Case No. ARB/02/16, paras. 197, 202 (2010) ('While some norms of customary law are peremptory (*jus cogens*), others are not, and States may contract otherwise'); *Azurix Corporation v. Argentina*, Decision on Application for Annulment, ICSID Case No. ARB/01/12, para. 90 (2009) (noting that a treaty is capable of modifying otherwise binding customary international law, to the exclusion of *jus cogens*); *Phoenix Action Limited v. Czech Republic*, Award, ICSID Case No. ARB/06/5, para. 77 (2009) ('This has been stated for the WTO law stemming from the Marrakech Agreements of 1994: States in their treaty relations can contract out of one, more or in theory, all rules of general international law (other than those of *jus cogens*)') (internal quotation marks omitted); *CMS Gas Transmission Company v. Argentina*, Award, ICSID Case No. ARB/01/8, IIC 65, para. 325 (2005) (finding that the defence of necessity requires impairment of 'the essential interest of the international community as a whole', or 'that a peremptory norm of international law [*jus cogens*] might have been compromised').

228 *Riveros v. Office of the Public Prosecutor*, Supreme Court of Justice (Argentina), M/2333/XLII, ILDC 1084, paras. 15, 32–8 (2007); *Chile v. Arancibia Clavel*, Supreme Court of Justice (Argentina), A/533/XXXVIII, ILDC 1082, para. 28 (2004); *Office of the Prosecutor v. Priebke*, Supreme Court of Justice (Argentina), P/457/XXXI, ILDC 1599, paras. 2–5 (1995); *Washington Cabrera J. E. c. Comisión Técnica Mixta de Salto Grande*, Supreme Court of Justice (Argentina), Fallas 1993-305-2150, Opinion of Guastavino and Gabrielli, paras. 9–11 (1983).

Australia,[229] Austria,[230] Belgium,[231] Bosnia and Herzegovina,[232] Canada,[233] Chile,[234] Colombia,[235] the Czech Republic,[236] France,[237] Germany,[238]

[229] *Habib v. Australia*, Federal Court of Australia Full Court, [2010] FCAFC 12, ILDC 1518; *Zhang v. Zemin*, New South Wales Court of Appeal (Australia), [2010] NSWCA 255; *Regina v. Tang*, High Court of Australia, [2008] HCA 39, paras. 110–17 (Kirby, J.); *Nulyarimma and Others v. Thompson / Buzzacott v. Minister for the Environment and Others*, Federal Court of Australia, [1999] FCA 1192, 120 ILR 353, paras. 57 (Whitlam, J.), 178, 186 (Merkel, J.) (1999).

[230] *A.A. v. Austria*, Supreme Court of Austria, No. 1Ob225/07f, para. 4.3 (2008); *Anita W. v. John Adam II (Prince of Liechtenstein)*, Supreme Court of Austria, No. 7Ob316/00x, ILDC 1, para. 13 (2001); Supreme Court of Austria, Decision No. 11Os139/98 (1998).

[231] *R.D. v. Belgium*, Court of Cassation (Belgium), No. P.04.1211.N, JT 2005, 322, ILDC 6, para. 24 (2004); *Re Sharon and Yaron*, Court of Cassation (Belgium), No. P.02.1139.F/2, JT 2003, 243, ILDC 5 (2003); Court of Appeal (Bruxelles), 127 ILR 110, 114, 120 (2002); Jugoslovenski *Aerotransport v. Belgium*, Court of Appeal (Bruxelles), No. 1998/KR/528, para. 3.2 (1999).

[232] *Prosecutor's Office v. Anić*, Court of Bosnia and Herzegovina (Section I for War Crimes), S1 1 K 005596 11 Kro, ILDC 1907, paras. 27–8 (2011).

[233] *Regina v. Munyaneza*, Montreal Superior Court (Criminal Division) (Canada), 2009 QCCS 2201, paras. 70–9 (2009); *Victoria (City) v. Adams*, Supreme Court of British Columbia (Canada), 2008 BCSC 1363, para. 162 (2008) (quoting *Suresh*, *infra*); *Bouzari v. Islamic Republic of Iran*, Court of Appeal for Ontario (Canada), 71 OR (3d) 675, paras. 57–73 (2004); *Suresh v. Canada (Minister of Citizenship and Immigration)*, Supreme Court (Canada), [2002] 1 SCR 3, paras. 46, 59–64; *Regina v. Finta*, Supreme Court (Canada), 1 SCR 701, 22 (1994).

[234] *Re Víctor Raúl Pinto v. Relatives of Tomás Rojas*, Supreme Court (Chile), Decision on Annulment, No. 3125–04, ILDC 1093, paras. 29–31 (2007).

[235] *Gallón Giraldo y Otros v. Colombia*, Constitutional Court (Colombia), No. C-370/2006, ILDC 660, para. 4.9.6 (2006); *Constitutional Case No. C-225/95*, Constitutional Court (Colombia), No. C-225/95 (1995) (quoted in *Mapiripán Massacre v. Colombia*, IACtHR Series C No. 134, para. 115 (2005)).

[236] *Novotný v. Ministry of Justice*, Constitutional Court of the Czech Republic, No. I ÚS 601/04, ILDC 990, para. 34 (2007).

[237] *Lydienne X v. Prosecutor*, Court of Cassation (Criminal Division) (France), No. 12-81676, ILDC 2035, paras. 10.4, 14 (2013); *Réunion Aérienne v. Socialist People's Libyan Arab Jamahiriya*, Court of Cassation (Civil Division) (France), No. 09-14743, 150 ILR 630, 634 (2011); *Ely Ould Dah Case*, Gard Assizes Court (France), No. 70/05 (Arrêt de condamnation) / No. 71/05 (Arrêt statuant sur les intérêts civils) (2005).

[238] *Attorney of the Federal Armed Forces v. Anonymous (a Major of the Armed Forces)*, Federal Administrative Court (Germany), 2 WD 12:04, ILDC 483, paras. 4.1.4.1.1, 4.1.6 (2005); *East German Expropriation Case, Mr von der M*, BVerfG [Constitutional Court] (Germany), 2 BvR 955/00, ILDC 66, paras. 97–8, 116 (2004); *Jorgic Case*, BVerfG [Constitutional Court] (Germany), 2 BvR 1290/99, ILDC 132, paras. 17, 26–7 (2000); *Former Syrian Ambassador to the German Democratic Republic*, BVerfG [Constitutional Court] (Germany), 2 BvR 1516/96, 115 ILR 596, 608–9, 613–14 (1997).

Greece,[239] Hong Kong,[240] Israel,[241] Italy,[242] Kenya,[243] Latvia,[244] Namibia,[245] The Netherlands,[246] New Zealand,[247] Peru,[248] The Philippines,[249]

[239] *Margellos v. Federal Republic of Germany*, *Anotato Eidiko Dikastirio* (Special Supreme Court) (Greece), No. 6/2002, 129 ILR 525, paras. 13–15 (2002); *Prefecture of Voiotia v. Federal Republic of Germany (Distomo Massacre Case)*, Court of Cassation (*Areios Pagos*) (Greece), No. 11/2000, 129 ILR 513, 521 (2000).

[240] *C, KMF and BF v. Director of Immigration and Secretary for Security*, Court of Final Instance (Hong Kong), FACV Nos. 18/19/20 2011 (2013); *C v. Director of Immigration*, Court of First Instance (Hong Kong), HCAL 132/2006, [2008] 2 HKC 165, ILDC 1119, paras. 78, 133–5 (2008).

[241] *Attorney-General (Israel) v. Eichmann*, Supreme Court (Israel), 36 ILR 5 (1962) (by inference).

[242] *Germany v. De Guglielmi et al.*, Court of Appeal (Italy), No. 941/2012, ILDC 1905, para. 15 (2012); *Lozano v. Italy*, Court of Cassation (First Criminal Chamber) (Italy), No. 31171/2008, ILDC 1085, para. 6 (2008); *Germany v. Mantelli and ors*, Court of Cassation (Italy), Preliminary Order on Jurisdiction, No. 14201/2008, ILDC 1037, para. 11 (2008); *Ferrini v. Germany*, Court of Cassation (Civil Section) (Italy), No. 5044/2004, ILDC 19 (2004); *Germany v. Milde*, Court of Cassation (First Criminal Section) (Italy), No. 1072/2009, ILDC 1224 (2009).

[243] *Kenya Section of the International Commission of Jurists v. Attorney General et al.*, High Court (Kenya), [2011] eKLR, ILDC 1804, paras. 64–7, 74–5, 99 (2011); *R.M. v. Attorney General*, High Court (Kenya), Civil Case 1351, AHRLR 256 (KeHC 2006), ILDC 699, paras. 47, 75 (2006).

[244] *Kariņš and ors v. Parliament of Latvia and Cabinet of Ministers of Latvia (Border Treaty)*, Constitutional Court (Latvia), No. 2007-10-0102, ILDC 884, paras. 10, 25.6 (2007).

[245] *Minister of Defence v. Mwandinghi*, High Court (Namibia), 1991 (1) SA 851 (Nm), 91 ILR 343, 352–4 (1990), *affirmed by* Supreme Court (Namibia), 1992 (2) SA 355 (NmS), 91 ILR 358 (1991).

[246] *Stichting Mothers of Srebrenica and ors v. Netherlands and United Nations*, Supreme Court (Netherlands), LJN: BW1999, ILDC 1760, paras. 4.3.7–4.3.14 (2012); *Association of Lawyers for Peace (Vereniging van Juristen voor de Vrede) and ors v. Netherlands*, Supreme Court (Netherlands), LJN: AN8071, ILDC 152, paras. 3.2–3.4 (2004); *Bouterse Case*, Amsterdam Court of Appeal (Netherlands), Nos. R 97/163/12 Sv & R 97/176/12 Sv, para. 5 (2000), *abrogated on other grounds by Bouterse Case*, Supreme Court (Netherlands), LJN: AB1471, ILDC 80 (2001).

[247] *Fang v. Jiang*, High Court (New Zealand), [2007] NZAR 420, ILDC 1226, para. 26 (2006); *Mansouri-Rad v. Department of Labour*, Refugee Status Appeals Authority (New Zealand), No. 74665/03, [2005] NZAR 60, ILDC 217, para. 63 (2005); *Attorney General v. Ahmed Zaoui and ors*, Supreme Court (New Zealand), SC CIV 19/2004, [2005] NZSC 38, ILDC 81, para. 51 (2005).

[248] *Rivera Lazo and ors*, Superior Court (Third Criminal Chamber) (Peru), No. 28-2001, ILDC 1887, para. 16 (2010); *Fujimori Case*, Supreme Court (Specialized Criminal Law Chamber) (Peru), No. 19-2001 AV, ILDC 1516, para. 711 (2009); *see Peru v. Chile*, Supreme Court (Chile), No. 2242-06, ILDC 1443 (2007).

[249] *Muna et al. v. Romulo et al.*, Supreme Court (Philippines), G.R. No. 159618, ILDC 2059, paras. 40–50, 89–94 (2011).

Poland,[250] Russia,[251] South Africa,[252] South Korea,[253] Spain,[254] Slovenia,[255] Switzerland,[256] the United Kingdom,[257] and

[250] *Natoniewski v. Germany*, Supreme Court (Poland), No. IV CSK 465/09, 2010 Polish Yearbook of International Law 299, 302, ILDC 1996 (2010).

[251] *H. v. Prosecutor General Office*, Supreme Court (Russia), N KAS06-129, ILDC 1361, Reference 5 (2006).

[252] *Mthembu v. State*, Supreme Court of Appeal (South Africa), No. 379/07, (2008) ZASCA 51, ILDC 958 (2008); *Van Zyl and ors v. Government of South Africa and ors*, North Gauteng High Court (South Africa), No. 20320/02, [2005] ZAGPHC 70, ILDC 171, paras. 20–1 (2005); *Kaunda v. President of South Africa and ors*, Constitutional Court (South Africa), No. CCT 23/04, 2005 (4) SA 235 (CC), ILDC 89, paras. 28–9 (2004).

[253] *Yeo and ors v. Nippon Steel & Sumitomo Metal*, High Court (South Korea), 2012 Na 44947, ILDC 2104, Reference 3 (2013).

[254] *Criminal Law Chamber of the Supreme Court et al. v. Garzón Real*, Supreme Court (Spain), No. 101/2012, ILDC 1855, para. 3 (2012); *Guatemala Genocide Case*, National Court (Spain), Response to the Guatemala Constitutional Court, No. 331/1999, 4 (2008); *Scilingo Manzorro v. Spain*, Supreme Court (Spain), No. 798/2007, ILDC 1430, paras. 6–7 (2007); *Guatemala Genocide Case (Menchú Tumn and ors v. Two Guatemalan Government Officials and Six Members of the Guatemalan Military)*, Constitutional Court (Criminal Chamber) (Spain), Spanish Constitutional Court Decision Accepting Jurisdiction, No. 237/2005, ILDC 137 (2005); *Public Prosecutor's Office and ors v. Scilingo Manzorro*, National Court (*Audiencia Nacional*) (Criminal Chamber) (Spain), No. 16/2005, ILDC 136, paras. B.1–B.2, B.4–B.5 (2005).

[255] *Arbitration Agreement Opinion Procedure*, Constitutional Court (Slovenia), Rm-1/09-26, ILDC 1485, para. 26 (2010); *One Third of the National Assembly Deputies*, Constitutional Court (Slovenia), Rm-1/00-29, ILDC 402, para. 14 (2001); *A.A. v. Germany*, Constitutional Court (Slovenia), Up-13/99-24, paras. 13–14 (2001).

[256] *A. (Kahled Nezzar) v. Office of the Attorney General*, Federal Criminal Court (Switzerland), No. BB.2011.140 (TRIAL trans. 2012); *A. v. State Secretariat for Economic Affairs and Federal Department of Economic Affairs*, First Public Law Chamber (Switzerland), No. 1A 48/2007, ILDC 1201, para. 7 (2008); *A. v. Federal Department of Economic Affairs*, Federal Supreme Court (Switzerland), No. 2A 783/2006, ILDC 1200, paras. 8.1–8.4, 9.2 (2008); *Nada v. State Secretariat for Economic Affairs and Federal Department of Economic Affairs*, Federal Supreme Court (Switzerland), No. 1A 45/2007, ILDC 461, paras. 7.3–7.4 (2007).

[257] *R. (on the application of Al-Jedda) v. Secretary of State for Defence*, House of Lords (UK) [2007] UKHL 58, para. 35 (Bingham, L.); *Jones v. Ministry of the Interior of Saudi Arabia and Lieutenant Colonel Abdul Aziz*, House of Lords (UK), [2006] UKHL 26; *R. (on the application of Hilal Abdul-Razzaq Ali Al-Jedda) v. Secretary of State for Defence*, Court of Appeal (UK), [2006] EWCA Civ 327, paras. 67, 75 (Brooke, L. J.); *K. v. Secretary of State for the Home Department*, House of Lords (UK), [2006] UKHL 46, para. 8 (Bingham, L.); *R. (on the application of Al Rawi and ors) v. Secretary of State for Foreign and Commonwealth Affairs et al.*, Court of Appeal (UK), [2006] EWCA Civ 1279, para. 102 (Laws, L. J.); *A. and Others v. Secretary of State for the Home Department (No. 2)*, House of Lords (UK), [2005] UKHL 71, paras. 30–4 (Bingham, L.); *R. (on the application of European Roma Rights Centre) v. Immigration Officer at Prague Airport*, House of Lords (UK), [2004] UKHL 55, para. 46 (Steyn, J.); *R. (on the application of Al-Skeini and ors) v. Secretary of State for Defence*, High Court of Justice (UK), [2004] EWHC 2911

Zimbabwe.[258] Federal courts of the United States have referred to causes of action for piracy,[259] slavery,[260] war crimes,[261] crimes against humanity,[262] genocide,[263] torture,[264] apartheid,[265] and terrorism,[266] as arising from *jus cogens* or, by proxy, the 'law of nations'.[267] Though not exhaustive, this survey indicates the breadth of jurisprudence that has evolved at the national level to further refine *jus cogens*, concerning not only the content of the category, but also its effects and limitations.[268] And, unlike cases before the International Court, which have primarily related to disputes arising from proceedings for violations of *jus cogens* norms, domestic cases concern the direct effect and enforcement of peremptory norms through criminal prosecutions and civil proceedings for *jus cogens* violations.

(Admin.), para. 216 (Rix, L. J.); *Kuwait Airways Corporation v. Iraqi Airways Company*, House of Lords (UK) [2002] UKHL 19, para. 114 (Steyn, L.); *Campaign for Nuclear Disarmament v. Prime Minister of the United Kingdom and ors*, High Court of Justice (UK), (2002) EWHC 2777 (Admin.), paras. 17, 47 (Brown, L. J.); *R. v. Bow Street Metropolitan Stipendiary Magistrate and Others, Ex parte Pinochet Ugarte (No. 3)*, House of Lords (UK), [2000] 1 A.C. 147, 38 ILM 581 (1999).

258 *Mann v. Republic of Equatorial Guinea*, High Court (Zimbabwe), No. CA 507/07, [2008] ZWHHC 1, 153 ILR 697, 711–12 (2008) (Patel, J.).

259 *Institute of Cetacean Research v. Sea Shepherd Conservation Society*, 725 F.3d 940, 943 (9th Cir. 2013); *United States v. Dire*, 680 F.3d 446, 454 (4th Cir. 2012) *cert. denied*, 133 S. Ct. 982 (2013).

260 *Doe I v. Unocal Corp.*, 395 F.3d 932, 945 (9th Cir. 2002) *on reh'g en banc sub nom. John Doe I v. Unocal Corp.*, 403 F.3d 708 (9th Cir. 2005); *Sampson v. Federal Republic of Germany*, 250 F.3d 1145, 1154, *n.* 5 (7th Cir. 2001).

261 *Sarei v. Rio Tinto, PLC*, 487 F.3d 1193, 1202 (9th Cir. 2007) *on reh'g en banc*, 550 F.3d 822 (9th Cir. 2008); *Kadic v. Karadzic*, 70 F.3d 232, 243 (2nd Cir. 1995).

262 *Sarei*, 487 F.3d at 1202; *Princz v. Federal Republic of Germany*, 26 F.3d 1166, 1182 (DC Cir. 1994) (Wald, J., Dissenting).

263 *Abelesz v. Magyar Nemzeti Bank*, 692 F.3d 661, 676 (7th Cir. 2012); *Sarei v. Rio Tinto, PLC*, 671 F.3d 736, 759 (9th Cir. 2011) *cert. granted, judgment vacated sub nom. Rio Tinto PLC v. Sarei*, 133 S. Ct. 1995 (2013) (citing *Bosnia v. Serbia*, 2007 ICJ Reports 91, para. 161).

264 *Unocal Corp.*, 395 F.3d at 945; *In re Estate of Ferdinand Marcos, Human Rights Litigation*, 25 F.3d 1467, 1475 (9th Cir. 1994).

265 *Sarei v. Rio Tinto, PLC*, 671 F.3d 736, 675 (9th Cir. 2011) *cert. granted, judgment vacated sub nom. Rio Tinto PLC v. Sarei*, 133 S. Ct. 1995 (2013); *In re South African Apartheid Litigation*, 617 F. Supp. 2d 228, 240–1 (SDNY 2009); *Sarei v. Rio Tinto, PLC*, 487 F.3d 1193, 1197 (9th Cir. 2007) *on reh'g en banc*, 550 F.3d 822 (9th Cir. 2008).

266 *Flatow v. Islamic Republic of Iran*, 999 F.Supp. 1, 23 (DDC 1998). *But see Tel-Oren v. Libyan Arab Republic*, 726 F.2d 774, 807 (DC Cir. 1984) (Bork, J., Concurring).

267 See discussion *infra*, 12.B (Individual Civil Responsibility).

268 For a description of the relevant holdings in the cases listed *supra nn.* 228–58, *see infra*, Chapter 20 (Annex).

Although judiciaries are not the delegated arbiters of *jus cogens*, a clear role for courts and tribunals has emerged in international law by which their pronouncements on the emergence of *jus cogens* carry particular weight. As the ICJ is 'the principal judicial organ of the United Nations', perhaps its legitimacy to speak for the international community with respect to *jus cogens* follows accordingly.[269] The *ad hoc* criminal tribunals, as 'organs' of the Security Council, might also be seen to enjoy unique authority as arbiters of international norms.[270] The SCSL, for example, was established pursuant to a request by the Security Council, to the UN Secretary-General, to establish 'a Tribunal based on the highest international standards of criminal justice';[271] the court viewed its own formation as 'an expression of the will of the international community'.[272]

Decisions rendered by regional and domestic courts have also been recognized as authoritative statements of the content and effects of *jus cogens*. For example, judgments by the US Second Circuit Court of Appeals,[273] and the UK House of Lords,[274] were recognized to be the authoritative pronouncements that the prohibition of torture belonged to *jus cogens*,[275] in addition to the *Furundžija* judgment by the ICTY,[276] and prior to the decision of the International Court in *Questions Relating to the Obligation to Prosecute or Extradite* (2012).[277] In this sense, the

[269] Charter of the United Nations, Article 92 (1945). *See* N. G. Onuf, *Further Thoughts on a New Source of International Law: Professor D'Amato's 'Manifest Intent'*, 65 AMERICAN JOURNAL OF INTERNATIONAL LAW 774, 778 (1971) ('the authoritative voice of the International Court of Justice, speaking, as it were, for the international community, seems to have affirmed the legitimacy of these general norms outside the conventional sources of international law. And this is another way of saying that the World Court is helping to legitimate a new source of law. This new source is seen in specific relation to general norm-creating treaty provisions, but it has been argued here that the latter are part of a generic class of community actions which also include certain General Assembly resolutions').

[270] *See Prosecutor v. Tadić*, Decision on the Defence Motion for Interlocutory Appeal on Jurisdiction, IT-94-1-A, paras. 28–47 (1995) (discussing UNSC Chapter VII authority to establish international tribunals).

[271] SC Res. 1757, UN Doc. S/Res/1757 (2007).

[272] *Prosecutor v. Taylor*, No. SCSL-03-01-I-059, Decision on Immunity from Jurisdiction, para. 38 (2004).

[273] *Filartiga v. Pena-Irala*, 630 F.2d 876 (2nd Cir. 1980).

[274] *R. v. Bow Street Metropolitan Stipendiary Magistrate and Others, Ex parte Pinochet Ugarte (No. 3)*, House of Lords (UK), [2000] 1 A.C. 147, 38 ILM 581 (1999).

[275] *Al-Adsani v. United Kingdom*, ECtHR, No. 35763/97 (2001).

[276] *Prosecutor v. Furundžija*, IT-95-17/1-T, paras. 153–4 (1998).

[277] *Questions Relating to the Obligation to Prosecute or Extradite (Belgium v. Senegal)*, Judgment, ICJ Reports 2012, p. 422, para. 99.

contribution of national courts to the jurisprudence of *jus cogens* suggests a particular role for judicial organs more generally that is not exclusive to organs of the international community. This is perhaps unsurprising given that the enforcement of *jus cogens* norms against individuals who commit international crimes necessarily resides primarily with domestic judiciaries as a practical matter, in addition to international criminal tribunals.[278] While the International Court recently referred to judgments of national courts as 'State practice of particular significance',[279] this observation may understate the role of domestic courts in contributing to an international jurisprudence of *jus cogens*.

More broadly, judicial practice indicates that, in the absence of an international legislative organ endowed with the authority to codify peremptory norms, evidence of their emergence through application by judicial organs at every level serves the function of effectuating *jus cogens* norms accepted and recognized by the international community.[280] In such instances, courts and tribunals are not exercising legislative competence in contradistinction to that of the State.[281] Rather, by basing their pronouncements in *opinio juris sive necessitatis* evidenced by State practice, judicial organs are best positioned, and have occasion, to articulate the existence of peremptory norms in their law-applying capacities. So long as the international community lacks formal legislative institutions, it is foreseeable that judicial organs will continue to play an important role in authoritatively recognizing the culmination of the customary process through which peremptory norms emerge. To ensure fidelity to the positive sources of international law,[282] it is critical that judiciaries are transparent in their

[278] *See* discussion *infra*, Part IV (Peremptory Norms and the Individual).

[279] *Jurisdictional Immunities of the State (Germany v. Italy: Greece Intervening)*, Judgment, ICJ Reports 2012, p. 99, para. 55.

[280] This function of courts is familiar to the common law tradition. *See* H. L. A. Hart, The Concept of Law 138 (Oxford: Clarendon Press 1961) ('The law . . . is what the courts say it is').

[281] *Cf.* Kolb, *Principles as Sources of International Law*, 10–11; Oscar Schachter, *The Nature and Process of Legal Development in International Society*, *in* The Structure and Process of International Law: Essays in Legal Philosophy, Doctrine and Theory 766 (The Hague: Martinus Nijhoff, Ronald St John Macdonald & Douglas Johnston eds., 1983); Charney, *Universal International Law*, 537–8.

[282] d'Aspremont, Formalism and the Sources of International Law 12–14 (namely, the ascertainment of rules and evidence of rules of international law).

application of the formal source of peremptory norms to orient *jus cogens* jurisprudence in the requisite *opinio juris sive necessitatis* and practice of States.[283]

[283] *Compare* STL Interlocutory Decision (2011), paras. 29–89 (undertaking an extensive survey of *opinio juris sive necessitatis* evidenced in the practice of States to confirm the international crime of terrorism had crystallized in customary international law), *with Siderman de Blake v. Republic of Argentina*, 965 F.2d 699, 717 (9th Cir. 1992) (citing repeated reference to the status of torture as an international crime without reference to formal sources, then concluding, '[i]n light of the unanimous view of these authoritative voices, it would be unthinkable to conclude other than that acts of official torture violate customary international law . . . Given this extraordinary consensus, we conclude that the right to be free from official torture is fundamental and universal, a right deserving of the highest status under international law, a norm of *jus cogens*').

9

Normativity and positivism: a reconciliation

Social contract theory provides a perspective for the way the legislative mechanism of *opinio juris sive necessitatis* incorporates the higher interests of the international community into norms belonging to *jus cogens*. The theory of the social contract is predicated upon the *idea* of a *contract*; that is, the expression of common interests of individuals through an instrument that establishes the authority of civil society formed to realize those interests. For early contractarians, consent was the linchpin to a historical narrative of the establishment of civil society in which parties to the social contract, by expression of their collective interest, enter into civil society and subject themselves to its associated norms. In practice, however, the notion of consent was generally taken to be interchangeable with tacit consent, compromising the social contract's claim to historicity. Ultimately, the notion of consent to a contract fell away completely, leaving the social contract without the explicit contractual element that had defined earlier theories. Rather, a legislative principle emerged based upon the interests that individuals comprising a community *ought* to agree to rather than what was (or might have been) explicitly or implicitly undertaken through consent. This principle, the general will, replaced consent in later contractarian thought and necessarily relinquishes any historical claim to the formation of civil society, taking its formation instead as given.

Hobbes's account of civil society relies upon consent as the legislative principle of the social contract. In accordance with the laws of nature, individuals enter into a contract with one another, through which they unite into a single will and submit to the leviathan – to whom sovereignty is transferred – in exchange for peace and security.[1] Contract, according to Hobbes, is understood as the 'mutual transferring of Right' and may be concluded either expressly or through

[1] Thomas Hobbes, LEVIATHAN II.17.85–8 (London: Penguin Books, C. B. McPherson ed., 1985 [1651]).

inference (i.e. tacit consent).[2] Locke similarly accounts for the formation of political society as the product of consent, defining political society as 'nothing but the consent of any number of free men capable of a majority to unite and incorporate into such a society'.[3] The purpose of this civil society is to enforce the law of nature, and individuals express this common interest by forfeiting their individual rights to enforce the law of nature, through the social contract, in exchange for political order guaranteeing their natural rights. In practice, the historicity of the operative principle of agreement in Locke's theory of the social contract is understood to constitute a form of tacit consent.[4] Tacit consent is conceptualized as a form of 'voluntary assent and acquiescence' by which individual participation in, and enjoyment of, aspects of civil society constitute an expression of their will to be bound.[5]

Rousseau and Kant employ an ostensibly dissimilar legislative principle that distances their social contract theories from notions of consent. According to Rousseau, the social contract between the individual and society is governed by neither explicit consent, nor tacit consent, but rather the general will of society as a whole.[6] Indeed, Rousseau's solution to the ills of the states of nature and society is a form of association by which its members unite not under their individual wills, but through a 'general will' which 'considers only the common interests' of the people as a whole.[7] A contractual aspect of Rousseau's theory is implicated by the way in which every member of society 'puts his person and all his power in common under the supreme direction of the general will', establishing a corporate personality under which every member is 'an indivisible part of the whole'.[8] However, the general will remains authoritative in its expression of the common interests that every member ought to share. Moreover, the social contract contains a

[2] *Ibid.*, II.14.66.

[3] John Locke, Two Treatises of Government II.8.99 (London: Everyman 2003 [1689]).

[4] *Ibid.*, II.8.119.

[5] *See* John Dunn, *Consent in the Political Theory of John Locke*, 10(2) The Historical Journal 153–82 (1967).

[6] *See* Jeremy Jennings, *Rousseau, Social Contract and the Modern Leviathan*, *in* The Social Contract from Hobbes to Rawls 120 (London: Routledge, David Boucher & Paul Kelly eds., 1994) (observing that Rousseau's social contract is in this sense 'anything but contractual').

[7] Jean-Jacques Rousseau, The Social Contract (Du Contract Social ou Principes Du Droit Politique) II.3 (London: Everyman 2003 [1762]).

[8] *Ibid.*, I.6.

'tacit undertaking' by which society as a whole is vested with the power to compel individuals who refuse to obey the general will to comply, which 'means nothing more than that he will be forced to be free'.[9] This understanding establishes collective reason, rather than consent, as the compelling legislative mechanism of the social contract, which in turn serves as the guiding principle of basic norms of civil society.

Kant adopts Rousseau's depiction of the general will as the legislative principle of civil society, finding that the 'original contract' constitutes the 'basic law, which can arise only from the general (united) will of the people'.[10] By linking social contract theory with his more general moral and political philosophy, Kant is able to develop the notion of the general will to a greater depth. For Kant, the general will (from which the content of public order derives) flows from the categorical imperative, the 'supreme principle of the doctrine of morals', which is expressed by the directive to use humanity, both in one's own person and in others, always as an end and never merely a means.[11] In consequence, norms that emerge through the general will conform to universal laws of practical reason (i.e. natural law). The original contract is the product of this general will, through which individuals escape the state of nature and enter political society by enshrining common interests they ought to share.

As noted above, a consequence of conceptualizing the contract as the product of a general will rather than consent is that such theories eventually abandoned any claim of historicity. For Kant, as for Rousseau, the contract is not intended to account for the origin of civil society, and the former repeatedly cautions against this; rather, it is a legislative concept that gives form to the civil society in which individuals ought to participate.[12] Freeing the original contract from historical fact allows the theory to provide a logical framework without compromising itself

[9] *Ibid.*, I.7.

[10] Immanuel Kant, On The Common Saying: That May Be Correct in Theory, But It Is of no Use in Practice [1793], *in* The Cambridge Edition of the Works of Immanuel Kant 8:295 (Cambridge University Press, Mary Gregor ed., 1996) [hereinafter, Kant, Theory and Practice]; Immanuel Kant, Metaphysics of Morals [1797], in The Cambridge Edition of the Works of Immanuel Kant 6.256 (Gregor ed.) [hereinafter, Kant, Metaphysics].

[11] Immanuel Kant, Groundwork of the Metaphysics of Morals [1795], in The Cambridge Edition of the Works of Immanuel Kant 4:429; 4:437–8 (Gregor ed.) [hereinafter, Kant, Groundwork]; Kant, Metaphysics 6:225–6.

[12] Kant, Theory and Practice 8:297; Kant, Metaphysics 6:315–16; 6:318–19.

with reaching notions of consent, relying instead upon a legislative principle expressing objective common interests (the general will) as its basis of legitimacy. Given the way in which tacit consent would operate in practice in the social contracts of Hobbes and Locke, it is not incomparable in effect to the general will as an expression of the common interests of society.

The legislative mechanism of the social contract offers a perspective from which to better understand the sources of *jus cogens*. In the previous chapter, it was demonstrated that *jus cogens* derives its peremptory authority as an expression of the higher interests of the international community as a whole. This relation corresponds to the way in which contractarianism depicts the basis of the social contract in the common interests of a community necessary to the maintenance of society. The legal category of *jus cogens* is, in this view, conceived to be a product of the socialization of the international community. Enlightenment contractarianism posits legislative mechanisms of tacit consent and general will as the vehicles by which fundamental values and interests of a community are translated into protections of its members through the social contract. By conceiving of imperative norms essential to the maintenance of a community in this way, contractarianism provides a tool that mediates protection of fundamental principles and the emergence of public order norms that ultimately bind all members of a community. A similar process is evidenced by the formation of *jus cogens*.

The normativity implicit in *peremptory* norms of general international law, and their categorical distinction as *jus cogens* from *jus dispositivum*, is evocative of the natural law tradition in international law. In this contemporary iteration, however, positive law admits this normativity through the incorporation of general principles of law, i.e. human dignity, in a way that admits a moral element which produces an imperative, universal quality to the positive law arising therefrom. A kind of inclusive positivism permits such considerations through *opinio juris sive necessitatis*, evidenced by the practice of States, pursuant to the emergence of peremptory norms. In the context of *jus cogens*, the social need depicted by *opinio juris sive necessitatis* is linked to human dignity, a phenomenon that has been referred to as the 'juridical conscience of mankind'.

The idea of the social contract offers a window into the way in which international law negotiates these ostensibly divergent traditions of natural law and legal positivism that converge with *jus cogens*. The social contract depicts the transcription of the most fundamental principles of a community into public order norms upheld by civil society. Tacit consent and general will account for the expression of higher interests that a community shares and characterize the legislative mechanisms through which public order norms emerge. In international law, theories of tacit consent and acquiescence akin to those found in the social contracts of Hobbes and Locke have been proposed, and largely rejected, as an explanation for the binding power of customary international law.[13] Of course, it is this very weakness of contractarianism that led its proponents to concede their claims to historicity and saw later contractarians abandon consent-based explanations altogether. In both instances, this parallel experience suggests that the articulation of public order norms is not a process amenable to reliance upon consent. On the one hand, this might be inferred from the emergence of the general will as a more suitable legislative mechanism in the work of later social contract theorists, one that avoids the pitfalls of a consent-based approach. On the other, this same shift is reflected by the way in which *opinio juris sive necessitatis* has emerged as the primary factor of customary international law, whereby State practice is relied upon for evidence of social need, rather than to document what was, or may have been, consented to implicitly through the practice of each State. Norms belonging to *jus cogens* have, in this view, been conceived as an expression of 'the general will of the international community'.[14] Therefore, '[t]he rise of *jus cogens* norms limits state sovereignty in the sense that the "general will" of the international community of states, and other actors, will take precedence over the individual wills of states to order their relations'.[15]

[13] *See* Jörg Kammerhofer, *Uncertainty in the Formal Sources of International Law: Customary International Law and Some of Its Problems*, 15(3) European Journal of International Law 523, 533 (2004); Stephen Hall, *The Persistent Spectre: Natural Law, International Order and the Limits of Legal Positivism*, 12(2) European Journal of International Law 269, 287–9 (2001); Jonathan Charney, *The Persistent Objector Rule and the Development of Customary International Law*, 56 British Yearbook of International Law 1, 16–21 (1985); James Brierly, The Law of Nations 51–3 (Oxford: Clarendon Press, 6th edn. 1963); Gerald Fitzmaurice, *The General Principles of International Law Considered from the Standpoint of the Rule of Law*, 92(II) Recueil des Cours 36–47 (1957).

[14] Andrea Bianchi, *Enforcing International Law Norms Against Terrorism: Achievements and Prospects*, *in* Enforcing International Law Norms against Terrorism 491, 526 (Oxford: Hart Publishing, Andrea Bianchi & Yasmin Naqvi eds., 2004) (with respect to the prohibition of terrorism).

[15] *Princz v. Federal Republic of Germany*, 26 F.3d 1166, 1182 (DC Cir. 1994) (Wald J., Dissenting) (internal quotation marks omitted).

This parallel is sharpened by the function of human dignity in both the doctrine of *jus cogens* and the Kantian social contract. According to the jurisprudence of *jus cogens*, *opinio juris sive necessitatis* is an expression of social need represented by general principles representative of the higher interests of the international community as a whole, namely, human dignity. This relation reflects the 'juridical conscience of mankind', pursuant to which the legal recognition of non-derogable peremptory norms emerges through customary international law. It may be recalled that, for Kant, the general will (from which the content of public order derives) is linked to the categorical imperative, the 'supreme principle of the doctrine of morals', which is expressed by the practical imperative to use humanity, both in one's own person and in others, always as an end and never merely a means. The categorical imperative, and in turn the Kantian general will, derives from the principle of human dignity, from which flows universal law as well as the moral quality of this law.[16] The Kantian social contract, in turn, is predicated upon a general will according to which human dignity mediates the interaction of individuals within a community by the establishment of civil society. Thus, in both the Kantian social contract and *jus cogens*, human dignity can be seen to underlie much: the higher interests of a community, the intrinsic worth of the individual that must be respected for the maintenance of social coexistence, the principle informing public order norms of society, the quality of the resultant norms as morally prescriptive values (or duties), and the dependence of the universal realization of these duties in a community upon respect owed to other human beings. The observation by the ICTY – that the 'humanisation' of international law, in the context of *jus cogens*, 'marks the translation into legal norms of the "categorical imperative" formulated by Kant in the field of morals' – reflects this understanding of *jus cogens* jurisprudence.[17]

The legislative mechanics of *jus cogens* resemble the way in which the social contract accounts for the emergence of civil society norms independent of the express consent of its members. As one member of the ILC observed during the drafting of the law of treaties, '[u]ltimately, it was more society and less the law itself which defined the content of *jus cogens*'.[18] The public order nature of peremptory norms and their prioritization of community interests over the contractual will of legal subjects

[16] See discussion *supra*, Chapter 5.A (Human Dignity as a Moral Concept).
[17] *Prosecutor v. Kupreškić*, IT-95-16-T, para. 518 (2000).
[18] [1963] I YbILC 73, para. 4 (685th Meeting, statement by Mr Rosenne).

demonstrates the way in which law emerging through this process is hierarchically superior to that concluded by legal subjects. Although *opinio juris sive necessitatis* is evidenced by the practice of States, this process is not bound by the formalism of 'constant and uniform' State practice. The practice of States need not be universal and often takes collective, rather than individual, form; the acts of an individual State, or group of States, are insufficient to affect the emergence of a peremptory norm or legal obligations arising therefrom. Together, the material and formal sources of peremptory norms reflect the public order character of *jus cogens* by elevating the social need of the international community *as a whole* over the preferences of the individual State.

In the context of material and formal sources in international law, this process at first appears to pose a challenge to legal positivism. However, this challenge does not require a departure from the recognized sources of international law. The emergence of peremptory norms is dependent upon *opinio juris sive necessitatis* evidenced by the practice *of States*, thereby orienting the emergence of peremptory norms with the State, the basis of formal sources of international law. And the process culminates in positive law in force in the international community, as reflected by the authoritative pronouncements of judicial organs. The incorporation of public order norms into positive international law thereby retains the formal dimension of positivism through the doctrine of customary international law whilst giving effect to normative considerations hitherto admitted exclusively by the direct influence of natural law. This process bypasses the supposed need to identify a 'new source' of international law to account for *jus cogens*. What is more, the role of State practice in evidencing *opinio juris sive necessitatis* pursuant to the formation of peremptory norms grants a historicity to *jus cogens* that social contract theory to varying degrees lacks. The source of *jus cogens* reflects a kind of general will expressed by the community of States, insofar as the collective interests of the international community of States as a whole are evidenced in, but not limited by, the practice of States. As such, the customary source of *jus cogens* is more closely related to an actual expression of the will of the community than the abstract general will is taken to be, yet is not dependent upon the consent, tacit or otherwise, of each member of the international community to have binding force.

In this sense, social contract theory and *jus cogens* exhibit a common shift away from theories of tacit consent and acquiescence unsustainable in practice towards an explanation of public order which emerges as a manifestation of the higher interests of a community. The legislative mechanism of the social contract is reflected in *jus cogens* as a bridge between divergent doctrinal positions of naturalism and positivism that helps to explain the incorporation of normative elements into positive law. Contractarianism accounts for the emergence of norms necessary to the maintenance of society through the shared values and higher interests of a community, rather than the direct consent of its individual members to such rules. In the context of *jus cogens*, a hybridized source of international law renders intelligible the way customary law and general principles, together, account for the emergence of norms necessary for the social existence of the international community apart from the direct consent of individual States. In practice, this process is based principally upon *opinio juris sive necessitatis*, expressive of the higher interests of the international community, as a proxy for mankind that gives rise to positive rules of *jus cogens*. As such, the emergence of peremptory norms is as much social contract as it is international law. Through its formal and material sources, *jus cogens* can be seen to parallel the social contract as a product of the protection of human dignity as necessary to preserve the society of the international community of States as a whole.

PART IV

Peremptory norms and the individual

A substantive conceptualization of the form and material content of *jus cogens* is elusive in contemporary jurisprudence. To address this lacuna, Chapter 10 identifies the developments of international human rights and international crimes as legal antecedents to contemporary peremptory norms. The conclusions of Part III concerning the sources of peremptory norms are then applied in Chapter 11 to guide a survey of peremptory norms accepted and recognized by the international community as a whole. The nature of individual responsibility arising under international law for violations of peremptory norms is considered in Chapter 12, with particular attention to the doctrines of immunity and amnesty. This part closes with Chapter 13, which relates the material content of *jus cogens* to the form of the social contract, which share key substantive elements signposted in the previous chapters: they both arise through social need, informed by common interests and values of the community, in response to historical exigencies, which give form to individual-oriented norms necessary to socialized coexistence within a community.

10

Contemporary legal foundations

Since its inception, *jus cogens* has been understood to constitute fundamental international norms concerning the individual. It therefore serves to evaluate *jus cogens* not as an isolated element of international law, but as one of a series of important, interrelated legal developments of the period. In the first place, the codification of a catalogue of individual rights, especially following the Second World War, expressed the gradual acceptance of the individual as a subject of legal rights and freedoms in international law. Concurrently, the recognition of individual criminal responsibility for violations of international law established the capacity of the individual to bear duties under international law. Following these developments, the doctrine of *jus cogens* was articulated by the Vienna Convention, evincing the existence of certain non-derogable norms articulating individual protections and duties. The following sections gloss these two aspects of the legal personality of the individual in international law – rights and duties – as presuppositions of *jus cogens.*

A Individual legal personality

It is axiomatic that the individual should have a place in any legal system, even one applying predominantly to States.

> There can be no law without human will. Individuals have always applied international law and individuals have always in the last resort been subjects of international law either directly (as pirates, officers, etc.) or indirectly (as citizens of the state against which sanctions of one kind are applied).[1]

While the debate over the status of the individual in international law was waged largely during the first part of the twentieth century,[2] the

[1] Edvard Hambro, *Individuals Before International Tribunals*, 35 Proceedings of the American Society of International Law at Its Annual Meeting 22, 23 (1941).

[2] *See, e.g.*, Wolfgang Friedmann, *The Changing Dimensions of International Law*, 62(7) Columbia Law Review 1147–65 (1962); Marek Korowicz, *The Problem of the International Personality of Individuals*, 50(3) American Journal of International Law

concept of individual legal personality began to take form at the end of the nineteenth century. One early recognition of the possession of rights by the individual under international law, as a legal person rather than channelled through the State, is found in *The Paquete Habana*, decided by the US Supreme Court in 1898.[3] The case concerned the seizure and sale of two Spanish fishing vessels, *The Paquete Habana* and *The Lola*, as prizes of war by the United States Navy during the Spanish-American War. Ultimately, the United States was obliged to restore the proceeds from the sale of the vessels and any cargo to the owners of the vessels, because they had been wrongly captured in violation of the rights of fishermen under customary international law.[4] In effect, the Court formally declared the actions of a State to have violated the legal rights of an individual, or group of individuals, as a matter of international law. As such, the case is perhaps the earliest expression of individual legal personality in contemporary international law.[5]

Decades later, the League of Nations reinforced this proposition by conferring a range of rights upon minorities through a series of treaties under its minorities protection system, including equality before the law, freedom to use native languages, the right to establish institutions, and the provision of education in native languages.[6] Although only member States could bring petitions alleging the violation of minority rights

533–62 (1956); George Manner, *The Object Theory of the Individual in International Law*, 46(3) AMERICAN JOURNAL OF INTERNATIONAL LAW 428–49 (1952); Philip Jessup, *The Subjects of a Modern Law of Nations*, 45 MICHIGAN LAW REVIEW 383–408 (1952); Lassa Oppenheim, I INTERNATIONAL LAW, A TREATISE 20, 579 (London: Longmans, Green & Company, Hersch Lauterpacht ed., 6th edn. 1947); Phillip Brown, *The Individual and International Law*, 18(3) AMERICAN JOURNAL OF INTERNATIONAL LAW 532–6 (1924).

3 *The Paquete Habana*, 175 US 677, 708 (1900) ('This review of the precedents and authorities on the subject appears to us abundantly to demonstrate that at the present day, by the general consent of the civilized nations of the world, and independently of any express treaty or other public act, it is an established rule of international law, founded on considerations of humanity to a poor and industrious order of men, and of the mutual convenience of belligerent states, that coast fishing vessels, with their implements and supplies, cargoes and crews, unarmed and honestly pursuing their peaceful calling of catching and bringing in fresh fish, are exempt from capture as prize of war').

4 *Ibid.*, 686, 712–14.

5 Mark Janis, *Individuals as Subjects of International Law*, 17 CORNELL INTERNATIONAL LAW JOURNAL 61, 64 (1984) (noting that this decision was rendered 'during the high tide of positivism', making it all the more remarkable).

6 Helmer Rosting, *Protection of Minorities by the League of Nations*, 17(4) AMERICAN JOURNAL OF INTERNATIONAL LAW 641–60 (1923).

before the Council, the rights were nevertheless directly and explicitly conferred upon individuals.

The early twentieth century saw the gradual development of the procedural capacity of the individual to act upon his rights before international judicial organs.[7] The Central American Court of Justice, established at Cartago in 1907 by the Convention of Washington, was the first international tribunal before which the individual had the capacity to make claims on his own behalf against the State. Though the individual could only bring claims against his home State, and the Court heard only five cases before it was dissolved in 1918 (all of which the individual claimants lost), the Court nevertheless represents an important procedural milestone.[8] Similarly, the International Prize Court was established in 1907 by the Hague Convention XII to hear appeals to decisions of national prize courts brought both by neutral States and by private individuals; however, the convention was never ratified.[9] And, following the First World War, Article 297 of the Treaty of Versailles (1919) permitted 'nationals of the Allied and Associated Powers' – i.e. individuals – to appear before Mixed Arbitral Tribunals to bring claims against Germany, thereby allowing nationals of victor States to take legal action against German nationals or the State itself.[10]

These examples demonstrate a nascent recognition of the international rights of the individual and his capacity to exercise them in an international context. Notwithstanding such procedural developments, the overwhelming reality prior to the Second World War remained that international law was concerned primarily with the rules and legal structures of interstate relations.[11] It has been suggested that it is precisely this State-oriented 'science' of international law that allowed for the

[7] P. K. Menon, *The Legal Personality of Individuals*, 6 Sri Lanka Journal of International Law 127, 132–5 (1994) (providing discussion of the examples found in this paragraph).

[8] *Ibid.*

[9] Convention (XII) Relative to the Creation of an International Prize Court, The Hague (18 October 1907), *in* Dietrich Schindler and Jiri Toman, The Law of Armed Conflicts: A Collection of Conventions, Resolutions, and Other Documents 825–36 (Dordrecht: Martinus Nijhoff 1988).

[10] Menon, *The Legal Personality of Individuals*, 127, 132–5 (citing *Lederer v. German Government* (in which the court explicitly recognized the procedural capacity granted to the individual) and *Sigwald v. Germany* (in which the French-German Mixed Arbitral Tribunal noted that, in the context of action brought by a French national, the French government need not intervene).

[11] Wolfgang Friedman, Legal Theory 551 (London: Stevens & Sons 1967).

outbreak of the world wars,[12] illustrative of the practical impact of the prevailing international normative system upon international relations. It comes as little surprise then that the response of the international community in the aftermath of the Second World War was to erect a new international system characterized by the introduction of natural law concepts into positive international law. This process embraced the emergent principle of individual legal personality to codify a catalogue of rights and duties borne by the individual directly, rather than (and indeed not conferred by) the State. The development of individual rights and the normalization of the individual as a legal person in international law are interdependent, mutually reinforcing elements that together established the status of the individual in modern international law.

B The human rights movement

The contemporary human rights regime is rooted in the normative value of human dignity and the codification of basic rights and freedoms common to all mankind. This movement, the legacy of a post-war spirit of cosmopolitanism and pacifism, has largely been realized through the UN system and its emphasis on the promotion and preservation of the dignity of the human person.[13] The commitment by the international community set forth in the UN Charter to promote the dignity and rights of the individual, and the universality of the instrument more generally, prominently establishes human rights as a fundamental priority of the international community.[14] Support for the idea of individual rights is reiterated throughout the instrument, particularly in Article 1(3), which expands the purposes of the United Nations to explicitly include the promotion of human rights.[15] The precedence of human rights in the

[12] Walter Schiffer, The Legal Community of Mankind 257 (New York: Columbia University Press 1954).

[13] *See* Theodor Meron, Human Rights Law-Making in the United Nations (Oxford: Clarendon Press 1986).

[14] Charter of the United Nations, Preamble (1945) ('We the peoples of the United Nations, Determined . . . To reaffirm faith in fundamental human rights, in the dignity and worth of the human person, in the equal rights of men and women and of nations large and small').

[15] *Ibid.*, Article 1(3) (establishing 'The Purposes of the United Nations' to include 'international co-operation in solving international problems of an economic, social, cultural, or humanitarian character, and in promoting and encouraging respect for human rights and for fundamental freedoms for all without distinction as to race, sex, language, or religion').

Charter is demonstrative of both the acknowledgement by States of the importance of the concept to international peace and security, and its overarching commitment to the promotion of those rights internationally, thereby establishing the foundation for human rights legislation of the twentieth century.

It is in the context of the UN system that the 'International Bill of Rights' evolved,[16] consisting of three landmark instruments supporting the development and preservation of individual rights:[17] the Universal Declaration of Human Rights (1948),[18] the International Covenant on Civil and Political Rights (1966),[19] and the International Covenant on Economic, Social and Cultural Rights (1966).[20] The Universal Declaration builds upon the mandate of the Charter by expounding various fundamental rights and freedoms deemed to be inalienable, universal, and conferred upon the individual. The instrument primarily establishes personal, legal, civil, and political rights and includes various social, economic, and cultural rights; many of these latter rights are considered to be aspirational in the sense that they represent a minimal standard of good governance that States are expected to achieve.[21] A similar observation applies to many of the provisions of the two Covenants that followed the Universal Declaration.[22] The ICCPR establishes the aforementioned right to self-determination and expands upon the various civil and political rights established by the Universal Declaration.[23] The Covenant also contains a monitoring mechanism in the form of

[16] Stephen Gardbaum, *Human Rights as International Constitutional Rights*, 19(4) European Journal of International Law 749–68 (2008).

[17] *See* Jack Donnelly, *International Human Rights: A Regime Analysis*, 40(3) International Organization 599–642 (1986); Taslim Elias, New Horizons in International Law 3–19 (The Hague: Martinus Nijhoff 1979).

[18] Universal Declaration of Human Rights, UNGA Res. 217 A (III), A/Res/217 (III) (1948) [hereinafter, Universal Declaration (1948)].

[19] International Covenant on Civil and Political Rights, 99 UNTS 171, Preamble (1966) (*entered into force* 23 March 1976) [hereinafter, ICCPR (1966)].

[20] International Covenant on Economic, Social and Cultural Rights, 993 UNTS 3, Preamble (1966) (*entered into force* 3 January 1976) [hereinafter, ICESCR (1966)].

[21] John Rawls, The Law of Peoples 80 *n*. 24 (Cambridge, MA: Harvard University Press 2001) (identifying UDHR Articles 3 to 18 as 'human rights proper', while clasing other rights delineated by the Declaration as 'liberal aspirations').

[22] Stephen Hall, *The Persistent Spectre: Natural Law, International Order and the Limits of Legal Positivism*, 12(2) European Journal of International Law 269, 302–4 (2001) (suggesting that the inclusion of politicized social and economic rights in the corpus of human rights law has the potential to undermine human rights proper).

[23] ICCPR (1966).

the Human Rights Committee, which is charged with examining State reports on the implementation of rights and investigating individual petitions alleging violations of Covenant provisions.[24] Interestingly, Article 16 restates the sixth Article of the Universal Declaration, 'Everyone shall have the right to recognition everywhere as a person before the law', explicitly denoting the international legal personality of the individual that the provisions of the ICCPR implicitly reinforce.[25] Finally, the ICESCR reiterates the foundational principles of the ICCPR and similarly expands upon the social, cultural, and economic rights articulated by the Universal Declaration.[26] Like the ICCPR, the ICESCR contains a review mechanism by which the Economic and Social Council (ECOSOC) receives and responds to State reports detailing the implementation of Covenant provisions.[27]

Taken together, these instruments affirm the participation of the individual in international law by possessing rights and freedoms directly rather than through the State as a conduit of individual protections. Individual legal personality was expressly confirmed in these terms by the International Court of Justice in *LaGrand (Germany v. United States)*, which concerned implementation of the Vienna Convention on Consular Relations (VCCR) by the United States.[28] With respect to notification requirements of the VCCR, the Court confirmed that such an international instrument 'creates individual rights', 'as opposed to individual rights derivative of the rights of States'.[29] This finding by the Court reflects the culmination of the post-war codification of individual protections in international law. To be sure, treaty-based individual rights are distinct in kind from *jus cogens* insofar as they are based in international conventions rather than customary international law.[30] However this expressly consent-based foundation of human rights legislation, from which individual legal personality definitively emerged, was a critical precursor to the future development of *jus cogens* because States accepted and recognized that international rights condition the relationship between State and individual. This capacity of the individual to possess rights and freedoms in international law is a central presupposition of *jus cogens*, and its development laid the necessary groundwork for the evolution of peremptory norms that transcend a rigid modality of State

[24] *Ibid.*, Articles 28, 40–2. [25] *Ibid.*, Article 16. [26] ICESCR (1966).
[27] *Ibid.*, Articles 16–22.
[28] *LaGrand (Germany v. United States of America)*, ICJ Reports 2001, p. 466.
[29] *Ibid.*, paras. 76–7. [30] *See* discussion *supra*, Chapter 8.A.i (Treaty Law).

consent.[31] The principal point of common relevance to both treaty-based and customary individual rights is that they attach to the individual directly rather than to the State. Without individual legal personality, individual rights under international law could only derive from rights of the State, effectively precluding individual protections that apply to individuals independent of the will of the State. It is for this reason that the gradual recognition of the individual as a subject of protections under international law substantively and structurally precedes the development of *jus cogens*.

C Individual responsibility in international law

Recalling the premise that the right of one individual constitutes the correlative duty of another,[32] implicit in the recognition of individual rights and freedoms in international law is the conception of individual responsibility arising from their violation.[33] Accountability and responsibility for the violation of law, even international law, can only in a literal sense be attributed to the individual who sets the unlawful act into motion, rather than a personified organization of individuals *in abstractum*. It follows from this proposition that sanctions for illicit conduct can only have the requisite effect – via deterrence, punishment, retribution, rehabilitation, and incapacitation – if applied to the individual directly. International criminal law has evolved to recognize the individual as the primary subject of particular duties under international law, identify contrary acts and omissions of the individual to be criminal in nature, and impose responsibility directly upon the individual for such violations of international law.[34] Consequently, the development of individual criminal responsibility has required international law to adopt structural

[31] *See* discussion *supra*, Chapter 10.A (Individual Legal Personality).

[32] Jan Gorecki, *Human Rights: Explaining the Power of a Moral and Legal Idea*, 32 The American Journal of Jurisprudence 153, 160 (1987) ('anyone's right implies someone else's duty').

[33] *See, e.g.*, William Schabas, *International Crimes*, *in* David Armstrong (ed.), Routledge Handbook of International Law (London: Routledge 2009); Bruce Broomhall, International Justice & the International Criminal Court (Oxford University Press 2003); Steven Ratner and Jason Abrams, Accountability for Human Rights Atrocities in International Law (Oxford: Clarendon Press 1987).

[34] Kate Parlett, The Individual in the International Legal System 229 (Cambridge University Press 2011); Roland Portmann, Legal Personality in International Law 162 (Cambridge University Press 2010); Hersch Lauterpacht, International Law and Human Rights 43 (London: Praeger 1950).

and procedural elements of municipal legal systems to accommodate the prosecution of international crimes.

Throughout the early twentieth century, increasing globalization and international interaction necessitated international cooperation to combat a range of 'ordinary' crimes of an inherently transnational nature. The International Criminal Police Congress was convened at Vienna in 1923, where the International Criminal Police Commission (which later took its telegraphic address, INTERPOL, as its common name) was established to promote transnational law enforcement cooperation to combat counterfeiting after the First World War.[35] A catalogue of crimes of an inherently transnational nature have since come to engage individual responsibility.[36] Additionally, the United Nations later articulated a range of crimes of a 'law-enforcement' nature, mostly established through UN conventions on penal matters, including human trafficking,[37] trade in narcotics,[38] organized crime,[39] financing terrorism,[40] and crimes against protected persons.[41] This range of transnational crimes illustrates the practical necessity of an international law that admits the capacity of the individual to bear responsibility for crimes not bound by the borders of the sovereign State yet of general concern to all States. To this end, INTERPOL continues to coordinate mutual assistance and develop institutions to prevent and suppress 'ordinary

[35] *See* Constitution of the International Criminal Police Organization – INTERPOL, Article 1 (*entered into force* 13 June 1956).

[36] For example, espionage, counterfeiting currency, illicit traffic in drugs, slave trading, trading in women and children, pollution of the seas, damaging submarine cable, offences against persons protected by international law, unlawful dispatch of explosives through post, pirate broadcasting, and theft of national and archaeological treasures. *See* Peter Andreas and Ethan Nadelmann, Policing the Globe 3 (Oxford University Press 2006) ('Policing transnational crime has evolved from a limited and ad hoc assortment of police actions and extradition agreements to a highly intensive and regularized collection of law enforcement mechanisms and institutions').

[37] Protocol to Prevent, Suppress and Punish Trafficking in Persons, Especially Women and Children, supplementing the United Nations Convention against Transnational Organized Crime, 2237 UNTS 319 (12 December 2000, *entered into force* 25 December 2003).

[38] Convention against Illicit Traffic in Narcotic Drugs and Psychotropic Substances, 1582 UNTS 95 (20 December 1988, *entered into force* 11 November 1990).

[39] Convention against Transnational Organized Crime, UN Doc. A/55/383 (15 November 2000, *entered into force* 29 September 2003).

[40] International Convention for the Suppression of the Financing of Terrorism, 2178 UNTS 197 (9 December 1999, *entered into force* 10 April 2002).

[41] Convention on the Prevention and Punishment of Crimes against Internationally Protected Persons, including Diplomatic Agents, 1035 UNTS 167 (14 December 1973, *entered into force* 20 February 1977).

crimes'.[42] Because the police functions of crime and punishment are inherently sovereign powers, international coordination in this area marked a significant development in international law and the relations of States.

Distinct from ordinary crimes of a transnational character, international crimes are conceived to be particularly serious violations of international law.[43] The aftermath of the First World War saw the developmental stages of individual criminal responsibility for serious violations of international law. The Treaty of Versailles (1919), which marked the end of the war, provides the conceptual origin of the prosecution of individuals for serious violations of international law, particularly those committed in the name of the State.[44] The Treaty adopted the premise, articulated several years prior in a 1915 Joint Declaration by France, Great Britain, and Russia condemning atrocities committed against Armenians by Turkey, that crimes under international law engage individual responsibility.[45] Articles 227–30 of the Treaty of Versailles delineated the authority of Allied military tribunals to prosecute violations of the laws and customs of war, predicated upon the responsibility of individuals for the most serious violations of humanitarian law.[46] The German Emperor, Wilhelm II, was arraigned under Article 227 'for a supreme offence against international morality and the sanctity of treaties'.[47]

[42] Constitution of the International Criminal Police Organization – INTERPOL, Article 2 (Identifying the 'aims' of Interpol '(1) To ensure and promote the widest possible mutual assistance between all criminal police authorities within the limits of the laws existing in the different countries and in the spirit of the "Universal Declaration of Human Rights"; (2) To establish and develop all institutions likely to contribute effectively to the prevention and suppression of ordinary law crimes').

[43] *See* Hans-Heinrich Jescheck, *International Crimes*, *in* II ENCYCLOPEDIA OF PUBLIC INTERNATIONAL LAW 1122–3 (Amsterdam: North-Holland, Rudolf Bernhard ed., 1995) (distinguishing between 'international crimes in the broad sense' and 'crimes against international law').

[44] Menon, *The Legal Personality of Individuals*, 133–4; Luigi Ferrari-Bravo, *International and Municipal Law: The Complementarity of Legal Systems*, *in* THE STRUCTURE AND PROCESS OF INTERNATIONAL LAW 731 (The Hague: Martinus Nijhoff, Ronald St John Macdonald & Douglas Johnston eds., 1983).

[45] Joint Declaration of France, Great Britain and Russia, RG 59, 867.4016/67 (29 May 1915) ('In view of those new crimes of Turkey against humanity and civilization, the Allied governments announce publicly to the Sublime-Porte that they will hold personally responsible [for] these crimes all members of the Ottoman government and those of their agents who are implicated in such massacres').

[46] The Treaty of Peace Between the Allied and Associated Powers and Germany, Articles 227–30 (signed at Versailles 28 June 1919).

[47] *Ibid.*, Article 227.

However, the Kaiser was never prosecuted, and the largely symbolic nature of the Treaty is demonstrative of the reality that a functional system of individual prosecution for international crimes had not yet reached fruition. A later attempt to establish an international criminal court to prosecute individuals for the international crime of terrorism met a similar fate. The Annex to the Convention for the Prevention and Punishment of Terrorism (1938) contained a Convention for the Creation of an International Court,[48] which provided for a court with jurisdiction over individuals accused of 'acts of terrorism';[49] however, the Convention never entered into force. Although largely unsuccessful, early efforts to prosecute international crimes highlight the recognition that serious violations of international law engage individual responsibility, an important development in the doctrine of responsibility under international law.

Individual criminal responsibility under international law became the legacy of reconciliation in the aftermath of the Second World War. An extensive structure of norms and forces relating to international criminal prosecution took shape, beginning with the Agreement for the Prosecution and Punishment of the Major War Criminals of the European Axis (1945).[50] The related Nuremberg Rules stipulated individual responsibility for certain core crimes – crimes against peace, war crimes, and crimes against humanity – falling within the jurisdiction of the International Military Tribunal (IMT) at Nuremberg,[51] which was established by the 1945 Agreement.[52] In its pioneering Judgment, the Tribunal explained its jurisdiction over individuals, rather than the State, as the parties accountable for grave violations of international law:

> It was submitted that international law is concerned with the actions of sovereign States, and provides no punishment for individuals; and further, that where the act in question is an act of State, those who carry it out are not personally responsible but are protected by the doctrine of the sovereignty of the State. In the opinion of the Tribunal, both these

[48] Convention for the Prevention and Punishment of Terrorism, League of Nations Doc. C.546(I).M.383(I).1937.V (16 November 1937), 19 LEAGUE OF NATIONS O.J. 23 (1938).

[49] *Ibid.*, Annex, Article 1.

[50] Agreement for the Prosecution and Punishment of the Major War Criminals of the European Axis (London Agreement), 82 UNTS 280 (signed at London 8 August 1945).

[51] Nuremberg Rules, *in* Agreement for the Prosecution and Punishment of the Major War Criminals of the European Axis, 82 UNTS 279 (signed at London 8 August 1945).

[52] Charter of the International Military Tribunal, *in* Agreement for the Prosecution and Punishment of the Major War Criminals of the European Axis, 82 UNTS 280 (signed at London 8 August 1945) [hereinafter, IMT Charter (1945)]; *see also* International Military Tribunal for the Far East Charter, TIAS No. 1589, 3, 4 Bevans 20 (19 January 1946).

> submissions must be rejected. That international law imposes duties and liabilities upon individuals as well as upon States has long been recognized . . . Crimes against international law are committed by men, not by abstract entities, and only by punishing individuals who commit such crimes can the provisions of international law be enforced.[53]

This understanding was reaffirmed the same year in a UN General Assembly Resolution adopting the principles recognized by the Nuremberg Charter and the Judgment of the Tribunal.[54] The Resolution called for the formulation of an 'International Criminal Code' on the basis of the principles established by the Charter and Judgment of the IMT. In 1947 this task was bifurcated, and the General Assembly directed the ILC to formulate the principles of the Nuremberg Charter and Judgment, as well as a draft code of offences against the peace and security of mankind.[55] By requesting the ILC to explain the relation of the Nuremberg principles to the draft code,[56] the General Assembly implicitly pointed to an expansion of international criminal law as a doctrine of greater breadth than the crimes prosecuted by the IMT.

In response to the first directive of the General Assembly, the ILC drafted the Principles of International Law recognized in the Charter of the Nuremberg Tribunal and in the Judgment of the Tribunal (1950),[57] which expands upon the regime of individual responsibility for international crimes established by the IMT.[58] Principle I provides that '[a]ny person who commits an act which constitutes a crime under international law is responsible therefor and liable to punishment'.[59] Individual criminal responsibility was also the cornerstone of the Draft Code of

[53] *Nazi Conspiracy and Aggression*, International Military Tribunal at Nuremberg, Opinion and Judgment, 52–3 (1946).

[54] Affirmation of the Principles of International Law Recognized by the Charter of the Nürnberg Tribunal, GA Res. 95 (I), UN Doc. A/Res/95(I) (11 December 1946).

[55] Formulation of the Principles Recognized in the Charter of the Nürnberg Tribunal and in the Judgment of the Tribunal, GA Res. 177 (II), UN Doc. A/Res/177(II) (21 November 1947).

[56] *Ibid.* (The General Assembly directed the Commission to '*(a)* Formulate the principles of international law recognized in the Charter of the Nürnberg Tribunal and in the judgment of the Tribunal, and *(b)* Prepare a draft code of offences against the peace and security of mankind, indicating clearly the place to be accorded to the principles mentioned in sub-paragraph *(a)* above').

[57] Report of the International Law Commission Covering the Work of its First Session, [1950] II YbILC 374–78 (Formulation of the Nürnberg Principles).

[58] Principles of International Law Recognized in the Charter of the Nürnberg Tribunal and in the Judgment of the Tribunal, UN Doc. A/CN.4/SER.A/1950/Add.1 (1950).

[59] *Ibid.*, Article I.

Offences against the Peace and Security of Mankind (1954), drafted in response to the second direction of the General Assembly.[60] The Draft Articles provide in Article 1 that '[o]ffences against the peace and security of mankind, as defined in this Code, are crimes under international law, for which the responsible individuals shall be punished'.[61] Although drafting was completed in 1954, the Code, which identifies some twenty international crimes and denies the defenses of sovereign immunity and superior orders in its final two Articles, did not immediately enter into force. The Code was not formally ratified until the end of the twentieth century, in its circumscribed form as the Draft Code of Crimes against the Peace and Security of Mankind (1996).[62] The catalogue of crimes in the final instrument is limited to five specific crimes – aggression, genocide, crimes against humanity, crimes against United Nations and associated personnel, and war crimes – and the instrument retained its focus on individual criminal responsibility, providing in Article 2(1) that '[a] crime against the peace and security of mankind entails individual responsibility'.[63] By this point, the concept of individual criminal responsibility under international law first expressed during the inter-war period had been given full effect.

Individual criminal responsibility was the procedural core of the international judicial organs created during the last decade of the twentieth century. The principle served as the basis for the International Criminal Tribunals for the former Yugoslavia (ICTY)[64] and Rwanda (ICTR),[65] *ad hoc* bodies established under the Chapter VII authority of the UN Security Council based upon the precedent established by the IMT at Nuremberg.[66] The tribunals reflect the widespread acceptance of

60 Report of the International Law Commission Covering the Work of its Sixth Session, [1954] II YbILC 149, para. 41 *et seq.* [hereinafter, Draft Code of Offences (1954)].

61 *Ibid.*, 150 (Article 1).

62 Report of the International Law Commission on the Work of its Forty-Eighth Session, [1996] II(2) YbILC 17.

63 *Ibid.*, 18–22 (Article 2); 42–56 (Articles 16–20).

64 Statute of the International Tribunal for the Prosecution of Persons Responsible for Serious Violations of International Humanitarian Law Committed in the Territory of the Former Yugoslavia since 1991, UN Doc. S/Res/827 (annex) (25 May 1993).

65 Statute of the International Criminal Tribunal for Rwanda, UN Doc. S/Res/955 (annex) (8 November 1994).

66 *See* James Crawford, THE INTERNATIONAL LAW COMMISSION'S ARTICLES ON STATE RESPONSIBILITY 423 (Cambridge University Press 2003); Christopher Greenwood, *The Development of International Humanitarian Law by the International Criminal Tribunal for the Former Yugoslavia*, 2 MAX PLANCK YEARBOOK OF UNITED NATIONS LAW 97–140 (1998); Payam Akhavan, *The International Criminal Tribunal for Rwanda: The*

individual responsibility for international crimes in contemporary international law. The 1996 Draft Code of Crimes against the Peace and Security of Mankind also contains a Draft Statute for an International Criminal Court based upon individual criminal responsibility, one durably articulated by the Rome Statute of the International Criminal Court (1998).[67] The Rome Statute established the International Criminal Count (ICC), the first permanent court with jurisdiction over international crimes committed by individuals.[68] The jurisdiction of the court is 'limited to the most serious crimes of concern to the international community as a whole' – genocide, crimes against humanity, war crimes, and aggression – and explicitly concerned with individual criminal responsibility.[69] Elements of Crimes (2000),[70] promulgated pursuant to Article 9 of the Rome Statute, augments the Statute by expounding the breadth of core crimes applicable to the individual under the jurisdiction of the ICC.[71] More recent *ad hoc* criminal tribunals, such as the Special Court for Sierra Leone (SCSL),[72] the Extraordinary Chambers in the Court of Cambodia (ECCC),[73] and the Special Tribunal for Lebanon (STL),[74] serve particular situations in which individual States have joined

Politics and Pragmatics of Punishment, 90(3) American Journal of International Law 501–10 (1996).

67 Rome Statute of the International Criminal Court, UN Doc. A/CONF.183.9 (17 July 1998, *entered into force* 1 July 2002) [hereinafter, Rome Statute (1998)].

68 *Ibid.*, Articles 1, 25.

69 *Ibid.*, Article 5. *See* Bruce Broomhall, International Justice & the International Criminal Court (2003).

70 Elements of Crimes, ICC-ASP/1/3(part II-B), UN Doc. PCNICC/2000/1/Add.2 (9 September 2002).

71 *See* ICC Review Conference, The Crime of Aggression, Resolution RC/Res.6 (11 June 2010).

72 On the Establishment of a Special Court for Sierra Leone, SC Res 1315, UN Doc. S/Res/1315 (14 August 2000); *see* Agreement Between the United Nations and the Government of Sierra Leone on the Establishment of a Special Court for Sierra Leone, 2178 UNTS 138 (16 January 2002, *entry into force* 12 April 2002) [hereinafter, SCSL Statute (2002)].

73 Khmer Rouge Trials, GA Res. 57/228 B, UN Doc. A/RES/57/228/B (22 May 2003) (with annex Draft Agreement between the United Nations and the Royal Government of Cambodia Concerning the Prosecution under Cambodian Law of Crimes Committed during the Period of the Democratic Kampuchea); *see* Agreement between the United Nations and the Royal Government of Cambodia Concerning the Prosecution under Cambodian Law of Crimes Committed during the Period of the Democratic Kampuchea, 2329 UNTS 117 (6 June 2003, *entered into force* 29 April 2005) [hereinafter, ECCC Statute (2003)].

74 On the Establishment of a Special Tribunal for Lebanon, SC Res. 1757, UN Doc. S/Res/1757 (30 May 2007) (with annex Agreement Between the United Nations and the Lebanese Republic on the establishment of a Special Tribunal for Lebanon); *see*

with the United Nations to promote the transparent and effective prosecution of international crimes.

Like other criminal courts and tribunals, the salient feature of the Rome Statute is its predication upon principles of individual criminal responsibility and the legal personality of the individual more generally, rather than any form of State responsibility. The ICC was structured to functionally mirror a domestic court,[75] whilst adopting the subject matter of international law,[76] and elements of international relations,[77] thereby merging international and municipal legal concepts. Moreover, the principle of 'complementarity' calls for cooperation between domestic legal orders and the international court, and defers prosecutorial jurisdiction to national courts where there exists sufficient confidence in the capacity of domestic legal orders.[78] Through complementarity, the Rome Statute integrates municipal and international legal systems in such a way as to create a unified legal mechanism designed to enhance the capacity of actors to prosecute certain international crimes. It is in this respect that the ICC, more than any other international judicial organ, has linked domestic and international modalities of prosecution for international crimes. A different synergy is seen in the recent generation of *ad hoc* criminal tribunals created through agreements between individual States and the United Nations to establish special courts with jurisdiction over specified international crimes and serious violations of domestic law.[79]

Agreement Between the United Nations and the Lebanese Republic on the establishment of a Special Tribunal for Lebanon (with Statute), 2461 UNTS 280 (22 January 2007 and 6 February 2007, *entered into force* 10 June 2007) [hereinafter, STL Statute (2007)].

[75] Rome Statute (1998), Articles 53–85 (V. Investigation and Prosecution; VI. The Trial; VII. Penalties; VIII. Appeal and Revision).

[76] *Ibid.*, Articles 5–10.

[77] *Ibid.*, Articles 86–112 (IX. International Cooperation and Judicial Assistance; X. Enforcement; XI. Assembly of States Parties).

[78] *See, e.g.*, *Arrest Warrant of 11 April 2000 (Democratic Republic of the Congo v. Belgium)*, ICJ Reports 2002, Dis. Op. Van Den Wyngaert, para. 37 (citing Rome Statute (1998), Article 17) ('The jurisdiction of an International Criminal Court, set up by the Rome Statute, is moreover conditioned by the principle of complementarity: primary responsibility for adjudicating war crimes and crimes against humanity lies with the States. The International Criminal Court will only be able to act if States which have jurisdiction are unwilling or unable genuinely to carry out investigation or prosecution'); Rome Statute (1998), Article 17 ('the International Criminal Court established under this Statute shall be complementary to national criminal jurisdictions').

[79] *See* STL Statute (2007), Article 2 (identifying the Lebanese Criminal Code and certain other provisions of Lebanese law as the applicable criminal law); ECCC Statute (2003),

The critical importance of the Nuremberg Principles and the legacy of international criminal responsibility is that the individual is recognized to possess duties, and responsibility for their violation, under international law. '[I]ndividuals have international duties which transcend the national obligations of obedience imposed by the individual State.'[80] The development of international criminality removes the veil of sovereignty that had previously shielded the individual from accountability for breaches of international law. Such a development follows reflexively from the recognition that the individual is capable of possessing rights under international law. That the individual is directly responsible under international law for violations of fundamental norms, and that these violations constitute international crimes, is a central component of *jus cogens*. In this sense, it has been observed that *jus cogens* is doctrinally linked to the Nuremberg Principles:

> The universal and fundamental rights of human beings identified by Nuremberg – rights against genocide, enslavement, and other inhumane acts – are the direct ancestors of the universal and fundamental norms recognized as *jus cogens*.[81]

What is more, international law now recognizes that a 'crime in this sense is seen as a violation of basic rules of *jus cogens*'.[82] The evolution of individual criminal responsibility was therefore a necessary precursor to the practical effect of peremptory norms.

Articles 1–2 (establishing subject-matter jurisdiction of the court through special legislative grant including international law and Cambodian penal law); SCSL Statute (2002), Articles 1–5 (establishing competence of the court to prosecute serious violations of international humanitarian law and Sierra Leonean law).

80 *Nazi Conspiracy and Aggression*, International Military Tribunal at Nuremberg, Opinion and Judgment, 53 (1946); *see Prosecutor v. Furundžija*, IT-95-17/1-T, para. 155 (1998).

81 *Siderman de Blake v. Republic of Argentina*, 965 F.2d 699, 715 (9th Cir. 1992) (internal citation omitted).

82 Jochen Frowein, *Jus Cogens*, *in* III ENCYCLOPEDIA OF PUBLIC INTERNATIONAL LAW 65, 68 (Amsterdam: North-Holland, Rudolf Bernhardt ed., 1997).

11

The content of *jus cogens*

The post-war developments in international law and politics glossed above provide the legal foundation for a system of peremptory norms denoting rights and duties that apply to the individual. The development of individual legal personality in international law enabled the conferral of rights and duties directly upon the individual, rather than application through the State as the exclusive conduit of international law protections and obligations.[1] The law of human rights is illustrative of the capacity of the individual to possess rights and freedoms in international law. The concurrent evolution of individual criminal responsibility for certain violations of international law is demonstrative of the capacity of the individual to bear duties under international law. These twin legal developments underlie the emergence of public order norms transcending both the law within States and that concluded between States, and it is in the context of these developments that procedural and substantive dimensions of *jus cogens* are best understood.

A Identifying peremptory norms

Since the formal establishment of *jus cogens* with the codification of the Vienna Convention, its substantive ambiguity has been the target of criticism and a source of scepticism towards the category as a meaningful classification. Brownlie, for example, observes that notwithstanding international consensus around particular norms, 'more authority exists for the category of *jus cogens* than exists for its particular content, and rules do not develop in customary law which readily correspond to the

[1] For two views on the monist-dualist distinction as it pertains to this development, *compare* Antônio Augusto Cançado Trindade, *International Law for Humankind: Towards a New Jus Gentium (II) – General Course on Public International Law*, 317 Recueil des Cours 108–15 (2005), *with* Louis Henkin, *General Course on Public International Law*, 216 Recueil des Cours 89–93 (1989).

new categories'.[2] The classic retort to Brownlie's point is that, even if the concept of *jus cogens* was merely 'an empty box, the category was still useful; for without the box, it cannot be filled'.[3] One reason for this substantive uncertainty is that the Vienna Convention formally lacks a list of peremptory norms. The ILC declined to formally include a catalogue of peremptory norms in the final text of the Vienna Convention, providing the following explanation in its commentary:

> The emergence of rules having the character of *jus cogens* is comparatively recent, while international law is in process of rapid development. The Commission considered the right course to be to provide in general terms that a treaty is void if it conflicts with a rule of *jus cogens* and to leave the full content of this rule to be worked out in State practice and in the jurisprudence of international tribunals.[4]

Such agnosticism has persisted to this day, a point reflected by the ILC in its commentary to the Articles on State Responsibility.[5] It should be noted, however, that the ILC offered some examples of treaties violating 'obvious and best settled rules of *jus cogens*' in its commentary to the Vienna Convention,[6] a practice mirrored in its commentary to the

[2] Ian Brownlie, Principles of Public International Law 516-17 (Oxford: Clarendon Press, 5th edn. 1998).

[3] Andrea Bianchi, *Human Rights and the Magic of* Jus Cogens, 19(3) European Journal of International Law 491 (2008) (internal quotation marks omitted) (quoting Georges Abi-Saab, *The Third World and the Future of the International Legal Order*, 29 Revue Egyptienne de Droit International 27, 53 (1973)).

[4] Humphrey Waldock, Fifth Report on the Law of Treaties, [1966] II YbILC 248, para. 3 (Commentary to Draft Article 50); *see* [1963] I YbILC 71, para. 53 (684th Meeting, statement by Mr Ago) ('But since it was intrinsically difficult to draw up a list of examples and since the peremptory norms might change, it would be better not to give any examples at all, and to allow the interpretation of the article to develop').

[5] International Law Commission, Responsibility of States for Internationally Wrongful Acts, Report of the International Law Commission on the Work of its Fifty-Third Session, [2001] II(2) YbILC 112, para 3 [hereinafter, ILC Articles on State Responsibility (2001)] (Commentary to Draft Article 40) ('It is not appropriate to set out examples of the peremptory norms referred to in the text of article 40 itself, any more than it was in the text of article 53 of the 1969 Vienna Convention. The obligations referred to in article 40 arise from those substantive rules of conduct that prohibit what has come to be seen as intolerable because of the threat it presents to the survival of States and their peoples and the most basic human values').

[6] Waldock, Fifth Report, [1966] II YbILC 248, para. 3 (Commentary to Draft Article 50) ('(*a*) a treaty contemplating an unlawful use of force contrary to the principles of the Charter, (*b*) a treaty contemplating the performance of any other act criminal under international law, and (*c*) a treaty contemplating or conniving at the commission of acts, such as trade in slaves, piracy, or genocide, in the suppression of which every State is called upon to co-operate').

Articles on State Responsibility.[7] Even so, this approach has precipitated an air of uncertainty with respect to the content of *jus cogens*.

Ostensibly, the lack of an authoritative list avoids the potentially damaging consequences of enumeration.[8] Disagreement regarding a declaration enumerating peremptory norms would conceivably have compromised the concept of *jus cogens* in international law altogether. Conversely, the absence of such a definitive list evades the exclusory effect of imperfectly categorizing particular norms as peremptory to the exclusion of others. Instead of a frozen catalogue of norms, extension of the concept is available to emergent peremptory norms as customary international law develops accordingly.

It was noted by the ILC in 1966 that 'there is no simple criterion by which to identify a general rule of international law as having the character of *jus cogens*',[9] and again in 1996, that it remained that 'the identification of these norms is not easy; this is in fact the main flaw in the notion of *jus cogens*'.[10] One consequence of this formal indeterminacy is a tendency to overstate the catalogue of *jus cogens* and blur the distinction between peremptory norms observable in positive law and those norms that perhaps ought to be peremptory.[11] Indeed, it has been observed that 'one of the major threats posed to the concept of *jus cogens*

[7] ILC Articles on State Responsibility (2001), 112–13 (Commentary to Article 40, paras. 4–5) (These include the prohibitions against aggression, slavery and slave trade, genocide, racial discrimination and apartheid, torture, and war crimes (grave violations of humanitarian law)).

[8] Some arguments disfavouring enumeration mirror those raised in the constitutional debates between the Federalists and Anti-Federalists in early United States history over ratification of a Bill of Rights. *See* THE FEDERALIST No. 84, at 513 (Alexander Hamilton) (New York: Penguin Books, Charles Kelser & Clinton Rossiter, eds., 2003) ('[B]ills of rights, in the sense and to the extent in which they are contended for, are not only unnecessary in the proposed Constitution, but would even be dangerous'); James Wilson, *Remarks on the Pennsylvania Ratifying Convention* (28 October 1787) ('If we attempt an enumeration, everything that is not enumerated is presumed to be given. The consequence is, that an imperfect enumeration would throw all implied power into the scale of the government, and the rights of the people would be rendered incomplete').

[9] Waldock, Fifth Report, [1966] II YbILC 247–8, para. 2 (Commentary to Draft Article 50).

[10] Gaetano Arangio-Ruiz, Eighth Report on State Responsibility, [1996] II(1) YbILC 64, para. 142.

[11] Alexander Orakhelashvili, PEREMPTORY NORMS IN INTERNATIONAL LAW 60, 65 (Oxford University Press 2006); Marjorie Whiteman, Jus Cogens *in International Law, with a Projected List*, 7 GEORGIA JOURNAL OF INTERNATIONAL AND COMPARATIVE LAW 609, 625–6 (1977) (producing a lengthy list of peremptory norms); *cf.* Anthony D'Amato, *It's a Bird, It's a Plane, It's* Jus Cogens*!*, 6(1) CONNECTICUT JOURNAL OF INTERNATIONAL LAW 1 (1991) (criticizing this tendency).

is the tendency . . . to see it everywhere'.[12] In response to this tendency, an early reflection by the ILC bears repeating: 'peremptory rules were rare, and it was unlikely that they would ever be very numerous in international law'.[13] The purpose of identifying the peremptory norms in international law is threefold: first, it demonstrates that, rather than an empty legal category, there are specific norms accepted and recognized in international law of peremptory status; second, it orients the material content of *jus cogens* in the conclusions of the previous chapters regarding authority and sources; and, finally, it permits a functional examination of peremptory norms as operative legal rules.

The method of identifying peremptory norms applied in this chapter is derived from the formal source of *jus cogens* identified in Chapter 8.[14] There, it was shown that peremptory norms are norms of customary international law influenced by general principles of law, namely human dignity. This understanding of the formal source of *jus cogens* derives from the construction of Article 53 of the Vienna Convention, as supported by the ILC drafting history, *travaux préparatoires* of the UN Conference on the Law of Treaties, and subsequent jurisprudence.[15] In this sense, peremptory norms arise from the social need of the international community, *opinio juris sive necessitatis*, which is linked to the general principle of human dignity.[16] Authoritative recognition of *opinio* resides in practice with international judicial organs, which look to resolutions of the UN General Assembly, the Security Council, and near-universal instruments of public international law as manifestations of the social need of the international community as a whole expressed through community-oriented channels.[17] This *opinio juris sive necessitatis* is evidenced in State practice, particularly where the State acts as an organ of the international community, and such practice includes codification of multilateral instruments, relevant practice of international institutions and organizations, and affirmative domestic legislative and judicial practice.[18] Finally, confirmation of the emergence of peremptory norms is often found in the pronouncements of judicial organs exercising their adjudicatory capacities.[19] As a doctrine of customary international

[12] Bianchi, *Human Rights and the Magic of* Jus Cogens, 506.
[13] [1963] I YbILC 75, para. 24 (685th Meeting, statement by Mr Ago).
[14] *See* discussion *supra*, Chapter 8.B (Article 53 of the Vienna Convention). [15] *Ibid.*
[16] *See* discussion *supra*, Chapter 8.B.i. (*Opinio Juris Sive Necessitatis*). [17] *Ibid.*
[18] *See* discussion *supra*, 8.B.ii (State Practice).
[19] *See* discussion *supra*, 8.D (Judicial Organs).

law, it follows that pronouncements by courts and tribunals are, in practice, the most authoritative articulations of peremptory norms. Consequently, the international law of *jus cogens* has evolved through the judgments of domestic and international courts as a kind of international common law, and courts frequently look to the assessments of customary international law carried out by other judicial organs to determine whether a peremptory norm has crystallized in international law.[20] These elements of the formal source of peremptory norms will be relied upon to identify peremptory norms accepted and recognized by the international community as a whole.

It should be noted that the catalogue to follow is not intended to be absolute: it is assumed that the development of the conscience of mankind will see this list modified over time in response to new threats to the interests of the international community.[21] Having acknowledged this, it also bears observing that, notwithstanding the absence of a formal catalogue of *jus cogens*, there has never been a formal dispute concerning the content of *jus cogens* or the status of a specific peremptory norm.[22] This indicates that, although not formalized as such, the catalogue of peremptory norms is indeed accepted and recognized by the international community as a whole, an indication of the declaratory nature of *jus cogens*.[23] Finally, the following examination is constrained in its treatment of domestic legislation. It is taken for granted that each of the acts identified below, prohibited as *jus cogens*, is also addressed by the national legal codes of the vast majority of States. Evidence of State practice is most relevant to the emergence of peremptory norms of general international law where the link between practice and *opinio*

[20] *See, e.g.*, *Al-Bihani v. Obama*, 619 F.3d 1, 17 (DC Cir. 2010) (Kavanaugh, J., concurring in denial of reh'g *en banc*) (describing customary international law as best understood as 'a kind of international common law').

[21] *Cf.* [1963] I YbILC 71, para. 53 (684th Meeting, statement by Mr Ago), *supra*, *n.* 4.

[22] International Law Commission (finalized by Martti Koskenniemi), *Fragmentation of International Law*, UN Doc. A/CN.4/L.682, para. 377 (2006) (quoting Antonio Cassese, INTERNATIONAL LAW 202 (Oxford University Press, 2nd edn. 2005)). Article 66(a) of the Vienna Convention provides a mechanism for adjudication of disputes arising from the content of peremptory norms of general international law as outlined in Articles 53 and 64; it has never been invoked.

[23] Though courts have invariably pronounced norms to belong to *jus cogens* without comment on the requisite *opinio juris sive necessitatis* evidenced by State practice. This, if anything, is a compelling reason for courts to apply a transparent analysis of the formal source of peremptory norms to thereby ensure that the category remains a product of the international community of States rather than judicial activism. *See supra*, Chapter 8, *n.* 283.

juris sive necessitatis is clearly drawn – frequently when the State acts in international fora – and the present survey is generally limited to practice of this nature.

i. Piracy

The oldest peremptory norm of international law accepted and recognized by the international community is the prohibition against piracy. Preceding the category of *jus cogens* by centuries, the outlaw of piracy is one of the earliest expressions of the interests of the international community as a whole, reflected in the mantra that a pirate is an enemy of mankind (*hostis humani generis*).[24] One early incidence of the notion is found in the charge to the jury in the 1718 trial of Stede Bonnet in Charleston, South Carolina:

> As to the heinousness or wickedness of the offence, it needs no aggravation, it being evident to the reason of all men. Therefore a pirate is called 'hostis humani generis,' with whom neither faith nor oath is to be kept. And in our law they are termed 'brutes,' and 'beasts of prey'; and that it is lawful for any one that takes them, if they cannot with safety to themselves bring them under some government to be tried, to put them to death.[25]

Piracy is in this sense regarded as the first international crime and,[26] accordingly, the first international norm to impute individual responsibility.[27] Most basically, piracy under international law entails violence, often for personal gain, in effectively lawless areas (on the high seas, in the air, or otherwise beyond the jurisdiction of the State) where the individual cannot be safeguarded by the State.[28] This particular nature of piracy, and its violent character, forms the basis of its prohibition as a

[24] *See, e.g.*, Philip Jessup, A MODERN LAW OF NATIONS 18 (London: Macmillan 1952).

[25] *Trials of Major Bonnet and others for Piracy*, 5 George I (1718), *in* 15 A COMPLETE COLLECTION OF STATE TRIALS AND PROCEEDINGS FOR HIGH TREASON AND OTHER CRIMES AND MISDEMEANORS FROM THE EARLIEST PERIOD TO THE YEAR 1783 1231, 1235 (London: T. C. Hansard, Thomas Howell ed., 1819).

[26] *United States v. Hasan*, 747 F. Supp. 2d 599, 605 (ED Va. 2010) *aff'd sub nom. United States v. Dire*, 680 F.3d 446 (4th Cir. 2012) ('by the Eighteenth Century, the international crime of piracy was well established as the *only* universal jurisdiction crime').

[27] Lauri Hannikainen, PEREMPTORY NORMS (*JUS COGENS*) IN INTERNATIONAL LAW 67-75 (Helsinki: Finnish Lawyers' Publishing Company 1988).

[28] *See United States v. Hasan*, 747 F. Supp. 2d 599, 630-37 (ED Va. 2010) *aff'd sub nom. United States v. Dire*, 680 F.3d 446 (4th Cir. 2012) (Piracy Under the Law of Nations in the Twenty-First Century).

peremptory norm in accordance with the higher interests of the international community.[29] In contemporary international law, piracy is defined to constitute illegal acts of violence or detention committed by individuals for private ends against a ship, aircraft, persons, or property, on the high seas, or outside the jurisdiction of any State.[30] The prohibition against piracy was an early exemplar of an accepted and recognized peremptory norm of general international law,[31] and an illustration of the way in which *jus cogens* constitutes 'a sphere in which [the] rules binding individuals for the benefit of other individuals overlapped with the norms of state relationships'.[32]

The inception of an *opinio juris sive necessitatis* of the international community prohibiting piracy predates codification of the doctrine of *jus cogens*. One clear articulation of *opinio* is found in the context of the 1926 League of Nations Committee of Experts for the Progressive Codification of International Law.[33] A response by Romania to the Committee drew attention to the 'special character' of the prohibition against piracy:

[29] *See* Kenneth Randall, *Universal Jurisdiction under International Law*, 66(4) TEXAS LAW REVIEW 785, 794 (1988).

[30] United Nations Convention on the Law of the Sea, 1833 UNTS 3, Article 101 (10 December 1982, *entered into force* 16 November 1994) (Definition of Piracy) [hereinafter, UNCLOTS (1982)]:

> Piracy consists of any of the following acts:
>
> (a) any illegal acts of violence or detention, or any act of depredation, committed for private ends by the crew or the passengers of a private ship or a private aircraft, and directed:
> (i) on the high seas, against another ship or aircraft, or against persons or property on board such ship or aircraft;
> (ii) against a ship, aircraft, persons or property in a place outside the jurisdiction of any State;
>
> (b) any act of voluntary participation in the operation of a ship or of an aircraft with knowledge of facts making it a pirate ship or aircraft;
>
> (c) any act of inciting or of intentionally facilitating an act described in subparagraph (a) or (b).

[31] *See, e.g.*, Brownlie, PRINCIPLES OF PUBLIC INTERNATIONAL LAW 515; Manfred Lachs, *The Development and General Trends of International Law in Our Time*, 169 RECUEIL DES COURS 206 (1980); United Nations Conference on the Law of Treaties, Vienna, 9 April–22 May 1969, A/CONF.39/11/Add.1 (1970), Second Session [hereinafter, UNCLOT, Second Session (1969)] 102, para. 21 (statement by the United States) ('It was easy to say that *jus cogens* existed because a treaty promoting slavery or piracy was clearly unenforceable in existing international life'); Hersch Lauterpacht, First Report on the Law of Treaties, [1953] II YbILC 155, para. 4.

[32] *Sosa v. Alvarez-Machain*, 542 US 692, 715 (2004) (in reference to the law of nations in 1789, which included the prohibition of piracy).

[33] *See* League of Nations Committee of Experts for the Progressive Codification of International Law, League of Nations Doc. C.196.M.70.1927.V (1926).

> Absolute piracy (piracy *jus gentium*) is regarded today as an offense of a special character, because it is *punishable wherever encountered.* We already see in embryo the principle – which, in future social relations will become the practice – of penalizing throughout the world violations of law which are common to every country.[34]

This universality of the prohibition against piracy was reiterated more recently by the UN Security Council in Resolution 1918 (2010) which, following a long series of resolutions concerning piracy, unanimously called upon all States to criminalize piracy under their national laws.[35] International practice expressing *opinio* pursuant to the prohibition against piracy is reflected most directly in the law of the sea, evidenced as early as the Paris Declaration Respecting Maritime Law (1865) and authoritatively codified in the UN Convention on the Law of the Sea (1982).[36] The *jus cogens* status of the prohibition against piracy has been articulated by international organs, particularly the ILC,[37] before which it was observed during the drafting of the law of treaties that the prohibition against piracy, alongside slavery, 'proved that there was such a thing as *jus cogens* and that States could not derogate from it'.[38]

The expression of the prohibition against piracy by judicial organs as a norm of concern to all States can also be traced back centuries.[39] In *United States v. Robins* (1799), for example, the District Court of the District of South Carolina described piracy as 'an offence against all and every nation, and therefore alike punishable by all':

> A pirate, under the law of nations, is an enemy of the human race. Being the enemy of all, he is liable to be punished by all. Any act which denotes this universal hostility, is an act of piracy . . . [P]iracy under the law of

[34] *Ibid.*, 202 (Reply of Romania to Questionnaire 6 (26 November 1926)), *in* Barry Dunbar, THE LAW OF INTERNATIONAL SEA PIRACY 95 (The Hague: Martinus Nijhoff 1980).

[35] SC Res. 1918, UN Doc. S/Res/1918, para. 2 (2010).

[36] UN Convention on the Law of the Sea, 1833 UNTS 3, Article 101 (10 December 1982, *entered into force* 16 November 1982).

[37] Waldock, Fifth Report, [1966] II YbILC 248, para. 3 (Commentary to Draft Article 50); [1963] I YbILC 63, para. 44 (683rd Meeting, statement by Mr Tabibi), 214, para. 68 (705th Meeting, statement by Mr El-Erian).

[38] [1966] I YbILC 38, para. 26 (828th Meeting, statement by Mr. Yasseen).

[39] *See United States v. Smith*, 18 US 153 (1820) (Story, J.) (finding piracy under the law of nations punishable in this case, noting that '[t]he common law, too, recognises and punishes piracy as an offense, not against its own municipal code, but as an offense against the law of nations, (which is part of the common law,) as an offense against the universal law of society, a pirate being deemed an enemy of the human race'); *United States v. Robins*, 27 F. Cas. 825, 862 (DSC 1799); *Trials of Major Bonnet and Others for Piracy*, 1231, 1235.

> nations, which alone is punishable by all nations, can only consist in an act which is an offence against all. No particular nation can increase or diminish the list of offences thus punishable.[40]

The Privy Council of the United Kingdom, in a 1934 Report on *Piracy Jure Gentium*, considered that the unique nature of crimes under international law, a system lacking its own mechanisms of enforcement, necessarily conferred upon all States jurisdiction over *hostis humani generis*.[41] The conceptualization of piracy as prohibited by an inviolable law of nations subject to universal enforcement is analogous to its contemporary status as *jus cogens*.[42] More recently, in *Regina v. Tang* (2008), the Australian High Court identified the *jus cogens* status of the prohibition against slavery by analogy to the prohibition of piracy.[43] Two recent cases before US Circuit Courts strike a similar tone to the 1799 *Robins* case, reiterating that the prohibition against piracy belongs to the 'law of nations', which in contemporary US jurisprudence is parlance for *jus cogens*.[44] Kenya has conducted a series of prosecutions of 'piracy by the law of nations' (piracy *jure gentium*), finding in one instance the critical elements of the crime to include seizure or attempt to seize a ship by sea 'by violence or by putting those in possession of such ship in fear

[40] *United States v. Robins*, 27 F. Cas. 825, 862 (DSC 1799) (quoting speech delivered to the US Congress by John Marshall).

[41] Report of the Lords of the Judicial Committee of the Privy Council, [1934] A.C. 586, 2 (26 July 1934) (citing Hugo Grotius, I De Jure Belli ac Pacis Libri Tres II.XX.XL) (Oxford: Clarendon Press, Francis Kelsey trans., James B. Scott ed., 1925 [1646]) ('With regard to crimes as defined by international law, that law has no means of trying or punishing them. The recognition of them as constituting crimes and the trial and punishment of the criminals are left to the municipal law of each country. But whereas according to international law the criminal jurisdiction of municipal law is ordinarily restricted to crimes committed on its terra firma or territorial waters or its own ships, and to crimes by its own nationals whenever committed, it is also recognized as extending to piracy committed on the high seas by any national on any ship, because a person guilty of such piracy has placed himself beyond the protection of any State. He is no longer a national but *hostis humani generis* and as such he is justiciable by any State anywhere').

[42] *See* discussion *infra*, Chapter 12.B (Individual Civil Responsibility) (discussing the relationship between the law of nations and *jus cogens* in US jurisprudence).

[43] *Regina v. Tang*, High Court of Australia, [2008] HCA 39, para. 111 (Kirby, J.) ('As stated in the Code, slavery, like piracy, is a crime against humanity. Thus those who engage in "slavery", piracy and other special crimes are enemies of mankind. Such offences arguably attract obligations that attach to crimes of universal jurisdiction. As a rule [of] *jus cogens*, slavery is prohibited as a peremptory norm from which no derogation is permitted').

[44] *Institute of Cetacean Research v. Sea Shepherd Conservation Society*, 725 F.3d 940, 943 (9th Cir. 2013); *United States v. Dire*, 680 F.3d 446, 454 (4th Cir. 2012) *cert. denied*, 133 S. Ct. 982 (2013).

[for their lives]'.[45] Similar proceedings have been conducted in the Netherlands[46] and Seychelles.[47]

ii. Slavery

The exercise of powers attached to the rights of ownership over a human being has been absolutely outlawed as contrary to the higher interests of the international community as a whole. Slavery and the slave trade quite obviously violate the respect owed to the intrinsic worth of the human person and contravene the interests of the international community.[48] As such, enslavement is commonly recognized as a crime against

[45] *See, e.g.*, *Regina v. Abdirahnam Isse Mohamud et al.*, High Court of Kenya, CR 72/2011, 5-6 (2011) (alongside a local dimension of piracy, 'an international dimension, coinciding with the demand of the law of nations, demand[s] that all States should protect the high seas against piracy. Thus, an element of international law was in this way, being grafted into the Kenyan machinery of criminal justice', rendering piracy actionable notwithstanding the repeal of section 69(1) of the Penal Code of Kenya, which had previously criminalized piracy *jure gentium*); *Kenya v. Aid Mohamed Ahmed et al.*, Chief Magistrate Court, CR 3486/2008, 22-23 (2008).

[46] *Samanyolu* Case, Rotterdam District Court, CR 10/600012-09, 2-3 (2010) (in criminal prosecution of five Somali pirates, the district court relied upon universal jurisdiction over piracy under international law as codified by Article 381 of The Criminal Code of The Netherlands).

[47] *See, e.g.*, *Regina v. Mohamed Ahmed Dahir & Ten (10) Others*, Supreme Court of Seychelles, CR 51/2009, paras. 61, 71 (2010) (convicting eight of piracy *jure gentium* while finding companion charges of terrorism unsubstantiated).

[48] Supplementary Convention on the Abolition of Slavery, the Slave Trade, and Institutions and Practices Similar to Slavery, 226 UNTS 3, Articles 1, 3 (7 September 1956, *entered into force* 30 April 1957) [hereinafter, Supplementary Slavery Convention (1956)]. Article 1 defines slavery as including:

(a) Debt bondage, that is to say, the status or condition arising from a pledge by a debtor of his personal services or of those of a person under his control as security for a debt, if the value of those services as reasonably assessed is not applied towards the liquidation of the debt or the length and nature of those services are not respectively limited and defined;
(b) Serfdom, that is to say, the condition or status of a tenant who is by law, custom or agreement bound to live and labour on land belonging to another person and to render some determinate service to such other person, whether for reward or not, and is not free to change his status;
(c) Any institution or practice whereby:
  (i) A woman, without the right to refuse, is promised or given in marriage on payment of a consideration in money or in kind to her parents, guardian, family or any other person or group; or
  (ii) The husband of a woman, his family, or his clan, has the right to transfer her to another person for value received or otherwise; or

humanity,[49] and its prohibition belongs to *jus cogens*.[50] The Australian High Court, in *Regina v. Tang* (2008) cited immediately above, drew attention to the mutually reinforcing nature of the legal prohibition against slavery and the gravity of the offence itself, which has culminated in its status as an 'extremely grave international crime':

> As stated in the Code, slavery, like piracy, is a crime against humanity. Thus those who engage in 'slavery', piracy and other special crimes are enemies of mankind. Such offences arguably attract obligations that attach to crimes of universal jurisdiction. As a rule [of] *jus cogens*, slavery is prohibited as a peremptory norm from which no derogation is permitted. This further reinforces the seriousness of slavery[.][51]

The prohibition against slavery is very clearly an expression of the values and interests of the international community, and its emergence as a peremptory norm of international law is demonstrable in *opinio juris sive necessitatis* evidenced by State practice.

Early articulation of an *opinio juris sive necessitatis* pursuant to the prohibition of slavery can be traced to the Congress of Vienna (1815), which adopted the Declaration Relative to the Universal Abolition of the

(iii) A woman on the death of her husband is liable to be inherited by another person;

Article 3(1) defines slave trade:

> The act of conveying or attempting to convey slaves from one country to another by whatever means of transport, or of being accessory thereto, shall be a criminal offence under the laws of the States Parties to this Convention and persons convicted thereof shall be liable to very severe penalties.

[49] Elements of Crimes, ICC-ASP/1/3(part II-B), UN Doc. PCNICC/2000/1/Add.2 (9 September 2002) [hereinafter, Elements of Crimes (2002)], Article 7(1)(c); Agreement Between the United Nations and the Government of Sierra Leone on the Establishment of a Special Court for Sierra Leone, 2178 UNTS 138 (16 January 2002, *entry into force* 12 April 2002) [hereinafter, SCSL Statute (2002)], Article 2(c); Statute of the International Criminal Tribunal for Rwanda, UN Doc. S/Res/955 (annex) (8 November 1994) [hereinafter, ICTR Statute (1994)], Article 3(c); Statute of the International Tribunal for the Prosecution of Persons Responsible for Serious Violations of International Humanitarian Law Committed in the Territory of the Former Yugoslavia since 1991, UN Doc. S/Res/827 (annex) (25 May 1993) [hereinafter, ICTY Statute (1993)], Article 5(c).

[50] Brownlie, PRINCIPLES OF PUBLIC INTERNATIONAL LAW 515; Hannikainen, PEREMPTORY NORMS (*JUS COGENS*) IN INTERNATIONAL LAW 75–87, 444–56; Lachs, *The Development and General Trends of International Law in Our Time* 205; Ulrich Scheuner, *Conflict of Treaty Provisions with a Peremptory Norm of General International Law*, 29(4) ZEITSCHRIFT FÜR AUSLANDISCHES OFFENTLISCHES RECHT UND VOLKERRECHT 28, 33 (1969).

[51] *Regina v. Tang*, High Court of Australia, [2008] HCA 39, paras. 110–17 (Kirby, J.).

Slave Trade.[52] The eight powers that signed the instrument declared the slave trade to be 'repugnant to the principles of humanity and universal morality'.[53] Toward the end of the nineteenth century, this *opinio* was articulated again by the signatories of the General Act of Berlin of 26 February 1885, in which the States exercising sovereignty in Africa agreed to 'bind themselves ... to help in suppressing slavery, and especially the Slave Trade',[54] a motivation reflected in the General Act for the Repression of the African Slave Trade (Brussels Act) of 1890.[55] The preamble of the Convention of Saint-Germain-en-Laye of 1919 is framed in terms of the application of 'general principles [established by the Acts of Berlin and Brussels] which should guide their commercial and civilizing action ... in a continent where slavery and the slave trade still flourished'.[56] Parties to the convention pledged to 'endeavor to secure the complete suppression of slavery in all its forms and of the slave trade by land and sea'.[57] Not long thereafter, the Slavery Convention of 1926 codified the objective 'to find a means of giving practical effect throughout the world to such intentions as were expressed in regard to slave trade and slavery by the signatories of the Convention of Saint-Germain-en-Laye'.[58]

The fruition of this *opinio* is evidenced in the preamble of the Supplementary Convention on the Abolition of Slavery, the Slave Trade, and Institutions and Practices Similar to Slavery (1956).[59] The instrument begins by orienting the prohibition in the consideration 'that freedom is the birthright of every human being' and that 'the peoples of the United Nations reaffirmed in the Charter their faith in the dignity and worth of the human person'.[60] The subsequent prohibition of slavery can be seen

[52] General Treaty of the Vienna Congress, 63 CTS 473, Act XV (Declaration of Eight European Courts on the Abolition of the Slave Trade) (signed at Vienna 8 February 1815).

[53] *Ibid.*

[54] General Act of Berlin relative to the Congo, Chapter 1 (VI), Chapter 2 (IX) (signed at Berlin 26 February 1885).

[55] General Act for the Repression of the African Slave Trade, 173 CTS 293 (signed at Brussels 2 July 1890).

[56] Convention revising the 1885 General Act of Berlin relative to the Congo, 8 LNTS 27 (signed at Saint-Germain-en-Laye 10 September 1919).

[57] *Ibid.*, Article 11.

[58] Slavery, Servitude, Forced Labour and Similar Institutions and Practices Convention of 1926, 60 LNTS 253, Preamble (25 September 1926, *entered into force* 9 March 1927) [hereinafter, Slavery Convention (1926)].

[59] Supplementary Slavery Convention (1956), Articles 1, 3.

[60] *Ibid.*, Preamble.

to derive precisely from these values and interests common to the international community as a whole. This *opinio* was reiterated as recently as 2010, when the UN General Assembly adopted a United Nations Global Plan of Action to Combat Trafficking in Persons, in which it affirmed that the trafficking of persons 'constitutes a serious threat to human dignity, human rights and development'.[61] The International Court effectively took note of this *opinio juris sive necessitatis* in *Barcelona Traction,* in which it observed that obligations arise from the prohibition against slavery 'towards the international community as a whole . . . [which] are the concern of all States'.[62]

This *opinio juris sive necessitatis* is evidenced by a substantial body of State practice, particularly where States operate as members of the international community. Following the entry into force of the British Abolition of Slavery Act (1833),[63] Britain concluded an array of bilateral treaties to suppress the practices of slavery and trade in slaves. However, the wider practice of States evidencing *opinio juris sive necessitatis* followed later through a series of multilateral agreements: the General Act of the Berlin Conference (1895), the General Act for the Repression of the African Slave Trade (Brussels Act) of 1890, the Convention of Saint-Germain-en-Laye of 1919, the Slavery, Servitude, Forced Labour and Similar Institutions and Practices Convention of 1926, the Protocol Amending the Slavery Convention (1953),[64] and the Supplementary Convention on the Abolition of Slavery, the Slave Trade, and Institutions and Practices Similar to Slavery (1956). The 1926 instrument was codified through the League of Nations, and the 1956 Convention was adopted by a Conference of Plenipotentiaries convened by the UN Economic and Social Council, illustrating the way in which relevant practice includes that of States acting as organs of the international community. Supplemental instruments have been concluded concerning particular aspects of slavery, such as traffic in white slaves,[65] and in

[61] GA Res. 64/293, UN Doc. A/Res/64/293 (30 July 2010).

[62] *Barcelona Traction, Light and Power Company, Limited (Belgium v. Spain)*, Judgment, ICJ Reports 1970, p. 3, para. 33.

[63] Abolition of Slavery Act, 3 & 4 Will. IV c. 73 (1833).

[64] Protocol Amending the Slavery Convention, 182 UNTS 51 (23 October 1953, *entered into force* 7 December 1953).

[65] Protocol, signed at Lake Success, New York, on 4 May 1949, amending the International Agreement for the Suppression of the White Slave Traffic, signed at Paris, on 18 May 1904, and the International Convention for the Suppression of the White Slave Traffic, signed at Paris, on 4 May 1910, 30 UNTS 23 (4 May 1949, *entered into force* 21 June

women and children.[66] The *jus cogens* character of the prohibition against slavery has been affirmed by international organs, notably the ILC,[67] and has been articulated by various judicial organs, including the circuit courts of the United States,[68] the Australian High Court,[69] the Inter-American Court of Human Rights,[70] and the International Court of Justice.[71]

iii. War crimes (serious violations of humanitarian law)

The laws and customs of war are articulated by international humanitarian law as protections afforded to individuals in armed conflict, with respect to particularly vulnerable persons, to mitigate unnecessary pain and suffering. As noted by the ICTY in the *Kupreškić* case, the development of international humanitarian law represented the incorporation of human-oriented moral obligations in international law, a departure from the State-oriented interests that generally characterize international law:

> The absolute nature of most obligations imposed by rules of international humanitarian law reflects the progressive trend towards the so-called 'humanisation' of international legal obligations, which refers to the general erosion of the role of reciprocity in the application of humanitarian law over the last century. The underpinning of this shift was that it became clear to States that norms of international humanitarian law were not intended to protect State interests; they were designed to benefit individuals *qua* human beings ... [C]ompliance with humanitarian rules could not be made dependent on a reciprocal or corresponding

1951); International Convention for the Suppression of the 'White Slave Traffic' (4 May 1910, *entered into force* 18 July 1905).

66 Protocol signed at Lake Success, New York, on 12 November 1947, to amend the Convention for the Suppression of the Traffic in Women and Children, concluded at Geneva on 30 September 1921, and the Convention for the Suppression of the Traffic in Women of Full Age, concluded at Geneva on 11 October 1933, 53 UNTS 13 (*entered into force* 24 April 1950); International Convention for the Suppression of the Traffic in Women and Children, 9 LNTS 415 (30 September 1921, *entered into force* 15 June 1922).

67 *See* ILC Articles on State Responsibility (2001), 248, para. 3 (Commentary to Article 50).

68 *Unocal Corp.*, 395 F.3d 932, 945 (9th Cir. 2002) *on reh'g en banc sub nom. John Doe I v. Unocal Corp.*, 403 F.3d 708 (9th Cir. 2005); *Sampson v. Federal Republic of Germany*, 250 F.3d 1145, 1154, *n.* 5 (7th Cir. 2001).

69 *Regina v. Tang*, High Court of Australia, [2008] HCA 39, para. 111 (Kirby, J.).

70 *Aloeboetoe et al. v. Suriname*, IACtHR Series C No. 15, paras. 56–7 (1993).

71 *Jurisdictional Immunities of the State (Germany v. Italy: Greece Intervening)*, Judgment, ICJ Reports 2012, p. 99, para. 93; *Barcelona Traction, Light and Power Company, Limited (Belgium v. Spain)*, Judgment, ICJ Reports 1970, p. 3, para. 33 (by inference).

> performance of these obligations by other States. This trend marks the translation into legal norms of the 'categorical imperative' formulated by Kant in the field of morals: one ought to fulfil an obligation regardless of whether others comply with it or disregard it.[72]

This premise of humanitarian law is expressed in the Commentary to common Article 3 of the Geneva Conventions, which establishes minimum standards for the treatment of persons *hors de combat* by defining activities that are 'prohibited at any time and in any place whatsoever':[73]

> [T]he object of the Convention is a purely humanitarian one, that it is in no way concerned with the internal affairs of States, and that it merely ensures respect for the few essential rules of humanity which all civilized nations consider as valid everywhere and under all circumstances and as being above and outside war itself.[74]

The interests of the international community are expressed through the protection of human dignity during times of war. The serious violation of humanitarian law constitutes a war crime.[75] The peremptory status of the

[72] *Prosecutor v. Kupreškić*, IT-95-16-T, para. 518 (2000).

[73] Geneva Convention (I) for the Amelioration of the Condition of the Wounded and Sick in Armed Forces in the Field, 75 UNTS 31, Article 3 (12 August 1949, *entered into force* 21 October 1950) [Hereinafter, Geneva Convention I (1949)]; Geneva Convention (II) for the Amelioration of the Condition of Wounded, Sick and Shipwrecked Members of Armed Forces at Sea, 75 UNTS 85, Article 3 (12 August 1949, *entered into force* 21 October 1950) [hereinafter, Geneva Convention II (1949)]; Geneva Convention (III) Relative to the Treatment of Prisoners of War, 75 UNTS 135, Article 3 (12 August 1949, *entered into force* 21 October 1950) [hereinafter, Geneva Convention III (1949)]; Geneva Convention (IV) Relative to the Protection of Civilian Persons in Time of War, 75 UNTS 287, Article 3 (12 August 1949, *entered into force* 21 October 1950) [hereinafter, Geneva Convention IV (1949)].

[74] Jean Pictet (ed.), I The Geneva Conventions of 12 August 1949 60 (Geneva: International Committee of the Red Cross 1952).

[75] Rome Statute (1998), Article 8(2) ('For the purpose of this Statute, "war crimes" means: (a) Grave breaches of the Geneva Conventions of 12 August 1949, namely, any of the following acts against persons or property protected under the provisions of the relevant Geneva Convention', as well as other 'serious violations of laws and customs' applicable in armed conflicts of various types); *see, e.g., Sarei v. Rio Tinto, PLC*, 671 F.3d 736, 763-4 (9th Cir. 2011) *cert. granted, judgment vacated sub nom.* (*on other grounds*) *Rio Tinto PLC v. Sarei*, 133 S. Ct. 1995 (US 2013) ('War crimes are defined primarily by the Geneva Conventions, to which the United States, along with at least 180 nations, is a party and which constitute part of customary international law'); *Lozano v. Italy*, Court of Cassation (First Criminal Chamber) (Italy), No. 31171/2008, ILDC 1085, paras. 6–7 (2008) (defining 'war crimes' as 'serious breaches' of international humanitarian law).

prohibition of war crimes as serious violations of humanitarian law is supported throughout the literature on the subject.[76]

An *opinio juris sive necessitatis* pursuant to the prohibition of war crimes was articulated at the Brussels Conference on the Laws and Customs of War in 1874, which produced a short Final Protocol,[77] as well as a longer catalogue of articles in the Declaration of Brussels.[78] In the Final Protocol, with reference to 'ideas of humanity', the fifteen signatories agreed:

> It had been unanimously declared that the progress of civilization should have the effect of alleviating, as far as possible, the calamities of war; and that the only legitimate object which States should have in view during war is to weaken the enemy without inflicting upon him unnecessary suffering.[79]

This *opinio*, based in the general principle of human dignity, was more broadly articulated by the international community through the Martens Clause of the Hague Conventions of 1899 and 1907, instruments codifying the law of war and particular humanitarian norms.[80] The Martens Clause expressly invokes moral obligations deriving from the international community oriented in basic considerations of humanity.[81]

[76] *See, e.g.*, Orakhelashvili, PEREMPTORY NORMS IN INTERNATIONAL LAW 61–4; Hannikainen, PEREMPTORY NORMS (*JUS COGENS*) IN INTERNATIONAL LAW 87–111, 620–713; Alfred Verdross, Jus Dispositivum *and* Jus Cogens *in International Law*, 60 AMERICAN JOURNAL OF INTERNATIONAL LAW 55, 59 (1966).

[77] Final Protocol, ACTES DE LA CONFÉRENCE DE BRUXELLES 307 (signed at Brussels 27 August 1874).

[78] Project of an International Declaration Concerning the Laws and Customs of War, ACTES DE LA CONFÉRENCE DE BRUXELLES 297 (signed at Brussels 27 August 1874).

[79] Final Protocol, ACTES DE LA CONFÉRENCE DE BRUXELLES 307, Preamble (signed at Brussels 27 August 1874).

[80] Hague Convention (II) with Respect to the Laws and Customs of War on Land and its annex, 32 Stat. 1803, 1 Bevans 247, 187 CTS 429 (29 July 1899, *entered into force* 4 September 1900) [hereinafter, Hague Convention II (1899)]; Hague Convention (IV) respecting the Laws and Customs of War on Land and its annex, 36 Stat. 2277, 1 Bevans 631, 205 CTS 277 (18 October 1907, *entered into force* 26 January 1910) [hereinafter, Hague Convention IV (1907)].

[81] Hague Convention IV (1907) ('Until a more complete code of the laws of war has been issued, the High Contracting Parties deem it expedient to declare that, in cases not included in the Regulations adopted by them, the inhabitants and the belligerents remain under the protection and the rule of the principles of the law of nations, as they result from the usages established among civilized peoples, from the laws of humanity, and the dictates of the public conscience'); Hague Convention II (1899) ('Until a more complete code of the laws of war is issued, the High Contracting Parties think it right to declare that in cases not included in the Regulations adopted by them, populations and belligerents

The Geneva Conventions share a common denunciation clause, whose final paragraph borrows from the Martens Clause of the Hague Conventions,[82] to reinforce the inviolable nature of the rules contained by the instruments as customary international law.[83] The *opinio juris sive necessitatis* reflected by the Geneva Conventions, 'the essential motive which had brought sixty-four nations together at Geneva', is documented in their Commentaries.[84] The Martens Clause is said to have 'inspired' the drafting of provisions concerning *jus cogens* in the Vienna Convention on the Law of Treaties by *special rapporteur* Waldock.[85]

This *opinio juris sive necessitatis* is expressed in the founding instruments of international courts and tribunals as well as their jurisprudence. The IMT at Nuremberg relied upon near-universal instruments of public international law, and the drafting of such instruments, as 'expressions of opinion' of 'the conscience of the world'.[86] The offences defined in the ICTY Statute, which include war crimes, have been identified by that Tribunal as 'Universally Condemned Offences ... of concern to the international community as a whole'.[87] And the Rome Statute incorporates those same 'most serious crimes of international concern'.[88] In *Military and Paramilitary Activities in and against Nicaragua* (1986), the International Court of Justice recognized that obligations arising

remain under the protection and empire of the principles of international law, as they result from the usages established between civilized nations, from the laws of humanity, and the requirements of the public conscience').

82 Geneva Convention I (1949), Article 63; Geneva Convention II (1949), Article 62; Geneva Convention III (1949), Article 142; Geneva Convention IV (1949), Article 158 ('The denunciation ... shall in no way impair the obligations which the Parties to the conflict shall remain bound to fulfil by virtue of the principles of the law of nations, as they result from the usages established among civilized peoples, from the laws of humanity and the dictates of the public conscience'). *See* discussion *supra*, Chapter 5, text accompanying *n.* 58.

83 *Ibid.*, 413 ('The clause shows clearly ... that a Power which denounced the Convention would nevertheless remain bound by the principles contained in it insofar as they are the expression of inalienable and universal rules of customary international law').

84 *See* discussion *supra*, Chapter 4, text accompanying *nn.* 87–94.

85 [1963] I YbILC 131, para. 31 (693rd Meeting, statement by *special rapporteur* Waldock); *see* Egon Schwelb, *Some Aspects of International Jus Cogens as Formulated by the International Law Commission*, 61 American Journal of International Law 946, 957 (1967).

86 *Nazi Conspiracy and Aggression*, Opinion and Judgment, International Military Tribunal at Nuremberg 51–2 (1946); *see supra*, Chapter 8, *n.* 88.

87 *Prosecutor v. Nikolić*, Decision on Interlocutory Appeal Concerning Legality of Arrest, IT-94-2-AR73, paras. 24–5 (2003).

88 Rome Statute (1998), Article 1.

from common Articles 1 and 3 of the Geneva Conventions derive not only from the 'Conventions themselves, but from the general principles of humanitarian law to which the Conventions merely give specific expression'.[89] Additionally, the 2005 World Summit Outcome document adopted by the UN General Assembly details obligations of the international community pursuant to the responsibility to protect populations from war crimes.[90] These examples illustrate the consistent expression of *opinio juris sive necessitatis* prohibiting war crimes by international organs.

This *opinio juris sive necessitatis* is evidenced in the practice of States, acting as organs of the international community. Broad ascendance to the Hague Conventions,[91] and the Geneva Conventions,[92] has been relied upon as State practice evidencing the *opinio* of the international community pursuant to the peremptory prohibition against war crimes (serious breaches of humanitarian law).[93] Additional practice evidencing the prohibition of war crimes may be derived from the series of instruments classifying the offence as an international crime, which includes the Nuremberg Charter,[94] the Tokyo Charter,[95] the Draft Code of Offences against the Peace and Security of Mankind,[96] the Charter of the ICTY,[97] the Charter of the ICTR,[98] the Draft Code of Crimes against the Peace

[89] *Military and Paramilitary Activities in and against Nicaragua (Nicaragua v. United States of America)*, Judgment, ICJ Reports 1986, p. 14, para. 220.

[90] 2005 World Summit Outcome, GA Res. 60/1, UN Doc. A/Res/60/1, paras. 138–9 (24 October 2005).

[91] Hague Convention IV (1907); Hague Convention II (1899).

[92] Geneva Convention I (1949), Articles 49–50; Geneva Convention II (1949), Articles 50–1; Geneva Convention III (1949), Articles 129–30; Geneva Convention IV (1949), Articles 146–7.

[93] *See, e.g., Sarei v. Rio Tinto, PLC*, 671 F.3d 736, 763–4 (9th Cir. 2011) *cert. granted, judgment vacated sub nom. (on other grounds) Rio Tinto PLC v. Sarei*, 133 S. Ct. 1995 (US 2013) ('War crimes are defined primarily by the Geneva Conventions, to which the United States, along with at least 180 nations, is a party and which constitute part of customary international law').

[94] Charter of the International Military Tribunal, *in* Agreement for the Prosecution and Punishment of the Major War Criminals of the European Axis, 82 UNTS 280 (signed at London 8 August 1945) [hereinafter, IMT Charter (1945)], Article 6(b).

[95] International Military Tribunal for the Far East Charter, TIAS No. 1589, 3, 4 Bevans 20 (19 January 1946) [hereinafter, IMTFE Charter (1946)], Article 5(b).

[96] Report of the International Law Commission Covering the Work of its Sixth Session, [1954] II YbILC 149, para. 41 *et seq.* [hereinafter, Draft Code of Offences (1954)], Article 2, paras. 11–12.

[97] ICTY Statute (1993), Articles 2–3.

[98] ICTR Statute (1994), Article 4.

and Security of Mankind,[99] the Rome Statute,[100] and the Statute for the SCSL.[101] The Convention on the Non-Applicability of Statutory Limitations to War Crimes and Crimes Against Humanity reflects the seriousness of the international community towards enforcing this prohibition through effective punishment.[102]

The *opinio juris sive necessitatis* supporting the prohibition of war crimes, evidenced by the practice of States, has been consistently expressed by judicial organs recognizing the *jus cogens* status of the norm. The IMT at Nuremberg, which preceded the formal inception of the category of *jus cogens*, observed that the law of war constitutes a custom of universal recognition arising from general principles of law expressed by the practice of States.[103] In *Legality of the Threat or Use of Nuclear Weapons* (1996), the International Court indicated the prohibition against war crimes to be part of the 'intransgressible principles of international customary law'.[104] The International Court also implied the *jus cogens* status of the prohibition of war crimes in the *Arrest Warrant Case*[105] and 'assumed' that the 'rules of the law of armed conflict' belong to *jus cogens* in *Jurisdictional Immunities of the State*.[106] The ICTY has articulated the *jus cogens* status of the prohibition of war crimes,[107] and explained that its jurisdiction over war crimes related to the 'special character of [such] offences'.[108]

[99] Report of the International Law Commission on the Work of its Forty-Eighth Session, [1996] II(2) YbILC 17 [hereinafter, Draft Code of Crimes (1996)], Article 20.

[100] Rome Statute of the International Criminal Court, UN Doc. A/CONF.183.9 (17 July 1998, *entered into force* 1 July 2002) [hereinafter, Rome Statute (1998)], Article 8; *see* Elements of Crimes (2002), Article 8.

[101] SCSL Statute (2000), Articles 3–4.

[102] Convention on the Non-Applicability of Statutory Limitations to War Crimes and Crimes Against Humanity, 754 UNTS 73 (16 December 1968, *entered into force* 11 November 1970); *see* European Convention on the Non-Applicability of Statutory Limitations to Crimes Against Humanity and War Crimes, ETS No. 82 (25 January 1974, *entered into force* 27 June 2003).

[103] *Nazi Conspiracy and Aggression*, International Military Tribunal at Nuremberg, Opinion and Judgment, 51 (1946).

[104] *Legality of the Threat or Use of Nuclear Weapons*, Advisory Opinion, ICJ Reports 1996, p. 226 paras. 79, 83 (without pronouncing on the *jus cogens* status of the norm); *see ibid.*, Decl. Bedjaoui, p. 268, para. 21; Dis. Op. Weeramantry, p. 429, § 10.

[105] *Arrest Warrant of 11 April 2000 (Democratic Republic of the Congo v. Belgium)*, ICJ Reports 2002, p. 3, paras. 56–60.

[106] *Jurisdictional Immunities of the State (Germany v. Italy: Greece Intervening)*, Judgment, ICJ Reports 2012, p. 99, para. 93.

[107] *Prosecutor v. Kupreškić*, IT-95-16-T, paras. 519–20 (2000).

[108] *Prosecutor v. Nikolić*, Decision on Interlocutory Appeal Concerning Legality of Arrest, IT-94-2-AR73, paras. 24–5 (2003).

And decisions by domestic courts in Argentina,[109] Bosnia and Herzegovina,[110] Canada,[111] Italy,[112] the Philippines,[113] and the United States[114] have recognized the *jus cogens* character of the prohibition against war crimes. Such judicial pronouncements authoritatively confirm that the prohibition of war crimes belongs to *jus cogens*.

iv. Crimes against humanity

By definition, crimes against humanity are contrary to the basic considerations of humanity and intrinsic worth of the human person that underpin *jus cogens*. Most of the peremptory norms identified herein have, at some juncture, themselves been referred to as crimes against humanity.[115] However, crimes against humanity constitute a discrete category of inhumane acts, targeting civilians, defined by their widespread and systematic nature.[116] As noted by Judge Cassese: 'These crimes are particularly odious offences in that they constitute a serious attack on human dignity or grave humiliation or a degradation of one or more human beings[.]'[117] It is in this sense that the prohibition of crimes against humanity has been identified as one of the 'least controversial examples' of *jus cogens*.[118] The emergence of the peremptory norm

109 *Chile v. Arancibia Clavel*, Supreme Court of Justice (Argentina), A/533/XXXVIII, ILDC 1082, para. 28 (2004).

110 *Prosecutor's Office v. Anić*, Court of Bosnia and Herzegovina (Section I for War Crimes), S1 1 K 005596 11 Kro, ILDC 1907, paras. 27–8 (2011).

111 *Regina v. Finta*, Supreme Court (Canada), 1 SCR 701, 22 (1994) (by inference).

112 *Lozano v. Italy*, Court of Cassation (First Criminal Section) (Italy), No. 31171/2008, ILDC 1085, para. 6 (2008); *Ferrini v. Germany*, Court of Cassation (Civil Section) (Italy), No. 5044/2004, ILDC 19, paras. 9–9.1 (2004).

113 *Muna et al. v. Romulo et al.*, Supreme Court (Philippines), G.R. No. 159618, ILDC 2059, para. 89 (2011).

114 *Sarei v. Rio Tinto, PLC*, 487 F.3d 1193, 1202 (9th Cir. 2007) *on reh'g en banc*, 550 F.3d 822 (9th Cir. 2008).

115 *See, e.g.*, *Regina v. Tang*, High Court of Australia, [2008] HCA 39, para. 111 (Kirby, J.) ('slavery, like piracy, is a crime against humanity'); *Ferrini v. Germany*, Court of Cassation (Civil Section) (Italy), No. 5044/2004, ILDC 19, paras. 9–9.1 (2004) (concerning deportation and slavery as war crimes and crimes against humanity).

116 *See, e.g.*, Rome Statute (1998), Article 7 (identifying criminal acts that constitute crimes against humanity 'when committed as part of a widespread or systematic attack directed against any civilian population, with knowledge of the attack').

117 Antonio Cassese, International Law 250 (Oxford University Press, 2nd edn. 2005).

118 Brownlie, Principles of Public International Law 515.

prohibiting crimes against humanity closely parallels the prohibition against war crimes, and its formal genesis is similarly traceable to the IMT at Nuremberg.

One early expression of an *opinio juris sive necessitatis* prohibiting crimes against humanity is found in a 1915 Joint Declaration by France, Great Britain, and Russia condemning atrocities committed against Armenians by Turkey. The declaration, sent via telegram by the US Department of State on behalf of the French Foreign Office, concludes by declaring:

> In view of those new crimes of Turkey against humanity and civilization, the Allied governments announce publicly to the Sublime-Porte that they will hold personally responsible [for] these crimes all members of the Ottoman government and those of their agents who are implicated in such massacres.[119]

Notably, the understanding articulated by this Joint Declaration that crimes under international law entail individual criminal responsibility preceded the Nuremberg Tribunal by three decades. As discussed above, the IMT at Nuremberg later relied upon near-universal instruments of public international law, and the drafting of such instruments, as 'expressions of opinion' of 'the conscience of the world' to justify prosecution of offences within its jurisdiction, including crimes against humanity.[120] A more general statement of *opinio juris sive necessitatis* is found with the first session of the UN General Assembly in 1946. The General Assembly, expressing the collective will of the international community, called for the incorporation of the Nuremberg Principles into international law 'as a matter of primary importance',[121] which included the prohibition of crimes against humanity as detailed in the Nuremberg Charter as an international crime.[122] This *opinio* is reflected much later in the jurisprudence of the ICTY, which by 2003 considered crimes against humanity to be 'Universally Condemned Offences . . . of concern to the international community as a whole'.[123] The Rome Statute

[119] Joint Declaration of France, Great Britain and Russia, RG 59, 867.4016/67 (29 May 1915).

[120] *Nazi Conspiracy and Aggression*, Opinion and Judgment, International Military Tribunal at Nuremberg 51–2 (1946); *see supra*, Chapter 8, *n.* 88.

[121] Affirmation of the Principles of International Law Recognized by the Charter of the Nürnberg Tribunal, GA Res. 95 (I), UN Doc. A/Res/95(I) (11 December 1946).

[122] Report of the International Law Commission Covering the Work of its First Session, [1950] II YbILC 374–8, Principle VI(c) (Formulation of the Nürnberg Principles).

[123] *Prosecutor v. Nikolić*, Decision on Interlocutory Appeal Concerning Legality of Arrest, IT-94-2-AR73, paras. 24–5 (2003).

incorporates those same 'most serious crimes of international concern'.[124] Additionally, the 2005 World Summit Outcome document adopted by the UN General Assembly details obligations of the international community pursuant to the responsibility to protect populations from crimes against humanity.[125] These examples illustrate the consistent expression of *opinio juris sive necessitatis* prohibiting crimes against humanity by international organs.

This *opinio juris sive necessitatis* is evidenced in a substantial body of State practice. Formally, the origin of the international crime is found in the Charter of the IMT at Nuremberg,[126] and the category has been reiterated with remarkable consistency throughout modern practice in the Tokyo Charter, [127] the Draft Code of Offences against the Peace and Security of Mankind,[128] the Statute of the ICTY,[129] the Statute of the ICTR,[130] the Draft Code of Crimes against the Peace and Security of Mankind,[131] the Rome Statute,[132] and the Statute for the SCSL.[133] As above, the Convention on the Non-Applicability of Statutory Limitations to War Crimes and Crimes Against Humanity reflects State practice pursuant to the effective enforcement of the prohibition of crimes against humanity.[134]

The emergence of the prohibition of crimes against humanity has been broadly recognized by international courts and tribunals as belonging to *jus cogens*. The International Court of Justice, confronted with the question of applicable immunities to crimes against humanity, has repeatedly recognized the *jus cogens* nature of the prohibition. In the *Arrest Warrant* case (2002), the Court implicitly accepted the *jus cogens* status of crimes against humanity,[135] and writing in Dissent, Judge

[124] Rome Statute (1998), Article 1.

[125] 2005 World Summit Outcome, GA Res. 60/1, UN Doc. A/Res/60/1, paras. 138–9 (24 October 2005).

[126] IMT Charter (1945), Article 6(c). [127] IMTFE Charter (1946), Article 5(c).

[128] Draft Code of Offences (1954), Article 2, para. 11.

[129] ICTY Statute (1993), Article 5. [130] ICTR Statute (1994), Article 3.

[131] Draft Code of Crimes (1996), Article 18.

[132] Rome Statute (1998), Article 7; *see* Elements of Crimes (2002), Article 7.

[133] SCSL Statute (2000), Article 2.

[134] Convention on the Non-Applicability of Statutory Limitations (1968); *see* European Convention on the Non-Applicability of Statutory Limitations (1974).

[135] *Arrest Warrant of 11 April 2000 (Democratic Republic of the Congo v. Belgium)*, ICJ Reports 2002, p. 3, paras. 56–60 (finding no exception to immunity *ratione personae* of foreign minister for *jus cogens* violations of war crimes and crimes against humanity).

Al-Khasawneh observed: 'The effective combating of grave crimes has arguably assumed a *jus cogens* character reflecting recognition by the international community of the vital community interests and values it seeks to protect and enhance.'[136] In *Jurisdictional Immunities of the State* (2012), Judge Cançado Trindade similarly took note of the *jus cogens* status of the prohibition of crimes against humanity.[137] The ICTY,[138] SCSL,[139] and IACtHR[140] have expressly recognized the prohibition of crimes against humanity as *jus cogens*. The historic lineage of the *jus cogens* status of the norm was clearly articulated by Judge Wald of the US Court of Appeals for the DC Circuit in *Princz v. Federal Republic of Germany* (1992): 'the Nuremberg Charter's definition of "crimes against humanity" includes what are now termed *jus cogens* norms'.[141] The *jus cogens* status of the norm prohibiting crimes against humanity has also been recognized in the decisions of domestic courts in Argentina,[142] Bosnia and Herzegovina,[143] Chile,[144] Italy,[145] the

[136] *Ibid.*, Dis. Op. Al-Khasawneh, p. 95, para. 7; *see Armed Activities on the Territory of the Congo (New Application: 2002) (Democratic Republic of the Congo v. Rwanda)*, Sep. Op. Dugard, ICJ Reports 2006, p. 86, para. 11.

[137] *Jurisdictional Immunities of the State (Germany v. Italy: Greece Intervening)*, Judgment, ICJ Reports 2012, p. 99, Dis. Op. Cançado Trindade, paras. 313–14.

[138] *Prosecutor v. Kupreškić*, IT-95-16-T, paras. 519–20 (2000).

[139] *Prosecutor v. Kallon and Kamara*, Decision on Challenge to Jurisdiction: Lomé Accord Amnesty, SCSL-04-15-PT-060-I, paras. 60, 66–71 (2004).

[140] *Miguel Castro-Castro Prison v. Peru*, IACtHR Series C No. 160, paras. 402–4 (2006); *Almonacid Arellano et al. v. Chile*, IACtHR Series C No. 154, paras. 99, 128–9 (2006).

[141] *Princz v. Federal Republic of Germany*, 26 F.3d 1166, 1182 (DC Cir. 1994) (Wald, J., Dissenting).

[142] *Riveros v. Office of the Public Prosecutor*, Supreme Court of Justice (Argentina), M/2333/XLII, ILDC 1084, paras. 15, 32–8 (2007); *Chile v. Arancibia Clavel*, Supreme Court of Justice (Argentina), A/533/XXXVIII, ILDC 1082, para. 28 (2004); *Office of the Prosecutor v. Priebke*, Supreme Court of Justice (Argentina), P/457/XXXI, ILDC 1599, paras. 2–5 (1995).

[143] *Prosecutor's Office v. Anić*, Court of Bosnia and Herzegovina (Section I for War Crimes), S1 1 K 005596 11 Kro, ILDC 1907, paras. 27–8 (2011).

[144] *Re Víctor Raúl Pinto v. Relatives of Tomás Rojas*, Supreme Court (Chile), Decision on Annulment, No. 3125-04, ILDC 1093, paras. 29–31 (2007).

[145] *Germany v. Milde*, Court of Cassation (First Criminal Section) (Italy), No. 1072/2009, ILDC 1224, paras. 5–6 (2009); *Germany v. Mantelli and ors*, Court of Cassation (Italy), Preliminary Order on Jurisdiction, No. 14201/2008, ILDC 1037, para. 11 (2008); *Ferrini v. Germany*, Court of Cassation (Civil Section) (Italy), No. 5044/2004, ILDC 19, paras. 9–9.1 (2004).

Netherlands,[146] the Philippines,[147] South Korea,[148] Spain,[149] and the United States.[150]

v. *Aggression*

The prohibition against the aggravated use of force is one of the oldest norms of the law of nations, one dating to the inception of *jus ad bellum* and the earliest application of natural law principles to mediate international relations.[151] The emergence of the concept of 'just war' in international law reflected the existence of an international community governed by higher interests and social values through *jus ad bellum* and *jus in bello*. These principles were directed at mediating warfare through a kind of international morality whose ultimate beneficiary was mankind and the individual, its unit and ultimate victim of warfare. The premise of just war is articulated in the Dedication of *De Jure Belli Ac Pacis* by Grotius:

> It is worthy of your devotion to duty, worthy of your exalted estate, *not to attempt to despoil anyone of his rights by force of arms*, not to disturb ancient boundaries; but in war to continue the work of peace, and not to commence war save with the desire to end it at the earliest possible moment[.][152]

Natural law was, therefore, applied as *jus ad bellum* to mitigate war itself, not for the benefit of principalities and States but for the protection of the human person, in order to guard the rights of individuals. As indicated by Grotius, respect for the dignity of the individual depends upon the

[146] *Bouterse Case*, Amsterdam Court of Appeal (Netherlands), Nos. R 97/163/12 Sv & R 97/176/12 Sv, para. 5 (2000) (prosecuting crimes against humanity as crimes under customary international law subject to universal jurisdiction).

[147] *Muna et al. v. Romulo et al.*, Supreme Court (Philippines), GR No. 159618, ILDC 2059, paras. 89–94 (2011).

[148] *Yeo and ors v. Nippon Steel & Sumitomo Metal*, High Court (South Korea), 2012 Na 44947, ILDC 2104, Reference 3 (2013).

[149] *Scilingo Manzorro v. Spain*, Supreme Court (Spain), No. 798/2007, ILDC 1430, paras. 6-7 (2007); *Public Prosecutor's Office et al. v. Scilingo Manzorro*, National Court (*Audiencia Nacional*) (Criminal Chamber) (Spain), No. 16/2005, ILDC 136, paras. B.1–B.2, B.4–B.5 (2005).

[150] *Sarei v. Rio Tinto, PLC*, 487 F.3d 1193, 1202 (9th Cir. 2007) *on reh'g en banc*, 550 F.3d 822 (9th Cir. 2008); *Princz v. Federal Republic of Germany*, 26 F.3d 1166, 1182 (DC Cir. 1994) (Wald, J., Dissenting).

[151] *See* discussion *supra*, Chapter 7, text accompanying *nn.* 19–22.

[152] Grotius, De Jure, Dedication 4-5 (emphasis added).

transcendence of *jus ad bellum* over *raison d'état*. This same logical strand is found in contemporary jurisprudence, notably in *Armed Activities on the Territory of the Congo*, where Judge Dugard referred, in the context of *jus cogens*, to 'the right to be free from aggression' as 'one of the most important rights of the international order' which 'affirm the high principles of international law'; the corollary of that right is that the prohibition of aggression is one of 'the most fundamental policies or goals of the international community'.[153] Aggression constitutes the unlawful and aggravated use of force,[154] and its prohibition is widely recognized as a peremptory norm.[155]

[153] *Armed Activities on the Territory of the Congo (New Application: 2002) (Democratic Republic of the Congo v. Rwanda)*, Sep. Op. Dugard, ICJ Reports 2006, p. 86, para. 10.

[154] An important distinction should be made between the use of force and aggression. In *Military and Paramilitary Activities in and against Nicaragua*, the International Court referred to the prohibition of the use of force as containing certain exceptions as provided in the UN Charter, notably individual and collective self-defence under Article 51. ICJ Reports 1986, p. 14, paras. 190–3. One might add to this use of force pursuant to Article 42 of the UN Charter. Consequently, because the prohibition of the use of force permits derogation under certain circumstances, such prohibition does not belong to *jus cogens*. To make such a claim results in a *reductio ad absurdum*, as demonstrated by one commentator who employs this norm just so in an attempt to discredit *jus cogens* as a legal categorization more generally: Ulf Linderfalk, *The Effect of Jus Cogens Norms: Whoever Opened Pandora's Box, Did You Ever Think about the Consequences?*, 18(5) European Journal of International Law 853–71 (2008). The ILC has consistently avoided this tension by referring to the unlawful use of force as aggression, the latter of which is properly considered to belong to *jus cogens*. For example, the Draft Code of Offences (1954) defined the first prohibited offence against the peace and security of mankind as aggression: 'Any act of aggression, including the employment by the authorities of a State of armed force against another State for any purpose other than national or collective self-defence or in pursuance of a decision or recommendation of a competent organ of the United Nations'. In the Articles on State Responsibility, the ILC delineated a series of circumstances precluding wrongfulness of the use of force: consent, self-defence, countermeasures, *force majeure*, distress, and necessity. *See* ILC Articles on State Responsibility (2001), 27–8 (Chapter V, Articles 20–5). Of course, none of these circumstances may be invoked if doing so would conflict with a peremptory norm. *Ibid.* (Article 26). The commentary to Article 26 of the Articles makes this distinction between the sanctioned use of force and obligations arising under peremptory norms: *Ibid.*, 85, para. 6. What this indicates is that international law admits the lawful use of force and specifically prohibits as *jus cogens* the aggravated use of force. Although the crime of aggression is included in the Draft Code of Crimes (1996), Article 16, and the Rome Statute (1998), Article 5, a definition of aggression was formally adopted only in 2010 by the Review Conference of the Rome Statute following the Report by the Working Group on the Crime of Aggression. *See* ICC Review Conference, The Crime of Aggression, Resolution RC/Res. 6 (11 June 2010).

[155] Orakhelashvili, Peremptory Norms in International Law 216; Michael Byers, *Conceptualising the Relationship between* Jus Cogens *and* Erga Omnes *Rules*, 66 Nordic

Opinio juris sive necessitatis supporting the prohibition against aggression is expansive. The preamble of the Kellogg–Briand Pact (1928), which marks the first formal prohibition of aggression by States, expresses the awareness of its signatories 'of their solemn duty to promote the welfare of mankind' and their hope of 'uniting the civilized nations of the world in a common renunciation of war as an instrument of their national policy'.[156] The IMT at Nuremberg looked to the drafting of the Pact, as well as relevant League of Nations statements (what it termed 'international history'), 'as strong evidence of the intention to brand aggressive war as an international crime' and thus the '*expressions of opinion*' of the criminalization of aggression: 'The prohibition of aggressive war demanded by the conscience of the world, finds its expression in the series of pacts and treaties to which the Tribunal has just referred.'[157] The United Nations was subsequently established 'to save succeeding generations from the scourge of war', and to this end established as a chief purpose in the first Article of its Charter, to prevent and suppress acts of aggression.[158] At its first session, the UN General Assembly adopted Resolution 95 (1946) affirming the Nuremberg Principles, which included the prohibition of aggression as a crime against peace.[159] Further expressions of this *opinio juris* by the General Assembly may be derived from Resolution 2625 (1970), which adopted the Declaration on Principles of International Law Concerning Friendly Relations and Co-operation among States in accordance with the Charter of the United Nations,[160] and Resolution 3314 (1974), adopting the Definition of Aggression.[161] Like the judicial practice of the IMT, the International Court of Justice has looked to such articulations as affirmation of *opinio*

JOURNAL OF INTERNATIONAL LAW 211, 219 (1997); Hannikainen, PEREMPTORY NORMS (*JUS COGENS*) IN INTERNATIONAL LAW 117–24, 178, 317, 323–56 (1988); Herman Mosler, *The International Society as a Legal Community*, 140 RECUEIL DES COURS 35–6 (1974); Ulrich Scheuner, *Conflict of Treaty Provisions with a Peremptory Norm of General International Law*, 29(4) ZEITSCHRIFT FÜR AUSLANDISCHES OFFENTLISCHES RECHT UND VOLKERRECHT 28, 33 (1969).

[156] The Kellogg–Briand Pact of Paris, 46 Stat. 2343, 94 LNTS 57, TS No. 796, Preamble (signed at Paris 27 August 1928, *entered into force* 24 July 1929).

[157] *Nazi Conspiracy and Aggression*, Opinion and Judgment, International Military Tribunal at Nuremberg 52 (1946); *see* discussion *infra*, text accompanying *n.* 175.

[158] Charter of the United Nations, Preamble, Article 1(1) (1945).

[159] Affirmation of the Principles of International Law Recognized by the Charter of the Nürnberg Tribunal, GA Res. 95 (I), UN Doc. A/Res/95(I) (11 December 1946).

[160] GA Res. 2625 (XXV), UN Doc. A/Res/25/2625 (24 October 1970) (like the Kellogg–Briand Pact, the Declaration refers to aggression as a crime against peace).

[161] GA Res. 3314 (XXIX), UN Doc. A/Res/3314 (XXIX) (1974).

juris sive necessitatis supporting the prohibition against aggression. In *Military and Paramilitary Activities in and against Nicaragua* (1986), for example, the International Court referred to *opinio* evidenced by the Declaration on Principles of International Law Concerning Friendly Relations and Co-operation among States as limiting the use of force in accordance with the Charter of the United Nations.[162] And in *Barcelona Traction*, the Court indicated the existence of *opinio* by observing that obligations arising from the prohibition against aggression 'towards the international community as a whole . . . are the concern of all States'.[163] In a similar sense, the Rome Statute identifies aggression as one of 'the most serious crimes of concern to the international community as a whole'.[164]

State practice evidencing the *opinio juris sive necessitatis* prohibiting aggression is equally vast. Relevant international instruments recognizing the prohibition of aggression as an international crime include the Kellogg–Briand Pact,[165] a series of multilateral conventions concluded pursuant to the Kellogg–Briand Pact,[166] the Nuremberg Charter,[167] the Tokyo Charter,[168] the Principles of International Law Recognized in the Charter of the Nuremberg Tribunal and in the Judgment of the Tribunal,[169] the Draft Code of Offences against the Peace and Security of Mankind,[170] the Draft Code of Crimes against the Peace and Security of Mankind,[171] the Rome Statute,[172] and The Crime of Aggression.[173]

162 *Military and Paramilitary Activities in and against Nicaragua (Nicaragua v. United States of America)*, Judgment, ICJ Reports 1986, p. 14, para. 191 ('As already observed, the adoption by States of this text affords an indication of their *opinio juris* as to customary international law on the question. Alongside certain descriptions which may refer to aggression, this text includes others which refer only to less grave forms of the use of force').

163 *Barcelona Traction, Light and Power Company, Limited (Belgium v. Spain)*, Judgment, ICJ Reports 1970, p. 3, para. 33.

164 Rome Statute (1998), Article 5.

165 *See supra, n.* 157.

166 *See, e.g.*, Convention for the Definition of Aggression, 147 LNTS 69, No. 3391 (signed at London 3 July 1933, *entered into force* 17 February 1934).

167 IMT Charter (1945), Article 6(a) (defining 'crimes against peace' in relation to 'a war of aggression' or other illegal war).

168 IMTFE Charter (1946), Article 5(a) (defining 'crimes against peace' in relation to 'a war of aggression' or other illegal war).

169 Report of the International Law Commission Covering the Work of its First Session, [1950] II YbILC 374–8, Principle VI(a) (Formulation of the Nürnberg Principles) (defining 'crimes against peace' in relation to 'a war of aggression' or other illegal war).

170 Draft Code of Offences (1954), Article 2, paras. 1–2.

171 Draft Code of Crimes (1996), Article 16 (Crime of Aggression).

172 Rome Statute (1998), Article 5(1)(d) (The Crime of Aggression).

173 ICC Review Conference, The Crime of Aggression, Resolution RC/Res.6 (11 June 2010).

With reference to the practice of international organs, the ILC has consistently referred to the prohibition of aggression as a peremptory norm.[174]

The *jus cogens* character of the prohibition of aggression has been reflected in international jurisprudence. In its Judgment, which preceded the category of *jus cogens*, the IMT made reference to the emergence of the prohibition against aggression indicative of its peremptory character:

> [I]t must be remembered that international law is not the product of an international legislature, and that such international agreements as the [Kellogg–Briand] Pact of Paris have to deal with general principles of law, and not with administrative matters of procedure. The law of war is to be found not only in treaties, but in the customs and practices of states which gradually obtained universal recognition, and from the general principles of justice applied by jurists and practiced by military courts. This law is not static, but by continual adaptation follows the needs of a changing world. Indeed, in many cases treaties do no more than express and define for more accurate reference the principles of law already existing.[175]

It is in this way that the prohibition of aggression emerged in contemporary international law, evidenced by State practice expressive of the social need of the international community (*opinio juris sive necessitatis*). By implication, the International Court indicated the peremptory nature of the prohibition against aggression in *Barcelona Traction* with reference to derivative obligations *erga omnes* arising from 'the outlawing of acts of aggression'.[176] And, as noted above, in his separate opinion in *Armed Activities on the Territory of the Congo*, Judge Dugard identified the prohibition against aggression as belonging to *jus cogens*.[177] Most conclusively, the International Court in 2010 referred to 'the unlawful use of force' as among 'egregious violations of norms of general international law, in particular those of a peremptory character (*jus cogens*)'.[178] Although it is rare for aggression to arise before domestic courts by

[174] *See* ILC Articles on State Responsibility (2001), 112, para. 4 (Commentary to Article 40); Waldock, Fifth Report, [1966] II YbILC 248, para. 3 (Commentary to Article 50).

[175] *Nazi Conspiracy and Aggression*, Opinion and Judgment, International Military Tribunal at Nuremberg 52 (1946).

[176] *Barcelona Traction, Light and Power Company, Limited (Belgium v. Spain)*, Judgment, ICJ Reports 1970, p. 3, para. 34.

[177] *Armed Activities on the Territory of the Congo (New Application: 2002) (Democratic Republic of the Congo v. Rwanda)*, Sep. Op. Dugard, ICJ Reports 2006, p. 86, para. 10.

[178] *Accordance with International Law of the Unilateral Declaration of Independence in Respect of Kosovo*, Advisory Opinion, ICJ Reports 2010, p. 403, para. 81.

virtue of a special regime of prosecution for the crime,[179] the House of Lords referred to the *jus cogens* status of the prohibition in *Kuwait Airways Corporation v. Iraqi Airways Company* (2002).[180] In that case, the status of the norm justified a public policy exception to the Act of State doctrine, explaining the invalidation of Iraqi legislation promulgated pursuant to the invasion and annexation of Kuwait.[181]

vi. Genocide

The recognition of genocide as an international crime by the international community can be viewed as a direct response to atrocities committed during the Second World War.[182] Its inception may be traced to a proposal by Raphael Lemkin, to the Fifth Conference for the Unification of Penal Law in Madrid, calling for a League of Nations convention prohibiting the 'crime of barbarity' and other 'offences against the law of nations', whose universal prohibition 'attests to the fact that there is a legal conscience of the civilized international community'.[183] Although the proposal was not adopted, the crime of genocide (a term also coined by Lemkin) eventually entered into international law as the outlaw of specific 'acts committed with intent to destroy, in whole or in part, a national, ethnic, racial, or

[179] Report of the International Law Commission on the Work of its Forty-Eighth Session, [1996] II(2) YbILC 30, para. 14 (Commentary to Article 8) ('The aggression attributed to a State is a *sine qua non* for the responsibility of an individual for his participation in the crime of aggression. An individual cannot incur responsibility for this crime in the absence of aggression committed by a State. Thus, a court cannot determine the question of individual criminal responsibility for this crime without considering as a preliminary matter the question of aggression by a State. The determination by a national court of one State of the question of whether another State had committed aggression would be contrary to the fundamental principle of international law *par in parem imperium non habet*').

[180] *Kuwait Airways Corporation v. Iraqi Airways Company*, House of Lords (UK) [2002] UKHL 19, para. 114 (Steyn, L.).

[181] *Ibid.* (Resolution 369, which purported to dissolve the Kuwait Airways Corporation and transfer its property to the Iraqi Airways Company, was therefore not given effect by UK courts).

[182] *See* GA Res. 96 (I), The Crime of Genocide, UN Doc. A/Res/96 (I) (1 December 1946).

[183] Raphael Lemkin, *Acts Constituting a General (Transnational) Danger Considered as Offences against the Law of Nations: Additional Explications to the Special Report presented to the 5th Conference for the Unification of Penal Law in Madrid (14–20 October 1933)*, *in* Key Writings of Raphael Lemkin on Genocide (James Fussell, trans.), *available at* www.preventgenocide.org (last accessed 15 August 2014).

religious group'.[184] Genocide is manifestly opposed to the higher interests of the international community, and its prohibition has been conceived in international law in these very terms by the International Court of Justice, with respect to the 1948 Genocide Convention:

> The Convention was manifestly adopted for a purely humanitarian and civilizing purpose. It is indeed difficult to imagine a convention that might have this dual character to a greater degree, since its object on the one hand is to safeguard the very existence of certain human groups and on the other to confirm and endorse the most elementary principles of morality. In such a convention the contracting States do not have any interests of their own; they merely have, one and all, a common interest, namely, the accomplishment of those high purposes which are the *raison d'être* of the convention. Consequently, in a convention of this type one cannot speak of individual advantages or disadvantages to States, or of the maintenance of a perfect contractual balance between rights and duties. The high ideals which inspired the Convention provide, by virtue of the common will of the parties, the foundation and measure of all its provisions.[185]

These 'high ideals', given effect through the prohibition of genocide, express the social need of the international community as a whole in a way that reflects common interests and values represented by human dignity. Contemporary doctrine universally recognizes the prohibition against genocide as a peremptory norm of general international law.[186]

The *opinio juris sive necessitatis* supporting the prohibition of genocide may be traced to UN General Assembly Resolution 96 (The Crime of Genocide), which was adopted at the institution's first session in 1946. The General Assembly identified 'the punishment of the crime of genocide [as] a matter of international concern' and, to this end, affirmed 'that genocide is a crime under international law which the civilized world

[184] Convention on the Prevention and Punishment of the Crime of Genocide, Article II, 78 UNTS 277, No. 1021 (9 December 1948, *entered into force* 12 January 1951) [hereinafter, Genocide Convention (1948)].

[185] *Reservations to the Genocide Convention*, Advisory Opinion, ICJ Reports 1951, p. 15, 23.

[186] Orakhelashvili, Peremptory Norms in International Law 216; Michael Byers, *Conceptualising the Relationship between* Jus Cogens *and* Erga Omnes *Rules*, 66 Nordic Journal of International Law 211, 219 (1997); Hannikainen, Peremptory Norms (*Jus Cogens*) in International Law 456–66; Lachs, *The Development and General Trends of International Law in Our Time*, 206; Scheuner, *Conflict of Treaty Provisions with a Peremptory Norm of General International Law*, 33.

condemns'.[187] The Convention on the Prevention and Punishment of the Crime of Genocide (1948) was subsequently adopted by the General Assembly to marshal international cooperation 'in order to liberate mankind from such an odious scourge'.[188] In its Advisory Opinion, *Reservations to the Genocide Convention* (1951), the International Court undertook a tacit examination of *opinio juris sive necessitatis* forbidding genocide by assessing the intent of the international community expressed by these two articulations by the General Assembly:

> The origins of the Convention show that it was the intention of the United Nations to condemn and punish genocide as 'a crime under international law' involving a denial of the right of existence of entire human groups, a denial which shocks the conscience of mankind and results in great losses to humanity, and which is contrary to moral law and to the spirit and aims of the United Nations. The first consequence arising from this conception is that the principles underlying the Convention are principles which are recognized by civilized nations as binding on States, even without any conventional obligation. A second consequence is the universal character both of the condemnation of genocide and of the co-operation required 'in order to liberate mankind from such an odious scourge'. The Genocide Convention was therefore intended by the General Assembly and by the contracting parties to be definitely universal in scope. It was in fact approved on December 9th, 1948, by a resolution which was unanimously adopted by fifty-six States.[189]

Subsequent expressions of this *opinio* may be gleaned from the Statute of the ICTY, adopted by the UN Security Council,[190] and its subsequent jurisprudence, which refers to genocide as a universally condemned offence,[191] and the 2005 World Summit Outcome document adopted by the UN General Assembly, which details obligations of the international community arising from the responsibility to protect populations from genocide.[192]

International practice of States evidencing the *opinio juris sive necessitatis* prohibiting genocide is expansive. International instruments criminalizing genocide include the Convention on the Prevention and

187 GA Res. 96 (I), The Crime of Genocide, UN Doc. A/Res/96 (I) (1 December 1946).

188 GA Res. 260 (III), UN Doc. A/Res/260 (III) (9 December 1948).

189 *Reservations to the Genocide Convention*, Advisory Opinion, ICJ Reports 1951, p. 15, 23.

190 ICTY Statute (1993), Article 4 (Genocide).

191 *Prosecutor v. Nikolić*, Decision on Interlocutory Appeal Concerning Legality of Arrest, IT-94-2-AR73, paras. 24–5 (2003).

192 2005 World Summit Outcome, GA Res. 60/1, UN Doc. A/Res/60/1, paras. 138–9 (24 October 2005).

Punishment of Genocide,[193] the Draft Code of Offences against the Peace and Security of Mankind,[194] the Statutes of the ICTY,[195] and ICTR,[196] the Draft Code of Crimes against the Peace and Security of Mankind,[197] and the Rome Statute.[198] The practice of international organs, such as the ILC, similarly evidences this *opinio juris*.[199]

Courts and tribunals have repeatedly recognized the *jus cogens* character of the prohibition of genocide. The International Court has consistently observed that genocide constitutes a universal prohibition arising from the higher interests of the international community, giving rise to obligations *erga omnes*,[200] though it explicitly referred to *jus cogens* only as recently as 2006 (which marked the Court's first formal recognition of *jus cogens*).[201] The ICTY,[202] and ICTR,[203] have also recognized the *jus cogens* nature of the prohibition of genocide. And domestic courts in Canada,[204] Germany,[205] Italy,[206] the Philippines,[207]

[193] Genocide Convention (1948), Article I.

[194] Draft Code of Offences (1954), Article 2, para. 10.

[195] ICTY Statute (1993), Article 4. [196] ICTR Statute (1994), Article 2.

[197] Draft Code of Crimes (1996), Article 17.

[198] Rome Statute (1998), Article 6; *see* Elements of Crimes (2002), Article 6.

[199] International Law Commission (finalized by Martti Koskenniemi), *Fragmentation of International Law*, UN Doc. A/CN.4/L.682, para. 374 (2006); ILC Articles on State Responsibility (2001), 112, para. 4 (Commentary to Article 40).

[200] *Application of the Convention on the Prevention and Punishment of the Crime of Genocide (Bosnia and Herzegovina v. Serbia and Montenegro)*, Judgment, ICJ Reports 2007, p. 43, paras. 147, 162; *Armed Activities on the Territory of the Congo (New Application: 2002) (Democratic Republic of the Congo v. Rwanda)*, Judgment, ICJ Reports 2006, p. 6, paras. 64, 125; *Barcelona Traction, Light and Power Company, Limited (Belgium v. Spain)*, Judgment, ICJ Reports 1970, p. 3, paras. 33–4.

[201] *Application of the Convention on the Prevention and Punishment of the Crime of Genocide (Bosnia and Herzegovina v. Serbia and Montenegro)*, Judgment, ICJ Reports 2007, p. 43, para. 161; *Armed Activities on the Territory of the Congo (New Application: 2002) (Congo v. Rwanda)*, ICJ Reports 2006, p. 3, paras. 64, 125; *Reservations to the Genocide Convention*, Advisory Opinion, ICJ Reports 1951, p. 15, 23.

[202] *Prosecutor v. Brđanin*, IT-99-36-T, para. 680 (2004); *Prosecutor v. Kristic*, IT-98-33-T, para. 541 (2001); *Prosecutor v. Jelisić*, IT-95-10-T, para. 60 (1999).

[203] *Prosecutor v. Kayishema and Ruzindana*, ICTR-95-1-T, para. 88 (1999).

[204] *Regina v. Munyaneza*, Montreal Superior Court (Criminal Division) (Canada), 2009 QCCS 2201, paras. 70–9 (2009).

[205] *Jorgic Case*, BVerfG [Constitutional Court] (Germany), 2 BvR 1290/99, ILDC 132, paras. 17, 26–7 (2000).

[206] *Lozano v. Italy*, Court of Cassation (First Criminal Chamber) (Italy), No. 31171/2008, ILDC 1085, para. 6 (2008).

[207] *Muna et al. v. Romulo et al.*, Supreme Court (Philippines), GR No. 159618, ILDC 2059, paras. 40–50, 89–94 (2011).

Spain,[208] and the United States[209] have recognized the *jus cogens* character of the prohibition of genocide.

vii. Torture

The etymology of torture, deriving from the Latin *tort*, is indicative of the nature of the act as causing harm or wrong to a human being through the infliction of pain or injury.[210] Torture is quite obviously contrary to respect for the intrinsic dignity and worth of the human person. The convergence of the prohibition of torture in international human rights law, international humanitarian law, and international criminal law is indicative of the higher interests of the international community in safeguarding the dignity of the human person through its prohibition. It is precisely through this convergence that the prohibition of torture has emerged as a discrete peremptory norm of general international law, one that has 'now become one of the most fundamental standards of the international community'.[211] As observed by Judge Cançado Trindade in *Questions Relating to the Obligation to Prosecute or Extradite* (2012):

> The basic principle of humanity, rooted in the human conscience, has arisen and stood against torture. In effect, in our times, the *jus cogens* prohibition of torture emanates ultimately from the universal juridical

208 *Guatemala Genocide Case (Menchú Tumn and ors v. Two Guatemalan Government Officials and Six Members of the Guatemalan Military)*, National Court (Spain), Response to the Guatemala Constitutional Court, No. 331/1999, 4 (2008); *Guatemala Genocide Case (Menchú Tumn and ors v. Two Guatemalan Government Officials and Six Members of the Guatemalan Military)*, Constitutional Court (Criminal Chamber) (Spain), Spanish Constitutional Court Decision Accepting Jurisdiction, No. 237/2005, ILDC 137 (2005).

209 *Abelesz v. Magyar Nemzeti Bank*, 692 F.3d 661, 676 (7th Cir. 2012); *Sarei v. Rio Tinto, PLC*, 671 F.3d 736, 759 (9th Cir. 2011) *cert. granted, judgment vacated sub nom. Rio Tinto PLC v. Sarei*, 133 S. Ct. 1995 (2013) (citing *Bosnia v. Serbia*, 2007 ICJ Reports 91, para. 161).

210 *See* Convention against Torture and Other Cruel, Inhuman or Degrading Treatment or Punishment, GA Res. 39/46, 1465 UNTS 85, Article 1 (12 December 1984, *entered into force* 26 June 1987) ('the term "torture" means any act by which severe pain or suffering, whether physical or mental, is intentionally inflicted on a person for such purposes as obtaining from him or a third person information or a confession, punishing him for an act he or a third person has committed or is suspected of having committed, or intimidating or coercing him or a third person, or for any reason based on discrimination of any kind, when such pain or suffering is inflicted by or at the instigation of or with the consent or acquiescence of a public official or other person acting in an official capacity') [hereinafter, Torture Convention (1984)].

211 *Prosecutor v. Furundžija*, IT-95-17/1-T, paras. 153–4 (1998).

> conscience, and finds expression in the *corpus juris gentium* . . . Identified with general principles of law enshrining common and superior values shared by the international community as a whole, *jus cogens* ascribes an ethical content to the new *jus gentium*, the International Law for humankind. In prohibiting torture in any circumstances whatsoever, *jus cogens* exists indeed to the benefit of human beings, and ultimately of humankind.[212]

Under international law, torture is understood to constitute the intentional infliction of severe physical or mental pain and suffering.[213] The prohibition against torture is widely recognized in doctrine as a norm of *jus cogens*.[214]

Indication of *opinio juris sive necessitatis* in support of the prohibition of torture is found in the Universal Declaration of Human Rights (1948),[215] which begins with a preambular statement articulating the inherent dignity and equal rights of all members of the human family. Further indication of this *opinio* may be drawn from Resolution 3452 (1975) adopted by the UN General Assembly, titled Declaration on the Protection of All Persons from Being Subjected to Torture and Other Cruel, Inhuman or Degrading Treatment or Punishment.[216] In its preambular statement, the General Assembly considered the higher interests underpinning the need to prohibit torture to constitute 'the inalienable rights of all members of the human family . . . [which] derive from the inherent dignity of the human person'. General Assembly Resolution 39/46 (1984), which adopted the Convention against Torture and opened the instrument for signature, recounted the sustained work of the GA towards the drafting of a Torture Convention in such a way as to express *opinio juris sive necessitatis*.[217] Taking note of a history of *opinio* concerning the prohibition against torture, the first *special rapporteur* on

212 *Questions Relating to the Obligation to Prosecute or Extradite (Belgium v. Senegal)*, Judgment, ICJ Reports 2012, Sep. Op. Cançado Trindade, p. 487, paras. 84, 182.

213 Torture Convention (1984), Article 1.

214 Orakhelashvili, Peremptory Norms in International Law 225; Erika De Wet, *The Prohibition of Torture as an International Norm of* Jus Cogens *and Its Implications for National and Customary Law*, 1(1) European Journal of International Law 97–121 (2004); Byers, *Conceptualising the Relationship between* Jus Cogens *and* Erga Omnes *Rules*, 219; Hannikainen, Peremptory Norms (*Jus Cogens*) in International Law 499–513.

215 Universal Declaration (1948), Article 5.

216 GA Res. 3452, UN Doc. A/Res/30/3452 (9 December 1975).

217 Torture Convention (1984), Article 1.

Torture appointed by the UN Commission on Human Rights concluded that the prohibition of torture belongs to *jus cogens*.[218]

This *opinio juris sive necessitatis* is evidenced in the practice of States, notably in codification of the International Covenant on Civil and Political Rights (1966),[219] and the Convention against Torture and Other Cruel, Inhuman or Degrading Treatment or Punishment (1984),[220] as well as the criminalization of torture in the statute of the Extraordinary African Chambers.[221] Regional practice has consistently supported the prohibition of torture,[222] further evidencing the prevailing *opinio juris* against torture. Various further practice is found in the prohibition of torture as a violation of international humanitarian law and a crime against humanity.[223] The

218 Pieter Kooijmans, Report of the *Special Rapporteur* on Torture, UN Doc. E/CN.4/1986/15, para. 3 (19 February 1986) ('Torture is now absolutely and without any reservation prohibited under international law whether in time of peace or of war. In all human rights instruments the prohibition of torture belongs to the group of rights from which no derogation can be made. The International Court of Justice has qualified the obligation to respect the basic human rights, to which the right not to be tortured belongs beyond any doubt, as obligations *erga omnes*, which a State has *vis-à-vis* the community of States as a whole and in the implementation of which every State has a legal interest. The International Law Commission ... has labeled serious violations of these basic human rights as "international crimes", giving rise to the specific responsibility of the States concerned. In view of these qualifications, the prohibition of torture can be considered to belong to the rules of *jus cogens*. If ever a phenomenon was outlawed unreservedly and unequivocally it is torture').

219 International Covenant on Civil and Political Rights, 99 UNTS 171, Preamble (1966) (*entered into force* 23 March 1976), Article 7.

220 Torture Convention (1984).

221 Agreement on the Establishment of the Extraordinary African Chambers within the Senegalese Judicial System between the Government of the Republic of Senegal and the African Union and the Statute of the Chambers, Article 4(d) (22 August 2012 and 30 January 2013), 52 ILM 1028 [hereinafter, EAC Statute (2013)].

222 African Charter on Human and Peoples' Rights, OAU Doc. CAB/LEG/67/3 rev. 5, Article 5 (27 June 1981, *entered into force* 21 October 1986); European Convention for the Prevention of Torture and Inhuman or Degrading Treatment or Punishment, ETS No. 126 (26 November 1987, *entered into force* 1 February 1989); Inter-American Convention to Prevent and Punish Torture, OAS TS No. 67 (9 December 1985, *entered into force* 28 February 1987); American Convention on Human Rights, OAS TS No. 36, Article 5(2) (22 November 1969, *entered into force* 18 July 1978); European Convention for the Protection of Human Rights and Fundamental Freedoms, as amended by Protocols Nos. 11 and 14, ETS No. 5, Article 3 (4 November 1950, *entered into force* 3 September 1953).

223 *See* Elements of Crimes (2002), Articles 7(1)(f), 8(2)(a)(ii); SCSL Statute (2000), Article 2(f); Rome Statute (1998), Article 7(1)(f), 8(2)(a)(ii); Draft Code of Crimes (1996), Articles 18(c), 20(a)(ii); ICTR Statute (1994), Article 3(f); ICTY Statute (1993), Articles 2(b), 5(f).

international practice of the UN Committee against Torture,[224] as well as the ILC, [225] indicates the *jus cogens* nature of the prohibition of torture.

The emergence of the prohibition of torture as *jus cogens* has been reflected extensively in international, regional, and domestic jurisprudence. The International Court of Justice had occasion to recognize the peremptory status of the prohibition, on the basis of *opinio juris sive necessitatis* evidenced by the practice of States, in *Questions Relating to the Obligation to Prosecute or Extradite* (2012).[226] Whilst indicating the source of the prohibition in *opinio* and State practice, the brevity of its treatment by the Court reflects the extent of existing jurisprudence on the prohibition of torture, which belayed the need for further investigation, and to which the pronouncement by the International Court is further testament. Such prior jurisprudence includes most notably the *Furundžija* decision,[227] though the ICTY also articulated the *jus cogens* status of the prohibition on numerous other occasions.[228] The IACtHR,[229] and the ECtHR,[230] have made similar pronouncements reflecting the *jus cogens* status of the prohibition of torture. Judgments by domestic courts recognizing the *jus cogens* character of the prohibition of torture include those in Australia,[231]

[224] Committee Against Torture, General Comment No. 2, Implementation of Article 2 by States Parties, CAT/C/GC/2/CRP.1/Rev.4, para. 1 (23 November 2007).

[225] ILC Articles on State Responsibility (2001), 113, para. 5 (Commentary to Article 40).

[226] *Questions Relating to the Obligation to Prosecute or Extradite (Belgium v. Senegal)*, Judgment, ICJ Reports 2012, p. 422, para. 99.

[227] *Prosecutor v. Furundžija*, IT-95-17/1-T, paras. 153–4 (1998).

[228] *Prosecutor v. Simić*, IT-95-9/2-S, para. 34 (2002); *Prosecutor v. Kunarac et al.*, IT-96-23-T / IT-96-23/1-T, para. 466 (2001); *Prosecutor v. Delalić et al.*, IT-96-21-T, para. 454 (1998).

[229] *See, e.g.*, *Bayarri v. Argentina*, IACtHR Series C No. 187, para. 81 (2008); *Servellón García and ors v. Honduras*, IACtHR Series C No. 152, paras. 89–97 (2006); *Ximenes-Lopes v. Brazil*, IACtHR Series C No. 149 (2006); *Baldeón García v. Peru*, IACtHR Series C No. 147, para. 117 (2006); *Ramírez v. Guatemala*, IACtHR Series C No. 126, para. 117 (2005); *Ceaser v. Trinidad and Tobago*, IACtHR Series C No. 123, para. 100 (2005); *Tibi v. Ecuador*, IACtHR, Series C No. 114, para. 143 (2004); *Brothers Gomez Paquiyauri v. Peru*, IACtHR Series C No. 110, paras. 111–12 (2004).

[230] *Jones v. United Kingdom*, ECtHR, Nos. 34356/06 & 40528/06, paras. 210–14 (2014); *Othman v. United Kingdom*, ECtHR, No. 8139/09, paras. 253–5, 266–7 (2012); *Demir and Baykara v. Turkey*, ECtHR, No. 34503/97, para. 73 (2009); *Al-Adsani v. United Kingdom*, ECtHR, No. 35763/97 (2001).

[231] *Habib v. Australia*, Federal Court of Australia Full Court, [2010] FCAFC 12, ILDC 1518.

Canada,[232] France,[233] Italy,[234] the Netherlands,[235] New Zealand,[236] South Africa,[237] the United Kingdom,[238] and the United States.[239]

viii. Apartheid (systematic racial discrimination)

The prohibition of apartheid in international law derives from the basic right to equality found in Article 1 of the Universal Declaration of Human Rights, whereby apartheid constitutes a fundamental violation of this right, of the dignity of the human person, and the higher interests of the international community.[240] Consequently, as a systematic and institutionalized programme of racial discrimination, apartheid constitutes a violation of human dignity.[241] The historical emergence of apartheid as a peremptory norm is inexorably linked to

[232] *Bouzari v. Islamic Republic of Iran*, Court of Appeal for Ontario (Canada), 71 OR (3d) 675, paras. 57–73 (2004); *Suresh v. Canada (Minister of Citizenship and Immigration)*, Supreme Court (Canada), [2002] 1 SCR 3, paras. 46, 59–64.

[233] *Lydienne X v. Prosecutor*, Court of Cassation (Criminal Division) (France), No. 12-81676, ILDC 2035, paras. 10.4, 14 (2013).

[234] *Lozano v. Italy*, Court of Cassation (First Criminal Chamber) (Italy), No. 31171/2008, ILDC 1085, para. 6 (2008).

[235] *Bouterse Case*, Amsterdam Court of Appeal (Netherlands), Nos. R 97/163/12 Sv & R 97/176/12 Sv, para. 5 (2000), *reversed by Bouterse Case*, Supreme Court (Netherlands), LJN: AB1471, ILDC 80 (2001).

[236] *Attorney General v. Ahmed Zaoui and ors*, Supreme Court (New Zealand), SC CIV 19/2004, [2005] NZSC 38, ILDC 81, para. 51 (2005).

[237] *Mthembu v. State*, Supreme Court of Appeal (South Africa), No. 379/07, (2008) ZASCA 51, ILDC 958 (2008).

[238] *Jones v. Ministry of the Interior of Saudi Arabia and Lieutenant Colonel Abdul Aziz*, House of Lords (UK), [2006] UKHL 26; *K. v. Secretary of State for the Home Department*, House of Lords (UK), [2006] UKHL 46, para. 8 (Bingham, L.); *R. (on the application of Al-Skeini and ors) v. Secretary of State for Defence*, High Court of Justice (UK), [2004] EWHC 2911 (Admin.), para. 216 (Rix, L.J.); *R. v. Bow Street Metropolitan Stipendiary Magistrate and Others, Ex parte Pinochet Ugarte (No. 3)*, House of Lords (UK), [2000] 1 A.C. 147, 38 ILM 581 (1999).

[239] *See, e.g.*, *Doe I v. Unocal Corp.*, 395 F.3d 932, 945 (9th Cir. 2002) *on reh'g en banc sub nom. John Doe I v. Unocal Corp.*, 403 F.3d 708 (9th Cir. 2005); *In re Estate of Ferdinand Marcos, Human Rights Litigation*, 25 F.3d 1467, 1475 (9th Cir. 1994); *Siderman de Blake v. Republic of Argentina*, 965 F.2d 699, 717 (9th Cir. 1992); *Filartiga v. Pena-Irala*, 630 F.2d 876 (2nd Cir. 1980).

[240] *See, e.g.*, GA Res. 395 (V), UN Doc. A/Res/395 (V) (2 December 1950) ('*Considering* that a policy of "racial segregation" (*Apartheid*) is necessarily based on doctrines of racial discrimination').

[241] *See* International Convention on the Suppression and Punishment of the Crime of Apartheid, 1015 UNTS 243 (30 November 1973, *entered into force* 18 July 1976), Article II:

> For the purpose of the present Convention, the term 'the crime of apartheid', which shall include similar policies and practices of racial

the condemnation of discriminatory practices of South Africa both within its borders and in then South West Africa (Namibia).[242] Such policies were recognized by the international community to be contrary to its higher interests:

> As is plain from the texts of its many resolutions, what decided the United Nations to penalize South Africa's conduct was much less the non-compliance over reports and petitions than the flagrant violation of the most essential principles of humanity, principles protected by the

segregation and discrimination as practised in southern Africa, shall apply to the following inhuman acts committed for the purpose of establishing and maintaining domination by one racial group of persons over any other racial group of persons and systematically oppressing them:

(a) Denial to a member or members of a racial group or groups of the right to life and liberty of person:
  (i) By murder of members of a racial group or groups;
  (ii) By the infliction upon the members of a racial group or groups of serious bodily or mental harm, by the infringement of their freedom or dignity, or by subjecting them to torture or to cruel, inhuman or degrading treatment or punishment;
  (iii) By arbitrary arrest and illegal imprisonment of the members of a racial group or groups;
(b) Deliberate imposition on a racial group or groups of living conditions calculated to cause its or their physical destruction in whole or in part;
(c) Any legislative measures and other measures calculated to prevent a racial group or groups from participation in the political, social, economic and cultural life of the country and the deliberate creation of conditions preventing the full development of such a group or groups, in particular by denying to members of a racial group or groups basic human rights and freedoms, including the right to work, the right to form recognized trade unions, the right to education, the right to leave and to return to their country, the right to a nationality, the right to freedom of movement and residence, the right to freedom of opinion and expression, and the right to freedom of peaceful assembly and association;
(d) Any measures, including legislative measures, designed to divide the population along racial lines by the creation of separate reserves and ghettos for the members of a racial group or groups, the prohibition of mixed marriages among members of various racial groups, the expropriation of landed property belonging to a racial group or groups or to members thereof;
(e) Exploitation of the labour of the members of a racial group or groups, in particular by submitting them to forced labour;
(f) Persecution of organizations and persons, by depriving them of fundamental rights and freedoms, because they oppose *apartheid.*

242 *Ibid. See, e.g., Legal Consequences for States of the Continued Presence of South Africa in Namibia (South West Africa) notwithstanding Security Council Resolution 276 (1970),* Advisory Opinion, ICJ Reports 1971, p. 16.

> sanction of international law: equality, of which *apartheid* is the negation ... and the dignity of the human person[.][243]

With respect to the non-compliance referred to by Judge Ammoun, the clearest examples of the inefficacy of the persistent objector exemption to legal obligations arising under general international law concern the international response to policies of apartheid imposed by South Africa and Rhodesia.[244] Contemporary international legal doctrine widely recognizes the prohibition against apartheid (racial discrimination) as a peremptory norm.[245]

Expressions of *opinio juris sive necessitatis* supporting the prohibition of apartheid demonstrate a consistent and sustained condemnation of such conduct by the international community. Following the Declaration on the Elimination of All Forms of Racial Discrimination (1963),[246] which was unanimously adopted by the General Assembly, a series of subsequent resolutions condemned racial discrimination and apartheid as 'a total negation of the purposes and principles of the Charter of the United Nations' and a crime against humanity.[247] Additionally, a long series of General Assembly resolutions addressed apartheid in the South African context, further indicating the *opinio juris sive necessitatis* of the international community through the identification of apartheid and racial discrimination as crimes against humanity.[248] The Security Council similarly declared its opposition to apartheid in South Africa and called for international action in connection to the situation in

243 *Ibid.*, Sep. Op. Ammoun, p. 55, para. 8.

244 Jonathan Charney, *The Persistent Objector Rule and the Development of Customary International Law*, 56 British Yearbook of International Law 1, 15 (1985).

245 Brownlie, Principles of Public International Law 515; Byers, *Conceptualising the Relationship between* Jus Cogens *and* Erga Omnes *Rules*, 219; Hannikainen, Peremptory Norms (*Jus Cogens*) in International Law 75–87, 467–89; Scheuner, *Conflict of Treaty Provisions with a Peremptory Norm of General International Law*, 33.

246 GA Res. 1904 (XVIII), UN Doc. A/Res/1904 (XVIII) (20 November 1963).

247 GA Res. 2106 (XX), UN Doc. A/Res/2106 (XX) (21 December 1965) (International Convention on the Elimination of All Forms of Racial Discrimination); GA Res. 2786 (XXVI), UN Doc. A/Res/2786 (XXVI) (6 November 1971); GA Res. 2922 (XXVII), UN Doc. A/Res/2922 (XXVII) (15 November 1972); GA Res. 3068 (XXVIII), UN Doc. A/Res/3068 (XXVIII) (30 November 1973).

248 GA Res. 1761 (XVII), UN Doc. A/Res/1761 (XVII) (6 November 1962); GA Res. 2074 (XX), UN Doc. A/Res/2074 (XX) (17 December 1965); GA Res. 2145 (XXI), UN Doc. A/Res/2145 (XXI) (27 October 1966); GA Res. 2307 (XXII), UN Doc. A/Res/2307 (XXII) (13 December 1967); GA Res. 2396, UN Doc. A/Res/2396 (XXIII) (2 December 1968); GA Res. 2506, UN Doc. A/Res/2506 (XXIV) (21 November 1969).

Namibia.[249] In *Legal Consequences for States of the Continued Presence of South Africa in Namibia (South West Africa) Notwithstanding Security Council Resolution 276 (1970)*, although the case concerned the illegality of South Africa's continued presence in Namibia following the end of its League of Nations mandate to administer the territory, the International Court of Justice took the occasion to pronounce on the nature of apartheid as contrary to the higher interests of the international community:

> Under the Charter of the United Nations, the former Mandatory had pledged itself to observe and respect, in a territory having an international status, human rights and fundamental freedoms for all without distinction as to race. To establish instead, and to enforce, distinctions, exclusions, restrictions and limitations exclusively based on grounds of race, colour, descent or national or ethnic origin which constitute a denial of fundamental human rights is a flagrant violation of the purposes and principles of the Charter.[250]

Further expression of the social need of the international community can be drawn from the preamble of the International Convention on the Suppression and Punishment of the Crime of *Apartheid* (1974), which invokes principles of international law and the purposes of the UN Charter to declare apartheid to constitute a crime against humanity, and recalls the preambular passage of the Universal Declaration, 'that all human beings are equal in dignity and rights'.[251] These measures are indicative of an *opinio juris* supporting the absolute prohibition of apartheid and racial discrimination as contrary to the interests of the international community.

The *opinio juris sive necessitatis* against apartheid is evidenced most clearly in the practice of States acting as organs of the international community, most notably through codification of the International Convention on the Elimination of all Forms of Racial Discrimination (1965),[252] and the International Convention on the Suppression and

[249] SC Res. 282, UN Doc. S/Res/282 (23 July 1970); SC Res. 283, UN Doc. S/Res/283 (29 July 1970).

[250] *Legal Consequences for States of the Continued Presence of South Africa in Namibia (South West Africa) notwithstanding Security Council Resolution 276 (1970)*, Advisory Opinion, ICJ Reports 1971, p. 16, para. 131.

[251] Apartheid Convention (1973), Preamble, Article I.

[252] International Convention on the Elimination of All Forms of Racial Discrimination, 660 UNTS 195 (7 March 1966, *entered into force* 4 January 1969) [hereinafter, CERD (1966)].

Punishment of the Crime of *Apartheid* (1976).[253] Further practice supporting the prohibition against apartheid may be derived from its international criminalization as a crime against humanity,[254] and a war crime.[255] In the practice of international organizations, various ILC commentaries have acknowledged the *jus cogens* status of the prohibition against apartheid and racial discrimination.[256]

With respect to relevant pronouncements of judicial organs, the International Court was restrained in its treatment of apartheid in the South African context.[257] The prohibition of apartheid and racial discrimination has since been articulated by the International Court to belong to *jus cogens* by implication,[258] identification,[259] and through dissent.[260] The IACtHR recognized the *jus cogens* status of the prohibition of racial discrimination in *The Juridical Condition and the Rights of Undocumented Migrants* (2003).[261] Courts in the United Kingdom[262] and the United States[263] have also referred to the *jus cogens* status of the

253 Apartheid Convention (1973).

254 Rome Statute (1998), Article 7(1)(j); Draft Code of Crimes (1996), Article 18(f).

255 Protocol Additional to the Geneva Conventions of 12 August 1949, and relating to the Protection of Victims of Non-International Armed Conflicts (Protocol I), 1125 UNTS 3, Article 85(4)(c) (8 June 1977, *entered into force* 7 December 1978) [hereinafter, Additional Protocol I (1977)].

256 ILC Articles on State Responsibility (2001), 112, para. 4 (Commentary to Article 40).

257 *See Legal Consequences for States of the Continued Presence of South Africa in Namibia (South West Africa) notwithstanding Security Council Resolution 276 (1970)*, Advisory Opinion, ICJ Reports 1971, p. 16, para. 131.

258 *Barcelona Traction, Light and Power Company, Limited (Belgium v. Spain)*, Judgment, ICJ Reports 1970, p. 3, para. 34 (with reference to *erga omnes* obligations arising from its prohibition).

259 *Armed Activities on the Territory of the Congo (New Application: 2002) (Congo v. Rwanda)*, ICJ Reports 2006, p. 3, para. 78 (with reference to systematic racial discrimination).

260 *Application of the International Convention on the Elimination of All Forms of Racial Discrimination (Georgia v. Russian Federation)*, Preliminary Objections, ICJ Reports 2011, p. 70, Dis. Op. Cançado Trindade, p. 239, para. 180.

261 *The Juridical Condition and the Rights of Undocumented Migrants*, IACtHR, Advisory Opinion OC-18/03, Series A No. 18, paras. 97–101, 110–11 (2003) ('[T]his Court considers that the principle of equality before the law, equal protection before the law and non-discrimination belongs to *jus cogens*, because the whole legal structure of national and international public order rests on it and it is a fundamental principle that permeates all laws').

262 *R. (on the application of European Roma Rights Centre) v. Immigration Officer at Prague Airport*, House of Lords (UK), [2004] UKHL 55, para. 46 (Steyn, J.).

263 *Sarei v. Rio Tinto, PLC*, 671 F.3d 736, 759 (9th Cir. 2011) *cert. granted, judgment vacated sub nom. Rio Tinto PLC v. Sarei*, 133 S. Ct. 1995 (2013); *In re South African Apartheid*

prohibition of systematic racial discrimination by reference to apartheid. In South Africa, however, domestic courts avoided the question of the effect of *jus cogens* upon its grant of amnesty for violations of the prohibition of apartheid by finding that an affirmative determination of the constitutionality of its amnesty law rendered any contrary international law obligation, even one arising from *jus cogens*, 'irrelevant'.[264]

ix. Terrorism

Substantial evidence indicates that the prohibition of terrorism belongs to *jus cogens*. Terrorism, the indiscriminate attack upon civilians to intimidate a population or coerce a government pursuant to political or ideological aims, constitutes a manifest violation of the dignity of the human person.[265] By definition, terrorism entails the use of human beings, through violence, as a means to achieve some end, thereby absolutely violating the principle of respect for the human person. The prohibition of terrorism in international law is therefore said to reflect 'the general will of the international community'.[266] As

Litigation, 617 F. Supp. 2d 228, 240-41 (SDNY 2009) (with reference to the law of nations); *Siderman de Blake v. Republic of Argentina*, 965 F.2d 699, 717 (9th Cir. 1992) (citing RESTATEMENT (THIRD) OF FOREIGN RELATIONS LAW OF THE UNITED STATES § 702, cmt. *n* (1987)).

264 *Azanian Peoples Organization ('AZAPO') and ors v. President of South Africa and ors*, Constitutional Court (South Africa), No. CCT 17/96, 1996 (4) SA 671 (CC), ILDC 648, paras. 26–7 (1996); *Azanian Peoples Organization and ors v. Truth and Reconciliation Commission and ors*, Cape Provincial Division of the Supreme Court (South Africa), 1996 (4) SA 562 (C) (1996) (after endorsing amnesty exception in Article 6(5) of Protocol II to the Geneva Conventions, the court found it unnecessary 'to consider further the applicability of the *jus cogens* to the interpretation to the constitution' (quoted in commentary by H. Strydom at ILDC 648 (12 April 2010))).

265 *See Prosecutor v. Ayyash et al.*, No. STL-11–01/I/AC/R17bis, Interlocutory Decision on the Applicable Law: Terrorism, Conspiracy, Homicide, Perpetration, Cumulative Charging, 145 ILR 232, para. 102 (2011) [hereinafter, STL Interlocutory Decision (2011)]; Office of the United Nations High Commissioner for Human Rights, *Human Rights, Terrorism and Counter-terrorism* [Fact Sheet No. 32], UN Doc DPI/2439B/Rev.2, 5-6 (December 2007); UN Working Group on a Draft Comprehensive Convention on International Terrorism, *Measures to Eliminate International Terrorism*, Report of the Working Group, UN Doc. A/C.6/56/L.9 (29 October 2001) (informal text of Article 2(1)).

266 Andrea Bianchi, *Enforcing International Law Norms Against Terrorism: Achievements and Prospects*, *in* ENFORCING INTERNATIONAL LAW NORMS AGAINST TERRORISM 491, 526 (Oxford: Hart Publising, Andrea Bianchi & Yasmin Naqvi eds., 2004).

contemplated in the *Arancibia Clavel* case (2004) before the Supreme Court of Argentina:

> [T]errorism involves the commission of cruelties upon innocent and defenseless people causing unnecessary suffering and danger against the lives of the civilian population. It is a system of subversion of order and public security that, although the commission of certain isolated events could be fixed to a particular State, has recently been characterized by ignoring the territorial limits of the affected State, constituting in this way a serious threat to the peace and security of the international community. This is why its prosecution is not the exclusive interest of the State directly injured by it, but rather it is an aim whose achievement benefits, ultimately, all civilized nations, who are thereby obligated to cooperate in the global fight against terrorism[.][267]

The delayed crystallization of the prohibition of terrorism is a result of the struggle by the international community to articulate a common definition of terrorism. In 1937, the League of Nations drafted the Convention for the Prevention and Punishment of Terrorism, to which was annexed a Convention for the Creation of an International Criminal Court with jurisdiction over individuals for crimes of terrorism.[268] The inability of States to reach an agreement over a definition of terrorism prevented the Convention from entering into force and stifled subsequent efforts to draft a comprehensive international convention on the prohibition of terrorism.[269] This definitional issue precluded the crime of terrorism from incorporation in the Rome Statute, despite recognition that 'terrorist acts ... are serious crimes of concern to the international community'.[270] While these impediments have not been absolute, the historic absense of a

[267] STL Interlocutory Decision (2011), para. 86 *n.* 133 (quoting *Chile v. Arancibia Clavel*, Supreme Court of Justice (Argentina), A/533/XXXVIII, 51–2, paras. 21–2 (2004) (Boggiano, J., concurring)).

[268] Convention for the Prevention and Punishment of Terrorism, League of Nations Doc. C.546(I).M.383(I).1937.V (16 November 1937), 19 League of Nations O.J. 23 (1938); *ibid.*, Annex, Article 1.

[269] *See* Robert Kolb, *Universal Criminal Jurisdiction in Matters of International Terrorism: Some Reflections on Status and Trends in Contemporary International Law*, 50 Revue Hellenique de Droit International 43, 48–58 (1997).

[270] Final Act of the United Nations Diplomatic Conference of Plenipotentiaries on the Establishment of an International Criminal Court, Annex 1, Resolution E, UN Doc. A/CONF.183/10 (17 July 1998) ('no generally acceptable definition of the crime[] of terrorism ... could be agreed upon for the inclusion, within the jurisdiction of the Court').

common definition is illustrated by the disparate criminalization of terrorism in three domains: domestic law,[271] the law of war,[272] and

[271] Virtually every State in the world has adopted domestic legislation criminalizing international terrorism. *See* United Nations Office on Drugs and Crime, *Electronic Legal Resources on International Terrorism*, *available at* www.unodc.org/tldb (last accessed 15 August 2014). This practice has been viewed as indicative of the 'international criminalization of terrorism', a crime which generally constitutes three elements under domestic law: (1) a criminal act, (2) intended to terrorize or coerce, (3) of a transnational nature. *See* STL Interlocutory Decision, paras. 89–93. United States law exemplifies this trend, which defines 'international terrorism' as activities that:

(A) involve violent acts or acts dangerous to human life that are a violation of the criminal laws of the United States or of any State, or that would be a criminal violation if committed within the jurisdiction of the United States or of any State;
(B) appear to be intended –
  (i) to intimidate or coerce a civilian population;
  (ii) to influence the policy of a government by intimidation or coercion; or
  (iii) to affect the conduct of a government by mass destruction, assassination, or kidnapping; and
(C) occur primarily outside the territorial jurisdiction of the United States, or transcend national boundaries in terms of the means by which they are accomplished, the persons they appear intended to intimidate or coerce, or the locale in which their perpetrators operate or seek asylum[.]

18 USC § 2331(1) (2001). Under the US Code, Domestic Terrorism is defined in identical terms, with the exception of the 'transnational' element (C), which is substituted with conduct 'occur[ing] primarily within the territorial jurisdiction of the United States'. 18 USC § 2331(5) (2001). Under such a definition, the *actus reas* and *mens rea* of terrorism are constant across terrorism of either a domestic or international nature.

[272] Geneva Convention IV (1949), Article 33; Additional Protocol I (1977), Article 51(2); Protocol Additional to the Geneva Conventions of 12 August 1949, and relating to the Protection of Victims of Non-International Armed Conflicts (Protocol II), (8 June 1977, *entered into force* 7 December 1978) [hereinafter, Additional Protocol II (1977)], Article 13(2). The international law of war prohibits terrorism in wartime as a specific protection of civilians during armed conflict. Terrorism is prohibited under the Geneva Conventions, *ibid.*, and therefore such acts constitute war crimes. *See* ICTR Statute (1994), Article 4(d) (Acts of terrorism); SCSL Statute (2000), Article 3(d) (Acts of terrorism); *Prosecutor v. Galić*, Judgment, IT-98-29-T, paras. 98, 133 (2003) (finding terrorism as a war crime to form a 'specific prohibition within the general prohibition of attack on civilians', and convicting Galić of crime of terrorism for sniping and bombing campaign on Sarajevo). In *Galić*, the Trial Chamber distilled the elements of the crime of terrorism as:

1. Acts of violence directed against the civilian population or individual civilians not taking direct part in hostilities causing death or serious injury to body or health within the civilian population.
2. The offender wilfully made the civilian population or individual civilians not taking direct part in hostilities the object of those acts of violence.

public international law.[273] The direct effect of distinct, and to some extent competing, definitions of the crime of terrorism in international law has been inconsistent precedent and prosecution of terrorism.[274]

In its 2011 Interlocutory Decision on the Applicable Law in *Prosecutor v. Ayyash et al.*, the Special Tribunal for Lebanon attempted to resolve the definitional issue by looking to *opinio juris sive necessitatis* and State practice to formulate a definition of the international crime of

3. The above offence was committed with the primary purpose of spreading terror among the civilian population.

On Appeal, the Appeals Chamber determined that the prohibition of terrorism enshrined in the Additional Protocols to the Geneva Conventions belonged to customary international law with sufficient precision to uphold the convition: *Prosecutor v. Galić*, Case No. IT-98-29-A, paras. 90–109 (2006).

273 International Convention for the Suppression of the Financing of Terrorism, 2178 UNTS 197, Article 2(1)(b) (10 December 1999, *entered into force* 10 April 2002); *See, e.g., Suresh v. Canada (Minister of Citizenship and Immigration)*, Supreme Court (Canada), [2002] 1 SCR 3, paras. 96–8 (finding the definition of international terrorism in the International Convention for the Suppression of the Financing of Terrorism (1999), ratified by 179 States at the time of writing, had been adopted as an authoritative definition of international terrorism). The Convention defines terrorism as:

> [Any] act intended to cause death or serious bodily injury to a civilian, or to any other person not taking an active part in the hostilities in a situation of armed conflict, when the purpose of such act, by its nature or context, is to intimidate a population, or to compel a government or an international organization to do or to abstain from doing any act.

The 1999 Convention definition contains elements of the wartime (law of war) and peacetime (domestic law) definitions of terrorism. The definition retains the civilian element embodying the humanitarian law principle of distinction between civilian and combatant, and omits the international locus element, while broadening the *mens rea* element include intimidation and coercion of a range of actors. As discussed below, combining the domestic and law of war definitions of terrorism to form an international standard risks obscuring the two distinct functions served – for example, this definition would exclude any non-civilian protection against terrorism. In the context of recent jurisprudence, it is unclear whether the conventional definition of the crime of terrorism adequately defines the international crime of terrorism. In the absense of a comprehensive convention addressing international terrorism, fourteen 'sectoral' multilateral conventions have been concluded regarding specific acts of terrorism. *See infra, n.* 288. In addition, every region of the world has concluded a multilateral treaty combatting terrorism. *See infra, n.* 289.

274 *See* Thomas Weatherall, *The Status of the Prohibition of Terrorism in International Law*, 46(2) Georgetown Journal of International Law 589–627 (2015).

terrorism.[275] Following a survey of State practice evidencing *opinio juris sive necessitatis* across the three domains discussed above – domestic, humanitarian, and international law – the STL concluded that State practice evidencing *opinio* 'share[s] a core concept: terrorism is a criminal action that aims at spreading terror or coercing governmental authorities and is a threat to the stability of society or the State'.[276] The Tribunal found sufficient evidence in the practice of States to support an *opinio juris sive necessitatis* criminalizing terrorism,[277] and the criminal elements set out by the Interlocutory Decision closely track the elements common to the domestic criminalization of international terrorism.[278] The year after the STL issued its Interlocutory Decision, in *Regina v. Gul*, the England Court of Appeal adopted the Tribunal's definition of a customary international law norm prohibiting terrorism, finding it equally applicable to armed conflict with no exception for 'freedom fighters'.[279]

[275] STL Interlocutory Decision (2011), paras. 29–89 (finding that 'a customary rule of international law regarding the international crime of terrorism, at least in time of peace, has indeed emerged').

[276] *Ibid.*, para. 97.

[277] *See ibid.*, paras. 91, 128–37 ('To turn into an international crime, a domestic offence needs to be regarded by the world community as an attack on universal values (such as peace or human rights) or on values held to be of paramount importance in that community; in addition, it is necessary that States and intergovernmental organisations, through their acts and pronouncements, sanction this attitude by clearly expressing the view that the world community considers the offence at issue as amounting to an international crime').

[278] *Ibid.*, para. 85 (finding the crime of terrorism under customary international law contains three elements:

(i) the perpetration of a criminal act . . . or threatening such an act;
(ii) the intent to spread fear among the population . . . or directly or indirectly coerce a national or international authority to take some action, or to refrain from taking it;
(iii) when the act involves a transnational element).

[279] *R. v. Gul*, [2012] EWCA Crim 280, 152 ILR 568 (2012) (appealing terrorism conviction in part on the basis that the definition of terrorism under international law 'excluded those engaged in an armed struggle against a government who attacked the armed forces of that government'. Citing the 2011 STL Interlocutory Decision, the Court of Appeal concluded that '[i]t was common ground that international law has developed so that there is an international crime of terrorism at least in time of peace[.]' *Ibid.*, paras. 32–5. The England Court of Appeal further determined that State practice and *opinio juris* had not established an exception for insurgent attacks on government forces from the definition of terrorism (that such attacks are *not* terrorism). *Ibid.*, paras. 37, 47. The breadth of the STL definition, when applied so generally to non-international armed conflict, effectively forecloses the legality of the use of force by individuals not qualifying for combatant status under the law of armed conflict (i.e. 'freedom fighters')). *See*

The *opinio juris sive necessitatis* of the international community pursuant to the prohibition of terrorism is evidenced by a series of UN General Assembly resolutions dating to 1972, under the respective headings of *Measures to Eliminate International Terrorism*[280] and *Measures to Prevent International Terrorism.*[281] The *opinio* of the international community is further evidenced by a succession of resolutions by the UN Security Council identifying terrorism as a threat to peace and security and reaffirming the imperative to combat terrorism in all its forms and manifestations by all means; since 2006, acts of terrorism have been identified by the Security Council as 'criminal and unjustifiable'.[282] Special note must be made of Resolution 1373 (2001), which constituted a legally binding Chapter VII resolution instructing States to prevent and punish acts of terrorism.[283] Judicial pronouncements have considered this extensive expression of *opinio juris sive necessitatis* to reflect the 'reasonable consensus of the international community' regarding the prohibition of terrorism.[284] Most recently, the Special Tribunal for Lebanon pronounced in favor of an *opinio juris sive necessitatis* of the prohibition against terrorism.[285]

Aleksandar Marsavelski, *The Crime of Terrorism and the Right of Revolution in International Law*, 28 Connecticut Journal of International Law 243, 246 (2013) (proposing defences applicable to acts falling within the scope of the international crime of terrorism).

280 A/Res/66/282 (2012); A/Res/66/105 (2011); A/Res/65/34 (2010); A/Res/64/118 (2009); A/Res/63/129 (2008); A/Res/62/71 (2007); A/Res/61/40 (2006); A/Res/60/43 (2005); A/Res/59/46 (2004); A/Res/58/81 (2003); A/Res/57/27 (2002); A/Res/56/88 (2001); A/Res/55/158 (2000); A/Res/54/110 (1999); A/Res/53/108 (1998); A/Res/52/165 (1997); A/Res/51/210 (1996); A/Res/50/53 (1995); A/Res/46/51 (1991).

281 A/Res/44/29 (1989); A/Res/42/159 (1987); A/Res/40/61 (1985); A/Res/38/130 (1983); A/Res/36/109 (1981); A/Res/34/145 (1979); A/Res/32/147 (1977); A/Res/31/102 (1976); A/Res/3034(XXVII) (1972).

282 S/Res/1963 (2010); S/Res/1904 (2009); S/Res/1822 (2008); S/Res/1787 (2007); S/Res/1735 (2006); S/Res/1624 (2005); S/Res/1566 (2004); S/Res/1540 (2004); S/Res/1456 (2003) (Adopting Declaration on the Issue of Combating Terrorism); S/Res/1373 (2001); S/Res/1267 (1999).

283 SC Res. 1373, UN Doc. S/Res/1373, Preamble (28 September 2001) ('such acts, like any act of international terrorism, constitute a threat to international peace and security').

284 *Zrig v. Canada (Minister of Citizenship and Immigration)*, Federal Court of Appeal (Canada), 2003 FCA 178, [2003] 3 F.C. 761, para. 179 (2002) (Decary, J. A., concurring); *see Italy v. Abdelaziz and ors*, Court of Cassation (First Criminal Section) (Italy), No. 1072, 17 Guida al Diritto 90, ILDC 559, para. 2.1 (2007).

285 STL Interlocutory Decision (2011), para. 100.

This *opinio juris sive necessitatis* of the prohibition against terrorism is expressed by extensive international practice. Virtually every State has adopted some form of domestic legislation concerning terrorism,[286] practice appropriately viewed in the context of reports by States to the Counter-Terrorism Committee to reflect the collective criminalization of terrorism.[287] Notwithstanding difficulty in reaching a comprehensive definition of terrorism, some fourteen 'sectoral' conventions prohibiting specific forms of terrorism reflect the practice of States acting on behalf of the international community.[288] Multilateral treaties to combat terrorism concluded in every region of the world

[286] *See* United Nations Office on Drugs and Crime, *Electronic Legal Resources on International Terrorism*, *available at* www.unodc.org/tldb (last accessed 15 August 2014).

[287] STL Interlocutory Decision (2011), para. 92 ('many States have reported back to the Counter-Terrorism Committee not only their success in doing so, but also their understanding that terrorism is an international crime and/or that their laws increasingly align with a global standard').

[288] International Convention for the Suppression of Acts of Nuclear Terrorism, 2445 UNTS 89 (13 April 2005, *entered into force* 7 July 2007); International Convention for the Suppression of the Financing of Terrorism, 2178 UNTS 197 (10 December 1999, *entered into force* 10 April 2002); International Convention for the Suppression of Terrorist Bombings, 2149 UNTS 256 (17 May 1997, *entered into force* 23 May 2001); Convention on the Safety of United Nations and Associated Personnel, 2051 UNTS 363 (9 December 1994, *entered into force* 15 January 1999); Convention on the Marking of Plastic Explosives for the Purpose of Detection, ICAO Doc. 9571 (1 March 1991, *entered into force* 21 June 1998); Protocol on the Suppression of Unlawful Acts of Violence at Airports Serving International Civil Aviation, ICAO Doc. 9518 (24 February 1988, *entered into force* 6 August 1989); Convention for the Suppression of Unlawful Acts against the Safety of Civil Aviation, 974 UNTS 177 (23 September 1971, *entered into force* 26 January 1973); Protocol for the Suppression of Unlawful Acts against the Safety of Fixed Platforms Located on the Continental Shelf, 1678 UNTS 304 (10 March 1988, *entered into force* 1 March 1992); Convention for the Suppression of Unlawful Acts against the Safety of Maritime Navigation, 1678 UNTS 201 (10 March 1988, *entered into force* 1 March 1992); Convention on the Physical Protection of Nuclear Material, 1456 UNTS 101 (3 March 1980, *entered into force* 8 February 1987); International Convention against the Taking of Hostages, 1316 UNTS 205 (17 December 1979, *entered into force* 3 June 1983); Convention on the Prevention and Punishment of Crimes against Internationally Protected Persons, Including Diplomatic Agents, 1035 UNTS 167 (14 December 1973, *entered into force* 20 February 1977); Convention for the Suppression of Unlawful Acts against the Safety of Civil Aviation, 2974 UNTS 177 (23 September 1971, *entered into force* 26 January 1973); Convention for the Suppression of Unlawful Seizure of Aircraft, 860 UNTS 105 (16 December 1970, *entered into force* 14 October 1971); Convention on Offences and Certain Other Acts Committed on Board Aircraft, 704 UNTS 219 (14 September 1963, *entered into force* 4 December 1969).

constitute corroborating practice,[289] many of which include explicit reference in their preambular statements to United Nations resolutions and instruments combatting terrorism that express *opinio juris sive necessitatis*.[290] Additional practice evidencing *opinio* may be derived from its prohibition under international humanitarian law.[291] The Statutes of the ICTR,[292] and the SCSL,[293] explicitly refer to acts of terrorism as falling within their jurisdiction as international crimes. The State practice of Canada bears special mention, where a 2007

289 Association of South East Asian Nations, ASEAN Convention on Counter Terrorism (27 May 2011); Council of Europe, Convention on the Prevention of Terrorism, CETS No. 196 (16 May 2005, *entered into force* 1 June 2007); South Asian Association for Regional Cooperation, Additional Protocol to the SAARC Regional Convention on Suppression of Terrorism Convention, SAARC/SUMMIT.12/SC.29/27, Annex-III (4 January 2004, *entered into force* 12 January 2006); Organization of the African Union, Protocol to the OAU Convention on the Prevention and Combating of Terrorism (8 July 2004); European Union, Protocol Amending the European Convention on the Suppression of Terrorism, CETS No. 190 (15 May 2003); Council of the European Union, Framework Decision 2002/475/JHA on Combating Terrorism, [2002] O.J. L 164/3 (13 June 2002); Organization of American States, Inter-American Convention Against Terrorism, AG/Res. 1840 (XXXII-O/02) (3 June 2002); Organization of the Islamic Conference, Convention of the Organization of the Islamic Conference on Combating International Terrorism, Annex to Resolution No. 59/26-P (1 July 1999); Organization of African Unity, OAU Convention on the Prevention and Combating of Terrorism (14 June 1999); Commonwealth of Independent States, Treaty on Cooperation among States members of the Commonwealth of Independent States in Combating Terrorism (4 June 1999); League of Arab States, The Arab Convention on the Suppression of Terrorism (22 April 1998); South Asian Association for Regional Cooperation, SAARC Regional Convention on Suppression of Terrorism (4 November 1987, *entered into force* 22 August 1988); European Convention on the Suppression of Terrorism, CETS No. 090 (27 January 1977, *entered into force* 4 August 1978); Organization of American States, Convention to Prevent and Punish Acts of Terrorism Taking the Form of Crimes against Persons and Related Extortion that Are of International Significance, OAS TS No. 37 (2 February 1971).

290 *See* ASEAN Convention on Counter Terrorism (2007); Additional Protocol to the SAARC Regional Convention on Suppression of Terrorism Convention (2004) (specifically referring to legally binding Security Council Resolution 1373); Protocol to the OAU Convention on the Prevention and Combating of Terrorism (2004) (specifically referring to legally binding Security Council Resolution 1373); Protocol Amending the European Convention on the Suppression of Terrorism (2003); Convention of the Organization of the Islamic Conference on Combating International Terrorism (1999); The Arab Convention on the Suppression of Terrorism (1998).

291 Geneva Convention IV (1949), Article 33; Additional Protocol I (1977), Article 51(2); Additional Protocol II (1977), Article 13(2).

292 ICTR Statute (1994), Article 4(d) (Acts of terrorism).

293 SCSL Statute (2000), Article 3(d) (Acts of terrorism).

amendment to its criminal code explicitly refers to the *jus cogens* status of the prohibition of terrorism in international law.[294]

Pronouncements by judicial organs have reflected the emergence of prohibition against terrorism as general international law,[295] most notably by the STL in its 2011 Interlocutory Decision:

> The conclusion is therefore warranted that a customary rule has evolved in the international community concerning terrorism . . . [I]t can be said that there is a settled practice concerning the punishment of acts of terrorism, as commonly defined, at least when committed in time of peace; in addition, this practice is evidence of a belief of States that the punishment of terrorism responds to a social necessity (*opinio necessitatis*) and is hence rendered obligatory by the existence of a rule requiring it (*opinio juris*).[296]

That this custom is *jus cogens* in character may be inferred from a later statement by the STL regarding its international criminalization.[297] The ICTY identified the prohibition against terrorism as peremptory by extension from international humanitarian law.[298] And domestic courts

[294] An Act to amend the State Immunity Act and the Criminal Code (deterring terrorism by providing a civil right of action against perpetrators and sponsors of terrorism), S.C. 2007 (Canada), Preamble ('WHEREAS the prohibition against terrorism, as well as the prevention, repression and elimination of terrorism, are peremptory norms of international law (*jus cogens*) accepted and recognized by the international community of States as a whole as norms from which no derogation is possible').

[295] *Italy v. Abdelaziz and ors*, Court of Cassation (First Criminal Section) (Italy), No. 1072, 17 Guida al Diritto 90, ILDC 559, para. 2.1 (2007).

[296] STL Interlocutory Decision (2011), para. 102 (citing *North Sea Continental Shelf (Federal Republic of Germany v. Denmark / Federal Republic of Germany v. Netherlands)*, Judgment, ICJ Reports 1969, p. 3, paras. 76–7).

[297] *Ibid.*, paras. 91, 104, 128–37 ('To turn into an international crime, a domestic offence needs to be regarded by the world community as an attack on universal values (such as peace or human rights) or on values held to be of paramount importance in that community; in addition, it is necessary that States and intergovernmental organisations, through their acts and pronouncements, sanction this attitude by clearly expressing the view that the world community considers the offence at issue as amounting to an international crime. . . In the case of terrorism, demonstrating the requisite practice and *opinio juris seu necessitatis*, namely the legal view that it is necessary and indeed obligatory to bring to trial and punish the perpetrators of terrorist acts, is relatively easy').

[298] *Prosecutor v. Galić*, Case No. IT-98-29-A, para. 98 (2006) ('the prohibition against terror is a specific prohibition within the general prohibition of attack on civilians. The general prohibition is a peremptory norm of customary international law. It could be said that the specific prohibition also shares this peremptory character, for it protects the same value').

in Argentina,[299] France,[300] Italy,[301] Mexico,[302] Spain,[303] and the United States[304] have recognized the *jus cogens* status of the prohibition of terrorism either explicitly or by reference to its legal effects. With potential resolution of the definitional issue that had long beleaguered jurisprudence in the area of terrorism, judicial organs can be expected to continue to express the *jus cogens* status of its prohibition.

B Self-determination

It follows next to consider whether other international law norms, recognized to have *erga omnes* effects, belong to *jus cogens*. The first such principle is self-determination, which concerns the right of peoples to freely determine their political status. The principle has been articulated prominently in two UN General Assembly resolutions, the first being the Declaration on the Granting of Independence to Colonial Countries and Peoples (1960), which emphasized the importance of

299 *Chile v. Arancibia Clavel*, Supreme Court of Justice (Argentina), A/533/XXXVIII, ILDC 1082, para. 28 (2004); *ibid.*, paras. 21–2 (Boggiano, J., concurring).

300 *Réunion Aérienne v. Socialist People's Libyan Arab Jamahiriya*, Court of Cassation (Civil Division) (France), No. 09-14743, 150 ILR 630, 634–5 (2011) (assuming 'that the prohibition on acts of terrorism can be ranked as a *jus cogens* norm of international law').

301 *Italy v. Abdelaziz and ors*, Court of Cassation (First Criminal Section) (Italy), No. 1072, 17 Guida al Diritto 90, ILDC 559, para. 2.1 (2007) (referring to the prohibition of terrorism as a customary international rule).

302 *Decision on the Extradition of Ricardo Miguel Cavallo*, Supreme Court (Mexico), No. 712/2003, 42 ILM 888, 908-9 (2003) (finding international crime of terrorism, alongside genocide, war crimes, and crimes against humanity, imposes obligation to extradite or prosecute that cannot be affected by domestic amnesty laws).

303 *Decision (Auto) of the Full Penal Chamber Confirming Spanish Jurisdiction to Investigate Crimes of Genocide and Terrorism Committed during the Chilean Dictatorship*, National Court (*Audiencia Nacional*) (Spain), No. 173/98, §§ 5–7, 119 ILR 331, 342–4 (1998); *see also Decision (Auto) of the Full Penal Chamber Confirming Spanish Jurisdiction over the Crimes of Genocide and Terrorism committed during the Argentine Dictatorship*, National Court (*Audiencia Nacional*) (Spain), No. 84/98, §§ 8–10 (1998) (asserting universal jurisdiction over crimes of genocide and terrorism notwithstanding domestic amnesties over those offences).

304 *Almog v. Arab Bank, PLC*, 471 F. Supp. 2d 257, 281, 284 (EDNY 2007) (finding certain acts of terrorism to be 'universally condemned'); *Flatow v. Islamic Republic of Iran*, 999 F. Supp. 1, 23 (DDC 1998) ('terrorism has achieved the status of almost universal condemnation, as have slavery, genocide, and piracy, and the terrorist is the modern era's *hosti humani generis* – an enemy of all mankind'); *United States v. Yunis*, 924 F.2d 1086, 1092 (DC Cir. 1991) (recognizing universal jurisdiction over certain acts of terrorism).

respect of the principles of equal rights and self-determination of peoples, identifying the latter to be a right of all peoples.[305] A decade later, the Declaration on Principles of International Law concerning Friendly Relations and Co-operation among States in accordance with the Charter of the United Nations (1970) identified the principle of equal rights and self-determination of peoples alongside other principles of the international system, such as the sovereign equality of States, good faith, and non-intervention.[306] The relevant Advisory Opinion of the period by the International Court of Justice, *Legal Consequences for States of the Continued Presence of South Africa in Namibia* (1971), was viewed as more a product of the coalescence of a prohibition against apartheid than a reflection of self-determination.[307] Moreover, the report of the UN *special rapporteur* of the Sub-Commission on Prevention of Discrimination and Protection of Minorities, titled *The Right to Self-Determination* (1981), concluded against the *jus cogens* status of the right to self-determination.[308] That the height of decolonization was evidently insufficient to generate a peremptory norm concerning self-determination is not insignificant, and at the close of the twentieth century, the status of the principle remained a matter for debate.[309]

The International Court contributed to the debate by pronouncing on the *erga omnes* status of the right to self-determination in *East Timor* (1995).[310] In its Judgment, the Court provided neither indication of the customary emergence of the norm in international law – through *opinio juris sive necessitatis* evidenced by State practice – nor a statement of its *jus cogens* status. An expression of such elements, found in other judicial pronouncements reflecting the emergence of peremptory norms, would

[305] Declaration on the Granting of Independence to Colonial Countries and Peoples, GA Res. 1514 (XV), UN Doc. A/Res/1514 (XV) (14 December 1960).

[306] GA Res. 2625 (XXV), UN Doc. A/Res/25/2625 (24 October 1970).

[307] *Legal Consequences for States of the Continued Presence of South Africa in Namibia (South West Africa) notwithstanding Security Council Resolution 276 (1970)*, Advisory Opinion, ICJ Reports 1971, p. 16, para. 131; *ibid.*, Sep. Op. Ammoun, p. 55, para. 7.

[308] Aureliu Cristescu, *The Right to Self-Determination (Report of the Special Rapporteur of the Sub-Commission on Prevention of Discrimination and Protection of Minorities)*, UN Doc. E/CN.4/Sub.2/404/Rev.1, para. 154 (1981) ('No United Nations instrument confers such a peremptory character on the right of peoples to self-determination').

[309] Hurst Hannum, AUTONOMY, SOVEREIGNTY, AND SELF-DETERMINATION 45 (Philadelphia: University of Pennsylvania Press 1996).

[310] *East Timor (Portugal v. Australia)*, Judgment, ICJ Reports 1995, p. 90, para. 29 (citing *Legal Consequences for States of the Continued Presence of South Africa in Namibia (South West Africa) notwithstanding Security Council Resolution 276 (1970)*, Advisory Opinion, ICJ Reports 1971, p. 16, paras. 52–3).

have been necessary where the status of a norm was as contested as that of self-determination. The International Court restated the position in a later Advisory Opinion, *Legal Consequences of the Construction of a Wall in the Occupied Palestinian Territory* (2004), by indicating that self-determination is an obligation *erga omnes* of concern to all States, while again declining to pronounce on its peremptory status.[311] The Court recognized the right of peoples to self-determination as 'one of the essential principles of contemporary international law';[312] however, its language is a departure from 'elementary considerations of humanity', a construction employed by the Court when referring to obligations *erga omnes* related to peremptory norms.[313] In fact, in *Legal Consequences of the Construction of a Wall in the Occupied Palestinian Territory*, the Court identified the *erga omnes* character of the principle of self-determination with respect to the UN Charter,[314] and only later in the next paragraph referred to 'elementary considerations of humanity' in reference to international humanitarian law and related obligations *erga omnes*.[315] The jurisprudence of the Court thereby appears to signal a distinction between the sources of the obligations *erga omnes* in question.[316] Accordingly, the pronouncements of the International Court concerning self-determination are perhaps better viewed as support for the *erga omnes* character of 'essential principles' of international law, such as those delineated in the 1970 Declaration on Principles, than as evidence that the right to self-determination is a peremptory norm of general international law.

When compared to the formal source of peremptory norms depicted in the previous chapter, self-determination does not appear to reflect the

311 *Legal Consequences of the Construction of a Wall in the Occupied Palestinian Territory*, Advisory Opinion, ICJ Reports 2004, p. 136, paras. 155–7.

312 *East Timor (Portugal v. Australia)*, Judgment, ICJ Reports 1995, p. 90, para. 29.

313 *Legal Consequences of the Construction of a Wall in the Occupied Palestinian Territory*, Advisory Opinion, ICJ Reports 2004, p. 136, para. 157; *Legality of the Threat or Use of Nuclear Weapons*, Advisory Opinion, ICJ Reports 1996, p. 226, paras. 79, 95; *Military and Paramilitary Activities in and against Nicaragua (Nicaragua v. United States of America)*, Judgment, ICJ Reports 1986, p. 14, para. 218; *Reservations to the Genocide Convention*, Advisory Opinion, ICJ Reports 1951, p. 15, 23; *The Corfu Channel Case (United Kingdom of Great Britain and Northern Ireland v. Albania)*, Judgment, ICJ Reports 1949, p. 4, 22.

314 *Legal Consequences of the Construction of a Wall in the Occupied Palestinian Territory*, Advisory Opinion, ICJ Reports 2004, p. 136, para. 156.

315 *Ibid.*, para. 157.

316 This distinction is consistent with the material source of *jus cogens*: *see* discussion *supra*, Chapter 3 (The Interests of the International Community).

standard set by other peremptory norms glossed in the present survey, which emerged through a clear *opinio juris sive necessitatis* evidenced in the practice of States and reflected by judicial organs, indicating decidedly the recognition and acceptance of a norm by the international community as belonging to *jus cogens*. The lack of practice expressing this *opinio*, highlighted by the International Court's pronouncements and compounded by linguistic differences, suggests that the right of peoples to self-determination may be dissimilar to norms belonging to *jus cogens*. The absence of identifiable legal effects – obligations to prevent and punish violations – and consequences – individual responsibility under international law – characteristic of other peremptory norms underscores this point.[317] The fact that there exists contrary evidence is also significant, as no other peremptory norm examined above exhibited any such disagreement.

The importance of the principle of self-determination to international relations is beyond question, and this much is reflected in the pronouncements of the International Court. Moreover, as a principle essential to friendly relations and cooperation among States, it is necessarily of concern to all States. However, there are many such principles of international law not subsumed by *jus cogens*. Jurisprudence indicates that it may yet be more accurate to regard self-determination as a political principle akin to others pronounced in the Declaration on Principles of International Law Concerning Friendly Relations and Co-operation among States, which sets out duties and obligations to be respected by all States. This would indicate that, although obligations *erga omnes* derive from peremptory norms and their performance has a particular meaning in the context of *jus cogens*, the concept of *erga omnes* may also be relevant to 'essential principles of contemporary international law' as distinct from peremptory norms of general international law (*jus cogens*).

C The common heritage of mankind

Another area of international law where obligations *erga omnes* have been articulated is the common heritage of mankind. Ancient Roman law conceived of a category of property to which private rights of ownership could not attach because the community as a whole retained

[317] *See* discussion *infra*, Chapter 12 (Individual Responsibility); Chapter 14.C (Punishment and Universal Jurisdiction).

control.[318] These areas constituted *res communis* – which included the air, waterways, ocean, and shorelines – and were considered *publica juris gentium* (common to all and proper to none).[319] This classical concept is recognized by international law as antecedent to the contemporary doctrine of 'the common heritage of mankind'.[320] Like *res communis*, the principle underlying the common heritage of mankind is that there are certain domains that fall beyond the sovereignty of the individual State which, therefore, are appropriately regulated by the international community as a whole.[321] As such, the common heritage of mankind is taken to reflect the interests of the international community and mankind as a whole.[322] The principle is peculiar in that it reflects broad concerns of both 'spatial and temporal dimensions' that require obligations in the present to preserve and protect objects and spaces for future generations.[323] In some instances, the 'common concern of mankind' is more appropriate in classifying the interest in question than common 'heritage', an alteration that alleviates any proprietary connotation. The 'commonness' central to the common heritage of mankind reflects considerations evocative of the doctrine of *jus cogens*.

> The conceptions of common heritage and of common concern of mankind embody universal solidarity and social responsibility (rather than competitiveness), emanate from human conscience (rather than from the

318 *See* Kemal Baslar, THE CONCEPT OF THE COMMON HERITAGE OF MANKIND IN INTERNATIONAL LAW 40–3 (The Hague: Martinus Nijhoff 1998).

319 Hugo Grotius, MARE LIBERUM Chapter V (Indianapolis, IN: Liberty Fund, Richard Hakluyt trans., David Armidate ed., 2004 [1609]).

320 Cançado Trindade, *International Law for Humankind: Towards a New Jus Gentium (I)*, 371 (quoting United Nations, Office of Legal Affairs, *The Law of the Sea – Concept of the Common Heritage of Mankind (Legislative History of Articles 133 to 150 and 311 (6) of the UN Convention on the Law of the Sea)* 1, 3 (1996) ("'It is difficult to say exactly when the concept of the common heritage of mankind first arose in human consciousness. The idea, in one form or another, could probably be traced to ancient times ... Suffice it to point out that in the 1830s a Latin American jurist, Andrés Bello, argued that those things which could not be held by one nation without detriment to the others ought to be considered by the international community as "common patrimony". In 1898, A. G. de Lapradelle, a French jurist, advanced the idea that the oceans should be "le patrimoine de l'humanité"'").

321 *See* Cançado Trindade, *International Law for Humankind: Towards a New Jus Gentium (I)*, 394–5.

322 Bruno Simma, *From Bilateralism to Community Interest in International Law*, 250 RECUEIL DES COURS 240–2 (1994); Christian Tomuschat, *Obligations Arising for States Without or Against their Will*, 241 RECUEIL DES COURS 226–7 (1993).

323 *See* Cançado Trindade, *International Law for Humankind: Towards a New Jus Gentium (I)*, 365–6.

> free 'will' of States), reflect basic values of the international community as a whole (rather than State interests), and strengthen the notion of an international *ordre public* (rather than a fragmented contractual vision).[324]

Unlike *jus cogens*, which constitutes protections related to the dignity of the human person, contemporary analogs of *res communis* refer to the management of domains reserved for the benefit of the whole of mankind beyond the sovereignty claims of individual States. The primary concern that arises in the context of the common heritage of mankind is the exploitation and development of such domains by individual States, to the exclusion of other States and detriment of future generations. Therefore, the functional focus of instruments and norms contemplating the common heritage of mankind is responsibility for the conservation and preservation of such objects for peaceful purposes, development, and the interests of mankind.[325] In contemporary international law, the common heritage of mankind encompasses the high seas, outer space, Antarctica, the environment, and cultural heritage; each will be considered briefly in turn, before presenting some general conclusions.

i. The high seas

The principle that State sovereignty cannot extend to the high seas was expressed in the writings of Grotius by the phrase *mare liberum*, meaning the free sea, in his work of that title.[326] The principle is enshrined in Part VII in the UN Convention on the Law of the Sea (1982).[327] The Preamble of the Convention calls for the development of principles embodied in GA Resolution 2749 (1970),[328] in which

> the General Assembly solemnly declared *inter alia* that the area of the seabed and ocean floor and the subsoil thereof, beyond the limits of national jurisdiction, as well as its resources, are the common heritage of mankind, the exploration and exploitation of which shall be carried out for the benefit of mankind as a whole, irrespective of the geographical location of States[.][329]

324 *Ibid.*, 391–2.

325 *See, e.g.*, Graham Nicholson, *The Common Heritage of Mankind and Mining: An Analysis of the Law as to the High Seas, Outer Space, the Antarctic and World Heritage*, 6(1) New Zealand Journal of Environmental Law 177, 183 (2002).

326 Grotius, Mare Liberum Chapter V.

327 UNCLOTS (1982), Part VII.

328 Declaration of Principles Governing the Sea-Bed and the Ocean Floor, and the Subsoil Thereof, Beyond the Limits of National Jurisdiction, GA Res. 2749 (XXV), UN Doc. A/Res/2749 (XXV), para. 1 (17 December 1970).

329 UNCLOTS (1982), Preamble.

According to the Convention, the legal right to the resources contained in this Area is reserved to 'mankind as a whole',[330] and all activities in the Area are limited to the benefit of mankind as a whole,[331] for peaceful purposes only.[332] The Deep Sea Bed Agreement (1994), which was adopted by the UN General Assembly to substantially restructure the Convention's development regime according to free market principles, reaffirms that 'the seabed and ocean floor and subsoil thereof . . . are the common heritage of mankind'.[333] Certain provisions of the law of the sea belong to customary international law, and the UN Convention on the Law of the Sea overlaps with customary international law to some extent.[334] The status of deep-sea resources as belonging to the common heritage of mankind appears well accepted in principle,[335] with 157 signatories to the 1982 Convention and 79 to the 1994 Agreement on Part XI as of 30 January 2013.[336] In *Responsibilities and Obligations of States Sponsoring Persons and Entities with Respect to Activities in the Area* (2011), the Seabed Disputes Chamber of the International Tribunal for the Law of the Sea (ITLOS) determined that obligations *erga omnes* arise from the reservation of the high seas and the Area to the common heritage of mankind:

> Each State Party may . . . be entitled to claim compensation in light of the *erga omnes* character of the obligations relating to preservation of the environment of the high seas and in the Area. In support of this view, reference may be made to article 48 of the ILC Articles on State Responsibility[.][337]

The International Court may find occasion to make a similar pronouncement in its decision concerning a dispute between Bolivia and Chile over Bolivia's access to the Pacific Ocean.[338]

330 *Ibid.*, Article 137. 331 *Ibid.*, Article 140. 332 *Ibid.*, Article 141.

333 Agreement Relating to the Implementation of Part XI of the United Nations Convention on the Law of the Sea of 10 December 1982, GA Res. 48/263, UN Doc. A/Res/48/263, Preamble (28 July 1994).

334 *See* James Harrison, Making the Law of the Sea: A Study in the Development of International Law 27–61 (Cambridge University Press 2011).

335 *Ibid.*, 38 (as possibly belonging to customary international law).

336 *See Multilateral Treaties Deposited with the Secretary-General*, United Nations Treaty Collection, *available at* http://untreaty.un.org (last accessed 15 August 2014).

337 *Responsibilities and Obligations of States Sponsoring Persons and Entities with Respect to Activities in the Area*, International Tribunal for the Law of the Sea (Seabed Disputes Chamber), Advisory Opinion, Case No. 17, para. 180 (2011) (citing ILC Articles on State Responsibility, Article 48 (Invocation of responsibility by a State other than an injured State)).

338 *Obligation to Negotiate Access to the Pacific Ocean (Bolivia v. Chile)*, Application Instituting Proceedings (*filed in the Registry of the Court* 24 April 2013).

ii. Outer space, the moon and other celestial bodies

Contemporary international law frequently equates outer space, the moon, and other celestial bodies with the common heritage of mankind. Following the post-war development of rocket propulsion and the ensuing Space Race between the United States and the Soviet Union, the UN General Assembly recognized 'the common interest of mankind as a whole in furthering the peaceful use of outer space' and established the Committee on the Peaceful Uses of Outer Space (COPUS) pursuant to this end.[339] The General Assembly unanimously determined that international law applies to outer space and celestial bodies in 1961,[340] and articulated a Declaration of Legal Principles Governing the Activities of States in the Exploration and Use of Outer Space two years later.[341] In its Declaration, the General Assembly determined that '[t]he exploration and use of outer space shall be carried on for the benefit and in the interests of all mankind' and, along with celestial bodies, shall be 'free for exploration and use by all States ... in accordance with international law ... [and are] not subject to national appropriation'.[342] More than one hundred General Assembly resolutions on the matter reflect the *opinio juris sive necessitatis* of the international community and 'the common interest of mankind in promoting and expanding the exploration and use of outer space, as the province of all mankind, for peaceful purposes and in continuing efforts to extend to all States the benefits derived therefrom'.[343] A series of multilateral treaties provides substantive support in the practice of States that space is 'the province of all mankind' and is 'not subject to national appropriation by claim of sovereignty'.[344] This foundation provides a basis for the claim that the reservation of outer space and celestial bodies to the common heritage of mankind generates obligations *erga omnes* owed by States to the international community as a whole. While there is support for the proposition that

[339] GA Res. 1472 (XIV), UN Doc. A/Res/1472(XIV) (12 December 1959).

[340] GA Res. 1721 (XVI) [A], UN Doc. A/Res/1721(XVI)[A] (20 December 1961).

[341] GA Res. 1962 (XVIII), UN Doc. A/Res/1962(XVIII) (13 December 1963).

[342] *Ibid.*, paras. 1–3.

[343] *See, e.g.*, GA Res. 65/97, UN Doc. A/Res/65/97 (20 January 2011).

[344] Treaty on Principles Governing the Activities of States in the Exploration and Use of Outer Space, Including the Moon and Other Celestial Bodies, 610 UNTS 205, Articles 1–2 (27 January 1967, *entered into force* 10 October 1967); Convention on International Liability for Damage Caused by Space Objects, 961 UNTS 187, Preamble (29 March 1972, *entered into force* 1 September 1972); Agreement Governing the Activities of States on the Moon and Other Celestial Bodies, 1363 UNTS 3, Article 11 (5 December 1979, *entered into force* 11 July 1984).

the reservation of outer space, the moon, and other celestial bodies to the common heritage of mankind belongs to *jus cogens*,[345] the observation by Judge Cançado Trindade that such obligations are more precicely characterized as obligations *erga omnes* only appears more consistent with the distinction between peremptory norms and obligations *erga omnes* in international law.[346]

iii. The Antarctic

It is commonly asserted that Antarctica, as part of the common heritage of mankind, is exempt from the exclusive control of individual States. The 1959 Antarctic Treaty, which was concluded by all 'interested parties', suspended claims of sovereignty over the Antarctic and demarcated the continent as a zone of peace.[347] In the Preamble to the instrument, the signatories recognized 'that it is in the interest of all mankind that Antarctica shall continue forever to be used exclusively for peaceful purposes and shall not become the scene or object of international discord', a principle given legal force by Article I of the Treaty.[348] The instrument also prohibited any future assertion of sovereignty claims over the Antarctic. The Protocol on Antarctic Environmental Protection (1991) reaffirmed that 'the protection of the Antarctic environment and dependent and associated ecosystems is in the interest of mankind as a whole',[349] and accordingly prohibited 'any activity relating to mineral resources' of the Antarctic, apart from scientific research, thereby inhibiting commercial development of the continent at least among the thirty-three States party to the Protocol.[350] While

345 *See* Francis Lyall and Paul Larsen, Space Law: A Treatise 80 (Burlington, VT: Ashgate 2013) ('There is therefore considerable strength in the argument . . . that fundamental principles of the OST now come into the category of *ius cogens*'); Carl Christol, *Judge Manfred Lachs and the Principle of* Jus Cogens, 22 Journal of Space Law 33, 41–5 (1994).

346 Cançado Trindade, *International Law for Humankind: Towards a New Jus Gentium (I)*, 368–9.

347 The Antarctic Treaty, 402 UNTS 71, Article IV (1 December 1959, *entered into force* 23 June 1961) (Argentina, Belgium, Chile, France, Japan, New Zealand, Norway, South Africa, the Soviet Union, the United Kingdom, and the United States are the original signatories to the treaty, to which forty-eight nations are current parties).

348 *Ibid.*, Preamble, Article I.

349 Protocol on Environmental Protection to the Antarctic Treaty, Preamble, 30 ILM 1455 (4 October 1991, *entered into force* 14 January 1998).

350 *Ibid.*, Article 7.

some authorities have asserted the *erga omnes* character of obligations arising from the reservation of the Antarctic to the common heritage of mankind,[351] the question remains whether the Antarctic truly belongs to the global commons, given the non-universality of the Antarctic Treaty and the fact that, notwithstanding the instrument, sovereignty claims, though frozen, continue to apply to much of the Antarctic.[352]

iv. The environment

Another domain often raised in the context of the common heritage of mankind is the environment. The 1972 Stockholm Declaration on the Human Environment articulates the goal of 'the identification, avoidance and control of environmental risks and the solution of environmental problems [] for the common good of mankind'.[353] More recently, environmental concerns, such as climate change, have been referred to as a 'common concern of mankind'.[354] These constructions distinguish the environment from the more proprietary connotation of 'heritage' applied to the domains of the high seas, outer space, and the Antarctic. Rather than necessarily reflecting a difference in kind, however, this reframing shifts the consideration from the common benefit of resource exploitation to the shared burden of protection.[355] Put differently, 'common concern' focuses on the nature of obligations arising with respect to the environment rather than the commonality of rights from which these obligations arise. There is some support in contemporary jurisprudence that the general obligation to protect the environment is an obligation *erga omnes* owed by States to the international community as a whole.[356] In the *Case Concerning the Gabčíkovo-Nagymaros Project* (1997) before the International Court, Vice-President Weeramantry considered the

351 *See, e.g.*, Jonathan Charney, *The Antarctic System and Customary International Law*, *in* INTERNATIONAL LAW FOR ANTARCTICA 101 (The Hague: Martinus Nijhoff, Francesco Francioni & Tullio Scovazzi eds., 1987).

352 Nicholson, *The Common Heritage of Mankind and Mining*, 191.

353 The Stockholm Declaration on the Human Environment, UN Doc. A/CONF.48/14/Rev.1, Principle 18 (16 June 1972).

354 *See, e.g.*, GA Res. 43/53, UN Doc. A/Res/43/53, para. 1 (6 December 1988) (Protection of Global Climate for Present and Future Generations of Mankind).

355 Cançado Trindade, *International Law for Humankind: Towards a New Jus Gentium (I)*, 381.

356 *See* Marina Spinedi, *Les conséquences juridiques d'un fait internationalement illicite causant un dommage à l'environnement*, *in* INTERNATIONAL RESPONSIBILITY FOR ENVIRONMENTAL HARM 75–124 (London: Graham & Trottman, Francesco Francioni & Tullio Scovazzi eds., 2001).

tension arising when considering obligations *erga omnes* in the context of an *inter parties* dispute:

> Yet this scarcely does justice to rights and obligations of an *erga omnes* character – least of all in cases involving environmental damage of a far-reaching and irreversible nature . . . We have entered an era of international law in which international law subserves not only the interests of individual States, but looks beyond them and their parochial concerns to the greater interests of humanity and planetary welfare.[357]

Although conservation and preservation of the environment undoubtedly occupy the 'common concern' of humanity, the status of obligations arising from this concern remains unsettled. Identification of discrete extra-State interests of humanity and planetary welfare also suggests a principled distinction between norms belonging to *jus cogens* and those concerning the common heritage of mankind, though such 'greater interests' are clearly interrelated.

v. Cultural heritage

The concept of cultural heritage is one closely related to the common heritage of mankind. This linkage was clearly articulated in the UNESCO Declaration on Principles of International Cultural Co-operation (1966), which states that 'all cultures form part of the common heritage belonging to all mankind'.[358] Perhaps to temper the proprietary implications of the application of this concept to areas within the sovereign control of States, the animating principle of cultural heritage as the common heritage of mankind is balanced by an emphasis on the common 'concern' of the international community in conservation and preservation. To this effect, parties to the 1972 Convention take care to acknowledge 'the sovereignty of the States on whose territory the cultural and natural heritage . . . is situated', whilst establishing that,

[357] *Gabčíkovo-Nagymaros Project (Hungary / Slovakia)*, Judgment, ICJ Reports 1997, Sep. Op. Weeramantry, p. 88, 117–18; *see Legality of the Threat or Use of Nuclear Weapons*, Advisory Opinion, ICJ Reports 1996, Dis. Op. Weeramantry, p. 429, 504 ('principles of environmental law thus do not depend for their validity on treaty provisions. They are part of customary international law. They are part of the *sine qua non* for human survival').

[358] Declaration on Principles of International Cultural Co-operation, UNESCO Standard-Setting Instruments, IV.C., Article 1 (4 November 1966).

> parts of the cultural or natural heritage . . . need to be preserved as part of the world heritage of mankind as a whole . . . [and] it is incumbent on the international community as a whole to participate in the protection of the cultural and natural heritage[.][359]

A similar sentiment is reflected in the Universal Declaration on Cultural Diversity (2001) adopted by the General Conference of UNESCO,[360] the Convention for the Protection of the Underwater Cultural Heritage (2001),[361] the Convention for the Safeguarding of Intangible Cultural Heritage (2003),[362] and the Convention on the Protection and Promotion of the Diversity of Cultural Expressions (2005).[363] Following the destruction of the Buddhas of the Bamiyan in March 2001 in Afghanistan, the UN General Assembly reiterated 'the need to respect the common heritage of mankind'.[364] The General Assembly of States Parties to the Convention Concerning the Protection of the World Cultural and Natural Heritage condemned the 'wilful destruction of the cultural heritage' as a 'crime against the common heritage of humanity'.[365] In a similar vein, as a matter of international humanitarian law, the 2003 UNESCO Declaration Concerning the Intentional Destruction of Cultural Heritage indicated that the prohibition against the 'international

[359] Convention Concerning the Protection of the World Cultural and Natural Heritage, 1037 UNTS 151, Preamble, Articles 6–7 (16 November 1972, *entered into force* 17 December 1975).

[360] UNESCO Universal Declaration on Cultural Diversity, UNESCO Doc. CLT-2002/WS/9 (2002), Article 1 (2 November 2001) (The 'uniqueness and plurality of the identities of the groups and societies making up humankind' form part of the 'common heritage of humanity').

[361] Convention for the Protection of the Underwater Cultural Heritage, UNESCO Doc. 31C/Resolution 24, Preamble, Article 2 (2 November 2001, *entered into force* 2 January 2009) (concerning underwater cultural heritage as 'an integral part of the cultural heritage of humanity').

[362] Convention for the Safeguarding of Intangible Cultural Heritage, 2368 UNTS 1 (17 October 2003, *entered into force* 20 April 2006) (referring to 'the universal will and the common concern to safeguard the intangible cultural heritage of humanity').

[363] Convention on the Protection and Promotion of the Diversity of Cultural Expressions, 2440 UNTS 311, Preamble, Article 2 (20 October 2005, *entered into force* 18 March 2007) ('cultural diversity forms a common heritage of humanity and should be cherished and preserved for the benefit of all').

[364] GA Res. 55/243, UN Doc. A/Res/55/243, Preamble (1 May 2001).

[365] Acts Constituting a Crime against the Common Heritage of Humanity, UNESCO Doc. 31C/Resolution 26 (2 November 2001); Resolution on the Protection of the Cultural Heritage of Afghanistan Adopted by the General Assembly of States Parties to the World Heritage Convention at its Thirteenth Session, UNESCO Doc. WHC-2001/CONF.206/8 Rev., Annex III (30–31 October 2001).

destruction of cultural heritage' had become part of customary international law and constitutes an international crime.[366] Indeed, the intentional destruction of cultural heritage constitutes a war crime.[367] Against this backdrop, authorities have concluded that the prohibition against the wilful destruction of cultural heritage, as part of the common heritage of mankind, generates obligations *erga omnes*.[368]

***

The common heritage of mankind is an expression of the interests of the international community as a whole. Contemporary jurisprudence evinces the *res communis* character of the domains recognized to belong to the common heritage of mankind through the emergence of legal obligations to preserve and protect such domains for present and future generations. These obligations vary dramatically across the law governing the high seas, outer space and celestial bodies, the Antarctic, the environment, and cultural heritage. The extent to which such obligations constitute obligations *erga omnes parties* – or further, *erga omnes* obligations owed by each State to the international community as a whole – remains an evolving area of international law.

Two observations are warranted based on the foregoing survey. First, the degree to which a domain is accepted to belong to the common heritage of mankind is proportionate to the legal support for the *erga omnes* character of associated *res communis* obligations. For example, relevant jurisprudence appears quite settled that the high seas and outer space belong to the common heritage of mankind; the obligations of States to preserve and protect these *res communis*-type domains have emerged most clearly as obligations *erga omnes* owed to the international community as a whole. By contrast, the environment is more often

366 UNESCO Declaration Concerning the Intentional Destruction of Cultural Heritage, UNESCO Doc. 32C/Resolution 39, Preamble, II para. 2 (17 October 2003) ('For the purposes of this Declaration "intentional destruction" means an act intended to destroy in whole or in part cultural heritage, thus compromising its integrity, in a manner which constitutes a violation of international law or an unjustifiable offence to the principles of humanity and dictates of public conscience, in the latter case in so far as such acts are not already governed by fundamental principles of international law').

367 *See, e.g.*, Hague Convention IV (1907), Articles 27 and 56; ICTY Statute (1993), Article 3(d); Rome Statute (1998), Articles 8(2)(b)(ix) and 8(2)(e)(iv).

368 *See* Roger O'Keefe, *World Cultural Heritage: Obligations to the International Community as a Whole?*, 53(1) International and Comparative Law Quarterly 189, 190, 196–7 (2004).

characterized as belonging to the common concern, rather than the heritage, of mankind, and the obligations of States to protect and preserve this domain, as a matter of law, have not clearly crystallized as obligations *erga omnes* under customary international law.

The second observation is that *jus cogens* and the common heritage of mankind remain discrete concepts in international law notwithstanding their similarities.[369] Like peremptory norms belonging to *jus cogens*, norms concerning the common heritage of mankind reflect interests of the international community as a whole that transcend individual sovereign States; each category of norms generates obligations *erga omnes*. However, the principles underlying each category are distinct: human dignity gives rise to peremptory norms, while a principle akin to *res communis* underpins the common heritage of mankind.[370] The norms of each category are different in kind. Quite clearly, *res communis* norms are derogable and arise almost exclusively as the product of international agreements reflecting the common concern of the international community. The extent to which these norms have entered into customary international law is yet evolving. Even the freedom of the high seas, perhaps the most well established of the *res communis* norms, has carved out of it an exception for the territorial waters of maritime States, over which States may project their sovereignty. Similarly, management of the resources contained by this domain is determined as a matter of treaty law. By contrast, *jus cogens* constitutes fundamental protections of the individual, the moral dimension of which renders their normative expressions peremptory. The positive obligations arising from *jus cogens*, the performance of which requires States to prevent and punish

369 While some authorities suggest that the common heritage of mankind is a part of *jus cogens*, others distinguish between the two concepts as a matter of law and principle. *Compare* Baslar, THE CONCEPT OF THE COMMON HERITAGE OF MANKIND IN INTERNATIONAL LAW 363–7 ('principles of peaceful uses and the non-appropriation of international spaces acquired the character of *jus cogens*'), *and* Hannikainen, PEREMPTORY NORMS (*JUS COGENS*) IN INTERNATIONAL LAW Chapter 11, *with* Cançado Trindade, *International Law for Humankind: Towards a New Jus Gentium (I)*, 389 ('The term *common* ... has brought to the fore the notion of obligations *erga omnes* ... the term *concern* has suggested a primary focus on the *causes* of problems and conflicts, the preventive character of regimes of protection and the general obligation of due diligence').

370 *See Gabčíkovo-Nagymaros Project (Hungary / Slovakia)*, Judgment, ICJ Reports 1997, Sep. Op. Weeramantry, p. 88, 118 (referring to 'the greater interests of humanity and planetary welfare', as reinforcing, but possibly distinct, forces underlying obgligations in international law).

violations as international crimes, are qualitatively distinct from obligations arising from the common heritage of mankind, which require States to respect and preserve those domains for present and future generations. While *jus cogens* protects the individual from affronts to their basic human dignity, the common heritage of mankind protects areas for generations of humanity not yet in being. And although the obligations arising from *jus cogens* are beyond question obligations *erga omnes*, relevant evidence suggests that the same cannot be claimed in every instance of obligations arising from the common heritage of mankind.

D The right to life

The right to life has been referred to as 'the most fundamental human right' and is also held by some to belong to *jus cogens*.[371] However, as a matter of legal construction, all rights are subject to limitation, most generally by the enjoyment of that right by others. Therefore, it is problematic to conceive of any 'right', even one so fundamental, as absolute, and the right to life is not a suitable candidate as a peremptory norm. In a similar sense, the principle of human dignity does not belong to *jus cogens*, even if it constitutes a material source of norms belonging to the category.[372] One prohibition related to the right to life concerns the death penalty;[373] however, judicial authorities are mixed in their assessment of whether the prohibition of the death penalty is sufficiently crystallized in customary international law to belong to *jus cogens*. For

371 Karen Parker and Lyn Beth Neylon, *Jus Cogens: Compelling the Law of Human Rights*, 12 Hastings International & Comparative Law Review 411, 431–2 (1988–9); Hannikainen, Peremptory Norms (*Jus Cogens*) in International Law 514–20 (in the context of large-scale and arbitrary killings); Paul Gormley, *The Right to Life and the Rule of Non-Derogability: Peremptory Norms of* Jus Cogens, *in* The Right to Life in International Law 120–59 (Dordrecht: Martinus Nijhoff, Bertrand Ramcharan ed., 1985); United Nations Commission on Human Rights, Protection of Human Rights in Chile, UN Doc. A/37/564, para. 22 (4 November 1982) (the right to life is 'a fundamental right in any society ... [and] forms part of *jus cogens* in international human rights law').

372 *Cf. Prosecutor v. Kallon and Kamara*, Decision on Challenge to Jurisdiction: Lomé Accord Amnesty, SCSL-04-15-PT-060-I, para. 71 (2004) (describing the obligation to protect human dignity as a peremptory norm).

373 *See* William Schabas, The Abolition of the Death Penalty in International Law 19, 376 (Cambridge University Press, 3rd edn. 2002) (the prohibition of the death penalty, in connection with the right to life, as 'a norm of *jus cogens*, may be envisaged in the not too distant future').

example, while the norm has been articulated to belong to *jus cogens* by the Inter-American Commission on Human Rights,[374] circuit courts of the United States have found, on the contrary, that the prohibition of the death penalty does not belong to *jus cogens*.[375] There is no evidence that the legal effects associated with *jus cogens*, or related obligations *erga omnes*, have emerged in relation to the prohibition of the death penalty.

[374] *Thomas v. United States*, No. 12.240, Inter-American Commission on Human Rights, Report No. 100/03, paras. 40–1 (2003); *Domingues v. United States*, No. 12.285, Inter-American Commission on Human Rights, Report No. 62/02, para. 85 (2000); *Roach and Pinkerton v. United States*, No. 9647, Inter-American Commission on Human Rights, Res. 3/87, para. 56 (1987) ('in the member States of the OAS there is recognized a norm of *jus cogens* which prohibits the State execution of children').

[375] *Hain v. Gibson*, 287 F.3d 1224, 1243-4 (10th Cir. 2002); *Buell v. Mitchell*, 274 F.3d 337, 373 (6th Cir. 2001) ('since the abolition of the death penalty is not a customary norm of international law, it cannot have risen to the level that the international community as a whole recognizes it as *jus cogens*').

12

Individual responsibility

To this point, it has been demonstrated that the individual is the primary subject of peremptory norms in international law. The material content of *jus cogens*, as protections of the dignity of the human person, indicates that the State is not the primary beneficiary of protections conferred by such norms. The law of international responsibility indicates the corollary, namely, that the individual is the sole bearer of criminal responsibility for violations of *jus cogens*. The classification of an offence as an international crime refers at once to the seriousness of the law violated – a peremptory norm belonging to *jus cogens* – and the subject of criminal responsibility for the breach: the individual.[1] To this effect, it has been observed that the justiciability of *jus cogens* norms against individuals is the lineage of the Nuremberg prosecutions that followed the Second World War.[2]

Moreover, the development of individual civil responsibility has dispelled the distinction between public and private acts in violation of peremptory norms, indicative of the way in which these duties

[1] This is distinct from the notion of transnational crime, which refers to the special scope of a crime rather than its gravity; e.g. espionage, counterfeiting currency, illicit traffic in drugs, slave trading, trading in women and children, pollution of the seas, damaging submarine cable, offences against persons protected by international law, unlawful dispatch of explosives through post, pirate broadcasting, and theft of national and archaeological treasures.

[2] *Siderman de Blake v. Republic of Argentina*, 965 F.2d 699, 715 (9th Cir. 1992) (quoting *Barcelona Traction*, ICJ Reports 1970, p. 3, para. 33); *C v. Director of Immigration*, Court of First Instance (Hong Kong), HCAL 132/2006, [2008] 2 HKC 165, ILDC 1119, para. 78 (2008) ('Much of the impetus for the recognition of *jus cogens* arose out of the state-sponsored atrocities of the Second World War. In plain terms, *jus cogens* seeks to be a supreme law, one which, recognising fundamental human rights, denies the unlimited will of the state. *Jus cogens* recognises that some deeds are so wrong, so abhorrent, that no legitimate legal order could fail to proscribe them').

are borne directly by the individual rather than through the State. The erosion of traditional immunities under international law for perpetrators of international crimes reflects the priority of the international community to deny impunity to individuals who violate peremptory norms. And the increasing invalidation and non-recognition under international law of domestic amnesties for international crimes demonstrates the inability of acts of the sovereign State to affect individual responsibility arising for violations of *jus cogens*. Each of these aspects of individual responsibility for violations of *jus cogens* is considered in turn.

A Individual criminal responsibility

As illustrated above, peremptory norms constitute protections of the individual when formulated as positive rights or freedoms; the corollary of this conceptualization is to formulate each peremptory norm as a duty of the individual, the violation of which constitutes an international crime imputing individual responsibility. This premise may be traced to the definition of 'international crime' established by the International Military Tribunal (IMT) at Nuremberg:

> An international crime is such an act universally recognized as criminal, which is considered a grave matter of international concern and for some valid reason cannot be left within the exclusive jurisdiction of the State that would have control over it under ordinary circumstances.[3]

Implicit in this formulation of an international crime, as one extending beyond the exclusive jurisdiction of an individual State, is that such conduct imposes criminal responsibility attaching to the individual rather than the State:

> Crimes against international law are committed by men, not by abstract entities, and only by punishing individuals who commit such crimes can the provisions of international law be enforced.[4]

[3] *United States v. List et al. (The Hostage Case)*, *in* 11 TRIALS OF WAR CRIMINALS BEFORE THE NUERNBERG MILITARY TRIBUNALS UNDER CONTROL COUNCIL LAW NO. 10 759, 1241 (Washington: GPO 1950).

[4] *Nazi Conspiracy and Aggression*, Opinion and Judgment, International Military Tribunal at Nuremberg 53 (1946).

The violation of each peremptory norm – piracy,[5] slavery,[6] crimes against humanity,[7] war crimes (grave violations of humanitarian law),[8]

[5] United Nations Convention on the Law of the Sea, 1833 UNTS 3, Articles 100, 101, and 105 (10 December 1982, *entered into force* 16 November 1994) [hereinafter, UNCLOTS (1982)]; *see, e.g.*, *United States v. Dire*, 680 F.3d 446, 454 (4th Cir. 2012) *cert. denied*, 133 S. Ct. 982 (2013); *Samanyolu* Case, Rotterdam District Court (Netherlands), CR 10/600012-09, 2–3 (2010); *Regina v. Mohamed Ahmed Dahir & Ten (10) Others*, Supreme Court (Seychelles), CR 51/2009, paras. 61, 71 (2010).

[6] Supplementary Convention on the Abolition of Slavery, the Slave Trade, and Institutions and Practices Similar to Slavery, 226 UNTS 3, Articles 3, 5 (7 September 1956, *entered into force* 30 April 1957; *see, e.g.*, *Prosecutor v. Charles Taylor*, Judgment, SCSL-03-01-T-1283, para. 6994(a) (2012); *Prosecutor v. Sesay, Kallon, and Gbao*, Judgment, SCSL-04-15-T, para. 76 (2009); *Regina v. Tang*, High Court of Australia, [2008] HCA 39 (paras. 110–17) (Kirby, J.).

[7] Agreement Between the United Nations and the Government of Sierra Leone on the Establishment of a Special Court for Sierra Leone, 2178 UNTS 138, Article 2 (16 January 2002, *entry into force* 12 April 2002)[hereinafter, SCSL Statute (2000)]; Rome Statute of the International Criminal Court, UN Doc. A/CONF.183.9 (17 July 1998, *entered into force* 1 July 2002) [hereinafter Rome Statute (1998)] Article 7; Report of the International Law Commission on the Work of its Forty-Eighth Session, [1996] II(2) YbILC 17 [hereinafter, Draft Code of Crimes (1996)], Article 18; Statute of the International Criminal Tribunal for Rwanda, UN Doc. S/Res/955 (annex) (8 November 1994) [hereinafter, ICTR Statute (1994)], Article 3; Statute of the International Tribunal for the Prosecution of Persons Responsible for Serious Violations of International Humanitarian Law Committed in the Territory of the Former Yugoslavia since 1991, UN Doc. S/Res/827 (annex) (25 May 1993) [hereinafter, ICTY Statute (1993)], Articles 2–3; Report of the International Law Commission Covering the Work of its Sixth Session, [1954] II YbILC 149, para. 41 *et seq.* [hereinafter, Draft Code of Offences (1954)], Article 2, para. 11; International Military Tribunal for the Far East Charter, TIAS No. 1589, 3, 4 Bevans 20 (19 January 1946) [hereinafter, IMTFE Charter (1946)], Article 5(c); Charter of the International Military Tribunal, *in* Agreement for the Prosecution and Punishment of the Major War Criminals of the European Axis, 82 UNTS 280 (signed at London 8 August 1945) [hereinafter, IMT Charter (1945)], Article 6(c); *see, e.g.*, *Prosecutor v. Gbagbo*, Decision on the Confirmation of Charges, ICC-02/11-01/11, paras. 251–2, 259–60 (2014); *Kenya Section of the International Commission of Jurists v. Attorney General et al.*, High Court (Kenya), [2011] eKLR, ILDC 1804, paras. 64–7, 74–5, 99 (2011); *Rivera Lazo and ors*, Superior Court (Third Criminal Chamber) (Peru), No. 28-2001, ILDC 1887, para. 16 (2010); *Kadic v. Karadzic*, Third Amended Indictment, IT-95-5/18-PT, paras. 48–75 (2009); *Scilingo Manzorro v. Spain*, Supreme Court (Spain), No. 798/2007, ILDC 1430, paras. 6–7 (2007); *Prosecutor v. Kambanda*, Judgment, ICTR-97-23-S, para. 40 (1998); *Nazi Conspiracy and Aggression*, Opinion and Judgment, International Military Tribunal at Nuremberg (1946).

[8] SCSL Statute (2000), Articles 3–4; Rome Statute (1998), Article 8; Draft Code of Crimes (1996), Article 20; ICTR Statute (1994), Article 4; ICTY Statute (1993), Articles 2–3; Draft Code of Offences (1954), Article 2, paras. 11–12; Geneva Convention I (1949), Articles 49–50; Geneva Convention II (1949), Articles 50–1; Geneva Convention III (1949), Articles 129–30; Geneva Convention IV (1949), Articles 146–7; IMTFE Charter (1946), Article 5 (b); IMT Charter (1945), Article 6(b); *see, e.g.*, *A. (Kahled Nezzar) v. Office of the Attorney*

aggression,[9] genocide,[10] torture,[11] apartheid (systematic racial

General, Federal Criminal Court (Switzerland), No. BB.2011.140 (2012); *Prosecutor v. Gaddafi et al.*, Pre-Trial Chamber I, ICC-01/11-01/11-T-1 (2011); *Prosecutor's Office v. Anić*, Court of Bosnia and Herzegovina (Section I for War Crimes), S1 1 K 005596 11 Kro, ILDC 1907, paras. 27–8 (2011); *Prosecutor v. Popović et al.*, Judgment, IT-05–88-T, paras. 2103–7, 2110 (2010); *Prosecutor v. Setako*, Judgment and Sentence, ICTR-04–81-T, paras. 483–91 (2010); *Prosecutor v. Norman et al.*, Judgment, SCSL-04-14-T, paras. 108, 978 (2007); *Chile v. Arancibia Clavel*, Supreme Court of Justice (Argentina), A/533/XXXVIII, ILDC 1082, para. 28 (2004); *Nazi Conspiracy and Aggression*, Opinion and Judgment, International Military Tribunal at Nuremberg (1946).

9 ICC Review Conference, The Crime of Aggression, Resolution RC/Res.6 (11 June 2010); Rome Statute, Article 5(1)(d); Draft Code of Crimes (1996), Article 16; Draft Code of Offences (1954); Report of the International Law Commission Covering the Work of its First Session, [1950] II YbILC 374–8, Principle VI(a) (Formulation of the Nürnberg Principles); IMTFE Charter (1946), Article 5(a) (defining 'crimes against peace' in relation to 'a war of aggression' or other illegal war); IMT Charter (1945), Article 6(a) (defining 'crimes against peace' in relation to 'a war of aggression' or other illegal war); Convention for the Definition of Aggression, 147 LNTS 69, No. 3391 (signed at London 3 July 1933, *entered into force* 17 February 1934); *Nazi Conspiracy and Aggression*, Opinion and Judgment, International Military Tribunal at Nuremberg (1946); *see supra*, Chapter 11, *n.* 179 (discussing individual prosecution for acts of aggression).

10 Rome Statute (1998), Article 6; Draft Code of Crimes (1996), Article 17; ICTR Statute (1994), Article 2; ICTY Statute (1993), Article 4; Convention on the Prevention and Punishment of the Crime of Genocide, Articles IV–VI, 78 UNTS 277, No. 1021 (9 December 1948, *entered into force* 12 January 1951); *see, e.g., Muna et al. v. Romulo et al.*, Supreme Court (Philippines), GR No. 159618, ILDC 2059, paras. 40–50, 89–94 (2011); *Prosecutor v. al Bashir*, Second Warrant of Arrest, No. ICC-02/05-01/09-95, 3 (2010); *Regina v. Munyaneza*, Montreal Superior Court (Criminal Division) (Canada), 2009 QCCS 2201, paras. 70–9 (2009); *Prosecutor v. Kristic*, IT-98-33-T, para. 541 (2001); *Jorgic Case*, BVerfG [Constitutional Court] (Germany), 2 BvR 1290/99, ILDC 132, paras. 17, 26–7 (2000); *Prosecutor v. Akayesu*, Judgment, ICTR-96-4-T (1998).

11 Agreement on the Establishment of the Extraordinary African Chambers within the Senegalese Judicial System between the Government of the Republic of Senegal and the African Union and the Statute of the Chambers (22 August 2012 and 30 January 2013), 52 ILM 1028 [hereinafter, EAC Statute (2013)], Article 4(d); SCSL Statute (2000), Article 2(f); Rome Statute (1998), Articles 7(1)(f), 8(2)(a)(ii); Draft Code of Crimes (1996), Articles 18(c), 20(a)(ii); ICTR Statute (1994), Article 3(f); ICTY Statute (1993), Articles 2(b), 5(f); Convention against Torture and Other Cruel, Inhuman or Degrading Treatment or Punishment, GA Res. 39/46, 1465 UNTS 85, Articles 4, 6, 7 (12 December 1984, *entered into force* 26 June 1987); *see, e.g., Lydienne X v. Prosecutor*, Court of Cassation (Criminal Division) (France), No. 12-81676, ILDC 2035, paras. 10.4, 14 (2013); *Questions Relating to the Obligation to Prosecute or Extradite (Belgium v. Senegal)*, Judgment, ICJ Reports 2012, p. 422, para. 121; *Bouterse Case*, Amsterdam Court of Appeal (Netherlands), Nos. R 97/163/12 Sv & R 97/176/12 Sv, para. 5 (International Commission of Jurists trans., 2000), *reversed by Bouterse Case*, Supreme Court (Netherlands), LJN: AB1471, ILDC 80 (2001); *R. v. Bow Street Metropolitan Stipendiary Magistrate and Others, Ex parte Pinochet Ugarte (No. 3)*, House of Lords (UK), [2000] 1 A.C. 147, 38 ILM 581 (1999).

discrimination),[12] and terrorism[13] – constitutes an international crime,[14] imputing individual criminal responsibility.[15] Although it has been suggested that *jus cogens* constitutes a broader legal category than that of

[12] Rome Statute (1998), Article 7(1)(j); Draft Code of Crimes (1996), Article 18(f); Protocol Additional to the Geneva Conventions of 12 August 1949, and relating to the Protection of Victims of Non-International Armed Conflicts (Protocol I), 1125 UNTS 3 (8 June 1977, *entered into force* 7 December 1978) [hereinafter, Additional Protocol I (1977)], Article 85 (4)(c); International Convention on the Suppression and Punishment of the Crime of Apartheid, 1015 UNTS 243 (30 November 1973, *entered into force* 18 July 1976) [hereinafter, Apartheid Convention (1973)], Articles I, III; GA Res. 2106 (XX), UN Doc. A/Res/2106 (XX), Article 2 (21 December 1965) (International Convention on the Elimination of All Forms of Racial Discrimination); *see, e.g.*, *Prosecutor v. Bikindi*, Judgment, ICTR-01-72-T, paras. 379–81, 433 (2008) (concerning persecution on the basis of race as a crime against humanity); *The State v. Walter Basson*, Judgment, Constitutional Court (South Africa), No. CCT 30/03, 2005 (1) SA 171 (CC), para. 37 (2004).

[13] Agreement Between the United Nations and the Lebanese Republic on the establishment of a Special Tribunal for Lebanon (with Statute), 2461 UNTS 280 (22 January 2007 and 6 February 2007, *entered into force* 10 June 2007) [hereinafter, STL Statute (2007)], Article 2(a); SCSL Statute (2000), Article 3(d); ICTR Statute (1994), Article 4(d); Geneva Convention IV (1949), Article 33; Additional Protocol I (1977), Article 51(2); Protocol Additional to the Geneva Conventions of 12 August 1949, and relating to the Protection of Victims of Non-International Armed Conflicts (Protocol II) (8 June 1977, *entered into force* 7 December 1978) [hereinafter, Additional Protocol II (1977)], Preamble, Article 13(2); Convention for the Prevention and Punishment of Terrorism, League of Nations Doc. C.546(I).M.383(I).1937.V (16 November 1937), 19 League of Nations O.J. 23 (1938) (never entered into force); *see, e.g.*, *Prosecutor v. Ayyash et al.*, No. STL-11-01/I/AC/R17bis, Interlocutory Decision on the Applicable Law: Terrorism, Conspiracy, Homicide, Perpetration, Cumulative Charging, 145 ILR 232 (2011) [hereinafter, STL Interlocutory Decision (2011)], para. 102; *Prosecutor v. Fofana and Kondewa*, Judgment, SCSL-04-14-T, para. 167 (2007); *Italy v. Abdelaziz and ors*, Court of Cassation (First Criminal Section) (Italy), No. 1072, 17 Guida al Diritto 90, ILDC 559, para. 2.1 (2007); *Chile v. Arancibia Clavel*, Supreme Court of Justice (Argentina), A/533/XXXVIII, ILDC 1082, para. 28 (2004); *ibid.*, paras. 21–2 (Boggiano, J., concurring); *Prosecutor v. Galić*, Judgment, IT-98-29-T, paras. 98, 769 (2003); *Decision (Auto) of the Full Penal Chamber Confirming Spanish Jurisdiction to Investigate Crimes of Genocide and Terrorism Committed during the Chilean Dictatorship*, National Court (*Audiencia Nacional*) (Spain), No. 173/98, §§ 5–7, 119 ILR 331, 342–4 (1998); *Decision (Auto) of the Full Penal Chamber Confirming Spanish Jurisdiction over the Crimes of Genocide and Terrorism committed during the Argentine Dictatorship*, National Court (*Audiencia Nacional*) (Spain), No. 84/98, §§ 8–10 (1998).

[14] Jochen Frowein, *Jus Cogens*, *in* III Encyclopedia of Public International Law 65, 68 (Amsterdam: North-Holland, Rudolf Bernhardt ed. 1997) ('A crime in this sense is seen as a violation of basic rules of *jus cogens*').

[15] *See, e.g.*, James Crawford, *International Crimes of States*, *in* The Law of International Responsibility 405, 405–14 (Oxford University Press, James Crawford, Alain Pellet & Simon Olleson eds., 2009) (noting that international law does not admit crimes of States).

international crimes,[16] jurisprudence has not borne out this position in practice.

As examined in Chapter 14, the performance of obligations *erga omnes* arising from peremptory norms requires the State, where possible, to extradite or prosecute individuals alleged to have violated peremptory norms.[17] Universal jurisdiction over such violations enables this duty by expanding the traditional bases of jurisdiction in international law to ensure that an individual who violates a peremptory norm can find no refuge from punishment.[18] In principle, by violating a peremptory norm, the individual commits a crime against the international community as a whole,[19] and prosecution by a custodial State is obligatory irrespective of the usual jurisdictional links of nationality or territory.[20] As much was observed to be a legal effect of *jus cogens* by the Trial Chamber of the ICTY in *Furundžija*:

> [A]t the individual level, that is, that of criminal liability, it would seem that one of the consequences of the *jus cogens* character bestowed by the international community upon the prohibition of torture is that every State is entitled to investigate, prosecute and punish or extradite individuals accused of torture, who are present in a territory under its jurisdiction. Indeed, it would be inconsistent on the one hand to prohibit torture to such an extent as to restrict the normally unfettered treaty-making power of sovereign States, and on the other hand bar States from prosecuting and punishing those torturers who have engaged in this odious

16 *See* ILC, Draft Articles on State Responsibility with Commentaries Thereto Adopted by the International Law Commission on First Reading 129–30, para. 62 (1997) (Commentary to Article 19) (Article 19 of the Draft Articles adopted in 1996 concerned the doctrine of 'international crimes of States', which was abandoned in the final version of the Articles on State Responsibility, therefore the expanded doctrine of international crimes found in the commentary to draft Article 19 is unavailing).

17 *See* discussion *infra*, Chapter 14.C (Punishment and Universal Jurisdiction).

18 *See ibid.*, text accompanying *nn.* 111–30.

19 *See, e.g.*, *Sánchez and ors v. Gibson and ors*, Supreme Court (Spain), No. 1240/2006, ILDC 993, para. 7 (2006) (discussing war crimes as 'crimes against the international community' under Spanish law); *Guatemala Genocide Case (Menchú Tumn and ors v. Two Guatemalan Government Officials and Six Members of the Guatemalan Military)*, Constitutional Court (Criminal Chamber) (Spain), Spanish Constitutional Court Decision Accepting Jurisdiction, No. 237/2005, ILDC 137, para. 6 (2005) (discussing regimes of universal jurisdiction over 'crimes against the international community' such as genocide, prohibited as *jus cogens*).

20 André De Hoogh, Obligations *Erga Omnes* and International Crimes 164 (The Hague: Martinus Nijhoff 1996); Steven Ratner and Jason Abrams, Accountability for Human Rights Atrocities in International Law 140–6 (Oxford: Clarendon Press 1987).

> practice abroad. This legal basis for States' universal jurisdiction over torture bears out and strengthens the legal foundation for such jurisdiction found by other courts in the inherently universal character of the crime. It has been held that international crimes being universally condemned wherever they occur, every State has the right to prosecute and punish the authors of such crimes.[21]

The obligation to extradite or prosecute individuals for violations of peremptory norms underscores individual criminal responsibility arising independently from State responsibility,[22] and irrespective of whether the individual acted as a State organ or a private individual.[23] This serves to locate primary, criminal responsibility for violations of peremptory norms with the individual whose agency set the illegal act into motion. Imputing responsibility upon the individual in such a way is necessary to the goals of criminal law.[24]

During drafting of the ILC Articles on State Responsibility, the proposition emerged that certain internationally wrongful acts of the State might constitute international crimes. Draft Article 19 of the first reading of the Draft Articles on State Responsibility adopted by the ILC in 1997 envisaged international crimes as acts of States:

> An internationally wrongful act which results from the breach by a State of an international obligation so essential for the protection of fundamental interests of the international community that its breach is recognized as a crime by that community as a whole constitutes an international crime.[25]

Taxonomically, the classification of international crime had been contrasted with international delict, defined by negation as any internationally wrongful act not constituting an international crime, thereby employing the distinction between 'delinquency' and 'crime' to reflect the gravity of an internationally wrongful act of the State.[26] Robert Ago,

21 *Prosecutor v. Furundžija*, IT-95-17/1-T, para. 156 (1998).

22 *See* discussion *infra*, Chapter 15.B (Dual Responsibility).

23 De Hoogh, OBLIGATIONS *ERGA OMNES* AND INTERNATIONAL CRIMES 164.

24 *Ewing v. California*, 538 US 11, 25 (2003) (citing Wayne LaFave & Austin Scott, 1 SUBSTANTIVE CRIMINAL LAW § 1.5, 30–6 (United States: West 1986)) (discussing goals of deterrence, punishment, retribution, rehabilitation, and incapacitation). *See* discussion *supra*, Chapter 10, text accompanying *nn.* 32–4.

25 ILC, Draft Articles on State Responsibility with Commentaries Thereto Adopted by the International Law Commission on First Reading 105 (Article 19(2)).

26 Robert Ago, Fifth Report on State Responsibility, [1976] II(1) YbILC 54, para. 153 (Commentary to Draft Article 17) ('As for the term to be used for denoting what are sometimes vaguely called "other" internationally wrongful acts, or "ordinary" or "simple" breaches of an international obligation, we believe that the classical term "delict" is

the second *special rapporteur* on State responsibility, intended for this distinction to reflect the 'normative differentiation' between two kinds of rules, *jus dispositivum* and *jus cogens*, in international law.[27] Draft Article 19 was ultimately omitted from the final version of the ILC Articles on States Responsibility (2001) because, in practice, only individuals have faced prosecution for international crimes; there 'has been . . . no development of penal consequences for States of breaches of these fundamental norms'.[28] Therefore, under the presumption that the subject of responsibility for international crimes is the individual, it was thought to be inappropriate to include such an article in a code of *State* responsibility.[29] As a result, State responsibility contemplated in the final version of the Articles is concerned exclusively with internationally wrongful acts of the State arising from attributable conduct in violation of its obligations under international law.[30]

The limitation of criminal responsibility in international law to the individual is reflected in practice. Apart from theoretical challenges facing the concept,[31] international law contains a paucity of practice in

especially appropriate. This term was commonly used in works on international law as a synonym for "internationally wrongful act" . . . it has the advantage of being customarily used, in the various legal systems, to denote wrongful acts less serious that those referred to by the word "crime"').

[27] *Ibid.*, 32, para. 99; 53, para. 151 ('The recognition in our draft that a distinction should be made between some internationally wrongful acts which are more serious and others which are less serious is comparable in importance to the recognition, in the Convention on the Law of Treaties, of the distinction to be made between "peremptory" norms of international law and those norms from which derogation through particular agreements is possible . . . By analogy, therefore, it might be useful to specify in the present draft that – apart from the indisputable case of the obligation to refrain from resorting to force in international relations – the breach of an international obligation relating to a given domain cannot be considered an international crime unless the norm out of which the obligation in question arises is a norm of general international law accepted and recognized as essential by the international community of States as a whole, that is to say, by all those which are today fundamental components of that community').

[28] Internationally Wrongful Acts, Report of the International Law Commission on the Work of its Fifty-Third Session, [2001] II(2) YbILC 26 *et seq.* [hereinafter, ILC Articles on State Responsibility (2001)], 111–12, paras. 5–7 (Commentary to Chapter III).

[29] *Ibid.*, para. 7 ('Accordingly, the present articles do not recognize the existence of any distinction between State "crimes" and "delicts" for the purposes of Part One. On the other hand, it is necessary for the articles to reflect that there are certain consequences flowing from the basic concepts of peremptory norms of general international law and obligations to the international community as a whole within the field of State responsibility').

[30] *Ibid.*, 26 (Articles 1–2).

[31] Theodor Meron, HUMAN RIGHTS AND HUMANITARIAN NORMS AS CUSTOMARY LAW 214 (Oxford: Clarendon Press 1989; *see* C. A. W. Manning, THE NATURE OF INTERNATIONAL

support of State criminality, with no development of penal consequences or application of criminal sanctions to States in relation to international crimes.[32] Instead, only the individual is subject to criminal responsibility under international law.[33] The ILC, taking note of these difficulties, reiterated the now-familiar statement by the IMT that international crimes are 'committed by men, not by abstract entities'.[34] The ILC further observed:

> The term 'individual responsibility' has acquired an accepted meaning in the light of the Rome Statute and other instruments; it refers to the responsibility of individual persons, including State officials, under certain rules of international law for conduct such as genocide, war crimes and crimes against humanity.[35]

The reference to 'certain rules of international law' may be inferred to contemplate peremptory norms *in toto*, violations of which constitute international crimes. The individual, by this view, is the sole subject of criminal responsibility in international law for violations of peremptory norms.

This conclusion by the ILC is derived from a legal history of accountability for violations of peremptory norms that provides concordant support. For example, International Military Tribunals at Nuremberg and Tokyo established to prosecute individuals for crimes carried out in their official capacities as State agents regarded neither Germany nor Japan as criminally responsible and made no attempt to apply penal consequences to either State as such. The *ad hoc* tribunals for Yugoslavia and Rwanda are characterized by the same emphasis on individual responsibility for international crimes, as the ICTY explicitly observed: 'Under present international law it is clear that States, by definition, cannot be the subject of criminal sanctions akin to those provided for in national criminal systems.'[36] The jurisdiction of the ICC is similarly addressed to individual, rather than State, criminal responsibility for

SOCIETY 61 (London: Macmillan 1975) (describing the concept as 'juridically speaking a nonsense').

32 Nina Jørgensen, THE RESPONSIBILITY OF STATES FOR INTERNATIONAL CRIMES 205 (Oxford University Press 2000).

33 *See, e.g.*, Crawford, *International Crimes of States*, 405–14.

34 ILC Articles on State Responsibility (2001), 111, para. 5 (Commentary to Chapter III).

35 *Ibid.*, 143, para. 4 (Commentary to Article 58).

36 *Prosecutor v. Blaškić*, Judgment on the Request of Croatia for Review of the Decision of Trial Chamber II of 18 July 1997, IT-95-14-AR108bis, para. 25 (1997); *see* ICTR Statute (1994); ICTY Statute (1993).

violations of peremptory norms.[37] And more recent *ad hoc* criminal tribunals, such as the Special Court for Sierra Leone (SCSL),[38] the Extraordinary Chambers in the Court of Cambodia (ECCC),[39] and the Special Tribunal for Lebanon (STL),[40] have been established by agreements between individual States and the United Nations to promote the transparent and effective prosecution of individuals for certain international crimes. Similarly, the Extraordinary African Chambers (*Chambres africaines extraordinaires* (CAE)) was established by agreement between Senegal and the African Union to prosecute individuals, particularly Hissène Habré, for war crimes, genocide, crimes against humanity, and torture that occurred in Chad between 7 June 1982 and 1 December 1990 'in accordance with Senegal's international commitments'.[41]

Targeting the individual directly as the subject of prosecution and sanction for violations of general international law serves a number of functional purposes essential to the operation of law. Most basically, accountability for illegal conduct is vital to the principle of justice and the function of legal order generally. By lifting the veil of State sovereignty that would otherwise shield the individual from responsibility, individual responsibility for international crimes carries the expectation of accountability, thereby deterring delinquent behaviour by combating impunity.[42] Developments in the international law of immunities and amnesty discussed below underscore this function of individual criminal responsibility.[43] And by facing punishment and incapacitation, individuals who violate peremptory norms are deprived of the capacity to commit such acts in the future. In practice, preventing the recurrence of the atrocities of the Second World War by establishing a viable

[37] Rome Statute (1998), Article 25 (establishing jurisdiction over 'natural persons pursuant to this Statute').

[38] SCSL Statute (2000). [39] ECCC Statute (2003). [40] STL Statute (2007).

[41] EAC Statute (2013) (this organ was established pursuant to the prosecution of Hissène Habré in response to the 2012 *Belgium v. Senegal* decision by the International Court: *see Questions Relating to the Obligation to Prosecute or Extradite (Belgium v. Senegal)*, Judgment, ICJ Reports 2012, p. 422, para. 121).

[42] Before the Second World War, there was no viable system of international justice or universal jurisdiction signalling to individuals that they would be held accountable for crimes of such a magnitude as today considered international crimes. This literal sense of 'lawlessness' is thought to have contributed to the horrors of the world wars, a condition which the post-war international community sought to eliminate directly, in part through the legal developments detailed in the previous sections.

[43] *See* discussion *infra*, Chapter 12.C. (Immunities); Chapter 12.D. (Amnesty).

deterrent was a key motivation behind the Nuremberg Trials,[44] and the subsequent evolution of individual responsibility for *jus cogens* violations has been viewed as a deterrent against international crimes.[45]

B Individual civil responsibility

Both international and domestic legal systems have recognized individual civil liability for *jus cogens* violations in relation to the criminal responsibility arising from such conduct. This follows naturally where legal systems permit parallel civil and criminal proceedings, or initiate civil claims in the context of criminal proceedings.[46] In many civil law countries, this process, *action civile*, enables plaintiffs to attach civil claims to criminal prosecutions.[47] France, for example, has on numerous occasions rendered civil awards concurrently alongside criminal judgments in cases involving *jus cogens* violations.[48] The Rome Statute provides for the award of reparations,[49] and the establishment of a trust

[44] De Hoogh, Obligations *Erga Omnes* and International Crimes 174.

[45] *See, e.g.*, *Prosecutor v. Furundžija*, IT-95-17/1-T, para. 154 (1998) ('Clearly, the *jus cogens* nature of the prohibition against torture . . . is designed to produce a deterrent effect, in that it signals to all members of the international community and the individuals over whom they wield authority that the prohibition of torture is an absolute value from which nobody must deviate').

[46] *See, e.g.*, Roman Kolodkin, Preliminary Report on Immunity of State Officials from Foreign Criminal Jurisdiction, UN Doc. A/CN.4/601, para. 54 (2008).

[47] International Bar Association, Report of the Task Force on Extraterritorial Jurisdiction 120–1 (London: International Bar Association 2009) ('In *actions civiles*, the court may order compensation even though it may not have had jurisdiction to do so had the plaintiff brought the claim in a purely civil action. Countries recognizing the *action civile* generally do not make distinctions according to the basis of the criminal court's jurisdiction . . . [These] countries includ[e] Argentina, Bolivia, Bulgaria, China, Colombia, Costa Rica, Denmark, Finland, France, Germany, Greece, Italy, Luxembourg, Myanmar, Netherlands, Norway, Panama, Poland, Romania, Russia, Senegal, Spain, Sweden and Venezuela'); Donald Donovan and Anthea Roberts, *The Emerging Recognition of Universal Civil Jurisdiction*, 100 American Journal of International Law 142, 154 (2006).

[48] *See, e.g.*, *Réunion Aérienne v. Socialist People's Libyan Arab Jamahiriya*, Court of Cassation (Civil Division) (France), No. 09-14743, 150 ILR. 630, 634 (2011) (Paris Assizes Court delivered both criminal and civil judgments against six Libyan nationals for *jus cogens* violation of terrorism in March 1999); *Ely Ould Dah Case*, Gard Assizes Court (France), No. 70/05 (Arrêt de condamnation) / No. 71/05 (Arrêt statuant sur les intérêts civils) (2005) (the Gard Assizes Court delivered criminal and civil judgments against Dah simultaneously on 1 July 2005); *Rwanda Genocide Case*, Court of Cassation (Criminal Division) (France), No. 96-82491 (1998) (permitting civil claims against participants in Rwandan Genocide).

[49] Rome Statute (1998), Article 75 (Reparations to Victims).

fund for the benefit of victims of international crimes.[50] In this sense, the ICC Prosecutor indicated that the Court could award civil damages in conjunction with criminal judgments against Saif Al-Islam Gaddafi and Abdullah Al-Senussi.[51] Writing in concurrence in *Sosa v. Alvarez-Machain* (2004), US Supreme Court Justice Stephen Breyer suggested that the same jurisdictional principles that enable prosecution for international crimes extend to civil responsibility:

> The fact that this procedural consensus exists suggests that recognition of universal jurisdiction in respect to a limited set of norms is consistent with principles of international comity. That is, allowing every nation's courts to adjudicate foreign conduct involving foreign parties in such cases will not significantly threaten the practical harmony that comity principles seek to protect. That consensus concerns criminal jurisdiction, but consensus as to universal criminal jurisdiction itself suggests that universal tort jurisdiction would be no more threatening ... That is because the criminal courts of many nations combine civil and criminal proceedings, allowing those injured by criminal conduct to be represented, and to recover damages, in the criminal proceeding itself ... Thus, universal criminal jurisdiction necessarily contemplates a significant degree of civil tort recovery as well.[52]

This observation was made in reference to the Alien Tort Statute (ATS) of the United States Code, through which a substantial jurisprudence of individual civil liability for *jus cogens* violations has developed, which warrants special attention.[53]

The ATS, enacted as part of the Judiciary Act by the First Congress in 1789, provides that district courts 'shall also have cognizance, concurrent with the courts of the several States, or the circuit courts, as the case may be, of all causes where an alien sues for a tort only in violation of the law of nations or a treaty of the United States'.[54] The historical context of the period reveals the kind of norms that would have been recognized at common law as belonging to the law of nations.[55] These were norms

[50] *Ibid.*, Article 79 (Trust Fund).

[51] Second Report to the Prosecutor of the International Criminal Court to the UN Security Council Pursuant to UN Security Council Resolution 1970, para. 13 (2 November 2011).

[52] *Sosa v. Alvarez-Machain*, 542 US 692, 762–3 (2004) (Breyer, J., Concurring).

[53] *See* Thomas Weatherall, *Lessons from the Alien Tort Statute*: Jus Cogens *as the Law of Nations*, 103(5) GEORGETOWN LAW JOURNAL (2015) (from which the discussion to follow has been excerpted).

[54] Act of Sept. 24, 1789, ch. 20, § 9, 1 Stat. 77.

[55] *Filartiga v. Pena-Irala*, 630 F.2d 876, 885 (2nd Cir. 1980) ('The constitutional basis for the Alien Tort Statute is the law of nations, which has always been part of the federal common law').

identified in Blackstone's Commentaries as offences against the law of nations included in the criminal law of England at the time: violation of safe conducts, infringement of the rights of ambassadors, and piracy.[56] While the ATS has since been amended, it still confers subject-matter jurisdiction to district courts over disputes between aliens arising under the law of nations: 'The district courts shall have original jurisdiction of any civil action by an alien for a tort only, committed in violation of the law of nations or a treaty of the United States.'[57] The statute reflects an early concern over respect for the law of nations with particular regard to foreigners. Notwithstanding the apparent importance of the ATS at the time of its enactment, only one case was heard under the statute in the 170 years following its ratification.[58] Jurisprudence under the ATS emerged not long after codification of *jus cogens* in the Vienna Convention on the Law of Treaties in 1969, and Federal courts have since broadly recognized the concept of *jus cogens.*[59] The fact that the ATS went virtually unused following its enactment in 1789, then burgeoned just a decade after the formal codification of this category of fundamental norms in international law, suggests a possible relationship between ATS jurisprudence and the doctrine of *jus cogens.* Indeed, it may be inferred that the establishment of a category of fundamental international rules, akin to the law of nations at the time the ATS was codified, provided a frame of reference by which US courts have ascertained with some confidence which norms of contemporary international law are comparable in stature to the eighteenth-century law of nations.[60]

The landmark case *Filartiga v. Pena-Irala* (1980) signalled the reintroduction of the ATS in a way that opened the US legal system to aliens as an avenue to redress violations of peremptory norms.[61] The case concerned Joelito Filártiga, a seventeen-year-old kidnapped and tortured to death in March 1976 by Américo Norberto Peña Irala, the Inspector General of Police in Asunción, Paraguay. The Second Circuit US Court of

[56] *Sosa*, 542 US at 715 (citing 4 Commentaries 68).

[57] 28 USC § 1350. *See Sosa*, 542 US at 713 ('As enacted in 1789, the ATS gave the district courts "cognizance" of certain causes of action, and the term bespoke a grant of jurisdiction, not power to mold substantive law').

[58] *See Sosa*, 542 US at 712.

[59] *See, e.g., Siderman de Blake v. Republic of Argentina*, 965 F.2d 699, 715 (9th Cir. 1992).

[60] *Sosa*, 542 US at 725 (a cause of action under ATS must 'rest on a norm of international character accepted by the civilized world and defined with a specificity comparable to the features of the 18th-century paradigms we have recognized').

[61] *Filartiga v. Pena-Irala*, 630 F.2d 876 (2nd Cir. 1980).

Appeals reversed a district court judgment dismissing the complaint on the basis of the norm in question, the prohibition against torture. The Second Circuit noted that the 'paucity of suits successfully maintained under the [ATS] is readily attributable to the statute's requirement of alleging a "violation of the law of nations" at the jurisdictional threshold'.[62] Nevertheless, the Circuit found that the prohibition of torture was universally recognized by all nations, thereby constituting a precept of the law of nations within the meaning of the ATS. Therefore, because 'courts must interpret international law not as it was in 1789, but as it has evolved and exists among the nations of the world today',[63] the district court ruled in favor of the Filártigas on remand and awarded $10.4 million (US).[64]

The Supreme Court decided its first ATS case in 2004, *Sosa v. Alvarez-Machain*, where it established a standard by which to identify causes of action falling within the scope of the ATS. The case was brought by Humberto Alvarez-Machain, a Mexican physician who had been abducted by a group of Mexican citizens, including Jose Francisco Sosa, in connection with the murder of a US Drug Enforcement Administration agent.[65] The Court reversed a judgment affirmed by the Ninth Circuit that had awarded damages to Alvarez for arbitrary arrest and detention in violation of the law of nations.[66] The Court based its ruling on the norm in question, which it held to fall outside a specific category of 'actionable norms' of a 'definable, universal, and obligatory' character.[67] This holding indicates that the law of nations is not equated without bound to contemporary international law but, rather, refers only to a particular subset of international law comparable to Blackstone's three offences.[68] A cause of action under the ATS must, according to the Court, 'rest on a norm of international character accepted by the civilized world and defined with a specificity comparable to the features of the 18th-century paradigms we have recognized'.[69] The standard established by the Court essentially imposes the object and purpose of the ATS as a guide to the international norms actionable under the statute, a position

62 *Ibid.*, 887. 63 *Ibid.*, 881.
64 *Filartiga v. Pena-Irala*, 577 F. Supp. 860, 867 (EDNY 1984).
65 *Sosa v. Alvarez-Machain*, 542 US 692 (2004).
66 *Alvarez-Machain v. United States*, 331 F.3d 604, 613–15, 620 (9th Cir. 2003) *rev'd sub nom. Sosa v. Alvarez-Machain*, 542 US 692 (2004) and *vacated*, 374 F.3d 1384 (9th Cir. 2004).
67 *Sosa*, 542 US at 732 (internal quotation marks omitted).
68 *Ibid.*, 715 (citing 4 Commentaries 68). 69 *Ibid.*, 725.

reiterated in the Court's subsequent treatment of the ATS, *Kiobel v. Royal Dutch Petroleum Co.*[70] However, the Court did little to specify which particular international norms fall within the contemporary law of nations, leaving the category to be borne out in application of the ATS by lower courts as a matter of federal common law.

The development of case law under the ATS illustrates the broader conclusions reached throughout this chapter regarding the individual as the primary subject of protections, as well as responsibility, under *jus cogens*. Though not always articulated as such, it may be inferred that the norms contemplated by the ATS are peremptory norms of general international law. To give effect to the 'definable, universal, and obligatory' standard for norms falling within the scope of the ATS, federal courts frequently look to whether the norm in question is a *jus cogens* norm.[71] This reliance is demonstrated both explicitly – by express reference to the category of *jus cogens* – and implicitly – by delineating a law of nations coextensive with *jus cogens* and actionable under the ATS. Each aspect is considered in turn.

Since the 1990s, several federal courts of appeals have expressly relied upon the doctrine of *jus cogens* to assess whether jurisdiction under the ATS is appropriate. One of the earliest references to *jus cogens* in ATS jurisprudence is *In re Estate of Ferdinand E. Marcos Human Rights Litigation*, which came before the Ninth Circuit in 1992. The *Marcos* litigation was brought by families of victims of torture, execution, and disappearance against the former President of the Philippines, Ferdinand Marcos,[72] and his daughter, Imee Marcos-Manotoc,[73] who fled to Hawaii in 1986. Claimants, as aliens – citizens of the Philippines living in Hawaii – relied upon the ATS to engage the jurisdiction of the Federal District Court for the District of Hawaii. In affirming judgment in favor

70 *Kiobel v. Royal Dutch Petroleum Co.*, 133 S. Ct. 1659, 1665 (2013).

71 *See, e.g., Sarei v. Rio Tinto, PLC*, 487 F.3d 1193, 1202 (9th Cir. 2007) *on reh'g en banc*, 550 F.3d 822 (9th Cir. 2008); *Taveras v. Taveraz*, 477 F.3d 767, 782 (6th Cir. 2007); *Princz v. Federal Republic of Germany*, 26 F.3d 1166, 1178 (DC Cir. 1994) (Wald, J., Dissenting) (referring to ATS jurisdiction over '*jus cogens* norms of the law of nations'); *In re Estate of Ferdinand E. Marcos Human Rights Litig*ation, 978 F.2d 493, 503 (9th Cir. 1992); *Adhikari v. Daoud & Partners*, 697 F. Supp. 2d 674, 686 (SD Tex. 2009); *Doe v. Qi*, 349 F. Supp. 2d 1258, 1277 (ND Cal. 2004); *Mehinovic v. Vuckovic*, 198 F. Supp. 2d 1322, 1344 (ND Ga. 2002); *Sandhu v. Burke*, No. 97 CIV. 4608 (JGK), 2000 WL 191707, *10 n.11 (SDNY 2000); *Xuncax v. Gramajo*, 886 F. Supp. 162, 183 (D Mass. 1995).

72 *In re Estate of Ferdinand Marcos, Human Rights Litigation*, 25 F.3d 1467, 1469 (9th Cir. 1994).

73 *In re Estate of Ferdinand E. Marcos Human Rights Litigation*, 978 F.2d at 495.

of the claimants in the 1992 litigation against Marcos–Manotoc, the Ninth Circuit concluded that the 'violation of a *jus cogens* norm of international law [] properly invokes the subject-matter jurisdiction of the federal courts under § 1350'.[74] Similarly, in the 1994 litigation against the former President Marcos, the Ninth Circuit affirmed subject-matter jurisdiction under the ATS by finding that '[t]he allegations in this case satisfy the specific, universal and obligatory standard. Under international law . . . official torture violates *jus cogens*'.[75]

The Ninth Circuit reiterated this position more than a decade later in *Sarei v. Rio Tinto, PLC*, a claim brought by residents of Papua New Guinea against the mining company Rio Tinto for, *inter alia*, crimes against humanity and war crimes – *jus cogens* violations – arising from a mine uprising and the ten-year civil war that followed.[76] The Ninth Circuit held in part that 'Plaintiffs here have alleged several claims asserting *jus cogens* violations that form the least controversial core of modern day AT[S] jurisdiction'.[77] The Sixth Circuit observed the converse in *Taveras v. Taveraz*, namely that where a *jus cogens* norm is not in question, then ATS jurisdiction is likely not properly engaged. The Sixth Circuit explained that the case, which concerned cross-border child abduction by a parent with full custody, 'does not present any *jus cogens* or otherwise binding customary norm of international law which gives rise to a violation of the law of nations under the ATS'.[78] These parameters set out by the Sixth and Ninth Circuits indicate that the violation of a *jus cogens* norm is at least sufficient to engage federal subject-matter jurisdiction under the ATS.[79] These cases also demonstrate the utility of reference to *jus cogens* by analogy to the law of nations, and as illustrated below, there is little indication in current jurisprudence that circuit courts are prepared to venture beyond the content of *jus cogens* to interpret 'the

74 *Ibid.*, 503.

75 *In re Estate of Ferdinand Marcos, Human Rights Litigation*, 25 F.3d at 1475 (internal quotation marks omitted).

76 *Sarei*, 487 F.3d at 1197.

77 *Ibid.*, 1202 ('including allegations of war crimes, crimes against humanity and racial discrimination').

78 *Taveras v. Taveraz*, 477 F.3d 767, 782 (6th Cir. 2007).

79 *See* Kurtis A. Kemper, *Annotation, Construction and Application of Alien Tort Statute (28 U.S.C.A. § 1350) – Tort in Violation of Law of Nations or Treaty of United States*, 64 ALR Fed. 2d 417 (2012) ('a *jus cogens* violation is sufficient, but not necessary, to state a claim under the ATS').

law of nations' for purposes of civil liability for violations of the law of nations under the ATS.

Federal district courts have mirrored the reasoning of the circuits by relying on *jus cogens* to interpret the law of nations under the ATS. In 1995, the District Court for the District of Massachusetts observed in *Xuncax v. Gramajo* that the case at bar, which concerned torture and other cruel, inhuman, and degrading treatment, 'concerns the proper characterization of the *kind* of wrongs meant to be addressed under § 1350: those perpetrated by *hostis humani generis* ("enemies of all humankind") in contravention of *jus cogens* (peremptory norms of international law)'.[80] The Southern District of New York interpreted *Filartiga* as linking ATS jurisdiction to *jus cogens* in *Sandhu v. Burke*, holding that '*Filartiga* recognized that the ATS granted federal courts jurisdiction to hear tort claims alleging violations of *jus cogens* norms of international law'.[81] The Northern District of California echoed this connection in *Doe v. Qi*, finding that '[c]onduct which violates *jus cogens* – norms of international law that are so fundamental and universally recognized that they are binding on nations even if they do not agree to them – constitutes a violation of the "law of nations"'.[82] In 2009, the Southern District of Texas concluded that, 'human trafficking and forced labor, whether committed by states or private individuals, have been recognized as violations of *jus cogens* norms, and therefore fall within the jurisdictional grant of the ATS'.[83] The Northern District of Georgia has suggested that the *jus cogens* status of a norm of international law is sufficient, but not necessary, to engage the jurisdiction of the ATS: 'To be actionable under the AT[S], these norms must be specific, universal and obligatory... A *jus cogens* violation satisfies, but is not required, to meet this standard.'[84] Thus, while district courts appear comfortable consulting *jus cogens* to determine the law of nations for the purposes of ATS jurisdiction, they have stopped short of expressly limiting jurisdiction under the ATS to violations of that category of norms.

Even so, ATS jurisdiction has not been extended to international norms beyond the category of *jus cogens*. To be sure, Federal courts do

80 *Xuncax v. Gramajo*, 886 F. Supp. 162, 183 (D Mass. 1995).

81 *Sandhu v. Burke*, 97 CIV. 4608 (JGK), 2000 WL 191707, *10 n.11 (SDNY 2000).

82 *Doe v. Qi*, 349 F. Supp. 2d 1258, 1277 (ND Cal. 2004).

83 *Adhikari v. Daoud & Partners*, 697 F. Supp. 2d 674, 686 (SD Tex. 2009).

84 *Mehinovic v. Vuckovic*, 198 F. Supp. 2d 1322, 1344 (ND Ga. 2002) (internal quotation marks omitted).

not in every instance expressly refer to *jus cogens* to interpret the law of nations for purposes of jurisdiction under the Alien Tort Statute. However broader judicial practice reinforces this connection for purposes of statutory construction insofar as the causes of action recognized by federal courts are coextensive with the doctrine of *jus cogens*. In contemporary international law, nine peremptory norms have been accepted and recognized by the international community as *jus cogens* from which no derogation is permitted: the prohibitions of piracy, slavery, war crimes (grave violations of humanitarian law), crimes against humanity, aggression, genocide, torture, apartheid (systematic racial discrimination), and terrorism.[85] Similarly, federal courts have identified the contemporary law of nations to provide causes of action for piracy, slavery, war crimes, crimes against humanity, genocide, torture, apartheid, and terrorism, eight of nine *jus cogens* norms.[86] In many of these cases, courts have recognized the *jus cogens* status of the relevant norm under international law. The exclusion of aggression from this list follows logically from the special regime of prosecution of the crime under international law arising from its immediate relation to State conduct and related denial of jurisdiction over the crime to third-States.[87] Importantly, courts have denied jurisdiction under the ATS for causes of action not belonging to *jus cogens*, such as illegal detention,[88] environmental abuse,[89] cultural genocide,[90] and child abduction.[91] This breadth of judicial practice supports the proposition that courts look to the doctrine of *jus cogens* to give meaning to the law of nations for purposes of the ATS. What is more, this jurisprudence suggests that while a *jus cogens* violation is sufficient to constitute a violation of the law of nations under the ATS, in practice, a *jus cogens* violation is also necessary to state a claim under the ATS. In *Kiobel v. Royal Dutch Petroleum Co.* (2013), the Supreme Court constrained access to US courts under the ATS by determining that a claim under the statute must sufficiently 'touch and concern' the United States to overcome a 'presumption against extraterritoriality'.[92]

[85] *See* discussion *supra*, Chapter 11.A (Identifying Peremptory Norms).
[86] *See* discussion *supra*, Chapter 8, *nn.* 259–66.
[87] Report of the International Law Commission on the Work of its Forty-Eighth Session, [1996] II(2) YbILC 30, para. 14 (Commentary to Article 8); *see supra*, Chapter 11, *n.* 179.
[88] *Sosa v. Alvarez-Machain*, 542 US 692, 738 (2004).
[89] *Beanal v. Freeport-McMoran, Inc.*, 197 F.3d 161, 167 (5th Cir. 1999).
[90] *Ibid.*, 167–8.
[91] *Taveras v. Taveraz*, 477 F.3d 767, 782 (6th Cir. 2007).
[92] *Kiobel v. Royal Dutch Petroleum Co.*, 133 S. Ct. 1659, 1669 (2013).

Given that the ATS is a jurisdiction-granting statute only, the *jus cogens* norms recognized in this context are part of US federal common law more broadly and are not limited to jurisdiction under the ATS. Therefore, according to the Supreme Court, 'a federal court could properly recognize [these international norms] as within the common law enforceable without any further statutory authority' beyond the ATS context.[93] Consequently, US district courts have expressed a willingness to 'imply the existence of a private right of action for violations of *jus cogens* norms of international law'.[94] It is in this sense that, as a matter of federal common law, '[i]t is clear that *jus cogens* norms of international law are part of the laws of the United States'.[95]

The justiciability of peremptory norms under the ATS is commensurate with offences – crimes against the law of nations – that the instrument was intended to circumscribe at the time of its enactment at the end of the eighteenth century.[96] While US law is unique in its provision of a

[93] *Sosa v. Alvarez-Machain*, 542 US 692, 729 (2004).

[94] *See Adamu v. Pfizer, Inc.*, 399 F. Supp. 2d 495, 501 (SDNY 2005) *rev'd and remanded sub nom. Abdullahi v. Pfizer, Inc.*, 562 F.3d 163 (2nd Cir. 2009) (citing *Sosa v. Alvarez-Machain*, 542 US 692, 694–5 (2004); *Bivens v. Six Unknown Named Agents of the Fed. Bureau of Narcotics*, 403 US 388 (1971)) ('federal courts have the authority to imply the existence of a private right of action for violations of *jus cogens* norms of international law'); *Benas v. Baca*, No. CV-00-11507 LGB (SHX), 2001 WL 485168, at *3 (CD Cal. 2001) *aff'd*, 30 F. App'x 753 (9th Cir. 2002) ('*Jus cogens* norms of international law do not in themselves create a private right of action for individual citizens ... Federal courts may, however, imply a private right of action for violations of *jus cogens* norms of international law ... Judicial authority to recognize implied remedies for violations of constitutional rights applies equally to violations of *jus cogens* norms such as those prohibiting genocide, torture, and slavery'); *Hawkins v. Comparet-Cassani*, 33 F. Supp. 2d 1244, 1255–6 (CD Cal. 1999) *rev'd in part*, 251 F.3d 1230 (9th Cir. 2001) (citing *The Paquete Habana*, 175 US 677, 700 (1900)) ('It is clear that *jus cogens* norms of international law are part of the laws of the United States. However, the law of nations does not in itself create a personal right of action for individual citizens ... It is also clear, however, that federal courts may imply a personal right of action for violations of *jus cogens* norms of international law'); *White v. Paulsen*, 997 F. Supp. 1380, 1383–4 (ED Wash. 1998) (citing *Bivens v. Six Unknown Named Agents of the Fed. Bureau of Narcotics*, 403 US 388 (1971)) ('Plaintiffs are correct in their general assertion that federal courts have the authority to imply the existence of a private right of action for violations of *jus cogens* norms of international law ... This Court can conceive of no adequate reason why the rationale supporting the existence of judicial authority to recognize implied remedies for constitutional rights does not apply with equal or greater force to *jus cogens* norms of international law, such as the prohibitions on genocide, torture, and slavery').

[95] *Hawkins v. Comparet-Cassani*, 33 F. Supp. 2d 1244, 1255–6 (CD Cal. 1999) *rev'd in part*, 251 F.3d 1230 (9th Cir. 2001) (citing *The Paquete Habana*, 175 US 677, 700 (1900)).

[96] *Sosa v. Alvarez-Machain*, 542 US 692, 715 (2004).

discrete jurisdictional statute enabling aliens to bring suit for *jus cogens* violations, as noted above many civil law countries implicitly permit similar recourse through *actione civile*.[97] Tortious consequences for violations of peremptory norms affirm the premise that *jus cogens* norms are individual-oriented in kind. As tort law expressly concerns wrongs towards other individuals, civil responsibility for the violation of peremptory norms reinforces the notion that the individual is the primary subject of protections and duties under peremptory norms and is to be 'made whole' in the event of their breach.

C Immunities

The doctrine of sovereign immunity derives from customary international law[98] and embodies the principle of *par in parem non habet imperium*: between equals no power.[99] As a doctrine based in 'comity', sovereign immunity emerged from a customary space between law and policy.[100] Three distinct elements can be distilled from the core principle of sovereign immunity. Immunity *ratione personae* refers to the immunity of certain high State officials, such as Heads of State, Heads of Government, and Ministers of Foreign Affairs because 'he or she is recognized under international law as representative of the State solely by virtue of his or her position'.[101] Immunity *ratione materiae* concerns the immunity enjoyed by organs of the State for acts performed in their official capacity which the 'State is entitled to claim ... [as acts]

[97] *See* discussion *supra*, text accompanying *nn*. 46–53.

[98] *See, e.g.*, *Jurisdictional Immunities of the State (Germany v. Italy: Greece Intervening)*, Judgment, ICJ Reports 2012, p. 99, paras. 53–4; UN Convention on Jurisdictional Immunities of States and their Property, UN Doc. A/59/508, Preamble (2 December 2004).

[99] *See, e.g.*, *Jurisdictional Immunities of the State (Germany v. Italy: Greece Intervening)*, Judgment, ICJ Reports 2012, p. 99, para. 57; *Schooner Exchange v. McFaddon*, 11 US 116, 134 (1812); Ian Sinclair, *The Law of Sovereign Immunity: Recent Developments*, 167 Recueil des Cours 197–9 (1980).

[100] *Jones v. United Kingdom*, ECtHR, Nos. 34356/06 & 40528/06, para. 188 (2014) ('sovereign immunity is a concept of international law, developed out of the principle *par in parem non habet imperium*, by virtue of which one State shall not be subject to the jurisdiction of another State. The grant of sovereign immunity to a State in civil proceedings pursues the legitimate aim of complying with international law to promote comity and good relations between States through the respect of another State's sovereignty'); *Hilton v. Guyot*, 159 US 113, 163–4 (1895).

[101] *Arrest Warrant of 11 April 2000 (Democratic Republic of the Congo v. Belgium)*, ICJ Reports 2002, p. 3, para. 53.

attributed to the State, so that the individual organ may not be held accountable for those acts or transactions'.[102] The jurisdictional immunity of the State refers to the underlying principle articulated above that one State shall not be subject to the jurisdiction of another State, which is conceived as both a right and a corresponding obligation incumbent 'upon other States to respect and give effect to that immunity'.[103]

Assessing the effect of *jus cogens* on these elements of sovereign immunity requires avoiding two common oversimplifications. First, the principle of sovereign immunity must be distinguished from its particular application as State and individual immunities.[104] Although deriving from the common principle of sovereign immunity, each form of immunity serves a specific purpose and operates in a procedurally distinct way. While there is some support for the proposition that 'the State' is defined to include any representative of the State 'acting in that capacity' for purposes of immunity[105] – and for practical purposes this relation is effectively borne out in many instances – both the US Supreme Court[106] and the ECtHR[107] have rejected this assumption in relation to *jus cogens*. Therefore, while State immunity is a consequence of sovereignty, just as immunities *ratione personae* and *ratione materiae*, individual immunities remain distinct from the jurisdictional immunity of the State and should not be prejudged by the question of State immunity. Second, treating sovereign immunity and *jus cogens* as distinctly procedural and substantive rules oversimplifies a dichotomy which,[108] in practice, is not so clear: one distinctly procedural aspect of *jus cogens* is its

102 *Prosecutor v. Blaškić*, Judgment on the Request of Croatia for Review of the Decision of Trial Chamber II of 18 July 1997, IT-95-14-AR108bis, para. 41 (1997).

103 *Jurisdictional Immunities of the State (Germany v. Italy: Greece Intervening)*, Judgment, ICJ Reports 2012, p. 99, para. 56.

104 *Cf.* Roger O'Keefe, *Jurisdictional Immunities*, *in* The Development of International Law by the International Court of Justice 107, 144–6 (Oxford University Press, Christian Tams & James Sloane eds., 2013).

105 UN Convention on Jurisdictional Immunities of States and their Property, UN Doc. A/59/508, Article 2(1)(b) (2 December 2004).

106 *Samantar v. Yousuf*, 560 US 305, 308 (2010) (finding State immunity not determinative of immunity of former State official because that individual is not a 'foreign State').

107 *Jones v. United Kingdom*, ECtHR, Nos. 34356/06 & 40528/06, para. 205 (2014) ('The fact that there is no general *jus cogens* exception as regards State immunity rules is therefore not determinative as regards claims against named State officials').

108 *Jurisdictional Immunities of the State (Germany v. Italy: Greece Intervening)*, Judgment, ICJ Reports 2012, p. 99, para. 93; *Arrest Warrant of 11 April 2000 (Democratic Republic of the Congo v. Belgium)*, ICJ Reports 2002, p. 3, para. 60 ('Immunity from criminal jurisdiction and individual criminal responsibility are quite separate concepts. While

relationship to universal jurisdiction, while a court's subject-matter jurisdiction cannot be completely divorced from substantive considerations. To simply dispense with the 'normative hierarchy' theory does not, therefore, sufficiently resolve the issue.[109] This section considers the way *jus cogens* interacts with immunities *ratione personae* and *ratione materiae*, while the jurisdictional immunity of the State will be taken up in Chapter 15.[110]

i. Immunity ratione personae

Immunity *ratione personae* is immunity 'granted to high State officials to guarantee the proper functioning of the network of mutual inter-State relations, which is of paramount importance for a well-ordered and harmonious international system'.[111] The protection of high officials from the jurisdiction of foreign States reflects a core premise underlying sovereign immunity, 'to promote comity among nations by ensuring that leaders can perform their duties without being subject to detention, arrest or embarrassment in a foreign country's legal system'.[112] Consequently, this procedural immunity extends to high officials 'recognized under international law as representative of the State solely by virtue of his or her office'.[113] While immunity *ratione personae* most clearly attaches to Heads of State,[114] the International Court of Justice has recognized the scope of immunity *ratione personae* to extend more broadly to 'certain

jurisdictional immunity is procedural in nature, criminal responsibility is a question of substantive law').

[109] *Compare Jurisdictional Immunities of the State (Germany v. Italy: Greece Intervening)*, Judgment, ICJ Reports 2012, p. 99, para. 93, *with Al-Adsani v. United Kingdom*, ECtHR, No. 35763/97, para. 3 (2001) (Rozakis & Caflisch, J. J., Dissenting) ('The acceptance ... of the *jus cogens* nature of the prohibition ... entails that a State allegedly violating it cannot invoke hierarchically lower rules (in this case, those on State immunity) to avoid the consequences of the illegality of its actions').

[110] *See* discussion *infra*, Chapter 15.D (Jurisdictional Immunity of the State).

[111] *Arrest Warrant of 11 April 2000 (Democratic Republic of the Congo v. Belgium)*, ICJ Reports 2002, Joint Sep. Op. Higgins, Kooijmans & Buergenthal, para. 75.

[112] *Yousuf v. Samantar*, 699 F.3d 763, 767 (4th Cir. 2012), *cert. denied*, 134 S. Ct. 897 (US 2014).

[113] *Arrest Warrant of 11 April 2000 (Democratic Republic of the Congo v. Belgium)*, ICJ Reports 2002, p. 3, paras. 51–3 ('in international law it is firmly established that ... certain holders of high-ranking offices in a State ... enjoy immunities from jurisdiction in other States').

[114] *Lafontant v. Aristide*, 844 F. Supp. 128, 132 (EDNY 1994) ('a state and its ruler are one for the purposes of immunity').

holders of high-ranking office in a State, such as the Head of State, Head of Government and Minister of Foreign Affairs'.[115] Immunity *ratione personae* is therefore a 'status' immunity.[116] Consequently, such immunity shields the office holder only during his or her tenure.[117] Moreover, the International Court considered immunity *ratione personae* to be subject to a number of limitations: (1) it cannot shield an official from prosecution in his home country, (2) it may be waived by the official's home State, (3) it terminates at the end of an officials tenure, and (4) an individual enjoying such immunity may nevertheless be subject to the jurisdiction of 'certain international criminal courts'.[118] This part considers the interaction of *jus cogens* with immunity *ratione personae* in three domains: criminal prosecution before international courts, criminal prosecution before domestic courts, and civil proceedings before domestic courts.

a. International criminal prosecution

It is uncontroversial that the State may waive *sua sponte* the immunity *ratione personae* enjoyed by its senior officials to confer jurisdiction to international criminal courts. The Foreign Minister of Côte d'Ivoire did just that with respect to Laurent Gbagbo, Côte d'Ivoire's then President.[119] Such waiver, alongside the Article 27 waiver by parties to the Rome Statute,[120] hails in State consent. However, the final limit to immunity *ratione personae* articulated by the International Court in Paragraph 61 of the *Arrest Warrant* case, cited immediately above, suggests a profound development in the interaction between *jus cogens* and immunities. Three examples illustrate the exception articulated by the Court. First, Charles Taylor, the incumbent Head of State of Liberia,

[115] *Arrest Warrant of 11 April 2000 (Democratic Republic of the Congo v. Belgium)*, ICJ Reports 2002, p. 3, para. 51.

[116] *See, e.g., R. v. Bow Street Metropolitan Stipendiary Magistrate and Others, Ex parte Pinochet Ugarte (No. 3)*, House of Lords (UK), [2000] 1 A.C. 147, 38 ILM 581, 644 (1999) (Millett, L.).

[117] *See ibid.*, 637 (Hutton, L.), 641 (Saville, L.), 653 (Phillips, L.), 644 (Millett, L.) ('This immunity is not in issue in the present case. Senator Pinochet is not a serving head of state. If he were, he could not be extradited').

[118] *Arrest Warrant of 11 April 2000 (Democratic Republic of the Congo v. Belgium)*, ICJ Reports 2002, p. 3, para. 61.

[119] *Prosecutor v. Gbagbo*, Decision Pursuant to Article 15 of the Rome Statute on the Authorisation of an Investigation into the Situation in the Republic of Côte d'Ivoire, No. ICC-02/11-14, paras. 12–15 (2011).

[120] Rome Statute (1998), Article 27.

was indicted on 7 March 2003 by the Prosecutor of the SCSL for crimes against humanity and war crimes committed in Sierra Leone during the civil war in that State.[121] While Taylor attempted to quash his indictment and set aside the outstanding arrest warrant on grounds of immunity *ratione personae*, the Appeals Chamber of the SCSL found such immunity inapplicable.[122] Second, following referral of the situation in Sudan to the Prosecutor of the ICC,[123] the Pre-Trial Chamber of the ICC issued two warrants for the arrest of Omar al-Bashir, the sitting Head of State of Sudan, on 14 July 2009 and 12 July 2010.[124] In disposing of al-Bashir's claim of immunity *ratione personae*, the Pre-Trial Chamber concluded that 'the current position of Omar Al Bashir as Head of a state *which is not party to the Statute*, has no effect on the Court's jurisdiction over the present case'.[125] Finally, following referral of the situation in Libya to the ICC Prosecutor by the UN Security Council on 26 February 2011,[126] the ICC Prosecutor brought a case against 'those who bear the greatest responsibility for the most serious crimes',[127] namely Moammar Gaddafi (*de facto* Head of State of Libya), Saif Al-Islam Gaddafi (*de facto* Prime Minister of Libya), and Abdullah Al-Senussi (the head of Military Intelligence).[128]

121 *See Prosecutor v. Taylor*, Judgment, No. SCSL-03-01-T-1283 (2012).

122 *Prosecutor v. Taylor*, Decision on Immunity from Jurisdiction, No. SCSL-03-01-I-059, para. 52 (2004) ('the principle seems now established that the sovereign equality of states does not prevent a Head of State from being prosecuted before an international criminal tribunal or court').

123 SC Res. 1593, UN Doc. S/Res/1593 (31 March 2005).

124 *Prosecutor v. Al Bashir*, First Warrant of Arrest, No. ICC-02/05-01/09-1 (4 March 2009) (two counts of war crimes and three counts of crimes against humanity); *Prosecutor v. Al Bashir*, Second Warrant of Arrest, No. ICC-02/05-01/09-95 (12 July 2010) (three counts of genocide).

125 *Prosecutor v. Al Bashir*, Decision on the Prosecution's Application for a Warrant of Arrest against Omar Hassan Ahmad Al Bashir, No. ICC-02/05-01/09-3, paras. 41–5 (4 March 2009) (the ICC justified this conclusion based on a 'core goal[] of the Statute ... to put an end to impunity', the principles articulated in Article 27(1) to achieve this end, the case law of the chamber, and the referral of the situation to the ICC by the Security Council).

126 SC Res. 1970, UN Doc. S/Res/1970, Preamble, paras 4–8 (26 February 2011); *see also* SC Res. 1973, UN Doc. S/Res/1973, Preamble (17 March 2011) ('those responsible for or complicit in attacks targeting the civilian population, including aerial and naval attacks, must be held to account').

127 First Report of the Prosecutor of the International Criminal Court to the UN Security Council Pursuant to UNSCR 1970, para. 25 (4 May 2011).

128 *Situation in the Libyan Arab Jamahiriya*, Decision on the 'Prosecutor's Application Pursuant to Article 58 as to Muammar Mohammed Abu Minyar Gaddafi, Saif Al-Islam Gaddafi and Abdullah Al-Senussi', No. ICC-01/11-01/11-1 (27 June 2011).

Instead of contemplating the immunity *ratione personae* of these officials, the instrumentalities of the international community appeared satisfied that the offences at issue justified the measures taken by the Security Council and the ICC.[129]

The actions by the SCSL and ICC in the cases concerning Taylor, al-Bashir, and Gaddafi indicate limitations to the immunity *ratione personae* that would otherwise shield incumbent Heads of State. Prosecution before international criminal organs does not implicate the same sovereignty concerns underlying the principle *par in parem non habet imperium* as does prosecution by the domestic courts of a foreign State. Even so, sovereignty considerations are not entirely alleviated by the involvement of international fora. In the *al-Bashir* case, for example, each arrest warrant issued by the Pre-Trial Chamber directed the ICC Registry to transmit 'a request for cooperation seeking the arrest and surrender' of al-Bashir to Sudanese authorities pursuant to rule 176(2) 'to all States Parties to the Statute and all the United Nations Security Council members that are not States Parties to the Statute'.[130] Further, the Registrar was directed in each instance 'to prepare and transmit *to any other State* any additional request for arrest and surrender which may be necessary'.[131] In the context of immunity *ratione personae*, such an order must be reconciled with Article 98 of the Rome Statute, which bars the ICC from issuing 'a request for surrender or assistance which would require the requested State to act inconsistently with its obligations under international law with respect to the State or diplomatic immunity of a person or property of a third State, unless the Court can first obtain the cooperation of that third State for the waiver of the immunity'.[132] This article, which contains a parallel provision concerning obligations arising

[129] UN Secretary-General, Secretary-General's Remarks to the General Assembly on Libya (1 March 2011) ('there is no impunity . . . those who commit crimes against humanity will be punished, [and] fundamental principles of justice and accountability shall prevail'); 6491st Meeting of the United Nations Security Council, UNSCOR, 6491st Meeting, UN Doc. S/PV.6491, 5 (26 February 2011) (statement by Mr Osorio) ('Reconciliation will require the establishment of responsibility, confronting impunity and ensuring that those who commit or have committed crimes against humanity are brought to justice').

[130] *Prosecutor v. Al Bashir*, Second Decision on the Prosecution's Application for a Warrant of Arrest against Omar Hassan Ahmad Al Bashir, No. ICC-02/05-01/09-94, 29 (12 July 2010); *Prosecutor v. Al Bashir*, Decision on the Prosecution's Application for a Warrant of Arrest against Omar Hassan Ahmad Al Bashir, No. ICC-02/05-01/09-3, 92–3 (4 March 2009).

[131] *Ibid.* (emphasis added).

[132] Rome Statute (1998), Article 98(1).

under international agreements,[133] would seem in the present context to require a waiver of immunity for execution of the warrants by national authorities to conform to immunity *ratione personae* under customary international law, unless an explanation can be provided for the non-recognition of such immunity.

To be sure, the arrest warrants issued by the SCSL and ICC are distinct from the Belgian arrest warrant at issue in the *Arrest Warrant* case by virtue of the source of the warrant: an international judicial organ rather than a domestic court. However, they do not differ in terms of their treatment of the immunity *ratione personae* normally enjoyed by the subjects of those arrest warrants. The distinguishing feature appears to relate to forum rather than consent. The ICC is an institution independent from the United Nations,[134] therefore membership of the United Nations does not imply consent to the jurisdiction of the ICC.[135] If referral of a situation to the ICC by the Security Council is sufficient to waive immunity *ratione personae*, then the Chapter VII power of the Security Council would effectively include the power to remove immunity *ratione personae* absent the consent (constructive or otherwise) of the State in question.[136] Vesting the Security Council with such power to

133 *Ibid.*, Article 98(2).

134 *Compare* Statute of the International Court of Justice, 15 UNCIO 355, Article 1 (1945) ('The International Court of Justice established by the Charter of the United Nations [is] the principal judicial organ of the United Nations'), *with* Negotiated Relationship Agreement between the International Criminal Court and the United Nations, ICC-ASP/3/Res.1, Article 2(1) (4 October 2004, *entered into force* 22 July 2004) ('The United Nations recognizes the Court as an independent judicial institution').

135 *See* Rome Statute (1998), Preamble, Articles 1–2.

136 Rome Statute (1998), Article 13 (Article 13 provides three avenues by which the ICC may exercise its jurisdiction: (a) referral of a situation to the Prosecutor by a State Party, (b) referral by the Security Council acting under Chapter VII of the UN Charter, or (c) *proprio motu* investigation by the ICC Prosecutor. Because the ICC is a treaty body of the Rome Statute, the authority granted to States Parties and the Prosecutor under the Statute would necessarily be limited to States parties to the Statute. The Chapter VII authority of the Security Council introduces a source of authority external to the Rome Statute with the power to subject non-parties to jurisdiction of the Rome Statute, because Chapter VII actions by the Security Council are binding upon all UN member States, and many members of the United Nations are not States parties to the Rome Statute. Since States not parties to the Rome Statute have not waived the immunity of its officials before the ICC under Article 27 of the Statute, an alternative explanation is required for the non-recognition of immunity *ratione personae*, given that the ICC can establish jurisdiction over individuals acting on behalf of non-States parties). *See* Dapo Akande, *The Jurisdiction of the International Criminal Court over Nationals of Non-Parties: Legal Basis and Limits*, 1(3) JOURNAL OF INTERNATIONAL CRIMINAL JUSTICE 618–50 (2003).

abrogate an immunity considered to be 'an extension of the immunity of the foreign state'[137] calls into question the 'principle of the sovereign equality of all its Members' upon which the UN Organization is based,[138] to which the doctrine of sovereign immunity gives effect.

Moreover, on a practical level, it is unclear how States might comply with a warrant to arrest and surrender a sitting Head of State while respecting that official's immunity *ratione personae*. Absent a waiver by Liberia, Sudan, or Libya disclaiming immunity *ratione personae* of its respective Head of State, the execution of those warrants by national authorities would appear to raise the same concerns of sovereign immunity implicated in the *Arrest Warrant* case. However, if such arrest warrants and requests for assistance are consistent with Article 98 of the Rome Statute in the case of warrants issued by the ICC, then State cooperation must be conceived to be consistent with the immunities of such officials.[139] As the principle of complementarity calls for cooperation between domestic legal orders and the ICC,[140] parsing domestic and international judicial processes is insufficient to alleviate this tension. Reframing such warrants as imposing obligations only upon the respective official's State is refuted by the object and purpose of such requests, which call on States broadly to cooperate in the detention and surrender of officials enjoying immunity *ratione personae*.[141] The notion that arrest

But see Prosecutor v. Al-Bashir, Decision on the Cooperation of the Democratic Republic of the Congo Regarding Omer Al-Bashir's Arrest and Surrender to the Court, No. ICC-02/05-01/09-195, para. 29 (2014) (Pre-Trial Chamber II determined that 'the SC implicitly waived the immunities granted to Omar Al-Bashir under international law and attached to his person as a Head of State').

137 *See* Restatement (Second) of Foreign Relations Law of the United States § 66 (1965) ('The immunity of a foreign state . . . extends to . . . its head of state').

138 Charter of the United Nations, Article 2(1) (1945); *see also* Declaration on Principles of International Law Concerning Friendly Relations and Co-operation among States in accordance with the Charter of the United Nations, GA Res. 2625, UN Doc. A/Res/25/2625, Annex (24 October 1970).

139 Rome Statute (1998) Article 98.

140 *See, e.g., Arrest Warrant of 11 April 2000 (Democratic Republic of the Congo v. Belgium)*, ICJ Reports 2002, p. 3, Dis. Op. Van den Wyngaert, p. 137, para. 37 ('The jurisdiction of an International Criminal Court, set up by the Rome Statute, is moreover conditioned by the principle of complementarity: primary responsibility for adjudicating war crimes and crimes against humanity lies with the States. The International Criminal Court will only be able to act if States which have jurisdiction are unwilling or unable genuinely to carry out investigation or prosecution') (citing Rome Statute (1998), Article 17).

141 For discussion of possible interactions between Articles 27 and 98 of the Rome Statute, *see* Dapo Akande, *International Law Immunities and the International Criminal Court*, 98(3) American Journal of International Law 407, 419–30 (2004).

and extradition is in any instance consistent with immunity *ratione personae* is at odds with the basic purpose of that immunity – to shield high officials from foreign judicial process.[142]

Any suggestion that international arrest warrants are conceived to be limited in any meaningful way by immunity *ratione personae* was decidedly refuted in the *Gaddafi* case. The ICC Prosecutor indicated that the Court was 'acting in real time', suggesting an exercise of law-enforcement-type capacities by the ICC to remove the individuals in question from power.[143] To this end, the ICC openly relied upon States to detain and transfer the individuals for whom it had issued arrest warrants.[144] Comments by members of the Security Council after adopting Resolution 1593, which referred the situation in Darfur to the ICC Prosecutor, were similarly revealing. The United States delegation maintained that, 'absent consent of the State involved, any investigations or prosecutions of nationals of non-party States should come only pursuant to a decision by the Council'.[145] By this reasoning, the Chapter VII authority of the Security Council includes the power to strip an official of immunity *ratione personae*, a position at odds with the principle of sovereignty underlying the UN Charter.[146] France, by contrast, emphasized that the nature of the offences in question, and the will of the international community to ensure accountability for such violations, was the basis of the denial of immunity, rather than the authority of the Security Council.[147]

According to either understanding, the international arrest warrants and subsequent criminal proceedings against Taylor, al-Bashir, and Gaddafi suggest that immunity *ratione personae* does not apply in proceedings for violations of *jus cogens* instituted by international judicial organs such as the ICC. This jurisprudence is consistent with the limitation to immunity *ratione personae* articulated by the International Court

[142] *See, e.g.*, *Ye v. Zemin*, 383 F.3d 620 (7th Cir. 2004).

[143] ICC Prosecutor Presents his Findings in Libya, 1 (16 May 2011).

[144] *Prosecutor v. Al Bashir*, Second Decision on the Prosecution's Application for a Warrant of Arrest against Omar Hassan Ahmad Al Bashir, No. ICC-02/05-01/09-94, 29 (12 July 2010); *Prosecutor v. Al Bashir*, Decision on the Prosecution's Application for a Warrant of Arrest against Omar Hassan Ahmad Al Bashir, No. ICC-02/05-01/09-3, 92–3 (4 March 2009).

[145] Press Release, Security Council, Security Council Refers Situation in Darfur, Sudan, to Prosecutor of the International Criminal Court, UN Press Release SC/8351 (31 March 2005) (statement by the United States).

[146] Charter of the United Nations, Article 2(1) (1945).

[147] UN Press Release SC/8351 (31 March 2005) (statement by France).

of Justice in the *Arrest Warrant* case.[148] The presumptive execution of such warrants by national authorities raises serious questions regarding the scope of immunity *ratione personae* for international crimes where proceedings are instituted by international courts and tribunals.

b. Criminal prosecution before domestic courts

In contrast to criminal proceedings instituted by international courts, there is no evidence that *jus cogens* violations affect immunity *ratione personae* for criminal prosecution before domestic courts. In *Pinochet*, the UK House of Lords noted that had Senator Pinochet held office at the time of litigation, his immunity *ratione personae* would have precluded British courts from asserting jurisdiction over the *jus cogens* violations at issue.[149] The French Court of Cassation reached a similar conclusion in the *Gaddafi* case, which concerned the 1989 bombing of a civilian airliner over Chad, overturning a 2000 judgment by the Court of Appeal of Paris finding that Head of State immunity does not apply in cases concerning violations of *jus cogens*.[150] In the *Arrest Warrant* case decided the following year, the International Court of Justice delineated the parameters of the immunity *ratione personae* articulated in the *Pinochet* and *Gaddafi* cases. The case concerned the legality of an international arrest warrant issued in absentia by a Belgian investigating magistrate against the incumbent Minister of Foreign Affairs of the Congo, Abdu aye Yerodia Ndombasi.[151] The International Court found that Yerodia, as an incumbent Foreign Minister, enjoyed 'immunity from criminal jurisdiction and ... inviolability' from prosecution, making no distinction between official acts and acts outside of Yerodia's official conduct.[152] Immunity *ratione personae* shielded Yerodia notwithstanding that the conduct in question violated *jus cogens* and constituted international crimes.[153] The Court of Cassation of Belgium subsequently recognized that the immunity *ratione personae* of Ariel Sharon, the sitting Prime

[148] *Arrest Warrant of 11 April 2000 (Democratic Republic of the Congo v. Belgium)*, ICJ Reports 2002, p. 3, para. 61.

[149] *R. v. Bow Street Metropolitan Stipendiary Magistrate and Others, Ex parte Pinochet Ugarte (No. 3)*, House of Lords (UK), [2000] 1 A.C. 147, 38 ILM 581 (1999), 641 (Saville, L.), 644 (Millett, L.), 653 (Phillips, L.), 673 (Hutton, L.).

[150] *Gaddafi Case*, Court of Appeal of Paris (*Chambre d'accusation*) (France), RGDIP 1999, p. 464 (2000), Court of Cassation (Criminal Chamber), RGDIP 2001, p. 473 (2001), 152 ILR 490, 491, 496.

[151] *Arrest Warrant of 11 April 2000 (Democratic Republic of the Congo v. Belgium)*, ICJ Reports 2002, p. 3.

[152] *Ibid.*, para. 51. [153] *Ibid.*, paras. 54–5.

Minister of Israel, rendered prosecution under Belgium's universal jurisdiction statute inadmissible.[154]

Judicial authority indicates that immunity *ratione personae* prevails as a rule of customary international law in domestic courts for the prosecution of international crimes. This illustrates that the principle at the heart of sovereign immunity, *par in parem non habet imperium*, endures at the national level to preclude incumbent high officials from appearing before domestic courts notwithstanding the offences with which they are accused. The divergence in application of immunity *ratione personae* between domestic and international criminal proceedings for *jus cogens* violations suggests that sovereign immunity is a peculiarly inter-State principle that is not absolute. The divergence between the *Pinochet* dicta, *Gaddafi* (I) case, *Arrest Warrant* decision, and *Sharon* case, and the three cases discussed above – *Taylor*, *al-Bashir*, and *Gaddafi* (II) – suggests a branch point in the application of immunity *ratione personae*, whose parameters remain to be completely determined. In any event, domestic attempts to prosecute sitting high officials for *jus cogens* violations have waned, perhaps due in part to the emergence of international judicial organs competent to undertake such proceedings, in addition to this negative precedent.

c. Civil proceedings before domestic courts

The recognition of immunity *ratione personae* in civil proceedings for *jus cogens* violations before domestic courts has mirrored its application in domestic criminal prosecution of incumbent high officials. United States law is fairly unique in providing express jurisdiction over civil claims by aliens for conduct amounting to *jus cogens* violations under the Alien Tort Statute (ATS),[155] yet even in this context the application of immunity *rationae personae* prevails. Federal courts of the United States deciding claims under the ATS have consistently recognized immunity *ratione personae* to shield high State officials for proceedings for damages arising from *jus cogens* violations: immunity *ratione personae* was applied in

[154] *Re Sharon and Yaron*, Court of Cassation (Belgium), P.02.1139.F/2, JT 2003, 243, 127 ILR 110, para. 21 (2003).

[155] 28 USC § 1350 ('The district courts shall have original jurisdiction of any civil action by an alien for a tort only, committed in violation of the law of nations or a treaty of the United States'). *See* discussion *supra*, Chapter 12.B (International Civil Responsibility); *Kiobel v. Royal Dutch Petroleum Co.*, 621 F.3d 111, 115 (2nd Cir. 2010) *aff'd*, 133 S. Ct. 1659 (US 2013) (describing ATS as 'a jurisdictional provision unlike any other in American law and of a kind apparently unknown to any other legal system in the world').

cases concerning Jean-Bertrand Aristide (sitting President of Haiti),[156] Robert Mugabe and Stan Mudenge (sitting President and Foreign Minister of Zimbabwe, respectively),[157] Jaing Zemin (sitting President of China),[158] Ariel Sharon (sitting Prime Minister of Israel),[159] and Paul Kagame (sitting President of Rwanda),[160] from civil claims for violations of *jus cogens* norms. In recognizing immunity *ratione personae*, US courts have clearly distinguished domestic civil proceedings from international criminal proceedings. As the US District Court for the District of DC recently observed, '[t]he application of immunity by international tribunals in criminal cases is irrelevant to the question of how individual nations treat each others' leaders in civil cases'.[161]

***

This final point by the district court is insightful because it casts sovereign immunity as a matter of inter-State relations – based in comity – that has crystallized as customary international law. It is likely for this reason that the treatment of immunity *ratione personae* in civil domestic proceedings mirrors its application in criminal prosecution at the domestic level, yet departs from prosecution at the international level. The principle that there exists no power among equals – *par in parem non habet imperium* –

156 *Lafontant v. Aristide*, 844 F.Supp. 128, 130 (EDNY 1994) (concerning torture and extrajudicial killing of a political opponent).

157 *Tachiona v. Mugabe*, 169 F. Supp. 2d 259, 316–17 (SDNY 2001) *aff'd in part, rev'd in part* and *remanded sub nom. Tachiona v. United States*, 386 F.3d 205 (2nd Cir. 2004) (the US District Court for the Southern District of New York initially found Mugabe and Mudenge protected by immunity *ratione personae* from charges including torture and terrorism; the Second Circuit found diplomatic immunity sufficient to warrant dismissing the claim without reaching the question of immunity *ratione personae*).

158 *Ye v. Zemin*, 383 F.3d 620, 625–7 (7th Cir. 2004) ('The Executive Branch's determination that a foreign leader should be immune from suit even when the leader is accused of acts that violate *jus cogens* norms is established by a suggestion of immunity').

159 *Doe I v. State of Israel*, 400 F. Supp. 2d 86, 105, 111 (DDC 2005) ('*Jus cogens* violations, without more, do not constitute an implied waiver of . . . immunity. . . Defendant Sharon is the recognized head of state for Israel, and . . . he is entitled to immunity under the head-of-state doctrine').

160 *Habyarimana v. Kagame*, 696 F.3d 1029, 1032 (10th Cir. 2012) *cert. denied*, 133 S. Ct. 1607 (US 2013) ('We must accept the United States' suggestion that a foreign head of state is immune from suit – even for acts committed prior to assuming office – as a conclusive determination by the political arm of the Government that the continued [exercise of jurisdiction] interferes with the proper conduct of our foreign relations' (internal citations omitted)).

161 *Manoharan v. Rajapaksa*, 845 F. Supp. 2d 260, 265–6 (DDC 2012) *aff'd*, 711 F.3d 178 (DC Cir. 2013).

that underlies sovereign immunity is implicated by domestic proceedings in a way it is not with respect to international fora. As a matter of principle, therefore, it seems that applicability of immunity *ratione personae* in domestic proceedings, yet not international prosecution, is a distinction dependent upon the forum – domestic or international – rather than the nature of the proceeding in question – civil or criminal.

If jurisprudence continues to develop along this trajectory, then the development of international criminal organs with competence to prosecute sitting officials who would otherwise enjoy immunity marks a critical benchmark in the interaction of *jus cogens* and sovereign immunity. This jurisprudence indicates that immunity *ratione personae*, though absolute when applied, is not absolutely applied. It further suggests that immunity *ratione personae* hails from sovereignty as *equality*, which resonates with the underling *par in parem non habet imperium* principle.[162] This provides a coherent explanation as to why international judicial organs, such as the SCSL and ICC, might prosecute sitting Heads of State, while domestic courts in the United Kingdom, France, and Belgium would be precluded from commencing those same proceedings.[163] The contrast between the 2001 *Gaddafi* case before the French Court of Cassation and the 2011 proceeding instituted before the ICC casts this point in sharp relief. The status and commensurate immunity of the official targeted had not changed, but the forum was crucially different. This supports the proposition that sovereign immunity, at least with respect to *jus cogens* violations, is an inter-State principle that does not apply to proceedings before international fora where sovereign equality is not at issue.

Without question, this recasting of sovereign immunity marks an erosion of the protection from personal jurisdiction afforded to high State officials by immunity *ratione personae*. Immunities are conceived to benefit that State, by shielding its highest representatives, and the

[162] *See* Roman Kolodkin, Second Report on Immunity of State Officials from Foreign Criminal Jurisdiction, UN Doc. A/CN.4/631, para. 63 n.141 (2010) ('immunity derives from the principle of the sovereign equality of States').

[163] *See* The AU–EU Expert Report on the Principle of Universal Jurisdiction, EU Doc. 8672/1/09 Rev 1, paras. 37–8 (16 April 2009) (To illustrate this point, African States have expressed their concern that '[i]ndictments issued by European states against officials of African states have the effect of subjecting the latter to the jurisdiction of European states, contrary to the sovereign equality and independence of states. For African states, this evokes memories of colonialism. In so far as the indictment of sitting state officials is concerned, there is disregard for immunities enjoyed by state officials under international law. Consequently, any such indictment severely constrains the capacity of African states to discharge the functions of statehood on the international plane').

international community, by ensuring harmonious relations among its members; the individual is strictly not the legal beneficiary of such immunities.[164] The Law Lords in *Pinochet* quoted from *Oppenheim's International Law* to place these developments in the doctrine of immunity into context:

> While no general rule of positive international law can as yet be asserted which gives to States the right to punish foreign nationals for crimes against humanity in the same way as they are, for instance, entitled to punish acts of piracy, there are clear indications pointing to the gradual evolution of a significant principle of international law to that effect. That principle consists both in the adoption of the rule of universality of jurisdiction and in the recognition of the supremacy of the law of humanity over the law of the sovereign state when enacted or applied in violation of elementary human rights in a manner which may justly be held to shock the conscience of mankind.[165]

This passage recalls that the State is not an abstract entity but a community of human beings.[166] Protection of international criminals such as al-Bashir and Gaddafi from international scrutiny under the guise of State dignity is an affront to the citizens against whom grave violations of human rights are perpetrated. As State sovereignty is increasingly viewed to be contingent upon respect for certain values common to the international community, it is perhaps unsurprising that bare sovereignty is no longer sufficient to absolutely shield incumbent high officials from prosecution for *jus cogens* violations. The extent to which sovereignty-based immunity defenses will be available in the future to high officials alleged to have committed *jus cogens* violations was called into question by the US District Court in the *Mugabe* case:

> These precedents instruct that resort to head-of-state and diplomatic immunity as a shield for private abuses of the sovereign's office is wearing thinner in the eyes of the world and waning in the cover of the law. The prevailing trend teaches that the day does come to pass when those who violate their public trust are called upon, in this world, to render account for the wrongs they inflict on innocents.[167]

164 Andrea Bianchi, *Immunity versus Human Rights: The Pinochet Case*, 10(2) EUROPEAN JOURNAL OF INTERNATIONAL LAW 237, 261 (1999).

165 Lassa Oppenheim, I OPPENHEIM'S INTERNATIONAL LAW 998 (London: Longman, Robert Jennings & Arthur Watts eds., 9th edn. 1992).

166 *See* discussion *supra*, Chapter 12.A (Individual Criminal Responsibility) (noting that the State is not the proper subject of criminal responsibility).

167 *Tachiona v. Mugabe*, 169 F. Supp. 2d 259, 317 (SDNY 2001) *aff'd in part, rev'd in part* and *remanded sub nom. Tachiona v. United States*, 386 F.3d 205 (2nd Cir. 2004).

Proceedings against Charles Taylor, Omar al-Bashir, and Moammar Gaddafi indicate this sense of a limitation of immunity *ratione personae*, yet the extent of this limitation is not yet fully formed. To be sure, it would go too far to conclude at present that there is no longer any sovereign immunity for *jus cogens* violations.[168] However, it remains an open question whether the institutional, forum-based qualification of immunity *ratione personae* marks an end point or simply one stage in an evolving interplay between *jus cogens* and sovereign immunity. That international courts have recently issued a series of warrants calling on States to arrest and extradite individuals ordinarily enjoying immunity *ratione personae* suggests dynamism rather than stasis.

ii. Immunity ratione materiae

Immunity *ratione materiae* is an element of sovereign immunity according to which State officials are exempt from prosecution for official acts attributable to the State.[169] The State is entitled to claim such acts as its own, 'so that the individual organ may not be held accountable for those acts or transactions'.[170] In effect, 'sovereign immunity, which belongs to a foreign *state*, extends to an individual *official* acting on behalf of that foreign state'.[171] This 'official acts' or 'functional' immunity is necessary to prevent the immunity of the State from circumvention by simply suing a named official in place of the State itself.[172] The implicit corollary of this reasoning is that an official is not protected by sovereign immunity for conduct exceeding the scope of his official duty,[173] where

168 Alexander Orakelashvili, Peremptory Norms in International Law 344, 358 (Oxford University Press 2006) (suggesting immunity cannot apply in proceedings for *jus cogens* violations); Bianchi, *Immunity versus Human Rights: The Pinochet Case*, 261 (same).

169 Hazel Fox, The Law of State Immunity 455 (Oxford University Press 2004) ('The doctrine of the imputability of the acts of the individual to the State ... in classical law ... imputes the act solely to the state, who alone is responsible for its consequences. In consequence, any act performed by the individual as an act of the State enjoys the immunity which the State enjoys').

170 *Prosecutor v. Blaškić*, Judgment on the Request of Croatia for Review of the Decision of Trial Chamber II of 18 July 1997, IT-95-14-AR108bis, para. 41 (1997).

171 *Yousuf v. Samantar*, 699 F.3d 763, 767 (4th Cir. 2012) *cert. denied*, 134 S. Ct. 897 (US 2014) (citing *Underhill v. Hernandez*, 168 US 250, 252 (1897)) (emphasis in original).

172 *Jones v. United Kingdom*, ECtHR, Nos. 34356/06 & 40528/06, para. 202 (2014).

173 *Ibid.*, para. 205 ('It is clear from the foregoing that individuals only benefit from State immunity *ratione materiae* where the impugned acts were carried out in the course of their official duties').

'the officer purports to act as an individual and not as an official, [because such] a suit directed against that action is not a suit against the sovereign'.[174] In contrast to immunity *ratione personae*, which is immunity from personal jurisdiction, immunity *ratione materiae* is a form of immunity from subject-matter jurisdiction that is conduct-based rather than office-based and, as such, attaches to conduct attributable to the State even after an individual's official status terminates.[175] Thus, while immunity *ratione personae* is limited by tenure in office, immunity *ratione materiae* is limited to official acts performed by State officials in their official capacity.[176]

Certain criminal acts are typically characterized to fall outside the scope of official conduct as acts, by definition, not sanctionable by the sovereign, even where such acts are carried out 'under the color of law'.[177] Consequently, acts outside the authority of the State are not properly attributed to the State for the purposes of State responsibility and,[178] as a result, the sovereign immunity of the State does not extend to confer immunity *ratione materiae* to such conduct.[179] This principle has

174 *Chuidian v. Philippine National Bank*, 912 F.2d 1095, 1106 (9th Cir. 1990) (internal quotation marks omitted).

175 This distinction between immunities of individual officials under customary international law is without comment to individual immunities established by treaties. However, 'diplomatic immunity' might be characterized as a form of immunity *ratione personae*. *See* Vienna Convention on Diplomatic Relations, 500 UNTS 95, Article 31 (18 April 1961, *entered into force* 24 June 1964). By contrast, 'consular immunity' is a form of functional immunity *ratione materiae*. *See* Vienna Convention on Consular Relations, 596 UNTS 661, Article 43, (24 April 1963, *entered into force* 19 March 1967).

176 *See* Roman Kolodkin, Preliminary Report on Immunity of State Officials from Foreign Criminal Jurisdiction, UN Doc. A/CN.4/601, paras. 78–83 (2008).

177 *See, e.g.*, *In re Doe*, 860 F.2d 40, 45 (2nd Cir. 1988) ('were we to reach the merits of the issue, we believe there is respectable authority for denying head-of-state immunity to a former head-of-state for private or criminal acts in violation of American law').

178 ILC Articles on State Responsibility (2001), Article 2 ('Elements of an Internationally Wrongful Act of a State: There is an internationally wrongful act of a State when conduct consisting of an action or omission: (a) is attributable to the State under international law; and (b) constitutes a breach of an international obligation of the State'); Article 5 ('Conduct of persons or entities exercising elements of governmental authority: The conduct of a person or entity which . . . is empowered by the law of that State to exercise elements of the governmental authority shall be considered an act of the State under international law, *provided the person or entity is acting in that capacity in the particular instance*' (emphasis added)).

179 *See, e.g.*, *Attorney-General (Israel) v. Eichmann*, Supreme Court (Israel), 36 ILR 5, 277, 310 (1962) ('Of such odious acts it must be said that in point of international law they are completely outside the "sovereign" jurisdiction of the State that ordered or ratified their commission, and therefore those who participated in such acts must personally

been applied to violations of *jus cogens* and international crimes: these grave violations of international law fall beyond the official capacity of State officials and, as such, are not protected from international or domestic criminal jurisdiction by immunity *ratione materiae* because they cannot be sanctioned by the sovereign.[180] Consequently, as the ICTY Appeals Chamber noted in *Blaškić*, 'those responsible for such crimes cannot invoke immunity from national or international jurisdiction even if they perpetrated such crimes while acting in their official capacity'.[181]

Because of its relation to substantive law,[182] immunity *ratione materiae* has been characterized as 'a substantive defense from liability' rather than a procedural defence on jurisdiction.[183] In the United States, for example, this approach is reflected in recent determinations by the US Department of State to suggest conduct-based immunity before domestic courts.[184] A substantive approach to immunity *ratione materiae* follows from the need to establish whether the conduct in question is 'official' as a preliminary matter necessarily precedent to a determination of whether immunity attaches to such conduct.[185] The alternative to this substantive

account for them and cannot shelter behind the official character of their task or mission, or behind the "Laws" of the State by virtue of which they purported to act . . . In other words, international law postulates that it is impossible for a State to sanction an act that violates its severe prohibitions, and from this follows the idea which forms the core of the concept of "international crime", that a person who was a party to such a crime must bear individual responsibility for it').

180 Roman Kolodkin, Second Report on Immunity of State Officials from Foreign Criminal Jurisdiction, UN Doc. A/CN.4/631, para. 57 (2010) ('The viewpoint, whereby grave crimes under international law cannot be considered as acts performed in an official capacity, and immunity *ratione materiae* does not therefore protect from foreign criminal jurisdiction exercised in connection with such crimes, has become fairly widespread') (internal citations omitted).

181 *Prosecutor v. Blaškić*, Judgment on the Request of Croatia for Review of the Decision of Trial Chamber II of 18 July 1997, IT-95-14-AR108bis, para. 41 (1997).

182 *See* Antonio Cassese, International Criminal Law 303–4 (Oxford University Press, 2nd edn. 2008).

183 Anthony Colangelo, *Jurisdiction, Immunity, Legality, and Jus Cogens*, 14(1) Chicago Journal of International Law 53, 57, 78–9, 91 (2013).

184 *Ibid.*, 79.

185 This operation of immunity *ratione materiae* in civil judicial proceedings does not raise 'practical difficulties' peculiar to *jus cogens*. The concern is that 'simply because plaintiffs allege . . . violations of so-called *jus cogens*' would be sufficient to hail foreign officials into court, compromising the 'effectiveness' of immunity. However pleading standards at least in US courts counsel that merely alleging a *jus cogens* violation would not have this effect because mere allegations cannot sustain a claim in the first instance. *Compare* David Stewart, Samantar *and the Future of Foreign Official Immunity*, 15(3) Lewis & Clark Law Review 633, 658 (2011), *with Ashcroft v. Iqbal*, 556 US 662, 678–9 (2009)

approach to immunity *ratione materiae* would transform official acts immunity into a form of immunity *ratione personae* that would bar any consideration of the conduct at issue when determining applicability of immunity *ratione materiae* to a State official.

Paralleling the discussion in subsection (i) above, the following segments address the interaction of *jus cogens* and sovereign immunity in the application of immunity *ratione materiae* in three areas: criminal prosecution before international judicial bodies, criminal prosecution before domestic courts, and civil proceedings before domestic courts.

a. International criminal prosecution

Since the end of the Second World War, international law has denied immunity *ratione materiae* in the prosecution of international crimes before international courts and tribunals.[186] The premise underlying the military tribunals at Nuremberg and Tokyo is that international crimes cannot properly be considered to fall within the official conduct of a State official because such acts exceed the scope of State conduct that may be sanctioned under international law. As articulated by the IMT at Nuremberg:

> The principle of international law, which under certain circumstances, protects the representatives of a State, cannot be applied to acts which are condemned as criminal by international law... [I]ndividuals have international duties which transcend the national obligations of obedience imposed by the individual State. He who violates the laws of war cannot obtain immunity while acting in pursuance of the authority of the State if the State in authorizing action moves outside its competence under international law.[187]

The principle has been articulated by present-day international tribunals, as illustrated by the ICTY in *Blaškić*.[188] The State is unable to claim

('the pleading standard ... demands more than an unadorned, the-defendant-unlawfully-harmed-me accusation ... a complaint must contain sufficient factual matter, accepted as true, to state a claim to relief that is plausible on its face' (internal quotation marks omitted) (citing *Bell Atlantic Corp. v. Twombly*, 550 US 544 (2007))).

186 *See* IMT Charter (1945), Article 7 ('The official position of defendants, whether as Heads of State or responsible officials in Government Departments, shall not be considered as freeing them from responsibility or mitigating punishment'); IMTFE Charter (1946), Article 6.

187 *Nazi Conspiracy and Aggression*, International Military Tribunal at Nuremberg, Opinion and Judgment, 53 (1946).

188 *Prosecutor v. Blaškić*, Judgment on the Request of Croatia for Review of the Decision of Trial Chamber II of 18 July 1997, IT-95-14-AR108bis, para. 41 (1997) ('those responsible

violations of *jus cogens* as its own for the purposes of sovereign immunity, and thereby extend immunity *ratione materiae* and shield State officials from international criminal prosecution, because the State is foreclosed from sanctioning violations of rules accepted and recognized by the international community as a whole from which no derogation is permitted. The conclusion that the State is deprived from permitting such conduct as a matter of international law is indicative of a normative hierarchy in international law.[189] Put differently, *jus cogens* violations, even when carried out under the color of law, are not attributable to the State as sovereign acts for purposes of immunity, therefore officials cannot benefit from immunity *ratione materiae* for *jus cogens* violations.

b. Criminal prosecution before domestic courts

Unlike the clear demarcation between the non-application of immunity *ratione personae* for *jus cogens* violations in international fora and its uniform application in domestic courts, the inapplicability of immunity *ratione materiae* before international courts and tribunals has been consistently affirmed in the criminal prosecution of international crimes before domestic courts. The seminal case establishing that functional immunity is unavailable to shield former officials from *jus cogens* violations is the *Pinochet* case.[190] In *Pinochet,* the House of Lords determined that *jus cogens* violations – in this instance the international crime of torture – could not be considered 'official acts' under international law for the purposes of immunity *ratione materiae* because such conduct cannot be officially authorized by the sovereign.[191] The House of Lords alluded to the attribution of official acts to the State as the mechanism by which immunity *ratione materiae* extends to State officials for official acts, and the corollary, that the effective immunity of the State from responsibility where conduct is not attributable to it exposes such acts to prosecution. As noted by Lord Millett:

> [A]cts which attract state immunity in civil proceedings because they are characterised as acts of sovereign power may, for the very same reason, attract individual criminal liability ... It is important to emphasise that

for such [international] crimes cannot invoke immunity from national or international jurisdiction even if they perpetrated such crimes while acting in their official capacity').

189 *Prosecutor v. Furundžija*, IT-95-17/1-T, para. 155 (1998).

190 *R. v. Bow Street Metropolitan Stipendiary Magistrate and Others, Ex parte Pinochet Ugarte (No. 3)*, House of Lords (UK), [2000] 1 A.C. 147, 38 ILM 581 (1999).

191 *Ibid.*, 594–5 (Browne-Wilkinson, L.), 626 (Hope, L.) 639 (Hutton, L.), 643 (Saville, L.), 651 (Millett, L.), 663 (Phillips, L.).

> Senator Pinochet is not alleged to be criminally liable because he was head of state when other responsible officials employed torture to maintain him in power. He is not alleged to be vicariously liable for the wrongdoing of his subordinates. He is alleged to have incurred direct criminal responsibility for his own acts in ordering and directing a campaign of terror involving the use of torture.[192]

The criminality of alleged conduct is alone insufficient to render immunity *ratione materiae* inapplicable, as the House of Lords made clear, because criminal acts can be carried out officially to give rise to attribution to the State and, in turn, immunity *ratione materiae*.[193]

The *jus cogens* status of the prohibition against torture under international law, and universal jurisdiction over prosecution of the crime, rendered Pinochet's conduct *ultra vires*. According to Lord Hope, although immunity *ratione materiae* would apply to all acts performed by a Head of State in the exercise of his government functions, it would not extend to acts undertaken under the colour of law for personal benefit or to violations of *jus cogens* norms.[194] In this vein, Lord Browne-Wilkinson asked rhetorically, '[h]ow can it be [that] international law purposes an official function to do something which international law itself prohibits and criminalises?'[195] To recognize immunity *ratione materiae* for such conduct would 'produce bizarre results' by immunizing all perpetrators of torture as defined by the Torture Convention from prosecution, rendering the instrument moot.[196] The House of Lords thus concluded Senator Pinochet did not enjoy immunity *ratione materiae* for conduct undertaken under the colour of law in violation of *jus cogens*, rendering him subject to detention and extradition to Spain.[197]

192 *Ibid.*, 651 (Millett, L.). It is evident from the opinions by the Law Lords in *Pinochet* that the Torture Convention and *jus cogens* were considered to be distinct, authoritative rationales for the denial of immunity *ratione materiae* for acts of torture. *See* Alexander Orakhelashvili, *State Immunity and Hierarchy of Norms: Why the House of Lords Got It Wrong*, 18(5) European Journal of International Law 955, 969 (2008).

193 *Ibid.*, 593 (Browne-Wilkinson, L.) ('It is not enough to say that it cannot be part of the functions of the head of state to commit a crime. Actions which are criminal under the local law can still have been done officially and therefore give rise to immunity *ratione materiae*. The case needs to be analysed more closely').

194 *Ibid.*, 622 (Hope, L.) (noting that these two exceptions are the 'only two exceptions to this approach which customary international law has recognised').

195 *Ibid.*, 594 (Browne-Wilkinson, L.) 196 *Ibid.*

197 *R. v. Bow Street Metropolitan Stipendiary Magistrate and Others, Ex parte Pinochet Ugarte (No. 3)*, House of Lords (UK), [2000] 1 A.C. 147, 38 ILM 581 (1999).

Non-recognition of immunity *ratione materiae* for violations of *jus cogens* has been evidenced in a line of domestic criminal proceedings for international crimes. In 2000, the Amsterdam Court of Appeal refused to grant immunity *ratione materiae* to Desi Bouterse, the former military ruler of the Republic of Suriname accused of the torture and summary execution of fifteen political opponents in December 1982,[198] because 'the commission of very serious offences as are concerned here – cannot be considered to be one of the official duties of a head of state'.[199] The Italian Court of Cassation, in the 2008 *Lozano* case, recognized that immunity *ratione materiae* does not apply to war crimes and crimes against humanity by virtue of their status as *jus cogens* norms, and because the violation of peremptory norms on behalf of the State constitutes 'an abuse of sovereignty'.[200] The French Court of Assizes similarly declined to recognize immunity *ratione materiae* from criminal prosecution for *jus cogens* violations in the 2005 *Ould Dah* case,[201] a conclusion subsequently endorsed by the ECtHR in 2009:

> The Court considers that, in agreement with ICTY jurisprudence, the prohibition against torture is an imperative norm, in otherwords *jus cogens*. Even if states can claim immunity from responsibility in civil cases for acts of torture allegedly perpetrated but not provided for in the forum state, this case deals with the criminal responsibility of an individual for acts of alleged torture and not with state immunity in a civil claim by a torture victim.[202]

198 *Bouterse Case*, Amsterdam Court of Appeal (Netherlands), Nos. R 97/163/12 Sv & R 97/176/12 Sv, para. 5 (International Commission of Jurists trans., 2000), *abrogated on other grounds by Bouterse Case*, Supreme Court (Netherlands), LJN: AB1471, ILDC 80 (2001).

199 *Ibid.*, para. 4.2.

200 *Lozano v. Italy*, Court of Cassation (First Criminal Chamber) (Italy), No. 31171/2008, ILDC 1085, para. 6 (2008). *See* Antonio Cassese, *The Italian Court of Cassation Misapprehends the Notion of War Crimes*, 6(5) JOURNAL OF INTERNATIONAL CRIMINAL JUSTICE 1077, 1082 (2008) (translating para. 6) (This rule, '[o]n account of the peremptory nature of international humanitarian law, which imposes respect for fundamental human rights and the possibility for universal values transcending individual state communities, aims at limiting the civil responsibility of a foreign state the organ of which, while performing acts *jure imperii* such as in military operations, has engaged in actions of such gravity as to undermine the very foundations of the coexistence of nations, actions that may therefore be classified as international crimes').

201 *Ely Ould Dah Case*, Gard Assizes Court (France), No. 70/05 (Arrêt de condamnation) / No. 71/05 (Arrêt statuant sur les intérêts civils) (2005); *see Ould Dah v. France*, No. 13113/03, 48 ILM 884, 884–5 (2009) (detailing an extensive procedural history in French courts).

202 *Ould Dah v. France*, No. 13113/03, 48 ILM 884, 894–6 (2009) (citing *Al-Adsani v. United Kingdom*, ECtHR, No. 35763/97, paras. 60–1, 66 (2001)).

In so finding, the court distinguished *Al-Adsani v. United Kingdom*, which concerned the jurisdictional immunity of the State itself from civil claims arising from *jus cogens* violations.[203] Applying this same principle in 2012, the Federal Criminal Court of Switzerland dismissed a claim of immunity in criminal proceedings against Kahled Nezzar, a former defence minister of Algeria,[204] because 'respect of humanitarian *jus cogens* rules and the existence of several judgments issued on this subject by national and international courts, has highlighted the emergence of an evolution towards an increase in the causes of exceptions to immunity from jurisdiction',[205] even in cases of 'the immunity of (former) Heads of State vis-à-vis crimes contrary to rules of *jus cogens*'.[206]

A final indication of the extent to which the inapplicability of immunity *ratione materiae* to criminal prosecution for *jus cogens* violations prevails in contemporary jurisprudence is the treatment of the matter by the International Court of Justice in *Questions Relating to the Obligation to Prosecute or Extradite*.[207] The case originated from a civil-party application filed in Belgium on 30 November 2000 against Hissène Habré, the former President of Chad, for torture, genocide, and serious violations of international humanitarian law.[208] The Minister of Justice of Chad reported to the Belgian investigating judge that Habré's Head of State immunity had been officially lifted by the Sovereign National Conference of Chad.[209] The investigating judge subsequently issued an international arrest warrant and indicted Habré for serious violations of international humanitarian law, torture, genocide, crimes against humanity, and war crimes.[210] On 22 September 2005, Belgium sought Habré's extradition from Senegal for prosecution under its international crimes statute, which in Article 5(3) provided that '[t]he immunity attaching to the official capacity of a person does not preclude the

203 *See Al-Adsani v. United Kingdom*, ECtHR, No. 35763/97, para. 61 (2001).

204 *A. (Kahled Nezzar) v. Office of the Attorney General*, Federal Criminal Court (Switzerland), No. BB.2011.140 (TRIAL trans. 2012).

205 *Ibid.* para. 5.3.4.

206 *Ibid.* paras. 5.3.5, 5.4.3 ('it is generally recognized that the prohibition of serious crimes against humanity, including torture ... genocide, crimes against humanity and war crimes is mandatory in nature (*jus cogens*) ... it would be difficult to admit that conduct contrary to fundamental values of the international legal order can be protected by rules of that very same legal order. Such situation would be paradoxical ... It follows that, in the present case, the suspect cannot claim any immunity *ratione materiae*').

207 *Questions Relating to the Obligation to Prosecute or Extradite (Belgium v. Senegal)*, Judgment, ICJ Reports 2012, p. 422.

208 *Ibid.*, para. 19. 209 *Ibid.*, para. 20. 210 *Ibid.*, para. 21.

application of this Act'.[211] The *Chambre d'accusation* of the Dakar Court of Appeal rejected Belgium's jurisdiction over Habré on 25 November 2005, because the alleged conduct was 'committed in the exercise of his functions' as President of Chad and thereby enjoyed jurisdictional immunity even after the termination of Habré's tenure in office.[212] Belgium instituted proceedings before the International Court in 2009 against Senegal concerning its compliance with its obligation to prosecute or extradite Habré for acts of torture committed as Head of State. In its judgment in the case, the International Court recalled that the Torture Convention – under which the dispute proceeded – is based on universal jurisdiction.[213] Moreover, it recognized the prohibition against torture as *jus cogens*,[214] and held that Senegal was in breach of its obligations *erga omnes* which required Senegal to prosecute or extradite Habré.[215] In ordering Senegal to submit the case to prosecution or extradite Habré, the International Court was silent on the issue of immunity *ratione materiae* raised by Senegal. One inference that may be drawn from this omission is that precedent had been sufficiently established by 2012 that immunity *ratione materiae* does not apply to the criminal prosecution of *jus cogens* violations before domestic courts.

The foregoing cases stand for the proposition that *jus cogens* violations, even if committed under the colour of law, are not 'official acts' for the purposes of applying immunity *ratione materiae* in criminal proceedings before domestic courts. Because violations of *jus cogens* cannot be sanctioned by the State as a matter of international law, such conduct cannot be attributed to the State as a sovereign act for purposes of immunity; consequently, sovereign immunity cannot extend from the State to shield officials alleged to have committed such acts from prosecution. Although this distinction has been criticized because 'such violations are, by definition, committed in the exercise of sovereign authority',[216] this critique fails to consider the

211 *Loi relative à la répression des violations graves de droit international humanitaire* [Act Concerning the Punishment of Grave Breaches of International Humanitarian Law] of 10 February 1999, Moniteur Belge [Official Gazette of Belgium] 23 March 1999, 9286 ('*L'immunité attachée à la qualité officielle d'une personne n'empêche pas l'application de la présente loi*').

212 *Questions Relating to the Obligation to Prosecute or Extradite (Belgium v. Senegal)*, Judgment, ICJ Reports 2012, p. 422, para. 22.

213 *Ibid.*, para. 75. 214 *Ibid.*, para. 99. 215 *Ibid.*, para. 117.

216 Sevrine Knuchel, *State Immunity and the Promise of* Jus Cogens, 9(2) Northwestern Journal of International Human Rights 149, 174 (2011).

underlying rationale by which *jus cogens* constrains what is within the power of the sovereign to authorize and, in turn, what may constitute an official act sanctioned by the sovereign. This conceptualization of the interaction between sovereign immunity and *jus cogens* in the *ratione materiae* context parallels its application before international criminal tribunals, unlike immunity *ratione personae* where a clear dichotomy prevails between criminal prosecution at the international and domestic levels.[217]

This procedural commonality between international and domestic proceedings is significant because it indicates that the sovereignty concerns which preserve immunity *ratione personae* in domestic criminal proceedings for *jus cogens* violations are not clearly implicated by the prosecution in domestic courts of individuals who are not protected by their status. This follows logically from the premise that *jus cogens* violations are not attributable to the State – prosecution of such acts is not thereby tantamount to impleading the State. Given the apparent clarity with which this 'fairly widespread' principle has emerged in domestic criminal proceedings,[218] it follows next to consider how domestic courts have applied this principle in civil proceedings, where jurisprudence has been less consistent.

c. Civil proceedings before domestic courts

Two divergent strands of jurisprudence have emerged with respect to the application of immunity *rationae materiae* in civil proceedings before domestic courts for *jus cogens* violations. These approaches are characterized by the *Samantar* case decided by the US Fourth Circuit in 2012,[219] and the *Jones* case decided by the House of Lords in 2006.[220]

[217] *See* discussion *supra*, Chapter 12.C.i. (Immunity *Ratione Personae*).

[218] Roman Kolodkin, Second Report on Immunity of State Officials from Foreign Criminal Jurisdiction, UN Doc. A/CN.4/631, para. 57 (2010) ('The viewpoint, whereby grave crimes under international law cannot be considered as acts performed in an official capacity, and immunity *ratione materiae* does not therefore protect from foreign criminal jurisdiction exercised in connection with such crimes, has become fairly widespread' (internal citations omitted)).

[219] *Yousuf v. Samantar*, 699 F.3d 763 (4th Cir. 2012) *cert. denied*, 134 S. Ct. 897 (US 2014); *see Samantar v. Yousuf*, 560 US 305 (2010).

[220] *Jones v. Ministry of the Interior of Saudi Arabia and Lieutenant Colonel Abdul Aziz*, House of Lords (UK), [2006] UKHL 26; *see Jones v. United Kingdom*, ECtHR, Nos. 34356/06 & 40528/06 (2014).

In *Samantar*, Somali natives brought a civil suit in US district court against the former Prime Minister of Somalia, Mohamed Ali Samantar, for *jus cogens* violations including acts of torture.[221] In the first phase of the case, the Supreme Court distinguished the acts of an individual official from those of the State for purposes of sovereign immunity under the Foreign Sovereign Immunities Act (FSIA).[222] The Court held that a foreign official, sued as an individual for conduct undertaken in his official capacity, is not a 'foreign State' for purposes of sovereign immunity and that the FSIA, in turn, is not controlling on the matter.[223] This follows, the Court reasoned, because 'the immunity of the foreign state extends to an individual for acts taken in his official capacity', but not to acts beyond this scope, indicating that an assessment of the individual conduct in question for the purposes of attribution must precede a determination of sovereign immunity.[224] The Court thus refuted the notion that foreign officials were to be automatically afforded immunity as States under the FSIA for *jus cogens* violations[225] and rejected the reasoning of the US Ninth Circuit Court of Appeals in *Chuidian*, which had found the FSIA inapplicable only to *ultra vires* conduct by State officials.[226] The same distinction between the individual and State conduct is implicit in the Torture Victim Protection Act, which provides a civil cause of action against individual officials for torture committed on behalf of the State under 'actual or apparent authority, or under color of

[221] *Samantar v. Yousuf*, 560 US 305, 308 (2010) (Samantar also held the rank of First Vice President and Minister of Defense).

[222] *Ibid.* In 1976, the US Congress enacted the FSIA to codify the 'restrictive theory' of sovereign immunity existing in common law. *See* 28 USC § 1602 *et seq*. The FSIA is 'the sole basis for obtaining [subject-matter] jurisdiction over a foreign state in our courts'. *Argentine Republic v. Amerada Hess Shipping Corp*., 488 US 428, 434 (1989).

[223] *Ibid*., 325 ('we think this case, in which respondents have sued petitioner in his personal capacity and seek damages from his own pockets, is properly governed by the common law because it is not a claim against a foreign state as the Act defines that term').

[224] *Ibid*., 322.

[225] *Cf. Matar v. Dichter*, 563 F.3d 6 (2nd Cir. 2009) (deference to executive branch recognition of immunity *ratione materiae* for *jus cogens* violations by former head of Israeli Security Agency); *Belhas v. Ya'alon*, 515 F.3d 1279 (DC Cir. 2008) (retired head of Israeli army intelligence granted State immunity under FSIA for *jus cogens* violations).

[226] *Chuidian v. Philippine National Bank*, 912 F.2d 1095, 1098 (9th Cir. 1990) *abrogated by Samantar v. Yousuf*, 560 US 305 (2010) ('Federal courts have jurisdiction over suits against foreign sovereigns under the Foreign Sovereign Immunity Act . . . Nevertheless, we do not base our jurisdiction on the Act. To do so would be insufficient for this case because some of the claims presented do not raise an issue of sovereign immunity [because they do not involve sovereign acts]').

law'.[227] The holding authoritatively rejected the proposition that suit against an official for conduct on behalf of the State automatically equates to a suit against that official's State,[228] an assertion that prejudges the question of attribution.

On remand from the Supreme Court, Samantar renewed his motion to dismiss his case based on immunity *ratione personae*, as he was Head of State of Somalia at the time of the offences, and immunity *ratione materiae*, given that the conduct in question was undertaken in the discharge of his official duties.[229] The Fourth Circuit, citing the application of immunities *ratione personae* and *ratione materiae* in domestic criminal proceedings for *jus cogens* violations, determined that 'American courts have generally followed the foregoing trend, concluding that *jus cogens* violations are not legitimate official acts and therefore do not merit foreign official immunity but still recognizing that head-of-state immunity, based on status, is of an absolute nature and applies even against *jus cogens* claims.'[230] Consequently, as in the criminal context, immunity *ratione materiae* was found inapplicable in civil proceedings for *jus cogens* violations because such acts cannot be considered 'official acts' for the purposes of responsibility and sovereign immunity:

> Unlike private acts that do not come within the scope of foreign official immunity, *jus cogens* violations may well be committed under color of law and, in that sense, constitute acts performed in the course of the foreign official's employment by the Sovereign. However, as a matter of international and domestic law, *jus cogens* violations are, by definition, acts that are not officially authorized by the Sovereign.[231]

The Fourth Circuit indicated that this must be so as a matter of logic, 'because no state officially condones' *jus cogens* violations, so 'few such acts, if any, would fall under the rubric of "official actions" taken in the course of an official's duties'.[232] In a different proceeding, the Ninth Circuit indicated that, regardless of whether such conduct is officially

227 *See* 28 USC § 1350 note § 2(a)(1) ('an individual who, under actual or apparent authority, or color of law, of any foreign nation . . . subjects an individual to torture shall, in a civil action, be liable for damages to that individual').

228 *Cf.* Curtis Bradley & Jack Goldsmith, *Foreign Sovereign Immunity, Individual Officials, and Human Rights Litigation*, 13 Green Bag 2D 9, 13 (2009) ('a suit against an individual official for actions carried out on behalf of the state is in reality a suit against the foreign state').

229 *Yousuf v. Samantar*, 699 F.3d 767 (4th Cir. 2012) *cert. denied*, 134 S. Ct. 897 (US 2014).

230 *Ibid.*, 776.

231 *Ibid.*, 775–6.

232 *Ibid.*, 777 (quoting Senate Report No. 102–249, 8 (1991) (regarding the Torture Victim Protection Act)).

condoned by the State, the controlling rationale is that '[i]nternational law does not recognize an act that violates *jus cogens* as a sovereign act'.[233] Adopting this reasoning, the Fourth Circuit concluded in *Samantar* that, 'under international and domestic law, officials from other countries are not entitled to foreign official immunity for *jus cogens* violations, even if the acts were performed in the defendant's official capacity'.[234] Samantar could not benefit from immunity *ratione personae* because he no longer occupied a position conferring such immunity. On 13 January 2014, the Supreme Court denied *certiorari* in the *Samantar* case, leaving the Fourth Circuit's holding intact.

The House of Lords reached a different conclusion in *Jones v. Ministry of the Interior of Saudi Arabia and Lieutenant Colonel Abdul Aziz*,[235] a claim brought in the courts of England against Saudi Arabia and Lieutenant Colonel Abdul Aziz in his individual capacity for acts of torture. The case concerned an appeal by the Kingdom of Saudi Arabia from a decision by the England Court of Appeal, which unanimously held that, while service against the State of Saudi Arabia was properly denied by the government, claims against the individual defendant for acts of torture were not precluded by immunity *ratione materiae* and must be allowed to proceed.[236] Departing from his own comments in *Pinochet*, Lord Justice Phillips, writing for the Court of Appeal, concluded:

> On reflection I have concluded that the argument does not run . . . If civil proceedings are brought against individuals for acts of torture in circumstances where the state is immune from suit *ratione personae*, there can be no suggestion that the state is vicariously liable. It is the personal responsibility of the individuals, not that of the state, which is in issue. The state is not indirectly impleaded by the proceedings.[237]

The House of Lords disagreed,[238] finding that acts of torture constitute official acts, given that the Torture Convention expressly envisages

233 *Siderman de Blake v. Republic of Argentina*, 965 F.2d 699, 718 (9th Cir. 1992).

234 *Yousuf v. Samantar*, 699 F.3d 763, 777 (4th Cir. 2012) *cert. denied*, 134 S. Ct. 897 (US 2014).

235 *Jones v. Ministry of the Interior of Saudi Arabia and Lieutenant Colonel Abdul Aziz*, House of Lords (UK), [2006] UKHL 26 (on appeal, a second claim was heard alongside that of Jones).

236 *Jones v. Ministry of the Interior of Saudi Arabia and Lieutenant Colonel Abdul Aziz*, [2004] EWCA Civ 1394, paras. 99 (Mance, L. J.), 100 (Neuberger, L. J.), 101 (Phillips, L. J.).

237 *Ibid.*, para. 128 (Phillips, L. J.).

238 *Jones v. Ministry of the Interior of Saudi Arabia and Lieutenant Colonel Abdul Aziz*, House of Lords (UK), [2006] UKHL 26., paras. 30–1 (Bingham, L.), 83–5 (Hoffmann, L.).

torture by a public official acting under colour of law.[239] The Lords distinguished *Pinochet* as a criminal case, which could have no bearing on immunity before civil proceedings,[240] and determined that acts of officials are equated with acts of the State itself, attracting 'an absolute preliminary bar, precluding any examination of the merits'.[241] Accordingly, the House of Lords reversed the Court of Appeal and restored the government's denial of permission to serve process against Aziz.[242]

Jones challenged the decision of the House of Lords before the ECtHR.[243] The case proceeded as one concerning the right of access to a court under Article 6 of the European Convention on Human Rights (ECHR),[244] and whether granting blanket State immunity to a State official for acts of torture disproportionately interfered with that right.[245] The ECtHR determined on 14 January 2014 that the UK had not breached the applicants' Article 6 right of access.[246] In considering the matter, the ECtHR discussed at length the absolute immunity of the State under the UK State Immunity Act (1978),[247] the European Convention on State Immunity (1972),[248] and the United Nations Convention on Jurisdictional Immunities of States and Their Property (2004),[249] the latter of which defines 'State' to include representatives of the State acting in that capacity and includes no '*jus cogens* exception'.[250] In considering whether acts of officials as individuals can be distinguished from acts of

239 *Ibid.*, paras. 19 (Bingham, L.), 83 (Hoffmann, L.). *See* Torture Convention (1984), Article 1(1) ('For the purposes of this Convention, the term "torture" means any act by which severe pain or suffering ... is inflicted by or at the instigation of or with the consent or acquiescence of a public official or other person acting in an official capacity').

240 *Ibid.*, paras. 19, 32 (Bingham, L.), 46, 71 (Hoffmann, L.).

241 *Ibid.*, paras. 33 (Bingham, L.), 68 (Hoffmann, L.) ('state immunity affords individual employees or officers of a foreign state protection under the same cloak as protects the state itself' (internal quotation marks omitted)).

242 *Ibid.*, paras. 35 (Bingham, L.), 102 (Hoffmann, L.), 103 (Rodger, L.), 104 (Walker, L.), 105 (Carswell, L.).

243 *Jones v. United Kingdom*, ECtHR, Nos. 34356/06 & 40528/06 (2014).

244 European Convention for the Protection of Human Rights and Fundamental Freedoms, as amended by Protocols Nos. 11 and 14, ETS No. 5, Article 3 (4 November 1950, *entered into force* 3 September 1953).

245 *Jones v. United Kingdom*, ECtHR, Nos. 34356/06 & 40528/06, para. 3 (2014).

246 *Ibid.*, para. 215. 247 State Immunity Act, 1978, c. 33, §§ 1–2 (UK).

248 European Convention on State Immunity, ETS No. 74, Article 15 (16 May 1972, *entered into force* 6 June 1976).

249 UN Convention on Jurisdictional Immunities of States and their Property, UN Doc. A/59/508, Article 2(1)(b) (2 December 2004).

250 *Jones v. United Kingdom*, ECtHR, Nos. 34356/06 & 40528/06, paras. 76–9 (2014).

the State, the ECtHR quoted the House of Lords, which reached the opposite outcome to the US Supreme Court in *Samantar I*:

> [C]ustomary international law did not admit of any exception – regarding allegations of conduct amounting to torture – to the general rule of immunity *ratione materiae* for State officials in the sphere of civil claims where immunity is enjoyed by the State itself.[251]

Because claims against a foreign official were viewed as tantamount to impleading the foreign State, which enjoys absolute State immunity, those claims were also barred by sovereign immunity,[252] practically transforming immunity *ratione materiae* into a form of immunity *ratione personae*. The ECtHR also distinguished between the application of immunity *ratione materiae* in the criminal and civil contexts and, citing 'little national case-law concerning civil claims lodged against named State officials for *jus cogens* violations', concluded that 'State practice on the question is in a state of flux'.[253] As such, the decision by the House of Lords was found neither arbitrary nor manifestly erroneous.[254]

The *Samantar* and *Jones* cases illustrate disharmony in contemporary jurisprudence regarding the applicability of immunity *ratione materiae* in civil proceedings against State officials for *jus cogens* violations. Both extraterritorial criminal and civil proceedings for *jus cogens* violations rely upon the same basis of jurisdiction: universal jurisdiction.[255] However, it would go too far to propose generally that universal jurisdiction 'prevail[s] over the prior rule according immunity *ratione materiae*',[256]

[251] *Ibid.*, para. 214. [252] *Ibid.*, paras. 175, 207. [253] *Ibid.*, paras. 210–13.

[254] *Ibid.*, para. 214.

[255] Roman Kolodkin, Second Report on Immunity of State Officials from Foreign Criminal Jurisdiction, UN Doc. A/CN.4/631, para. 66, *n.* 159 (2010) ('The question arises as to whether it can in principle be said that the consequences for immunity of prohibiting grave international crimes by *jus cogens* norms may be different depending on what kind of jurisdiction is being exercised – civil or criminal. Neither practice nor logic appear to show that such consequences would differ... If a peremptory norm prevails over immunity, then immunity from which jurisdiction – civil or criminal – is of no account. And vice versa. All the more so since sometimes the two types of jurisdiction exercised are very close – for example, when a civil action is brought and is considered within the scope of a criminal case'). *See Sosa v. Alvarez-Machain*, 542 US 692, 762–3 (2004) (Breyer, J., Concurring).

[256] *See* Dapo Akande, *International Law Immunities and the International Criminal Court*, 98(3) American Journal of International Law 407, 415 (2004); *R. v. Bow Street Metropolitan Stipendiary Magistrate and Others, Ex parte Pinochet Ugarte (No.* 3*)*, House of Lords (UK), [2000] 1 A.C. 147, 38 ILM 581, 661 (1999) (Phillips, L.) ('Once

for, as the International Court has noted, 'jurisdiction does not imply absence of immunity, while absence of immunity does not imply jurisdiction'.[257] Therefore, what is at issue remains the immunity applicable where jurisdiction lies.

Resolution of this issue appears to turn, in part, on whether or not there is a meaningful distinction between the immunities applicable to criminal and civil proceedings. Writing in dissent in *Jones*,[258] Judge Kaaydjiva found 'it difficult to accept that general differences between criminal and civil law justif[y] a distinction in the application of immunity in the two contexts'.[259] The Judge also expressed scepticism over how civil proceedings against a State official constituted a greater interference with the State than criminal proceedings,[260] a premise necessary to recognize immunity from civil suit notwithstanding the obligation *erga omnes* to extradite or prosecute under the Torture Convention.[261] The US approach denies such a distinction,[262] which parallels immunities jurisprudence from criminal prosecutions before domestic courts.[263] This approach is implicit in civil law countries such as France,[264] where civil and criminal proceedings may commence together.[265]

Conversely, Commonwealth courts, as affirmed by the ECtHR in *Jones*, have maintained a distinction in the application of immunities between criminal and civil proceedings. One would presume that the determination of an 'official act' should not depend on whether the

extra-territorial jurisdiction is established, it makes no sense to exclude from it acts done in an official capacity').

257 *Arrest Warrant of 11 April 2000 (Democratic Republic of the Congo v. Belgium)*, ICJ Reports 2002, p. 3, para. 59; *see* Anthony Colangelo, *Jurisdiction, Immunity, Legality, and Jus Cogens*, 14(1) Chicago Journal of International Law 53, 81 (2013) ('This sort of heaping implication upon implication strains the international lawyer's fidelity to discerning international law from actual state practice and *opinio juris*').

258 *Jones v. United Kingdom*, ECtHR, Nos. 34356/06 & 40528/06 (2014) (Kalaydjieva, J., Dissenting).

259 *Ibid.* (internal quotation marks omitted).

260 *Ibid.*

261 Torture Convention (1984), Article 5(2).

262 *Yousuf v. Samantar*, 699 F.3d 763, 776 (4th Cir. 2012) *cert. denied*, 134 S. Ct. 897 (US 2014).

263 *See, e.g., R. v. Bow Street Metropolitan Stipendiary Magistrate and Others, Ex parte Pinochet Ugarte (No. 3)*, House of Lords (UK), [2000] 1 A.C. 147, 38 ILM 581 (1999).

264 *See, e.g., Ely Ould Dah Case*, Gard Assizes Court (France), No. 70/05 (Arrêt de condamnation) / No. 71/05 (Arrêt statuant sur les intérêts civils) (2005); *see Ould Dah v. France*, No. 13113/03, 48 ILM 884, 885 (2009).

265 *See* discussion *supra*, text accompanying *nn.* 46–53.

proceeding against an individual is criminal or civil.[266] But this distinction prevails where immunity *ratione materiae* has barred civil litigation for *jus cogens* violations. Lords Bingham and Hoffmann concluded in *Jones* that, because the Torture Convention applied specifically to torture by 'a public official or other person acting in an official capacity',[267] all such acts must fall within the scope of immunity *ratione materiae* as official acts.[268] Immunity *ratione materiae* in civil proceedings for torture, by this reasoning, is coextensive with the crime: 'if they are official enough to come within the Convention, I cannot see why they are not official enough to attract immunity'.[269] This is an express departure from the position taken by the House of Lords in *Pinochet*, where Lord Millett concluded that 'there was no immunity to be waived' because immunity *ratione materiae* 'could not possibly be available [to a *jus cogens* violation]'.[270] In effect, the House of Lords found the *jus cogens* violation of torture in *Pinochet* could not constitute an 'official act' in a criminal prosecution yet in *Jones* concluded that torture by State officials is always an 'official act' attracting immunity in a civil proceeding.

One point of departure between *Samantar* and *Jones* is the legal explanation for the inapplicability of immunity: whether the Torture Convention or *jus cogens* does the heavy lifting. While reliance on the Torture Convention cabins the inapplicability of immunity *ratione materiae* to criminal proceedings, domestic proceedings contemplating immunity for *jus cogens* violations frequently rely on the *jus cogens* nature of the norm to justify non-recognition of immunity *ratione materiae*.[271] A second point of departure between the two proceedings is that the Fourth Circuit's 2012 decision in *Samantar* was preceded by

[266] *But see Jones v. Ministry of the Interior of Saudi Arabia and Lieutenant Colonel Abdul Aziz*, House of Lords (UK), [2006] UKHL 26, para. 32 (Bingham, L.) ('the distinction between criminal proceedings ... and civil proceedings ... was fundamental to [the *Pinochet*] decision').

[267] Torture Convention (1984), Article 1(1).

[268] *Jones v. Ministry of the Interior of Saudi Arabia and Lieutenant Colonel Abdul Aziz*, House of Lords (UK), [2006] UKHL 26., paras. 19 (Bingham, L.), 83 (Hoffmann, L.).

[269] *Ibid.*, para. 83 (Hoffmann, L.).

[270] *R. v. Bow Street Metropolitan Stipendiary Magistrate and Others, Ex parte Pinochet Ugarte (No. 3)*, House of Lords (UK), [2000] 1 A.C. 147, 38 ILM 581 (1999), 651 (Millett, L.) ('International law cannot be supposed to have established a crime having the character of a *jus cogens* and at the same time to have provided an immunity which is co-extensive with the obligation it seeks to impose').

[271] *See* Orakhelashvili, *State Immunity and Hierarchy of Norms*, 969 (noting that the Law Lords considered the Torture Convention and *jus cogens* to be distinct, authoritative rationales for the denial of immunity *ratione materiae* for acts of torture).

the Supreme Court's determination that acts of the individual are distinguishable from those of the State.[272] Commonwealth countries have not reached the conclusions of the *Samantar* holding in the civil context, a critical step towards the conclusion that *jus cogens* violations cannot constitute 'official acts'. Instead, courts in those countries have ruled consistently with *Jones* in New Zealand,[273] and Australia,[274] that immunity *ratione materiae* is 'incidentally conferred' by the jurisdictional immunity of the State. The US approach, a structural analysis focusing on the subjects of suit – the individual or the State – rather than the nature of the suit – civil or criminal, alleviates tensions arising in this area of jurisprudence. The Commonwealth approach, by contrast, lends itself to the legal error of lumping individual immunity from subject-matter jurisdiction together with the jurisdictional immunity of the State,[275] insofar as the procedural immunity of the State from civil suit before domestic courts is taken to be determinative of the immunity *rationae materiae* of State officials in civil suits for *jus cogens* violations,[276] a linkage rejected by the ECtHR in *Jones*.[277]

Reconciliation of this divergence is complicated by the fact that each approach involved the statutory interpretation of domestic legislation purporting to codify customary international law.[278] This context explains why *Samantar* concerned the application of immunity under common law in the absense of a controlling statute, while

[272] *Samantar v. Yousuf*, 560 US 305, 325 (2010).

[273] *Fang v. Jiang*, High Court (New Zealand), [2007] NZAR 420, ILDC 1226 (2006) (civil claims against former members of Chinese government for *jus cogens* violations dismissed).

[274] *Zhang v. Zemin*, New South Wales Court of Appeal (Australia), [2010] NSWCA 255 (civil claim for *jus cogens* violations against the former President of China dismissed).

[275] *See Jones v. Ministry of the Interior of Saudi Arabia and Lieutenant Colonel Abdul Aziz*, House of Lords (UK), [2006] UKHL 26, para. 84 (Hoffman, L.), paras. 18, 25 (Bingham, L.) ('The Grand Chamber's decision in *Al-Adsani* is very much in point, since it concerned the grant of immunity to Kuwait under the 1978 [State Immunity] Act, which had the effect of defeating the applicant's claim in England for damages for torture allegedly inflicted upon him in Kuwait').

[276] Bradley & Goldsmith, *Foreign Sovereign Immunity, Individual Officials, and Human Rights Litigation*, 13 (favouring this position).

[277] *Jones v. United Kingdom*, ECtHR, Nos. 34356/06 & 40528/06, para. 205 (2014) ('The fact that there is no general *jus cogens* exception as regards State immunity rules is therefore not determinative as regards claims against named State officials').

[278] *Compare* Foreign Sovereign Immunity Act, 28 USC § 1602 *et seq.* (1976), *with* State Immunity Act, 1978, c. 33, §§ 1–2 (UK) *and* European Convention on State Immunity, ETS No. 74, Article 15 (16 May 1972, *entered into force* 6 June 1976).

Jones concerned exceptions to a statute found to be controlling. Which approach more closely conforms to the application of immunity *ratione materiae* under customary international law might be inferred from consistency with the application of immunity *ratione materiae* in domestic criminal prosecutions for *jus cogens* violations, which too is governed by customary international law.

***

The jurisprudence of criminal prosecution for *jus cogens* violations, before both international and domestic fora, supports the proposition that such conduct does not constitute 'official acts' of State officials because *jus cogens* violations cannot be sanctioned by the sovereign as a matter of international law. As such, the immunity *ratione materiae* that shields the official acts of individuals does not extend to *jus cogens* violations, even if such acts are undertaken 'under the color of law'.[279] The common application of this principle across both international and domestic fora suggests that the principle underlying sovereign immunity, *par in parem non habet imperium*, is not implicated where State officials are prosecuted for *jus cogens* violations. Immunity *ratione materiae* prevents the immunity of the State from being bypassed by simply naming State officials; however, because *jus cogens* violations fall beyond the official conduct of the State, they are not properly considered sovereign acts. Therefore, prosecution of such acts does not implicitly implead the State in criminal proceedings, this accounting for the common inapplicability of immunity *ratione materiae* in criminal proceedings in domestic as well as international courts. This conclusion presupposes that *jus cogens* limits sovereignty in such a way as to preclude the State from officially authorizing violations of peremptory norms.

The ILC *special rapporteur* on jurisdictional immunities rejected a distinction based on the criminal or civil nature of proceedings as

[279] *See, e.g.*, Orakhelashvili, Peremptory Norms in International Law 325 ('if foreign courts adjudicate a breach of *jus cogens* such as torture they do not infringe on the sovereignty of the State in which that breach took place: a violation of *jus cogens* is not a sovereign act and attracts no immunity'); Salvatore Zappalà, *Do Heads of State in Office Enjoy Immunity from Jurisdiction for International Crimes? The* Ghaddafi *Case before the French* Cour de Cassation, 12(3) European Journal of International Law 595, 601 (2001) ('It is generally agreed that an exception to functional immunity exists in cases where the individual is responsible for crimes under international customary law').

contrary to both practice and logic.[280] Those arguing otherwise maintain that civil proceedings more directly implead the State than criminal prosecution because the former more closely resemble proceedings that might be brought against the State itself; therefore civil immunities should accordingly be broader.[281] Importantly, however, some legal systems conduct parallel civil and criminal proceedings, or initiate civil claims in the context of criminal proceedings.[282] In many civil law countries, this process, *action civile*, enables plaintiffs to attach civil claims to criminal prosecutions.[283] Divergence between immunities applicable to criminal and civil proceedings for *jus cogens* violations would produce the absurd result of immunizing State officials from such civil proceedings brought in conjunction with criminal charges for which no such immunity would apply.

The outcome reached by the House of Lords in *Jones*, which relies on just such a distinction, might best be viewed through a political lens. While the government retains control over public criminal indictments, it does not retain that control over private civil litigation,[284] creating potentially 'serious consequences for both the development and expression of the Nation's foreign policy'.[285] The United States has mitigated this lack of control by deferring to statements of immunity by the Department of State in civil proceedings, although this authority was called into question vis-à-vis *jus cogens* violations by the *Samantar* decision.[286] Without the ability to assert immunity, there is no 'safety

[280] Roman Kolodkin, Second Report on Immunity of State Officials from Foreign Criminal Jurisdiction, UN Doc. A/CN.4/631, para. 66, *n.* 159 (2010).

[281] *See, e.g., Jones v. Ministry of the Interior of Saudi Arabia and Lieutenant Colonel Abdul Aziz*, House of Lords (UK), [2006] UKHL 26, paras. 30–1 (Bingham, L.).

[282] Roman Kolodkin, Preliminary Report on Immunity of State Officials from Foreign Criminal Jurisdiction, UN Doc. A/CN.4/601, para. 54 (2008).

[283] *See* discussion *supra*, Chapter 12.B (Individual Civil Responsibility).

[284] *See* Curtis Bradley, *The Costs of International Human Rights Litigation*, 2 CHICAGO JOURNAL OF INTERNATIONAL LAW 457, 460 (2001) (civil litigation 'shifts responsibility for official condemnation and sanction of foreign governments away from elected political officials to private plaintiffs and their representatives').

[285] Reply Brief for the United States as Respondent Supporting Petitioner, 7, *Sosa v. Alvarez-Machain*, 542 US 692 (2004) (No. 03–339) (internal quotation marks omitted); *see* Brief for the United States as *Amicus Curiae* Supporting Affirmance, 1–2, *Samantar v. Yousuf*, 560 US 305 (2010) (No. 08–1555) (contemplating 'significant implications' of sovereign immunity 'for the reciprocal treatment of United States officials and for our Nation's foreign relations').

[286] *Yousuf v. Samantar*, 699 F.3d 763, 773 (4th Cir. 2012) *cert. denied*, 134 S. Ct. 897 (U.S. 2014) ('In sum, we give absolute deference to the State Department's position on

valve' by which a State government might ameliorate the potential foreign policy complications that may arise from civil suits by private individuals against State officials. Variation in State practice in the area of immunity *ratione materiae* in civil litigation for *jus cogens* might therefore reflect political reservations inherent in opening national courts to such litigation. The amicus brief submitted by former Attorneys General of the United States in support of Samantar outlines the underlying policy concerns: the application of such precedent to US officials in foreign courts, the uncertainty of immunities jurisprudence, the effect on decision-making by government officials, etc.[287] Such a policy would deny all prospect of relief to victims of *jus cogens* violations, a troubling outcome if a central function of legal order is to 'make whole' persons injured by tortious conduct. Moreover, whatever its merits, this approach raises the very real question of whether immunities should be the domain of law or policy. Today, the doctrine of immunities belongs to customary international law.[288] Policy preferences are improperly imposed under the guise of legal principle in 'a state of flux'.[289]

D Amnesty

Unlike immunities arising in international law, amnesty is a sovereign act under domestic law.[290] Even so, the interaction of *jus cogens* with

status-based immunity doctrines such as head-of-state immunity. The State Department's determination regarding conduct-based immunity, by contrast, is not controlling, but it carries substantial weight in our analysis of the issue [of foreign official immunity for violations of *jus cogens* norms]'). This is not the first time that the discretion of the executive branch to determine the application of immunity has been curtailed: *see* 28 USC § 1602 ('Claims of foreign states to immunity should henceforth be decided by courts of the United States and of the States in conformity with the principles set forth in this chapter').

287 *See* Brief of Amici Curiae Former Attorneys General of the United States in Support of Petitioner, *Yousuf v. Samantar*, 699 F.3d 763 (4th Cir. 2012) *cert. denied*, 134 S. Ct. 897 (US 2014) (No. 12–1078).

288 *Jurisdictional Immunities of the State (Germany v. Italy: Greece Intervening)*, Judgment, ICJ Reports 2012, p. 99, para. 54; *see, e.g.*, David Stewart, Samantar *and the Future of Foreign Official Immunity*, 15(3) Lewis & Clark Law Review 633, 648 (2011) ('International immunities can no longer be considered discretionary or merely a question of grace, comity, or convenience ... such decisions must be founded on a clear relationship to customary international law').

289 *Jones v. United Kingdom*, ECtHR, Nos. 34356/06 & 40528/06, para. 213 (2014).

290 *See* Office of the United Nations High Commissioner for Human Rights, *Rule-of-Law Tools For Post-Conflict States, Amnesties*, UN Doc. HR/PUB/09/1 (2009); Faustin

domestic amnesty laws is no less fraught with considerations of political necessity and comity. An amnesty is a government pardon generally for political offences extended to an entire class, group, or community.[291] Amnesty is generally granted to 'political' crimes against the State and, as such, represents an exercise of sovereign power to forgive political offences. Such an amnesty is distinct from a pardon, which exempts an individual convicted of a crime from punishment, without effect on the underlying offence itself. The implicit rationale underlying amnesty is that forgiveness of political offences on a large scale is more beneficial to a community than prosecution and punishment of the offences themselves.

The application of amnesty to violations of *jus cogens* raises two obvious issues. The first is that violations of *jus cogens* constitute international crimes that are not crimes against the State per se, but rather, crimes against the international community as a whole.[292] Therefore the application of amnesty, as an act of sovereign forgiveness to crimes under international law is inapposite. The second issue, which follows from the first, is that an act of sovereign power by the State is insufficient to affect the obligations *erga omnes* arising from *jus cogens*, the performance of which requires the State to punish violations of *jus cogens* through prosecution or extradition.[293] An individual State lacks the power to relieve itself of obligations arising from peremptory norms, owed to the international community as a whole, just as no derogation is permitted from *jus cogens* by the unilateral conduct of the State.[294] Therefore, a domestic amnesty law that constitutes a serious breach of the obligations *erga omnes* of a State would trigger, under Article 41(2) of the ILC Articles on State Responsibility, 'the obligation of collective non-recognition by the international community as a whole of the legality of situations resulting directly from serious breaches' of such obligations.[295]

Historically, there is substantial practice in which States have granted broad amnesties as part of peace and reconciliation processes.[296] With

Ntoubandi, Amnesty for Crimes against Humanity under International Law 9–38 (Leiden: Martinus Nijhoff 2007) (The Concept of Amnesty).

291 Black's Law Dictionary (West Group, 9th edn. 2009) (Amnesty).

292 *See* discussion *supra*, Chapter 12.A (Individual Criminal Responsibility).

293 *See* discussion *infra*, Chapter 14.C (Punishment and Universal Jurisdiction).

294 *See* discussion *supra*, Chapter 5.C.i (Non-Derogation).

295 ILC Articles on State Responsibility (2001), 114, para. 5 (Commentary to Article 41).

296 *See* Tricia Olsen *et al.*, Transitional Justice in Balance: Comparing Processes, Weighing Efficacy (Washington, DC: United States Institute of Peace Press 2010).

particular respect to the relation of amnesty and *jus cogens*, Judge Cassese presented in his 2003 edition a cautious vision of international law: a State is not precluded from granting domestic amnesty for international crimes, while third-States are under no obligation to recognize such amnesty by refraining from prosecution.[297] According to this view, States as a matter of domestic law are free to grant amnesty for international crimes, but because domestic legislation cannot apply extraterritorially, third-States need not recognize such amnesty. By 2013, however, Judge Cassese had added that *jus cogens* 'may be construed as imposing' an obligation upon States to refrain from granting amnesty to violations of peremptory norms.[298] As a matter of principle and practice, it is necessary to revisit the interaction between *jus cogens* and amnesty in light of subsequent developments before international and domestic courts.

In principle, the grant of amnesty by a State to *jus cogens* violations is invalid insofar as it purports to absolve covered individuals from responsibility for international crimes and is to be accorded no recognition by third-States as a breach of the obligation of the State to punish such offences. These parameters were set out in *dicta* by the ICTY in *Furundžija*, which concluded that an amnesty law that covers *jus cogens* violations exceeded that power of the State and 'would not be accorded international legal recognition'.[299] The tribunal wrote, in the context of the prohibition against torture:

> The fact that torture is prohibited by a peremptory norm of international law has other effects at the inter-state and individual levels. At the inter-state level, it serves to internationally de-legitimise any legislative, administrative or judicial act authorising torture. It would be senseless to argue, on the one hand, that on account of the *jus cogens* value of the prohibition against torture, treaties or customary rules providing for torture would be null and void *ab initio*, and then be unmindful of a State say, taking national measures authorising or condoning torture or absolving its

[297] Antonio Cassese, INTERNATIONAL CRIMINAL LAW 315 (Oxford University Press, 1st edn. 2003) ('There is not yet any general obligation for States to refrain from amnesty laws on these crimes. Consequently, if a State passes any such law, it does not breach a customary rule. Nonetheless if a court of another State having in custody persons accused of international crimes decides to prosecute them although in their national State they would benefit from an amnesty law, such court would not thereby act contrary to general international law, in particular to the principle of respect for the sovereignty of other States').

[298] Antonio Cassese, INTERNATIONAL CRIMINAL LAW 312 (Oxford University Press, 3rd edn. 2013).

[299] *Prosecutor v. Furundžija*, IT-95-17/1-T, para. 155 (1998).

> perpetrators through an amnesty law. If such a situation were to arise, the national measures ... would not be accorded international legal recognition. Proceedings could be initiated by potential victims if they had *locus standi* before a competent international or national judicial body with a view to asking it to hold the national measure to be internationally unlawful; or the victim could bring a civil suit for damage in a foreign court, which would therefore be asked *inter alia* to disregard the legal value of the national authorising act. What is even more important is that perpetrators of torture acting upon or benefiting from those national measures may nevertheless be held criminally responsible for torture, whether in a foreign State, or in their own State under a subsequent regime.[300]

The tribunal's description of the effects of *jus cogens* upon a domestic amnesty law purporting to apply to violations of *jus cogens* reflects legal effects anticipated by the normative hierarchy implicit in *jus cogens*. Amnesty would be invalid as a matter of international law, and would not affect individual criminal responsibility arising under international law; therefore such amnesty would not preclude prosecution before foreign or international courts and tribunals.

The interaction between *jus cogens* and amnesties depicted by the ICTY has been borne out in the practice of international and domestic courts. The following subsections consider jurisprudence concerning the two effects of *jus cogens* on amnesty articulated in *Furundžija*: invalidity of amnesty for purposes of individual criminal responsibility, and non-recognition through the exercise of universal jurisdiction by third-States.

i. Invalidation

Since *Furundžija*, the non-applicability of amnesty to violations of *jus cogens* has been expressly articulated by another international judicial organ, the SCSL. The jurisdiction of the Court was challenged by objections in several proceedings based on the amnesty provisions of Article IX of the Lomé Agreement. In *Prosecutor v. Kallon and Kamara*, defendants claimed that the domestic amnesty of Article IX of the Lomé Agreement precluded international criminal prosecution.[301] The Court disagreed, finding that the grant of amnesty, a sovereign act, was

[300] *Ibid.* (internal citations omitted); para. 157 (noting that statutes of limitations would be similarly inapplicable to *jus cogens* violations).

[301] *Prosecutor v. Kallon and Kamara*, Decision on Challenge to Jurisdiction: Lomé Accord Amnesty, SCSL-04-15-PT-060-I, paras. 60, 66–71 (2004).

insufficient to cover crimes subject to universal jurisdiction.[302] In response to another jurisdictional challenge on the basis of amnesty two months later, the SCSL Appeals Chamber found support in international law 'that there is a crystallized international norm to the effect that a government cannot grant amnesty for serious crimes under international law'.[303] The tribunal therefore concluded that Article IX of the Lomé Agreement could not apply to *jus cogens* violations because States were under a duty to prosecute international crimes, an understanding shared by both the UN Secretary-General as well as Sierra Leone.[304] In a separate decision rendered the same day, the Appeals Chamber determined that a domestic amnesty covering *jus cogens* violations 'would not be accorded legal recognition'.[305] The Court observed that 'state practice is changing to conform with the consistent view' that amnesties for *jus cogens* violations are impermissible.

The inapplicability of domestic amnesties to *jus cogens* violations has also been reflected in several cases before the IACtHR, which has repeatedly found domestic amnesties inapplicable to *jus cogens* violations. Though not a criminal court with jurisdiction over natural persons, the IACtHR has the authority to require States to compensate individuals for certain conduct attributable to the State in accordance with the obligation of the State to prosecute and punish human rights violations.[306] *Barrios Altos v. Peru* (2001) concerned a massacre of fifteen people by the Peruvian army in the *Barrios Altos* neighborhood of Lima, Peru, on 3 November 1991.[307] The Congress of Peru adopted Amnesty Law No. 26479, covering human rights violations from 1980 to 1995, pursuant to which the *Barrios Altos Case* was stayed in Peru. The IACtHR found that

> all amnesty provisions, provisions on prescription and the establishment of measures designed to eliminate responsibility are inadmissible, because they are intended to prevent the investigation and punishment of . . . non-derogable rights recognized by international human rights law.[308]

302 *Ibid.*, para. 71.

303 *Prosecutor v. Gbao*, Decision on Preliminary Motion on the Invalidity of the Agreement between the United Nations and the Government of Sierra Leone on the Establishment of the Special Court for Sierra Leone, SCSL-04-15-PT-141, para. 9 (2004).

304 *Ibid.*, para. 10.

305 *Prosecutor v. Kondewa*, Decision on Lack of Jurisdiction/Abuse of Process, Amnesty Provided by the Lomé Accord, SCSL-0414-T-128-7347, paras. 45–52 (2004) (quoting *Prosecutor v. Furundzija*, IT-95-17/1, para. 155 (1998)).

306 *See* Jo Pasqualucci, The Practice and Procedure of the Inter-American Court of Human Rights 226 (Cambridge University Press 2012).

307 *Barrios Altos Case*, IACtHR Series C No. 75 (2001).

308 *Ibid.*, 41.

The Court reached a similar conclusion in *Almonacid Arellano et al. v. Chile*, which concerned the murder of Almonadic Arellano by Chilean police on 16 September 1973, prior to Chile's ratification of the American Convention on Human Rights (ACHR) and recognition of IACtHR jurisdiction.[309] Chile, moreover, had since enacted Decree Law No. 2.191, purporting to grant amnesty to those responsible for crimes against humanity.[310] The Court found that the prohibition of crimes against humanity belonged to *jus cogens* at the time of the offence at issue, and therefore the general and systematic attack against portions of the civilian population in Chile fell within the Court's jurisdiction.[311] Moreover, the Court found that the domestic amnesty law, to the extent that it presumed to apply to crimes against humanity, had no legal effect.[312] In 2010, the IACtHR considered the validity of Brazil's 1979 amnesty law, Law No. 6.683, which applied to human rights violations 'carried out with political motivation' between 2 September 1961 and 15 August 1979.[313] Shortly before the IACtHR judgment, on 29 April 2010, the Federal Supreme Court of Brazil affirmed the constitutionality of the Amnesty Law.[314] In rendering its judgment, the IACtHR reviewed a substantial body of jurisprudence in which analogous amnesties had been found to be inconsistent with the obligations of States under international law to investigate and, where necessary, prosecute international crimes.[315] The Court linked those obligations to *jus cogens*,[316] and found Brazil's amnesty law to 'lack legal effect' due to 'its express non-compatibility' with the ACHR.[317] Finally, the Court reached a similar conclusion in *Gelman v. Uruguay*, with respect to the Expiry Law of Uruguay, which had prevented investigation into the forced disappearance of María Claudia García Gelman by State officials.[318] Following a review of extensive practice prohibiting amnesty for international crimes in international law,[319] as well as domestic practice across the region,[320] and after recalling the *jus cogens* prohibition of the offence in question,[321] the Court found found Uruguay in breach of its obligation to investigate, prosecute, and punish violations of the ACHR.[322] 'One after another',

[309] *Almonacid Arellano et al. v. Chile*, IACtHR Series C No. 154 (2006).
[310] *Ibid.*, paras. 128–9. [311] *Ibid.*, para. 99. [312] *Ibid.*, paras. 128–9.
[313] *Gomes-Lund et al. (Guerrilha do Araguaia) v. Brazil*, IACtHR Series C No. 219, paras. 134–7 (2010).
[314] *Ibid.*, para. 136. [315] *Ibid.*, paras. 140–71. [316] *Ibid.*, para. 137.
[317] *Ibid.*, para. 174. [318] *Gelman v. Uruguay*, IACtHR Ser. C No. 221 (2011).
[319] *Ibid.*, paras. 195–214. [320] *Ibid.*, paras. 215–24. [321] *Ibid.*, para. 183.
[322] *Ibid.*, para. 240.

domestic amnesty laws have been repealed across the region as a result of the rulings of the IACtHR.[323]

Before domestic courts, the Spanish National Court and Supreme Court of Mexico provide instances of domestic courts finding the amnesty laws of another State in contravention of obligations under international law. In the landmark *Audiencia Nacional* decisions of 4 and 5 November 1998, the Spanish National Court determined that courts of Spain had authority to exercise universal jurisdiction over the international crimes of genocide and terrorism committed in Argentina and Chile.[324] In its reasoning, the National Court found the amnesty laws of those countries to be contrary to *jus cogens* and therefore invalid, apart from the inability of domestic law of third-States to pardon or decriminalize an offence under Spanish (and international) law.[325] 'Irrespective' of whether such a law violated *jus cogens*, the Court wrote, foreign amnesty laws could have no extraterritorial effect to preclude the exercise of universal jurisdiction in Spain.[326] The Supreme Court of Mexico, in *Decision on the Extradition of Ricardo Miguel Cavallo* (2003), similarly determined that the amnesty laws of Argentina, the 'laws of full stop' and the 'law of owed obedience' (*Leyes de Punto Final y Obediencia Debida*), did not preclude Mexico from fulfilling an extradition request by Spain.[327] In recognition that the decision not to respect Argentina's amnesty laws 'harmed the sovereignty of Argentina', the Mexico Supreme Court explained that domestic legislation of Argentina could have no extraterritorial effect in Mexico that would preclude Mexico from discharging its obligation to extradite or prosecute under international law.[328] The Court then went further to observe that each of the

[323] Pasqualucci, The Practice and Procedure of the Inter-American Court of Human Rights 323. *See* discussion *infra*, text accompanying notes 331–43.

[324] *Decision (Auto) of the Full Penal Chamber Confirming Spanish Jurisdiction to Investigate Crimes of Genocide and Terrorism Committed during the Chilean Dictatorship*, National Court (*Audiencia Nacional*) (Spain), No. 173/98, §§ 5–7, 119 ILR 331, 342–4 (1998); *see also Decision (Auto) of the Full Penal Chamber Confirming Spanish Jurisdiction over the Crimes of Genocide and Terrorism committed during the Argentine Dictatorship*, National Court (*Audiencia Nacional*) (Spain), No. 84/98, §§ 8–10 (1998).

[325] *Decision (Auto) of the Full Penal Chamber Confirming Spanish Jurisdiction to Investigate Crimes of Genocide and Terrorism Committed during the Chilean Dictatorship*, National Court (*Audiencia Nacional*) (Spain), No. 173/98, § 8, 119 ILR 331, 344 (1998).

[326] *Ibid.*

[327] *Decision on the Extradition of Ricardo Miguel Cavallo*, Supreme Court (Mexico), No. 712/2003, 42 ILM 888 (2003).

[328] *Ibid.*, 908–9.

States involved was under an obligation to extradite or prosecute war crimes and crimes against humanity under international law, rendering the amnesty law of Argentina in breach of those obligations:

> [T]hese laws were considered contrary to Conventions advanced with the objective of assuring the prosecution and punishment of those responsible for war crimes and crimes against humanity, among which provided for genocide and terrorism. For this reason those amnesty laws were not binding on other member States such as Mexico and Spain, who, in the name of the international community, could exercise extraterritorial jurisdiction, given that in complying with the obligatory rules of international law, this did not constitute a legal authority but rather an obligation . . . With the result that if a State passed laws pursuant to its legislation that contravened these international instruments, these laws would not be binding on other States that had the obligation of prosecuting and punishing those responsible for the international crimes, and since the laws of 'full stop' and the law of 'owed obedience' ('Leyes de Punto Final y Obediencia Debida') are in contravention of the provisions recognized by international law, they could not be recognized and accepted by the Mexican State.[329]

Unlike the Spanish National Court before it, the Supreme Court of Mexico couched non-recognition of the domestic amnesty law in terms of the invalidity of such an amnesty as a violation of the obligation under international law to extradite or prosecute war crimes and crimes against humanity. Although the implications of this linkage will be discussed further below,[330] the reasoning of the Supreme Court of Mexico parallels that of the ICTY in *Furundžija* and the IACtHR in *Barios Altos*, as well as subsequent decisions by the SCSL.

Latin-American jurisprudence demonstrates a concurrent trend in domestic courts towards critical self-evaluation, and rejection, of domestic amnesty laws contrary to obligations arising under international law. In Colombia, following review of the constitutionality of the Rome Statute,[331] both the Constitutional Court[332] and the Supreme Court of Justice[333]

[329] *Ibid.*, 909. [330] *See* discussion *infra*, text accompanying *nn.* 389–92.

[331] *Review of the Constitutionality of the Rome Statute of the International Criminal Court*, Constitutional Court (Colombia), No. C-578/2002, para. 2 (2002) (finding that the protection of human dignity by international law strengthens the normative value of the Constitution of Colombia).

[332] *Gallón Giraldo y Otros v. Colombia*, Constitutional Court (Colombia), No. C-370/2006, ILDC 660, para. 4.9.6 (2006).

[333] *Segovia Massacre Case*, Supreme Court of Justice (Colombia), No. 156, 68 (2010) (*reproduced in Gomes-Lund et al. (Guerrilha do Araguaia) v. Brazil*, IACtHR Series

recognized that amnesty laws to promote the demobilization of paramilitary and guerrilla groups must conform with Colombia's obligations under international law, with specific reference to *jus cogens*. The Supreme Court of Argentina similarly found amnesty laws promulgated following Argentina's period of dictatorship to be in breach of Argentina's international law obligations and, therefore, invalid and unconstitutional[334]; Justices Boggiano and Maquedo, writing in concurrence, indicated that the amnesty laws violated *jus cogens* insofar as the prohibition of crimes against humanity was in force as a matter of customary international law at the time of the crimes, and therefore obligated prosecution.[335] The Constitutional Court of Peru found that amnesty laws applied to human rights violations during the Fujimori regime exceeded the domestic authority to grant amnesty by contravening the obligation to guarantee and protect rights arising from human dignity under international law (a principle also enshrined in the Constitution of Peru),[336] and were thereby null and void.[337] This determination was responsive to the judgment by the IACtHR in *Barios Altos*, which found the amnesty law of Peru to be invalid under international law.[338] The Supreme Court of Chile nullified its Pinochet-era amnesty law in 2007, finding that obligations arising under international law – particularly obligations arising from the Geneva Conventions and *jus cogens* to prevent and punish crimes against humanity – were beyond the scope of such domestic amnesty,[339] with amnesty in such circumstances constituting an 'affront to human dignity'[340] that 'offend[ed] the human conscience'.[341] Finally, in view of this precedent, the Uruguay Supreme Court of Justice determined that an amnesty provision enacted to shield military and police officials from prosecution for human rights violations was an unconstitutional

C No. 219, para. 169 (2010) ('the norms related to [h]uman [r]ights form part of the great group of provisions of General International Law, those of which are recognized as *ius cogens* norms, [the] reason for which, they are irrevocable, imperative . . . and non-disposable').

334 *Simón v. Office of the Public Prosecutor*, Supreme Court of Justice (Argentina), S/1767/XXXVIII, ILDC 579 (2005) (concerning the 1986 Full Stop Law and the 1987 Law of Due Obedience).

335 *Ibid.*, paras. 40–3 (Boggiano, J., Concurring), 45 (Maqueda, J., Concurring).

336 *Case of Santiago Martín Rivas*, Supreme Court (Peru) (Constitutional and Social Chamber), No. 679-2005-PA/TC, ILDC 960, paras. 26–33, 58 (2007) (concerning Laws 26479 and 26492).

337 *Ibid.*, para. 60.

338 *Barrios Altos Case*, IACtHR Series C No. 75 (2001).

339 *Re Víctor Raúl Pinto v. Relatives of Tomás Rojas*, Supreme Court (Chile), Decision on Annulment, No. 3125-04, ILDC 1093, paras. 23, 39 (2007) (concerning Decree Law 2191).

340 *Ibid.*, para. 27.

341 *Ibid.*, para. 31.

infringement on the judicial authority to regulate the expiry of criminal proceedings[342] and contravened human rights originating beyond the sovereignty of the State.[343]

Two exceptions to this trend of self-invalidation of domestic amnesty laws in relation to international law obligations are found in South Africa and Spain. In 1996 – prior to each of the decisions discussed in this part above – the Constitutional Court of South Africa considered whether its amnesty laws following the end of apartheid conformed to its international law obligations.[344] The Azanian Peoples Organization challenged the constitutionality of the amnesty provision under international law, as incorporated by the 1996 Constitution of South Africa.[345] The Constitutional Court considered that, because the amnesty law was promulgated pursuant to a directive in the Constitution of South Africa, the amnesty law itself came into force through authority of the Constitution.[346] Therefore, the amnesty law was by its nature consistent with the Constitution, a finding that rendered any consideration of international law obligations 'irrelevant'.[347] Although the Constitutional Court avoided the issue of *jus cogens* entirely, the lower Cape Provisional Division of the Supreme Court found it unnecessary by the same

342 *Case of de Nibia Sabalsagaray Curutchet*, Supreme Court of Justice (Uruguay), No. 365/09, paras. 13, 15 (2009) (concerning Law 15.848 (Expiry Law): 'the unlawfulness of an amnesty law enacted ... [contrary to human rights protections under international law] has been declared by courts, of both the international community and the States that went through similar processes experienced by Uruguay during the same period in time') (*reproduced in Gomes-Lund et al. (Guerrilha do Araguaia) v. Brazil*, IACtHR Series C No. 219, para. 167 (2010)).

343 *Ibid.*, para. 6 ('current regulation of human rights is not based on the position of sovereign States, but in the person as holder, given his or her status as such, of essential rights that can not be ignored based on the exercise of the constituent power, neither original nor derivative').

344 Promotion of National Unity and Reconciliation Act, No. 34 of 1995 (promulgated by the South African National Assembly to investigate human rights violations committed during the apartheid period between March 1960 and May 1994, the Act created an Amnesty Committee with the power to grant civil and criminal amnesty to individuals disclosing human rights violations committed in relation to apartheid).

345 *Azanian Peoples Organization ('AZAPO') and ors v. President of South Africa and ors*, Constitutional Court (South Africa), No. CCT 17/96, 1996 (4) SA 671 (CC), ILDC 648 (1996).

346 *Ibid.*, para. 14.

347 *Ibid.*, para. 26 ('The issue which falls to be determined in this Court is whether section 20 (7) of the Act is inconsistent with the Constitution. If it is, the enquiry as to whether or not international law prescribes a different duty is irrelevant to that determination. International law ... [is] relevant only in the interpretation of the Constitution itself').

reasoning 'to consider further the applicability of [] *jus cogens* to the interpretation of the constitution'.[348] This approach to obligations arising under international law, as 'trumped' by contrary provisions of constitutional law, is backward with respect to obligations *erga omnes* arising from *jus cogens* owed to the international community.[349] To support its finding, the Constitutional Court looked to similar laws enacted in Chile, Argentina, and El Salvador,[350] all of which have since been found to be inconsistent with obligations related to *jus cogens* under international law.[351] The Court narrowly consulted obligations arising under the Geneva Conventions, where it endorsed an exception for amnesty following non-international armed conflict in Additional Protocol II to the Geneva Conventions,[352] while maintaining that such rules were nevertheless irrelevant given the constitutionality of the act.[353] The Court made no attempt to reconcile its holding with South Africa's obligation to prosecute international crimes, and its treatment of amnesty in this context was contemporaneously described as 'a disregard for international law'.[354] Although the ruling was clearly a pragmatic response to challenges facing the newly formed democratic government of South Africa,[355] the

[348] *Azanian Peoples Organization and ors v. Truth and Reconciliation Commission and ors*, Cape Provincial Division of the Supreme Court (South Africa), 1996 (4) SA 562 (C) (1996) (quoted in commentary by H. Strydom at ILDC 648 (12 April 2010)).

[349] Constitution of the Republic of South Africa, No. 108 of 1996, § 232 ('Customary international law is law in the Republic unless it is inconsistent with the Constitution or an Act of Parliament').

[350] *Azanian Peoples Organization ('AZAPO') and ors v. President of South Africa and ors*, Constitutional Court (South Africa), No. CCT 17/96, 1996 (4) SA 671 (CC), ILDC 648, paras. 22–4 (1996).

[351] *See* discussion *supra*, Chapter 12.D.i (Invalidation).

[352] Additional Protocol II (1977), Article 6(5).

[353] *Azanian Peoples Organization ('AZAPO') and ors v. President of South Africa and ors*, Constitutional Court (South Africa), No. CCT 17/96, 1996 (4) SA 671 (CC), ILDC 648, paras. 28–31 (1996).

[354] John Dugard, *Kaleidoscope: International Law and the South African Constitution*, 1 European Journal of International Law 77, 88–91 (1997).

[355] *Azanian Peoples Organization ('AZAPO') and ors v. President of South Africa and ors*, Constitutional Court (South Africa), No. CCT 17/96, 1996 (4) SA 671 (CC), ILDC 648, para. 45 (1996) ('The election made by the makers of the Constitution was to permit Parliament to favour "the reconstruction of society" involving in the process a wider concept of "reparation", which would allow the state to take into account the competing claims on its resources but, at the same time, to have regard to the "untold suffering" of individuals and families whose fundamental human rights had been invaded during the conflict of the past').

reasoning of the Court is inconsistent with subsequent jurisprudence on the relation of *jus cogens* and domestic amnesty.

While the decision by the Constitutional Court of South Africa had the benefit of preceding international jurisprudence that would directly refute its reasoning, the same is not true of a 2012 decision by the Supreme Court of Spain, which is ironic given that a 1998 decision by the Spanish National Court began the movement towards judging domestic amnesties against international law obligations.[356] In a complex decision rendered on 27 February 2012,[357] the Supreme Court considered criminal charges arising from acts of genocide, torture, and terrorism committed during the Spanish Civil War and the Franco dictatorship. At issue was a 2008 Order issued by Judge Baltasar Garzón instituting criminal proceedings against leaders of the Franco regime, applying treaty and customary international law to crimes committed in Spain between 1936 and 1952.[358] Among the obstacles to the 2008 Order was Spain's 1977 amnesty law, Law 46/1977, which was enacted by the country's first democratic parliament to facilitate political transition in Spain by precluding investigation of political crimes committed before 15 December 1976.[359] In quashing Judge Garzón's 2008 Order, the Court determined in part that the Spanish judiciary lacked the authority to apply customary international law for the purposes of criminal prosecution.[360] It further concluded that, even if *jus cogens* rendered the grant of amnesty to international crimes invalid, the Court lacked the authority to annul the amnesty law, which could be repealed only by an act of the legislature.[361] The Court's decision exposes the political challenges arising from the interrelation of amnesty with international law

[356] *Decision (Auto) of the Full Penal Chamber Confirming Spanish Jurisdiction to Investigate Crimes of Genocide and Terrorism Committed during the Chilean Dictatorship*, National Court (*Audiencia Nacional*) (Spain), No. 173/98, § 8, 119 ILR 331, 342–4 (1998); *Decision (Auto) of the Full Penal Chamber Confirming Spanish Jurisdiction over the Crimes of Genocide and Terrorism committed during the Argentine Dictatorship*, National Court (*Audiencia Nacional*) (Spain), No. 84/98, §§ 8–10 (1998) (holding that Spanish courts can exercise jurisdiction committed in Chile and Argentina under universal jurisdiction, and finding amnesty laws of those countries of no relevance).

[357] *Criminal Law Chamber of the Supreme Court et al. v. Garzón Real*, Supreme Court (Spain), No. 101/2012, ILDC 1855 (2012).

[358] *Ibid.*, para. 3.

[359] Amnesty Act, No. 46/1977, Article 1 (15 December 1976) ('Amnesty Act').

[360] *Criminal Law Chamber of the Supreme Court et al. v. Garzón Real*, Supreme Court (Spain), No. 101/2012, ILDC 1855, para. 3 (2012).

[361] *Ibid.*

obligations, even where a judiciary is otherwise supportive of *jus cogens*. The judgment is at odds with Spain's own jurisprudence regarding the invalidity of domestic amnesty for violations of *jus cogens*.

ii. Non-recognition

Insofar as the application of amnesty to *jus cogens* violations constitutes a serious breach of the obligations *erga omnes* of a State arising from *jus cogens*, the performance of which requires the State to prosecute *jus cogens* violations, third-States are obligated not to recognize the legality of the situation arising from such a breach.[362] As discussed above, the ICTY reasoned in *Furundžija* that an amnesty law that covers *jus cogens* violations 'would not be accorded international legal recognition'.[363] This proposition has since been applied by the SCSL. In *Prosecutor v. Kallon and Kamara*, defendants claimed that the domestic amnesty of Article IX of the Lomé Agreement precluded international criminal prosecution.[364] The Court rejected that defence, because 'a state cannot sweep such crimes into oblivion and forgetfulness which other states have jurisdiction to prosecute'.[365] According to the Court, notwithstanding whatever domestic effect the Lomé Agreement had on the prosecution of *jus cogens* violations in the national courts of Sierra Leone, it had no effect on the universal jurisdiction of foreign and international courts to prosecute those crimes, and need not be recognized as such.[366] In response to a similar challenge to the Court's jurisdiction in *Prosecutor v. Allieu Kondewa*, the Appeals Chamber went beyond this premise of ineffectiveness and determined that a domestic amnesty covering *jus cogens* violations 'would not be accorded legal recognition'.[367]

The ECtHR has similarly indicated that domestic amnesty for *jus cogens* violations need not be afforded legal recognition by the courts of third-States. In the *Ould Dah* case discussed above,[368] the ECtHR endorsed the decision by the French Court of Assizes to decline to

362 ILC Articles on State Responsibility (2001), Article 41.
363 *Prosecutor v. Furundžija*, IT-95-17/1-T, para. 155 (1998).
364 *Prosecutor v. Kallon and Kamara*, Decision on Challenge to Jurisdiction: Lomé Accord Amnesty, SCSL-04-15-PT-060-I, paras. 60, 66–71 (2004).
365 *Ibid.*, para. 71. 366 *Ibid.*, para. 88.
367 *Prosecutor v. Kondewa*, Decision on Lack of Jurisdiction/Abuse of Process, Amnesty Provided by the Lomé Accord, SCSL-04-14-T-128-7347, paras. 45–52 (2004) (quoting *Prosecutor v. Furundžija*, IT-95-17/1, para. 155 (1998)).
368 *See Ould Dah v. France*, No. 13113/03, 48 ILM 884 (2009).

recognize a domestic amnesty in a criminal prosecution for *jus cogens* violations.[369] Dah participated in an 'ethnic purge' and 'campaign of oppression' in the suppression of a coup in Mauritania, and was later convicted by the French Court of Assizes for acts of torture on 1 July 2005.[370] The case was the first to be brought under the universal jurisdiction provision of the French penal code, which grants French courts jurisdiction where a defendant is present on French territory and the claim is based on certain international conventions.[371] Importantly, on 14 June 1993, prior to these proceedings, Mauritius passed an amnesty law, Law No. 93-23, barring proceedings arising from suppression of the coup. Dah challenged his conviction under Article 7 of the European Convention on Human Rights,[372] claiming that the Mauritian amnesty law had been inappropriately displaced by the French penal code, which was being applied retroactively because French law at the time of the acts did not conceive of a separate crime of torture.[373] The ECtHR dismissed the retroactivity claim given the nature of the offence in question and, finding that the criteria of the French penal code had been satisfied, determined that the Mauritian amnesty law did not preclude application of the French universal jurisdiction provision.[374]

The Montpellier Court of Appeal in France, which heard an earlier phase of the *Dah* case, explicitly denied recognition of the 1993 amnesty law, which purported to extend to the international crime of torture in question.[375] The judge in that opinion determined that such a domestic amnesty provision was not enforceable in third-States and, therefore, could not affect the application of international law in France.[376] The Supreme Court of Mexico, in the above-mentioned *Decision on the*

[369] *Ely Ould Dah Case*, Gard Assizes Court, No. 70/05 (Arrêt de condamnation) / No. 71/05 (Arrêt statuant sur les intérêts civils) (2005); *see Ould Dah v. France*, No. 13113/03, 48 ILM 884, 885 (2009).

[370] *Ould Dah v. France*, No. 13113/03, 48 ILM 884, 885 (2009).

[371] *Ibid.*, 894.

[372] European Convention for the Protection of Human Rights and Fundamental Freedoms, as amended by Protocols Nos. 11 and 14, ETS No. 5, Article 7 (4 November 1950, *entered into force* 3 September 1953).

[373] *Ould Dah v. France*, No. 13113/03, 48 ILM 884, 891 (2009).

[374] *Ibid.*, 894–5.

[375] *Ely Ould Dah Case*, Montpellier Assize Court (Court of Appeal) (France), Indictment and Partial Dismissal, No. 99/14445, 4/99/48 (2001).

[376] *Ibid.*, § 4 (*L'amnistie*) ('Quelle que soit la légitimité d'une telle amnistie, dans le cadre d'une politique locale de réconciliation, cette loi n'a d'effet que sur le territoire de l'État concerné et n'est pas opposable aux pays tiers, dans le cadre de l'application du droit international. Elle n'a en conséquence aucune incidence sur l'action publique pour l'application de la loi en France').

Extradition of Ricardo Miguel Cavallo (2003), provided a similar explanation for its decision not to recognize the application of Argentina's amnesty law:

> The fact that a State decided not to exercise jurisdiction in order to prosecute crimes subject to international jurisdiction did not prevent any other State of an international agreement to exercise its own jurisdiction. This is so because international treaties that are applicable to the present case recognized the jurisdiction of any State party to those treaties, namely, jurisdiction to prosecute them, judge them and punish them in conformity with their domestic law and the treaties themselves, with the purpose of preventing impunity... Argentinean laws could not be binding on another State nor would they have the legal effect of depriving it from exercising jurisdiction[.][377]

Importantly, the Supreme Court of Mexico went further to suggest that it had an obligation not to recognize such an amnesty in order to prosecute international crimes on behalf of the international community.[378] The implication of such an obligation of non-recognition is that amnesty for *jus cogens* violations, by a State bound by those same duties to prosecute and punish international crimes, would necessarily constitute a breach of those duties, as the Supreme Court of Mexico did find with respect to Argentina.[379]

The Supreme Court's decision to justify its non-recognition of Argentina's grant of amnesty raises the issue of international comity, a principle that counsels deference to the executive, legislative, and judicial decisions of other States.[380] The treatment of the South African amnesty by one US court suggests that considerations of comity may inform the decision to recognize, or not, domestic amnesty. In *In re S. African Apartheid Litigation*, the Southern District of New York considered civil actions brought by individuals under the ATS against multinational corporations that had violated international law by doing business with South Africa during the apartheid period.[381] The District Court

377 *Decision on the Extradition of Ricardo Miguel Cavallo*, Supreme Court (Mexico), No. 712/2003, 42 ILM 888, 908–9 (2003).

378 *Ibid.*, 909; *see* discussion *supra*, text accompanying *n*. 329.

379 *Ibid.*

380 *See, e.g., Hilton v. Guyot*, 159 US 113, 163–4 (1895) ('"Comity," in the legal sense, is neither a matter of absolute obligation, on the one hand, nor of mere courtesy and good will, upon the other. But it is the recognition which one nation allows within its territory to the legislative, executive, or judicial acts of another nation, having due regard both to international duty and convenience, and to the rights of its own citizens, or of other persons who are under the protection of its laws').

381 *In re S. African Apartheid Litigation*, 617 F. Supp. 2d 228 (SDNY 2009).

determined that, because businesses had neither sought nor been granted amnesty, it was appropriate for those claims to be adjudicated outside the Truth and Reconciliation process.[382] 'Therefore international comity d [id] not require dismissal of this suit.'[383] The implication of the District Court's reasoning is that, had the corporations received amnesty, or had the case concerned individuals granted amnesty under the Truth and Reconciliation Commission Act (TRC), then the Court would have been precluded from hearing the claim. By contrast, in 2004, the US District Court for the Eastern District of California rendered its judgment in a case brought against the former chief of security for the head of El Salvadorian paramilitary groups for crimes against humanity.[384] An El Salvadorian judge had applied the 1993 amnesty law to dismiss the parallel proceeding brought in El Salvador with prejudice.[385] The District Court, instead of dismissing the case in consideration of international comity, recalled the findings of the IACtHR in a related proceeding[386] and found the application of the amnesty law to constitute an exhaustion of domestic remedies, thereby allowing suit to proceed in the United States under the ATS.[387] Thus, the application of an amnesty law by El Salvador produced the opposite response to the potential application of amnesty by South Africa.

***

Linking non-recognition of domestic amnesty laws to the invalidity of amnesty applied to *jus cogens* violations – as did the ICTY and SCSL – serves in part to alleviate whatever comity concerns may arise from non-recognition of a domestic grant of amnesty. In the 1998 *Audiencia Nacional* decisions, the Spanish National Court considered the inability of domestic law of third-States to pardon or decriminalize an offence under Spanish (and international) law to be distinct from

382 *Ibid.*, 279–80. 383 *Ibid.*, 286.

384 *Doe v. Rafael Saravia*, 348 F. Supp. 2d 1112 (ED Cal. 2004). 385 *Ibid.*, 1153.

386 *Ibid.* (quoting *Monsenor Oscar Arnulfo Romero and Galdamez v. El Salvador*, Case 11.481, Report No. 37/00, OEA/Ser.L/V/II.106 Doc. 3 rev. at 671, para. 25 (1999) ('The above-noted judicial decrees dismissing charges, adopted under the General Amnesty Law, have had the effect of deciding the instant case in the domestic jurisdiction. Once this domestic means of settling the matter posed is exhausted in the internal jurisdiction of El Salvador, the mechanisms of international protection established in the American Convention are triggered')).

387 *Ibid.*, 1159 (The Court awarded a judgment in the amount of $10 million against defendant).

the inherent invalidity of those amnesty laws as contrary to *jus cogens*.[388] 'Regardless' of whether such a law violated *jus cogens*, the Court wrote, that law in any event could have no extraterritorial effect to preclude the exercise of universal jurisdiction in Spain. If, however, instead of being a mere discretionary measure, invalidity provided a justification for non-recognition of domestic amnesty for *jus cogens* violations, then concerns over comity and 'harm' to foreign sovereignty may largely be alleviated.

To this end, recent practice in international and domestic courts supports the proposition 'that there is a crystallized international norm to the effect that a government cannot grant amnesty for serious crimes under international law'.[389] While the principle that third-States need not recognize domestic amnesties appears to be well accepted, the invalidity of amnesty laws covering *jus cogens* violations is a comparatively recent development.[390] The liberty of a third-State to decline to recognize the domestic amnesty of a State with respect to international crimes follows as a matter of legal hierarchy: law of a domestic system can neither modify nor absolve legal responsibility arising under peremptory international law, nor affect the jurisdiction of third-States under international law to prosecute on the basis of that responsibility. If, however, a domestic amnesty provision applied to *jus cogens* violations

[388] *Decision (Auto) of the Full Penal Chamber Confirming Spanish Jurisdiction to Investigate Crimes of Genocide and Terrorism Committed during the Chilean Dictatorship*, National Court (*Audiencia Nacional*) (Spain), No. 173/98, § 8, 119 ILR 331, 342–4 (1998); *Decision (Auto) of the Full Penal Chamber Confirming Spanish Jurisdiction over the Crimes of Genocide and Terrorism Committed during the Argentine Dictatorship*, National Court (*Audiencia Nacional*) (Spain), No. 84/98, §§ 8–10 (1998) (holding that Spanish courts can exercise jurisdiction committed in Chile and Argentina under universal jurisdiction, and finding amnesty laws of those countries of no relevance).

[389] *Prosecutor v. Gbao*, Decision on Preliminary Motion on the Invalidity of the Agreement between the United Nations and the Government of Sierra Leone on the Establishment of the Special Court for Sierra Leone, SCSL-04-15-PT-141, para. 9 (2004).

[390] *See, e.g.*, Mark Freeman and Max Pensky, *The Amnesty Controversy in International Law*, *in* AMNESTY IN THE AGE OF HUMAN RIGHTS ACCOUNTABILITY 53 (Cambridge University Press, Francesca Lessa & Leigh Payne eds., 2012) ('An argument can therefore be mounted that amnesties covering such offenses would deviate from this obligation [*erga omnes*], and indeed much of the legal opinion that holds domestic amnesties as contrary to *customary* international law infers such a status from these peremptory universal obligations to outlaw and punish'); Leila Sadat, *Competing and Overlapping Jurisdictions*, *in* II INTERNATIONAL CRIMINAL LAW: MULTILATERAL AND BILATERAL ENFORCEMENT MECHANISMS 227 (Leiden: Brill, M. Cherif Bassiouni ed., 2008) ('a prohibition against the grant of blanket amnesties for the commission of *jus cogens* crimes may now have crystallized as a matter of general customary international law').

is conceived to be invalid insofar as it constitutes a serious breach of obligations *erga omnes*, then third-States would be under an *obligation* not to recognize such amnesty.[391] Non-recognition of domestic amnesties for *jus cogens* violations by virtue of their invalidity is doctrinally consistent with obligations owed by the State to the international community as a whole.

There are many reasons why the invalidity of amnesty laws for *jus cogens* violations in recent jurisprudence is a positive practical development. With respect to self-invalidation by national courts, particularly in Latin America, the nullification of amnesty provisions reflects a high degree of transparency and accountability. While judicial decisions to this effect in Colombia, Argentina, Peru, Chile, and Uruguay were largely responsive to jurisprudence of the IACtHR, those internal determinations nevertheless indicate the perceived invalidity of amnesty provisions for *jus cogens* violations. Although Spain reached no clear decision in this regard – its Supreme Court lacked the authority to annul its domestic amnesty provision 'even if' it conflicted with *jus cogens* – Spain has been less reticent to determine the invalidity of such amnesties granted by other countries. Moreover, as a prudential matter, the invalidity of domestic amnesty with respect to *jus cogens* violations alleviates concerns over international comity that necessarily arise when a domestic court considers whether or not to recognize relevant legislation of another sovereign State by providing third-States a rationale – and an obligation under international law – upon which not to recognize such amnesty. A linkage between invalidity and non-recognition also resolves 'double jeopardy' considerations inherent in prosecuting an individual abroad for conduct for which he has been granted amnesty by his country of nationality, as demonstrated by the ruling of the Constitutional Court of Peru in *Rivas*.[392]

Limiting the scope of permissible domestic amnesties raises the fear that *jus cogens* may inhibit future reconciliation processes and unravel those of the past. It is conceivable, on the contrary, that 'blanket' amnesties themselves undermine sustainable peace. In a 2009

[391] ILC Articles on State Responsibility (2001), Article 41(2).

[392] *Case of Santiago Martín Rivas*, Supreme Court (Peru) (Constitutional and Social Chamber), No. 679-2005-PA/TC, ILDC 960, paras. 13–18, 50 (2007) (finding that any *res judicata* effect arising from the amnesty in question was merely 'apparent' or 'fraudulent' because the amnesty had exceeded the limits of domestic authority under international law).

report, entitled *Amnesty*, UN High Commissioner for Human Rights Navi Pillay suggests:

> The United Nations policy of opposing amnesties for war crimes, crimes against humanity, genocide or gross violations of human rights, including in the context of peace negotiations, represents an important evolution, grounded in long experience. Amnesties that exempt from criminal sanction those responsible for atrocious crimes in the hope of securing peace have often failed to achieve their aim and have instead emboldened their beneficiaries to commit further crimes. Conversely, peace agreements have been reached without amnesty provisions in some situations where amnesty had been said to be a necessary condition of peace and where many had feared that indictments would prolong the conflict.[393]

The Lomé Agreement serves as one such indication that amnesty provisions may be included in peace agreements with exceptions for *jus cogens* violations, and that such a substantive restriction is not preclusive of amnesty. It seems, moreover, that such a condition, which was included in the Lomé Agreement at the behest of the UN Security Council, may feature in future amnesty agreements brokered by the United Nations.[394] To this end, for example, the Report of the International Commission of Inquiry on Libya noted that Libya must '[e]nsure that any amnesty process conforms to Libya's obligations under international law by holding accountable all perpetrators of serious crimes'.[395] Provisions establishing the nullity of amnesty have been common across the most recent generation of *ad hoc* courts,[396] though the Rome Statute and the statutes of the ICTY and ICTR are silent on the issue of amnesty.

[393] Office of the United Nations High Commissioner for Human Rights, *Rule-of-Law Tools For Post-Conflict States, Amnesties*, UN Doc. HR/PUB/09/1, V (2009).

[394] Report of the Secretary-General to the United Nations Security Council, *The Rule of Law and Transitional Justice in Conflict and Post-Conflict Societies*, UN Doc. S/2004/616, para. 10 (2004) ('United Nations-endorsed peace agreements can never promise amnesties for genocide, war crimes, crimes against humanity or gross violations of human rights').

[395] Report of the International Commission of Inquiry to Investigate All Alleged Violations of International Law in Libya, UN Doc. A/HRC/19/68, para. 127(p) (2012) (It is not clear that Law 35 (On Granting Amnesty for Some Crimes), promulgated by the National Transitional Council on 2 May 2012, entirely conforms to this directive).

[396] CAE Statute (2013), Article 20 ('An amnesty granted to any person falling within the jurisdiction of the Extraordinary African Chambers with respect to the crimes referred to in articles 5 to 8 of this Statute shall not be a bar to prosecution'); STL Statute (2007), Article 6 ('An amnesty granted to any person for any crime within the jurisdiction of the Special Tribunal shall not be a bar to prosecution'); ECCC Statute (2003), Article 11 (agreement by Cambodia not to request a pardon or amnesty for any individual who

The obligation of States to prosecute grave violations of international law and the extension of amnesty are not mutually exclusive, even if *jus cogens* precludes 'blanket' amnesties. As supported by significant State practice in recent years,[397] in view of the obligations *erga omnes* arising from peremptory norms, the invalidity of amnesty for *jus cogens* violations necessarily follows. Conformity to *erga omnes* obligations owed to the international community cannot be contracted out by States; therefore, insofar as States have a duty to prevent and punish international crimes, amnesty laws inclusive of *jus cogens* violations constitute a breach of those obligations. Doctrinally, such amnesty is invalid *ab initio* and warrants non-recognition by third-States.

may be investigated or convicted for a crime within the scope of the agreement); SCSL Statute (2002), Article 10 ('An amnesty granted to any person falling within the jurisdiction of the Special Court in respect of the crimes referred to in articles 2 to 4 of the present Statute shall not be a bar to prosecution').

397 Freeman and Pensky, *The Amnesty Controversy in International Law*, 54 ('Crystallization is, crucially, in the eye of the beholder ... When it comes to amnesty, in particular, even disinterested parties looking at the same facts can come to opposite conclusions').

13

The form of *jus cogens*

A The individual as the subject of peremptory norms

The centrality of the individual in *jus cogens* doctrine is well established in contemporary international law and is recognized in both legal discourse and practice. Fitzmaurice, in one of the earliest articulations of the concept of *jus cogens* in international law, referred for illustrative purposes to 'cases where the position of the individual is involved, and where the rules contravened are rules instituted for the protection of the individual'.[1] Verdross concurred that 'all rules of general international law created for a humanitarian purpose' constitute *jus cogens*.[2] This position is supported by the material content of *jus cogens*, which constitutes norms under which only the individual can be a subject proper. It should be noted that 'collective' or 'group' rights are taken to refer to rights accruing to the individual as a member of that group.[3] Every peremptory norm thus constitutes a protection of the basic dignity of the human person, directly or as a member of some (e.g. ethnic, political, or racial) group, which has emerged in response to egregious acts contrary to the interests of the international community.

[1] Gerald Fitzmaurice, Third Report on the Law of Treaties, [1958] II YbILC 40–1, para. 76.

[2] Alfred Verdross, Jus Dispositivum *and* Jus Cogens *in International Law*, 60 American Journal of International Law 55, 59 (1966) (This is one of three groups of *jus cogens* proposed by Verdross, the others being the prohibition of treaties infringing upon the rights of third-States and rules regarding the use of force in the UN Charter).

[3] It stands to reason that 'group' or 'collective' simply denotes a subset of individuals apart from whom the rights of the group have no meaning. Norm construction in terms of collectivity underscores the nature of the protection afforded by the norm rather than denoting *sui generis* subjects of rights and duties. Individuals that make up a group – whether national, ethnic, religious, or racial – are protected by group rights in just the same way that legal rights and freedoms apply directly to individuals rather than to States as political collectives. *See* Michael Smith, Human Dignity and the Common Good in the Aristotelian-Thomistic Tradition 175–9 (Lewiston, NY: Mellen University Press 1995).

Conversely, the law of international responsibility confirms the individual to be the sole bearer of criminal responsibility for the violation of peremptory norms. In fact, the term 'international crime' captures at once the seriousness of the international norm violated – a peremptory norm – as well as the subject of international responsibility for the violation: the individual. The development of individual civil responsibility, particularly in the United States, reinforces this premise by illuminating the way in which rights and duties stipulated by peremptory norms are borne directly by the individual in tort vis-à-vis other individuals. The erosion of traditional individual immunities from both criminal and civil responsibility for *jus cogens* violations demonstrates the priority placed upon individual responsibility by the international community. And the increasing non-recognition and invalidity of domestic amnesty for *jus cogens* violations underscores the inability of the State to affect the responsibility of its own citizens for international crimes. At this, it is reasonable to conclude that a homocentric approach to the study of *jus cogens* is not only appropriate, but also necessary to understand the concept both substantively and functionally.[4]

Consequently, *jus cogens* departs from the traditional notion of subjects and objects in international law, by which the State is recognized as the primary subject of legal rights and duties. The syntax of peremptory norms illuminates this point. The rights and duties denoted by peremptory norms are depicted as two-term relations between a subject (of a right or duty) and an object (the right or duty itself).[5] That is, individual A (the subject of a right) has a claim to some protection B (the object of a right); or individual A (the subject of a duty) bears a duty not to commit some act B (the object of a duty). One can logically place each peremptory norm identified above into such a formulation. In order to operationalize these norms, however, two-term formulations must then be translated into three-term relations which denote correlatives. Judge Dugard alluded to this bifurcated nature of peremptory norms, as

[4] Julius Stone, *A Sociological Perspective On International Law*, *in* THE STRUCTURE AND PROCESS OF INTERNATIONAL LAW 263 (The Hague: Martinus Nijhoff, Ronald St John Macdonald & Douglas Johnston eds., 1983) ('It is only a heuristic implication from the general assumption which must be made by sociological enquiries, that international law is a law made by and for human beings – that state entities in some manner and degree represent their human populations – in short, that international law is a homocentric law, to be studied as such').

[5] John Finnis, NATURAL LAW AND NATURAL RIGHTS 201–2 (Oxford: Clarendon Press 1980).

constituting both rights and duties, in *Armed Activities on the Territory of the Congo*:

> On the one hand, [norms of *jus cogens*] affirm the high principles of international law, which recognize the most important rights of the international order – such as the *right to be free* from aggression, genocide, torture and slavery and the right to self-determination; while, on the other hand, they give legal form to the most fundamental policies or goals of the international community – *the prohibitions on* aggression, genocide, torture and slavery and the advancement of self-determination.[6]

The importance of a three-term construction is that it relates the right or freedom of one individual to the correlative duty of another.

Just such a formulation was authoritatively articulated by Wesley Hohfeld in a pair of essays published in the early twentieth century, where the term 'right' was constructed as the correlative of 'duty'.[7] Identifying both the beneficiary of a right as well as the bearer of its correlative duty is necessary to translate a norm into an operative legal rule.[8] Having established in the previous chapters that the subject of both rights and duties of peremptory norms is the individual, the three-term form of peremptory norms is rightly constructed in terms of the individual. Specifically, the formulation is structured as follows: individual A (the subject of a right) has a claim to protection B (the object of a right), against individual C (the bearer of the correlative duty).[9] To clarify the relation between individual A and individual C, it is helpful to refer to the schema Hohfeld proposes in his second essay, in which he distinguishes between paucital rights (rights *in personam*) and mutual rights (rights *in rem*):

[6] *Armed Activities on the Territory of the Congo (New Application: 2002) (Democratic Republic of the Congo v. Rwanda)*, Sep. Op. Dugard, ICJ Reports 2006, p. 86, para. 10 (emphasis added).

[7] Wesley Hohfeld, *Some Fundamental Legal Conceptions as Applied in Judicial Reasoning*, 23 Yale Law Journal 16, 32 (1913); Wesley Hohfeld, *Fundamental Legal Conceptions as Applied in Judicial Reasoning*, 26 Yale Law Journal 710, 717 (1917) (In his first essay, Hohfeld develops a 'scheme of "opposites" and "correlatives"' to clarify what he identifies as loose and imprecise legal terminology. In doing so, he establishes eight conceptions that constitute the 'lowest common denominators of the law'. These are namely right, privilege, powers, and immunities, whose respective correlates are duty, 'no-right', liabilities, and disabilities).

[8] Finnis, Natural Law and Natural Rights 218–20.

[9] R. J. Vincent, *The Idea of Rights in International Ethics*, *in* Traditions of International Ethics 253 (Princeton University Press, Terry Nardin & David Mapel eds., 1992).

> A paucital right, or claim, (right *in personam*) is either a unique right residing in a person (or group of persons) and availing against a single person (or single group of persons); or else it is one of a *few* fundamentally similar, yet separate, rights availing respectively against a few definite persons. A mutual right, or claim, (right *in rem*) is always *one* of a large *class* of *fundamentally similar* yet separate rights, actual and potential, residing in a *single* person (or single group of persons) but availing *respectively* against persons constituting a very large and indefinite class of people.[10]

Individual protections delineated by peremptory norms are best conceived in this sense as mutual rights; in effect, such rights constitute not one single right or one single correlative duty, but rather, 'many separate and distinct rights, actual and potential, each one of which has a correlative duty resting upon some one person'.[11] It is in this sense that the individual is the subject of protections and duties under peremptory norms.

B Social contract through historical exigencies

The individual-oriented norms of *jus cogens* can be viewed through the substantive lens of the social contract. The social contract articulates fundamental individual protections recognized by society that, conversely, connote obligations to respect those rights in other members of society. Dramatic variation in the substance of rights across different theories of social contract is the culmination of different conceptualizations of the 'state of nature' that reflect distinct historical and political contexts that condition the prevailing social contract. Corresponding variation across prescribed governance structures is related to needs arising from contrasting conceptualizations of the human condition that determine the character of civil society. Nevertheless, the basic outcome of the social contract remains establishing civil society as the mechanism through which to protect the fundamental rights of the individual vis-à-vis other individuals.[12]

Hobbes, for example, holds individual physical security – 'the security of a man[']s person' – to be the fundamental protection established and enforced by political society.[13] By virtue of its importance to social

[10] Hohfeld, *Fundamental Legal Conceptions as Applied in Judicial Reasoning*, 718 (internal citations omitted).

[11] *Ibid.*, 740–4.

[12] Michael Lessnoff (ed.), Social Contract Theory 3 (Oxford: Basil Blackwell 1991).

[13] Thomas Hobbes, Leviathan II.14.66 (London: Penguin Books, C. B. Macpherson ed., 1985 [1651]).

coexistence, in historical context, this protection transcends all other rights and duties in society, a reflection of man's destructive natural state and the paramount need to escape it through civil society. Locke, by contrast, takes the broader series of life, liberty, and property to be fundamental individual rights of man, those basic rights observable but insecure in man's natural state.[14] Through this vision of the social contract, proper political order exists principally to realize the basic rights of the individual, necessary to human flourishing, in a community among other individuals. This distinctly liberal depiction of the product of the social contract is a reflection of the prior elements of Locke's social contract theory, by which natural law informs a 'common good' through (tacit) consent to basic individual protections. According to Rousseau, man exchanges natural liberty for civil liberty through the social contract, giving rise to a civil state in which the individual rights of man are protected.[15] In contrast to the security-oriented social contract depicted by Hobbes, there is no sacrifice of freedom or liberty by entering into the social contract,[16] a vision that follows from Rousseau's depiction of the natural state of man as one of pure freedom and equality. For Kant, the product of the original contract is a series of normative rights, with correlative moral duties protecting the individual human being, which constitute the foundation of the civil condition.[17] As defined by Kant,

> *Right* is the limitation of the freedom of each to the condition of its harmony with the freedom of everyone insofar as this is possible in accordance with a universal law; and *public* right is the sum of *external laws* which make such a thoroughgoing harmony possible.[18]

[14] John Locke, Two Treatises of Government II.7.87, II.9.124 (London: Everyman, 2003 [1689]).

[15] Jean-Jacques Roussseau, The Social Contract (du Contract Social ou Principes du Droit Politique) I.8 (London: Everyman 2003 [1762]).

[16] Jeremy Jennings, *Rousseau, Social Contract and the Modern Leviathan*, *in* The Social Contract from Hobbes to Rawls 117 (London: Routledge, David Boucher & Paul Kelly eds., 1994).

[17] Immaneul Kant, On the Common Saying: That May Be Correct in Theory, but It Is of no Use in Practice [1793], in The Cambridge Edition of the Works of Immaneul Kant 8:289, 8:295 (Cambridge University Press, Mary Gregor ed., 1996) [hereinafter, Kant, Theory and Practice].

[18] *Ibid.*, 8:290.

A natural right is understood to be one 'which can be derived from *a priori* principles for a civil constitution',[19] a relation that directly links the public right generated by the original contract to natural law. Kant identifies the natural rights of the citizen as lawful freedom, equality, and civil independence.[20] These principles form the basis of the civil condition as a rightful condition, a relation that orients the product of the social contract in the common will that all individuals ought to share, by virtue of the importance of these values to social coexistence.

There are a number of key substantive points of similarity between *jus cogens* and the social contract, the most obvious of which is their individual-oriented content. Maximizing the well-being of the individual through civil society by defining basic rights and duties necessary to coexistence with other individuals in a community is, according to the narrative of contractarianism, the reason individuals unite through the social contract.[21] Analogously, in the context of *jus cogens*, the higher interests of the international community are represented by the principle of human dignity which, through the mechanics of customary international law, gives rise to individual-oriented peremptory norms. *Jus cogens* constitutes primary rights and duties of the individual which, by virtue of their importance to international society, permit no derogation. With reference to the norms belonging to *jus cogens*, the 'state of nature' of international relations can be depicted as a condition in which piracy, slavery, war crimes, crimes against humanity, aggression, genocide, torture, apartheid, and terrorism could be freely carried out. International society has progressively outlawed such conduct through *jus cogens* norms.

Like the social contract, the material content of *jus cogens* is a product of historical exigencies. The social contract is at its core a quasi-historical narrative that conceives of human beings uniting through common interests and values to recognize basic norms pursuant to the protection of those interests through society. The norms defined by those common interests and values respond to historical conditions – the 'state of nature' – that give rise to the social contract, as demonstrated by the

[19] Kant, Theory and Practice 8:290; Immanuel Kant, Metaphysics of Morals [1797], in The Cambridge Edition of the Works of Immanuel Kant 6:256 (Gregor ed.) [hereinafter, Kant, Metaphysics].

[20] Kant, Theory and Practice 8:290; Kant, Metaphysics 6:314.

[21] *See* discussion *supra*, Chapter 6 (Expression of an International Social Contract).

diversity of contractarianism.[22] A similar narrative is implicit in the emergence of *jus cogens* norms. The interests of the international community as a whole shape *opinio juris sive necessitatis* in response to conduct abhorrent to those interests, giving rise to peremptory norms. The recognition and acceptance of each peremptory norm by the international community therefore evinces distinct historical narratives that, together, define the material content of *jus cogens*. In this sense, alongside the Mayflower Compact,[23] *jus cogens* provides a rare example of the operation of a social contract in practice.

The inherently social dimension of peremptory norms provides another layer of similarity with the social contract. *Jus cogens*, like the social contract, gives rise to norms protected to ensure social coexistence. This social nature of higher interests, in both contractarianism and *jus cogens*, is reflected in the norms themselves as well as the processes through which normative content is generated.[24] The formulation of non-derogable peremptory norms in response to historical exigencies by the international community as a whole suggests a social weight akin to rights and duties of the social contract that emerge in response to the 'state of nature'. As a matter of international law, the State can neither limit the protections enjoyed by the individual under *jus cogens*, nor affect the responsibility that arises for violations of those protections. Moreover, the expression of *opinio juris sive necessitatis* by States reflects interests and values common to the international community *as a whole*, a juridical entity representing the social need of mankind, rather than the mere aggregation of State interests. This *opinio* is expressed largely before international fora – through resolutions by the United Nations and near-universal instruments of public international law – where States function as constituents of the international community. The socialization of the international community has, consequently, provided a mechanism through which to articulate norms constituting the requisites for international social coexistence.

[22] *See* discussion *supra*, Chapter 6, text accompanying *nn.* 1–28.

[23] Alexander Young, Chronicles of the Pilgrim Fathers of the Colony of Plymouth from 1602 to 1625 120–1, *n.* 3 (Boston: Charles C. Little & James Brown 1841) (The Mayflower Compact was signed on 11 November 1620 aboard the *Mayflower* as the first governing instrument of the American colony at Plymouth: 'Here, for the first time in the world's history, the philosophical fiction of the social contract was realized in practice').

[24] See discussion *supra*, Chapter 9 (Normativity and Positivism: A Contractarian Reconciliation).

The individual-oriented, historical, and social aspects of *jus cogens* evidenced throughout this part build upon prior conclusions pertaining to the authority and sources of *jus cogens*. These conclusions further indicate the way in which *the international community of States as a whole* depicts a layered concept that encapsulates both procedural and substantive elements.[25] As demonstrated in the survey of the material content of *jus cogens*, procedurally, peremptory norms emerge through articulations of *opinio juris sive necessitatis* by States, principally in some international capacity, and this *opinio* is evidenced by the practice of States largely acting as organs of the international community. At the same time, this *opinio juris sive necessitatis* is informed by the higher interests of the international community as a whole, represented by the general principle of human dignity. The normative product of this process constitutes fundamental protections of the human person. Here again, the relationship between the procedural and substantive dimensions of the international community indicates that the State, and the international community more generally, serves the higher interests of mankind. This relation between the individual and institutions of governance reflects the premise of the social contract, namely, to promote a *raison d'être* of governance structures that safeguards existential protections of the individual.

Individual responsibility, in turn, is an important corollary of the individual-oriented protections denoted by *jus cogens* norms. Early expressions of international criminal law were linked to notions of juridical conscience in much the same way as *jus cogens*, as observed in 1928 by Vespasian Pella, President of the International Association of Penal Law:

> The proposition for the creation of an International Criminal Code can no longer be regarded as utopian. On the contrary they are concrete manifestations of a powerful *desideratum* of the contemporary judicial conscience.[26]

Moreover, M. Cherif Bassiouni has observed that the regime of international criminal justice reflects an international social contract in the sense that the 'inherent and inalienable' rights of victims depend upon the enforcement of international criminal law because individual respect

[25] See discussion *supra*, Chapter 3.A (The International Community of States as a Whole).

[26] M. Cherif Bassiouni, A Draft International Criminal Code and Draft Statute for an International Criminal Tribunal XII (Alphen aan den Rijn: Sijthoff & Noordhoff 1987) (quoting Vespasian Pella, Revue Internationale De Droit Pénal 275 (1928)).

for peremptory norms is implicitly dependent upon (and exchanged for) enforcement by the international community.[27] In a penological sense, enforcement is required to reinforce and reaffirm the value of human dignity that gives rise to peremptory norms, a value undermined by international criminal conduct:

> Punishment for *jus cogens* international crimes helps restore the human dignity of the specific victim and symbolically reaffirms the value of human dignity of human genre and, in the Kantian sense, it restores the human dignity of the perpetrator.[28]

Civil liability for such conduct reinforces a dignitarian conceptualization of fundamental duties owed to other members of society.[29] In this vein, the erosion of individual immunities from both criminal prosecution and civil proceedings for *jus cogens* violations reveals the priority that the international community has vested in a system of responsibility for international crimes.[30] There is further support for the proposition that obligations arising from *jus cogens*, which place significant weight upon international criminal responsibility, preclude the grant of blanket amnesties.[31] Recalling that immunities under international law are conceived to be a direct extension of the sovereignty of the State itself, and that amnesty constitutes an exercise of pure sovereignty, it is clear that the limits placed upon State sovereignty by *jus cogens* are significant.[32] The performance of obligations *erga omnes* arising from *jus cogens*, discussed in the following chapter, requires States as constituents of the international community to prosecute or extradite individuals who commit international crimes, further enforcing this contractarian structure of *jus cogens*.

[27] M. Cherif Bassiouni, *The Philosophy and Policy of International Criminal Justice, in* MAN'S INHUMANITY TO MAN 108–18 (The Hague: Martinus Nijhoff, Antonio Cassese & Lal Chand Vohrah eds., 2003).

[28] *Ibid.*, 115–16 ('This is why punishment for such crimes cannot be compromised by the political practice of blanket amnesties').

[29] *See* discussion *supra*, Chapter 12.B (Individual Civil Responsibility).

[30] *See* discussion *supra*, Chapter 12.C (Immunities).

[31] M. Cherif Bassiouni, *The Philosophy and Policy of International Criminal Justice*, 116. *See* discussion *supra*, Chapter 12.D (Amnesty).

[32] *See* discussion *supra*, Chapter 12.C (Immunities).

PART V

Peremptory norms and the State

Part V considers the legal effects of *jus cogens* through obligations *erga omnes* arising from peremptory norms and the allocation of State responsibility for their violation. If individual-oriented legal elements are the 'primary' effects of *jus cogens*, then these State-based aspects may be conceived as the 'secondary' effects of *jus cogens*. This relation is not one of hierarchy but rather of succession. This part begins, in Chapter 14, by considering obligations *erga omnes* arising from peremptory norms, a status that denotes the legal indivisibility of obligations arising under *jus cogens*. Chapter 15 assesses State responsibility under *jus cogens*, which contributes to an understanding of the duality expressed by *the international community as a whole*. Then, Chapter 16 presents a case study on the international response to the 2011 Libyan uprising, which illustrates the way in which the legal effects of obligations *erga omnes*, and peremptory norms more broadly, operate within the governance structures of existing international institutions. Chapter 17 concludes this part by considering the way in which the State-based legal order arising from *jus cogens* reflects the culmination of a social contract in the form of international civil society.

14

The enforcement of *jus cogens*: obligations *erga omnes*

The legal effects of *jus cogens* are actualized through obligations arising from peremptory norms – obligations *erga omens* – through which a civil society function is conceived in international law.[1] While *jus cogens* contains norms directed towards the individual, obligations *erga omnes* specifically concern the enforcement of those norms by the State. As the ICTY observed in *Furundžija*, 'a peremptory norm or *jus cogens* ... enjoys a higher rank in the international hierarchy than treaty law and even "ordinary" customary rules', whereas obligations '*erga omnes* ... appertain[] to the area of international enforcement (*lato sensu*)'.[2] Translating to mean 'against all', an *erga omnes* obligation is one owed by each State to the international community as a whole.[3] The doctrine of obligations *erga omnes* was first articulated by the International Court of Justice in *Barcelona Traction* (1970),[4] where it distinguished State-to-State obligations from those 'toward the international community as a whole', and interpreted the latter to arise from peremptory norms:

> In particular, an essential distinction should be drawn between the obligations of a State towards the international community as a whole, and those arising vis-à-vis another State in the field of diplomatic protection. By their very nature the former are the concern of all States. In view of the importance of the rights involved, all States can be held to have a legal interest in their protection; they are obligations *erga omnes*.[5]

1 *See* discussion *supra*, Chapter 1.B (Obligations *Erga Omnes*).

2 *Prosecutor v. Furundžija*, IT-95-17/1-T, para. 153 (1998).

3 *See* Christian Tams, Enforcing Obligations *Erga Omnes* in International Law (Cambridge University Press 2005); Maurizio Ragazzi, The Concept of International Obligations *Erga Omnes* (Oxford University Press 1997); André De Hoogh, Obligations *Erga Omnes* and International Crimes (The Hague: Martinus Nijhoff 1996).

4 *Barcelona Traction, Light and Power Company, Limited (Belgium v. Spain)*, Judgment, ICJ Reports 1970, p. 3.

5 *Ibid.*, para. 33.

Functionally, the classification *erga omnes* denotes a general legal interest of all States as members of the international community in the performance of these obligations. Such a general legal interest has been reiterated by the ILC to be the distinguishing feature of *erga omnes* obligations, most succinctly in the Fourth Report on State Responsibility (1992) by *special rapporteur* Arangio-Ruiz:

> It is well known ... that the concept of *erga omnes* obligation is not characterized by the importance of the interest protected by the norm (as is typical of *jus cogens*) but rather by the 'legal indivisibility' of the content of the obligation, namely by the fact that the rule in question provides for obligations which bind simultaneously each and every State concerned with respect to all the others.[6]

This legal indivisibility is a product of the importance of the interests of the international community protected by peremptory norms, which are given legal effect through *erga omnes* obligations.

The practice of States, acting as organs of the international community, has defined the role of the State with respect to *jus cogens.*[7] Peremptory norms emerge through the practice of States in their capacity as organs of the international community, articulating and reflecting the higher interests of the international community as a whole. Obligations arising from peremptory norms demonstrate a further sense in which the State acts as such an instrument of the international community in the realization of these higher interests through enforcement. Obligations *erga omnes* are conceived to derive not from the consent or will of the State, but from norms of *jus cogens* themselves, which arise from the *opinio juris sive necessitatis* of the international community evidenced by the practice of States in their capacity as organs of the international community. By extension, then, obligations *erga omnes* arising from peremptory norms are a product of the same *opinio* that gives form to *jus cogens*, expressive

[6] Gaetano Arangio-Ruiz, Fourth Report on State Responsibility, [1992] II(1) YbILC 34, para. 92; *see* Robert Ago, Fifth Report on State Responsibility, [1976] II(1) YbILC 29, para. 89; *Prosecutor v. Furundžija*, IT-95-17/1-T, para. 151 (1998) ('Furthermore, the prohibition of torture imposes upon States obligations *erga omnes*, that is, obligations owed towards all the other members of the international community, each of which then has a correlative right. In addition, the violation of such an obligation simultaneously constitutes a breach of the correlative right of all members of the international community and gives rise to a claim for compliance accruing to each and every member, which then has the right to insist on fulfillment of the obligation or in any case to call for the breach to be discontinued').

[7] *See* discussion *supra*, Chapter 8.B.ii (State Practice).

of social need informed by the higher interests of the international community (represented by human dignity) in response to historical exigencies. It is in this sense that norms of *jus cogens* are sometimes identified as obligations *erga omnes*, which reflects their practical linkage but confuses this functional distinction. As the International Court has repeatedly stated, 'intransgressible principles of international customary law ... incorporate obligations which are essentially of an *erga omnes* character ... to be observed by all States'.[8] As obligations arising from the higher interests of the international community as a whole, their respect and enforcement is owed by every State to the international community by virtue of their membership in the international community.

The imposition of obligations arising from peremptory norms is understood to entail 'a number, albeit a small one, of international obligations which, by reason of the importance of their subject-matter for the international community as a whole, are – unlike the others – obligations in whose fulfillment all States have a legal interest'.[9] Obligations *erga omnes* are 'virtually coextensive' with *jus cogens*,[10] and it is in this sense that obligations of the State arise from peremptory norms, not

[8] *Legal Consequences of the Construction of a Wall in the Occupied Palestinian Territory*, Advisory Opinion, ICJ Reports 2004, p. 136, para. 157 ('With regard to international humanitarian law, the Court recalls that in its Advisory Opinion on the *Legality of the Threat or Use of Nuclear Weapons* it stated that a great many rules of humanitarian law applicable in armed conflict are so fundamental to the respect of the human person and "elementary considerations of humanity", that they are to be observed by all States whether or not they have ratified the conventions that contain them, because they constitute intransgressible principles of international customary law. In the Court's view, these rules incorporate obligations which are essentially of an *erga omnes* character' (internal quotation marks omitted)); *Legality of the Threat or Use of Nuclear Weapons*, Advisory Opinion, ICJ Reports 1996, p. 226, paras. 79, 95; *Military and Paramilitary Activities in and against Nicaragua (Nicaragua v. United States of America)*, Judgment, ICJ Reports 1986, p. 14, para. 218; *Reservations to the Genocide Convention*, Advisory Opinion, ICJ Reports 1951, p. 15, 23; *The Corfu Channel Case (United Kingdom of Great Britain and Northern Ireland v. Albania)*, Judgment, ICJ Reports 1949, p. 4, 22.

[9] Report of the International Law Commission on the Work of its Twenty-Eighth Session, [1976] II(2) YbILC 99, para. 10 (Commentary to Draft Article 19 adopted by the ILC at its 28th Session).

[10] James Crawford, Third Report on State Responsibility, [2000] II(1) YbILC 34, para. 106 (a); James Crawford, Fourth Report on State Responsibility, [2001] II(1) YbILC 13, para. 49 ('even if the two are not different aspects of the one underlying idea, the two substantially overlap'). However, obligations *erga omnes* are not necessarily the exclusive domain of *jus cogens* and may also arise from other 'essential principles of contemporary international law', such as the right of peoples to self-determination and the common heritage of mankind: *see* discussion *supra*, Chapter 11 (The Material Content of *Jus Cogens*).

as the subject of protections and duties, but as the mechanism necessary for their realization. Although obligations *erga omnes* have been recognized repeatedly by the ICJ,[11] their practical effect remains a progressive area of international law and has only recently come into focus. Consequently, the work of the ILC remains central to an understanding of obligations *erga omnes*, particularly the scope and consequences of the general legal interest in their fulfilment.

The performance of obligations *erga omnes* is increasingly articulated in practice to constitute positive duties to prevent and punish violations of peremptory norms. Specific obligations *erga omnes partes* to prevent and punish are found variously in the conventions codifying each of the peremptory norms examined above, instruments otherwise concerned with the definition and individual criminality of peremptory norms.[12]

[11] *See supra*, Chapter 1, *n*. 25.

[12] Rome Statute of the International Criminal Court, UN Doc. A/CONF.183.9, [hereinafter, Rome Statute (1998)], Articles 86–90 (17 July 1998, *entered into force* 1 July 2002); Report of the International Law Commission on the Work of its Forty-Eighth Session, [1996] II(2) YbILC 17 [hereinafter, Draft Code of Crimes (1996)], Article 9; Convention against Torture and Other Cruel, Inhuman or Degrading Treatment or Punishment, GA Res. 39/46, 1465 UNTS 85 [hereinafter, Torture Convention (1984)], Article 7(1) (12 December 1984, *entered into force* 26 June 1987); United Nations Convention on the Law of the Sea, 1833 UNTS 3 [hereinafter, UNCLOTS (1982)], Articles 100, 105 (10 December 1982, *entered into force* 16 November 1994) (Definition of Piracy); International Convention on the Suppression and Punishment of the Crime of *Apartheid*, 1015 UNTS 243 [hereinafter, Apartheid Convention (1976)], Articles IV, VI (30 November 1973, *entered into force* 18 July 1976); International Convention on the Elimination of All Forms of Racial Discrimination, 660 UNTS 195 [hereinafter, CERD (1966)], Articles 2–3 (7 March 1966, *entered into force* 4 January 1969); Supplementary Convention on the Abolition of Slavery, the Slave Trade, and Institutions and Practices Similar to Slavery, 226 UNTS 3, Articles 1, 3, 8 (7 September 1956, *entered into force* 30 April 1957); Report of the International Law Commission Covering the Work of its Sixth Session, [1954] II YbILC 149 [hereinafter, Draft Code of Offences (1954)], Article 2, paras. 11–12; Geneva Convention (I) for the Amelioration of the Condition of the Wounded and Sick in Armed Forces in the Field, 75 UNTS 31, Article 49 (12 August 1949, *entered into force* 21 October 1950) [Hereinafter, Geneva Convention I (1949)]; Geneva Convention (II) for the Amelioration of the Condition of Wounded, Sick and Shipwrecked Members of Armed Forces at Sea, 75 UNTS 85 [hereinafter, Geneva Convention II (1949)], Article 50 (12 August 1949, *entered into force* 21 October 1950); Geneva Convention (III) Relative to the Treatment of Prisoners of War, 75 UNTS 135 [hereinafter, Geneva Convention III (1949)], Article 129 (12 August 1949, *entered into force* 21 October 1950); Geneva Convention (IV) Relative to the Protection of Civilian Persons in Time of War, 75 UNTS 287 [hereinafter, Geneva Convention IV (1949)], Article 146 (12 August 1949, *entered into force* 21 October 1950); Convention on the Prevention and Punishment of the Crime of Genocide [hereinafter, Genocide Convention (1948)], Articles IV–VII, 78 UNTS 277, No. 1021 (9 December 1948, *entered into force* 12 January 1951); Slavery, Servitude, Forced Labour and Similar

The broad ascendance of States to these conventions, the accepted customary nature of the norms they codify, and the recognized peremptory nature of these norms all indicate that obligations *erga omnes* arising therefrom are (like the norms themselves) not limited by the scope of relevant conventions.[13] Simply put, if a norm is recognized to be universal and non-derogable as *jus cogens*, it follows that obligations arising from that norm, necessary to its fulfilment, must similarly be universal as obligations *erga omnes*. That performing obligations *erga omnes* requires States to prevent and punish violations of peremptory norms, and that these obligations extend beyond treaty instruments articulating such duties, was introduced by the International Court of Justice in *Application of the Genocide Convention*:

> [G]enocide [is] a crime under international law ... It follows that the rights and obligations enshrined by the Convention are rights and obligations *erga omnes*. The Court notes that the obligation each State thus has to prevent and to punish the crime of genocide is not territorially limited by the Convention.[14]

In the context of obligations *erga omnes* more generally, such a formulation underlies the premise that *jus cogens* depends upon the functional capacity of the State to realize peremptory norms. The present chapter reflects a standard in contemporary jurisprudence whereby the performance of obligations *erga omnes* is increasingly viewed in terms of the prevention and punishment by the State of *jus cogens* violations.

A Prevention and consequences for third-States

Preventing violations of peremptory norms is conceived to be an aspect of the performance of obligations *erga omnes* owed to the international

Institutions and Practices Convention of 1926, 60 LNTS 253, Preamble [hereinafter, Slavery Convention (1926)], Articles 2, 6 (25 September 1926, *entered into force* 9 March 1927); *supra*, Chapter 11, *n.* 289 (various provisions of sectoral terrorism conventions).

13 *See* Arangio-Ruiz, Fourth Report, [1992] II(1) YbILC 34, para. 92 (identifying a common legal structure to obligations *erga omnes* and obligations *erga omnes partes*).

14 *Application of the Convention on the Prevention and Punishment of the Crime of Genocide (Bosnia and Herzegovina v. Serbia and Montenegro)*, Preliminary Objections, Judgment, ICJ Reports 1996, p. 595, para. 31 (internal quotation marks omitted). *See Armed Activities on the Territory of the Congo (New Application: 2002) (Congo v. Rwanda)*, ICJ Reports 2006, p. 3, para. 64; *Reservations to the Genocide Convention*, Advisory Opinion, ICJ Reports 1951, p. 15, 23 ('The first consequence arising from this conception is that the principles underlying the [Genocide] Convention are principles which are recognized by civilized nations as binding on States, even without any conventional obligation').

community as a whole. This functional element indicates that each State is bound to prevent violations of peremptory norms within its jurisdiction.[15] It is in this sense that prevention constitutes an expectation of due diligence upon the State.[16] The general legal interest in the fulfilment of obligations *erga omnes* extends its scope to mean that every State has a legal interest in the prevention of violations of peremptory norms in each State. At once, this reflects an aim of obligations *erga omnes* – to preempt and suppress violations of peremptory norms – as well as their scope: to be performed everywhere irrespective of divergent interests of the State.

While the functional element of prevention is uncontroversial, the aspect of generality is unorthodox and warrants further attention. The work of the ILC contributed significantly to an understanding of the legal effects of this aspect of obligations *erga omnes* in the Articles on State Responsibility. By delineating particular consequences for serious breaches of obligations arising from peremptory norms, it may be inferred that the ILC contemplated the prevention of violations of peremptory norms.[17] Such an understanding follows from the commentary to Article 40, which considers consequences in terms of the magnitude of a 'breach of peremptory norms' and conceives of the seriousness of a breach of obligations *erga omnes* in terms of the organization or intensity of 'the violation ... of the peremptory norms in question'.[18] Moreover, the particular consequences delineated in Article 41 of the instrument are clearly intended to address the failure to prevent violations of peremptory norms. The ILC considered breaches of obligations *erga omnes* in this sense in its Commentary to the Articles:

> While peremptory norms of general international law focus on the scope and priority to be given to a certain number of fundamental obligations, the focus of obligations to the international community as a whole is essentially on the legal interest of all States in compliance – i.e. in terms of the present articles, in being entitled to invoke the responsibility of any State in breach. Consistently with the difference in their focus, it is

15 *Application of the Convention on the Prevention and Punishment of the Crime of Genocide (Bosnia and Herzegovina v. Serbia and Montenegro)*, Judgment, ICJ Reports 2007, p. 43, para. 432.

16 *See* discussion *infra*, Chapter 15.A.i (International Responsibility for Breaches of Obligations *Erga Omnes*).

17 International Law Commission, Responsibility of States for Internationally Wrongful Acts, Report of the International Law Commission on the Work of its Fifty-Third Session, [2001] II(2) YbILC 26, Article 41 [hereinafter, ILC Articles on State Responsibility (2001)].

18 *Ibid.*, 113, paras. 7–8 (Commentary to Article 40).

> appropriate to reflect the consequences of the two concepts in two distinct ways. First, serious breaches of obligations arising under peremptory norms of general international law can attract additional consequences, not only for the responsible State but for all other States. Secondly, all States are entitled to invoke responsibility for breaches of obligations to the international community as a whole.[19]

Here, the ILC draws attention to consequences arising from the legal interest of all States in the fulfilment of obligations arising from peremptory norms: as *erga omnes* denotes the scope of obligations owed to all States, the corollary is that all States have an interest in compliance and are consequently entitled to act pursuant to this end.

As obligations *erga omnes* are owed to the international community as a whole, and all States have a legal interest in their fulfilment, their violation is conceived to affect all States. A breach of obligations *erga omnes* permits third-States to respond to suppress the breach, as noted among other examples in the ruling of the ICTY in *Furundžija*.[20] Moreover, in the event of a breach of obligations *erga omnes* arising from peremptory norms, particular consequences are defined for third-States to take action on behalf of the international community pursuant to the positive duty of each State to suppress such conduct. The seed of the concept, *actio popularis*, is found in the Separate Opinion of Judge Ammoun in *Barcelona Traction*, who identified a legal right or interest in 'an action brought in defence of a collective or general interest, the objective being to safeguard legality or the respect due to principles of an international or humane nature, translated into imperative legal norms (*jus cogens*)'.[21] The rationale for States to respond to serious breaches of obligations *erga omnes* was reflected by the International Court in *Legal Consequences for States of the Continued Presence of South Africa in Namibia (South West Africa)* (1971): 'As to the general consequences resulting from the illegal [situation] . . . all States should bear in mind that the injured entity is a people which must look to the international community for assistance'.[22] Not long thereafter, the ILC acknowledged that a possible consequence of legal obligations deriving from the

[19] *Ibid.*, 111–12, para. 7 (Commentary to Chapter III).

[20] *Prosecutor v. Furundžija*, IT-95-17/1-T, para. 151 (1998).

[21] *Barcelona Traction, Light and Power Company, Limited (Belgium v. Spain)*, Judgment, ICJ Reports 1970, Sep. Op. Ammoun, p. 286, para. 34.

[22] *Legal Consequences for States of the Continued Presence of South Africa in Namibia (South West Africa) notwithstanding Security Council Resolution 276 (1970)*, Advisory Opinion, ICJ Reports 1971, p. 16, para. 127.

normative distinction between *jus cogens* and *jus dispositivum* is that a breach of the former might entail *actio popularis*.[23] *Special rapporteur* Riphagen followed this line of reasoning to its logical conclusion in his Third Report on State Responsibility:

> [T]he introduction of extra-State interests as the object of protection by rules of international law tends towards the recognition of an *actio popularis* of every State having participated in the creation of such extra-State interests, the other possibilities of enforcement being either only self-enforcement, or enforcement by the subject to which this extra-State interest is allocated for this purpose.[24]

The observations by the International Court and the ILC reflect the reality that, in many cases, only third-States have the capacity to redress violations of peremptory norms where such violations are enabled by the failure of the first-State to fulfil its obligations *erga omnes* through prevention. In this context, as the sole entities materially capable in the last instance of countermanding circumstances permitting the violation of peremptory norms, third-States are empowered to respond to serious violations of peremptory norms. This contemporary development abandons the earlier position of the Court in the *South West Africa Cases* (1966), which initially denied the existence of *actio popularis* in international law.[25]

The International Court has clearly articulated three particular consequences arising for third-States from breaches of obligations *erga omnes*. Most immediately, third-States are obligated not to recognize the legality of a situation resulting from, or maintained by, the breach of obligations *erga omnes*.[26] Third-States are under a parallel obligation not to aid or assist in the maintenance of such a situation.[27] While these consequences were articulated in cases concerning ongoing breaches of obligations *erga omnes*, such consequences may apply in principle to situations arising from breaches of obligations *erga omnes* whether or not the breaches

[23] Ago, Fifth Report, [1976] II(1) YbILC 50, para. 141 (without endorsement).

[24] Willem Riphagen, Third Report on State Responsibility, [1982] II(1) YbILC 37, para. 94.

[25] *South West Africa Cases (Ethiopia v. South Africa / Liberia v. South Africa) (Second Phase)*, Judgment, ICJ Reports 1966, p. 6, para. 88.

[26] *Legal Consequences of the Construction of a Wall in the Occupied Palestinian Territory*, Advisory Opinion, ICJ Reports 2004, p. 136, para. 159; *Legal Consequences for States of the Continued Presence of South Africa in Namibia (South West Africa) notwithstanding Security Council Resolution 276 (1970)*, Advisory Opinion, ICJ Reports 1971, p. 16, para. 126.

[27] *Ibid.*

themselves are continuing.[28] Finally, third-States are under an obligation to cooperate to bring an end to serious breaches of obligations *erga omnes*, within the limits of the Charter of the United Nations and international law.[29] It is in this sense that a form of *actio popularis* has been directly linked to obligations *erga omnes* arising from peremptory norms in international law.

The ILC articulated these same legal consequences for third-States arising from serious breaches of obligations *erga omnes* in Article 41 of the Articles on State Responsibility.[30] Article 41(2) denotes a duty to abstain from maintaining or recognizing the legality of a situation arising from serious breaches of obligations arising from peremptory norms. Article 41(1) articulates an extension of the duty to prevent violations of peremptory norms in the form of suppression: 'States shall cooperate to bring to an end through lawful means any serious breach' of oblgiations arising from peremptory norms.[31] By this view, where a State has breached its obligation to prevent violations of peremptory norms, it is the *positive duty* of third-States to suppress that breach by virtue of the *erga omnes* character of the obligation breached and the values the norm in question protects.[32] Thus, consequences arising for third-States from

[28] *See Legal Consequences of the Construction of a Wall in the Occupied Palestinian Territory*, Advisory Opinion, ICJ Reports 2004, p. 136, paras. 88, 155–7; *Legal Consequences for States of the Continued Presence of South Africa in Namibia (South West Africa) notwithstanding Security Council Resolution 276 (1970)*, Advisory Opinion, ICJ Reports 1971, p. 16, para. 126.

[29] *Legal Consequences of the Construction of a Wall in the Occupied Palestinian Territory*, Advisory Opinion, ICJ Reports 2004, p. 136, para. 159; *Legal Consequences for States of the Continued Presence of South Africa in Namibia (South West Africa) notwithstanding Security Council Resolution 276 (1970)*, Advisory Opinion, ICJ Reports 1971, p. 16, para. 126.

[30] ILC Articles on State Responsibility (2001), Article 41 (Particular consequences of a serious breach of an obligation under this chapter):

1. States shall cooperate to bring to an end through lawful means any serious breach within the meaning of article 40.
2. No State shall recognize as lawful a situation created by a serious breach within the meaning of article 40, nor render aid or assistance in maintaining that situation.
3. This article is without prejudice to the other consequences referred to in this Part and to such further consequences that a breach to which this chapter applies may entail under international law.

[31] *Ibid.*

[32] *Ibid.*, 114, para. 2 (Commentary to Article 41) ('States are under a positive duty to cooperate in order to bring to an end serious breaches in the sense of article 40').

the breach of obligations *erga omnes* may themselves be contemplated as an extension of the same obligations breached.[33]

According to the ILC, in order to engage particular legal consequences for breaches of obligations *erga omnes*, the breach must satisfy a threshold of seriousness defined by its 'gross or systematic' character,[34] as set out in Article 40 of the Articles on State Responsibility.[35] This threshold would not exonerate the State for breaches of *erga omnes* obligations that are neither gross nor systemic in nature but, rather, aims to reserve the consequences for breaches of obligations *erga omnes* for those of a magnitude necessitating an *actio popularis* response.[36] While it is perhaps desirable for third-States to be bound by a positive duty to suppress only serious breaches of obligations *erga omnes* arising from peremptory norms, whether the obligations of non-recognition and non-maintenance should also be so limited is less clear. The International Court, when it has articulated legal consequences for third-States arising from breaches of obligations *erga omnes*, related those consequences to the *erga omnes* character of the obligations breached rather than the 'seriousness' of those breaches.[37] More generally – beyond the limited

[33] *See* Anne-Laure Vaurs-Chaumette, *Peoples and Minorities*, *in* The Law of International Responsibility 999–1002 (Oxford University Press, James Crawford, Alain Pellet & Simon Olleson eds., 2009).

[34] ILC Articles on State Responsibility (2001), Article 40 (Application of this chapter):

1. This chapter applies to the international responsibility which is entailed by a serious breach by a State of an obligation arising under a peremptory norm of general international law.
2. A breach of such an obligation is serious if it involves a gross or systematic failure by the responsible State to fulfil the obligation.

[35] *Ibid.*, 113, para. 8 (Commentary to Article 40) ('To be regarded as systematic, a violation would have to be carried out in an organized and deliberate way. In contrast, the term "gross" refers to the intensity of the violation or its effects; it denotes violations of a flagrant nature, amounting to a direct and outright assault on the values protected by the rule. The terms are not of course mutually exclusive; serious breaches will usually be both systematic and gross. Factors which may establish the seriousness of a violation would include the intent to violate the norm; the scope and number of individual violations; and the gravity of their consequences for the victims').

[36] James Crawford, *International Crimes of States*, *in* The Law of International Responsibility 410 (Crawford *et al.* eds.).

[37] *Legal Consequences of the Construction of a Wall in the Occupied Palestinian Territory*, Advisory Opinion, ICJ Reports 2004, p. 136, para. 159; *Legal Consequences for States of the Continued Presence of South Africa in Namibia (South West Africa) notwithstanding Security Council Resolution 276 (1970)*, Advisory Opinion, ICJ Reports 1971, p. 16, para. 126.

category of obligations arising from peremptory norms to which Articles 40 and 41 expressly refer – the ILC provides a more general savings clause under Article 54 for 'Measures taken by States other than an injured State',[38] envisaging countermeasures by non-injured States that follow where the obligation breached is owed to a group of States or 'to the international community as a whole'.[39]

Practice indicates that responses to breaches of obligations arising from peremptory norms are context-dependent and may constitute a range of policy options.[40] For example, in *Legal Consequences for States of the Continued Presence of South Africa in Namibia (South West Africa) notwithstanding Security Council Resolution 276 (1970)* (1971), the International Court outlined measures for UN member States to refrain from lending support or assistance to the maintenance of apartheid in Namibia, abstain from entering into treaty relations where South Africa acted on behalf of Namibia, withhold diplomatic recognition through establishing missions, and forgo entering into economic relationships.[41] The case concerned the 'illegality and invalidity' of South Africa's continued presence in Namibia following the end of its League of Nations mandate to administer the territory. The Court, however, based its Judgment not merely on the dissolution of the mandate but, more importantly, on the ongoing policy of apartheid.[42] Apartheid, Judge Ammoun noted in his Separate Opinion, is an offence against the 'dignity of the human person' that constitutes a violation of international law commensurate with war crimes, genocide, and crimes against

[38] ILC Articles on State Responsibility (2001), Article 54 ('This chapter does not prejudice the right of any State, entitled under article 48, paragraph 1, to invoke the responsibility of another State, to take lawful measures against that State to ensure cessation of the breach and reparation in the interest of the injured State or of the beneficiaries of the obligation breached'). *See ibid.*, 139, para. 6 (Commentary to Article 54).

[39] *Ibid.*, Article 48 (Invocation of responsibility by a State other than an injured State) (while the Articles refer only to the invocation of responsibility by States, rather than international organizations, actions by States undertaken individually and collectively through international organizations would in principle fall within this same conceptualization).

[40] Lionos-Alexandre Sicilanos, *Countermeasures in Response to Grave Violations of Obligations Owed to the International Community, in* THE LAW OF INTERNATIONAL RESPONSIBILITY 1137–48 (Crawford *et al.* eds.).

[41] *Legal Consequences for States of the Continued Presence of South Africa in Namibia (South West Africa) notwithstanding Security Council Resolution 276 (1970)*, Advisory Opinion, ICJ Reports 1971, p. 16, paras. 119, 122–4.

[42] *Ibid.*, paras. 127–33; Sep. Op. Ammoun, p. 55, paras. 6–8. (suggesting that the legal consequences outlined by the court were informed by the policy of apartheid practised by South Africa).

humanity.[43] Consequently, the *erga omnes* nature of the obligations breached required the international community to take action in response to the ongoing administration of apartheid by South Africa, which the International Court described as 'a denial of fundamental human rights [which] is a flagrant violation of the purposes and principles of the [UN] Charter.[44] Discrete examples of collective action, undertaken by States in response to serious breaches of obligations *erga omnes*, are available with respect to each norm of *jus cogens*: for example, the coordinated response to combat piracy off the Horn of Africa;[45] ongoing efforts to suppress human trafficking in the Greater-Mekong Sub-region;[46] the use of force to reverse North Korean aggression against South Korea,[47] and Iraqi aggression in Kuwait;[48] humanitarian intervention in response to genocide in Kosovo;[49] suppression of war crimes and crimes against humanity in Libya;[50] various efforts to deter apartheid in South Africa;[51] international pressure for the United States to halt alleged torture at Bagram Air Force Base, Afghanistan, and Guantanamo Bay,

43 *Ibid.*, para. 8.

44 *Legal Consequences for States of the Continued Presence of South Africa in Namibia (South West Africa) notwithstanding Security Council Resolution 276 (1970)*, Advisory Opinion, ICJ Reports 1971, p. 16, paras. 126–31

45 SC Res. 1851, UN Doc. S/Res/1851 (16 December 2008) (one among a series of related resolutions, for example, '[c]alls upon States, regional and international organizations that have the capacity to do so, to take part actively in the fight against piracy and armed robbery at sea off the coast of Somalia, in particular, consistent with this resolution, resolution 1846 (2008), and international law', and seeks to coordinate action among States engaged in combatting piracy).

46 *See, e.g.*, United Nations Inter-Agency Project on Human Trafficking in the Greater Mekong Sub-region (UNIAP), PHASE III (2007–10) MIDTERM EVALUATION REPORT (Paul Cunnington and Samantha Hung eds., 2009).

47 SC Res. 84, UN Doc. S/Res/84 (7 July 1950) (authorizing use of force to repel invasion of South Korea).

48 SC Res. 678, UN Doc. S/Res/678 (29 November 1990) (authorizing use of force to repel invasion of Kuwait).

49 SC Res. 1244, UN Doc. S/Res/1244, para. 5 (10 June 1999) (authorizing intervention in Kosovo; however, the resolution followed the use of force).

50 SC Res. 1973, UN Doc. S/Res/1973 (17 March 2011) (authorizing States to take 'all necessary measures . . . to protect civilians and civilian populated areas'); SC Res. 1970, UN Doc. S/Res/1970 (26 February 2011).

51 *See, e.g.*, SC Res. 554, UN Doc. S/Res/554 (17 August 1984) (declaring Constitution of South Africa 'null and void'); SC Res. 418, UN Doc. S/Res/418 (4 November 1977) (imposing a mandatory arms embargo on South Africa in place of prior voluntary measures); GA Res. 2396, UN Doc. A/Res/2396 (2 December 1968) (restricting cultural contacts with South Africa); GA Res. 1899, UN Doc. A/Res/1899 (13 November 1963) (imposing voluntary oil embargo on South Africa).

Cuba;[52] and the UN-endorsed military response to Afghanistan's failure to prevent and punish terrorism.[53]

B Protection and the use of force

One issue deserving special attention is whether humanitarian intervention through the use of force constitutes a 'lawful means ... [by which] to bring an end' to a serious breach of obligations owed to the international community as a whole, within the meaning of Article 41 (1) of the Articles on State Responsibility. Humanitarian operations in Kosovo in 1999[54] and Libya in 2011[55] are notable instances in which third-States resorted to the use of force to suppress serious breaches of obligations *erga omnes*. The doctrine of humanitarian intervention arose in the writings of Grotius, who endorsed action taken on behalf of basic interests of humanity as the 'most wide-reaching' cause for war:

> The final and most wide-reaching cause for undertaking wars on behalf of others is the mutual tie of kinship among men, which of itself affords sufficient ground for rendering assistance ... This includes intervening against wrongs committed to one's own people.[56]

This same idea of undertaking action 'on behalf of others' on the basis of basic humanity is reflected in the interests of the international

[52] *See* Detainee Treatment Act of 2005, Pub. L. No. 109–148, 119 Stat. 2739 (prohibits the 'cruel, inhumane, or degrading treatment or punishment' of any detainee in US Government custody, 'regardless of nationality or physical location').

[53] SC Res. 1386, UN Doc. S/Res/1386 (20 December 2001); SC Res. 1383, UN Doc. S/Res/1383 (6 December 2001); SC Res. 1378, UN Doc. S/Res/1378 (14 November 2001); SC Res. 1377, UN Doc. S/Res/1377 (12 November 2001); SC Res. 1373, UN Doc. S/Res/1373 (28 September 2001); SC Res. 1368, UN Doc. S/Res/1368 (12 September 2001) (calling on 'the international community to redouble their efforts to prevent and suppress terrorist attacks including by increased cooperation').

[54] SC Res. 1244, UN Doc. S/Res/1244, para. 5 (10 June 1999) (authorizing intervention in Kosovo, however the resolution followed the use of force).

[55] SC Res. 1973, UN Doc. S/Res/1973, para. 4 (17 March 2011) (authorizing 'all necessary measures ... to protect civilians and civilian populated areas' in Libya); SC Res. 1970, UN Doc. S/Res/1970 (26 February 2011). *See* discussion *infra*, Chapter 16 (An Illustration: The Libya Crisis).

[56] Hugo Grotius, De Jure Belli ac Pacis Libri Tres II.XXV.VI, II.XXV.VIII (Oxford: Clarendon Press, Francis Kelsey trans., James B. Scott ed., 1925 [1646]) [hereinafter, Grotius, De Jure].

community, expressed through *jus cogens* and given effect by obligations *erga omnes*.

The proposition that States have a legal *right* to undertake humanitarian intervention remains a controversial one; even more so that States have a legal *obligation* to do so.[57] In 1986, the UK Foreign Office observed that 'the best case that can be made in support of humanitarian intervention is that it cannot be said to be unambiguously illegal';[58] however, international law in this area has evolved over the past three decades. The debate over the legality of humanitarian intervention was cast into sharp relief following the use of chemical weapons by the Syrian government against its own citizens in August 2013.[59] Although the commission of war crimes and crimes against humanity had been prevalent throughout the course of the Syrian civil war,[60] the use of chemical weapons by the Assad regime marked a turning point in the international response to the conflict. Throughout the civil war, collective action by the United Nations under the authority of the Security Council's Chapter VII powers had been prevented by political interests of certain members of the Council.[61] Following the use of chemical weapons, international discourse took a more urgent tone, and three distinct positions emerged in the debate surrounding the legality of humanitarian intervention in international law.

[57] *Compare* Ian Brownlie and C. J. Apperley, *Kosovo Crisis Inquiry: Memorandum on the International Law Aspects*, 49(4) International and Comparative Law Quarterly 878, 886–94 (2000) ('there is very little evidence to support assertions that a new principle of customary law legitimating humanitarian intervention has crystallised'), *with* Christopher Greenwood, *International Law and the NATO Intervention in Kosovo Memorandum submitted to the Foreign Affairs Committee of the House of Commons*, 49(4) International and Comparative Law Quarterly 926, 929–34 (2000) ('In my opinion modern customary international law does not exclude all possibility of military intervention on humanitarian grounds by States, or by an organisation like NATO').

[58] British Foreign Office, Foreign Policy Document No. 148, 57 British Yearbook of International Law 614 (1986).

[59] The White House, Office of the Press Secretary, US Government Assessment of the Syrian Government's Use of Chemical Weapons on August 21, 2013 (30 August 2013).

[60] *See, e.g.*, Office of the High Commissioner for Human Rights, Report of the Independent International Commission of Inquiry on the Syrian Arab Republic, UN Doc. A/HRC/21/50 (16 August 2012).

[61] *See* Draft Resolution S/2011/612 (4 October 2011), Draft Resolution S/2012/77 (2 February 2012), and Draft Resolution S/2012/538 (19 July 2012) (each invoking Chapter VII of the UN Charter and vetoed by both Russia and China).

i. The conservative position

The UN Charter expressly provides for the use of force in two contexts: self-defence,[62] or pursuant to a Security Council resolution.[63] Article 51 permits recourse to individual or collective self-defence, while the Security Council may authorize the use of force pursuant to Article 42 of the UN Charter more generally. A conservative position maintains that these provisions reflect the universe of possible avenues to use force under international law. In this sense, for example, collective action was authorized in Libya under Chapter VII of the UN Charter through Security Council Resolutions 1970[64] and 1973;[65] the latter authorized the use of force by the international community on behalf of the civilian population of Libya. In the Syria context, the Russian Federation was particularly forceful in its articulation of this classical position, declaring in an official statement by its Ministry of Foreign Affairs that any intervention outside the authorization of the Security Council would constitute a 'direct violation' of international law.[66] Russian President Vladimir Putin went further: 'Under current international law, force is permitted only in self-defense or by the decision of the Security Council. Anything else is unacceptable under the United Nations Charter and would constitute an act of aggression.'[67] Setting aside the credibility of the advocate, whose annexation of Crimea the following year was condemned by the United Nations[68] and classified as an act aggression by US Secretary of State John Kerry,[69] the conservative position serves as a baseline from which to consider humanitarian intervention. While it is beyond question that humanitarian intervention can be undertaken legally under Chapter VII of the UN Charter, whether the Security Council is the *exclusive* legal avenue for humanitarian intervention in international law remains in

62 Charter of the United Nations, Article 51 (1945). 63 *Ibid.*, Article 42.

64 SC Res. 1970, UN Doc. S/Res/1970 (26 February 2011).

65 SC Res. 1973, UN Doc. S/Res/1973 (17 March 2011).

66 Ministry of Foreign Affairs of Russia, Statement of 30 August 2013 by the official representative of the Ministry of Foreign Affairs of Russia Alexander Lukashevich regarding the statements of the United States about the forceful action against Syria, 1655-30-08-2013 (30 August 2013).

67 Vladimir Putin, Editorial, *A Plea for Caution From Russia*, The New York Times, A31 (11 September 2013).

68 GA Res. 68/262, UN Doc. A/Res/68/262 (27 March 2014) (Territorial Integrity of Ukraine).

69 *See* Will Dunham, *Kerry Condemns Russia's 'Incredible Act of Aggression' in Ukraine*, Reuters, *available at* www.reuters.com/article/2014/03/02/us-ukraine-crisis-usa-kerry-idUSBREA210DG20140302 (2 March 2014).

question. The conservative position answers this question in the affirmative, recognizing no legal use of force beyond self-defence and Security Council authorization. Given the ability of a single State to obstruct authorization,[70] and effectively dictate the legality of such use of force, alternative modes of legal recourse are desirable, particularly in response to serious breaches of obligations owed to the international community.

ii. The interventionist position

The converse of the conservative position is that the breach of certain obligations owed to the international community as a whole constitutes a sufficient justification under international law to permit intervention. To this end, US Secretary of State John Kerry utilized language common to discourse on *jus cogens* to justify a unilateral response to the violation of particular 'international norms'.

> What we saw in Syria last week should shock the conscience of the world. It defies any code of morality . . . The indiscriminate slaughter of civilians, the killing of women and children and innocent bystanders by chemical weapons is a moral obscenity. By any standard, it is inexcusable . . . this international norm cannot be violated without consequences. And there is a reason why no matter what you believe about Syria, all peoples and all nations who believe in the cause of our common humanity must stand up to assure that there is accountability for the use of chemical weapons so that it never happens again.[71]

However, it is not immediately clear that this sentiment, which expresses the *moral* legitimacy of the use of force in response to such humanitarian distress, is sufficient to establish *legal* justification without further qualification. In a Joint Statement released by the White House on 6 September 2013, a group of G-20 States expressed their support for the use of force by the United States in Syria without UN authorization due to 'paralysis' of the Security Council.[72] This statement too presents

[70] *See supra, n.* 61.

[71] Federal News Service, *Transcript: Secretary of State John Kerry's Remarks on Alleged Syria Chemical Attack News Conference by Secretary of State John Kerry*, THE WASHINGTON POST, *available at* www.washingtonpost.com/world/national-security/transcript-secretary-of-state-john-kerrys-remarks-on-alleged-syria-chemical-attack/2013/08/26/40b0b4ea-0e8b-11e3-bdf6-e4fc677d94a1_story.html (26 August 2013).

[72] The White House, Joint Statement on Syria, *available at* www.whitehouse.gov/the-press-office/2013/09/06/joint-statement-syria (6 September 2013) (signed by Australia, Canada, France, Italy, Japan, South Korea, Saudi Arabia, Spain, Turkey, the United Kingdom, and

arguments in favour of the perceived legitimacy of the use of force, yet neglects presenting any legal justification beyond a moral claim.

The 'Responsibility to Protect' suggests one possible avenue by which to contemplate the legality of the interventionist position. The doctrine is the creation of the United Nations and has gained increasing traction over the past decade as a safeguard against mass atrocities.[73] The principle articulates the obligation of the State to protect its population against violations of particular peremptory norms, failing which collective action by the international community is mandated. At present, the mandate of the responsibility to protect is formally extended to three peremptory norms of general international law.[74] In effect, the responsibility to protect reiterates the obligations *erga omnes* of the State, arising from peremptory norms and owed to the international community as a whole, as well as legal consequences arising from their breach. In principle, the responsibility to protect implicates the principle of *actio popularis*, action undertaken by third-States in response to serious breaches of obligations *erga omnes*. However, the responsibility to protect does not expressly entitle States to use force, as noted by Secretary-General Ban Ki-moon:

> RtoP is not a new code for humanitarian intervention. Rather, it is built on a more positive and affirmative concept of sovereignty as responsibility ... the responsibility to protect does not alter the legal obligation of Member States to refrain from the use of force except in conformity with the Charter. Rather, it reinforces this obligation.[75]

the United States: 'We call for a strong international response to this grave violation of the world's rules and conscience that will send a clear message that this kind of atrocity can never be repeated. Those who perpetrated these crimes must be held accountable. Signatories have consistently supported a strong UN Security Council Resolution, given the Security Council's responsibilities to lead the international response, but recognize that the Council remains paralyzed as it has been for two and a half years. The world cannot wait for endless failed processes that can only lead to increased suffering in Syria and regional instability. We support efforts undertaken by the United States and other countries to reinforce the prohibition on the use of chemical weapons').

[73] 2005 World Summit Outcome, GA Res. 60/1, UN Doc. A/Res/60/1, paras. 138–9 (24 October 2005); *see* SC Res. 1674, UN Doc. S/Res/1674, para. 4 (2006) (reaffirming the provisions of paragraphs 138 and 139 of the 2005 World Summit Outcome Document).

[74] *Ibid.* (These are genocide, war crimes, and crimes against humanity, with the addition of ethnic cleansing, which would be generally subsumed by one of the three enumerated core crimes).

[75] UN Secretary-General Ban Ki-moon, *Remarks at 'Responsible Sovereignty: International Cooperation for a Changed World'*, UN Doc. SG/SM/11701 (15 July 2008).

The statement by the Secretary-General opposes the possibility that the responsibility to protect provides a discrete legal justification for the use of force outside Article 51 of the UN Charter.

Even so, the principles underlying the responsibility to protect suggest that the use of force may constitute a lawful response to serious breaches of obligations owed to the international community, by virtue of the magnitude of those breaches and the interest of the international community in bringing them to a halt. The prohibition against the use of force derives from respect for the sovereignty of the State,[76] which is conceived as sovereignty delegated to the State by its citizens.[77] The doctrine of responsibility to protect accordingly indicates the State is bound to respect certain international norms arising from the interests of the international community as a whole. 'Sovereignty as responsibility', a corollary of the responsibility to protect, is a principle whereby sovereignty is conditioned upon responsibility.[78] These increasingly accepted international principles support the conclusion that 'international law does not require that respect for the sovereignty and integrity of a State must in all cases be given priority over the protection of human rights and human life'.[79] Therefore, under this theory, where third-States have a legal interest in the performance of obligations *erga omnes* and 'shall' take action to bring an end to serious breaches of those obligations,[80] and the conduct of the first-State has undermined its claim to sovereignty, then the pallet of lawful means by which third-States may respond would include the use of force by virtue of the nature of the breaches in question.

[76] Charter of the United Nations, Article 2 (1945); *see also* Declaration on Principles of International Law Concerning Friendly Relations and Co-operation among States in accordance with the Charter of the United Nations, GA Res. 2625, UN Doc. A/Res/25/2625, Annex, Principle a (24 October 1970).

[77] *See* discussion *supra*, Chapter 3.A.ii ('of States').

[78] *See* Francis Deng, Donald Rothchild, Sadikei Kimaro, I. William Zartman & Terrence Lyons, SOVEREIGNTY AS RESPONSIBILITY: CONFLICT MANAGEMENT IN AFRICA 32–3 (Washington, DC: Brookings Institution Press 1996) ('sovereignty carries with it responsibilities for the population. It is from acceptance of this responsibility that the legitimacy of a government derives. The relationship between the controlling authority and the populace should ideally ensure the highest standards of human dignity').

[79] Christopher Greenwood, *International Law and the NATO Intervention in Kosovo Memorandum submitted to the Foreign Affairs Committee of the House of Commons*, 49 (4) INTERNATIONAL AND COMPARATIVE LAW QUARTERLY 926, 929 (2000).

[80] *See* discussion *supra*, text accompanying *nn.* 20–53.

iii. The hybrid position: 'humanitarian self-defence'

The United Kingdom articulated a variant of the interventionist position that attempts to bring humanitarian intervention, absent Security Council authorization, within the scope of Article 51 of the UN Charter as a form of self-defence. According to this legal justification for humanitarian intervention, 'if the Security Council is blocked', then 'humanitarian intervention' constitutes a discrete 'legal basis' for the use of force.[81] The UK Government articulated three conditions that must be met to engage the doctrine of humanitarian self-defence:

> (i) there is convincing evidence, generally accepted by the international community as a whole, of extreme humanitarian distress on a large scale, requiring immediate and urgent relief;
> (ii) it must be objectively clear that there is no practicable alternative to the use of force if lives are to be saved; and
> (iii) the proposed use of force must be necessary and proportionate to the aim of relief of humanitarian need and must be strictly limited in time and scope to this aim (i.e. the minimum necessary to achieve that end and for no other purpose).[82]

Interestingly, these conditions largely adopt the language of self-defence, whereby an imminent threat, the absense of an alternative, and proportionality condition unilateral recourse to the use of force. These elements were articulated in 2004 by the UN High Level Panel on Threats, Challenges, and Change: '[A] threatened State, according to long established international law, can take military action as long as the threatened attack is imminent, no other means would deflect it and the action is proportionate'.[83] By appropriating these elements into a legal justification for humanitarian intervention, the UK Government effectively defines humanitarian intervention as a form of self-defence, which would thereby fall within Article 51 of the UN Charter and permit the use of force without Security Council authorization.[84]

81 Prime Minister's Office, 10 Downing Street, *Chemical Weapons Use by Syrian Regime: UK Government Legal Position*, para. 4 (29 August 2013).

82 *Ibid.*

83 UN Secretary-General, Report of the High Level Panel on Threats, Challenges and Change, UN Doc. A/59/565, para. 188 (2004) (emphasis omitted).

84 This formulation echoes the doctrine of 'preventive self-defense' set out by the 'Caroline Test', articulated by US Secretary of State Daniel Webster in relation to the 1837 *Caroline* Affair, who called upon Great Britain to show:

Under the UK Government's legal justification for the use of force, the threshold condition of imminence for resort to self-defence is modified in part using the language of *jus cogens* by adding 'extreme humanitarian distress on a large scale ... *accepted by the international community as a whole*'. The requirement that such force be necessary and proportionate is further modified as 'strictly limited in time and scope ... to the relief of humanitarian need'. The UK Government thereby articulated a form of 'humanitarian self-defence' that, if accepted, would alleviate the need to define legal recourse to the use of force beyond Article 51 of the UN Charter. This legal justification is consistent with the concept of a common interest in the performance of obligations *erga omnes*. It suggests that serious breaches of obligations owed to the international community as a whole, to the extent that they produce 'extreme humanitarian distress', constitute an imminent threat to the interests of the international community warranting the use of force as a form of self-defence.[85]

***

According to the ILC, 'States are under a positive duty to cooperate in order to bring to an end serious breaches' of obligations owed to the international community as a whole,[86] yet they shall do so only 'through lawful means'.[87] Three distinct positions have emerged with respect to the legality of the use of force as a response to serious breaches of

> [The] necessity of self-defence [was] instant, overwhelming, leaving no choice of means, and no moment of deliberation ... [and that the British force], even supposing the necessity of the moment authorized them to enter the territories of the United States at all, did nothing unreasonable or excessive; since the act, justified by the necessity of self-defence, must be limited by that necessity, and kept clearly within it.

Letter from Daniel Webster, US Secretary of State, to Henry Fox, British Minister in Washington, 24 April 1841, *in* 1 British Documents on Foreign Affairs: Reports and Papers from the Foreign Office Confidential Print, Pt. I, Series C 153, 159 (Frederick, MD: University Publications of America, Kenneth Bourne ed., 1986). This standard was reiterated by the IMT at Nuremberg in its 1946 judgment: 'preventive action in foreign territory is justified only in case of "an instant and overwhelming necessity for self-defense, leaving no choice of means and no moment of deliberation"'. *Nazi Conspiracy and Aggression*, International Military Tribunal at Nuremberg, Opinion and Judgment, 36 (1946) (quoting The *Caroline* case).

85 *See* discussion *supra*, Chapter 14.B.i (The Convervative Position).

86 ILC Articles on State Responsibility (2001), 114, para. 2 (Commentary to Article 41).

87 *Ibid.*, Article 41(1).

obligations *erga omnes*. While the UK Government theory of 'humanitarian self-defence' offers a persuasive negotiation between the 'conservative' and 'interventionist' positions, its precise contours remain to be established through practice.

C Punishment and universal jurisdiction

The punishment of violations of peremptory norms is conceived to be a practical aspect of the performance of obligations *erga omnes* arising from *jus cogens*.[88] This functional element indicates the expectation that each State punish violators of peremptory norms within its territory. The Special Court for Sierra Leone referred to this duty when the power of Sierra Leone to prosecute international crimes was challenged following the conclusion of the Lomé Agreement,[89] the 1999 peace accord that ended that country's civil war and granted broad amnesty. The Court rejected the challenge, holding:

> Under international law, states are under a duty to prosecute crimes whose prohibition has the status of *jus cogens*. It is for this reason that the Special Representative of the United Nations Secretary-General asserted the UN's understanding of Article IX of the Lomé Agreement as excluding the international crimes of genocide, crimes against humanity, war crimes and other serious violations of international humanitarian law. Furthermore, at the time of the Special Court Agreement, Sierra Leone concurred with the position of the UN that the amnesty was not applicable to international crimes.[90]

Like preventing violations of peremptory norms, punishment is conceived as a form of due diligence on the part of the State.[91] The generality of obligations *erga omnes* extends to each State a legal interest in the punishment of violators of peremptory norms in every State. In practice, the principle of *aut dedere aut judicare* refers to the duty of the State to either prosecute or extradite suspected violators of peremptory norms in

[88] Colleen Enache-Brown and Ari Fried, *Universal Crime, Jurisdiction and Duty: The Obligation of* Aut Dedere Aut Judicare *in International Law*, 53 McGill Law Journal 613, 631 (1998); M. Cherif Bassiouni, *International Crimes:* Jus Cogens *and* Obligatio Erga Omnes, 59(4) Law and Contemporary Problems 63, 65–6 (1996).

[89] *Prosecutor v. Gbao*, Decision on Preliminary Motion on the Invalidity of the Agreement between the United Nations and the Government of Sierra Leone on the Establishment of the Special Court for Sierra Leone, SCSL-04-15-PT-141, paras. 9–10 (2004).

[90] *Ibid.*, para. 10.

[91] *See* discussion *supra*, Chapter 14.A (Prevention and Consequences for Third-States).

its custody irrespective of conventional bases of jurisdiction.[92] The premise of this alternative obligation,[93] by which the State must discharge its obligations *erga omnes* by prosecuting or extraditing such individuals for prosecution elsewhere, is to prevent impunity for violations of peremptory norms. Once again, the sentiment captured by the obligation can be found in the writings of Grotius, who envisaged just such an obligation *aut dedere aut punire*:

> [T]he state in which he who has been found guilty dwells ought to do one of two things. When appealed to it should either punish the guilty person as he deserves, or it should entrust him to the discretion of the party making the appeal.[94]

In practice, the contemporary expression of the obligation constitutes a broader duty centered on prosecution. It is an obligation that reflects the aim of this aspect of obligations *erga omnes* to punish violations of peremptory norms wherever possible.

As with the prevention aspect of obligations *erga omnes*, the functional element of punishment arising from *jus cogens* is uncontroversial in theory. However, the aspect of generality requires further attention and, again, the work of the ILC is helpful to an understanding of the performance of obligations *erga omnes* relating to punishment expressed by *aut dedere aut judicare*. The obligation to extradite or prosecute was adopted as a topic for study by the ILC in 2004, which in 2005 appointed a *special rapporteur* who has since submitted a series of reports to the UN General Assembly,[95] in addition to an extensive survey of relevant multilateral conventions conducted by the UN Secretariat,[96] and the establishment of a working group in 2008.[97]

[92] *See* discussion *infra*, text accompanying *nn.* 111–30.

[93] Zdzislaw Galicki, Preliminary Report on the Obligation to Extradite or Prosecute ("*aut dedere aut judicare*"), UN Doc. A/CN.4/571, para. 49 (2006).

[94] Grotius, De Jure, II.XXI.III–IV (at IV, para. 1). *See* Galicki, Preliminary Report on the Obligation to Extradite or Prosecute ("*aut dedere aut judicare*"), paras. 8–9.

[95] Zdzislaw Galicki, Fourth Report on the Obligation to Extradite or Prosecute (*aut dedere aut judicare*), UN Doc. A/CN.4/648 (2011); Third Report on the Obligation to Extradite or Prosecute (*aut dedere aut judicare*), UN Doc. A/CN.4/603 (2008); Second Report on the Obligation to Extradite or Prosecute (*aut dedere aut judicare*), UN Doc. A/CN.4/585 (2007); Preliminary Report on the Obligation to Extradite or Prosecute ("*aut dedere aut judicare*").

[96] UN Secretariat, Survey of Multilateral Conventions which may be of Relevance for the Commission's Work on the Topic 'The Obligation to Extradite or Prosecute (*aut dedere aut judicare*)', UN Doc. A/CN.4/630 (2010).

[97] Galicki, Fourth Report on the Obligation to Extradite or Prosecute (*aut dedere aut judicare*), para. 3.

The majority of the ILC's work on the obligation has to date centred on its basis in treaty law which, despite broad variation, shares two common features: the objective to punish particular conduct at the international level and a mechanism that obligates the custodial State to act pursuant to this end.[98] It may be recalled that obligations to this effect are contained in the various conventional expressions of peremptory norms.[99] Perhaps the clearest illustration of the obligation to extradite or prosecute is found in the Draft Code of Crimes against the Peace and Security of Mankind (1996), which in Article 9 articulates this obligation arising from the prohibitions of war crimes, crimes against humanity, and genocide.

Article 9. Obligation to extradite or prosecute

> Without prejudice to the jurisdiction of an international criminal court, the State Party in the territory of which an individual alleged to have committed a crime set out in article 17, 18, 19 or 20 is found shall extradite or prosecute that individual.[100]

In its Commentary, the ILC noted that 'the fundamental purpose' of including the *aut dedere aut judicare* principle in the Draft Code was 'to ensure that individuals who are responsible for particularly serious crimes are brought to justice by providing for the effective prosecution and punishment of such individuals by a competent jurisdiction'.[101] The Commission indicated no preference to prosecution or extradition.[102]

In *Questions Relating to the Obligation to Prosecute or Extradite* (2012), with respect to obligations *erga omnes partes* arising from the prohibition against torture, the International Court of Justice indicated that a preference for prosecution is implicit in the fulfilment of the obligation.

> [I]f the State in whose territory the suspect is present has received a request for extradition in any of the cases envisaged in the provisions of the Convention, it can relieve itself of its obligation to prosecute by acceding to that request. It follows that the choice between extradition

[98] UN Secretariat, Survey of Multilateral Conventions which may be of Relevance for the Commission's Work on the Topic 'The Obligation to Extradite or Prosecute (*aut dedere aut judicare*)', UN Doc. A/CN.4/630, para. 150 (2010).

[99] *See supra*, *n.* 12.

[100] Draft Codes of Crimes (1996), Article 9.

[101] *Ibid.*, 31, para. 2 (Commentary to Article 9).

[102] *Ibid.*, para. 6 ('Article 9 does not give priority to either alternative course of action'); *see ibid.*, 32, para. 8 (indicating that transfer of such an individual to an international criminal court would also satisfy the *aut dedere aut judicare* obligation).

> or submission for prosecution, pursuant to the Convention, does not mean that the two alternatives are to be given the same weight. Extradition is an option offered to the State by the Convention, whereas prosecution is an international obligation under the Convention, the violation of which is a wrongful act engaging the responsibility of the State.[103]

Applying this reasoning of the Court, with respect to obligations *erga omnes parties*, to obligations *erga omnes* more generally appears unobjectionable given that the issue turned on the effect of the *erga omnes* character of the obligation in question. It is in the sense of this obligation to extradite or prosecute that the generality of this aspect of obligations *erga omnes* becomes clear: if a State is in custody of an individual suspected of violating a peremptory norm, it is under a *positive duty* to see the individual brought to justice irrespective of nationality or the territory in which the crime was committed.[104] In principle, questions remain unanswered following the Court's decision in *Questions Relating to the Obligation to Prosecute or Extradite*, notably, whether and how obligations *erga omnes* might be enforced in the absense of a controlling treaty framework such as that provided in this instance by the Torture Convention. However, the preference for prosecution articulated by the International Court provides one possible solution, by casting extradition as not strictly a part of the primary obligation to prosecute, but merely an alternative alongside transfer to an international court, by which the primary obligation may be discharged.

The work of the ILC has considered the multitude of conventional expressions of the obligation to extradite or prosecute as a possible basis for a more general customary provision to this effect.[105] This proposal, however, appears to have been abandoned in favour of a content-based approach that focuses on 'particular categories of crimes which may create such a customary obligation, recognized as binding by the international community of States, though limited as to its scope and substance'.[106] This reflects the relation of punishment to obligations *erga omnes* arising from peremptory norms. Indeed, the ILC cites the obligation to extradite or prosecute articulated in the 1996 Draft Code as an

103 *Questions Relating to the Obligation to Prosecute or Extradite (Belgium v. Senegal)*, Judgment, ICJ Reports 2012, p. 422, para. 95.
104 *See* discussion *infra*, text accompanying *nn.* 131–40.
105 *See* Galicki, Third Report on the Obligation to Extradite or Prosecute (*aut dedere aut judicare*), paras. 88–9, 125.
106 Galicki, Fourth Report on the Obligation to Extradite or Prosecute (*aut dedere aut judicare*), para. 86.

exemplar of the customary obligation to punish violations of the prohibitions against war crimes, crimes against humanity, and genocide.[107] Early in its discussions on the matter, there was support for the limitation of the obligation to 'crimes that affect the international community as a whole', including war crimes, crimes against humanity, genocide, torture, and terrorism, in addition to multilateral conventions that employ the mechanism.[108] Belgium in particular articulated the justification for such a restriction.[109] Support for this proposition culminated in Draft Article 4 on the Obligation to Extradite or Prosecute, which delimits the generality of the obligation as arising from peremptory norms:

Article 4. International custom as a source of the obligation *aut dedere aut iudicare*

1. Each State is obliged either to extradite or to prosecute an alleged offender if such an obligation is deriving from the customary norm of international law.
2. Such an obligation may derive, in particular, from customary norms of international law concerning [serious violations of international humanitarian law, genocide, crimes against humanity and war crimes].
3. The obligation to extradite or prosecute shall derive from the peremptory norm of general international law accepted and recognized by the international community of States (*jus cogens*), either in the form of international treaty or international custom, criminalizing any one of acts listed in paragraph 2.[110]

Draft Article 4 expresses the obligation to extradite or prosecute as arising from peremptory norms, incumbent upon every State, just as the construction of Article 9 in the 1996 Draft Code.

107 *Ibid.*, para. 91.

108 Galicki, Second Report on the Obligation to Extradite or Prosecute (*aut dedere aut judicare*), para. 31.

109 Report of the International Law Commission on the Work of its Sixty-First Session, UN Doc. A/CN.4/612, para. 33 (Comments and Information Received from Governments) ('Belgium considers that all States must cooperate in suppressing certain extremely serious crimes – particularly crimes of international humanitarian law (crimes against humanity, genocide and war crimes) – since such crimes pose a threat, both qualitatively and quantitatively, to the most fundamental values of the international community. This contribution to the suppression effort may take the form of direct prosecution of the alleged perpetrators of such crimes or of extradition of those responsible to any State that wishes to prosecute them').

110 Galicki, Fourth Report on the Obligation to Extradite or Prosecute (*aut dedere aut judicare*), paras. 95–6 (The *special rapporteur* immediately notes that the catalogue of offences listed in paragraph 2 is not exhaustive and remains open to consideration).

The obligation to extradite or prosecute is predicated upon the principle of universal jurisdiction.[111] Universal jurisdiction over international crimes can be viewed as a product of the general legal interest of the international community as a whole in the fulfilment of obligations *erga omnes* arising from peremptory norms.[112] Universal jurisdiction constitutes a juridical principle distinct from other bases of jurisdiction – territory, nationality, protective, and passive personality – that permits States to assert jurisdiction over claims in their absence.[113] As it arises in customary international law,[114] the principle of universal jurisdiction permits any State, absent other bases of jurisdiction, to prosecute individuals for violations of peremptory norms.[115] While the obligation to extradite or prosecute is compulsory, the principle of universal jurisdiction is permissive and necessary to fulfil the obligation.[116] Moreover, universal jurisdiction is conceived to be a direct effect of the obligation to extradite or prosecute, as noted by the Institute of International Law in 2005:

> Universal jurisdiction is primarily based on customary international law. It can also be established under a multilateral treaty in the relations

[111] *See* Luc Reydams, UNIVERSAL JURISDICTION 28–80 (Oxford University Press 2003); Bruce Broomhall, INTERNATIONAL JUSTICE & THE INTERNATIONAL CRIMINAL COURT 105–27 (Oxford University Press 2003); Kenneth Randall, *Universal Jurisdiction under International Law*, 66(4) TEXAS LAW REVIEW 785–841 (1988).

[112] The crimes over which universal jurisdiction is recognized are coextensive with the catalogue of peremptory norms: *compare* discussion *supra*, Chapter 11.A (Identifying Peremptory Norms), *with* The AU–EU Expert Report on the Principle of Universal Jurisdiction, EU Doc. 8672/1/09 Rev 1, paras. 8–9 (16 April 2009); Stephen Macedo (ed.), UNIVERSAL JURISDICTION: NATIONAL COURTS AND THE PROSECUTION OF SERIOUS CRIMES UNDER INTERNATIONAL LAW 22 (Philadelphia, PA: University of Pennsylvania Press 2006) (The 'Princeton Principles of Universal Jurisdiction'), *and* RESTATEMENT (THIRD) OF FOREIGN RELATIONS LAW OF THE UNITED STATES § 404 (1987) (Universal Jurisdiction to Define and Punish Certain Offences).

[113] The AU–EU Expert Report on the Principle of Universal Jurisdiction, EU Doc. 8672/1/09 Rev 1, paras. 8–9 (16 April 2009); RESTATEMENT (THIRD) OF FOREIGN RELATIONS LAW OF THE UNITED STATES § 404 (1987) (Universal Jurisdiction to Define and Punish Certain Offences).

[114] *Cf.* The AU–EU Expert Report on the Principle of Universal Jurisdiction, EU Doc. 8672/1/09 Rev 1, paras. 9–11 (16 April 2009) (distinguishing treaty-based regimes of universal jurisdiction among States parties).

[115] De Hoogh, OBLIGATIONS *ERGA OMNES* AND INTERNATIONAL CRIMES 164; Steven Ratner and Jason Abrams, ACCOUNTABILITY FOR HUMAN RIGHTS ATROCITIES IN INTERNATIONAL LAW 140–6 (Oxford: Clarendon Press 1987).

[116] Galicki, Second Report on the Obligation to Extradite or Prosecute (*aut dedere aut judicare*), para. 34; Report of the International Law Commission on the Work of its Forty-Eighth Session, [1996] II(2) YbILC 32, para. 7 (Commentary to Article 9 of the Draft Code of Crimes (1996)).

> between the contracting parties, in particular by virtue of clauses which provide that a State party in the territory of which an alleged offender is found shall either extradite or try that person.[117]

Consequently, the duty to punish violations of peremptory norms is enabled through universal jurisdiction.[118] High-profile examples of the exercise of universal jurisdiction in contemporary international law include the prosecution of Adolf Eichmann by Israel in 1968,[119] proceedings against Augusto Pinochet in the United Kingdom in 1999,[120] and the universal jurisdiction statutes of Spain,[121] Belgium,[122] and the United

[117] Institute of International Law, *Universal Criminal Jurisdiction with Regard to the Crime of Genocide, War Crimes, and Crimes against Humanity*, para. 2 (Christian Tomuschat *rapporteur*, 2005); *see* Galicki, Third Report on the Obligation to Extradite or Prosecute (*aut dedere aut judicare*), para. 47 (endorsing this conclusion).

[118] *See, e.g.*, The AU–EU Expert Report on the Principle of Universal Jurisdiction, EU Doc. 8672/1/09 Rev 1, para. 11 (16 April 2009).

[119] *Attorney-General (Israel) v. Eichmann*, Supreme Court (Israel), 36 ILR 18, paras. 7, 12 (1961) (The District Court of Israel prosecuted and convicted the Head of the Jewish Office of the Gestapo on charges of genocide, war crimes, and crimes against humanity on the basis of the nature of the crimes themselves as 'crimes under the laws of all civilized nations', from which universal jurisdiction over their prosecution derives: 'The jurisdiction to try crimes under international law is *universal*').

[120] *R. v. Bow Street Metropolitan Stipendiary Magistrate and Others, Ex parte Pinochet Ugarte (No. 3)*, House of Lords (UK), [2000] 1 A.C. 147, 38 ILM 581, 589 (1999) (Millett, J.) ('The *jus cogens* nature of the international crime of torture justifies states in taking universal jurisdiction over torture wherever committed') (In this case, not only was the principle of universal jurisdiction invoked, but the doctrine of sovereign immunity was found inapplicable in the context of responsibility for the violation of peremptory norms).

[121] *Ley Orgánica del Poder Judicial* [Law on the Judiciary], 6/1985, Article 23(4) (Providing universal jurisdiction over a range of violations of international law. The law has been amended twice to require a territorial nexus to Spain that requires the suspect in question to be Spanish, a foreigner in Spain, or a foreigner whose extradition has been denied. Although Law 1/2009 (effective 4 November 2009) initially applied this limitation prospectively to allow ongoing investigations to proceed, the restriction was applied retroactively by Law 1/2014 (effective 15 March 2014) in response to proceedings against former Chinese president Hu Jintao and six other former high-ranking Chinese government officials. *See* Case No. 63/2008 (concerning charges of genocide in Tibet against Hu Jintao and others)).

[122] *Loi relative à la répression des violations graves de droit international humanitaire* [Act Concerning the Repression of Grave Breaches of International Humanitarian Law] of 16 June 1993 (concerning twenty 'crimes under international law' and requiring no territorial nexus to Belgium), *amended* 10 February 1999, MONITEUR BELGE [Official Gazette of Belgium] 23 March 1999, 9286 (adding genocide and crimes against humanity and denying immunity under the Act). On 23 April 2003, the Act was amended to limit the justiciability of complaints in the absense of a territorial nexus with Belgium. *See Loi de*

States.[123] Domestic codification of universal jurisdiction over international crimes, and the exercise of that jurisdiction, has become commonplace.[124]

While universal jurisdiction is elemental to the performance by States of obligations *erga omnes* arising from peremptory norms, the applicability of the principle itself is limited to this function of ensuring that domestic courts may establish jurisdiction over individuals alleged to have violated *jus cogens*. Universal jurisdiction is therefore separate from the question of immunity, and the two concepts should not be conflated.[125] As the International Court of Justice noted in the *Arrest Warrant* case, 'jurisdiction does not imply absence of immunity, while absence of immunity does not imply jurisdiction'.[126] And, although the most obvious examples of universal jurisdiction would at first seem to be found in the jurisprudence of international courts and tribunals,[127] the jurisdiction of such organs is distinct from universal jurisdiction '[a]s a technical and

1993 telle que modifiée par la loi du 23 avril 2003 relative à la répression des violations graves du droit international humanitaire et l'article 144 ter du Code judiciaire. The 1993 Act was repealed and replaced by Title 1 *bis* of the Criminal Code, which incorporates the same offences as the 1993 law, but restricts that jurisdiction to theories of active or passive personality (where the plaintiff or defendant is a citizen or resident of Belgium), or universal jurisdiction (where international treaty or custom requires prosecution). *See Loi du 5 août 2003 relative à la répression des infractions graves au droit international humanitaire; Nouveau titre I bis du Code penal*, L. 5 août 2003, article 5).

123 28 USC § 1350 (The Alien Tort Statute); *Sosa v. Alvarez-Machain*, 542 US 692, 762–3 (2004) (Breyer, J., Concurring) ('universal criminal jurisdiction necessarily contemplates a significant degree of civil tort recovery as well'); *Kiobel v. Royal Dutch Petroleum Co.*, 133 S. Ct. 1659, 1669 (2013) (Access to US courts under the ATS was restricted in *Kiobel*, where the Supreme Court determined that a claim under the statute must sufficiently 'touch and concern' the United States to overcome a 'presumption against extraterritoriality'); *see* discussion *supra*, Chapter 12.B (Individual Civil Responsibility).

124 For a survey of African and European practice, for example, *see* The AU–EU Expert Report on the Principle of Universal Jurisdiction, EU Doc. 8672/1/09 Rev 1, paras. 15–27 (16 April 2009).

125 *Compare* Anthony Colangelo, *Jurisdiction, Immunity, Legality, and Jus Cogens*, 14(1) Chicago Journal of International Law 53, 81 (2013) ('This sort of heaping implication upon implication strains the international lawyer's fidelity to discerning international law from actual state practice and *opinio juris*'), *with R. v. Bow Street Metropolitan Stipendiary Magistrate and Others, Ex parte Pinochet Ugarte (No. 3)*, House of Lords (UK), [2000] 1 A.C. 147, 38 ILM 581, 661 (1999) (Phillips, L.) ('Once extra-territorial jurisdiction is established, it makes no sense to exclude from it acts done in an official capacity').

126 *Arrest Warrant of 11 April 2000 (Democratic Republic of the Congo v. Belgium)*, ICJ Reports 2002, p. 3, para. 59.

127 *See* discussion *supra*, Chapter 12.A (International Criminal Responsibility).

conceptual matter'.[128] Moreover, the universal jurisdiction of domestic judicial organs over individuals alleged to have committed international crimes is wholly unrelated to the question of a State's consent to the jurisdiction of the Court. In this sense, neither the violation of a norm belonging to *jus cogens*,[129] nor the breach of obligations *erga omnes*,[130] is sufficient to engage the jurisdiction of the International Court of Justice.

Having considered the function and limitations of universal jurisdiction, and its role in the broader obligation of a custodial State to extradite or prosecute individuals alleged to have violated *jus cogens*, it follows to address the scope of this latter aspect of the performance of obligations *erga omnes* and the ability of third-States to exercise their general legal interest in its performance. The link between the obligation to extradite or prosecute and the performance of obligations *erga omnes* has been articulated repeatedly by the International Court.[131] A question arising frequently in contemporary jurisprudence is the scope of this aspect of obligations *erga omnes* and the extent to which third-States may demand the extradition of individuals suspected of violating peremptory norms where a custodial State is unwilling or unable to prosecute.

One such instance is the *Guatemala Genocide Case*, in which charges were brought in Spain against eight former high-ranking Guatemalan officials, including *de facto* president Efrain Rios Montt, for acts of genocide, torture, terrorism, and violations of humanitarian law committed during the country's 36-year civil war. Prosecution was made possible by the findings of the Commission for Historical Clarification,[132] and the

[128] The AU–EU Expert Report on the Principle of Universal Jurisdiction, EU Doc. 8672/1/09 Rev 1, para. 29 (16 April 2009) ('Universal jurisdiction relates to the competence of a state to prosecute persons before its own courts, rather than to the prosecution of those same persons before an international judicial body').

[129] *Armed Activities on the Territory of the Congo (New Application: 2002) (Congo v. Rwanda)*, ICJ Reports 2006, p. 3, para. 64 ('the fact that a dispute relates to compliance with a norm having such a [*jus cogens*] character ... cannot of itself provide a basis for the jurisdiction of the Court to entertain that dispute').

[130] *East Timor (Portugal v. Australia)*, Judgment, ICJ Reports 1995, p. 90, para. 29 ('the *erga omnes* character of a norm and the rule of consent to jurisdiction are two different things').

[131] *Questions Relating to the Obligation to Prosecute or Extradite (Belgium v. Senegal)*, Judgment, ICJ Reports 2012, p. 422, para. 68 (as obligations *erga omnes partes*); *Application of the Convention on the Prevention and Punishment of the Crime of Genocide (Bosnia and Herzegovina v. Serbia and Montenegro)*, Preliminary Objections, Judgment, ICJ Reports 1996, p. 595, para. 31.

[132] Guatemalan Commission for Historical Clarification, GUATEMALA: MEMORY OF SILENCE: REPORT OF THE COMMISSION FOR HISTORICAL CLARIFICATION, paras. 80–146

Recovery of Historical Memory Project,[133] which stretched their fact-finding mandates by identifying possible individual (as well as State) responsibility for violations of peremptory norms.[134] The Spanish Constitutional Court affirmed the assertion of universal jurisdiction by Spanish courts to prosecute the accused on the basis of the *jus cogens* norms in question in 2005,[135] reversing in part a 2003 Supreme Court decision that had found that Spanish law required a link of nationality to exercise universal jurisdiction where such extraterritoriality is not expressly provided for by international convention or UN authorization.[136] In December 2007, however, the Constitutional Court of Guatemala denied the jurisdiction of Spain to proceed with the case and declined to cooperate further with the Spanish investigation.[137] The Spanish judge leading the case responded with a statement in which he linked the obligation to extradite or prosecute to the performance of obligations *erga omnes*:

> The Court finds that Spain does not have jurisdiction to investigate said crimes, even though said crimes involve crimes of universal [prosecution]. They consequently negate the constant, settled, and well-established international doctrine in such cases, subscribed to by those countries that guarantee the defense of human rights. At the same time, with this decision, the Constitutional Court lets it be known that the State of Guatemala assumes full responsibility for violating its international obligations and its own national laws, by ignoring the *erga omnes* (universally applicable) international obligation *aut dedere aut judicare* (extradite or prosecute) recognized by most authoritative doctrines since it was established in the XVII century by Grotius and, today, incorporated into both customary and

(Washington, DC: American Association for the Advancement of Sciences, Christian Tomuschat, Otilia Lux de Coti & Alfredo Balsells Tojo eds., 1999). *See* Daniel Rothenberg (ed.), MEMORY OF SILENCE: THE GUATEMALAN TRUTH COMMISSION REPORT (New York: Palgrave Macmillan 2012).

133 Recovery of Historical Memory Project, GUATEMALA: NEVER AGAIN!: THE OFFICIAL REPORT OF THE HUMAN RIGHTS OFFICE, ARCHDIOCESE OF GUATEMALA 206–42, 289–301 (New York: Orbis Books 1999).

134 *See* Hilde Salvesen, GUATEMALA: FIVE YEARS AFTER THE PEACE ACCORDS 31 (Oslo: International Peace Research Institute 2002).

135 *Guatemala Genocide Case (Menchú Tumn and ors v. Two Guatemalan Government Officials and Six Members of the Guatemalan Military)*, Constitutional Court (Criminal Chamber) (Spain), Spanish Constitutional Court Decision Accepting Jurisdiction, No. 237/2005, ILDC 137, paras. 5–6 (2005).

136 *Guatemala Genocide Case (Menchú Tumn and ors v. Two Guatemalan Government Officials and Six Members of the Guatemalan Military)*, Constitutional Court (Criminal Chamber) (Spain), No. 237/2003, 42 ILM 686 (2003).

137 *Guatemala Genocide Case*, Judgment No. 3380–2007, Constitutional Court (Guatemala) (2007).

> conventional International Law and International Criminal Law ... In spite of this obligation *erga omnes*, applicable to all international crimes that are *ius cogens* in nature, like those here charged, the highest Guatemalan court says or insinuates nothing about the full effect of these laws and of the obligation of its courts to execute them, and thus Guatemala incurs [] a flagrant violation of its international obligations as a State.[138]

In effect, Spain invoked the international responsibility of Guatemala for breaching its obligations *erga omnes* arising from the peremptory norms at issue, which, according to Spain, required Guatemala to extradite or prosecute the individuals in question.[139]

The International Court of Justice pronounced on the scope of the obligation to extradite or prosecute as one arising *erga omnes* in *Questions Relating to the Obligation to Prosecute or Extradite*.[140] In 2009, Belgium instituted proceedings against Senegal regarding its compliance with the obligation to extradite or prosecute former Chadian President Hissène Habré for acts of torture. Given Senegal's failure to prosecute Habré, Belgium invoked what it claimed to be its right to pursue extradition to prosecute Habré pursuant to Senegal's performance of its obligations *erga omnes* arising from the prohibition against torture.[141] During oral proceedings at the merits stage, the generality of the obligation to

138 *Guatemala Genocide Case (Menchú Tumn and ors v. Two Guatemalan Government Officials and Six Members of the Guatemalan Military)*, Response of Spanish Constitutional Court Judge Santiago Pedraz to the Guatemala Constitutional Court Decision of 12 December 2007, para. 5 (Center for Justice & Accountability trans., 2008).

139 In January 2012, a Guatemalan court recognized the State's obligations arising from the peremptory norms in question and indicted Montt and three other former generals for genocide and crimes against humanity. Two months later, a Guatemalan judge refused to grant Montt immunity, clearing the way for his prosecution to proceed in Guatemala.

140 *Questions Relating to the Obligation to Prosecute or Extradite (Belgium v. Senegal)*, Judgment, ICJ Reports 2012, p. 422. *See* Mads Andenas & Thomas Weatherall, *II. International Court of Justice: Questions Relating to the Obligation to Extradite or Prosecute (Belgium v. Senegal), Judgment of 20 July 2012*, 62(3) International and Comparative Law Quarterly 753–69 (2013).

141 *Questions Relating to the Obligation to Prosecute or Extradite (Belgium v. Senegal)*, Public sitting held on Tuesday 7 April 2009, CR 2009/10, para. 12 (Introductory Presentation of Belgium's Responses) ('Turning from the source to the content of the right invoked by Belgium, this right is none other than that contained in conventional international law, namely the right for Belgium to see States fulfil their obligation to prosecute or extradite the perpetrator of a crime under international law. This right is ultimately nothing more than the transposition into law by the international community of a fundamental moral and social value which has now become a legal requirement – not to let some of the very gravest of crimes go unpunished').

punish violations of peremptory norms was viewed to be connected to the performance of obligations *erga omnes*, an understanding uncontested even where performance of that obligation was being disputed.[142] In its judgment in the case, the International Court recognized the link between obligations *erga omnes* and the duty to extradite or prosecute in the context of obligations *erga omnes partes* arising from the prohibition of torture codified by the Convention against Torture.[143] The Court found the claims of Belgium admissible on the basis of the right of standing arising from the general legal interest in the performance of obligations *erga omnes* (*partes*), which in this instance permitted Belgium to invoke the responsibility of Senegal for breaching its obligations *erga omnes*, the performance of which required Senegal to prosecute or extradite Habré.[144] Senegal, according to the Court, had breached its relevant obligations *erga omnes partes*,[145] the purpose of which was to ensure that acts of torture are punished and that its perpetrators find no safe haven from States parties to the Convention.[146] The Court held that 'Senegal must therefore take without further delay the necessary measures to submit the case to its competent authorities for the purpose of

[142] *Ibid.*, para. 14 (In response to a question from Judge Simma regarding the *erga omnes* character of the obligation to extradite or prosecute, Belgium stated: 'Belgium thinks it possible to reply in the affirmative. Moreover, Senegal appears to share that view, since . . . if one reads the statement of grounds for the Senegalese law which brings the main crimes under international humanitarian law within the Senegalese Penal Code, it states that this represents the "incorporation of international rules of conventional and customary origin"... The customary rules to which Senegal is referring are general customary rules, not local or regional ones. Even better, by stating that these rules have "the character of *jus cogens*", still in the statement of grounds for its law, Senegal too implicitly acknowledges their *erga omnes* character . . . So, even though some may debate the meaning and scope of custom, it is in any event clear that, as regards the customary and *erga omnes* character of the rule *aut dedere aut judicare* or *judicare vel dedere*, Belgium is pleased to note that in fact it shares the same belief as Senegal' (footnotes omitted)). *See Questions Relating to the Obligation to Prosecute or Extradite (Belgium v. Senegal)*, Provisional Measures, Order of 28 May 2009, Diss. Op. Cançado Trindade, ICJ Reports 2009, p. 165, paras. 65–91.

[143] *Questions Relating to the Obligation to Prosecute or Extradite (Belgium v. Senegal)*, Judgment, ICJ Reports 2012, p. 422, para. 72 (namely, obligations arising under Articles 5(2), 6(2), and 7(1) of the Torture Convention (1984)). *See* Andonas and Weatherall, *II. International Court of Justice: Questions Relating to the Obligation to Extradite or Prosecute*, 769 ('The obligations to prevent and punish violations of the Torture Convention are *erga omnes* by virtue of their origin from a norm belonging to *jus cogens*, obligations codified, but not created, by the convention'). *See* discussion *intra*, Chapter 15, *nn*. 84–9.

[144] *Ibid.* [145] *Ibid.*, para. 117. [146] *Ibid.*, paras. 119–20.

prosecution, if it does not extradite Mr. Habré'.[147] In so finding, the International Court confirmed the *erga omnes* character of the obligation to extradite or prosecute and pronounced for the first time on one legal effect of *erga omnes* for purposes of standing before the International Court,[148] as discussed further below.[149]

The generality of this aspect of obligations *erga omnes* arising from peremptory norms reflects the principle of accountability and the political goal to end impunity for serious violations of international law. In his address to the 2010 Review Conference on the International Criminal Court in Kampala, the UN Secretary-General declared 'the birth of a new Age of Accountability' through 'civil society' by 'the international community coming together in concert' to 'reject impunity'.[150] This principle of accountability underpins the obligation to extradite or prosecute.[151] Peremptory norms protect the higher interests of the international community as a whole and the obligation to punish violations of these norms can be seen as a manifestation of the general legal interest in the fulfilment of obligations arising therefrom. Accountability for violations of peremptory norms can only be reached through a durable and effective system of prosecution that denies violators safe haven in any corner of the world. To this end, the performance of obligations *erga omnes* may be seen to impose a positive duty upon each State to extradite or prosecute violators of peremptory norms and prescribe a general legal interest in the performance of such obligations.

147 *Ibid.*, para. 121. 148 *Ibid.*, paras. 67–70.

149 *See* discussion *infra*, Chapter 15.C (Standing before the International Court of Justice).

150 UN Secretary-General Ban Ki-moon, *An Age of Accountability*, Address at the Review Conference on the International Criminal Court 1, 4–5 (31 May 2010).

151 *See, e.g.*, Report of the International Law Commission on the Work of its Sixty-Third Session (2011), Topical Summary of the Discussion held in the Sixth Committee of the General Assembly during its Sixty-Sixth Session, UN Doc. A/CN.4/650, para. 46 (20 January 2012).

15

State responsibility and *jus cogens*

A State responsibility for internationally wrongful acts

State responsibility in international law is defined in terms of internationally wrongful acts. According to the ILC Articles on State Responsibility, an act or omission attributable to the State under international law that breaches an international obligation constitutes an internationally wrongful act that engages the international responsibility of the State.[1] In the context of peremptory norms, State responsibility for an internationally wrongful act may arise in two ways: the first concerns the breach of obligations *erga omnes* arising from peremptory norms; the second entails the attribution of conduct of an individual in violation of a peremptory norm. This section considers each aspect of State responsibility in turn.

i. International responsibility for breaches of obligations erga omnes

The State is internationally responsible for a breach of obligations *erga omnes* arising from peremptory norms. This aspect of responsibility arises where the apparatus of the State has failed, through will or negligence, to prevent the violation of a peremptory norm, through preemption or suppression, or to punish such a violation, through extradition or prosecution.[2] This is a consequence of the way in which the performance of obligations *erga omnes* imposes positive duties upon the State as a kind of due diligence.[3] As such, obligations *erga omnes* constitute obligations

[1] International Law Commission, Responsibility of States for Internationally Wrongful Acts, Report of the International Law Commission on the Work of its Fifty-Third Session, [2001] II(2) YbILC 26, Articles 1–2 [hereinafter, ILC Articles on State Responsibility (2001)].

[2] *See* discussion *supra*, Chapter 14 (The Enforcement of *Jus Cogens*: Obligations *Erga Omnes*).

[3] *See* Susan Marks and Fiorentina Azizi, *Responsibility for Violations of Human Rights Obligations: International Mechanisms*, *in* The Law of International Responsibility 728–32 (Oxford University Press, James Crawford, Alain Pellet & Simon Olleson eds., 2009).

of result rather than mere conduct, by virtue of their necessity to the fulfilment of the higher interests of the international community. This linkage was noted by Judge Cançado Trindade in *Questions Relating to the Obligation to Prosecute or Extradite*:

> One of such principles is that of respect of the dignity of the human person. Thus, in so far as the safeguard of the fundamental rights of the human person is concerned, the obligations of the State – conventional and of general international law – are of *result*, and not of simple conduct, so as to secure the effective protection of those rights. The absolute prohibition of grave violations of human rights ... entails obligations which can only be of *result*, endowed with a necessarily objective character, and the whole conceptual universe of the law of the international responsibility of the State has to be reassessed in the framework of the international protection of human rights, encompassing the origin as well as the implementation of State responsibility, with the consequent and indispensable duty of reparation.[4]

State responsibility for the failure to prevent and punish violations of peremptory norms was invoked most clearly in this sense by the International Court of Justice in *Application of the Genocide Convention* (2007),[5] and *Questions Relating to the Obligation to Prosecute or Extradite* (2012).[6] Precedent of State responsibility for the violation of positive duties arising from individual rights can be traced back several decades to judgments by the Inter-American Court of Human Rights and the European Court of Human Rights.

The Inter-American Court, in *Velásquez-Rodríguez v. Honduras* (1988), ruled on a case concerning the disappearance of Manfredo Velásquez with the tolerance of the Honduran government in September 1981.[7] The disappearance and associated acts were held to constitute violations of the rights to life, humane treatment, and liberty under the American Convention on Human Rights (ACHR) as well as a crime against humanity.[8] In its Judgment, the Inter-American Court

[4] *Questions Relating to the Obligation to Prosecute or Extradite (Belgium v. Senegal)*, Judgment, ICJ Reports 2012, Sep. Op. Cançado Trindade, p. 487, para. 49.

[5] *Application of the Convention on the Prevention and Punishment of the Crime of Genocide (Bosnia and Herzegovina v. Serbia and Montenegro)*, Judgment, ICJ Reports 2007, p. 43, paras. 469, 471.

[6] *Questions Relating to the Obligation to Prosecute or Extradite (Belgium v. Senegal)*, Judgment, ICJ Reports 2012, p. 422, paras. 121–2.

[7] *Velásquez-Rodríguez v. Honduras*, IACtHR Series C No. 4 (1988).

[8] *Ibid.*, paras. 153–60.

emphasized the basis of the rights in question, which is relevant to the nature of the obligations arising therefrom:

> The State is subject to law and morality. Disrespect for human dignity cannot serve as the basis for any State action ... The exercise of public authority has certain limits which derive from the fact that human rights are inherent attributes of human dignity and are, therefore, superior to the power of the State.[9]

According to the Inter-American Court, the nature of rights deriving from basic human dignity is such that they impose particular obligations upon the State. The fulfilment of these obligations requires the State to exercise its capacity to prevent, investigate, and punish violations of such rights, and State responsibility arises for a breach of these obligations.[10] The Inter-American Court pointedly distinguished State responsibility in the realm of protection and reparation from the criminal responsibility of those guilty of human rights violations.[11] The nature of State responsibility in this context concerns acts or omissions on the part of the State that created the circumstances under which the illegal acts transpired with impunity. Consequently, this basis of responsibility is distinct from the attribution of illegal acts of the individual in violation of international law to the State:

> Thus, in principle, any violation of rights recognized by the Convention carried out by an act of public authority or by persons who use their position of authority is imputable to the State. However, this does not define all the circumstances in which a State is obligated to prevent, investigate and punish human rights violations, nor all the cases in which the State might be found responsible for an infringement of those rights. An illegal act which violates human rights and which is initially not directly imputable to a State (for example, because it is the act of a private person or because the person responsible has not been identified) can lead to international responsibility of the State, not because of the act itself, but because of the lack of due diligence to prevent the violation or to respond to it as required ... The State has a legal duty to take reasonable steps to prevent human rights violations and to use the means at its disposal to carry out a serious investigation of violations committed within its jurisdiction, to identify those responsible, to impose the appropriate punishment and to ensure the victim adequate compensation.[12]

Here, the performance of obligations arising from protections of the individual was conceived as a kind of due diligence, failing which the

[9] *Ibid.*, paras. 154, 168. [10] *Ibid.*, paras. 166, 174. [11] *Ibid.*, para. 134.
[12] *Ibid.*, paras. 172, 174.

responsibility of the State is engaged. And indeed, the Inter-American Court found Honduras in breach of its obligations arising from the basic rights enshrined in the ACHR for failing to prevent and punish those responsible for the disappearance of Velásquez.[13]

A similar position emerged in two cases before the European Court of Human Rights (ECtHR) concerning State responsibility for the violation of obligations arising from Article 3 of the European Convention on Human Rights (ECHR), which prohibits torture and inhuman or degrading treatment.[14] The first, *A. v. United Kingdom* (1998),[15] involved the finding of State responsibility for the abuse of a child. The plaintiff in the case alleged that the State had failed to protect him from certain conduct amounting to a breach of its obligations under Articles 3 and 8 of the ECHR.[16] In holding the State in violation of its obligations arising under Article 3 of the ECHR, the ECtHR observed:

> [T]he obligation on the High Contracting Parties under Article 1 of the Convention to secure to everyone within their jurisdiction the rights and freedoms defined in the Convention, taken together with Article 3, requires States to take measures designed to ensure that individuals within their jurisdiction are not subjected to torture or inhuman or degrading treatment or punishment, including such ill-treatment administered by private individuals . . . In the circumstances of the present case, the failure to provide adequate protection constitutes a violation of Article 3 of the Convention.[17]

The Court ruled similarly in *Z. and Others v. The United Kingdom* (2001), another case concerning the failure of the State to take adequate measures to prevent the ill-treatment of children.[18] The applicants in the case alleged that this failure constituted a violation of Article 3 of the ECHR, an opinion shared unanimously by the European Commission of Human Rights,[19] which 'considered that there was a positive obligation on the Government to protect' against treatment contrary to Article 3.[20] In its ruling against the State, the Court restated its reasoning in *A. v. The United Kingdom*.[21] The precedent has emerged before the ECtHR that

[13] *Ibid.*, paras. 180, 188, 194.
[14] European Convention for the Protection of Human Rights and Fundamental Freedoms, as amended by Protocols Nos. 11 and 14, ETS No. 5, Article 3 (4 November 1950, *entered into force* 3 September 1953).
[15] *A. v. The United Kingdom*, ECtHR, No. 25599/94 (1998). [16] *Ibid.*, para. 16.
[17] *Ibid.*, paras. 22–4.
[18] *Z. and Others v. The United Kingdom*, ECtHR, No. 29392/95 (2001).
[19] *Ibid.*, para. 69. [20] *Ibid.*, para. 70. [21] *Ibid.*, para. 73.

State responsibility may be engaged for failure to prevent and punish violations of fundamental human rights, which constitutes a breach of obligations upon the State arising from such rights.

The reasoning employed in the rulings of the Inter-American and European Courts is mirrored in the Articles on State Responsibility, which conceive of State responsibility for the breach of obligations arising from peremptory norms, as well as particular legal consequences arising therefrom.[22] The UN Human Rights Committee (HRC) adopted this framework of State responsibility for breaches of obligations *erga omnes* in its 2004 General Comment on the legal obligations arising under the ICCPR.[23] The General Comment seizes on the obligations arising under Article 2 of the Covenant to prevent and punish violations of the rights enshrined in the instrument.[24] The HRC linked prevention and punishment to the fulfilment of obligations *erga omnes* arising from 'rules concerning the basic rights of the human person', the invocation of which is regarded as 'a reflection of legitimate community interest'.[25] Importantly, the HRC reiterated the way in which failure to fulfil these obligations constitutes a violation of international law by the State:

> [T]he positive obligations on States parties to ensure Covenant rights will only be fully discharged if individuals are protected by the State, not just against violations of Covenant rights by its agents, but also against acts committed by private persons or entities that would impair the enjoyment of Covenant rights in so far as they are amenable to application between private persons or entities. There may be circumstances in which a failure to ensure Covenant rights as required by article 2 would give rise to violations by States parties of those rights, as a result of States parties' permitting or failing to take appropriate measures or to exercise due diligence to prevent, punish, investigate or redress the harm caused by such acts by private persons or entities.[26]

[22] ILC Articles on State Responsibility (2001), Articles 40–1.

[23] UN Human Rights Committee, CCPR General Comment 31: Nature of the General Legal Obligation Imposed on States Parties to the Covenant (2004), *in* I COMPILATION OF GENERAL COMMENTS AND GENERAL RECOMMENDATIONS ADOPTED BY HUMAN RIGHTS TREATY BODIES 342, UN Doc. HRI/GEN/1/Rev.9 (Vol. I) (2008).

[24] International Covenant on Civil and Political Rights, 99 UNTS 171, Article 2 (1966) (*entered into force* 23 March 1976).

[25] UN Human Rights Committee, CCPR General Comment 31: Nature of the General Legal Obligation Imposed on States Parties to the Covenant (2004), 342, para. 2.

[26] *Ibid.*, 244–5, para. 8.

Taken together, the General Comment associates the performance of obligations arising from fundamental individual protections with the prevention and punishment of violations, characterizes these as due diligence obligations, and conceives their breach to engage State responsibility. This articulation reflects the operative legal formulation of State responsibility for breaches of obligations *erga omnes* arising from peremptory norms.

Relatedly, the principle of *non-refoulement* implicates the due diligence obligations incumbent upon the State arising from fundamental protections of the individual to preclude States from exposing individuals to certain inhuman treatment. The 1951 Convention on the Status of Refugees provides:

> No Contracting State shall expel or return ('refouler') a refugee in any manner whatsoever to the frontiers of the territories where his life or freedom would be threatened on account of his race, religion, nationality, membership of a particular social group or political opinion.[27]

More generally, *non-refoulement* applies to deportation, extradition, and expulsion,[28] and it is not exclusive to the 1951 Convention (nor subject to its exceptions).[29] The principle applies beyond the refugee context; for example, it is often found in instruments concerning torture, prohibiting States from exposing any individual to the risk of treatment contrary to human dignity.[30] This is evident from the case law of the Convention

[27] Convention Relating to the Status of Refugees, 189 UNTS 150, Article 33 (28 July 1951, *entered into force* 22 April 1954) (Article 33(2) delineates two exceptions to the prohibition against *non-refoulement* that a State may exercise in the interest of national security or community protection); *see* GA Res. 2312 (XXII) (Declaration on Territorial Asylum), UN Doc. A/Res/2312 (XXII), Article 3(1) (14 December 1967).

[28] UN Human Rights Committee, CCPR General Comment 20: Article 7 (prohibition of torture, or other cruel, inhuman or degrading treatment or punishment) (1982), *in* I Compilation of General Comments and General Recommendations Adopted by Human Rights Treaty Bodies 200, 201, para. 9, UN Doc. HRI/GEN/1/Rev.9 (Vol. I) (2008) ('In the view of the Committee, States parties must not expose individuals to the danger of torture or cruel, inhuman or degrading treatment or punishment upon return to another country by way of their extradition, expulsion or refoulement').

[29] *Chahal v. United Kingdom*, ECtHR, No. 22414/93, para. 80 (1996) ('The protection afforded by [ECHR] Article 3 (art. 3) is thus wider than that provided by Articles 32 and 33 of the United Nations 1951 Convention on the Status of Refugees').

[30] *See, e.g.*, Charter of Fundamental Rights of the European Union, 2000/C 364/01, Article 19 (2000); Inter-American Convention to Prevent and Punish Torture, OAS TS No. 67 (9 December 1985, *entered into force* 28 February 1987); Convention against Torture and Other Cruel, Inhuman or Degrading Treatment or Punishment, GA Res. 39/46, 1465 UNTS 85, Article 3 (12 December 1984, *entered into force* 26 June 1987) [hereinafter, Torture Convention (1984)].

against Torture Committee.[31] Although the principle is not itself a peremptory norm,[32] it admits no exception where *refoulement* would subject an individual to treatment forbidden by *jus cogens*. To this end, jurisprudence of the ECtHR has conceived *non-refoulement* to arise in the context of the ECHR Article 3 prohibition against torture,[33] and the African Court on Human and Peoples' Rights (ACtHPR) has concluded similarly.[34] The Inter-American Commission on Human Rights (IACHR) has contemplated *non-refoulement* as a State obligation arising from the *jus cogens* prohibition against torture,[35] a relation echoed by the

[31] *See, e.g.*, *Tapia Paez v. Sweden*, Communication No. 39/1996, UN Doc. CAT/C/18/D/39/1996, para. 14.5 (1997) ('The Committee considers that the test of article 3 of the [Torture] Convention is absolute. Whenever substantial grounds exist for believing that an individual would be in danger of being subjected to torture upon expulsion to another State, the State party is under obligation not to return the person concerned to that State. The nature of the activities in which the person concerned engaged cannot be a material consideration when making a determination under article 3 of the Convention'); *M.B.B. v. Sweden*, Communication No. 104/1998, UN Doc. CAT/C/22/D/104/1998, paras. 6.4–6.5 (1999)); *Agiza v. Sweden*, Communication No. 233/2003, UN Doc. CAT/C/34/D/233/2003, para. 13.8 (2005).

[32] *C, KMF and BF v. Director of Immigration and Secretary for Security*, Court of Final Instance (Hong Kong), FACV Nos. 18/19/20 2011 (2013) (in the case of 'C', finding that *non-refoulement*, as articulated in Article 33 of the UN Refugee Convention, had entered into customary international law but is not a peremptory norm); *C v. Director of Immigration*, Court of First Instance (Hong Kong), HCAL 132/2006, [2008] 2 HKC 165, ILDC 1119, paras. 133–5 (2008) (finding *non-refoulement* has not 'acquired the status of a peremptory norm'); *Attorney General v. Ahmed Zaoui and ors*, Supreme Court (New Zealand), SC CIV 19/2004, [2005] NZSC 38, ILDC 81, para. 51 (2005) ('While there is overwhelming support for the proposition that the prohibition on torture itself is *ius cogens*, there is no support in the state practice, judicial decisions or commentaries to which we were referred for the proposition that the prohibition on refoulement to torture has that status'). *Cf.* Jean Allain, *The* Jus Cogens *Nature of* Non-Refoulement, 13(4) International Journal of Refugee Law 533, 538 (2002); Cartagena Declaration on Refugees, para. 5 (22 November 1984) ('the principle of non-refoulement ... *should be* acknowledged and observed as a rule of *jus cogens*' (emphasis added)).

[33] *Soering v. United Kingdom*, ECtHR, No. 14038/88, paras. 85–91, 111 (1989) ('[An] inherent obligation not to extradite also extends to cases in which the fugitive would be faced in the receiving State by a real risk of exposure to inhuman or degrading treatment or punishment proscribed by that Article (art. 3)'); *Ahmed v. Austria*, ECtHR, No. 25964/94, paras. 39–47 (1996); *Chahal v. United Kingdom*, ECtHR, No. 22414/93, para. 80 (1996).

[34] *Modise v. Botswana*, ACHPR, Communication. No. 97/93, 2000 AHRLR 25, para. 91 (1996) ('[Complainant's repeated deportation] exposed him to personal suffering and indignity in violation of the right to freedom from cruel, inhuman or degrading treatment guaranteed under Article 5 of the [African] Charter').

[35] Inter-American Commission on Human Rights, *Report on the Situation of Human Rights of Asylum Seekers within the Canadian Refugee Determination System*, OEA/Ser.L/V/II.106,

Supreme Court of Canada in *Suresh*.[36] It is conceivable that *non-refoulement* is a corollary to *jus cogens* protections of the individual insofar as it is implicated by obligations of the State arising from peremptory norms, the performance of which requires States to prevent violations of *jus cogens*.[37] 'Foreseeably and necessarily' exposing an individual to conduct prohibited by *jus cogens* would logically violate the principle of *non-refoulement*.[38] Jurisprudence supports the proposition that the principle of *non-refoulement* is a 'due diligence' obligation incumbent upon the State that bars the State from taking actions towards an individual that would subject that person to certain forms of inhuman or degrading treatment.[39]

ii. International responsibility for violations of peremptory norms

In addition to State responsibility for the violation of obligations *erga omnes*, the State may incur international responsibility for violations of peremptory norms. The international law of State responsibility maintains that the conduct of an individual carried out in a public capacity (i.e. as a State organ), or otherwise attributable to the State, in violation of a peremptory norm constitutes an internationally wrongful act that engages the international responsibility of the State.[40] Under this rubric of State responsibility, the State may face liability

Doc. 40 rev., para. 154 (2000) ('As noted above, the prohibition of torture as a norm of *jus cogens* – as codified in the American Declaration generally, and Article 3 of the UN Convention against Torture in the context of expulsion – applies beyond the terms of the 1951 [Refugee] Convention. The fact that a person is suspected of or deemed to have some relation to terrorism does not modify the obligation of the State to refrain from return where substantial grounds of a real risk of inhuman treatment are at issue').

36 *Suresh v. Canada (Minister of Citizenship and Immigration)*, 2002 SCC 1, [2002] 1 SCR 3, paras. 46, 59–66, 75.

37 *See* Elihu Lauterpacht and Daniel Bethlehem, *The Scope and Content of the Principle of* Non-Refoulement*: Opinion*, *in* Refugee Protection in International Law 87, 158–64 (Cambridge University Press, Erika Feller, Volker Türk, & Frances Nicholson eds., 2003) (considering *non-refoulement* as an '*implied* component of the prohibition of torture' under customary international law).

38 *See, e.g., M.B.B. v. Sweden*, Communication No. 104/1998, UN Doc. CAT/C/22/D/104/1998, para. 6.5 (1999) (articulating a 'foreseeable and necessary consequence' standard under the performance of this obligation).

39 *See* Antônio Augusto Cançado Trindade, *International Law for Humankind: Towards a New Jus Gentium (II) – General Course on Public International Law*, 317 Recueil des Cours 165 (2005) (finding, in this sense, that 'the principle of *non-refoulement* falls under the domain of *jus cogens*').

40 *See* ILC Articles on State Responsibility (2001), Articles 4–8.

for violations of peremptory norms in the form of compensation, restitution, or satisfaction. This formulation of State responsibility is well established by customary international law, as expressed in the ILC Articles on State Responsibility: the State is responsible for any conduct attributable to it in breach of its obligations under international law.[41] This requires no further elaboration. However, it serves to differentiate between State and individual responsibility for the violation of a peremptory norm, which is relevant to the distinction between international crimes and internationally wrongful acts more generally.

First, State responsibility through attribution for *jus cogens* violations depends upon antecedent conduct of the individual, a practical point elucidated in the ILC Commentary to the Articles on State Responsibility:

> For particular conduct to be characterized as an internationally wrongful act, it must first be attributable to the State. The State is a real organized entity, a legal person with full authority to act under international law. But to recognize this is not to deny the elementary fact that the State cannot act of itself. An 'act of the State' must involve some action or omission by a human being or group: 'States can act only by and through their agents and representatives.'[42]

Thus, where an internationally wrongful act concerns the violation of a peremptory norm, it can arise only through the action of an individual in violation of that norm. The action must be committed by an individual acting in such a way as for his conduct to be attributable to the State. For example, the assessment of State responsibility for genocide in *Application of the Genocide Convention* was based upon the relevant findings of the ICTY concerning individual responsibility for the crime of genocide.[43] Of course, in the context of obligations *erga omnes*, a State breaches such obligations where it has failed to prevent or punish violations of peremptory norms – this too can only follow the violation of a peremptory norm by an individual.

Second, while individual responsibility is criminal in nature, State responsibility arising for internationally wrongful acts is of a different

[41] *Ibid.*, Articles 1–2.

[42] *Ibid.*, 35, para. 5 (Commentary to Article 2) (quoting *German Settlers in Poland*, 1923 PCIJ Series B, No. 6, 22).

[43] *Application of the Convention on the Prevention and Punishment of the Crime of Genocide (Bosnia and Herzegovina v. Serbia and Montenegro)*, Judgment, ICJ Reports 2007, p. 43.

character and bears no such criminality.[44] This is true for breaches of obligations *erga omnes* as well as violations of peremptory norms attributed to the State. The difference between individual and State responsibility for the violation of peremptory norms was clearly articulated by the International Court of Justice in *Application of the Genocide Convention*:

> The Court accordingly concludes that Contracting Parties to the Convention are bound not to commit genocide, *through the actions of their organs or persons or groups whose acts are attributable to them* ... It would however not be in keeping with the object and purpose of the Convention to deny that the international responsibility of a State – even though quite different in nature from criminal responsibility – can be engaged[.][45]

This observation affirms that the development of individual criminal responsibility has no analogue in the regime of State responsibility and that the attribution of individual acts that are criminal in nature attaches no such criminality to the State. So follows the pronouncement by the ICTY: 'Under present international law it is clear that States, by definition, cannot be the subject of criminal sanctions akin to those provided for in national criminal systems.'[46] Indeed, the idea of collective punishment implicit in the attribution of State criminal responsibility is itself deeply problematic in both theory and practice.[47] This fundamentally disparate nature of individual and State responsibility is implicit in the distinction between international crimes and internationally wrongful acts.[48]

Third, where State responsibility is established and reparation due for an internationally wrongful act, in the context of peremptory norms, the beneficiary of compensation is to be the individual whose basic dignity was compromised. This expectation would apply with equal force to internationally wrongful acts deriving from the violation of peremptory

44 *See* discussion *supra*, Chapter 12.A (Individual Criminal Responsibility).

45 *Application of the Convention on the Prevention and Punishment of the Crime of Genocide (Bosnia and Herzegovina v. Serbia and Montenegro)*, Judgment, ICJ Reports 2007, p. 43, paras. 166–7 (emphasis added).

46 *Prosecutor v. Blaškić*, Judgment on the Request of Croatia for Review of the Decision of Trial Chamber II of 18 July 1997, IT-95-14-AR108bis, para. 25 (1997).

47 *See Application of the Convention on the Prevention and Punishment of the Crime of Genocide (Bosnia and Herzegovina v. Serbia and Montenegro)*, Preliminary Objections, Judgment, ICJ Reports 1996, J. Decl. Shi and Vereshchetin, p. 631, 632 ('There can be no reconciliation unless individual guilt for the appalling crimes of the last few years replaces the pernicious theory of collective guilt on which so much racial hatred hangs' (quoting Hartley Shawcross, UK Chief Prosecutor at Nuremberg)).

48 *See* discussion *supra*, Chapter 12.A (Individual Criminal Responsibility).

norms as well as the breach of obligations *erga omnes*. This principle was articulated by the International Court in *Ahmadou Sadio Diallo*[49] and finds support in the ILC Commentary to the Articles on State Responsibility.[50] This practical point indicates that, while the primary responsibility for the violation of peremptory norms rests with the individual, the consequences of State responsibility might also be most appropriately directed towards the individual. These distinctions between individual and State responsibility arising with respect to peremptory norms reinforce the proposition that *jus cogens* is a fundamentally individual-oriented category of international law in both substance and application.

B Dual responsibility

The law of international responsibility conceives of individual and State responsibility as distinct, though often concurrent, forms of responsibility arising from the violation of peremptory norms. The Rome Statute of the International Criminal Court stipulates in Article 25(4) that 'No provision in this Statute relating to individual criminal responsibility shall affect the responsibility of States under international law.'[51] Article 4 of the Draft Code of Crimes against the Peace and Security of Mankind (Responsibility of States) provides for the same distinction.[52] Article 58 of the Articles on State Responsibility establishes the corollary: 'These articles are without prejudice to any question of the individual responsibility under international law of any person acting on behalf of a

[49] *Ahmadou Sadio Diallo (Republic of Guinea v. Democratic Republic of the Congo)*, Compensation, Judgment, ICJ Reports 2012, p. 324, para. 57 ('The Court recalls that the sum awarded to Guinea in the exercise of diplomatic protection of Mr. Diallo is intended to provide reparation for the latter's injury').

[50] ILC Articles on State Responsibility (2001), 95, para. 3 (Commentary to Article 33) ('When an obligation of reparation exists towards a State, reparation does not necessarily accrue to that State's benefit. For instance, a State's responsibility for the breach of an obligation under a treaty concerning the protection of human rights may exist towards all the other parties to the treaty, but the individuals concerned should be regarded as the ultimate beneficiaries and in that sense as the holders of the relevant rights. Individual rights under international law may also arise outside the framework of human rights').

[51] Rome Statute of the International Criminal Court, UN Doc. A/CONF.183.9 (17 July 1998, *entered into force* 1 July 2002) [hereinafter, Rome Statute (1998)], Article 25(4).

[52] Report of the International Law Commission on the Work of its Forty-Eighth Session, [1996] II(2) YbILC 17, Article 4 ('The fact that the present Code provides for the responsibility of individuals for crimes against the peace and security of mankind is without prejudice to any question of the responsibility of States under international law').

State.'[53] The duality of responsibility illuminated by these three articles is that by which the individual faces criminal and civil responsibility for violations of peremptory norms constituting international crimes, while the State faces responsibility for internationally wrongful acts deriving from the failure to fulfil obligations *erga omnes* arising from peremptory norms or through conduct attributable to the State in violation of a peremptory norm.

The duality of responsibility for violations of peremptory norms unfolded over fourteen years before the International Court of Justice in *Application of the Genocide Convention*,[54] which reached its final Judgment in 2007. The case concerned a claim by Bosnia and Herzegovina alleging acts of genocide had been committed against the Muslim population of Bosnia by Serb military and paramilitary forces under the direction of the Republic of Yugoslavia (Serbia and Montenegro) in violation of the Genocide Convention.[55] The Court based its jurisdiction on the compromisory clause of the Genocide Convention, to which both parties were regarded as signatories:

> Disputes between the Contracting Parties relating to the interpretation, application or fulfilment of the present Convention, *including those relating to the responsibility of a State for genocide* or for any of the other acts enumerated in article III, shall be submitted to the International Court of Justice at the request of any of the parties to the dispute.[56]

A principal issue of discord in the case involved the interpretation of 'the responsibility of a State', a reference absent from similar compromisory clauses in other texts codifying peremptory norms.[57] In his Separate Opinion to the Provisional Measures Order, Judge *ad hoc* Lauterpacht attempted to elucidate the meaning of this clause in the context of dual responsibility, observing first that the purpose of the Convention is

[53] ILC Articles on State Responsibility (2001), Article 58.

[54] *Application of the Convention on the Prevention and Punishment of the Crime of Genocide (Bosnia and Herzegovina v. Serbia and Montenegro)*, Judgment, ICJ Reports 2007, p. 43.

[55] *Application of the Convention on the Prevention and Punishment of the Crime of Genocide*, Provisional Measures, Order of 8 April 1993, ICJ Reports 1993, p. 3, paras. 1–2.

[56] Convention on the Prevention and Punishment of the Crime of Genocide, Article IX, II78 UNTS 277, No. 1021 (9 December 1948, *entered into force* 12 January 1951) (emphasis added).

[57] *See, e.g.*, Torture Convention (1984), Article 30; Supplementary Convention on the Abolition of Slavery, the Slave Trade, and Institutions and Practices Similar to Slavery, 226 UNTS 3, Article 10 (7 September 1956, *entered into force* 30 April 1957).

directed at individual criminal responsibility for the crime of genocide and also that the performance of corollary obligations requires States to prevent and punish the crime of genocide.[58] Lauterpacht then interpreted 'the responsibility of a State for genocide' to indicate that the Convention 'contemplates the possibility that a State may commit genocide', for a State, according to the Judge *as hoc*, can only logically be held responsible under general international law (through attribution) if it can be conceived to have committed the act itself.[59]

The International Court compounded its interpretive quandary in its Preliminary Objections Judgment. After recognizing the *erga omnes* character of obligations arising from the prohibition of genocide,[60] the Court observed that, beyond responsibility for the violation of obligations *erga omnes*, 'the responsibility of a State for genocide' conceived in Article IX of the Convention 'does not exclude *any* form of State responsibility'.[61] This Statement by the Court, more reaching than Lauterpacht's interpretation, prompted a flurry of separate and dissenting opinions concerning the nature of the rights and duties borne by individuals and States respectively under the prohibition of genocide.[62] The salient point of contention was the inappropriate interpretation of the compromisory clause of the Convention as creating by inference a new regime of State criminality distinct from the purpose of the instrument and contrary to the established principles of responsibility under international law more generally. In its final Judgment, the Court attempted to clarify the duality of responsibility for the violation of the peremptory norm prohibiting genocide, explicitly referring to the principle of 'duality of responsibility' as a 'constant feature of international law'.[63] The Court, however, affirmed its prior articulation and held that the obligation to prevent genocide 'necessarily *implies* the prohibition of the commission of

58 *Application of the Convention on the Prevention and Punishment of the Crime of Genocide*, Provisional Measures, Order of 8 April 1993, ICJ Reports 1993, Sep. Op. Lauterpacht, p. 407, paras. 109–10.

59 *Ibid.*, para. 111.

60 *Application of the Convention on the Prevention and Punishment of the Crime of Genocide (Bosnia and Herzegovina v. Serbia and Montenegro)*, Preliminary Objections, Judgment, ICJ Reports 1996, p. 595, para. 31.

61 *Ibid.*, para. 32.

62 *Ibid.*, Decl. Oda, p. 625, paras. 6–7; J. Decl. Shi and Vereshchetin, p. 631; Diss. Op. Kreca, p. 658, paras. 103–5.

63 *Application of the Convention on the Prevention and Punishment of the Crime of Genocide (Bosnia and Herzegovina v. Serbia and Montenegro)*, Judgment, ICJ Reports 2007, p. 43, para. 173.

genocide' bearing upon the State.[64] Cautious of misinterpretation, the Court repeated at numerous points that this form of State responsibility, while distinct from the obligations *erga omnes* relating to prevention and punishment, is explicitly not criminal and therefore different in kind from individual criminal responsibility.[65] This can be reasonably interpreted to refer to State responsibility by attribution under general international law, suggesting that the 'State prohibition' simply serves as a construction to link acts of the individual to the State through attribution.

As much was expressed, albeit tenuously, by the International Court. While the Court concluded that 'the obligation to prevent genocide necessarily implies the prohibition of the commission of genocide', it followed this immediately by observing:

> The Court accordingly concludes that Contracting Parties to the Convention are bound not to commit genocide, *through the actions of their organs or persons or groups whose acts are attributable to them* ... It would however not be in keeping with the object and purpose of the Convention to deny that the international responsibility of a State – even though quite different in nature from criminal responsibility – can be engaged through one of the acts, other than genocide itself, enumerated in Article III.[66]

Thus, State responsibility for the acts prohibited in Article III can only be engaged through the attribution of individual conduct in violation of the prohibition against genocide; the State cannot commit such acts itself. Ultimately, the Court failed to find State responsibility through attribution, determining that Serbia neither committed nor conspired to commit genocide, nor was it complicit in genocide.[67] However, the Court did find that Serbia had breached its obligations *erga omnes* by failing to prevent and punish acts of genocide and take adequate measures to suppress genocide in accordance with the provisional measures ordered in 1993.[68] These assessments were based on prior findings of individual criminal responsibility for genocide by the ICTY.[69]

This ruling by the International Court in *Application of the Genocide Convention* illustrates the principle of dual responsibility. The criminal responsibility of the individual is recognized as the primary locus of

[64] *Ibid.*, para. 166. [65] *Ibid.*, paras. 167, 170, 178.
[66] *Ibid.*, paras. 166–7 (emphasis added). [67] *Ibid.*, para. 471. [68] *Ibid.*
[69] *Application of the Convention on the Prevention and Punishment of the Crime of Genocide (Bosnia and Herzegovina v. Serbia and Montenegro)*, Judgment, ICJ Reports 2007, p. 43 (throughout the entire judgment).

accountability for violations of peremptory norms. Derivative obligations *erga omnes* impose upon the State positive obligations, the performance of which requires the State to prevent and punish violations of peremptory norms. The State bears international responsibility for breaches of obligations *erga omnes*, as well as responsibility under general international law for individual acts attributable to it, in violation of international law, all of which constitute internationally wrongful acts.[70] The separate opinions attached to the 2007 Judgment of the International Court indicate the piecemeal implementation of this framework in its judicial reasoning. In fact, only one judge outlined the duality of responsibility in its entirety,[71] indicating a prevailing uncertainty surrounding the jurisprudence of international responsibility for violations of peremptory norms.

C Standing before the International Court of Justice

The general legal interest of all States in the performance of obligations *erga omnes* confers the legal right of States to invoke the international responsibility of a State in breach of such obligations, which in turn informs the question of standing.[72] The general legal interest in the performance of obligations *erga omnes* entitles any State, according to the ILC, to invoke the responsibility of the State in breach, as indicated in Article 48(1)(b) of the Articles on State Responsibility.[73] In its Commentary to that article, the ILC notes:

> In case of breaches of obligations under article 48, it may well be that there is no State which is individually injured by the breach, yet it is highly desirable that some State or States be in a position to claim reparation, in

[70] *See* discussion *infra*, Chapter 15.D (Jurisdictional Immunity of the State).

[71] *Application of the Convention on the Prevention and Punishment of the Crime of Genocide (Bosnia and Herzegovina v. Serbia and Montenegro)*, Judgment, ICJ Reports 2007, Sep. Op. Tomka, p. 310, para. 61.

[72] *See* discussion *supra*, Chapter 14 (The Enforcement of *Jus Cogens*: Obligations *Erga Omnes*).

[73] ILC Articles on State Responsibility (2001), Article 48 (Invocation of responsibility by a State other than an injured State):

> 1. Any State other than an injured State is entitled to invoke the responsibility of another State in accordance with paragraph 2 if:
>   (*a*) the obligation breached is owed to a group of States including that State, and is established for the protection of a collective interest of the group; or
>   (*b*) the obligation breached is owed to the international community as a whole.

> particular restitution ... such a claim must be made in the interest of the injured State, if any, or of the beneficiaries of the obligation breached.[74]

This construction by the ILC reflects the general legal interest of all States in the fulfilment of obligations *erga omnes*: in the event of their breach, the legal interest of every State is effected, and therefore States are entitled to invoke the responsibility of the breaching State.[75] As with the legal consequences for third-States in response to serious breaches of obligations *erga omnes* noted above,[76] the invocation of international responsibility by third-States supports the individual protections delineated by peremptory norms undermined by the breach of related obligations *erga omnes*.[77]

The scope of obligations *erga omnes*, and judicial standing in the event of breach of such obligations, was the focal point of the dispute between Belgium and Senegal in *Questions Relating to the Obligation to Prosecute or Extradite*.[78] In its Judgment in the case, the International Court of Justice recognized the link between obligations *erga omnes* and the duty to extradite or prosecute in the context of obligations *erga omnes partes* arising from the Convention against Torture,[79] and affirmed the effect of the concept of *erga omnes* on standing.[80] The Court found the claims of Belgium admissible on the basis of the right of standing arising from the general legal interest in the performance of obligations *erga omnes* (*partes*), which in this instance permitted Belgium to invoke the responsibility of Senegal for breaching its obligations *erga omnes*, the performance of which required Senegal to prosecute or extradite Hissène Habré.[81]

[74] *Ibid.*, 127, para. 12 (Commentary to Article 48).
[75] *See* discussion *supra*, text accompanying Chapter 14, *nn.* 1–8.
[76] *See* discussion *supra*, Chapter 14.A (Prevention and Consequences for Third-States).
[77] *See, e.g.*, *Questions Relating to the Obligation to Prosecute or Extradite (Belgium v. Senegal)*, Judgment, ICJ Reports 2012, p. 422, paras. 67–70 (holding that the existence of a common interest in the performance of an obligation grants legal standing to third-States with respect to breaches of such an obligation).
[78] *Questions Relating to the Obligation to Prosecute or Extradite (Belgium v. Senegal)*, Judgment, ICJ Reports 2012, p. 422. *See* Mads Andenas & Thomas Weatherall, *II. International Court of Justice: Questions Relating to the Obligation to Extradite or Prosecute (Belgium v. Senegal), Judgment of 20 July 2012*, 62(3) International and Comparative Law Quarterly 753–69 (2013) (from which portions of this discussion derive).
[79] *Questions Relating to the Obligation to Prosecute or Extradite (Belgium v. Senegal)*, Judgment, ICJ Reports 2012, p. 422, para. 72 (namely, obligations arising under Articles 5(2), 6(2), and 7(1) of the Torture Convention (1984)).
[80] *Ibid.*, paras. 68–70. [81] *Ibid.*

In so finding, the Court pronounced for the first time on one legal effect of obligations *erga omnes* for third parties: the existence of a common interest in the performance of an obligation, as an obligation *erga omnes*, is alone sufficient to grant standing before the Court to third-States with respect to breaches of such an obligation.[82] According to the International Court, the common interest of States parties in certain obligations under the Torture Convention – as obligations *erga omnes partes* – was sufficient to establish the standing of Belgium before the Court:

> The obligations of a State party to conduct a preliminary inquiry into the facts and to submit the case to its competent authorities for prosecution are triggered by the presence of the alleged offender in its territory, regardless of the nationality of the offender or the victims, or of the place where the alleged offences occurred. All the other States parties have a common interest in compliance with these obligations by the State in whose territory the alleged offender is present. That common interest implies that the obligations in question are owed by any State party to all the other States parties to the Convention. All the States parties 'have a legal interest' in the protection of the rights involved.[83]

The 'common interest in compliance with the relevant obligations' under the Torture Convention, particularly those arising under Article 6 (paragraph 2) and Article 7 (paragraph 1) of the instrument, was sufficient to establish the admissibility of Belgium's claims, apart from whatever special interest Belgium might have had with respect to Senegal's compliance.[84]

It is certainly not the case that all obligations under multilateral conventions constitute obligations *erga omnes* (*partes*) conferring standing to all States parties, and the Court made no such claim; however, the demarcation of conventional obligations that are *erga omnes* from those that are not required a principled distinction. Tellingly, in distinguishing the obligations at issue from other multilateral convention obligations, the Court invoked its prior rulings in *Reservations to the Genocide Convention* (1951) and *Barcelona Traction* (1970).[85] However, another

[82] *Ibid.*, paras. 67–70.

[83] *Ibid.*, para. 68 (citing *Barcelona Traction, Light and Power Company, Limited (Belgium v. Spain)*, Judgment, ICJ Reports 1970, p. 3, para. 33; *Reservations to the Genocide Convention*, Advisory Opinion, ICJ Reports 1951, p. 15, 23).

[84] *Ibid.*, paras 67–70.

[85] *Ibid.*, para. 68 (citing *Barcelona Traction, Light and Power Company, Limited (Belgium v. Spain)*, Judgment, ICJ Reports 1970, p. 3, para. 33; *Reservations to the Genocide Convention*, Advisory Opinion, ICJ Reports 1951, p. 15, 23).

passage in the International Court's jurisprudence necessary for purposes of this distinction would appear to be *Military and Paramilitary Activities in and against Nicaragua* (1986), where the Court found that 'simply because' principles of general international law, 'recognized as such, have been codified or embodied in multilateral conventions does not mean that they cease to exist and to apply as principles of customary law, even as regards countries that are parties to such conventions'.[86] To maintain otherwise would suggest that obligations to prevent and punish articulated by instruments codifying peremptory norms, such as the Torture Convention, may limit the *erga omnes* obligations to which they give expression. The International Court rejected such a regressive understanding of the conventional expression of obligations arising from a peremptory norm in this instance,[87] as it did more generally in the 1986 *Nicaragua* case.[88] It is therefore possible to conclude that, because obligations in the Torture Convention which parallel obligations *erga omnes* have, at a minimum, a legal effect commensurate to the obligations *erga omnes* they codify, the availability of standing before the International Court to any State to which the obligation is owed to invoke the international responsibility of a State in breach is a feature of the *erga omnes* character of such obligations.

In this sense, the *erga omnes* character of obligations to prevent (through necessary legislative means) and punish (through extradition or prosecution) violations of the prohibition of torture codified by the Torture Convention was identified by the International Court, so too the legal effect in the area of standing arising from a breach of these obligations, namely standing of any party to which the obligation is owed to bring a claim against the offending State. These findings were integral to the standing of Belgium before the Court and arise as a consequence of

[86] *Military and Paramilitary Activities in and against Nicaragua (Nicaragua v. United States of America)*, Judgment, ICJ Reports 1986, p. 14, para. 174 (quoting *Military and Paramilitary Activities in and against Nicaragua (Nicaragua v. United States of America)*, Jurisdiction and Admissibility, Judgment, ICJ Reports 1984, p. 392, para. 73).

[87] *See Questions Relating to the Obligation to Prosecute or Extradite (Belgium v. Senegal)*, Judgment, ICJ Reports 2012, Sep. Op. Cançado Trindade, p. 487, paras. 134–5, 158.

[88] *Military and Paramilitary Activities in and against Nicaragua (Nicaragua v. United States of America)*, Judgment, ICJ Reports 1986, p. 14, paras. 174–8 ('there are no grounds for holding that when customary international law is comprised of rules identical to those of treaty law, the latter "supervenes" the former, so that the customary international law has no further existence of its own').

the *jus cogens* status of the prohibition against torture.[89] However, it bears noting that standing arising from the *erga omnes* character of the obligations in question is wholly unrelated to the question of a State's consent to the jurisdiction of the International Court. In this sense, neither the violation of a norm belonging to *jus cogens*,[90] nor the breach of an obligation *erga omnes*,[91] is sufficient to engage the jurisdiction of the International Court.

D Jurisdictional immunity of the State

The jurisdictional immunity of the State refers to the principle that one State shall not be subject to the jurisdiction of another State, which is conceived as both a right and a corresponding obligation incumbent 'upon other States to respect and give effect to that immunity'.[92] As an element of sovereign immunity, the jurisdictional immunity enjoyed by one State before the courts of another is based in customary international law.[93] The doctrine embodies the principle of *par in parem non habet imperium* (between equals no power)[94] and originated from considerations of 'comity'.[95] While the jurisdictional immunity of the State was initially characterized by an 'absolute' theory of immunity,[96] that

[89] *See* Andenas & Weatherall, *II. International Court of Justice: Questions Relating to the Obligation to Extradite or Prosecute (Belgium v. Senegal)*, 753, 765–6.

[90] *Armed Activities on the Territory of the Congo (New Application: 2002) (Congo v. Rwanda)*, ICJ Reports 2006, p. 3, para. 64 ('the fact that a dispute relates to compliance with a norm having such a [*jus cogens*] character . . . cannot of itself provide a basis for the jurisdiction of the Court to entertain that dispute').

[91] *East Timor (Portugal v. Australia)*, Judgment, ICJ Reports 1995, p. 90, para. 29 ('the *erga omnes* character of a norm and the rule of consent to jurisdiction are two different things').

[92] *Jurisdictional Immunities of the State (Germany v. Italy: Greece Intervening)*, Judgment, ICJ Reports 2012, p. 99, para. 56.

[93] *Ibid.*, paras. 53–4; UN Convention on Jurisdictional Immunities of States and their Property, UN Doc. A/59/508, Preamble (2 December 2004).

[94] *Jurisdictional Immunities of the State (Germany v. Italy: Greece Intervening)*, Judgment, ICJ Reports 2012, p. 99, para. 57; *Schooner Exchange v. McFaddon*, 11 US 116, 134 (1812); Ian Sinclair, *The Law of Sovereign Immunity: Recent Developments*, 167 Recueil des Cours 197–9 (1980).

[95] *Jones v. United Kingdom*, ECtHR, Nos. 34356/06 & 40528/06, para. 188 (2014); *Hilton v. Guyot*, 159 US 113, 163–4 (1895).

[96] *See, e.g.*, *Spanish Government v. Lambege et Pujol*, Court of Cassation (France), D. 1849 1 (1849); *Schooner Exchange v. McFaddon*, 11 US 116, 134 (1812) ('Sovereigns are equal. It is the duty of a sovereign, not to submit his rights to the decision of a *co-sovereign*. He is the sole arbiter of his own rights. He acknowledges no superior, but God alone. To his equals, he shows respect, but not *submission*').

approach was gradually supplanted by a 'restrictive' theory of immunity that recognizes State immunity only for sovereign or public acts (*acte jure imperii*), and not for non-sovereign conduct akin to that of a private individual (*acte jure gestionis*).[97] In *Jurisdictional Immunities of the State* (2012), the International Court of Justice found that, 'even on the assumption that the [domestic] proceedings ... involved violations of *jus cogens* rules, the applicability of the customary international law on State immunity was not affected'.[98] In so finding, the Court determined that State immunity, as an expressly preclusive procedural rule,[99] bars proceedings for the violation of a substantive rule, even where that rule belongs to *jus cogens*.[100] Although such a rigid dichotomy is suspect,[101] the more general determination by the Court underscores the conclusion that sovereign immunity applies to proceedings against individuals and States in different ways.[102] Interestingly, this affirmation of the jurisdictional immunity of the State in cases concerning *jus cogens* may be viewed as consistent with the same reasoning by which individual immunities have eroded with respect to *jus cogens* violations.

The rationale underlying State immunity in cases arising from violations of *jus cogens* hails from a personal-jurisdiction-type immunity which shields one State absolutely from involuntary subjugation to the jurisdiction of another State even for *jus cogens* violations. Given this preclusive procedural immunity, akin to the immunity *ratione personae* of the individual, 'there is no substantive content in the procedural plea of State immunity upon which a *jus cogens* mandate can bite'.[103] If the observation in Chapter 12 is correct,[104] and sovereign immunity is rooted in equality as per the underlying principle *par in parem non habet imperium*, then the principle of sovereignty underpinning the

[97] *See, e.g., Jurisdictional Immunities of the State (Germany v. Italy: Greece Intervening)*, Judgment, ICJ Reports 2012, p. 99, paras. 59–61; *Société Anonyme des Chemins de Fer Liégeois-Luxembourgeois v. The Netherlands*, Supreme Court (Belgium), Pasicrisie Belge, I, p. 294 (1903).

[98] *Jurisdictional Immunities of the State (Germany v. Italy: Greece Intervening)*, Judgment, ICJ Reports 2012, p. 99, para. 97.

[99] *Ibid.*, para. 82. [100] *Ibid.*, paras. 93–7.

[101] As noted above, in practice, such a dichotomy is not so clear: one distinctly procedural aspect of *jus cogens* is its relationship to universal jurisdiction, while a court's subject-matter jurisdiction cannot be completely divorced from substantive considerations.

[102] *See* discussion *supra*, Chapter 12.C (Immunities).

[103] Hazel Fox, The Law of State Immunity 525 (Oxford University Press 2004).

[104] *See* discussion *supra*, Chapter 12.C.i (Immunity *Ratione Personae*).

jurisdictional immunity of the State would be accommodated by proceedings before an international judicial organ such as the International Court.[105] Alternatively, a State may consent to suit before the jurisdiction of another State by treaty or other *ad hoc* arrangement as a way of waiving its procedural, personal-jurisdiction-type immunity before the domestic court of another State.

Approached as a form of subject-matter immunity, the jurisprudence of international and domestic courts indicates that *jus cogens* violations do not constitute 'official acts' for purposes of sovereign immunity.[106] Importantly, *jus cogens* violations are not merely an excess of authority or contravention of instructions.[107] As a matter of international law, the sovereign does not possess the authority to authorize *jus cogens* violations in the first instance, therefore such conduct cannot constitute 'official acts' attributable to the State for purposes of individual responsibility, even if committed 'under the color of law'.[108] If *jus cogens* violations were attributable to the State in this sense, it would seem that the classical doctrine of sovereign immunity would then apply to shield those individuals who commit such conduct from criminal and civil responsibility while exposing the State to responsibility. Instead, the distinction that violations of *jus cogens* committed 'under the color of law' do not constitute 'official acts' is determinative in denying immunity *ratione materiae* for purposes of both individual criminal responsibility and civil liability.[109] Taken together, immunity *ratione personae* is the procedural effect and immunity *ratione materiae* is the substantive result of the same principle of sovereign immunity, elements which apply equally to the State to provide effectively complete jurisdictional immunity for *jus*

[105] *See, e.g.*, *Application of the Convention on the Prevention and Punishment of the Crime of Genocide (Bosnia and Herzegovina v. Serbia and Montenegro)*, Judgment, ICJ Reports 2007, p. 43.

[106] *See, e.g.*, *Yousuf v. Samantar*, 699 F.3d 763, 776 (4th Cir. 2012) *cert. denied*, 134 S. Ct. 897 (US 2014); *R. v. Bow Street Metropolitan Stipendiary Magistrate and Others, Ex parte Pinochet Ugarte (No. 3)*, House of Lords (UK), [2000] 1 A.C. 147, 38 ILM 581 (1999). *See* discussion *supra*, Chapter 12.C.ii (Immunity *Ratione Materiae*).

[107] ILC Articles on State Responsibility (2001), Article 7 (Excess of authority or contravention of instructions) ('The conduct of an organ of a State or of a person or entity empowered to exercise elements of the governmental authority shall be considered an act of the State under international law if the organ, person or entity acts in that capacity, even if it exceeds its authority or contravenes instructions').

[108] *See* discussion *supra*, 12.C.ii (Immunity *Ratione Materiae*).

[109] Roman Kolodkin, Second Report on Immunity of State Officials from Foreign Criminal Jurisdiction, UN Doc. A/CN.4/631, para. 57 (2010).

cogens violations before domestic courts. This reasoning may explain the broad recognition of State immunity before domestic courts in cases concerning *jus cogens* violations.[110]

On the other hand, the international responsibility of the State can be engaged by attribution of conduct committed 'under the color of law',[111] notwithstanding that the individual cannot benefit from that attribution for purposes of immunity *ratione materiae*. The regime of the international responsibility of the State appears to differ sufficiently from criminal and civil responsibility in the realm of individual responsibility in such a way that internationally wrongful acts committed 'under the color of law' are attributable to the State for purposes of international responsibility, while those same acts are insufficient to engage immunity *ratione materiae* as 'official acts' in individual proceedings. The ILC indicated the possibility of such a relation in its commentary to the Articles on State Responsibility, observing that conduct undertaken under 'official capacity *or under the color of authority*' is attributable to the State when assessing international responsibility.[112] This position would partially achieve the same practical effect as the rejected 'normative hierarchy' theory that *jus cogens* 'trumps' immunity,[113] insofar as the State and individual may be dually responsible for the same conduct, albeit in different respects.[114]

Given that the State cannot be the subject of criminal responsibility for violations of *jus cogens*, and the premise that the State incurs international responsibility for internationally wrongful acts attributable to it is well accepted, the area in which a substantial volume of jurisprudence has emerged concerns the immunity of the State from domestic civil liability.[115] The jurisdictional immunity of the State has been found to shield a State from civil liability for *jus cogens* violations in the United

110 *See* discussion *infra*, text accompanying *nn.* 116–31.

111 ILC Articles on State Responsibility (2001), 42, para. 13 (Commentary to Article 4).

112 *Ibid.* (emphasis added).

113 *Compare Jurisdictional Immunities of the State (Germany v. Italy: Greece Intervening)*, Judgment, ICJ Reports 2012, p. 99, para. 93, *with Al-Adsani v. United Kingdom*, ECtHR, No. 35763/97, para. 3 (2001) (Rozakis & Caflisch, J. J., Dissenting) ('The acceptance ... of the *jus cogens* nature of the prohibition ... entails that a State allegedly violating it cannot invoke hierarchically lower rules (in this case, those on State immunity) to avoid the consequences of the illegality of its actions').

114 *See* discussion *supra*, Chapter 15.B (Dual Responsibility).

115 As an aside, imputing direct civil or criminal liability upon the State for violations of *jus cogens* appears to depart from the principle of dual responsibility that distinguishes

States,[116] United Kingdom,[117] Canada,[118] Greece,[119] Slovenia,[120] Poland,[121] and France.[122] Findings of State immunity in these cases centred on considerations of State equality in accordance with the principle *par in parem non habet imperium*, which recognizes no exception for *jus cogens* violations. The ECtHR has repeatedly pronounced on the immunity of the State from domestic civil litigation for *jus cogens* violations, perhaps most notably in *Al-Adsani v. United Kingdom*.[123] The International Court affirmed the immunity of the State from civil liability in *Jurisdictional Immunities of the State*,[124] where it effectively reversed those exceptional instances, namely in Greece,[125] and Italy,[126] in which domestic courts had recognized an exception to State immunity for *jus*

individual responsibility – criminal and civil – from the international responsibility of the State.

116 *Sampson v. Germany*, 250 F.3d 1145, 1154–5 (7th Cir. 2001); *Smith v. Libya*, 101 F.3d 239, 245 (2nd Cir. 1996); *Princz v. Federal Republic of Germany*, 26 F 3d 1166, 1174 (DC Cir. 1994); *Siderman de Blake v. Argentina*, 965 F 2d 699, 718–19 (9th Cir. 1992).

117 *Jones v. Ministry of the Interior of Saudi Arabia and Lieutenant Colonel Abdul Aziz*, House of Lords (United Kingdom) [2006] UKHL 26 (2006), paras. 35 (Bingham, L.), 102 (Hoffmann, L.), 103 (Rodger, L.), 104 (Walker, L.), 105 (Carswell, L.).

118 *Bouzari v. Islamic Republic of Iran*, Court of Appeal for Ontario (Canada), 71 OR (3d) 675, paras. 86–95 (2004).

119 *Margellos v. Federal Republic of Germany, Anotato Eidiko Dikastirio* (Special Supreme Court) (Greece), No. 6/2002, 129 ILR 525, paras. 13–15 (2002).

120 *A.A. v. Germany*, Constitutional Court (Slovenia), Up-13/99-24, paras. 13–14 (2001).

121 *Natoniewski v. Germany*, Supreme Court (Poland), No. IV CSK 465/09, 2010 Polish Yearbook of International Law 299, 302, ILDC 1996 (2010).

122 *Bucheron v. Germany*, Court of Cassation (France), No. 02-45961, Bull. Civ., 2003, I, No. 258 (2003).

123 *Jones v. United Kingdom*, ECtHR, Nos. 34356/06 & 40528/06, paras. 210–14 (2014); *Kalogeropoulou v. Greece and Germany*, ECtHR, No. 59021/00 (2002); *Al-Adsani v. United Kingdom*, ECtHR, No. 35763/97, para. 61 (2001).

124 *Jurisdictional Immunities of the State (Germany v. Italy: Greece Intervening)*, Judgment, ICJ Reports 2012, p. 99, paras. 92–7.

125 *Prefecture of Voiotia v. Federal Republic of Germany (Distomo Massacre Case)*, Court of Cassation (*Areios Pagos*) (Greece), No. 11/2000, 129 ILR 513, 521 (2000) (recognizing exception to State immunity from civil suit where *jus cogens* violation at issue); *but see Margellos v. Federal Republic of Germany, Anotato Eidiko Dikastirio* (Special Supreme Court) (Greece), No. 6/2002, 129 ILR 525, paras. 13–15 (2002) (foreign State continued to enjoy sovereign immunity irrespective of *jus cogens* violations at issue).

126 *Germany v. Prefecture of Voiotia*, Court of Cassation (Italy), No. 11163/2011, 150 ILR 706 (2011) (enforcement proceeding of judgments rendered in Greek courts); *Germany v. Mantelli and ors*, Court of Cassation (Italy), Preliminary Order on Jurisdiction, No. 14201/2008, ILDC 1037, para. 11 (2008); *Ferrini v. Germany*, Court of Cassation (Civil Section) (Italy), No. 5044/2004, ILDC 19 (2004); *Germany v. Milde*, Court of Cassation (First Criminal Section) (Italy), No. 1072/2009, ILDC 1224 (2009).

cogens violations. Voices in both the academy,[127] and the judiciary,[128] have objected to this proposition on the basis that *jus cogens* should overcome sovereign immunity as a matter of normative hierarchy.[129] Nevertheless, the Italian Parliament subsequently enacted legislation giving effect to the 2012 ICJ decision,[130] and Italian courts have recognized jurisdictional immunity in civil proceedings against a State for *jus cogens* violations.[131]

Therefore, sovereign immunity as a principle and its application to the State are not interchangeable because sovereign immunity clearly applies in particular ways to individuals and States.[132] Commentators have criticized such a bifurcation of individual and State immunities because

[127] *See, e.g.*, Alexander Orakhelashvili, *State Immunity and Hierarchy of Norms: Why the House of Lords got it Wrong*, 18(5) European Journal of International Law 955–70 (2008).

[128] *Jurisdictional Immunities of the State (Germany v. Italy: Greece Intervening)*, Judgment, ICJ Reports 2012, Diss. Op. Cançado Trindade, p. 179, para. 316 ('*Jus cogens* stands above the prerogative or privilege of State immunity, with all the consequences that ensue therefrom, thus avoiding denial of justice and impunity').

[129] *See, e.g.*, Alexander Orakhelashvili, Peremptory Norms in International Law 344 (Oxford University Press 2006) ('Therefore, the prohibition on torture prevails over State immunity and this happens because of the normative characteristics of that prohibition, not because the "rules" on State immunity shall or actually do allow this'); Orakhelashvili, *State Immunity and Hierarchy of Norms*, 966 ('A state committing the breach of *jus cogens* waives the entitlement of sovereign immunity for those breaches').

[130] *Legge* 14 January 2013, n. 5/2013 (Italy) (requiring courts to deny jurisdiction where the ICJ, 'in a judgment settling a dispute in which Italy is a party, excluded the possibility of subjecting a specific conduct of another State to civil jurisdiction').

[131] *Frascà v. Germany and Giachini (guardian of Priebke) and Italy (joining)*, Court of Cassation (Italy), Preliminary Order on Jurisdiction, No. 4284/2013, ILDC 1998 (2013) (recognizing the jurisdictional immunity of Germany from civil proceedings for *jus cogens* violations in accordance with the 2012 ICJ decision *Jurisdictional Immunity of the State* and Article 3(1) of Law No. 5/2013); *Military Prosecutor v. Albers and ors and Germany (joining)*, Court of Cassation (Italy), No. 32139/2012, ILDC 1921 (2012) (recognizing immunity of German State from civil proceeding awarding damages to *partie civile* in conjunction with criminal proeedings against individual perpetrators of *jus cogens* violations committed in the San Terenzo Monti massacre during the Second World War).

[132] *See* discussion *supra*, Chapter 12.C (Immunities); *cf.* Roger O'Keefe, *Jurisdictional Immunities*, in The Development of International Law by the International Court of Justice 107, 144–6 (Oxford University Press, Christian Tams & James Sloane eds., 2013) (O'Keefe seems to refer to sovereign immunity and State immunity interchangeably. Moreover, he posits the immunity of the State and its officials to be the same – the latter is 'an instantation of state immunity pure and simple' – and refers to the distinction, particularly in the United States, between the immunity of the State from suit and the immunity of acts of individual officials from suit as 'idiosyncratic national approaches').

it 'would eviscerate the responsibility of states for the crimes committed by their organs'.[133] But here it should be recalled that there is little to eviscerate. A State cannot be criminally prosecuted for *jus cogens* violations before any forum as a matter of international law.[134] And civil liability for States before domestic courts has been rejected by the International Court,[135] with notable outliers in US and Canadian terrorism exceptions[136] of admittedly limited effectiveness.[137] What remains is the international responsibility of the State for *jus cogens* violations, as considered by the International Court in *Application of the Genocide Convention* (2007).[138]

The divergence in immunities for States and individuals in proceedings for *jus cogens* violations demonstrates a nuanced interaction between the doctrines of sovereign immunity and *jus cogens*. This interaction suggests that sovereignty is a doctrine of equality, not supremacy, and that the power of sovereign authority to sanction official conduct is limited. These findings are consistent with *jus cogens* as a constraint on the sovereignty of the State by permitting no derogation. Moreover, these conclusions resonate with other legal effects of *jus cogens* – obligations *erga omnes* requiring the State to prevent and punish, and the obligation to extradite or prosecute given effect by universal jurisdiction – by lowering the barrier of sovereign immunity that would otherwise impede the performance of these obligations vis-à-vis individuals. Taken together, the contemporary regime of international law immunities exposes individual violators to both criminal responsibility and civil liability before a range of international and domestic fora, while effectively limiting State responsibility to international responsibility for internationally wrongful acts.

133 *See, e.g.*, Sevrine Knuchel, *State Immunity and the Promise of* Jus Cogens, 9(2) NORTHWESTERN JOURNAL OF INTERNATIONAL HUMAN RIGHTS 149, 165 (2011).

134 *See* discussion *supra*, Chapter 12.A (Individual Criminal Responsibility).

135 *Jurisdictional Immunities of the State (Germany v. Italy: Greece Intervening)*, Judgment, ICJ Reports 2012, p. 99, paras. 92–7.

136 28 USC § 1605A (Terrorism exception to the jurisdictional immunity of a foreign state); State Immunity Act, RSC 1985, c S-18, para. 6.1 (Canada) (Support of terrorism).

137 *In re Islamic Republic of Iran Terrorism Litigation*, 659 F. Supp. 2d 31, 137–40 (DDC 2009).

138 *See Application of the Convention on the Prevention and Punishment of the Crime of Genocide (Bosnia and Herzegovina v. Serbia and Montenegro)*, Judgment, ICJ Reports 2007, p. 43, para. 471.

16

An illustration: the Libya crisis

The self-immolation of Mohammed Bouazizi in Tunisia in December 2010 sparked a popular movement that swept through the Arab world in the spring of 2011. On 15 February that movement reached the Libyan city of Benghazi, where several hundred demonstrators rallied against the authoritarian regime of Colonel Moammar Gaddafi. The violent suppression of the protest instigated nationwide demonstrations that were met with indiscriminate force by the Libyan State, fuelling a protracted conflict between an armed citizenry demanding liberal reform and a recalcitrant regime grasping desperately to power.[1] The international community condemned the use of lethal force against the Libyan population and reacted swiftly to the crisis. World leaders demanded that Libya fulfil its responsibility under international law to protect its population and put an end to violence targeting civilians. Under the mandate of the United Nations Security Council, an international coalition ultimately resorted to the use of force to defend the Libyan people. The International Criminal Court issued arrest warrants for principal members of the Gaddafi regime in connection with crimes against humanity.

The International Commission of Inquiry on Libya observed in its 2012 Report that 'the legal regimes applicable to the crimes and violations under review here comprise a complex arena of international law and the jurisprudence on some issues is not altogether settled'.[2] The purpose of this chapter is to consider the extent to which the legal framework of *jus cogens* developed above might be applied as a structure to elucidate the policy response of the international community to the Libya crisis. Correspondence between *jus cogens* and the international

[1] *See* UN Human Rights Council, Report of the International Commission of Inquiry to Investigate All Alleged Violations of International Law in Libya, UN Doc. A/HRC/19/68, paras. 75–104 (2012) [hereinafter, 2012 UNHRC Report].

[2] *Ibid.*, para 8.

response to the situation in Libya serves at once to highlight the relevance of *jus cogens* in contemporary international relations and illustrate the implementation of *jus cogens* in practice through existing institutional mechanisms. Harmonization in these areas demonstrates that the legal effects and structural implications of *jus cogens* are consistent with the governing institutions of the international community.

A The violation of peremptory norms

On 15 February 2011, civilians in the Libyan city of Benghazi protested against the regime of Colonel Moammar Gaddafi. An increasingly violent crowd of several hundred demonstrators clashed with Libyan security forces, prompting the use of non-lethal force to contain the situation. In response to the government's crackdown, and inspired by uprisings in neighbouring Tunisia and Egypt, the National Conference for the Libyan Opposition called for a nationwide 'Day of Rage' on 17 February to commemorate demonstrations in Benghazi five years earlier. The use of lethal violence by the Libyan State to suppress the 17 February protests resulted in civilian casualties across the country, fuelling a full-scale uprising that was met with force by the Libyan State. On 22 February, Gaddafi appeared on Libyan State television to declare that he would lead 'millions to purge Libya inch by inch, house by house, household by household, alley by alley, and individual by individual [to] purify this land'.[3] Gaddafi referred to demonstrators as '"rats" who needed to be executed' and, to this end, brought to bear the full capabilities of the military apparatus of the Libyan State. The ensuing violence was characterized as 'widespread and systematic and in furtherance of a State policy . . . [where] the targeted population was civilians demonstrating against Muammar Gaddafi's regime or those perceived to be dissidents to the regime'.[4]

On 26 February 2011, the UN Security Council referred the situation in Libya to the Prosecutor of the ICC, who was tasked with investigating the nature and magnitude of the violence in Libya.[5] According to

[3] UN Human Rights Council, Report of the High Commissioner under Human Rights Council Resolution S-15/1, UN Doc. A/HRC/17/45, para. 5 (2011) [hereinafter, 2011 UNHRC Report].

[4] *Situation in the Libyan Arab Jamahiriya*, Decision on the 'Prosecutor's Application Pursuant to Article 58 as to Muammar Mohammed Abu Minyar Gaddafi, Saif Al-Islam Gaddafi and Abdullah Al-Senussi', No. ICC-01/11-01/11-1, para. 35 (27 June 2011).

[5] *See* First Report of the Prosecutor of the International Criminal Court to the UN Security Council Pursuant to UNSCR 1970 (2011) (4 May 2011).

Prosecutor Luis Moreno-Ocampo, in his First Report to the UN Security Council, evidence indicated that war crimes and crimes against humanity were ongoing in Libya.[6] The initial findings of the Commission in its investigation pursuant to HRC Resolution S-15/1 corroborated the ICC investigation, which found evidence of grave violations of human rights and international humanitarian law.[7] The initial report of the High Commissioner cited 'serious human rights violations' resulting in hundreds of deaths, thousands of arrests, and hundreds more unaccounted for, as well as reports of 'serious breaches of international humanitarian law'.[8] The Second Report of the ICC Prosecutor adopted these figures with the caveat that they represented only a period of less than two weeks at the end of February 2011; more accurate figures were unknown due to efforts to conceal the commission of atrocities.[9]

The atrocities committed in Libya, as crimes against humanity and war crimes, constitute violations of peremptory norms. As detailed by the ICC Prosecutor, crimes against humanity had been committed in Libya as defined by the Rome Statute, including murder, imprisonment or other severe deprivation of physical liberty, other inhumane acts, torture, and persecution,[10] as well as rape and deportation or forcible transfer.[11] As the situation developed into armed conflict, war crimes were committed as defined by the Rome Statute, including violence to life and person, intentionally directing attacks against civilians not taking a direct part in hostilities, and intentionally directing attacks against protected objects.[12] Following an extensive investigation into violations of international law committed by all parties during the Libya crisis, the International Commission of Inquiry on Libya released its findings on 2 March 2012.[13] The Commission corroborated the findings of the ICC Prosecutor and confirmed the conclusions presented in its 2011 report.[14] The Commission determined that Libyan forces violated international law through

[6] *Ibid.* [7] 2011 UNHRC Report, paras. 22–51. [8] *Ibid.* para 67.

[9] Second Report to the Prosecutor of the International Criminal Court to the United Nations Security Council Pursuant to UNSCR 1970 (2011), para. 16 (2 November 2011).

[10] *See* First Report of the Prosecutor of the International Criminal Court to the UN Security Council Pursuant to UNSCR 1970 (2011), para. 11 (4 May 2011) (citing Rome Statute of the International Criminal Court, UN Doc. A/CONF.183.9 (17 July 1998, *entered into force* 1 July 2002) [hereinafter, Rome Statute (1998)], Articles 7(1)(a), 7(1)(e), 7(1)(k), 7 (1)(f), and 7(1)(h), respectively).

[11] *Ibid.*, para. 12 (citing Rome Statute (1998), Articles 7(1)(g) and 7(1)(d), respectively).

[12] *Ibid.* (citing Rome Statute (1998), Articles 8(2)(c)(i), 8(2)(e)(i), and 8(2)(e)(iv), respectively).

[13] 2012 UNHRC Report. [14] 2011 UNHRC Report, paras. 22–51.

excessive use of force, unlawful killing, arbitrary detentions and enforced disappearances, torture and other forms of ill-treatment, sexual violence, and attacks on civilians, civilian objects, protected persons and objects.[15] It confirmed that crimes against humanity,[16] and violations of international humanitarian law amounting to war crimes, had been committed by Libyan forces.[17]

B Breaches of obligations *erga omnes* arising from peremptory norms

As elaborated above,[18] the State is bound by obligations *erga omnes* arising from peremptory norms, the performance of which requires the State to prevent and punish violations of peremptory norms. Implicit in widespread violations of peremptory norms by individuals is the corollary failure on the part of the State to prevent and punish such violations in breach of its obligations *erga omnes*. This is particularly clear where conduct in violation of peremptory norms is carried out through the apparatus of the State. As obligations owed to the international community as a whole, any State is entitled to invoke the responsibility of the State for their breach, as indicated in Article 48(1)(b) of the Articles on State Responsibility,[19] and conceivably undertake countermeasures in such instances as permitted by international law.[20] Furthermore, the Articles on State Responsibility distinguish particular legal consequences for serious breaches of obligations *erga omnes*.[21]

15 2012 UNHRC Report, paras. 15–81. 16 *Ibid.*, para 118.

17 *Ibid.*, para 119 (It bears noting that the Commission found that *thuwar*, the opposition forces fighting against the Gaddafi regime, also committed war crimes and crimes against humanity during the course of the conflict with some degree of impunity. As troubling as this last finding is, the scope of the present discussion is limited to those offences carried out by the Libyan regime that precipitated international action).

18 *See* discussion *supra*, Chapter 14 (The Enforcement of *Jus Cogens*: Obligations *Erga Omnes*).

19 International Law Commission, Responsibility of States for Internationally Wrongful Acts, Report of the International Law Commission on the Work of its Fifty-Third Session, [2001] II(2) YbILC 26, Article 48 (Invocation of responsibility by a State other than an injured State) [hereinafter, ILC Articles on State Responsibility (2001)] (while the Articles refer only to the invocation of responsibility by States, rather than international organizations, this discussion refers to actions by States undertaken individually and collectively through international organizations).

20 *Ibid.*, Article 54 ('Measures taken by States other than an injured State').

21 *Ibid.*, Articles 40–1 (Chapter III: Serious Breaches of Obligations under Peremptory Norms of General International Law).

Each of these procedural aspects of breaches of obligations *erga omnes* was expressed in the Libyan crisis.

The violation of peremptory norms in Libya was a direct result of State policy, the furtherance of which constituted war crimes and crimes against humanity.[22] Consequently, by inference, Libya was manifestly in breach of its obligations to the international community as a whole arising from peremptory norms. Article 48(1)(b) of the Articles on State Responsibility reflects the entitlement of any State to invoke the responsibility of Libya for breaching its obligations to prevent and punish war crimes and crimes against humanity. To this end, the international community broadly called upon Libya to fulfil its obligations arising under international law. This call was largely articulated in terms of the 'responsibility to protect', the language by which the United Nations refers to obligations *erga omnes* to protect civilian populations from violations of particular peremptory norms.[23] The President of the Security Council,[24] African Union (AU),[25] UN Human Rights Council,[26] and Organization of the Islamic Conference (OIC)[27] each issued statements calling upon Libya to fulfil its obligations arising under international law to protect its civilian population from human rights violations. Perhaps the most powerful statement to this effect came directly from the Security Council in Resolution 1970, '*recalling* the Libyan authorities' responsibility to protect its population'.[28] In other instances, particularly later in the crisis, parties invoked the responsibility of Libya for *failure* to fulfil its responsibility to protect the Libyan people, as did the US Ambassador to the United

[22] *See* discussion *infra*, *nn.* 110–21; *see* Chapter 15.A (State Responsibility for Internationally Wrongful Acts).

[23] The invocation of 'international responsibility of the State' and the 'Responsibility to Protect' reflect distinct uses of 'responsibility'. The former constitutes responsibility for internationally wrongful acts, while the latter reflects an international law obligation. Implicit in invoking the failure of the latter is the invocation of the former, as the failure to protect a population from violations of peremptory norms constitutes a breach of the obligations owed by the State to the international community.

[24] United Nations Security Council Press Statement on Libya, UN Doc. SC/10180 (22 February 2011).

[25] Communiqué of the 261st Meeting of the Peace and Security Council of the African Union, AU Doc. PSC/PR/COMM(CCLXI) (23 February 2011).

[26] UN Human Rights Council, Situation of Human Rights in the Libyan Arab Jamahiriya, UN Doc. A/HRC/S-15/2 (25 February 2011).

[27] Statement of Professor Ekmeleddin Ihsanoglu, OIC Secretary General, to the Meeting of the Permanent Representatives on the Situation in the Libyan Jamahiriya (8 March 2011).

[28] SC Res. 1970, UN Doc. S/Res/1970, Preamble (26 February 2011).

Nations,[29] the G8,[30] and the Council of Europe.[31] States invoking the responsibility of Libya for breaching its obligations owed to the international community were arguably entitled to undertake countermeasures to bring such breaches to a halt.[32]

With respect to particular consequences delineated in the Articles on State Responsibility for breaches of obligations arising from peremptory norms, the magnitude of the breach was recognized as 'serious'.[33] To engage particular consequences for *serious* breaches of obligations *erga omnes*, the Articles on State Responsibility indicate that a breach must meet a threshold of seriousness defined by the 'gross or systematic' character of the breaches.[34] Although Article 40 does not explicitly establish any objective criteria for determining the seriousness of such a breach, it anticipates that such breaches 'are likely to be addressed by the competent international organizations, including the Security Council and the General Assembly'.[35] It is relevant in this sense to recall that the Security Council deplored 'the gross and systematic violation' of human rights in Resolutions 1970 and 1973.[36]

Moreover, investigations by 'competent international organizations' into the violations perpetrated in Libya indicated that the failure of the Libyan State to uphold its obligations arising from peremptory norms satisfied the threshold of seriousness. Perhaps the most relevant finding in this regard was the unanimous order of provisional measures against Libya by the African Court on Human and Peoples' Rights (ACtHPR) on 25 March 2011, to address 'serious and massive human rights violations' in Libya.[37] The application had been submitted to the Court by the African Commission on Human and Peoples' Rights (ACHPR), which itself concluded that actions by the Libyan security forces 'amount[ed] to serious and widespread violations of the rights enshrined in Articles 1, 2,

[29] 6491st Meeting of the United Nations Security Council, UNSCOR, 6491st Meeting, UN Doc. S/PV.6491 (26 February 2011) (statement by Ms. Rice).

[30] Group of Eight, Deauville G8 Declaration: Renewed Commitment for Freedom and Democracy (26–27 May 2011).

[31] Council of the European Union, Council Conclusions on Libya, para. 2 (20 June 2011).

[32] ILC Articles on State Responsibility (2001), Article 54; *see ibid.*, 137, paras. 1–3 (Commentary to Article 54) (noting that the Articles conceive only of action taken by States and not through international organizations).

[33] *Ibid.*, Article 40. [34] *Ibid.*, para. 8 (Commentary to Article 40). [35] *Ibid.*, para 9.

[36] SC Res. 1973, UN Doc. S/Res/1973, Preamble (17 March 2011); SC Res. 1970, UN Doc. S/Res/1970, Preamble (26 February 2011).

[37] *African Commission on Human and Peoples' Rights v. Great Socialist People's Libyan Arab Jamahiriya*, ACtHPR, Order for Provisional Measures, No. 004/2011 (2011).

4, 5, 9, 11, 12, 13, and 23 of the [African] Charter' on Human and Peoples' Rights,[38] which would appear to indicate that the failure on the part of the State to fulfil its obligations *erga omnes* was gross and systematic. Accordingly, the Court stated, 'there is therefore a situation of extreme gravity and urgency, as well as a risk of irreparable harm to persons who are the subject of the application, in particular, in relation to the rights to life and to physical integrity of persons as guaranteed in the Charter'.[39] Interestingly, although the ACHPR had not requested provisional measures, the Court exercised its authority to do so '*proprio motu* "in cases of extreme gravity and urgency and when necessary to avoid irreparable harm to persons" and "which it deems necessary to adopt in the interest of the parties or of justice"'.[40] The ACtHPR thereby ordered:

> (1) The Great Socialist People's Libyan Arab Jamahiriya must immediately refrain from any action that would result in loss of life or violation of physical integrity of persons, which could be a breach of the provisions of the Charter or of other international human rights instruments to which it is a party.
> (2) The Great Socialist People's Libyan Arab Jamahiriya must report to the Court within a period of fifteen (15) days from the date of receipt of the Order, on the measures taken to implement this Order.[41]

In the present context, it might reasonably be inferred that 'measures taken to implement this Order' as envisaged in paragraph 2 would include the performance of Libya's obligations *erga omnes*. The order was the first ruling by the ACtHPR against a State party.

The investigation by the ICC also indicated that crimes against humanity and war crimes perpetrated in Libya met the threshold of seriousness set out by Article 40(2) of the Articles on State Responsibility,[42] a further indication that the State had seriously breached its relevant obligations *erga omnes*.[43] Similarly, the 7 June Report by the High Commissioner of the Human Rights Council documented conditions indicative of a gross and systematic failure on the part of Libya to

[38] *Ibid.*, para. 3. [39] *Ibid.*, para. 22. [40] *Ibid.*, para. 10. [41] *Ibid.*, para. 25.

[42] *Situation in the Libyan Arab Jamahiriya*, Decision on the 'Prosecutor's Application Pursuant to Article 58 as to Muammar Mohammed Abu Minyar Gaddafi, Saif Al-Islam Gaddafi and Abdullah Al-Senussi', No. ICC-01/11-01/11-1, para. 5 (27 June 2011).

[43] First Report of the Prosecutor of the International Criminal Court to the UN Security Council Pursuant to UNSCR 1970, paras. 15–20 (4 May 2011) (discussing the 'Gravity' requirement for jurisdiction of the ICC under the Rome Statute).

perform its obligations *erga omnes*.[44] In confirming these initial findings, the 2012 Report of the International Commission of Inquiry on Libya determined that these serious and widespread violations of international law amounted to crimes against humanity and war crimes.[45] And of course, crimes against humanity are by their very nature 'widespread and systematic' and imply a commensurately serious failure on the part of the State with respect to its relevant obligations.

Taken together, the position of the ACHPR and subsequent order of provisional measures by the ACtHPR, the finding of crimes against humanity and war crimes by the ICC, and the investigation by the Human Rights Council culminating in the Report of the International Commission of Inquiry, all indicate the gross and systematic failure of the Libyan State to fulfil its obligations arising from peremptory norms. The breaches of obligations *erga omnes* by Libya were, in effect, recognized by 'competent international organizations' to meet the threshold of seriousness set out in Article 40(2) of the Articles on State Responsibility. Thus, in the Libya context, the invocation of responsibility and recognition of seriousness regarding breaches of obligations arising from peremptory norms are consistent with the elements set forth in Articles 48 and 54 of the Articles on State Responsibility, regarding countermeasures in relation to obligations owed to the international community as a whole, as well as the parameters of Articles 40 and 41, which delineate particular consequences for breaches of obligations arising from peremptory norms.[46]

C Consequences for breaches of obligations *erga omnes*

A palette of legal options arose as a consequence of the duty of third-States to respond to breaches of obligations *erga omnes* owed to the international community.[47] All States are obligated to abstain from the recognition and maintenance of illegal situations arising from violations of peremptory norms, as well as to cooperate to bring an end to such

[44] 2011 UNHRC Report, para. 67. [45] 2012 UNHRC Report, paras. 118–19.

[46] Because the availability of countermeasures under Article 54 is framed only as a 'savings clause', and would presumably be subsumed by the particular consequences defined in Article 41 in this context, the following discussion will focus on the particular consequences for breaches of obligations *erga omnes* derived from the jurisprudence of the International Court. *See* ILC Articles on State Responsibility (2001), 139, para. 6 (Commentary to Article 54).

[47] *See* discussion *supra*, Chapter 14.A (Prevention and Consequences for Third-States).

breaches.[48] Collective action to suppress such breaches may in some instances include the use of force.[49] Additionally, members of the international community share a common legal interest in the prosecution of individuals for international crimes.[50] The present section considers the extent to which the response of the international community to the Libya crisis may be conceived in terms of these particular consequences arising for third-States in response to violations of peremptory norms: namely, non-recognition and non-assistance, collective action, and extradition and prosecution.

i. Non-recognition and non-assistance

All States are subject to obligations under international law not to recognize the legality of a situation resulting from, or maintained by, the breach of obligations *erga omnes* arising from peremptory norms,[51] and not to aid or assist in the maintenance of such a situation.[52] In the Libya context, it may be recalled that the purpose of conduct in violation of peremptory norms was to quell civilian demonstrations, and ultimately, subdue an uprising against the Libyan regime by force against the civilian population.[53] The effect of the serious breaches of obligations *erga omnes* in question was therefore to preserve the rule of the Libyan regime against the will of its civilian population. Consequently, fulfilling the duty of non-recognition may be conceived through the collective

48 *Ibid. See Legal Consequences of the Construction of a Wall in the Occupied Palestinian Territory*, Advisory Opinion, ICJ Reports 2004, p. 136, para. 159; *Legal Consequences for States of the Continued Presence of South Africa in Namibia (South West Africa) notwithstanding Security Council Resolution 276 (1970)*, Advisory Opinion, ICJ Reports 1971, p. 16, para. 126.

49 *See* discussion *supra*, Chapter 14.B (Protection and the Use of Force).

50 *See* discussion *supra*, Chapter 14.C (Punishment and Universal Jurisdiction).

51 *Legal Consequences of the Construction of a Wall in the Occupied Palestinian Territory*, Advisory Opinion, ICJ Reports 2004, p. 136, para. 159; *Legal Consequences for States of the Continued Presence of South Africa in Namibia (South West Africa) notwithstanding Security Council Resolution 276 (1970)*, Advisory Opinion, ICJ Reports 1971, p. 16, para. 126.

52 *Ibid. See* ILC Articles on State Responsibility (2001), Article 41 (Particular consequences of a serious breach of an obligation under this chapter).

53 *Situation in the Libyan Arab Jamahiriya*, Decision on the 'Prosecutor's Application Pursuant to Article 58 as to Muammar Mohammed Abu Minyar Gaddafi, Saif Al-Islam Gaddafi and Abdullah Al-Senussi', No. ICC-01/11-01/11-1, para. 35 (27 June 2011) ('the targeted population was civilians demonstrating against Muammar Gaddafi's regime or those perceived to be dissidents to the regime').

non-recognition of the legitimacy of the Libyan regime, in effect denying the legality of the situation resulting from the breach of obligations arising from peremptory norms. This denouncement was the initial response of the international community to the escalation of the crisis in Libya. Statements that the Gaddafi regime had lost the legitimacy to rule were made across the international community: by the US[54] and Libyan[55] representatives to the United Nations, by the Council of the League of Arab States,[56] the Chairman of the London Conference on Libya (which involved more than forty foreign ministers and representatives, including the UN Secretary-General, OIC Secretary-General, members of NATO, and the Arab League),[57] the Libya Contact Group (which included the Arab League, European Union, Gulf Cooperation Council, NATO, Organization of Islamic Cooperation, and more than forty States),[58] the European Council,[59] NATO,[60] the Joint Council and Ministerial Meeting of the EU and Gulf Cooperation Council,[61] the G8,[62] and the Council of the European Union.[63] Non-recognition of the legitimacy of the Libyan regime and, by extension, non-assistance in maintaining the situation in Libya arising from serious breaches of obligations *erga omnes* often directly followed the invocation of responsibility. Legally, because the Gaddafi regime had seriously breached its

[54] 6491st Meeting of the United Nations Security Council, UNSCOR, 6491st Meeting, UN Doc. S/PV.6491 (26 February 2011) (statement by Ms Rice).

[55] *Ibid.* (statement by Mr Dabbashi).

[56] Council of the League of Arab States, Res. No. 7360, para. 2 (12 March 2011), *in* Letter Dated 14 March 2011 from the Permanent Observer of the League of Arab States to the United Nations addressed to the President of the Security Council, UN Doc. S/2011/137 (15 March 2011).

[57] William Hague, London Conference on Libya (Chair's Statement) (29 March 2011); *see* Catherine Ashton, A Statement by the High Representative following the London Conference on Libya, No. 129/11 (29 March 2011).

[58] William Hague, Libya Contact Group (Chair's Statement), para. 2 (13 April 2011). *See* Contact Group on Libya, Chair's Conclusions, para. 4 (5 May 2011); Statement by the Co-Chairs of the Third Meeting of the Libya Contact Group, para. 2 (9 June 2011).

[59] European Council Decision, EUCO 7/1/11 REV 1, para. 7 (20 April 2011).

[60] NATO, Statement on Libya Following the Working Lunch of NATO Ministers of Foreign Affairs with non-NATO Contributors to Operation Unified Protector, Press Release (2011) 045 (14 April 2011).

[61] 21st EU–GCC Joint Council and Ministerial Meeting, Joint Communique, Ref. CL11-058EN, para. 8 (20 April 2011).

[62] Group of Eight, Deauville G8 Declaration: Renewed Commitment for Freedom and Democracy (26–27 May 2011).

[63] Council of the European Union, Council Conclusions on Libya, para. 2 (20 June 2011).

obligations *erga omnes* with the purpose of retaining power, its control over Libya was appropriately not recognized. A similar position was advanced by the International Court of Justice in its 1971 *Legal Consequences for States of the Continued Presence of South Africa in Namibia (South West Africa)* Advisory Opinion, in the context of a policy of apartheid administered by the government of South Africa.[64] While the situation in Namibia concerned a different context, the administration of territory by a former Mandatory under the UN Charter, the same approach appears applicable.

ii. Collective action

States are under an obligation to cooperate to bring an end to serious breaches of obligations *erga omnes*, within the limits of the Charter of the United Nations and international law.[65] According to the ILC, where a State has seriously (grossly or systematically) breached its obligations *erga omnes*, it is the *positive duty* of third-States to undertake collective action to suppress such a breach.[66] The UN Secretary-General clearly articulated this duty in his call for the international community to undertake collective action:

> I strongly believe that the first obligation of the international community is to do everything possible to ensure the immediate protection of civilians at demonstrable risk ... [W]hen a State manifestly fails to protect its population from serious international crimes, the international community has the responsibility to step in and take protective action in a collective, timely and decisive manner.[67]

[64] *Legal Consequences for States of the Continued Presence of South Africa in Namibia (South West Africa) notwithstanding Security Council Resolution 276 (1970)*, Advisory Opinion, ICJ Reports 1971, p. 16, paras. 128–33.

[65] *Legal Consequences of the Construction of a Wall in the Occupied Palestinian Territory*, Advisory Opinion, ICJ Reports 2004, p. 136, para. 159; *Legal Consequences for States of the Continued Presence of South Africa in Namibia (South West Africa) notwithstanding Security Council Resolution 276 (1970)*, Advisory Opinion, ICJ Reports 1971, p. 16, para. 126.

[66] ILC Articles on State Responsibility (2001), Articles 40–1; *ibid.*, 14, para. 2 (Commentary to Article 41) ('States are under a positive duty to cooperate in order to bring to an end serious breaches in the sense of article 40').

[67] UN Secretary-General Ban Ki-moon, Secretary-General's Briefing on Libya, UN Doc. S/PV.6490 (25 February 2011).

To this effect, the Security Council authorized collective action under Chapter VII of the UN Charter with the unanimous passage of Resolution 1970 on 26 February 2011.[68]

Resolution 1970 invoked the responsibility of the Libyan State for widespread and systematic violence perpetrated against civilians and recalled the responsibility of Libyan authorities to protect its population.[69] The resolution directed Libyan authorities to conform with their obligations by putting an immediate end to the violence, taking steps to fulfil the legitimate demands of its population, and acting with restraint and respect for human rights.[70] The Security Council referred the situation to the ICC, imposed a general arms embargo, called for a travel ban and asset freeze on particular individuals connected to the regime, established a new sanctions committee, and called upon States to cooperate to provide humanitarian assistance.[71] Days later, the UN General Assembly suspended Libya's membership to the Human Rights Council, an indication that Libya remained in breach of its relevant obligations notwithstanding the action taken by the Security Council.[72] The Libyan Opposition, in its Founding Statement, '[requested] the international community to fulfil its obligations to protect the Libyan people from any further genocide and crimes against humanity'.[73]

The Security Council responded to the ongoing crisis in Libya on 17 March 2011 with the passage of stronger language in Resolution 1973.[74] Acting again under Chapter VII of the UN Charter, the Security Council reiterated 'the responsibility of the Libyan authorities to protect the Libyan population' and condemned 'the gross and systematic violation of human rights',[75] while expressly calling on Libya to fulfil its obligations under international law.[76] Resolution 1973 strengthened the measures in Resolution 1970, took the additional step of imposing a no-fly zone over Libya, and authorized the use of force by the international community.[77]

68 SC Res. 1970, UN Doc. S/Res/1970 (26 February 2011). 69 *Ibid.*, Preamble.

70 *Ibid.*, paras. 1–2. 71 *Ibid.*, paras. 4–26.

72 GA Res. 65/265, UN Doc. A/Res/65/265 (1 March 2011).

73 Interim National Transitional Council, Founding Statement of the Interim Transitional National Council (TNC) (5 March 2011) (although the invocation of genocide in this instance is unsubstantiated as a matter of law).

74 SC Res. 1973, UN Doc. S/Res/1973 (17 March 2011). 75 *Ibid.*, Preamble.

76 *Ibid.*, para. 3.

77 *Ibid.*, paras. 4–6 (emphasis added) ('*The Security Council* ... *[a]uthorizes* Member States that have notified the Secretary-General, acting nationally or through regional organizations or arrangements, and acting in cooperation with the Secretary-General, *to take all necessary measures*, notwithstanding paragraph 9 of resolution 1970 (2011),

This authorization falls within the 'conservative' approach to the use of force for humanitarian purposes.[78] NATO commenced an alliance operation, 'Operation Unified Protector', pursuant to Resolutions 1970 and 1973 on 23 March 2011 to enforce the arms embargo, later expanding its mission to enforce the no-fly zone, and ultimately taking control of all military operations to protect civilians.[79] By 24 March, the United Kingdom, France, the United States, Denmark, Canada, Italy, Qatar, Belgium, Norway, Spain, and the United Arab Emirates had informed the Secretary-General of their use of force in Libya.[80] The European Union proposed to conduct its own military operation, 'EUFOR Libya', if requested by the UN Office for the Coordination of Humanitarian Affairs.[81] Other measures taken against the Gaddafi regime included restricting access to Libyan ports by the United Kingdom,[82] supplying light infantry weapons to Libyan opposition forces by France,[83] and an Egyptian court order to cease broadcasting Libyan State Television.[84]

Although the immediate goal of the military campaign was cessation of violence against the civilian population in Libya, the 'preferred outcome' of the operation was to facilitate political transition.[85] In the weeks following the initiation of the Libyan campaign, participants in the operation articulated this objective: the UN Secretary-General,[86]

to protect civilians and civilian populated areas under threat of attack in the Libyan Arab Jamahiriya').

[78] *See* discussion *supra*, Chapter 14.B.i (The Conservative Position).

[79] NATO, Operation UNIFIED PROTECTOR Final Mission Stats (2 November 2011); UN Secretary-General Ban Ki-moon, Secretary-General's Briefing to the Security Council on the Situation in Libya (24 March 2011).

[80] UN Secretary-General Ban Ki-moon, Secretary-General's Briefing to the Security Council on the Situation in Libya (24 March 2011).

[81] Council of the European Union, Council Decision 2011/210/CFSP, [2011] O. J. L 89/17, Article 1 (1 April 2011).

[82] Council of the European Union, Council Conclusions on Libya, para. 6 (20 June 2011).

[83] Colonel Thierry Burkhard, Statement to Agence France-Presse, BBC News, *available at* www.bbc.co.uk/news/mobile/world-africa-13955751 (29 June 2011).

[84] Fourth Meeting of the Libya Contact Group Chair's Statement, para. 9 (15 July 2011).

[85] *See, e.g.*, House of Commons, Interpretation of Security Council Resolution 1973 on Libya, SN/IA/5916, § 9 (6 April 2011) (What is the ultimate goal of the military action?).

[86] UN Secretary-General Ban Ki-moon, Secretary-General's Statement to the Libya Contact Group on the next steps in Implementing Security Council Resolution 1973 [As delivered] (13 April 2011).

European Council,[87] and Chair of the Libya Contact Group[88] planned next steps for the political transition of Libya. The G8 linked this objective to the invocation of responsibility for violations of international law and non-recognition of the situation arising therefrom:

> Qadhafi and the Libyan government have failed to fulfil their responsibility to protect the Libyan population and have lost all legitimacy. He has no future in a free, democratic Libya. He must go. We are committed to supporting a political transition that reflects the will of the Libyan people.[89]

NATO issued a statement to similar effect.[90] The call for political transition follows logically from the previous aspects of the international response assessed above. Following the invocation of Libyan responsibility for serious breaches of obligations owed to the international community, and non-recognition of the legality of the resultant political situation, collective action aimed to put an end to the breaches in question as well as the situation arising therefrom.[91] Even so, government transition by use of force is perhaps the most extreme example of collective action in response to violations of obligations arising from peremptory norms within the meaning of Article 41 of the Articles on State Responsibility.

iii. Extradition and prosecution

The performance of obligations *erga omnes* imposes a duty upon the State to punish transgressions of peremptory norms through prosecution or extradition.[92] Pursuant to its call 'to hold to account those responsible for attacks, including by forces under their control, on civilians', the UN

87 European Council Decision, EUCO 7/1/11 REV 1, para. 8 (20 April 2011); Council of the European Union, Council Conclusions on Libya, paras. 1, 7 (20 June 2011).

88 Second Meeting of the Libya Contact Group, Chairs' Conclusions, para. 3 (5 May 2011); Fourth Meeting of the Libya Contact Group, Chair's Statement, para. 8 (15 July 2011).

89 Group of Eight, Deauville G8 Declaration: Renewed Commitment for Freedom and Democracy, paras. 64–5 (26–27 May 2011).

90 NATO, Statement on Libya Following the Working Lunch of NATO Ministers of Defence with non-NATO Contributors to Operation Unified Protector, Press Release (2011) 071 (8 June 2011).

91 *See* Assembly of the African Union, Decision on the Peaceful Resolution of the Libyan Crisis, AU Doc. EXT/ASSEMBLY/AU/DEC/(01.2011), paras. 7–8 (25 May 2011) (expressing concern over the use of force pursuant to Security Council Resolutions 1970 and 1973).

92 *See* discussion *supra*, Chapter 14.C (Punishment and Universal Jurisdiction).

Security Council referred the situation in Libya to the ICC Prosecutor on 26 February.[93] The importance of prosecuting international crimes was noted by the ICC Prosecutor in the Libyan context:

> Arresting those who ordered the commission of crimes will contribute to the protection of civilians in Libya because it will deter ongoing crimes. It will deter crimes by removing those who ordered the crimes, and by sending a serious message to other potential perpetrators, in Libya and in other situations, that the international community will not condone such crimes.[94]

The First Report of the ICC Prosecutor detailed the procedural processes associated with the Libya crisis and the decision to focus the investigation 'on those who bear the greatest responsibility for the most serious crimes', without prejudice to violations committed by those not under investigation by the ICC.[95] The ICC limited its initial investigation to the responsibility of three individuals: Moammar Gaddafi (the effective Head of State of Libya), his eldest son Saif Al-Islam Gaddafi (the *de facto* Prime Minister of Libya), and Abdullah Al-Senussi (Gaddafi's brother-in-law and the Head of Military Intelligence).[96] The Pre-Trial Chamber of the ICC issued arrest warrants accordingly in the case of *Prosecutor v. Muammar Mohammed Abu Minyar Gaddafi, Saif Al-Islam Gaddafi and Abdullah Al-Senussi* (2011).[97] The Third Report of the ICC Prosecutor evaluated the extent of international cooperation towards the prosecution of international crimes committed in Libya.[98]

D Individual and State responsibility

International responsibility for the violation of peremptory norms is characterized by a 'duality of responsibility' according to which both

93 SC Res. 1970, UN Doc. S/Res/1970, Preamble, paras. 4–8 (26 February 2011).

94 ICC Prosecutor, Statement to the United Nations Security Council on the Situation in the Libyan Arab Jamahiriya, pursuant to UNSCR 1970 (2011), para. 25 (4 May 2011).

95 First Report of the Prosecutor of the International Criminal Court to the UN Security Council Pursuant to UNSCR 1970, para. 25 (4 May 2011).

96 *See* ICC Prosecutor, Statement to the United Nations Security Council on the Situation in the Libyan Arab Jamahiriya, pursuant to UNSCR 1970 (2011), para. 20 (4 May 2011); *see Situation in the Libyan Arab Jamahiriya*, Decision on the 'Prosecutor's Application Pursuant to Article 58 as to Muammar Mohammed Abu Minyar Gaddafi, Saif Al-Islam Gaddafi and Abdullah Al-Senussi', No. ICC-01/11-01/11-1 (27 June 2011).

97 Warrants of Arrest in respect of Muammar Gaddafi, Saif Al-Islam Gaddafi and Abdullah Al-Senussi, Nos. ICC-01/11-01/11-2, ICC-01/11-01/11-3, ICC-01/11-01/11-4 (27 June 2011).

98 Third Report of the Prosecutor of the International Criminal Court to the UN Security Council Pursuant to UNSCR 1970, paras. 5–13 (16 May 2012).

the individual and the State face distinct, though often concurrent, forms of responsibility.[99] The criminal responsibility of the individual is recognized as the primary locus of accountability for violations of peremptory norms. The State bears responsibility for breaches of obligations *erga omnes* and individual conduct attributable to it in violation of peremptory norms, all of which constitute internationally wrongful acts. This section contemplates the way in which each of these elements of responsibility was engaged in connection with the Libya crisis.

Individual conduct in violation of a peremptory norm constitutes an international crime engaging individual criminal responsibility.[100] The most prominent example of individual criminal responsibility in the Libya crisis is the indictment of three named officials for crimes against humanity before the ICC in *Prosecutor v. Gaddafi et al.*[101] The ICC Prosecutor conceived that reparations might be awarded with the personal assets of Saif Al-Islam Gaddafi and Abdullah Al-Senussi,[102] implying a degree of civil liability against the two individuals. More broadly, the Security Council stressed in Resolution 1970 'the need to hold to account those responsible for attacks ... on civilians',[103] and it was anticipated that a judicial process would be carried out by the new Libyan State to bring individuals who violated peremptory norms – on either side of the conflict – to justice.[104] This process would conceivably focus broadly on the prosecution of individuals for international crimes,[105]

[99] *See* discussion *supra*, Chapter 15.B (Dual Responsibility).

[100] *See* discussion *supra*, Chapter 12.A (Individual Criminal Responsibility).

[101] *Prosecutor v. Gaddafi et al.*, ICC-01/11-01/11-T-1 (2011); *see Prosecutor v. Gaddafi et al.*, Decision to Terminate the Case Against Muammar Mohammed Abu Minyar Gaddafi, ICC-01/11-01/11-28 (2011) (terminating the case against Moammar Gaddafi following his death on 22 November 2011).

[102] *See* ICC Prosecutor, Statement to the United Nations Security Council on the Situation in the Libyan Arab Jamahiriya, pursuant to UNSCR 1970 (2011), para. 13 (2 November 2011).

[103] SC Res. 1973, UN Doc. S/Res/1973, Preamble (17 March 2011); SC Res. 1970, UN Doc. S/Res/1970, Preamble (26 February 2011).

[104] Third Report of the Prosecutor of the International Criminal Court to the UN Security Council Pursuant to UNSCR 1970, paras. 36–41 (16 May 2012); *but see* 2012 UNHRC Report, paras. 799–800 (expressing concern over the unequal application of criminal law in post-conflict Libya).

[105] *See, e.g.*, UN Secretary-General, Secretary-General's Remarks to the General Assembly on Libya (1 March 2011) ('there is no impunity ... those who commit crimes against humanity will be punished, [and] fundamental principles of justice and accountability shall prevail'); 6491st Meeting of the United Nations Security Council, UNSCOR, 6491st Meeting, UN Doc. S/PV.6491, 5 (26 February 2011) (statement by Mr Osorio) ('Reconciliation will require the establishment of responsibility, confronting impunity and

irrespective of any amnesty process.[106] To this end, the NTC adopted Law No. 5 of 2011, which included the Transitional Justice Law and created a National Fact-Finding and Reconciliation Commission.[107] Moreover, in its 2 March 2012 Report, the International Commission of Inquiry on Libya recalled its mandate 'to identify those responsible, to make recommendations, in particular, on accountability measures, all with a view to ensuring that those individuals responsible are held accountable'.[108] Pursuant to its charge, the Commission identified, where possible, individuals guilty of violations of international law, either directly or through command responsibility, and transmitted that information to the UN High Commissioner for Human Rights.[109]

The State is responsible for internationally wrongful acts constituting, in the present context, either individual conduct in violation of peremptory norms attributed to the State or the breach of obligations *erga omnes*. The international law of State responsibility provides that conduct of an individual attributable to the State, in violation of obligations of the State under international law, constitutes an internationally wrongful act that engages the international responsibility of the State.[110] Should the findings of the pre-trial investigation of the ICC be confirmed, conduct of Moammar Gaddafi, Saif Al-Islam Gaddafi, and Abdullah Al-Senussi in violation of peremptory norms would in principle be attributable to Libya and, in turn, constitute internationally wrongful acts engaging Libya's international responsibility. The attribution of individual responsibility to the State is not, however, limited to the highest levels of government. Of particular relevance in this sense is the conclusion by the ICC Prosecutor that international crimes carried out in Libya were 'systematic, following the same *modus operandi* in multiple locations and executed through Security Forces'.[111] The 2012 Report of the International Commission of Inquiry on Libya similarly 'concluded that international crimes, specifically crimes against humanity and war crimes, were committed

ensuring that those who commit or have committed crimes against humanity are brought to justice').

106 2012 UNHRC Report, para. 795 ('It is important to ensure that the amnesty law is applied in a manner consistent with Libya's obligations under international law'). *See* discussion *supra*, Chapter 12.D (Amnesty).

107 *Ibid*., paras. 790–2. 108 *Ibid*., para. 95. 109 *Ibid*., para. 110.

110 ILC Articles on State Responsibility (2001), Articles 4–11.

111 First Report of the Prosecutor of the International Criminal Court to the UN Security Council Pursuant to UNSCR 1970, para. 17 (4 May 2011).

by Qadhafi forces in Libya'.[112] And the ACtHPR endorsed the conclusions of the ACHPR, which held that widespread and systematic violence against civilians had been perpetrated by the security forces of Libya.[113] A competent international judicial organ might therefore determine that the international responsibility of the Libyan State was engaged for internationally wrongful acts by the attribution of such violations of peremptory norms to the State under customary international law.[114]

A breach of obligations *erga omnes* arising from peremptory norms attributable to the State constitutes an internationally wrongful act engaging international responsibility.[115] Every indication supports the conclusion that violations of peremptory norms were committed systematically in Libya pursuant to or in furtherance of 'a State policy designed at the highest level of the State machinery'.[116] State policy, the furtherance of which constitutes violations of peremptory norms, is irreconcilable with obligations *erga omnes*, and obviously and manifestly breaches obligations arising from peremptory norms. Irrespective of the formal policy of the State, the gross and systematic character of war crimes and crimes against humanity perpetrated in Libya is indicative of serious breaches of the State's obligations arising from peremptory norms.[117] That Libya breached its obligations *erga omnes* was underscored by the broad invocation of the responsibility of the Libyan State for failing to protect its population.[118] The nature and seriousness of the breaches was indicated by the ACHPR, the ICC Prosecutor, and the International Commission of Inquiry on Libya.[119] This seriousness was emphasized by the provisional measures order of

[112] 2012 UNHRC Report, paras. 118–19.

[113] *African Commission on Human and Peoples' Rights v. Great Socialist People's Libyan Arab Jamahiriya*, ACtHPR, Order for Provisional Measures, No. 004/2011, paras. 2–3 (2011).

[114] *See* discussion *supra*, 15.A.ii (International Responsibility for Violations of Peremptory Norms).

[115] *See* discussion *supra*, 15.A.i (International Responsibility for Breaches of Obligations *Erga Omnes*).

[116] Second Report to the Prosecutor of the International Criminal Court to the United Nations Security Council Pursuant to UNSCR 1970 (2011), para. 14 (2 November 2011); First Report of the Prosecutor of the International Criminal Court to the UN Security Council Pursuant to UNSCR 1970, para. 17 (4 May 2011).

[117] *See* discussion *supra*, Chapter 14.A (Prevention and Consequences for Third-States).

[118] *See* discussion *supra*, text accompanying *nn.* 23–36.

[119] *See* discussion *supra*, text accompanying *nn.* 37–46.

the ACtHPR,[120] and the countermeasures authorized by the UN Security Council permitting the international community to protect civilians.[121] Although an international judicial organ might conclude that breaches by Libya of obligations *erga omnes* arising from peremptory norms constitute internationally wrongful acts engaging international responsibility – which legally justified the countermeasures undertaken by the international community to bring an end to those breaches – it is unlikely that international reasonability would be invoked against the 'new' Libyan regime.

***

By the summer of 2011, resolution emerged in the Libya crisis. On 3 August, the Interim Transitional National Council of Libya issued a Constitutional Declaration,[122] bringing a formal end to the State regime that facilitated serious violations of international law. Acting under Chapter VII of the UN Charter, the Security Council unanimously adopted Resolution 2009 on 16 September, relaxing its emergency countermeasures and establishing a Support Mission (UNSMIL) to assist and support the Libyan transition.[123] That same day, the General Assembly formally recognized the transitional government of Libya by seating the representative of the National Transitional Council (NTC) as the country's representative for its sixty-sixth session.[124] The NTC declared the full liberation of Libya on 23 October,[125] to which the Security Council responded by lifting the no-fly zone over Libya and terminating its mandate for collective action.[126]

The legal framework of *jus cogens* can be applied to structure the policy response of the international community to violations of

[120] *African Commission on Human and Peoples' Rights v. Great Socialist People's Libyan Arab Jamahiriya*, ACtHPR, Order for Provisional Measures, No. 004/2011, para. 25 (2011).

[121] SC Res. 1973, UN Doc. S/Res/1973, Preamble (17 March 2011); SC Res. 1970, UN Doc. S/Res/1970, Preamble (26 February 2011).

[122] Interim Transitional National Council, The Constitutional Declaration (3 August 2011).

[123] SC Res. 2009, UN Doc. S/Res/2009 (2011).

[124] UN General Assembly, After Much Wrangling, General Assembly Seats National Transitional Council of Libya as Country's Representative for Sixty-Sixth Session, Press Release GA/11137 (16 September 2011).

[125] UN Secretary-General Ban Ki-moon, Statement of the Secretary-General on the Declaration of the Liberation of Libya (23 October 2011).

[126] SC Res. 2016, UN Doc. S/Res/2016, paras. 5–6 (27 October 2011).

peremptory norms prohibiting war crimes and crimes against humanity in Libya. Implicit in the widespread and systematic violation of peremptory norms in Libya was a corollary breach of Libya's obligations *erga omnes*. Consequently, third-States were entitled to invoke the responsibility of the Libyan State and demand cessation of breaches of obligations owed to the international community. The serious nature of Libya's breaches permitted a range of legal options implemented by the international community through the United Nations, including non-recognition of the legality of the ensuing political situation, collective action countermeasures to suppress violations of peremptory norms, and cooperation towards the prosecution of international crimes in Libya. Dual responsibility is evident in the way individuals, particularly leaders of the Gaddafi regime, faced criminal responsibility for their violations of international law, while the international responsibility of the former Libyan State for internationally wrongful acts was effectively invoked through the attribution of illegal individual conduct and for breaches of obligations *erga omnes*.

The Libya experience indicates that, in practice, the elements of the framework of *jus cogens* are interconnected and overlapping. Peremptory norms were violated by individuals, entailing individual criminal responsibility, the scale of which indicated that the Libyan State had failed to protect its population. Consequently, State responsibility arose for illegal individual conduct attributable to the State in violation of peremptory norms as well as for breaches of its obligations *erga omnes*. The international community as a whole was entitled to invoke this responsibility and, given the seriousness of the breaches, third-States were empowered to respond accordingly. This response was immediately directed towards cessation of violations of peremptory norms, which were enabled by Libya's failure to prevent and punish such acts. Most basically then, individual conduct in violation of peremptory norms engaged a particular legal framework with the proximate objective of suppressing such acts. In this sense, determining a degree of individual responsibility, which is traditionally assessed in the aftermath of a crisis, was a precondition to resolution of the situation in Libya. This case study illustrates that violations of peremptory norms, the performance of obligations *erga omnes* arising therefrom, the response of the international community to serious breaches of those obligations, and international responsibility are concurrent rather than sequential elements of a complex normative regime through which the common interests of the international community are enforced.

The Libyan episode reveals that the source of this complexity lies in the reality that the doctrine of responsibility is no longer solely a post-conflict tool. The ICC Prosecutor noted in May 2011 that, unlike prior episodes of violations of peremptory norms and serious breaches of obligations *erga omnes* in Yugoslavia and Rwanda, the ICC and UN Security Council were 'acting in real time'.[127] Instead of merely undertaking investigations of individual and State responsibility for the commission of atrocities following an international crisis, the investigations of international courts and institutions – the ICC, and ACtHPR, the UNHRC – were integral to the policy response of the international community. The findings of these international organs enabled an interventionist response by the international community to suppress serious breaches of international law. This active role of judicial and investigatory organs represents a milestone for the institutions of the international community.

This case study also illustrates a palette of policy choices where obligations owed to the international community are breached. While the international response to the Libya episode highlights both the legal implications of *jus cogens* and the way in which these implications coincide with established legal mechanisms, it is an example that is neither exhaustive nor necessarily applicable to every instance of *jus cogens* violations. For example, the same framework could readily be applied to international intervention in the Kosovo War in 1998–9, notwithstanding key distinctions, such as the use of force outside Chapter VII authorization by the United Nations,[128] and the establishment of an *ad hoc* tribunal to prosecute international crimes.[129] By contrast, although the same legal framework is applicable to the civil war in Syria, where war crimes and crimes against humanity have gone unchecked and the responsibility of Syria for serious breaches of its obligations under international law has been invoked,[130] there has been little direct response by the international community and no action by the UN

[127] ICC Prosecutor Presents his Findings in Libya, 1 (16 May 2011).

[128] SC Res. 1244, UN Doc. S/Res/1244, para. 5 (10 June 1999) (authorizing intervention in Kosovo; however, the resolution followed the use of force).

[129] Statute of the International Tribunal for the Prosecution of Persons Responsible for Serious Violations of International Humanitarian Law Committed in the Territory of the Former Yugoslavia since 1991, UN Doc. S/Res/827 (annex) (25 May 1993).

[130] *See, e.g.*, Office of the High Commissioner for Human Rights, REPORT OF THE INDEPENDENT INTERNATIONAL COMMISSION OF INQUIRY ON THE SYRIAN ARAB REPUBLIC, UN Doc. A/HRC/21/50 (16 August 2012).

Security Council under Chapter VII due to political paralysis.[131] These episodes capture the degree to which the integrity of *jus cogens*, as an expression of the interests of the international community, is dependent upon the will of the international community where obligations arising from peremptory norms are breached. However, their divergence precludes dispositive guidance on the degree to which the legal consequences of *jus cogens* can, or must, be carried out in every instance through institutional authorities such as the United Nations acting under Chapter VII authority. Critically, the Libya crisis in particular demonstrates that the legal effects and structural implications of *jus cogens* are consistent with the governing institutions of the international community.

[131] *See* Draft Resolution S/2011/612 (4 October 2011), Draft Resolution S/2012/77 (2 February 2012), and Draft Resolution S/2012/538 (19 July 2012).

17

Realizing the international social contract

The enforcement of *jus cogens* through obligations *erga omnes* reflects elements of civil society established by the social contract. The purpose of the social contract is to safeguard fundamental protections of the individual, necessary for coexistence with other individuals in a community, through the establishment of civil society. Civil society is both defined through, and authoritative by virtue of, its realization of the common interests and values of a community. Depictions of civil society by social contract theorists are conditioned by distinct social and historical features that define prior aspects of the social contract, which accounts for the diversity of contract theory more generally. Nevertheless, the common outcome that social contract theory seeks to explain is the establishment of civil society as the mechanism through which to protect the fundamental rights of the individual.[1]

According to Hobbes, the formation of civil society entails the submission of wills to a common will in the interest of peace and safety which constitutes 'a real unity of them all'.[2] The Commonwealth, or *Civitas*, is in turn the product of man's self-interested union through the social contract to preserve this basic and fundamental right to security. The 'essence of the Commonwealth' is, according to Hobbes,

> One Person, of whose Acts a great Multitude, by mutual Covenants one with another, have made themselves every one the Author, to the end he may use the strength and means of them all, as he shall think expedient, for their Peace and Common Defence.[3]

The depiction of civil society by Hobbes is that of an indivisible body defined by the social contract and empowered to enforce the common interests of individuals united through it. The common interest in

[1] Michael Lessnoff (ed.), Social Contract Theory 3 (Oxford: Basil Blackwell 1991).

[2] Thomas Hobbes, Leviathan II.17.87 (London: Penguin Books, C. B. Macpherson ed., 1985 [1651]).

[3] *Ibid.*, II.17.87–8.

physical security leads, in the Hobbesian vision, to the establishment of a Leviathan as the sovereign power charged with its defence.

Locke submits that, by entering into the social contract, individuals establish civil society as the instrument through which to realize their fundamental rights to life, liberty, and property.[4] The preservation of these individual rights, which are guaranteed by establishing political order capable of enforcing the law of nature, is the 'great and chief end' of civil society. This distinctly liberal depiction of civil society is a reflection of the prior elements of Locke's social contract theory, whereby elements of natural law inform a legislative principle defined by consent to yield basic individual protections enforced by civil society. Notwithstanding its opposing character to the protections and structures conceived by Hobbes, the two similarly envisage governance directed towards the fundamental wellbeing of the individual.

According to Rousseau, man exchanges natural liberty for civil liberty through the social contract, resulting in a civil state defined by the general will and characterized as a moral state in which the individual rights of man are protected.[5] This narrative of the social contract envisages a form of association whereby man is able to 'remain as free as before'.[6] In contrast to Hobbes, there is no sacrifice of freedom or liberty by entering into the social contract,[7] a vision that follows from Rousseau's depiction of the natural state of man as one of pure freedom and equality. Therefore civil society is established to provide security unknown in the state of nature and alleviate the negative passions of the social state, ultimately creating a condition conducive to the development of 'rational natural law' in the form of basic individual protections.[8] Civil society is accordingly charged with the defence of these individual rights and freedoms. The power vested in civil society is that by which to compel individuals who refuse to obey the general will to comply with

[4] John Locke, Two Treatises of Government II.7.87, II.9.124 (London: Everyman 2003 [1689]).

[5] Jean-Jacques Rousseau, The Social Contract (du Contract Social ou Principes du Droit Politique) I.8 (London: Everyman 2003 [1762]) [hereinafter, Rousseau, Social Contract].

[6] *Ibid.*, Ch. 6 (The Social Compact).

[7] Jeremy Jennings, *Rousseau, Social Contract and the Modern Leviathan*, *in* The Social Contract from Hobbes to Rawls 117–20 (London: Routledge, David Boucher & Paul Kelly eds., 1994).

[8] Stanley Hoffmann and David Fidler, *Introduction*, *in* Rousseau on International Relations, xlii–xliii (Oxford: Clarendon Press, Stanley Hoffmann & David Fidler eds., 1991).

the common interests of the community; this 'means nothing more than that he will be forced to be free'.[9]

For Kant, the original contract produces normative rights with correlative moral duties protecting the individual human being that constitute the foundation of the civil condition.[10] The union established by the original contract pursuant to this end constitutes that end which individuals ought to share as the 'unconditional first duty' of those whose external relations mutually affect one another; it is society in the form of a civil condition, a commonwealth.[11] This duty leads to the establishment of a rightful condition of 'public right' at the national, inter-State, and global levels.[12] As defined by Kant,

> *Right* is the limitation of the freedom of each to the condition of its harmony with the freedom of everyone insofar as this is possible in accordance with a universal law; and *public* right is the sum of *external laws* which make such a thoroughgoing harmony possible.[13]

A natural right is understood to be one 'which can be derived from *a priori* principles for a civil constitution', [14] and Kant identifies the natural rights of the citizen to be lawful freedom, equality, and civil independence.[15] These principles form the basis of the civil condition as a rightful condition, a relation that orients civil society in the protection of the common will that all individuals ought to share.

The contractarian nature of obligations arising from peremptory norms is manifest. Civil society, according to contractarianism, is the institutional mechanism established through the social contract to guarantee the common interests and values of a community. It is precisely in such a capacity that the international community is charged to uphold *jus cogens* through obligations *erga omnes*. This aspect of international law represents a marked contrast to State interests and the international community as a system concerned exclusively with mediating bilateral

[9] Rousseau, Social Contract I.7.

[10] Immanuel Kant, On the Common Saying: That May Be Correct in Theory, but It Is of No Use in Practice [1793], *in* The Cambridge Edition of the Works of Immanuel Kant 8:289, 8:295 (Cambridge University Press, Mary Gregor ed., 1996) [hereinafter, Kant, Theory and Practice].

[11] *Ibid.*

[12] Immanuel Kant, Metaphysics of Morals [1797], *in* The Cambridge Edition of the Works of Immanuel Kant 6:309–72 (Gregor ed.) [hereinafter, Kant, Metaphysics] ('Public Right').

[13] Kant, Theory and Practice 8:290. [14] *Ibid.*; Kant, Metaphysics 6:256.

[15] Kant, Theory and Practice 8:290; Kant, Metaphysics 6:314.

relations.[16] While State-centric dimensions continue to define most international law, obligations *erga omnes* connote an international community that represents the whole of mankind to which obligations are owed by each State as constituent organs. In a contractarian sense, obligations *erga omnes* give effect to *jus cogens* by defining civil society duties directed to the State, apart from its particular interests, as a member of the international community.

Consequently, through obligations *erga omnes*, a civil society role is defined for the State as the instrument through which to uphold protections and duties of a public order character in international law. The legal category of *jus cogens* prescribes a State-based legal regime of obligations *erga omnes* pursuant to the enforcement of peremptory norms. These obligations, which derive from peremptory norms, impose upon the State positive duties owed to the international community as a whole, the performance of which requires the State to prevent and punish violations of peremptory norms. Thus, while peremptory norms constitute protections and duties accruing to the individual, the State is obligated as a member of the international community to implement and enforce peremptory norms. Obligations *erga omnes* therefore give effect to peremptory norms by requiring the State to function as the instrument of *jus cogens*. By virtue of the importance of the fulfilment of these obligations to the international community, *erga omnes* denotes a general legal interest of every other State in their performance. In this way, obligations *erga omnes* can be seen to delineate a civil society function to be fulfilled in the first instance by the State as a member of the international community of States as a whole.

It bears recalling that State responsibility arising with respect to violations of peremptory norms is most directly incurred by the State for breaches of obligations *erga omnes*. Responsibility by attribution of

[16] Bruno Simma, *From Bilateralism to Community Interest in International Law*, 250 Recueil des Cours 233–4 (1994); Christian Tomuschat, *Obligations Arising for States Without or Against their Will*, 241 Recueil des Cours 211 (1993) ('According to this interpretation, States live, as from their birth, within a legal framework of a limited number of basic rules which determines their basic rights and obligations with or without their will, leaving them, however, sufficient room for self-responsible action within the openings of that legal edifice. One may call this framework, from which every State receives its legal entitlement to be respected as a sovereign entity, the constitution of international society or, preferably, the constitution of the international community, community being a term suitable to indicate a closer union than between members of a society').

individual conduct aside, the international responsibility of the State arises in international law where the State has failed in its capacity as the organ of the international community to perform obligations arising from peremptory norms. This conceptualization of international responsibility, when contrasted with the survey of individual responsibility in Chapter 12, is revealing. While the individual bears direct criminal and civil responsibility for the violation of peremptory norms under international law (the State is not subject to the former form and at least immune from the latter), the international responsibility of the State arises directly where it has breached its obligations to the international community arising from peremptory norms. The international responsibility of the State for breaches of obligations *erga omnes* indicates the expectation that the State, as a matter of international law, fulfil its civil society function through the performance of obligations arising from peremptory norms. While a breach of these obligations constitutes an internationally wrongful act, as noted above, a widespread and systematic breach engages the duty of third-States to cooperate to bring such a breach to a halt.

In this last sense, the civil society capacity of the international community of States as a whole may be viewed as a result of the general legal interest of all States in the performance of obligations arising from peremptory norms. A practical effect of this generality is to impose particular duties upon all States with respect to violations of peremptory norms. A duty for third-States arises to undertake collective action to suppress serious breaches of obligations *erga omnes*, as a form of *actio popularis*, on behalf of the international community in defence of its higher interests. Pursuant to the enforcement of peremptory norms, States are directed to cooperate as members of the international community to uphold peremptory norms where a first-State is unwilling or unable to perform its obligations owed to the international community. Just as civil society arises from the social contract to enforce the common interests of the community, obligations *erga omnes* provide the basis for the international community to respond to violations of *jus cogens* where constituent States have failed to fulfil their obligations under peremptory norms.

Implicit in the authority of the international community to respond to serious breaches of obligations *erga omnes* is the removal of the ability of States to unilaterally enforce such obligations. In this regard, the social contract promotes stability by facilitating the forfeit of the power of members of the community to enforce their individual rights in exchange for the guarantee of their protection and enforcement by civil society. In much the same way, collective action by the international community is clearly viewed under international law as the appropriate response to violations of *jus cogens* vis-à-vis serious breaches of obligations *erga omnes*. This is the case with respect to countermeasures envisaged by Article 41 of the ILC Articles on State Responsibility, measures authorized under Chapter VII of the UN Charter, and the emergent doctrine of humanitarian self-defence as justification for the use of force. Therefore, third-States acting pursuant to obligations *erga omnes* in this regard discharge their civil society capacity as members of the international community. The liberty of members of the international community to unilaterally respond to breaches of obligations *erga omnes* would therefore seem to be constrained analogously to the way the social contract restricts the freedom of members of a community to enforce their individual rights in civil society. As much is evidenced in the most dramatic instance with the use of force, where legality even in the context of *jus cogens* seems to require some authorization by the international community. Thus, while obligations *erga omnes* impose a duty upon third-States to respond to serious breaches, this capacity is restricted in practice to actions undertaken on behalf of the international community as a whole.

This distinct role of the State arising under *jus cogens* demonstrates that the State is the functional object of *jus cogens*. The performance of obligations *erga omnes* requires the State to prevent and punish violations of peremptory norms because, for all practical purposes, only the State possesses the functional ability to uphold *jus cogens*, the material capability to respond to violations, and the procedural capacity to execute the relevant law.[17] Although obligations *erga omnes* are subsidiary to the primary protections and duties denoted by *jus cogens* – in the same sense that civil society can be seen as secondary to the primary protections delineated by the social contract – these obligations are essential to the practical operation of peremptory norms. Interestingly, obligations *erga omnes* of the State have been expressed through international political

[17] *See* Report of the Lords of the Judicial Committee of the Privy Council, [1934] AC 586, 2 (26 July 1934) (citing Grotius, De Jure II.XX.XL; *see* Hugo Grotius, De Jure Belli ac Pacis Libri Tres II.XX.XL (Oxford: Clarendon Press, Francis Kelsey trans., James B. Scott ed., 1925 [1646])) ('With regard to crimes as defined by international law, that law has no means of trying or punishing them. The recognition of them as constituting crimes and the trial and punishment of the criminals are left to the municipal law of each country').

initiatives promoting a 'responsibility to protect' in an 'age of accountability'. Responsibility and accountability, particularly in the context of peremptory norms, have been identified as landmark goals of the international community in the twenty-first century. Given that law is an expression of the values and aims of society – *ubi societas, ibi jus* – it is perhaps unsurprising that public order elements of international law should be reflected in the high politics of international relations. Particular significance lies in the distinctly societal character of these concepts. Responsibility and accountability are powerful social ideas that in this instance are wielded to define fundamental and universal obligations owed by every State to the international community as a whole. It may be recalled from Chapter 3 that the idea of the international community is bifurcated and contains a dual meaning. While in a procedural sense the State is the subject of duties of responsibility and accountability, these are substantive obligations owed to an international community representing mankind as the beneficiary of those obligations.

The legal effects of *jus cogens* delineated by obligations *erga omnes* reflect a contractarian approach to the enforcement of peremptory norms. As obligations owed to the international community, their breach permits a community-based response in terms of both the invocation of responsibility and the suppression of serious breaches. Obligations *erga omnes* reflect a civil society character of *jus cogens* that binds the State by common interests and values of mankind. During the drafting of the law of treaties, this particular form of socialization was recognized to be implicit in the codification of *jus cogens* in international law:

> While not opposed to the idea that the sovereignty of States was the basis of the international community ... sovereignty could [not] be absolute now that the international community had become organized ... There was not necessarily a surrender of national sovereignty, but membership of a community required the respect of certain rules. If that were not so, society would remain in the condition of savagery described by the phrase *homo homini lupus*, which had lasted until the First World War and had prevailed almost unchallenged in the inter-war period. By becoming members of the international society, States recognized the existence of a minimum international order, which was none other than *jus cogens*. The abstract notions of absolute freedom and absolute sovereignty were not compatible with the existence of international society.[18]

[18] [1966] I(1) YbILC 39, para. 40 (828th Meeting, statement by Mr Bartoš).

Obligations *erga omnes* deriving from peremptory norms are the culmination of this social evolution of a contractarian public order in international law. These obligations, like the civil society established by the social contract, are community-based and, through *opinio juris sive necessitatis*, express fundamental interests of the international community. By establishing obligations owed to the international community to enforce peremptory norms akin to the structures of civil society, obligations *erga omnes* can be seen as the essence of an international social contract.

PART VI

International law and social contract

This part consolidates the findings of the previous chapters by first presenting the legal observations that constitute the primary focus of this book. Specifically, Chapter 18 reviews the authority, sources, content, and enforcement of *jus cogens* and the way in which individual-oriented peremptory norms occupy a coherent State-based legal framework. Following these legal findings, Chapter 19 considers the broader theoretical implications of this book teased out by reference to the social contract. This entails a gloss of academic frameworks relevant to *jus cogens*, the way in which its defining features are consistent with the social contract, and finally, implications of a contractarian public order in international law.

18

Legal observations

A An individual-oriented *jus cogens*

This book confronted four interrelated aspects of *jus cogens*. The first of these is the peremptory authority of *jus cogens*, which derives from the interests of the international community of States as a whole. The construction *international community of States as a whole* is a layered concept containing both procedural and substantive elements of a juridical entity expressing the interests and values of an international society, comprising States, representing the social need of mankind. In practice, the interests and values of mankind are realized through States acting collectively as organs of the international community to establish peremptory norms of general international law. To this end, the higher interests of the international community of States as a whole are best conceived in terms of the individual, as the unit of mankind, rather than by the metrics of the State. The interests of the international community can be represented by human dignity, which refers most simply to the intrinsic worth of the human person. The operation of human dignity as an animating principle in the spheres of constitutional law, European Union law, public international law, and *jus cogens* underscores its validity as an expression of the higher interests of the international community.

The two aspects of human dignity are each of particular significance to *jus cogens*. The first is that human dignity is a quality of the individual that denotes his inalienable standing as a human being deserving respect from other human beings in society. This dignity, based in the autonomy of the individual, derives from the worth of the human person. It is in this sense that human dignity operates as a general principle of law to inform protections of the individual. The second aspect of human dignity is a moral quality that denotes duties of respect towards other individuals in society. Consequently, laws enshrining the first aspect of human dignity through protections of the intrinsic value of the human person are necessarily imbued with this second aspect that denotes corollary moral obligations. Both elements of human dignity are expressed in the jurisprudence of *jus cogens*, underlying the emergence of the prescriptive norms themselves as well as the moral quality of the duties they impose. This moral aspect accounts for the peremptory status of norms of *jus cogens*. Peremptory norms are non-derogable rules, universal in application and inviolable by contrary precepts of treaty and custom. In this context, human dignity arises not by virtue of human nature, divine origin, or *a priori* reason, but rather, as an expression of the higher interests of the international community. As such, the principle is the basis of norms deemed to be essential to the maintenance of social coexistence in the international community. It is by virtue of this social dimension that morality, and in turn the authority of *jus cogens*, can be understood in terms of the general legal principle of human dignity.

If norms of *jus cogens* derive their authority as expressions of the higher interests of the international community, it is necessary to understand precisely how these interests – the material source of *jus cogens* – are translated into public order norms through a formal source of positive international law. Normativity is a virtually constant aspect of the evolution of international law, one traditionally incorporated through natural law as a legal source. Under a positivist approach, normativity was formally introduced into international law by conceiving of public order norms deriving from the higher interests of the international community as *jus cogens*. A positivist account, derived from the construction of Article 53 of the Vienna Convention, indicates that peremptory norms emerge through a customary process influenced by general principles of law. The higher interests of the international community, represented by the general principle of human dignity, inform *opinio juris sive necessitatis* in response to historical exigencies, a relation that has been referred to as the 'juridical conscience of mankind'. This *opinio juris sive necessitatis*, evidenced by the practice of States, gives rise to peremptory norms of general international law. The outcome of this process is often confirmed in practice by the pronouncements of judicial organs in their enforcement capacities.

While noted above that the *international community of States as a whole* is a layered construct that contains both procedural and substantive dimensions, the formal and material sources of peremptory norms indicate stratification within the concept. On the one hand, the emergence of peremptory norms is dependent upon *opinio juris sive necessitatis* evidenced by the practice *of States*, thereby orienting the emergence of peremptory norms with the State. And the process culminates in positive law in force in the international community, as reflected by authoritative pronouncements of courts and tribunals. On the other hand, the emergence of peremptory norms depends upon State practice only as evidence of *opinio juris sive necessitatis*. The practice of States need not be universal, and the practice of an individual State, or group of States, is insufficient to affect *jus cogens* or the legal obligations arising therefrom. In this way, the formal source of peremptory norms reflects the public order character of *jus cogens* by elevating the material source, the higher interests of the international community of States *as a whole*, through *opinio juris sive necessitatis*, over the practice of the individual State. This normativity, implicit in the concept of *peremptory* norms of general international law, accounts for the categorical distinction of *jus cogens* from *jus dispositivum*.

The formal source of *jus cogens* evidences nine peremptory norms accepted and recognized by the international community of States as a whole: the prohibitions of piracy, slavery, war crimes, crimes against humanity, aggression, genocide, torture, apartheid, and terrorism. Each of these norms constitutes a fundamental protection of the human being under which only the individual can be considered a subject proper. This follows naturally given that peremptory norms derive from the higher interests of the international community implicated by the relations of States, represented by the general principle of human dignity, and an *opinio necessitatis* that defines standards necessary to the social coexistence of the international community as the juridical expression of mankind. This individual-oriented character of peremptory norms is reflected by the way in which the classification of an offence as an international crime refers at once to the seriousness of the law violated – a norm belonging to *jus cogens* – and the subject of criminal responsibility for the breach, the individual. The individual is the bearer of both criminal and civil responsibility for violations of *jus cogens*. The erosion of individual immunities under customary international law in the context of international crimes, and the trend towards invalidity and non-recognition of amnesty for such offences, underscores the priority placed by the international community upon individual accountability for *jus cogens* violations.

This individual-oriented content of *jus cogens* allows for the construction of a three-term formulation of peremptory norms operationalized through the identification of the individual as, at once, the primary beneficiary of peremptory norms as well as the subject of direct responsibility for their violation. This conclusion is the culmination of the authority and sources of peremptory norms. This individual-oriented form reflects the basis of the authority of *jus cogens* in the higher interests of the international community – i.e. mankind – represented by the general legal principle of human dignity. It is the product of a formal source of international law that incorporates these interests into positive law through *opinio juris sive necessitatis* as an element of normativity that supersedes State practice as the principal determinant of legal norms and related obligations. Given these elements, it follows logically that the resultant norms of *jus cogens* concern the individual as their primary beneficiary and legal subject. Taken together, these aspects of *jus cogens* reveal an individual-oriented sphere of international law that liberates the dignity of the individual, as a citizen of mankind, from the will of the State.

B The State-based legal framework of peremptory norms

Jus cogens, while individual-oriented, occupies a State-based legal framework. As much is indicated by the customary formation of peremptory norms 'accepted and recognized by the international community *of States* as a whole'. The construct, *international community of States as a whole*, indicates a procedural aspect by which peremptory norms emerge through the practice of States acting collectively as organs of the international community. Substantively, the construct reflects the collective social need of mankind, implicated by the relations of States, in furtherance of a common good based upon the wellbeing of the individual. This bifurcated understanding of the concept of the international community contains complementary aspects by which its procedural dimension serves its substantive end. This is to suggest that the collective social need of mankind is realized through the practice of States, acting through the international community, pursuant to the values and interests of mankind. As much is indicated by the formal source of *jus cogens*.

Moreover, in practice, the implementation and enforcement of peremptory norms depend entirely upon a State-based legal framework of obligations *erga omnes*. The performance of obligations arising from peremptory norms is increasingly conceived in practice to constitute positive duties to prevent and punish violations of peremptory norms. These obligations bind each State and, as obligations owed to the international community as a whole, have the effect of extending a general legal interest in their fulfilment to every State. In effect, the State is the subject of secondary obligations arising from primary rights and duties delineated by *jus cogens*. This relation reflects the reality that, in most instances, only the State possesses the material ability to suppress breaches of peremptory norms and the capacity to execute the law.

The general legal interest of all States in the fulfilment of obligations *erga omnes* denotes particular legal effects that require every State to act pursuant to these obligations. One result of this general legal interest is a series of particular consequences for third-States to respond collectively through *actio popularis*, on behalf of the international community, to serious violations of peremptory norms arising from a breach of obligations *erga omnes* by a first-State. Moreover, this generality indicates that each State has a legal interest in the punishment of violators of peremptory norms, wherever that violation occurred. Consequently, an obligation *aut dedere aut judicare* arises in practice whereby each State is under a duty to either extradite or prosecute suspected violators of peremptory norms in their territory on the basis of universal jurisdiction. These State-based legal effects derive from the *erga omnes* nature of obligations arising from peremptory norms and constitute a community-oriented regime of protection and enforcement.

The international responsibility of the State may arise with respect to *jus cogens* violations in two ways – from a breach of obligations *erga omnes*, or individual conduct attributable to the State in violation of peremptory norms – each of which constitutes an internationally wrongful act. State responsibility arising with respect to violations of peremptory norms is therefore only directly incurred by the State for breaches of obligations *erga omnes*. Responsibility by attribution aside, the international responsibility of the State under international law is engaged in this sense where the State has failed to prevent and punish violations of peremptory norms. This conceptualization of international responsibility, when contrasted with individual responsibility, is revealing. While the individual bears criminal and civil responsibility for the violation of peremptory norms in international law, State responsibility arises primarily where it has breached obligations owed to the international community arising from peremptory norms.

The effect of this State-based framework of obligations *erga omnes* is to clearly demarcate expectations upon the State to ensure that violations of peremptory norms are suppressed, that their effects are not recognized, and that those guilty of crimes contrary to the higher interests of the international community are brought to justice. This legal mechanism provides a structure of implementation and enforcement directed towards realizing the public order of *jus cogens*. Importantly, this regime demonstrates that the understanding of *jus cogens* developed in this book is consistent with, and indeed dependent upon, a State-based framework of international law. Although the beneficiary of rights and duties of *jus cogens* is the individual, the emergence and enforcement of these norms are dependent upon the State. Consequently, *jus cogens* is necessarily conceived in the context of a State-based system of international law.

19

Theoretical implications

A Frameworks relevant to *jus cogens*

The legal conclusions above draw attention to three schools of thought relevant to the concept of peremptory norms: the philosophy of normative individualism, the legal school of international constitutionalism, and the political doctrine of cosmopolitanism. This book touched upon various ways in which each of these frameworks is expressed through *jus cogens*, and those linkages are explicated in this section.

Normative individualism. Law is an expression of the goals and values of society and, as such, the institution of law is an instrument through which a community promotes its common good. The essential premise of normative individualism is variation of this truism, which holds that the fundamental purpose of law is the good of the individual. Although international law is generally understood as a legal order of States, normative individualism takes the State to be a collective of individuals for whom it is an instrument. Rather than a personified entity with its own interests, this philosophy regards the State, even in the context of international law, as an apparatus that exists to advance a common good defined in terms of the individual. This suggests that, irrespective of whether the international community as a whole is envisaged to represent all States or the whole of mankind, its *raison d'être* remains fundamentally the same. Conceiving of the State as an instrument of individual wellbeing is therefore a logical bridge between the general purpose of law and *jus cogens* of international law.

The philosophy of normative individualism has been adopted by the fields of international relations and international law, where the fundamental interests of the international community are frequently linked to humanity. In international relations, for example, Hedley Bull,[1] Terry

[1] Hedley Bull, THE ANARCHICAL SOCIETY 12, 25 (New York: Columbia University Press 1977).

Nardin,[2] and Philip Allott[3] all draw attention to political order at the global level concerned with the basic wellbeing of the individual. In International law, Judge Herman Mosler,[4] Judge Bruno Simma,[5] Judge A. A. Cançado Trindade,[6] C. Wilfred Jenks,[7] Fernando Tesón,[8] and Andreas Paulus,[9] among many others, depict an international law where the interests of the international community as a whole are oriented in the good of mankind through normative protections of the individual. Moreover, normative individualism is a hallmark of the New Haven School, which orients its legal philosophy in the premise that law exists to serve human beings through the preservation and advancement of basic human dignity.[10] What is common across each of these accounts is that the interests of the international community cannot be captured in terms of States *qua* States. These interests concern, most fundamentally, humanity, and are best conceived in terms of the individual as the unit of mankind rather than through the metrics of the State. The philosophy of normative individualism underlies the development of *jus cogens* in contemporary international law.

International constitutionalism. Since the Second World War, international law has evolved in a direction that recognizes core values common to the international community as a whole, admits obligations that bind the State beyond the traditional requirement of consent, and embraces extra-State legal interests and mechanisms of enforcement. The doctrine of *jus cogens* is an expression of the evolution of the

[2] Terry Nardin, LAW, MORALITY, AND THE RELATIONS OF STATES 44 (Princeton University Press 1983).

[3] Philip Allott, EUNOMIA 410–11 (Oxford University Press 1990).

[4] Herman Mosler, *The International Society as a Legal Community*, 140 RECUEIL DES COURS 70 (1974).

[5] Bruno Simma, *From Bilateralism to Community Interest in International Law*, 250 RECUEIL DES COURS 233–4 (1994).

[6] Antônio Augusto Cançado Trindade, *International Law for Humankind: Towards a New Jus Gentium (II) – General Course on Public International Law*, 317 RECUEIL DES COURS 19–20, 272 (2005).

[7] C. Wilfred Jenks, LAW, FREEDOM AND WELFARE, 99–100 (London: Stevens & Sons 1963).

[8] Fernando Tesón, A PHILOSOPHY OF INTERNATIONAL LAW 1 (Boulder, CO: Westview Press 1998).

[9] Andreas Paulus, Jus Cogens *in a Time of Hegemony and Fragmentation*, 74(2) NORDIC JOURNAL OF INTERNATIONAL LAW 297, 309 (2005).

[10] *See* Michael Reisman *et al.*, *The New Haven School: A Brief Introduction*, 32 YALE JOURNAL OF INTERNATIONAL LAW 575, 580 (2007); Myres McDougal, Harold D. Lasswell, and Lung-chu Chen, HUMAN RIGHTS AND WORLD PUBLIC ORDER: THE BASIC POLICIES OF AN INTERNATIONAL LAW OF HUMAN DIGNITY (New Haven, CT: Yale University Press 1980).

international community as a legal community, one regulated by a defined structure of norms and forces captured by the concept of international constitutional law.[11] Contemporary international law now regards the State to be embedded within an international constitutional framework that regards State sovereignty as part and parcel of legal order. There is an obvious paradox in the way that sovereignty is constrained, yet reinforced, through this notion of international constitutionalism and, since 1945, sovereignty has come to mean something very different from what it did after 1648. Sovereignty is no longer conceived to represent absolute freedom in the internal and external affairs of the State; rather, it is understood to be delegated by the individuals within its borders and contingent upon responsibilities owed to them. As recent history has demonstrated, the international community may be empowered to respond on behalf of citizenries towards whom the State has grossly failed to fulfil its obligations under international law.

Consequently, in contrast to the dictates of classical sovereignty, the State can no longer be considered an independent 'metaphysical entity' or a 'discrete political world'.[12] Rather, the contemporary international community is defined by interdependence and interconnection through which the actions of one State affect all the others, and elements of public order have evolved accordingly to mediate this developing social space. Peremptory norms, and the obligations *erga omnes* arising therefrom, have time and again been viewed through a constitutional lens as norms operating both procedurally and substantively as constitutional norms in international law.[13] Like constitutional law, *jus cogens* substantively

[11] *See* Marc Weller, *The Struggle for an International Constitutional Order*, *in* David Armstrong (ed.), Routledge Handbook of International Law (London: Routledge, David Armstrong ed., 2009); Stephen Gardbaum, *Human Rights as International Constitutional Rights*, 19(4) European Journal of International Law 749–68 (2008); Anne Peters, *Compensatory Constitutionalism: The Function and Potential of Fundamental International Norms and Structures*, 19 Leiden Journal of International Law 579–610 (2006); Christian Tomuschat, *Obligations Arising for States Without or Against their Will*, 241 Recueil des Cours 211 (1993).

[12] Marc Weller, *The Reality of the Emerging Universal Constitutional Order: Putting the Pieces of the Puzzle Together*, 10(2) Cambridge Review of International Affairs 40, 45 (1997).

[13] Alexander Orakhelashvili, Peremptory Norms in International Law 9–10 (Oxford University Press 2006); Michael Byers, *Conceptualising the Relationship between* Jus Cogens *and* Erga Omnes *Rules*, 66 Nordic Journal of International Law 211, 212 (1997); [1963] I YbILC 72, para. 65 (685th Meeting, statement by Mr de Luna).

enshrines basic requisites of human dignity and represents the highest level of a stratified legal hierarchy. Procedurally, peremptory norms are resistant to modification or repeal and prevail over conventional law. The legal conclusions developed in this book appeal to the international constitutionalist school of legal theory as one adding conceptual depth to *jus cogens* as a category of international law.

Cosmopolitanism. Cosmopolitanism is a political philosophy that combines elements of normative individualism with international constitutionalism in a progressive theory about the form of global governance. The term 'cosmopolitan' refers to the most basic and fundamental rights, moral in origin yet legal in nature, that transcend the boundaries of the State and accrue to the individual. Cosmopolitanism is held variously to be a political doctrine that depicts a moral sphere of justice,[14] applying to human beings, sometimes regarded as citizens[15] of a global polis or civil society,[16] that defines requirements of individual autonomy and equality,[17] expressive of values common to international society.[18] The primary focus of cosmopolitanism is the fate of mankind in an increasingly globalized world, a condition that necessitates a sphere of order atop a stratified legal hierarchy that constitutes universal legal principles of a humanitarian character.

The origin of contemporary cosmopolitanism can be traced to Kant's theory of perpetual peace. Kant refers to 'three relations' of public right as 'the right of a State, the right of nations, and cosmopolitan right'.[19] These three phases correspond to the organizational levels of the definitive articles of 'perpetual peace', with the first concerning domestic constitutional law, the second the law between States, and the third a cosmopolitan law binding all individuals. In terms familiar to the previous theoretical frameworks glossed above, Kant promotes the premise of cosmopolitanism:

[14] Nadia Urbinati, *Can Cosmopolitan Democracy be Democratic?*, *in* DEBATING COSMOPOLITICS 75 (London: Verso, Daniele Archibugi ed., 2003).

[15] Daniele Archibugi and David Held, *Introduction*, *in* COSMOPOLITAN DEMOCRACY 13 (Cambridge: Polity Press, Daniele Archibugi & David Held eds., 1995).

[16] Selya Benhabib, ANOTHER COSMOPOLITANISM 16 (Oxford University Press, Robert Prost ed., 2006).

[17] David Held, *Violence, Law and Justice in a Global Age*, *in* DEBATING COSMOPOLITICS 200 (Archibugi ed.).

[18] David Held, *Law of States, Law of Peoples: Three Models of Sovereignty*, 8(2) LEGAL THEORY 1, 31 (2002).

[19] Immanuel Kant, TOWARD PERPETUAL PEACE [1795], *in* THE CAMBRIDGE EDITION OF THE WORKS OF IMMANUEL KANT 8:365 (Cambridge University Press, Mary Gregor ed., 1996).

> Since the (narrower or wider) community of the nations of the earth has now gone so far that a violation of right on *one* place of the earth is felt in *all*, the idea of a cosmopolitan right is no fantastic and exaggerated way of representing right; it is, instead, a supplement to the unwritten code of the right of a state and the right of nations necessary for the sake of any public rights of human beings and so for perpetual peace[.][20]

The rationale underlying Kant's three-tier division is simple: because individuals interact, they are bound by civil law, taking the form of the State; because States also interact they too have developed a legal order between them through international law. And as peoples increasingly form an interdependent global society of individuals with common interests, this interaction is mediated by cosmopolitan law establishing basic standards of conduct. At each level of interaction, a condition of public right is achieved through protections necessary to the maintenance of social coexistence.[21] The cosmopolitan law that emerges pursuant to perpetual peace is described by Kant as an extension of the just nation-State that concerns individuals as citizens of a global civil society.[22]

The central premise common across all conceptualizations of cosmopolitan law is that its subject is the individual, as a member of a global civil society, rather than the State, which functionally comprises the international community. In practice, cosmopolitan law is envisaged as a division of contemporary international law, thereby employing a distinction between inter-State law – like *jus dispositivum* concluded by States – and law of a cosmopolitan nature, akin to *jus cogens* that binds all States and applies to every individual. Moreover, cosmopolitan law is conceived to express the common values of the international community in such a way that its violation in one place is felt everywhere, a construction echoed by the general legal interest in the performance of obligations *erga omnes* arising from peremptory norms. The premise of cosmopolitan law, as the final phase of lasting peace everywhere, is similarly reflected in *jus cogens* directed towards the universal protection of human dignity as the means to advance the peace and security of mankind. Thus, the development of *jus cogens* in international law can be regarded as an expression of cosmopolitanism and an indication of the evolutionary trajectory of contemporary international law.

[20] *Ibid.*, 8:360.

[21] *See* Immanuel Kant, METAPHYSICS OF MORALS [1797] *in* THE CAMBRIDGE EDITION OF THE WORKS OF IMMANUEL KANT 6:309–72 (Gregor ed.) ('Public Right').

[22] *See* Pavlos Eleftheriadis, *Cosmopolitan Law*, 9(2) EUROPEAN LAW JOURNAL 241–63 (2003).

B The social contract

The theoretical antecedents related to peremptory norms indicate the nature of an emerging social structure at the global level: the philosophy of normative individualism, the law of international constitutionalism, and the politics of cosmopolitanism are all expressive of a progressive, socialized sphere of political order. However, the task set out at the introduction of this book was not simply to make political observations, but to elucidate the formation and function of public order norms of *jus cogens*. The social contract was selected as an appropriate framework through which to approach this goal because contractarianism is designed to provide just such a narrative of the origin of civil society from the common interests of a community, and consequently, it offers a more complex understanding of public order than the theories glossed above.

The application of the social contract in this context is to reconcile individual-oriented *jus cogens* with a State-based legal order. Given the way contractarianism accounts for political authority in the context of individual wellbeing, a proposition that hinges on the idea and effect of society, the social contract is well suited to the task. The premise reflected by *jus cogens*, in the broadest sense, is the advancement of the most basic social goals of the international community as a whole, as observed by the ILC in 1963: 'Ultimately, it was more society and less the law itself which defined the content of *jus cogens*.'[23] In historical context, the absence of a substantive international legal society prompted the codification of *jus cogens* in the wake of the Second World War, notwithstanding the doctrines of positivism and Statism that had defined the international system to that point. Through a construction of the international community of States as a civil society encompassing the whole of mankind, it is possible to understand the public order defined by *jus cogens*. The social contract helps render intelligible the diverse and peculiar legal developments of the period arising from this international public order.

Social contract theory of the Enlightenment era was devised to account for the authority and content of public order. Notwithstanding profound differences in substance and philosophy across the principal theories of the period, their common contractarian framework is unified by central elements: the protection of the common interests of a community; the

[23] [1963] I YbILC 73, para. 4 (685th Meeting, statement by Mr Rosenne).

expression of social need conditioned by these common interests through tacit consent or general will; the delineation of basic individual rights and correlative duties necessary to coexistence; and the establishment of civil society pursuant to the protection of these public order norms. The social contract, however, need not be a historical instrument (in fact, Rousseau and Kant explicitly cautioned against this), and it would be folly to try to identify the Treaties of Westphalia, the UN Charter, or perhaps some other instrument, as *the* social contract of the international community.[24] As a *social* contract, its existence is manifest by society itself. The power of the social contract is that it predicates the emergence of political order upon the protection of societal values necessary to safeguard individual wellbeing within a community.

Contractarianism identifies 'parties' to the social contract to define the relation between individuals and society as well as its governance structures; just such a relation is defined in practice in the context of *jus cogens*. Practice reveals the relationship between the individual and the State through *the international community of States as a whole*, according to which the social need of mankind (*opinio juris sive necessitatis*) is expressed through the practice of States acting as organs of the international community. The construct of the *international community of States as a whole* thereby reflects a particular relation between the individual and the State by which the purpose of political organization is to safeguard the basic dignity of the human person. The expression of the idea of the social contract in the organization of the international community through the doctrine of *jus cogens* is at once intriguing and encouraging.

The impetus behind the organization of civil society through social contract is to protect norms necessary for coexistence. Moreover, contractarianism indicates that these shared values and interests are expressed through principles regarded to be moral in character and evocative of natural law. As public order norms, the category of *jus cogens* is an expression of common interests and values necessary for the social coexistence of mankind, implicated by the relations of States,

[24] *Cf.* Loius Henkin, *The Mythology of Sovereignty*, *in* Essays in Honour of Wang Tieya 351, 357 (London: Martinus Nijhoff, Ronald St John Macdonald ed., 1994) ('The international system has had a social contract at least since the seventeenth century, reflected in a network of international law ... The end of the Second World War saw a new social contract represented in the UN Charter. The Charter (I note) is a social contract of States').

within the international community. The 'higher interests' of the international community are 'extra State' in the sense that they concern the whole of mankind, of which the individual human being is the ultimate beneficiary. These interests may therefore be represented by the general principle of human dignity. Implicit in the concept of human dignity is a doctrine of morality, which arises in this instance as social obligations of respect owed universally to all members of the international community. It is in this context that *jus cogens*, as a category of norms accepted and recognized by the international community of States as a whole, can be viewed to permit no derogation.

The expression of higher interests of the international community as peremptory norms can be understood by analogy to the social contract, where the social need of a community dictates the form of civil society in response to historical exigencies (the 'state of nature'). Historical exigencies emerge where the interests of the international community are challenged by the relations of States, giving rise to *jus cogens* as 'a sphere in which [the] rules binding individuals for the benefit of other individuals overlap[] with the norms of state relationships'.[25] This quality is reflected both in the inception of the category of *jus cogens* following the Second World War and in the customary emergence of discrete peremptory norms in international law. Consequently, like the social contract, *jus cogens* establishes a particular relation of the individual, as the unit of mankind, to governance structures of States, by which the authority of the latter is contingent upon certain protections of the former necessary for the coexistence of mankind. With the emergence of *jus cogens* in international law, it becomes possible to envisage a social contract of the international community.

Contractarianism of the late Enlightenment employed the social contract to cognize how the most fundamental principles of a community are transcribed into public order norms upheld by civil society. (Tacit) consent and the general will characterize legislative mechanisms rooted in the expression of social need by which public order norms emerge to reflect the higher interests that a community shares. According to the jurisprudence of *jus cogens*, *opinio juris sive necessitatis* expresses social need reflecting the higher interests of the international community as a whole. The general principle of human dignity guides this *opinio juris sive necessitatis* as a kind of 'juridical conscience of mankind', which

[25] *Sosa v. Alvarez-Machain*, 542 US 692, 715 (2004) (with respect to the law of nations).

operates like a general will expressed by consent through State practice, from which emerges the legal recognition of non-derogable norms. This *opinio* is often articulated through institutional bodies competent to 'speak for' the international community and evidenced in the practice of States, particularly where States act as organs of the international community. Contractarianism can be brought to bear to cognize a legislative dynamic by which customary international law and general principles, together, account for the emergence of rules necessary to the maintenance of international society. Through the lens of the social contract, the development of *jus cogens* can be viewed as a product of the social need of the international community, evidenced by the practice of States, which together constitute the principal material and formal sources of peremptory norms.

The content of the social contract is the articulation of fundamental individual protections recognized by society that constitute corollary duties to respect those rights in other members of society. These protections and duties are defined through, and authoritative by virtue of, the common interests and values of a community. Similarly, norms of *jus cogens* are a product of *opinio juris sive necessitatis* conditioned by the higher interests of the international community which, as evidenced by the practice of States, constitute protections of the human being indisposable to the social coexistence of the international community as a matter of international law. Each peremptory norm accepted and recognized by the international community is linked to the dignity of the human person in such a way as to denote its indispensability to social coexistence of the international community. That these protections of the dignity of the human person manifest as non-derogable norms that cannot be affected by will of the individual State indicates that the State, and the international community more generally, serves the higher interests of mankind. Historically, establishing such a relation between the individual and governance structures is the political objective of contractarianism, whereby the social contract denotes a particular *raison d'être* of the latter in the fulfilment of the existential interests of the former.

Finally, the social contract is realized through the establishment of civil society as the mechanism by which to safeguard the fundamental rights of the individual, expressed through the common interests of a community, and necessary to the social coexistence of its members. Civil society is both defined through, and authoritative by virtue of, its realization of the common interests and values of a community, and individuals forfeit their freedom to enforce these interests through the social contract in exchange for the guarantee of their protection by civil society. A civil society capacity of the international community of States arises from the general legal interest of all States in the performance of obligations arising from peremptory norms. The practical effect of this generality is to impose particular duties upon *all States* with respect to violations of peremptory norms. A duty for third-States arises to undertake collective action to suppress serious breaches of obligations *erga omnes*, as a form of *actio popularis*, on behalf of the international community in defence of its higher interests. The obligation *aut dedere aut judicare* imposes the positive duty upon States to exercise their capacity to punish violators of peremptory norms on the basis of universal jurisdiction, denying impunity for violations of *jus cogens*. Obligations *erga omnes* have been expressed through international political initiatives promoting a 'responsibility to protect' in an 'age of accountability', which evoke inherently community-oriented values. Pursuant to the enforcement of peremptory norms, States are directed to cooperate, as members of the international community, to uphold peremptory norms where others are unwilling or unable to perform their obligations owed to the international community. The international responsibility of the State, which arises from breaches of obligations *erga omnes*, reinforces the expectation for the State to fulfil its civil society duties. By establishing obligations owed to the international community to enforce peremptory norms akin to the structures of civil society, obligations *erga omnes* represent the culmination of an international social contract.

C Final remarks

The social contract illuminates the way in which socialization links the interests of the international community of States as a whole with the fundamental wellbeing of the individual. This relation is essentially an extension of the basic premise of the State as an instrument of the protection of individuals within its borders. By applying this proposition to international politics, a conceptualization emerges through which a State-based legal order culminates in an individual-oriented *jus cogens* of inviolable rights and duties through the organization of international society. It is in this sense that contemporary international law and politics increasingly regard State sovereignty to be contingent upon a catalogue of basic humanitarian obligations representative of common values recognized by the international community as a whole. Such a relation is implicit in the incorporation of *jus cogens* in international law.[26] However, conditioning sovereignty in this way ought not to be conceived as an erosion of sovereignty but as a complement to it. Given the existential purpose of the State, it follows that the idea of sovereignty is merely one of a series of institutional mechanisms by which the ends of the State are protected. In this sense, the development of public order norms of *jus cogens* advances the basic directive of the State and, in the context of the international community as a legal community, reinforces sovereignty everywhere it succeeds in its *raison d'être*, whilst reserving the capacity of the international community to check sovereignty where it has strayed, through a general legal interest in obligations that require the State to prevent and punish violations of public order norms.

The higher interests of the international community of States as a whole consist in preserving the basic dignity of the human being, which exemplifies the character of the social evolution of the international system. It is a reality that links *jus cogens* with the tradition of the law of nations, the power of constitutionalism, and the philosophy of ancient law. In part because the inter-State system now addresses the individual, States are increasingly viewed as interdependent communities serving the wellbeing of human beings rather than insulated political spheres. Following the organization of international society in view of this end, the realization of *jus cogens* remains ongoing. In the context of one peremptory norm, it was observed, 'it is true that in the world, as we know it, departures from this norm are only too many. But the international community has signed up to it. The moral norm has ripened into a rule of customary international law. It is binding on all states.'[27] In view of this reality of peremptory norms generally, obligations *erga omnes* take on critical importance to contemporary international law and politics.

To this end, the legal framework of obligations *erga omnes* that evolved concurrently with *jus cogens* is evocative of a social contract of the international community that States are bound to uphold. Under the international public order defined by *jus cogens*, the State may not legitimately act, even on a democratic mandate, to carry out violations of *jus cogens*. At the same time, the international community as a whole

[26] [1966] I(1) YbILC 39, para. 40 (828th Meeting, statement by Mr Bartoš); *see supra*, Chapter 17, *n.* 18.

[27] *R. et al. v. Immigration Officer at Prague Airport*, House of Lords (UK), [2004] UKHL 55, para. 46 (2004) (Steyn, J.).

is empowered to respond to humanitarian atrocities within the boundaries of a State in the name of sovereignty.[28] This political reality echoes Rousseau's depiction of the power vested in society as a whole to compel the individual who refuses to obey the general will to comply, which 'means nothing more than that he will be forced to be free'. In the context of *jus cogens*, this sentiment is profound. But however powerful the legal effects arising from *jus cogens* may be – permitting universal jurisdiction, eroding immunity from prosecution, denying amnesty, and condoning *actio popularis* – these effects alone are not the solution to egregious violations of international law. Instead, *jus cogens* relies fundamentally upon the international social contract for respect of peremptory norms by the international community of States as a whole. This contractarian proposition is expressed by very real social and political expectations facing governments today. It is one that encourages a re-imagination of sovereignty and redefinition of traditional understandings of the international community.

[28] *See, e.g.*, SC Res. 1973, UN Doc. S/Res/1973, Preamble (17 March 2011) (In its preambular statement, the Security Council '*reaffirm*[*s*] its strong commitment to the sovereignty, independence, territorial integrity and national unity of the Libyan Arab Jamahiriya' while paragraph 4 '*Authorizes* Member States ... to take all necessary measures ... to protect civilians and civilian populated areas under threat of attack in the Libyan Arab Jamahiriya'. The compatibility of these statements is dependent upon a contingent understanding of sovereignty).

20

Annex

This annex constitutes a non-exhaustive summary of reported decisions by domestic courts regarding *jus cogens*. Its content is intended to serve as a resource to supplement the discussion of domestic jurisprudence in Chapter 8.D (Judicial Organs). Although this annex does not include the entire universe of domestic judgments concerning *jus cogens*, it does contain a representative sample of the breadth and substance of national jurisprudence on the subject.

Argentina

Riveros v. Office of the Public Prosecutor, Supreme Court of Justice (Argentina), M/2333/XLII, ILDC 1084, paras. 15, 32–8 (2007).	The Supreme Court of Justice determined that the prohibition of crimes against humanity belongs to *jus cogens* and that 1989 amnesty Decree 1002/89 was contrary to *jus cogens* because it violated the duty to investigate, prosecute, and punish crimes against humanity. The Court found these obligations sufficient to overcome the principle *ne bis in idem* (*res judicata*), statutes of limitations, and amnesties, enabling the Court to find the amnesty law in question unconstitutional.
Chile v. Arancibia Clavel, Supreme Court of Justice (Argentina), A/533/XXXVIII, ILDC 1082, para. 28 (2004).	In a proceeding against a Pinochet regime intelligence official, the Supreme Court of Justice found that war crimes and crimes against humanity pre-existed the Statutory Limitations Convention as customary international law to which a statute of limitations could not apply.

Office of the Prosecutor v. Priebke, Supreme Court of Justice (Argentina), P/457/XXXI, ILDC 1599, paras. 2–5 (1995).	The Supreme Court of Justice granted a request by Italy for extradition of a former German Officer under an arrest warrant issued in Rome in 1944 because crimes against humanity, as *jus cogens*, are not subject to statutes of limitations.
Washington Cabrera J. E. c. Comisión Técnica Mixta de Salto Grande, Supreme Court of Justice (Argentina), Fallos 1993-305-2150, Opinion of Guastavino and Gabrielli, paras. 9–11 (1983).	The Supreme Court of Justice invalidated an investment treaty pursuant to Article 53 of the Vienna Convention on the Law of Treaties, finding that the treaty abrogated due process protections considered by the court to belong to *jus cogens*.

Australia

Habib v. Australia, Federal Court of Australia Full Court, [2010] FCAFC 12, ILDC 1518 (2010).	The Federal Court of Australia Full Court found the 'Act of State' doctrine inapplicable to acts of torture, as violations of *jus cogens*, perpetrated while the claimant was in US custody in Pakistan, Egypt, and Guantánamo Bay, Cuba.
Zhang v. Zemin, New South Wales Court of Appeal (Australia), [2010] NSWCA 255 (2010).	The New South Wales Court of Appeal dismissed a civil claim against the former President of China arising from certain *jus cogens* violations.
Regina v. Tang, High Court of Australia, [2008] HCA 39, paras. 110–17 (Kirby, J. (2008)).	The High Court of Australia, in restoring the conviction of a brothel owner for slavery under international law, recognized the prohibition of slavery to belong to *jus cogens*.
Nulyarimma and Others v. Thompson / Buzzacott v. Minister for the Environment and Others, Federal Court of Australia, [1999] FCA 1192, 120 ILR 353, paras. 57 (Whitlam, J.), 178, 186 (Merkel, J. (2009)).	The Federal Court of Australia acknowledged that the prohibition of genocide belongs to *jus cogens*; however, judges Whitlam and Merkel disagreed over whether that status granted Australian courts the authority to prescribe genocide as a crime under the common law of Australia.

Austria

A.A. v. Austria, Supreme Court of Austria, No. 1Ob225/07f, para. 4.3 (2008).	The Supreme Court of Austria found that Security Council resolutions are to be measured against a minimum *jus cogens* standard of due process, in the context of employment termination pursuant to Chicago Convention.
Anita W. v. John Adam II (Prince of Liechtenstein), Supreme Court of Austria, No. 7Ob316/00x, ILDC 1, para. 13 (2001).	The Supreme Court of Austria acknowledged the interaction of *jus cogens* and sovereign immunity.
Supreme Court of Austria, Decision No. 11Os139/98 (1998).	The Supreme Court of Austria considered the denial of extradition due to threat of a *jus cogens* violation facing the petitioner.

Belgium

R.D. v. Belgium, Court of Cassation (Belgium), No. P.04.1211.N, JT, 2005, 322, ILDC 6, para. 24 (2004).	In the broader context of a European Council Framework Decision, the Court of Cassation found that the Treaty on Extradition and Mutual Assistance in Criminal Matters Between Belgium, Luxembourg, and the Netherlands (1962) had not been invalidated by the emergence of a peremptory norm under Article 64 of the Vienna Convention.
Re Sharon and Yaron, Court of Cassation (Belgium), P.02.1139.F/2, JT 2003, 243, ILDC 5 (2003); Court of Appeal (Bruxelles) (2002), 127 ILR 110, 114, 120.	The Court of Cassation of Belgium recognized the immunity *ratione personae* of Israeli Prime Minister Ariel Sharon to quash criminal proceedings under Belgium's universal jurisdiction statute; the Court of Appeal of Brussels had previously held that legislation providing for universal jurisdiction was not contrary to *jus cogens*, and that *jus cogens* did not require a State to extend its jurisdiction over an individual not present on its territory accused of international crimes.

Jugoslovenski Aerotransport v. Belgium, Court of Appeal (Bruxelles), No. 1998/KR/528, para. 3.2 (1999).	The Brussels Court of Appeal found in part that an embargo did not violate a *jus cogens* norm of international law.

Bosnia and Herzegovina

Prosecutor's Office v. Anić, Court of Bosnia and Herzegovina (Section I for War Crimes), S1 1 K 005596 11 Kro, ILDC 1907, paras. 27–8 (2011).	In the conviction of a member of the Yugoslav National Army, the Court of Bosnia and Herzegovina found the prohibitions of war crimes and crimes against humanity to belong to *jus cogens* and, therefore, actionable as customary international law at the time of the conduct at issue.

Canada

Regina v. Munyaneza, Montreal Superior Court (Criminal Division) (Canada), 2009 QCCS 2201, paras. 70–9 (2009).	The Montreal Superior Court, exercising universal jurisdiction in the prosecution of a Rwandan national for participation in the Rwandan Genocide, found that the international crime of genocide belongs to *jus cogens*.
Victoria (City) v. Adams, Supreme Court of British Columbia (Canada), 2008 BCSC 1363, para. 162 (2008).	The Supreme Court of British Columbia considered that '[t]he inquiry into the principles of fundamental justice is informed not only by Canadian experience and jurisprudence, but also by international law, including *jus cogens*'.
Bouzari v. Islamic Republic of Iran, Court of Appeal for Ontario (Canada), 71 OR (3d) 675, paras. 57–73 (2004).	The Court of Appeal for Ontario found the jurisdictional immunity of the State applicable to shield Iran from civil litigation notwithstanding the *jus cogens* status of the norms at issue in the case.
Suresh v. Canada (Minister of Citizenship and Immigration), Supreme Court (Canada), [2002] 1 SCR 3, paras. 46, 59–64.	In a case concerning deportation of a refugee who faced a risk of torture upon *refoulement*, the Supreme Court of Canada considered torture with reference to international law because '[t]he inquiry into the principles of

	fundamental justice is informed not only by Canadian experience and jurisprudence, but also by international law, including *jus cogens*'.
Regina v. Finta, Supreme Court (Canada), 1 SCR 701, 22 (1994).	The Supreme Court obliquely referred to *jus cogens* in its acquittal of the commander of the Gendarmerie in Szeged, Hungary, for war crimes perpetrated during the Second World War.

Chile

Re Víctor Raúl Pinto v. Relatives of Tomás Rojas, Supreme Court (Chile), Decision on Annulment, No. 3125–04, ILDC 1093, paras. 29–31 (2007).	The Supreme Court of Chile found that a domestic amnesty law could not be applied to *jus cogens* violations of crimes against humanity or the obligation to prosecute such offences which, as part of the domestic law of Chile, prevailed over Chilean legislation.

Colombia

Gallón Giraldo y Otros v. Colombia, Constitutional Court (Colombia), No. C-370/2006, ILDC 660, para. 4.9.6 (2006).	The Constitutional Court of Colombia evaluated the compatibility of domestic amnesties and pardons for political crimes with *jus cogens*.
Constitutional Case No. C-225/95, Constitutional Court (Colombia), No. C-225/95 (1995) (quoted in *Mapiripán Massacre v. Colombia*, Series C No. 134, para. 115 (2005)).	In this case concerning State responsibility of Colombia for conduct of the Revolutionary Armed Forces of Colombia (FARC), the Constitutional Court of Colombia recognized international humanitarian law as part of Colombia's 'constitutional block', and mandatory for all States, as well as State and non-State armed forces engaged in armed conflict.

Czech Republic

Novotný v. Ministry of Justice, Constitutional Court of the Czech	The Constitutional Court of the Czech Republic considered that

Republic, No. I ÚS 601/04, ILDC 990, para. 34 (2007).	*pacta sunt servanda* calls for the good faith expectation that international obligations are to be fulfilled, but only within the limits of *jus cogens*.

France

Lydienne X v. Prosecutor, Court of Cassation (Criminal Division) (France), No. 12-81676, ILDC 2035, paras. 10.4, 14 (2013).	The Court of Cassation recognized that torture belongs to *jus cogens* and that the investigation of international crimes occurring in Cameroon perpetrated against a French citizen did not breach the immunity of Cameroon or its representatives.
AFP and PLO v. Alstom and Veolia, Versailles Court of Appeal (France), No. 11-05331, 52 ILM 1161, 1181 (2013).	Expressing scepticism for the application of *jus cogens* to French corporations, the Versailles Court of Appeal held, '[t]he existence of a superior international public policy characterised as "*jus cogens*" to which the humanitarian rules invoked would belong and which should be mandatorily applied, is not established. Therefore, it cannot be argued that domestic courts should apply the humanitarian norms invoked against the French corporations in the name of international public policy derived from *jus cogens*'.
Réunion Aérienne v. Socialist People's Libyan Arab Jamahiriya, Court of Cassation (Civil Division) (France), No. 09-14743, 150 ILR 630, 634 (2011).	The Court of Cassation in this case declined to impose State civil liability for the *jus cogens* violation of terrorism, while reserving the right to do so where a sufficient degree of moral culpability is present.
Ely Ould Dah Case, Gard Assizes Court (France), No. 70/05 (Arrêt de condamnation) / No. 71/05 (Arrêt statuant sur les intérêts civils) (2005).	French courts in the *Ely Ould Dah Case* declined to recognize the immunity *ratione materiae* of a Mauritanian officer in his prosecution for *jus cogens* violations committed during an 'ethnic purge' in suppression of a coup in Mauritania.

Germany

Attorney of the Federal Armed Forces v. Anonymous (a Major of the Armed Forces), Federal Administrative Court (Germany), 2 WD 12:04, ILDC 483, paras. 4.1.4.1.1, 4.1.6 (2005).	The German Federal Administrative Court considered the prohibition of 'any' threat and use of military force to belong to *jus cogens*. The Court therefore allowed the appeal of a disciplinary conviction by a member of the German armed forces who refused to participate in Germany's use of force in Iraq due to its illegality under international law.
East German Expropriation Case, Mr von der M, BVerfG [Constitutional Court] (Germany), 2 BvR 955/00, ILDC 66, paras. 97–8, 116 (2004).	The Constitutional Court of Germany found that *jus cogens* was incorporated into the Basic Law of Germany, but that the protection of the property of a State's citizens is not part of *jus cogens*.
Jorgic Case, BVerfG [Constitutional Court] (Germany), 2 BvR 1290/99, ILDC 132, paras. 17, 26–7 (2000).	The German Constitutional Court applied universal jurisdiction over the crime of genocide to convict a Bosnian Serb for ethnic-cleansing in Bosnia and Herzegovina in 1992.
Former Syrian Ambassador to the German Democratic Republic, BVerfG [Constitutional Court] (Germany), 2 BvR 1516/96, 115 ILR 596, 608–9, 613–14 (1997).	The German Constitutional Court considered a challenge to an arrest warrant for a former Syrian Ambassador implicated in a bombing in central Berlin. The Court distinguished the effect of *jus cogens* upon the immunity of States and their organs, and that enjoyed by diplomats, the former being unavailable to the diplomat at the time of litigation.

Greece

Margellos v. Federal Republic of Germany, Anotato Eidiko Dikastirio (Special Supreme Court) (Greece), No. 6/2002, 129 ILR 525, paras. 13–15 (2002).	The Special Supreme Court of Greece recognized the jurisdictional immunity of Germany irrespective of the *jus cogens* character of the norms at issue.
Prefecture of Voiotia v. Federal Republic of Germany (Distomo	The Court of Cassation recognized an exception to the jurisdictional

Massacre Case), Court of Cassation (*Areios Pagos*) (Greece), No. 11/2000, 129 ILR 513, 521 (2000). — immunity of the State from civil suit where *jus cogens* violations are at issue. *See Jurisdictional Immunities of the State (Germany v. Italy: Greece Intervening)*, Judgment, ICJ Reports 2012, p. 99.

Hong Kong

C, KMF and BF v. Director of Immigration and Secretary for Security, Court of Final Instance (Hong Kong), FACV Nos. 18/19/20 2011 (2013). — In the case of 'C', the Court of Final Instance of Hong Kong found that *non-refoulement*, as articulated in Article 33 of the UN Refugee Convention, had entered into customary international law but is not a peremptory norm belonging to *jus cogens*.

C v. Director of Immigration, Court of First Instance (Hong Kong), HCAL 132/2006, [2008] 2 HKC 165, ILDC 1119, paras. 78, 133–5 (2008). — While endorsing the concept of *jus cogens*, the Court of First Instance considered *non-refoulement* to fall outside the category ('Much of the impetus for the recognition of *jus cogens* arose out of the state-sponsored atrocities of the Second World War. In plain terms, *jus cogens* seeks to be a supreme law, one which, recognising fundamental human rights, denies the unlimited will of the state. *Jus cogens* recognises that some deeds are so wrong, so abhorrent, that no legitimate legal order could fail to proscribe them').

Israel

Attorney-General (Israel) v. Eichmann, Supreme Court (Israel), 36 ILR 5 (1962). — The Supreme Court of Israel relied upon concepts implicit in the doctrine of *jus cogens* to justify Israel's prosecution of Adolf Eichmann in 1962, though the proceedings preceded the codification of the Vienna Convention in 1969 and did not expressly invoke *jus cogens*.

Italy

Germany v. De Guglielmi et al., Court of Appeal (Italy), No. 941/2012, ILDC 1905, para. 15 (2012).	The Court of Appeal of Italy applied the 2012 ICJ Judgment, *Jurisdictional Immunities of the State*, and recognized State immunity from jurisdiction notwithstanding the *jus cogens* character of the norms at issue in the case.
Germany v. Milde, Court of Cassation (First Criminal Section) (Italy), No. 1072/2009, ILDC 1224 (2009).	The Court of Cassation denied State immunity due to the *jus cogens* status of violations of crimes against humanity. *See Jurisdictional Immunities of the State (Germany v. Italy: Greece Intervening)*, Judgment, ICJ Reports 2012, p. 99.
Lozano v. Italy, Court of Cassation (First Criminal Chamber) (Italy), No. 31171/2008, ILDC 1085, para. 6 (2008).	The Court of Cassation identified the prohibitions against genocide, torture, and war crimes as belonging to *jus cogens*, to which immunity *ratione materiae* is inapplicable, but found the conduct in question did not constitute such an offence.
Germany v. Mantelli and ors, Court of Cassation (Italy), Preliminary Order on Jurisdiction, No. 14201/2008, ILDC 1037, para. 11 (2008).	The Court of Cassation denied the jurisdictional immunity of Germany due to the *jus cogens* status of norms violated.
Ferrini v. Germany, Court of Cassation (Civil Section) (Italy), No. 5044/ 2004, ILDC 19 (2004).	The Court of Cassation denied the jurisdictional immunity of Germany due to the *jus cogens* status of norms violated.

Kenya

Kenya Section of the International Commission of Jurists v. Attorney General et al., High Court (Kenya) [2011] eKLR, ILDC 1804, paras. 64–7, 74–5, 99 (2011).	The High Court of Kenya found, on the basis of *jus cogens*, the issuance of two arrest warrants for Omar Al Bashir, and their enforcement by any legal person with the capacity to do so, to be consistent with international law notwithstanding Al Bashir's Head-of-State status. The Court referred to obligations under the Rome Statute and commensurate obligations

arising for all States, pursuant to public order norms of *jus cogens*, under which all States have a duty to prosecute via universal jurisdiction.

R.M. v. Attorney General, High Court (Kenya), Civil Case 1351, AHRLR 256 (KeHC 2006), ILDC 699, paras. 47, 75 (2006).

The High Court of Kenya, in a case concerning parental responsibility in the face of discrimination against a child born out of wedlock, found that such responsibility did not belong to *jus cogens* and could therefore not be enforced by the Court. However, the Court indicated that the prohibition against racial discrimination belongs to *jus cogens*.

Latvia

Kariņš and ors v. Parliament of Latvia and Cabinet of Ministers of Latvia (Border Treaty), Constitutional Court (Latvia), No. 2007-10-0102, ILDC 884, paras. 10, 25.6 (2007).

In a proceeding concerning the legality of territory attained through USSR aggression in Latvia in 1940, the Constitutional Court of Latvia indicated that the prohibition against the unlawful use of force belongs to *jus cogens*.

Namibia

Minister of Defence v. Mwandinghi, High Court (Namibia), 1991 (1) SA 851 (Nm), 91 ILR 343 (1990), *affirmed by* Supreme Court (Namibia), 1992 (2) SA 355 (NmS), 91 ILR 35 (1991).

The High Court of Namibia considered that Article 145(1)(b) of the Constitution of Namibia, which accepted State responsibility for conduct by the prior regime that 'would not otherwise have been recognized by international law', referred to *jus cogens* violations. The Court found such conduct, in practice, to constitute acts or contracts based in, or giving rise to, racial discrimination, and considered this acceptance of responsibility to bind successor State Namibia.

The Netherlands

Stichting Mothers of Srebrenica and ors v. Netherlands and United Nations,

The Supreme Court of the Netherlands found that the *jus cogens* status of

Supreme Court (Netherlands), LJN: BW1999, ILDC 1760, paras. 4.3.7–4.3.14 (2012).	norms violated was insufficient to overcome immunity of the Netherlands and the United Nations in litigation arising from the massacre at Srebrenica.
Association of Lawyers for Peace (Vereniging van Juristen voor de Vrede) and ors v. Netherlands, Supreme Court (Netherlands), LJN: AN8071, ILDC 152, paras. 3.2–3.4 (2004).	The Supreme Court of the Netherlands found that the prohibition of the use of force belongs to *jus cogens*, yet Article 2(4) of the UN Charter could not be invoked by an individual.
Bouterse Case, Amsterdam Court of Appeal (Netherlands), Nos. R 97/163/12 Sv & R 97/176/12 Sv, para. 5 (2000), *abrogated on other grounds by Bouterse Case*, Supreme Court (Netherlands), LJN: AB1471, ILDC 80 (2001).	The Amsterdam Court of Appeal permitted prosecution of the former military ruler of the Republic of Suriname for crimes against humanity and torture on the basis of universal jurisdiction and concepts related to *jus cogens*, without expressly invoking the doctrine.
New Zealand	
Fang v. Jiang, High Court (New Zealand), [2007] NZAR 420, ILDC 1226, para. 26 (2006).	The High Court of New Zealand recognized the crime of torture as belonging to *jus cogens*, though ultimately dismissed civil claims against former members of the Chinese government for such offences.
Attorney General v. Ahmed Zaoui and ors, Supreme Court (New Zealand), SC CIV 19/2004, [2005] NZSC 38, ILDC 81, para. 51 (2005).	The Supreme Court of New Zealand recognized the *jus cogens* status of the prohibition of torture, while denying that the prohibition of *refoulement* to torture shares that status.
Mansouri-Rad v. Department of Labour, Refugee Status Appeals Authority (New Zealand), No. 74665/03, [2005] NZAR 60, ILDC 217, para. 63 (2005).	The Appeals Authority of New Zealand discussed the difficulty of identifying *jus cogens* norms in a case concerning the determination of refugee status.
Peru	
Rivera Lazo and ors, Superior Court (Third Criminal Chamber) (Peru),	In convicting members of the death squad *Colina Group*, the Superior Court of Peru found that the

No. 28-2001, ILDC 1887, para. 16 (2010).	prohibition of crimes against humanity bound Peru as a *jus cogens* norm of customary international law, notwithstanding the absence of legislative incorporation, and found a statute of limitations inapplicable to such norms.
Fujimori Case, Supreme Court (Specialized Criminal Law Chamber) (Peru), No. 19-2001 AV, ILDC 1516, para. 711 (2009).	The Supreme Court of Peru convicted former President Alberto Fujimori for a campaign against domestic terrorist groups in violation of the prohibition of crimes against humanity under customary international law, notwithstanding the non-incorporation of such norms into the Criminal Code of Peru. The Court recognized the obligation to prosecute and non-applicability of a statute of limitations.

The Philippines

Muna et al. v. Romulo et al., Supreme Court (Philippines), G.R. No. 159618, ILDC 2059, paras. 40–50, 89–94 (2011).	The Supreme Court of the Philippines found that a Non-Surrender Agreement with the United States did not defeat the object and purpose of the Rome Statute, in part because the *jus cogens* status of war crimes, crimes against humanity, and genocide enabled prosecution of these crimes in the United States through incorporation and universal jurisdiction even in the absence of US domestic legislation.

Poland

Natoniewski v. Germany, Supreme Court (Poland), No. IV CSK 465/09, 2010 Polish Yearbook of International Law 299, 302, ILDC 1996 (2010).	The Supreme Court of Poland recognized the jurisdictional immunity of Germany in a civil suit for *jus cogens* violations committed during World War II.

Russia

H. v. Prosecutor General Office, Supreme Court (Russia), N KAS06–129, ILDC 1361, Reference 5 (2006).	The Supreme Court of Russia recognized *jus cogens* to be incorporated into domestic law of the Russian Federation as a matter of constitutional law.

Slovenia

Arbitration Agreement Opinion Procedure, Constitutional Court (Slovenia), Rm-1/09–26, ILDC 1485, para. 26 (2010).	The Constitutional Court of Slovenia found that the *uti possidetis* principle is not a *jus cogens* norm.
One Third of the National Assembly Deputies, Constitutional Court (Slovenia), Rm-1/00–29, ILDC 402, para. 14 (2001).	The Constitutional Court of Slovenia found that the *uti possidetis* principle is not a *jus cogens* norm.
A.A. v. Germany, Constitutional Court (Slovenia), Up-13/99–24, paras. 13–14 (2001).	The Constitutional Court of Slovenia denied the existence of a principle under customary international law that would allow Slovenian courts to prosecute other States for *jus cogens* violations.

South Africa

Mthembu v. State, Supreme Court of Appeal (South Africa), No. 379/07, (2008) ZASCA 51, ILDC 958 (2008).	The Supreme Court of Appeal of South Africa found that the prohibition of torture, a *jus cogens* norm, had been incorporated into the constitution of South Africa, and that evidence obtained through torture must therefore be absolutely excluded from judicial proceedings.
Van Zyl and ors v. Government of South Africa and ors, North Gauteng High Court (South Africa), No. 20320/02, [2005] ZAGPHC 70, ILDC 171, paras. 20–1 (2005).	The North Gauteng High Court rejected the proposition that the State is obligated to espouse the claims of its citizens arising from violations of *jus cogens* norms as without 'judicial imprimatur'.
Kaunda v. President of South Africa and ors, Constitutional Court (South Africa), No. CCT 23/04, 2005 (4) SA 235 (CC), ILDC 89, paras. 28–9 (2004).	The Constitutional Court of South Africa denied a legal duty to exercise diplomatic protection where the injury is the result of a violation of *jus cogens* norms.

South Korea

Yeo and ors v. Nippon Steel & Sumitomo Metal, High Court (South Korea), 2012 Na 44947, ILDC 2104, Reference 3 (2013).	The High Court of South Korea found the prohibition of crimes against humanity as *jus cogens* in force during Japanese colonial rule over Korea. Therefore, a Japanese corporation's participation in forced labour during that time was subject to compensation.

Spain

Criminal Law Chamber of the Supreme Court et al. v. Garzón Real, Supreme Court (Spain), No. 101/2012, ILDC 1855, para. 3 (2012).	The Supreme Court of Spain found that Spanish law did not allow its domestic amnesty law to be annulled by the Court, notwithstanding any inconsistency with *jus cogens*.
Guatemala Genocide Case, National Court (Spain), Response to the Guatemala Constitutional Court, No. 331/1999, 4 (2008).	The prosecuting judge in the case, in response to Guatemala's denial of Spanish jurisdiction, invoked the international responsibility of Guatemala for violating its obligations *erga omnes* arising from the *jus cogens* norms at issue.
Scilingo Manzorro v. Spain, Supreme Court (Spain), No. 798/2007, ILDC 1430, paras. 6–7 (2007).	The Supreme Court of Spain affirmed the exercise of universal jurisdiction to convict an Argentinian national for crimes against humanity, in violation of *jus cogens*, committed during the 1976 Argentina coup.
Guatemala Genocide Case (Menchú Tumn and ors v. Two Guatemalan Government Officials and Six Members of the Guatemalan Military), Constitutional Court (Criminal Chamber) (Spain), Spanish Constitutional Court Decision Accepting Jurisdiction, No. 237/2005, ILDC 137 (2005).	The Constitutional Court of Spain removed the prior territorial nexus requirement to the application of universal jurisdiction to prosecute *jus cogens* violations.
Public Prosecutor's Office and ors v. Scilingo Manzorro, National Court (*Audiencia Nacional*) (Criminal Chamber) (Spain), No. 16/2005,	The National Court of Spain exercised universal jurisdiction to convict an Argentine national for crimes against humanity, as prohibited by customary

ILDC 136, paras. B.1-B.2, B.4-B.5 (2005).	international law and therefore part of the Spanish legal order, prior to codification of that crime in the Criminal Code of Spain.

Switzerland

A. (Kahled Nezzar) v. Office of the Attorney General, Federal Criminal Court (Switzerland), No. BB.2011.140 (2012).	The Federal Criminal Court of Switzerland dismissed a claim of immunity *ratione materiae* in criminal proceedings against a former Algerian minister of defence on the basis of the *jus cogens* status of the norms breached.
A. v. State Secretariat for Economic Affairs and Federal Department of Economic Affairs, First Public Law Chamber (Switzerland), No. 1A 48/2007, ILDC 1201, para. 7 (2008).	The First Public Law Chamber of Switzerland found that *jus cogens* constitutes a limit to the application of UN Security Council resolutions, but that no such norm was implicated by Resolutions 1267 and 1333.
A. v. Federal Department of Economic Affairs, Federal Supreme Court (Switzerland), No. 2A 783/2006, ILDC 1200, paras. 8.1–8.4, 9.2 (2008).	In the broader context of enforcement of a UN sanctions regime under Security Council Resolution 1483, the Federal Supreme Court of Switzerland found the procedural guarantees under ECHR Articles 6 and 13, and ICCPR Article 14, did not belong to *jus cogens*.
Nada v. State Secretariat for Economic Affairs and Federal Department of Economic Affairs, Federal Supreme Court (Switzerland), No. 1A 45/2007, ILDC 461, paras. 7.3–7.4 (2007).	The Federal Supreme Court of Switzerland recognized a broad category of *jus cogens* norms, but denied a claim that the asserted due process protections implicated by a UN Security Council Resolution belong to *jus cogens*.

United Kingdom

R. (on the application of Al-Jedda) v. Secretary of State for Defence, House of Lords (UK), [2007] UKHL 58, para. 35 (Bingham, L.).	The House of Lords concluded that Chapter VII UN Security Council resolutions supersede all treaty commitments, except where such an obligation also belongs to *jus cogens*.

Jones v. Ministry of the Interior of Saudi Arabia and Lieutenant Colonel Abdul Aziz, House of Lords (UK), [2006] UKHL 26.	The House of Lords recognized the sovereign immunity of Saudi Arabia, as well as its agent, notwithstanding allegations of *jus cogens* violations of torture at issue.
R. (on the application of Ali Al-Jedda) v. Secretary of State for Defence, Court of Appeal (UK), [2006] EWCA Civ 327, paras. 67, 75 (Brooke, L.J.).	The Court of Appeal of the UK discussed the interaction of Security Council Resolutions with *jus cogens.*
K. v. Secretary of State for the Home Department, House of Lords (UK), [2006] UKHL 46, para. 8 (Bingham, L.).	The House of Lords considered FGM to be a form of torture thereby violating the *jus cogens* prohibition of torture.
R. (on the application of Al Rawi and ors) v. Secretary of State for Foreign and Commonwealth Affairs et al., Court of Appeal (UK), [2006] EWCA Civ 1279, para. 102 (Laws, L.J.).	The Court of Appeal discussed the legal effects of *jus cogens* as 'a powerful constellation' that includes special standing, non-derogation, absoluteness of prohibitions, invalidity of authorizations, and universal jurisdiction.
A. and Others v. Secretary of State for the Home Department (No 2), House of Lords (UK), [2005] UKHL 71, paras. 30–4 (Bingham, L.).	The House of Lords denied the admissibility of evidence procured through torture in contravention of *jus cogens.*
R. (on the application of European Roma Rights Centre) v. Immigration Officer at Prague Airport, House of Lords (UK), [2004] UKHL 55, para. 46 (Steyn, J.).	The House of Lords found that British immigration officers at Prague Airport violated the Race Relations Act, and that the prohibition against systematic racial discrimination belongs to *jus cogens.*
R. (on the application of Al-Skeini and ors) v. Secretary of State for Defence, High Court of Justice (UK), [2004] EWHC 2911 (Admin.), para. 216 (Rix, L.J.).	The High Court of Justice found that the prohibition of torture belongs to *jus cogens* and falls within the jurisdiction of the UK and the Torture Convention, in a case concerning the death of an individual while in the custody of British forces in Iraq.
Kuwait Airways Corporation v. Iraqi Airways Company, House of Lords (UK), [2002] UKHL 19, para. 114 (Steyn, L.).	The House of Lords recognized a public policy exception to the Act of State doctrine was justified in the context of aggression as a violation of

	jus cogens. Accordingly, the Court declined to give effect to Iraqi Resolution 369, which furthered the invasion and annexation of Kuwait.
Campaign for Nuclear Disarmament v. Prime Minister of the United Kingdom and ors, High Court of Justice (UK), [2002] EWHC 2777 (Admin.), paras. 17, 47 (Brown, L. J.).	In litigation concerning the legality of the interpretation of UN Security Council Resolution 1441, which concerned the use of force in Iraq, the High Court of Justice recognized the prohibition of unlawful use of force belongs to *jus cogens*, but denied jurisdiction to determine the meaning of an instrument not incorporated into domestic law.
R. v. Bow Street Metropolitan Stipendiary Magistrate and Others, Ex parte Pinochet Ugarte (No. 3), House of Lords (UK), [2000] 1 A.C. 147, 38 ILM 581 (1999).	The House of Lords permitted the extradition of Augusto Pinochet for the international crime of torture and recognized the *jus cogens* status of the prohibition as a rationale for denying immunity *ratione materiae*.
United States	
See discussion *supra*, Chapter 12.B (Individual Civil Responsibility).	
Zimbabwe	
Mann v. Republic of Equatorial Guinea, High Court (Zimbabwe), No. CA 507/07, [2008] ZWHHC 1, 153 ILR 697, 711–12 (2008) (Patel, J.).	Judge Patel, for the High Court of Zimbabwe, recognized that the *jus cogens* prohibition of torture imposes certain duties upon States. Extradition with the belief that an individual would be in danger of torture would violate such obligations.

INDEX

Note: Author names are indexed only where there is significant discussion or citation.

Lightning Source UK Ltd.
Milton Keynes UK
UKHW03n0643190318
319631UK00013B/167/P

9 781107 081765